The Spectralities Reader

The Spectralities Reader

Ghosts and Haunting in Contemporary Cultural Theory

Edited by
María del Pilar Blanco
and
Esther Peeren

BLOOMSBURY
LONDON • NEW DELHI • NEW YORK • SYDNEY

Bloomsbury Academic
An imprint of Bloomsbury Publishing Plc

1385 Broadway	50 Bedford Square
New York	London
NY 10018	WC1B 3DP
USA	UK

www.bloomsbury.com

Bloomsbury is a registered trade mark of Bloomsbury Publishing Plc

First published 2013
© María del Pilar Blanco and Esther Peeren, 2013

Library of Congress Cataloging-in-Publication Data
The spectralities reader : ghosts and haunting in contemporary cultural theory / edited by María del Pilar Blanco and Esther Peeren.
pages cm
ISBN 978-1-4411-3860-6 (hardback)– ISBN 978-1-4411-0559-2 (paperback)– ISBN 978-1-4411-3689-3 (e-pub) 1. Ghosts in literature. 2. Supernatural in literature. 3. Other (Philosophy) in literature. 4. Culture--Philosophy. I. Blanco, María del Pilar. II. Peeren, Esther.
PN56.S8S64 2013
809.2'51209375--dc23
2013021064

ISBN: HB: 978-1-4411-3860-6
PB: 978-1-4411-0559-2
e-pdf: 978-1-4411-2478-4
e-pub: 978-1-4411-3689-3

Typeset by Fakenham Prepress Solutions, Fakenham, Norfolk NR21 8NN
Printed and bound in the United States of America

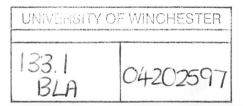

CONTENTS

ACKNOWLEDGMENTS

The materialization of *The Spectralities Reader* was a gradual process that we could not have completed on our own. First and foremost, we want to thank Katie Gallof, our wonderful editor at Bloomsbury, who believed in the project from the beginning and was always at hand to help. Claire Cooper and Kim Storry were instrumental in guiding the *Reader* through the production process, while Laura Murray provided invaluable marketing assistance. We also want to express our appreciation for the supportive responses of the authors of the texts we have included (and would have liked to include), which spurred us on in the early stages.

The necessary task of obtaining permissions to reprint the texts was made much less arduous and costly than it could have been by Anne Rocklein and Curtis Scott at the Clark Institute; Diane Grossé at Duke University Press; Kate Caras at Indiana University Press; Vicki Lee and Ruth Tellis at Palgrave Macmillan; Sarah Dodgson and Jenny Seabrook at Polity Press; Valérie Bernard at SAGE Publications; Ariane de Pree at Stanford University Press; Shannon A. Jackson and Kelly L. Rogers at The Johns Hopkins University Press; Pamela Quick and Nicholas Yeaton at The MIT Press; Jeff Moen at The University of Minnesota Press; Rebecca Soares at The University of Wisconsin Press; Deborah J. Gray at The University Press of New England; and Verity Butler, Richard S. Jones, and Emma Willcox at Wiley-Blackwell.

Permission to use indispensible images was kindly provided by Emilie Keldie at the Felix Gonzalez-Torres Foundation; Mikael Levin; and Kerry Schauber and Sue Nurse at the Memorial Art Museum at University of Rochester.

The funding provided by Bloomsbury for the permissions was supplemented by a generous grant from the Amsterdam School for Cultural Analysis (ASCA) at the University of Amsterdam. We are intensely grateful to ASCA's director, Christoph Lindner, and managing director, Eloe Kingma, for this invaluable assistance, without which this volume would not be here today.

Juliën Staartjes, student-assistant for the Department of Literary Studies at the University of Amsterdam, provided meticulous assistance scanning documents and retyping sections that refused to be electronically converted.

Finally, we thank David James and Naj Ghosheh for enduring the way this project has haunted us over the past few years, and in particular its possessive inhabitation of 2012's Christmas and New Year's Eve celebrations.

PERMISSIONS

Texts

Images

Beard, James Henry (1814–93). The Night Before the Battle. 1865. Oil on canvas. 30½ × 44½ in. (77.5 × 113 cm). Image copyright © The Memorial Art Gallery of the University of Rochester. Reprint permission granted by The Memorial Art Gallery of the University of Rochester.

Gonzalez-Torres, Felix. "Untitled", 1989. C-print jigsaw puzzle in plastic bag. 7½ × 9½ in. Edition of 3, 1 AP. © The Felix Gonzalez-Torres Foundation. Courtesy of Andrea Rosen Gallery, New York.

Homer, Winslow (1836–1910). Searchlight on Harbor Entrance, Santiago de Cuba. 1901. Oil on canvas, 30½ × 50½ in. (77.5 × 128.3 cm). Gift of George A. Hearn, 1906 (06.1282). The Metropolitan Museum of Art, New York, NY, U.S.A. Image copyright © The Metropolitan Museum of Art. Image source: Art Resource, NY.

Levin, Mikael. "Untitled" from War Story, 1995–6. © Mikael Levin. Reprinted with permission of Mikael Levin.

All images from Collier's Weekly that appear in Alexander Nemerov's essay are in the public domain and (as noted in the image credits within the essay) were generously supplied to the author by the Beinecke Rare Book & Manuscript Library, Yale University, New Haven, Connecticut.

Editors' Note

Spelling, punctuation, and references have been retained as they appear in the original texts. All footnotes have, however, been converted to endnotes and titles, headings, and epigraphs have been printed in accordance with Bloomsbury Academic's house style. For copyright reasons, (additional) images included in the original texts by Derrida and Stiegler, Gordon, Lippit, Matless, Richardson, and Sconce have been left out. For reasons of space, acknowledgments have also been left out. In texts that could not be included in their entirety, [...] is used to mark elided parts.

Introduction: Conceptualizing Spectralities

María del Pilar Blanco and Esther Peeren

a specter does not only cause séance tables to turn, but sets heads spinning.[1]

Ghosts, spirits, and specters have played vital roles in oral and written narratives throughout history and across cultures, appearing as anything from figments of the imagination, divine messengers, benign or exacting ancestors, and pesky otherworldly creatures populating particular loci to disturbing figures returned from the dead bent on exacting revenge, revealing hidden crimes, continuing a love affair or simply searching for a way to pass on. Their representational and socio-cultural functions, meanings, and effects have been at least as manifold as their shapes— or non-shapes, as the case may be—and extend far beyond the rituals, traditions, ghost stories, folktales, and urban legends they populate.

It is part of this beyond that *The Spectralities Reader* seeks to address by focusing on how, at the end of the twentieth century, a specific metamorphosis occurred of ghosts and haunting from possible actual entities, plot devices, and clichés of common parlance ("he is a ghost of himself," "we are haunted by the past") into influential conceptual metaphors permeating global (popular) culture and academia alike. A conceptual metaphor, Mieke Bal suggests, differs from an ordinary one in evoking, through a dynamic comparative interaction, not just another thing, word or idea and its associations, but a discourse, a system of producing knowledge.[2] Besides fulfilling an aesthetic or semantic function, then, a conceptual metaphor "performs theoretical work."[3] The ghost's emerging status as an analytical tool that *does* theory—and thereby, as Derrida notes in the above epigraph, "sets heads spinning"—was signaled and delineated by the sudden preference expressed in 1990s cultural criticism for the somewhat archaic terms "specter" and "spectrality" over the more mundane "ghost" and "ghost-liness."[4] "Specter" and "spectrality" not only have a more serious, scholarly ring to them, but specifically evoke an etymological link to visibility and vision, to that which is both *looked at* (as fascinating spectacle) and *looking* (in the sense of examining), suggesting their suitability for exploring and illuminating phenomena other than the putative return of the dead. In their new spectral guise, certain features of ghosts and haunting—such as their liminal position between visibility and invisibility, life and death, materi-ality and immateriality, and their association with powerful affects like fear and obsession—quickly came to be employed across the humanities and social sciences to theorize a variety of social, ethical, and political questions. These questions include, among others, the temporal and spatial sedimen-tation of history and tradition, and its impact on possibilities for social change; the intricacies of memory and trauma, personal and collective; the workings and effects of scientific processes, technologies, and media; and the exclusionary, effacing dimensions of social norms pertaining to gender, race, ethnicity, sexuality, and class.

The publication of Jacques Derrida's *Spectres de Marx* in 1993 (and its English translation, *Specters of Marx*, in 1994) is commonly considered the catalyst for what some have called the "spectral turn," marking the appearance of a new area of investigation of which the past two decades represent an apogee and of which this *Reader* collects a number of influ-ential texts, chosen to display the extent of spectrality's critical scope in contemporary cultural theory. Before charting this still-developing area in more detail and specifying the distinctive trajectories of spectrality explored in the six parts that constitute this *Reader*, it is first necessary to look back further than the 1990s in order to ask what changed at this time with regard to the critical perception of ghosts and haunting, and how this change was precipitated.

The ghost as actuality, metaphor, and concept

As noted, the figure of the ghost has haunted human culture and imagi-nation for a long time, perhaps even forever, although more insistently in certain societies and periods than in others. One of its heydays in the western world came in the late nineteenth century, when the literary fashion for ghost stories (developed in Romanticism and the genres of the Gothic and the fantastic) intersected with the effort to unlock other worlds and dimensions—material, psychic, and supernatural—that characterized both spiritualism, in its entanglement with new religious movements, the emergent discipline of psychology, and the professionalization of science in general, and the invention of penetrating yet intangible new media such as telegraphy, photography, and cinema.[5] In this era, the ghost already operated as a powerful metaphor for encounters with disturbing forms of otherness (including that contained inside the self, the home, and the homeland), the obfuscations inherent to capitalist commodity production (as outlined by Marx and Engels), and the ungraspable operations of newly discovered particles and microbes, as well as technological processes such as X-rays. This figurative use, however, remained grounded, to an extent, in the ghost's possible reality as an empirically verifiable supernatural phenomenon, making it less a tool for obtaining insight into something else than itself an object of knowledge and scientific experimentation (as, for example, in spirit photography and the exploits of the Society for Psychical Research, founded in 1882). In a way, the widespread obsession with proving or disproving the reality of spiritualist feats and related phenomena such as telepathy and *clairvoyance* prevented the ghost's figurative potential from fully emancipating itself.

Although the inclination to take the ghost literally largely abated over the course of the twentieth century, turning believing in actual ghosts (as the dead returned to life or able to communicate with the living) into something of a fringe eccentricity, its lingering association with such notions seems to have rendered the ghostly somewhat toxic for scholars seeking to be taken seriously. A case in point is Freud's famous 1919 elaboration of the *unheimlich* or uncanny, which meticulously seeks to avoid this concept's contamination with anything potentially supernatural. While admitting that "spirits and ghosts" would have been a suitable and logical starting point—"We might indeed have begun our investigation with this example, perhaps the most striking of all, of something uncanny"—Freud notes how he decided against this in order to avoid intermixing the uncanny with "what is purely gruesome."[6] Ostensibly, then, ghosts and spirits are deferred because of their lack of ambiguity and singular frightfulness, a rather strange position to take given the variety of shapes and affective reactions these figures could be seen to take on and elicit in the literature, other arts, and society of the time (as, for example, the welcomed, often comforting ghosts of spiritualism). From the remainder of Freud's text, we might surmise that what he finds truly "gruesome" is the fact that too many people remain susceptible to the backward attitude of considering ghosts a possible actuality. While this lingering susceptibility is not considered surprising, it is marked as something that ought, in time, to pass:

> In our great cities, placards announce lectures that undertake to tell us how to get into touch with the souls of the departed; and it cannot be denied that not a few of the most able and penetrating minds among our

men of science have come to the conclusion, especially towards the close of their own lives, that a contact of this kind is not impossible. Since almost all of us still think as savages do on this topic, it is no matter for surprise that the primitive fear of the dead is still so strong within us and always ready to come to the surface on any provocation.[7]

Here, the universal inability to grasp the idea of one's own mortality is—in what could be seen as a redoubled disavowal—displaced onto an equally repressed "primitive fear *of the dead*" that locates the demise outside the self in the other and explains why ghosts can only ever be threatening. Paradoxically, where repression is usually presented by Freud as withholding something important that ought to be accessed and worked through, the rejection of the belief "that the dead can become visible as spirits" is considered a commendable sign of having outgrown savage animism and primary narcissism. In this case, the content of the repressed is identified as a risible falsehood, the definitive dismissal of which is only being prevented, for the moment, by biology—which "has not yet been able to decide whether death is the inevitable fate of every living being or whether it is only a regular but yet perhaps avoidable event in life"—and by religion and government, which benefit from keeping intact the expectation of an afterlife.[8] Once rationality prevails and animistic beliefs are overcome by all, the uncanny associated with the resurfacing of animistic beliefs— clearly considered inferior to that proceeding from "repressed infantile complexes, from the castration complex, womb-phantasies, etc." and involving "an actual repression of some content of thought and a return of this repressed content, not a cessation of *belief in the reality* of such a content"—will happily be surrendered.[9]

Freud illustrates the uncanny feeling that arises "when something that we have hitherto regarded as imaginary appears before us in reality" with a story about a young married couple staying in a house with a table, the carvings on which come alive at night as "ghostly crocodiles." This particular instance of the uncanny is associated with an "infantile element" consisting of "the over-accentuation of psychical reality in comparison with material reality," while the story itself, which Freud apparently found in *Strand Magazine*, is called "naïve enough," yet capable of producing a "quite remarkable" sense of the uncanny.[10] Here, the susceptibility to the uncanny is explicitly related to *not* believing in the actuality of the ghostly events, for if they were acknowledged as real, there would be no repression (no element of really knowing better than to believe in ghosts) and consequently no uncanny effect. Only someone who has at least partially superseded what are seen as primitive or childish notions, then, has access to the uncanny, making it, as Brian McCuskey notes, "a mark of superior education" serving, in particular, to distinguish superstitious servants from their sophisticated masters: "it ... goes without saying—and Freud does not—that a superstitious person, whose mind readily accommodates occult phenomena, will not experience the frisson of the uncanny, feeling instead only fatalism or fear."[11] In the end, for Freud's theory to be accepted as rational and properly scientific, it has to dissociate itself thoroughly not only from literal ghosts (by grudgingly allowing a lingering belief in them, already tempered by rationality and destined to disappear), but equally from the ghost as metaphor—hence Freud's regret that the German "an *unheimlich* house" cannot be translated otherwise, in English, than as "a haunted house."[12] Lest the serious aesthetic study of the uncanny raise the crude specter of actual ghosts and the associated animistic worldview, it cannot in any way be linked with them.

From a different vantage point, but in a similar vein, Theodor Adorno rejects the ghostly in his "Theses against Occultism," where occultism is declared "a symptom of a regression in consciousness" leading to an illicit mixing of the conditional and the unconditional.[13] For Freud, too, the uncanny has to be exorcised—cleansed of ghosts—precisely because, to maintain its status as a normal, even privileged experience, it cannot, at least not exclusively, be associated with the (non-repressed) primitive "animistic conception of the universe."[14] For Adorno, it is indeed such a "reborn animalism" that, in a sweep of "panic," undoes the gains of enlightenment and establishes, in the wake of the death of God, a "second mythology."[15] In pre-capitalist society, he states, occultism may have had a valid function in explaining the unfathomable elements of nature by assigning them an anthropomorphic subjectivity; now, however, it has become merely another way to conceal the alienation produced by the subject's reification in capitalist production:

> The occultist draws the ultimate conclusion from the fetish-character of commodities: menacingly objectified labour assails him on all sides from demonically grimacing objects. What has been forgotten in a world congealed into products, the fact that it has been produced by men, is split off and misremembered as a being-in-itself added to that of the objects and equivalent to them. Because objects have frozen in the cold light of reason, lost their illusory animation, the social quality that now animates them is given an independent existence both natural and super-natural, a thing among things.[16]

Rather than remembering, in good Marxist fashion, that the laborer is the one who produces the object and its (added) value, the occultist takes the object for an autonomous agent, enhancing its status as a fetish while seeking to deny it. Historical processes and the fact that it is people who oppress people are obfuscated, Adorno suggests, by fortune-tellers, psychic researchers, and "astrological hocus-pocus," all working to transfer agency and responsibility to an external, ungraspable, non-material force.[17]

Adorno's rather hyperbolic rant against occult practices that were, by the time of writing in the 1940s, already rather marginal, but which are nevertheless likened to Fascism and seen to wield a totalitarian power, leaves little room for understanding the reasons why people invest themselves in these beliefs. He goes as far as to dismiss the fear of death he, like Freud, recognizes might underlie "the woeful idiocy they practice" as itself "crass."[18] The elided material diagnosis of the collective catastrophe society is heading towards is seen to invalidate any personal longing for hope or comfort as a childish indulgence, generating more than a whiff of the same elitism pervading Freud's discussion of the uncanny. If mediums convey "nothing more significant than the dead grandmother's greetings and the prophecy of an imminent journey," this can have no possible value for Adorno.[19] It merely marks those who take them seriously as "dunces," who, instead of challenging the way capitalism deprives their existence of worth, revel in its "everyday dreariness."[20]

While the occult is condemned for mixing the conditional and unconditional, Adorno praises the traditional religions for stressing the "inseparability of the spiritual and the physical": soul and body should not be thought apart from each other, as the supposed freedom of the soul (or mind) serves merely to conceal the unfreedom of the laboring body.[21] Only by thinking the spiritual as part of the physical, subsumed under it, does it become amenable to materialist critique. As in Freud, then, it is not just the supposed existence of actual ghosts that Adorno derides, but also the figurative use of spirit, from which the dangerous belief in the autonomous material reality of the ghost and the soul alike is seen to originate: "The doctrine of the existence of the Spirit, the ultimate exaltation of bourgeois consciousness, ... bore teleologically within it the belief in spirits, its ultimate degradation."[22] The only possible conclusion, drawn in Adorno's final sentence, is that there must not be *any* ghost or spirit, actual *or* metaphorical: "No spirit exists."[23]

How can the change from this reluctance to appeal to the figure of the ghost to Derrida's—and others'—wholehearted embrace of it at the end of the twentieth century be explained? What is striking in this respect is that Derrida's rehabilitation of the ghostly takes inspiration from precisely the two systems of thought represented by Freud and Adorno: psychoanalysis and Marxism. The latter, as is well known, provides the main impetus for *Specters of Marx*, which endeavors to conjure not only the multiple legacies of Marx's thought in the present—its haunting survival beyond the fall of the Berlin Wall and Francis Fukuyama's proclamation of the "end of history"—but also Marx's own alleged obsession with getting rid of ghosts. Following this line of thought, Adorno's dismissal of the occult as *occultus*, as concealing the secret that is the real condition of the material world, can be seen to restage Marx's ghostbusting stance, which, according to Derrida, is similarly aimed at making visible what is actually present:

Marx is very firm: when one has destroyed a phantomatic body, the real body remains. When the *ghostly* body (*die gespenstige Leibhaftigkeit*) of the emperor disappears, it is not the body that disappears, merely its phenomenality, its phantomality (*Gespensterhaftigkeit*). The emperor is then more real than ever and one can measure better than ever his actual power (*wirkliche Macht*).[24]

While Derrida's re-reading of Marx's work—especially his assertion that deconstruction "has remained faithful to a certain spirit of Marxism, to at least one of its spirits" and enables its "radicalization"[25]—can (and has been) critiqued,[26] his suggestion that rather than being expelled, the ghost should remain, be lived *with*, as a conceptual metaphor signaling the ultimate disjointedness of ontology, history, inheritance, materiality, and ideology, has been widely taken up. As related to "the deconstructive thinking of the trace, of iterability, of prosthetic synthesis, of supplementarity, and so forth," the ghost ceases to be seen as obscurantist and becomes, instead, a figure of clarification with a specifically ethical and political potential.[27]

The second, psychoanalytical locus of inspiration for Derrida's summoning of the spectral is found in the two forewords he wrote in the 1970s to Nicolas Abraham and Maria Torok's *The Wolf Man's Magic Word: A Cryptonymy* and Abraham's "The Shell and the Kernel," respectively entitled "Fors" and "Me-Psychoanalysis."[28] What attracts him in the work of these Hungarian-born psychoanalysts is their untying of sense from that which is present or presentable: besides the visible shell, the kernel, as that which is "inaccessible" and marked "with absolute non-presence," also becomes a carrier of meaning.[29] Moreover, the meanings contained in the kernel-like psychic formations of the crypt (an incorporated traumatic secret or loss of the self) and the phantom (an incorporated traumatic secret or loss of the other) are heterogeneous and consequently not amenable to systematic, instantaneous decoding; instead, they require multiple, laborious, and creative processes of translation or "analytico-poetic transcription."[30] It is easy to see how these ideas chime with Derrida's elaboration of, for instance, *différance*, even though, as Colin Davis explains in the article reprinted in this *Reader*, within Abraham and Torok's clinical orientation the process of deferred meaning is supposed to come to an eventual standstill in the curative moment. While no explicit mention of spectrality is made by Derrida in either foreword, the stated appreciation of the radically non-present(ational) figure of "the heterocryptic ghost that *returns* from the unconscious *of* the other, according to what might be called the law of *another generation*"[31] strongly foreshadows *Specters of Marx*'s discussion of the specter as a figuration of presence-absence, the negotiation of which compels a "*politics* of memory, of inheritance, and of generations."[32]

Abraham himself, in "Notes on the Phantom: A Complement to Freud's Metapsychology," does not hesitate to employ ghosts metaphorically, confident as he is of their ultimate unreality: "It is a fact that the 'phantom,' whatever its form, is nothing but an invention of the living."[33] Although the need to state this explicitly and his choice to place the term "phantom" – the synonym for ghost most intimately associated with the illusionary – between quotation marks may indicate an element of caution, the psychic formation it describes is unabashedly said to haunt. In fact, embodied ghosts are seen to derive from a more fundamental psychic figuration: "The phantoms of folklore merely objectify a metaphor active within the unconscious: the burial of an unspeakable fact *within the loved one*."[34] This resembles Adorno's insistence that *Geist* (spirit) becomes ghost, only here it leads to the positive conclusion that looking at objectified ghosts and their antics can elucidate the workings of the mind: "Here we are in the midst of clinical psychoanalysis and still shrouded in obscurity, an obscurity, however, that the nocturnal being of phantoms (if only in the metapsychological sense) can, paradoxically, be called upon to clarify."[35] What ensues is a consideration of intergenerational trauma as a haunting force, where the notion of haunting, as site of comparison, clarifies both the temporal and spatial aspects of the affliction, while its resolution is described as the phantom being "successfully exorcised."[36]

Yet another early engagement on Derrida's part with the ghost is found in *Of Spirit: Heidegger and the Question* from 1987. In contrast to Adorno's indictment of the metaphorical use of Spirit as generating its embodied counterparts—he calls occultism "the *enfant terrible* of the mystical moment in Hegel"[37]—Derrida insists that the two cannot be fully separated (which, incidentally, does not amount to their equation). Heidegger's vacillating between refusing spirit as anti-ontological and appealing to it as a non-religious form of spirituality that founds the world, without being able to keep the different meanings of *Geist* from infecting each other, is described through recourse to the vocabulary of the ghost and haunting:

> *Geist* is always haunted by its *Geist*: a spirit, or in other words, in French [and English] as in German, a phantom, always surprises by returning to be the other's ventriloquist. Metaphysics always returns, I mean in the sense of a *revenant* [ghost], and *Geist* is the most fatal figure of this *revenance* [returning, haunting]. Of the double who can never be separated from the single.[38]

The spirit, in its lexical link to the ghost, exhibits a "spectral duplicity," a self-haunting that "allows neither analysis nor dissolution into the simplicity of a perception."[39] Not only can the metaphorical and the literal sense of *Geist* not be kept apart, the metaphysical ghost and its penchant for haunting now becomes the basis for the concept of this inseparability, for the single that is always already double, the "*origin-heterogeneous*" [*hétérogène à l'origine*]."[40] The latter will, in *Specters of Marx*, where the ghost completes its transition from potential actuality to ordinary metaphor to conceptual metaphor, re-emerge as the "*more than one/no more one* [*le plus d'un*]" of hauntology.[41]

For Derrida, as Fredric Jameson notes, "spectrality does not involve the conviction that ghosts exist."[42] In its capacity as a figuration that *does* theory, it critiques precisely what both Adorno, in his quest for the material, and Freud, in his desire to unambiguously define the ambiguity of the uncanny, seek to preserve: "the 'unmixed': what is somehow pure and self-sufficient or autonomous, what is able to be disengaged from the general mess of mixed, hybrid phenomena all around it and named with the satisfaction of a single conceptual proper name."[43] Thus, even though he uses the literal ghost of Hamlet's father as a paradigmatic example and inveighs traditional scholars for not believing in ghosts, when Derrida proposes the possibility of "another 'scholar'" open to spectrality, this is not someone who trusts in the return of the dead; rather, it is someone "capable, beyond the opposition between presence and non-presence, actuality and inactuality, life and non-life, of thinking the possibility of the specter, the specter as possibility."[44] To believe or not believe in ghosts no longer involves a determination about the empirical (im)possibility of the supernatural, but indicates contrasting validated attitudes—a welcoming seen as ethical and enabling, and a rejection considered unethical and dispossessing—towards the uncertainty, heterogeneity, multiplicity, and indeterminacy that characterize language and Being because of their inevitable entanglement with alterity and difference. Derrida, then, far from being a ghostbuster like Freud, Adorno, and Abraham and Torok, uses the figure of the ghost to pursue (without ever fully apprehending) that which haunts *like a ghost* and, by way of this haunting, demands justice, or at least a response.

This quest cannot be called a science, or even a method, as the ghost or specter is seen to signify precisely that which escapes full cognition or comprehension: "One does not know: not out of ignorance, but because this non-object, this non-present present, this being-there of an absent or departed one no longer belongs to knowledge."[45] Hence our pluralization of "spectralities" in the title of this *Reader* and our hesitancy in presenting the spectral investigations gathered here as a new field or discipline (both of which imply delineation and control). The ghost, even when turned into a conceptual metaphor, remains a figure of unruliness pointing to the tangibly ambiguous. While it has insight to offer, especially into those matters that are commonly considered not to matter and into the ambiguous itself, its own status as discourse or epistemology is never stable, as the ghost also questions the formation of knowledge itself and specifically invokes what is placed outside it, excluded from perception and, consequently, from both the archive as the depository of the sanctioned, acknowledged past and politics as the (re)imagined present and future.

Although *Specters of Marx* is often seen to stand at the origin of the so-called "spectral turn" (a turn of phrase whose aptness and risks are at stake in the first part of this *Reader*), it would go against the spirit of the specter—and Derrida's elaboration of it—to assign a unitary genesis to what was in fact a diffuse, extended cultural moment. We have already seen that Derrida's ideas can be traced back to at least the 1970s and are predicated on the work of others.[46] In addition, his elaboration of spectrality coincided with further conceptual investigations of ghosts and haunting that opened up different avenues of inquiry. One example is Terry Castle's *The Apparitional Lesbian* (1993), which, by exploring the pervasive cultural disavowal of lesbianism through acts of "ghosting" (rendering lesbian sexuality invisible by associating it with the ephemeral) and thus emphasizing the ghost's association with dispossession, disappearance, and social erasure, provides an important counterweight to Derrida's emphasis on the specter as a powerful haunting force.[47] Another early conceptual exploration of the ghostly is found in Anthony Vidler's *The Architectural Uncanny* (1992), from which a section is included here. By way of an architectural consideration of notions of house and home, Vidler brings the uncanny (presented as a metaphor or trope that exceeds its Freudian elaboration) together with the ghost to suggest that "the uncanny might regain a political connotation as the very condition of contemporary haunting."[48] The specific architectural projects analyzed, which explore the possibility of making absence present through materializations of invisibility, translucency, and transparency, concretize what Derrida would call the "non-sensuous sensuous."[49] Moreover, Vidler's attention for the spatial dimension of haunting—its association with displacement and the out-of-place—marks a different path from *Specters of Marx*'s focus on the ghost's temporality, its tendency to put time out of joint.

The renewed conceptual interest in ghosts and haunting that characterized the 1990s has also been linked to a broader (and somewhat earlier) turn to history and memory, concentrating in particular on dealing with personal and collective trauma. Jeffrey Andrew Weinstock, for instance, connects "spectral discourse" with "the recent preoccupation with 'trauma' in which the presence of a symptom demonstrates the subject's failure to internalize a past event, in which something from the past emerges to disrupt the present."[50] The next section explores how certain elaborations of spectrality do indeed dovetail with the concerns of trauma studies, while at the same time insisting that, as a cross-disciplinary concept used to tackle a wide variety of phenomena, it goes beyond them.

Spectrality and trauma studies

Already in his *Cultural Semantics* from 1998, Martin Jay was speaking out about the "uncanny nineties," a particular *Zeitgeist* that described the "current obsession with the troubled interface between history and memory" and the concern with "the way the past makes cultural demands on us we have difficulty fulfilling."[51] In this academic milieu of saturated ghostliness, Jay perceived a problem in the collapsing of "the metaphoric and the real, the symbolic and the literal," claiming that it was "now the height of canniness to market the uncanny."[52] The disdain for any lingering belief in actual returnees from the dead or other supernatural entities that led Freud and Adorno to shy away from even metaphorical uses had apparently reversed into an uncritical and undifferentiated acceptance of any and all figurative ghosts. This pervasive haunting of the academy, according to Jay, had echoes in the "recent debates over alleged repressed memory" that were occupying scholars in the field of psychology.[53] As Abraham and Torok's notion of the phantom (as unconsciously inherited loss or secret) already indicated, the conceptual metaphor of spectrality is deeply embedded within the discourse of loss, mourning, and recovery that delineated the multidisciplinary project of trauma studies as it emerged in the 1980s. To be traumatized, as Cathy Caruth has explained, is to be "possessed by an image or event" located in the past.[54] To be "possessed"—gripped indefinitely by an anachronistic event—also describes the condition of being haunted, as it has been commonly construed. In other words, when we think of ghost stories (traditional ones, at least), it is the haunting of the present by the past that emerges as the most insistent narrative. The mode of expression that many scholars use to describe the spectral, then, is similar to, if not fully consonant with, the terms used to describe the affective qualities of trauma. Take, for instance, Ulrich Baer's chapter from *Spectral Evidence* reprinted here, in which he discusses Mikael Levin's and Dirk Reinartz's strikingly analogous photographs of contemporary landscapes growing in the areas where Nazi concentration camps use to stand. These are places that "[have] not been fully mastered and contained," characterized by their "enigmatic structure," and which confront us with the limits of historicization.[55] Baer addresses these photographs as traumatic and ghostly, given that, as spectators, we have arrived late at the scene of a "retained past" that nevertheless reminds us of its absence in our present.[56]

As Roger Luckhurst has outlined in *The Trauma Question*, the history of this disorder can be traced back to its physical origins in the 1600s, to the rise of psychology in the Victorian period, and, later, its reemergence at the end of the 1970s with the coinage of the term "post-traumatic stress disorder" (PTSD)—a diagnosis used for Vietnam veterans suffering from hallucinations, shell shock, and other forms of post-combat stress.[57]

Critics within trauma studies have expanded on this paradigm to address catastrophic personal and collective experiences, and the acts of witnessing and testimony related to them. Ranging from colonial violence and the genocides that transpired, for example, during the Holocaust and in Rwanda during the early 1990s, to the events of 9/11, these experiences are seen as eliding and literally rupturing comprehension; they are past acts which we would like to access again in order to attempt changing them, and which the traumatized often relive compulsively, but that remain locked in their inaccessibility and relentless repetition.

Scholars like Caruth have come to understand post-traumatic duress as not simply a "symptom of the unconscious," but "a symptom of history" as well.[58] Here we can see how the condition of the traumatized individual is catapulted into the larger, multi-subjective experience of a global culture in which the avant-garde dream of the revolutionary new is being replaced with, following Dominick LaCapra, the "memory-work" of studies of the past conducted in earnest during the final decades of the last century and the beginning of the twenty-first.[59] Thus, Caruth describes traumatized individuals as historical subjects, in the sense that, much like Abraham and Torok's phantom-laden patients, they "carry an impossible history within them or they become themselves the symptom of a history that they cannot entirely possess."[60] Trauma, as Caruth describes it, is forever engaged in the quest for an answer, an evanescent truth. Such is the case with ghosts that arrive from the past, seeking to establish an ethical dialogue with the present. Ghosts, in this case, are part of a symptomatology of trauma, as they become both the objects of and metaphors for a wounded historical experience.

Within the growing fields of memory and trauma studies, different and divergent arguments have emerged, especially with respect to the palliative possibilities of memory-work (which tends to envision a conjuration of the past's truth, primarily through giving a voice to its victims, which is subsequently laid to rest as traumatic repetition is foreclosed and the memory integrated into a narrative account[61]). As Richard Crownshaw has recently pointed out, the reliance of certain branches of trauma studies on "individual psychological and psychoanalytic definitions of experience" may drive the field into an "overpersonalisation" and, subsequently, "dehistoricis[ation]" of collective experience.[62] One of trauma studies' most outspoken critics has been Andreas Huyssen. In "Present Pasts: Media, Politics, Amnesia," he speaks of a "globalization paradox" of traumatic events like the Holocaust, whereby this event has become an absolute "cipher for the twentieth century as a whole."[63] What Huyssen describes here is a singular model of trauma (and its potential resolution) that is subsequently applied to other situations that, while perhaps similar in some ways, are nevertheless historically, culturally, and politically removed from the experiences of the Jews under Nazism. This "totalization" risks erasing the Holocaust's specificity, as well as locking other experiences of catastrophe and loss within a distant, now universalized and universalizing, model. Instead, Huyssen argues for a conception of remembrance in which memory and trauma are not treated as synonymous:

> It has been all too tempting to some to think of trauma as the hidden core of all memory. After all, both memory and trauma are predicated on the absence of that which is negotiated in memory or in the traumatic symptom. Both are marked by instability, transitoriness, and structures of repetition. But to collapse memory into trauma ... would unduly confine our understanding of memory, marking it too exclusively in terms of pain, suffering, and loss.[64]

The danger in marking all remembering with the affective registers of melancholia is that we may come to understand memory as working solely on the basis of repetition and negativity, rather than on its progressive (future) productivity. Here, we may remember Freud's equally singular association of the ghost with the gruesome and begin to be reminded of the innovation inherent in Derrida's conceptualization of the specter—which is always both *revenant* (invoking what was) and *arrivant* (announcing what will come)—as operating on a number of temporal planes, most crucially the future and its possible interactions with the present and the past. Derrida's specter not only "signals the unbidden imposition of parts of the past on the present, and the way in which the future is always already populated with certain possibilities derived from the past," but also, through its association with the messianic, or, less enigmatically, with Gayatri Spivak's ghost dance as future anterior, the potential for different re-articulations of these possibilities.[65] Unlike traumatic repetition, after all, the ghost is a figure of surprise that does not necessarily reappear in exactly the same manner or guise. Moreover, it provokes the one it haunts to a response or reaction, leading Avery F. Gordon to note that "haunting, unlike trauma, is distinctive for producing a something-to-be-done."[66]

Analyzing the problems of contemporary historiography, LaCapra seeks a way out of trauma discourse's melancholic conundrum by separating loss from absence. In its persistent reference to the missing object, loss can transform into nostalgia or, worse, a "utopian politics in quest of a new totality or fully unified community" when it is conflated with a conception of absence.[67] Put simply, absence that is interiorized as loss entails a process of incessant mourning and melancholia, as well as an overlaying of the planes of the then with those of the now. Absence describes something related, but quite different, to loss: we can understand it as transhistorical (structural) trauma, according to LaCapra, while loss must retain its historical specificity. As he explains:

Something of the past always remains, if only as a haunting presence or revenant. Moreover, losses are specific and involve particular events, such as the death of loved ones on a personal level or, on a broader scale, the losses brought about by apartheid or by the Holocaust in its effects on Jews and other victims of the Nazi genocide, including both the lives and cultures of affected groups. I think it is misleading to situate loss on a transhistorical level, something that happens when it is conflated with absence and conceived as constitutive of existence.[68]

In an argument that resonates with Huyssen's critique of the trauma paradigm, LaCapra argues for an understanding of trauma as grounded in the specific event, and the experiences that surround it.

LaCapra's prescription to work through the dialectics of absence and loss, and thus to produce "a condition of possibility of historicity,"[69] in many ways echoes Derrida's injunction to learn to "live otherwise, and better" by learning "to live *with* ghosts," and the latter's insistence that a history conceived as spectral would necessitate a reflection of how the past is both absent and present within the now moment, but also how the past can open up the possibilities for the future.[70] However, at the same time, Derrida could be said to be guilty of a similar dehistoricizing conflation to that between loss and absence. Hauntology, as a disjointed, non-foundational alternative ontology, rivals LaCapra's notion of absence in its tendency towards universality and transhistoricism, as becomes clear when Derrida states that "it is necessary to introduce haunting into the very construction of a concept. Of every concept, beginning with the concepts of being and time."[71] Undoubtedly, such a generalized notion of haunting has its uses, as does the idea of structural trauma. A distinction, however, must be maintained between the ghost as "only one in a series of deconstructive tropes," a meta-concept that comes to possess virtually everything, and its more specific conceptualizations, where ghosts and haunting are taken up as historically and culturally particular, and where they may even be re-supernaturalized.[72]

For Derrida, hauntology reshapes history by disrupting its conventional structure of chronology: "haunting is historical, to be sure, but it is not *dated*, it is never docilely given a date in the chain of presents, day after day, according to the instituted order of a calendar."[73] This may serve to counter the historical overdetermination (the search for truth in a fixed point of origin) that characterizes certain incarnations of trauma studies, but it also causes the specters he conjures to remain strangely unmoored from historical contexts, as all ghosts, by being reduced to their most general characteristics, become essentially the same (as do all exorcists). Ghosts, then, are not only apt embodiments and figurations of trauma, but trauma theory also provides valuable lessons as it responds to and takes on board critiques equally applicable to certain elaborations of spectrality. As the texts collected in this *Reader* show, a large part of the effort in the wake of *Specters of Marx* has been to specify the ghost's conceptual potential in relation to history and memory by pointing out, for example, that historical events or memories, even when ostensibly similar in kind, may give rise to vastly different hauntings, and that even the same event may not return in identical ways across time. All history and memory may indeed be spectral in some sense, but understanding the effects of particular instances requires careful contextualization and conceptual delimitation.

Having sketched the contact zone between trauma studies and theories of spectrality, it is important to avoid the impression that the ghost as conceptual metaphor is limited to elucidating issues of memory and history (whether traumatic or not); while these are important—perhaps even dominant—areas of investigation, spectrality has proven useful in addressing many other issues, to the point of seeming ubiquitous. While the extent of its scholarly reach will be outlined at the end of this introduction, the penultimate section explores the familiar danger of a newly popular academic concept turning into a bandwagon.

Stretching the ghost

The multidisciplinary applicability of trauma scholarship, and spectrality studies more broadly, means that terms developed within one field of study are employed in others. This transferability, while opening up interdisciplinary opportunities, may also result in rather cyclical, if not overstretched, interpretations of the uses, meanings, and possibilities of haunting. Recently, Roger Luckhurst has noted that "the ghost as figure of trauma has become almost a cliché, reinforced as it was throughout the 1990s by an elaborate critical discourse of spectres and 'spectrality.'"[74] Already in his critique of "the spectral turn" from 2002 (excerpted in this volume), he describes a body of London-based works of fiction, non-fiction, and criticism that he terms "the London Gothic" (marking another important intersection for spectral studies) in the following terms:

> Unable to discriminate between instances and largely uninterested in historicity (beyond its ghostly disruption), the discourse of spectralized modernity risks investing in the compulsive repetitions of a structure of melancholic entrapment. In this mode, to suggest an inevitably historicized mourning-work that might actually seek to lay a ghost to rest would be the height of bad manners. And because the spectral infiltrates the hermeneutic act itself, critical work can only replicate tropes from textual sources, punning spiritedly around the central terms of the Gothic to produce a curious form of meta-Gothic that elides object and instrument.[75]

If narrative language and the language of trauma are intimate bedfellows, given that both can play and experiment on the idea of overcoming the aporias left behind by the past, then it should be no wonder that the tropes of literary texts should find a home in the body of criticism that accompanies it. What Luckhurst describes in the passage above, however, does go to the heart of the evolution of the field of spectrality studies. This area of scholarly focus is often considered as a response, and antidote, to our alleged age of amnesia, and its emphasis on the duty to remember and acknowledge the past (to keep ghosts alive) can indeed seem overly judgmental of processes of closure and forgetting. Yet at the same time, living *with* ghosts does not have to entail "melancholic entrapment," since the spectral return, as noted earlier, is capable of exceeding pure replication. Conversant with nostalgia studies, yet another current within contemporary cultural theory,[76] studies of ghosts and haunting can do more than obsessively recall a fixed past; in an active, dynamic engagement, they may reveal the insufficiency of the present moment, as well as the disconsolations and erasures of the past, and a tentative hopefulness for future resolutions.

Still, despite the presence of a discourse that, generalizing the haunted experience, may resonate with and speak to other disciplines, histories, and languages, the problem of the ghost's specificity and its localized futurities continues to gnaw at the very idea of the absent present. As we read through the ever-growing pile of works on haunting and observe the continuing manifestation of ghosts in popular culture and the aesthetics and politics of the everyday, we must ask whether the trope of haunting and spectrality has reached its apotheosis, or (more optimistically) whether there are new ways in which we can continue to grow the field without rehearsing the registers we have been relying on for the past decades. The very appearance of this *Reader* signals our belief that scholarly work on spectrality has achieved a critical mass, making anthologization not only possible, but useful. This volume, however, was not undertaken in the mode of the traditional archive; we do not aim to definitively define or delimit a field, but rather to display the diverse fertility of the ghost and haunting as conceptual metaphors over a particular period, in the hope of revealing some influential trajectories and prompting future innovations (through inclusion *and* omission; after all, as Derrida argues in *Archive Fever*, archives are inevitably haunted by what they exclude).[77] Some effort of discrimination is inevitable, though, as we have reached an important (and perhaps slightly *unheimlich*) moment of self-inspection about our fascination with our condition as recovering amnesiacs and investigators of the spectral. Besides asking after the opportunities the spectral offers, this moment equally prompts us to gauge its limitations.

The 2010 *Haunted: Contemporary Photography / Video / Performance* exhibition at the Solomon R. Guggenheim Museum in New York struck us as coming up against the point where a concept threatens to break as it is stretched too thin. Curators Jennifer Blessing and Nat Trotman channeled Roland Barthes's idea that the medium of photography (which they extend to video and performance), especially in our post-capitalist age, is essentially a haunted one. However, where Barthes carefully elaborates the metaphor and, crucially, distinguishes the moving image as non-spectral,[78] the blurb on the cover of the exhibition catalogue appears to turn any invocation of the past or tradition, and any form of reproduction, into a haunting: "Much contemporary photography and video seems haunted—by the history of art, and by the ghostly apparitions that are reanimated in reproductive mediums, live performance, and the virtual world." At the same time, it confines the meaning of haunting to melancholic nostalgia: "By using dated, passé, or quasi-extinct stylistic devices, subject matter, and technologies, such melancholic art embodies a longing for an otherwise unrecuperable past."[79] The tension between an overly general interpretation—not everything that returns or is repeated is necessarily ghostly or uncanny—and a restricted reading of ghosts as figures of documentation, preservation, and remembrance pervaded the exhibition, which, despite bringing together an impressive collection of works from the 1960s to the 2000s, refused to congeal around its titular concept. Works that seem to invoke haunting only through their medium,

Figure 1   Felix Gonzalez-Torres, "Untitled", 1989. © The Felix Gonzalez-Torres Foundation. Courtesy of Andrea Rosen Gallery, New York.

their representation of something from the past, or their use of repetition or dated technologies were mixed with works that evoke more concrete, complex senses of ghostliness, such as the Cuban-born American visual artist Felix Gonzalez-Torres's 1989 *"Untitled,"* a chromogenic jigsaw puzzle enveloped in plastic (Figure 1).

This image speaks to the ghost first of all thematically, in *what* it depicts: the rather shapeless backlit shadow figure, further deformed by the creases in the curtain, appears as an unidentifiable ghostly visitor able, as per Derrida's visor effect (the power to see without being seen), to peek through the curtain at us, while we are left to wonder at its motivations. Our propensity to interpret the image as disturbing invokes the relationship between ghosts and the gruesome (on which, as we saw, Freud insists), as well as their tendency to induce paranoia and self-doubt: are we seeing something that is not actually there? While the visitor could indeed be supernatural, the everydayness of the curtain and the fragment of the chair visible in the lower left-hand corner suggests that the socio-political relations of the material world may also produce a sense of haunting. Issues of vulnerability, invasiveness, and hospitality are hinted at, yet any unequivocal signification is foreclosed by the fact that we cannot establish whether the curtain constitutes a protective or exclusionary barrier, and whether the ghostly figure is inside or outside, a threat or the one at risk of exposure. As such, the image foregrounds the in-between or undecidable as something that may unsettle us but nevertheless cannot be banished from our lives. This idea is reinforced at the formal level, as the plastic bag interferes with our ability to see the image clearly, while its composition from puzzle pieces confronts us simultaneously with our desire for completeness and identification, and with the fact that these will never be fully achieved—the outlined edges of the pieces forever render the image interrupted, fragmented.

Gonzalez-Torres's artwork, then, counters the dilution and non-differentiation of the notion of haunting that the *Haunted* exhibition at large facilitated, and may also be taken to visualize our conception of this *Reader*, which, like the plastic bag, provides a tentative—by no means impenetrable—casing for a collection of texts that interconnect and are ordered, but could well be shuffled and rearranged. The puzzle pieces, in turn, convey our desire to stress the multiplicity and heterogeneity of recent conceptualizations of spectrality, which originate in different disciplines and approach ghosts and haunting from numerous angles in order to elucidate a variety of cultural objects, histories, and socio-political issues. This multiplicity, as the outline below explicates, includes considerations of ghosts and haunting at a general level (as something that, per Derrida's *hauntology*, is inherent to Being) and more specific ones, but insists, in both cases, on careful conceptual specification. Ghostliness, haunting, and spectrality are not just fashionable terms to be thrown about at random, but difficult-to-grasp phenomena that require precise delineation as they enter different contexts and scholarly frameworks.

Outline

In order to remain readable, a *Reader* requires some sort of grouping of its collected texts, and this volume is no exception. The groupings chosen—after a process of selection that inevitably entailed some regrettable losses—are not intended to impose a singular structure on the materials, but should be taken as flexible signposts offering one way of broaching an area of thought characterized by multiple intersections and convergences, and not yet fully crystallized (if any scholarly area, disciplinary or interdisciplinary, ever is). Each part—as well as the texts contained in them—will be introduced separately, so here we confine ourselves to indicating the general motivation for and import of the six chosen foci.

The first part, entitled "The Spectral Turn," presents a logical starting point in reflecting on the spread of spectrality as cross-disciplinary instrument of analysis in the humanities and social sciences between the early 1990s and the present, which constitutes the *raison d'être* for this volume. It gathers together texts by Jacques Derrida, Colin Davis, Jeffrey Andrew Weinstock, Julian Wolfreys, and Roger Luckhurst that were either instrumental in inaugurating the interest in the ghost or specter as conceptual metaphor and developing this interest across different academic fields, or engage with the risks of its newfound prominence and status as an academic trend.

"Spectropolitics: Ghosts of the Global Contemporary" focuses on those recent explorations of spectrality that emphasize how, if ghosts and haunting are to be employed as conceptual metaphors, two aspects need to be taken into account. First, there is the fact that these phenomena are culturally specific, with non-western traditions yielding considerably different epistemological frameworks and critical possibilities than the western conceptions that initially dominated the spectral turn. Second, it is vital to acknowledge that notions of spectrality may facilitate the understanding and addressing of not only historical injustices and their commemoration in personal and/or collective memory, but also of situations of injustice and disempowerment arising in and from a present characterized by diffuse processes of globalization. The texts by Avery F. Gordon, Achille Mbembe, Arjun Appadurai, and Peter Hitchcock that make up this part propose, each in its own way, a "spectropolitics"—which may be a politics *of* or *for* specters—designed to address how, in different parts of the world, particular subjects become prone to social erasure, marginalization, and precarity. By analyzing how such processes can be thought in terms of spectralization or "ghosting," and by imagining counter-conjurations that refuse straightforward notions of rematerialization or exorcism, these critics appeal to spectrality as an alternative to or reconceptualization of the frameworks of postmodernism, postcoloniality, materialism, nationalism, and globalization.

Another dominant concern in recent considerations of spectrality has been the way in which the workings and socio-cultural impact of various media (from the telegraph and the X-ray to cinema, television, radio, and the internet) and their associated senses (most importantly vision and hearing) can be illuminated by exploring how their invention, establishment, and global consolidation was—and to some extent remains—intimately linked with the circulation of practices and discourses of the supernatural. The historical depth and cultural breadth of this particularly fruitful area of spectral investigation is represented, in the third part, "The Ghost in the Machine: Spectral Media," by Tom Gunning, Jeffrey Sconce, Akira Mizuta Lippit, Allen S. Weiss, and David Toop.

Taking up the direction indicated by Terry Castle's *The Apparitional Lesbian*, a number of critics have been engaged in exploring the specific ramifications of spectrality for questions of gender, sexuality, and race. Not only can these categories of social differentiation be seen as themselves spectral, in the sense that they are based on retrospectively naturalized, performatively ingrained distinctions that require continuous rematerialization, but they also stratify spectrality, as those excluded from the norm are likely to have greater difficulty in effectively asserting themselves as haunting forces than, for example, the sovereign subject that is Hamlet's father. The attempt to refashion spectrality as a more differentiated concept—and as such more relevant to the specific past, present, and future struggles for recognition, respect, and justice of those identified as non-masculine, non-heterosexual, and/or non-white—is central to the fourth part of this *Reader* on "Spectral Subjectivities: Gender, Sexuality, and Race," which gathers work by Gayatri Chakravorty Spivak, Carla Freccero, Sharon Holland, and Renée L. Bergland.

The spatial dimension of the ghost—which, although central to Gothic studies, threatened to become overshadowed by the focus on temporality within Derrida's work as well as within memory and trauma studies— is addressed in the fifth part, entitled "Possessions: Spectral Spaces," where Anthony Vidler, Ulrich Baer, David Matless, and Giorgio Agamben demonstrate how haunting, as a conceptual metaphor, can elucidate the way architecture, landscape, geography, and tourism mediate particular presences and absences, both material and in the less apprehensible form of dealing with traumatic or oppressive pasts.

The fifth part—in particular the texts by Baer and Agamben—already makes clear that any attempt to rigorously separate the spatial from the temporal dimension of spectrality is futile; ghosts and haunting invariably involve a complication of both realms, as well as of their interaction.

Therefore, the sixth and final part, "Haunted Historiographies," should be seen not as a counterpoint to the fifth, but as its continuation, just as it has strong links with the differentiated histories—and their haunting legacies—of particular subjects as delineated in the fourth one. Where the final part places its own emphasis, however, is in its focus not so much on specific histories as on the notion of historiography—the *making* of history and the way this process becomes entangled, as explicated by Judith Richardson, Jesse Alemán, and Alexander Nemerov, with notions of possession, the gothic and uncanny, and of the fine line that separates presence from absence, evidence from the barely perceptible.

Together, the six parts show the fecundity of the post-1990 use of the ghost as no longer primarily a literal phenomenon requiring empirical verification (although some do remain interested in this possibility, as is clear from the fact that the Society for Psychical Research survives until today[80]), but a conceptual metaphor capable of bringing to light and opening up to analysis hidden, disavowed, and neglected aspects of the social and cultural realm, past and present. As such, spectrality seeks less to take the place of other approaches or concepts than to supplement them with another dimension (a twilight zone, if you will) by offering a new, truly *other* perspective.

Notes

1   Jacques Derrida, *Specters of Marx: The State of the Debt, the Work of Mourning, & the New International*, trans. Peggy Kamuf (1993; New York and London: Routledge, 1994), 127.

2   Mieke Bal, "Exhibition Practices," *PMLA* 125, no. 1 (2010): 10.

3   Catherine Lord, "Set Adrift in Style: The Scholar as Fiction and Film-Maker in Jacob's Room," in *In(ter)discipline: New Languages for Criticism*, ed. Gillian Beer, Malcolm Bowie, and Beate Perrey (London: LEGENDA, 2007), 92. Teri Reynolds, whose work on cognitive metaphors Bal references, employs concepts from one field (physics) to elucidate another (narrative), stipulating that "these theories are not templates that constrain texts to correspond to the physics. Far from merely illustrating what is already known, they shape and articulate new critical possibilities." The "new critical possibilities" uncovered by spectrality as a cognitive or conceptual metaphor are what *The Spectralities Reader* seeks to present. Teri Reynolds, "Spacetime and Imagetext," *The Germanic Review* 73, no. 2 (2001): 161.

4   The *Oxford English Dictionary* confines the use of "spectre" and "spectrality" for matters related to ghostly apparitions to the (late) nineteenth century, with scientific uses based on its link to "spectrum"—in biology, chemistry, mathematics, and physics—extending to the present. A cursory search on *Google Scholar* confirms that spectrality's recent popularity in

the humanities and social sciences has barely dented the dominance of its deployment in the natural sciences.

5   For in-depth discussions of the late nineteenth- and early twentieth-century culture of ghosts and its legacies, see Janet Oppenheim, *The Other World: Spiritualism and Psychical Research in England, 1850–1914* (Cambridge: Cambridge University Press, 1985); Roger Luckhurst, *The Invention of Telepathy: 1870–1901* (Oxford: Oxford University Press, 2002); Pam Thurschwell, *Literature, Technology and Magical Thinking, 1880–1920* (Cambridge: Cambridge University Press, 2001); Marina Warner, *Phantasmagoria: Spirit Visions, Metaphors, and Media into the Twenty-First Century* (Oxford: Oxford University Press, 2006).

6   Sigmund Freud, "The Uncanny," in *Writings on Art and Literature* (Stanford: Stanford University Press, 1997), 218.

7   Ibid., 219.

8   Ibid., 218. Significantly, Freud devotes a large part of *Beyond the Pleasure Principle* (London: W. W. Norton, 1989) to establishing, by reference to biological experiments with single-cell organisms, precisely that death is "the inevitable fate of every living being." The dread this knowledge might evoke is assuaged by the proposition of the death drive, which makes death, as long as it occurs naturally, a (secretly) desirable end that, moreover, does not lead to another world but to a return to pre-birth inertia. In this manner, literal ghosts (those returned from the dead) are rendered not only impossible, but placed beyond human desire and impulse.

9   Freud, "Uncanny," 225, italics in the original. Our reading of Freud differs from that of Renée L. Bergland, who argues that "the long bizarre catalogue of the weird that he presents to his readers in 'The Uncanny' betrays a willingness more to entertain ghosts and horrors than to exorcize them." This ignores the divergent valuations Freud gives to the repressed and the surmounted. See Bergland, *The National Uncanny: Indian Ghosts and American Subjects* (Hanover, NH: University Press of New England, 2000), 12.

10   Freud, "Uncanny," 221.

11   Brian McCuskey, "Not at Home: Servants, Scholars, and the Uncanny," *PMLA* 121, no. 2 (2006): 429, 428.

12   Freud, "Uncanny," 218.

13   Theodor Adorno, "Theses against Occultism," in *Minima Moralia: Reflections from Damaged Life*, trans. E. F. N. Jephcott (1951; London and New York: Verso, 2005), 238.

14   Freud, "Uncanny," 216.

15   Adorno, "Theses," 239.

16   Ibid.

17   Ibid., 241.

18   Ibid.

19   Ibid.

20 Ibid., 242.

21 Ibid.

22 Ibid., 244. Adorno also notes how, in occultist thought, "only in the metaphor of the body can the concept of pure spirit be grasped at all, and is at the same time cancelled" (242). The spirit (here referring to the soul) should not be figuratively turned *into* a body, but has to stay located *within* the actual body as a bodily aspect, since any metaphorization indicates a departure from the material. Unlike Freud, then, Adorno might be considered hostile to metaphor in general as itself a spectralizing practice akin to the capitalist system that makes everything solid melt into air.

23 Ibid. Avery Gordon argues that in *Dialectic of Enlightenment*, Horkheimer and Adorno work towards establishing a Theory of Ghosts that would enable a "more complex understanding of the generative structures and moving parts of historically embedded social formations in a way that avoids the twin pitfalls of subjectivism and positivism." *Ghostly Matters: Haunting and the Sociological Imagination* (1997; Minneapolis: University of Minnesota Press, 2008), 19. However, although Horkheimer and Adorno do indeed agitate against the "disturbed relationship to the dead" that leaves them "forgotten and embalmed"—paralleled by a rejection of personal history "as something irrational, superfluous, utterly obsolete"—their argument in favor of remembering the dead and (personal) history is graphically separated, in a section entitled "Postscript," from the main section, "The Theory of Ghosts." *Dialectics of Enlightenment: Philosophical Fragments*, trans. Edmund Jephcott (Stanford: Stanford University Press, 2002), 178–9. There, a "unity" with the dead is proposed as "the proper relationship" to them, but this unity is explicitly not one that admits of any literal ghosts, which are seen to sublimate our dread of "death as absolute nothingness" (178). Rather, it entails a recognition—beyond the ghostly—of the "horror of annihilation" that marks both the living and the dead as "victims of the same conditions and of the same disappointed hope" (178). Thus, the metaphorical use of the ghost—which returns in the "Postscript" only once (and with a noticeable shift in terminology) to figure emigrants as "spectral intruders"—remains predicated on the need to reject its literal invocation (179).

24 Derrida, *Specters*, 131.

25 Ibid., 75, 92.

26 See Michael Sprinker, ed., *Ghostly Demarcations: A Symposium on Jacques Derrida's Specters of Marx* (London and New York: Verso, 1999) for a number of early critiques of Derrida's interpretation of Marx and Marxism in *Specters of Marx* by, among others, Antonio Negri, Pierre Macherey, Terry Eagleton, and Aijaz Ahmad. The main objections concern Derrida's elision of issues of class and class struggle, the non-concreteness of his concept of the New International, and his elaboration of the messianic. A response by Derrida is included that also takes up Spivak's review of *Specters of Marx* in "Ghostwriting," *Diacritics* 25, no. 2 (1995): 64–84, excerpted here. For a refutation of the idea that Derrida's notion of spectrality falls short of political engagement, see Stella Gaon, "'Politicizing Deconstruction': On Not

Treating *Specters of Marx*," *Rethinking Marxism: A Journal of Economics, Culture & Society*, 11, no. 2 (1999): 38–48.

27 Derrida, *Specters*, 75.

28 Nicolas Abraham and Maria Torok, *The Wolf Man's Magic Word: A Cryptonymy*, trans. Nicholas Rand (1976; Minneapolis: University of Minnesota Press, 1986); Nicolas Abraham, "The Shell and the Kernel: The Scope and Originality of Freudian Psychoanalysis," in *The Shell and the Kernel. Renewals of Psychoanalysis, Volume 1*, trans. Nicholas Rand (1968; Chicago and London: The University of Chicago Press, 1994), 79–98; Jacques Derrida, "Me-Psychoanalysis: An Introduction to the Translation of 'The Shell and the Kernel' by Nicolas Abraham," trans. Richard Klein, *Diacritics* 9, no. 1 (1979): 3–12; Jacques Derrida, "Foreword: *Fors*: The Anglish Words of Nicolas Abraham and Maria Torok," trans. Barbara Johnson, in *The Wolf Man's Magic Word: A Cryptonymy*, Nicolas Abraham and Maria Torok (Minneapolis: University of Minnesota Press, 1986), xi–xlviii.

29 Derrida, "Me-Psychoanalysis," 10.

30 Derrida, "Foreword: *Fors*," xxxiii.

31 Ibid., xxxi, italics in the original.

32 Derrida, *Specters*, xix, italics in the original.

33 Nicolas Abraham, "Notes on the Phantom: A Complement to Freud's Metapsychology," trans. Nicholas Rand, *Critical Inquiry* 13, no. 2 (1987): 287.

34 Ibid., 288, italics in the original.

35 Ibid.

36 Ibid., 292.

37 Adorno, "Theses," 244.

38 Jacques Derrida, *Of Spirit: Heidegger and the Question*, trans. Geoffrey Bennington and Rachel Bowlby (1987; Chicago and London: The University of Chicago Press, 1989), 40, italics in the original.

39 Ibid., 62.

40 Ibid., 107, italics in the original.

41 Derrida, *Specters*, xx, italics in the original.

42 Fredric Jameson, "Marx's Purloined Letter," in *Ghostly Demarcations: A Symposium on Jacques Derrida's Specters of Marx*, ed. Michael Sprinker (London and New York: Verso, 1999), 39.

43 Ibid., 44–5.

44 Derrida, *Specters*, 12.

45 Ibid., 6. In "Spectrographies," collected here, Derrida notes that his statement in Ken McMullen's film *Ghost Dance* that "psychoanalysis plus film equals … a science of ghosts" cannot hold because "there is something which, as soon as one is dealing with ghosts, exceeds, if not scientificity in general, at least what, for a very long time, has modeled scientificity on the real, the objective,

which is not or should not be, precisely, phantomatic." Jacques Derrida and Bernard Stiegler, "Spectrographies," in *Echographies of Television*, trans. Jennifer Bajorek (Cambridge: Polity Press, 2002), 118.

46 Besides Abraham and Torok and Heidegger, another important influence is the Czech philosopher Jan Patočka, whose *Heretical Essays on the Philosophy of History* is analyzed in Jacques Derrida, *The Gift of Death*, trans. David Wills (1992; Chicago and London: The University of Chicago Press, 1995). This analysis prompts an early formulation of what, in *Specters of Marx*, would become the visor effect, marking the ghostly ability to see without being seen: "The genesis of responsibility that Patočka proposes will not simply describe a history of religion or religiousness. It will be combined with a genealogy of the subject who says 'myself,' the subject's relation to itself as an instance of liberty, singularity, and responsibility, the relation to self as being before the other: the other in its relation to infinite alterity, one who regards without being seen but also whose infinite goodness *gives* in an experience that amounts to a *gift of death* [*donner la mort*]" (3).

47 Terry Castle, *The Apparitional Lesbian: Female Homosexuality and Modern Culture* (New York: Columbia University Press, 1993).

48 Anthony Vidler, *The Architectural Uncanny: Essays in the Modern Unhomely* (Cambridge, MA: The MIT Press, 1992), 14.

49 Derrida, *Specters*, 7.

50 Jeffrey Andrew Weinstock, ed., *Spectral America: Phantoms and the National Imagination* (Madison: University of Wisconsin Press, 2004), 5.

51 Martin Jay, *Cultural Semantics: Keywords of our Time* (London: The Athlone Press, 1998), 163–4.

52 Ibid., 163.

53 Ibid., 164.

54 Cathy Caruth, ed., *Trauma: Explorations in Memory* (Baltimore: Johns Hopkins University Press, 1995), 5.

55 Ulrich Baer, *Spectral Evidence: The Photography of Trauma* (Cambridge, MA and London: The MIT Press, 2002), 63, 69.

56 Ibid., 76.

57 Roger Luckhurst, *The Trauma Question* (Abingdon and New York: Routledge, 2008).

58 Caruth, *Trauma*, 5.

59 Dominick LaCapra, "Trauma, Absence, Loss," *Critical Inquiry* 25, no. 4 (1999): 713.

60 Caruth, *Trauma*, 5.

61 See, for example, Cathy Caruth, *Unclaimed Experience: Trauma, Narrative, and History* (Baltimore: Johns Hopkins University Press, 1996).

62 Richard Crownshaw, Jane Kilby, and Antony Rowland, eds., *The Future of Memory* (New York and Oxford: Berghahn Books, 2010), 10. Interestingly, Abraham and Torok's theory of the phantom has been seen as a way to

historicize Freudian psychoanalysis. In addition to tracing the incorporated secret to specific social norms (such as the disapproval of extra-marital births) rather than invariable psychic structures, Abraham suggests that "shared or complementary phantoms" that escape exorcism can be "established as social practices." Abraham, "Notes," 292.

63 Andreas Huyssen, "Present Pasts: Media, Politics, Amnesia," *Public Culture* 12, no. 1 (2000): 24.

64 Andreas Huyssen, *Present Pasts: Urban Palimpsests and the Politics of Memory* (Palo Alto, CA: Stanford University Press, 2003), 8.

65 Wendy Brown, "Specters and Angels at the End of History," in *Vocations of Political Theory*, ed. Jason A. Frank and John Tamborino (Minneapolis: University of Minnesota Press, 2000), 36.

66 Avery F. Gordon, "Introduction to the New Edition," in *Ghostly Matters: Haunting and the Sociological Imagination* (Minneapolis: University of Minnesota Press, 2008), xvi.

67 LaCapra, "Trauma," 698.

68 Ibid., 700–1.

69 Ibid., 727.

70 Derrida, *Specters*, xviii.

71 Ibid., 161.

72 Nicola Bown, Carolyn Burdett, and Pamela Thurschwell, "Introduction" in *The Victorian Supernatural*, ed. Nicola Bown, Carolyn Burdett, and Pamela Thurschwell (Cambridge: Cambridge University Press, 2004), 12. In their introduction, Bown, Burdett, and Thurschwell indict "the metaphorical supernatural" for "unify[ing] and flatten[ing] out the supernatural: [such theories] move too seamlessly over the supernatural into what it signifies" (10, 12). They proceed to ask: "How might we historicise a central aspect of the fascination of the supernatural—the desire to confound history and turn back time, to eschew the material world in favour of an ethereal, magic realm?" (12).

73 Derrida, *Specters*, 4.

74 Luckhurst, *Trauma Question*, 93.

75 Roger Luckhurst, "Contemporary London Gothic and the Limits of the 'Spectral Turn,'" *Textual Practice* 16, no. 3 (2002): 535. The Gothic is arguably the most common term used to describe geographies (textual or other) in which the past somehow intrudes upon the present. It is therefore not surprising that the Gothic has also seen a revival in scholarship over the past two decades. With some exceptions (e.g. Jesse Alemán's essay in this *Reader*), it predominantly explains an Anglo-American and European understanding of haunting and haunted experience. As we have explained in *Popular Ghosts: The Haunted Spaces of Everyday Culture*, although ghosts are a staple of the Gothic, which can itself be seen as haunted in that it constantly invokes its own generic origins in order to seek its definition, a conflation of the Gothic and the spectral should be avoided. María del Pilar

Blanco and Esther Peeren, eds., *Popular Ghosts: The Haunted Spaces of Everyday Culture* (New York: Continuum, 2010), xvi–xvii.

76 See, for example, Svetlana Boym, *The Future of Nostalgia* (New York: Basic Books, 2001) and Peter Fritzsche, *Stranded in the Present: Modern Time and the Melancholy of History* (Cambridge, MA: Harvard University Press, 2004).

77 Jacques Derrida, *Archive Fever: A Freudian Impression*, trans. Eric Prenowitz (1995; Chicago: University of Chicago Press, 1998). As with all volumes of this type, the process of selection for *The Spectralities Reader* was guided by our interests and familiarities, as well as by the constraints of the book format and factors of language and cost.

78 Barthes writes: "in the cinema, no doubt, there is always a photographic referent, but this referent shifts, it does not make a claim in favor of its reality, it does not protest its former existence; it does not cling to me: it is not a *specter.*" *Camera Lucida: Reflections on Photography*, trans. Richard Howard (1980; London: Vintage, 2000), 89.

79 Jennifer Blessing and Nat Trotman, eds., *Haunted: Contemporary Photography / Video / Performance* (New York: Guggenheim Museum, 2010).

80 See Ralph Noyes, "The Other Side of Plato's Wall," in *Ghosts: Deconstruction, Psychoanalysis, History*, ed. Peter Buse and Andrew Stott (Basingstoke: Palgrave Macmillan, 1999), 244–62.

PART ONE

The Spectral Turn

1

The Spectral Turn / Introduction

María del Pilar Blanco and Esther Peeren

What does it mean to think scholarly research, especially regarding ghosts and haunting, in terms of various "turns"? What does this metaphor imply? A turn can be a move towards or away from something (even both at the same time), a tightening or a loosening, a new departure or a revisiting. In academia, naming and claiming a "turn" tends to indicate a foregrounding of an aspect hitherto ignored or under-illuminated: the role of language in the linguistic turn, that of culture in the cultural turn, that of materiality in the material turn, etc. Yet the potentially expansive effect is tempered by an implication of exclusivity: instead of *also* looking at the highlighted aspect, it becomes (or is taken as) a looking *only* at this aspect, necessitating another turn to address newly emerged blind spots. In addition, the rhetoric of the turn suggests a decisive change of direction accompanied by a distancing from the starting point; after all, a "turn in place" is not really a turn at all. Real turns follow on each other and are therefore conceptualized as reactions or ordered in terms of cause and effect; they cannot be thought in concert with each other. Thus, while in *The Affect Theory Reader*, Gregory J. Seigworth and Melissa Gregg try to move away from the turn as a single decisive moment—"No one 'moment' or key 'theorist' inaugurated 'a' 'turn' 'to' affect; like others, we have been caught and enamored of affect *in turns*, in conjunction with new quotidian realities"[1]—their temporalizing pluralization reinforces rather than overcomes the ultimate singularity of the turn: only one can be taken at a time.

The ghost, as a figure of multiplicity that has turned (from being alive to living-dead) and, as a haunting force, keeps turning up, turning into, and returning in unpredictable and not always easily demarcated ways, could inaugurate an alternative logic of the turn as something not necessarily definitive or revolutionary in the sense of radically new. Instead of demanding a distancing, the twists and turns of haunting manifest as a layering, a palimpsestic thinking together, simultaneously, rather than a thinking against or after (as in the plethora of *counters* and *posts* each scholarly turn tends to precipitate). The spectral turn, then, may be read not only as a turn *to* the spectral, but also as the spectralization *of* the turn—its unmooring from defined points of departure, notions of linear progress, and fixed destinations.

Rather curiously, the spectral turn has not been as prominently or enthusiastically adopted as a site of academic affiliation as other critical reorientations. In fact, in a perhaps strangely fitting anachronism, a full two years before Jeffrey Andrew Weinstock's affirmative use of the term to title his introduction to the edited volume *Spectral America: Phantoms and the National Imagination* (2004), it featured in Roger Luckhurst's critical article "The Contemporary London Gothic and the Limits of the 'Spectral Turn'" (2002). This article, while apparently the first to name it, already marks the spectral turn—emphatically placed between quotation marks— as having outlived its use. Since then, an ambiguous attitude towards the notion of a spectral turn has persisted: the continued and spreading interest in matters ghostly is either not specifically referred to in these terms, or a certain prevarication is indicated by retaining Luckhurst's quotation marks or preceding it with a "so-called."[2] While such evasions and expressions of skepticism do not invalidate the idea of a surge in scholarly attention for ghosts and haunting, they do indicate a degree of self-reflexivity with respect to the established, non-spectralized logic of the turn. Accordingly, this first part of *The Spectralities Reader* shows the existence, survival, scope, uses, and effects of what appears as "the spectral turn" to be up for debate.

The opening gambit, ardently proclaiming spectrality's wide-ranging conceptual potential, almost unavoidably involves Jacques Derrida. "Spectrographies" is part of a transcribed "improvised interview" with Derrida conducted by Bernard Stiegler. Filmed in 1993 by Jean-Christophe Rosé for the INA (Institut National de l'Audiovisuel), it was published in *Echographies of Television: Filmed Interviews*.[3] Only slightly trailing the French publication of *Specters of Marx*, which, as we noted in our general introduction, is generally considered the main catalyst for the late-twentieth-century surge in explorations of ghosts and haunting, "Spectrographies" condenses the most vital aspects of the theorization of spectrality and hauntology delineated in the longer, less accessible work. It also installs a useful distance between Derrida's thinking of spectrality and his much-contested reading of Marx (without, however, completely excluding it).

The interview starts from a discussion of Derrida's statement "The future belongs to ghosts," made in Ken McMullen's 1983 experimental film *Ghost Dance*, which invokes an intricate discourse of ghosts and haunting predicated on technological advancement (by way of references to cargo cults), the living on of the past in the present, and psychic dissolution.[4] It proceeds to conjure a complex configuration of spectral meditations pertaining to death and mourning, technology and technics, (in)visibility, inheritance, justice and respect, messianicity, history, and Heidegger. Holding this ostensibly far-flung constellation together is the notion of the specter as that which, in its paradoxical invisible visibility—"it is the visibility of a body which is not present in flesh and blood"—proposes "a deconstructive logic" that, by insisting on "heteronomy," undoes established binaries and challenges foundational, presentist, and teleological modes of thinking.[5] The specter is always already before us, confronting us with what precedes and exceeds our sense of autonomy, seeing us without being seen, and demanding a certain responsibility and answerability, making Derrida's theory, besides an alternative ontology, also an ethics: "There is no respect and, therefore, no justice possible without this relation of fidelity or of promise, as it were, to what is no longer living or living yet, to what is not simply present."[6] What is at stake, ultimately, is the specter as a figure of absolute alterity (existing both outside and within us) that should, as emphasized in *Specters of Marx*, not be assimilated or negated (exorcized), but lived *with*, in an open, welcoming relationality.

Derrida's penchant for thinking (through) ghosts—which inhabited his work from long before *Specters of Marx* up to his death in 2004[7]— has received much comment, from the mostly critical responses focusing on Derrida's interaction with Marx gathered in Sprinker's *Ghostly Demarcations: A Symposium on Jacques Derrida's Specters of Marx* (1995) and the special issue of *Parallax* on the New International (2001) to works that specifically seek to take up and elaborate on his engagement with the specter, including Nicholas Royle's "Phantom Review" (1997), Jodey Castricano's *Cryptomimesis: The Gothic and Jacques Derrida's Ghost Writing* (2003), and David Appelbaum's *Jacques Derrida's Ghost: A Conjuration* (2009).[8] Since this part of the *Reader* is dedicated to exploring the spectral turn as a heterogeneous formation—as itself, in a way, spectralized: *"more than one/no more one [le plus d'un]"*[9]—we have chosen to follow Derrida's text with Colin Davis's "État Présent: Hauntology, Spectres and Phantoms." In this lucid essay, of which an extended version is included in *Haunted Subjects: Deconstruction, Psychoanalysis and the Return of the Dead* (2007), Davis bifurcates the spectral turn by arguing that the current fascination with ghosts and haunting is traceable to two models.[10] Rather than being conflated, these models—the deconstructive,

Derridean thinking of the ghost and its prior psychoanalytical elaboration by Nicolas Abraham and Maria Torok—should be carefully distinguished on the basis of contrasting attitudes towards the secret it embodies. For Derrida, this secret should remain at least partially inscrutable to ensure respect for otherness and to be of value for discovering what it means to learn to live; Abraham and Torok, on the other hand, conceive of their phantom as a lying intruder to be exposed and expelled through psychotherapy. In pointing to this contrast, Davis does not seek to identify either model as superior, but suggests that, when transposed to literary studies, each has value in facilitating a particular type of textual analysis.

Whereas neither Derrida nor Davis speaks in so many words of a spectral turn, this part would be incomplete without an excerpt from Weinstock's aforementioned introduction, which takes the term for its title and charts its progression through popular culture (from the 1980s resurgence in cinema ghosts to the apparitions crowding 1990s fiction, television, and theater) and, subsequently, academia. Noting the ghost's affinity—as a figure of undecidability as well as one that persistently demands attention—with poststructuralism and revisionist tendencies in history, Weinstock effectuates a necessary historical and cultural specification of spectrality by inquiring after the reason for the renewed prevalence of ghosts and haunting in late-twentieth-century American culture. Narrowing the focus to "America's Spectral Turn" suggests other possible ghostly turns elsewhere, provoked by different preoccupations than a "postmodern suspicion of meta-narratives accentuated by millennial anxiety" and a unique national history of ethnic diversity and cultural amnesia.[11] It also challenges the generalizing tendency of Derrida's account, which leaves unacknowledged its reliance on a western, Judeo-Christian conception of haunting.[12]

Following Weinstock's specification of the spectral turn—replicable for other nations or areas, as well as periods, media, genres, etc.—is Julian Wolfreys's "Preface: On Textual Haunting," from *Victorian Hauntings: Spectrality, Gothic, the Uncanny and Literature* (2002). Wolfreys, who conceives of literature in general as a haunting structure, has been accused of moving in the direction of broadening spectrality's reach to the point where everything becomes ghostly. It is worth pointing out, though, that while the preface indeed posits that all literature and storytelling is marked by the power of the text, its author/speaker, and characters to be reanimated again and again in a way that blurs or suspends "categories such as the real or the imaginary," subsequent chapters carefully trace the ways in which individual Victorian writers (Dickens, Tennyson, Eliot, and Hardy) mobilize specific forms of haunting—in the divergent modes of the gothic, the uncanny, and the spectral.[13] Wolfreys's book, therefore, shows how spectrality may operate, simultaneously, at different levels, without the making of a general point precluding more precise uses.

Closing the first part is an excerpt from Roger Luckhurst's critical contemplation of the limits of the spectral turn—the very turn this article, ironically, seems to have been the first to proclaim. In response to Martin Jay's question of why the uncanny has begun to function as a "master trope," Luckhurst critiques "the generalized economy of haunting" he feels inhabits the work of Derrida and Wolfreys, while arguing for a renewed focus on the "generative loci" that prompt specific Gothic apparitions, in this case in tales set in contemporary London.[14] Certain accounts of spectrality may indeed be faulted for ignoring historical, cultural, and geographical specificities—the way ghosts and haunting do not function the same, or elicit the same affective responses, in all contexts—as well as eliding significant differences between concepts like the uncanny, the Gothic, and the spectral. Yet at the same time the construction of a "meta-Gothic discourse" or the contemplation of the "ghostly disruption" of historicity itself are not without merit, as they enable us to think about the structuring role of forms of repetition and return in our contemporary postcolonial, globalizing, and increasingly re- and pre-mediated world.[15]

As subsequent parts of this *Reader* will show, far from finding its limit in Luckhurst's text, the spectral turn persists, not as a unified whole, but in (at least) two interdependent guises. The expansive adoption of the specter as able to (re)configure fundamental aspects of our culture and existence—always perilously close to overstretching the concept and ignoring local variations in the way ghosts and haunting are apprehended and employed—may have been what prompted the spectral turn and ensured its cross-disciplinary reach, yet its perpetuation and continued fecundity has largely depended on attempts to more precisely orient and differentiate spectrality.

Notes

1   Gregory J. Seigworth and Melissa Gregg, "An Inventory of Shimmers," in *The Affect Theory Reader*, ed. Melissa Gregg and Gregory J. Seigworth (Durham: Duke University Press, 2010), 19, italics in the original.

2   See, for example, Julian Holloway and James Kneale, "Locating Haunting: A Ghost-Hunter's Guide," *Cultural Geographies* 15 (2008): 297–312; Emilie Cameron, "Indigenous Spectrality and the Politics of Postcolonial Ghost Stories," *Cultural Geographies* 15 (2008): 383–93; Christine Ferguson, "Recent Studies in Nineteenth-Century Spiritualism," *Literature Compass 9*, no. 6 (2012): 431–40.

3   Jacques Derrida and Bernard Stiegler, "Spectrographies," in *Echographies of Television: Filmed Interviews*, trans. Jennifer Bajorek (1996; Cambridge: Polity Press, 2006), 31.

4   For an extended discussion of Derrida's appearance in this film, see Laurence Simmons, "Jacques Derrida's Ghostface," *Angelaki* 16, no. 1 (2011): 129–41.

5   Derrida and Stiegler, "Spectrographies," 115, 117, 122.

6   Ibid., 123–4.

7   See our general introduction for a discussion of the works leading up to *Specters of Marx*. Following that text, the specter reappears most insistently in Jacques Derrida, *Archive Fever: A Freudian Impression*, trans. Eric Prenowitz (1995; Chicago and London: The University of Chicago Press, 1998) and Jacques Derrida, *Learning to Live Finally: The Last Interview*, trans. Pascale-Anne Brault and Michael Naas (Hoboken: Melville House Publishing, 2007).

8   Michael Sprinker ed., *Ghostly Demarcations: A Symposium on Jacques Derrida's* Specters of Marx (London and New York: Verso, 1999); *The New International*, spec. issue of *Parallax* 7, no. 3 (2001): 1–137; Nicholas Royle, "Phantom Review," *Textual Practice* 11, no. 2 (1997): 386–98; Jodey Castricano, *Cryptomimesis: The Gothic and Derrida's Ghost Writing* (Montréal: McGill-Queen's University Press, 2001); David Appelbaum, *Jacques Derrida's Ghosts: A Conjuration* (Albany: SUNY Press, 2009).

9   Jacques Derrida, *Specters of Marx: The State of the Debt, the Work of Mourning, & the New International*, trans. Peggy Kamuf (1993; London and New York: Routledge, 1994), xx.

10   Colin Davis, *Haunted Subjects: Deconstruction, Psychoanalysis and the Return of the Dead* (Basingstoke: Palgrave MacMillan, 2007).

11   Jeffrey Andrew Weinstock, *Spectral America: Phantoms and the National Imagination* (Madison: University of Wisconsin Press, 2004), 5.

12   For a discussion of Derrida's Eurocentrism, seen as particularly jarring in view of his ties to Algeria, see Christopher Wise, "Saying 'Yes' to Africa: Jacques Derrida's *Specters of Marx*," *Research in African Literatures* 33, no. 4 (2002): 124–42.

13   Julian Wolfreys, *Victorian Hauntings: Spectrality, Gothic, the Uncanny and Literature* (Basingstoke: Palgrave, 2002), xiii.

14   Roger Luckhurst, "The Contemporary London Gothic and the Limits of the 'Spectral Turn,'" *Textual Practice* 16, no. 3 (2002): 527, 534, 528.

15   Luckhurst, "Contemporary London Gothic," 536, 535. On re- and pre-mediation, see Jay David Bolter and Richard Grusin, *Remediation: Understanding New Media* (Boston: The MIT Press, 2000) and Richard Grusin, *Premediation: Affect and Mediality after 9/11* (Basingstoke: Palgrave MacMillan, 2010).

2

Spectrographies

Jacques Derrida and Bernard Stiegler

BERNARD STIEGLER *I would like nonetheless to come back to the question of death, with or without direct or explicit reference to* Being and Time *– let's at least say that it would be necessary in certain respects to go there – insofar as, in Barthes, the analysis of photographic intentionality is inscribed in the question of narcissism and of mourning. Narcissism would be radically affected by the photographic experience in its strictly technical dimension. We have talked a lot about Barthes, whom I would like to cite so that I may then cite you, not from a book, but from a film in which you played yourself –* Ghostdance[1] *– and in which you say a number of things about film and ghosts. There is a thematic of the ghost and of the specter which is at the very heart of your book on Marx, but which has been insistent in your work for a very long time, which incessantly comes back there. Barthes writes, in* Camera Lucida: *"I call 'photographic referent,' not the optionally real thing to which an image or sign refers, but the necessarily real thing that was placed before the lens, without which there would be no photograph. Painting, on the other hand, can feign reality without having seen it." He adds, a bit further on: "[I]n photography, I can never deny that the thing was there. Past and reality are superimposed. . . . The photo is literally an emanation of the referent. From a real body which was there proceed radiations that come to touch me, I who am here. The duration of the transmission doesn't matter. The photo of the departed being comes to touch me like the delayed rays of a star. A kind of umbilical cord ties the body of the photographic thing to my gaze: light, though impalpable, is really a carnal medium here, a skin that I share with the one who was photographed. . . . The bygone thing has really touched, with its immediate radiations (its luminances), the surface that is in turn touched by my gaze."[2]*

Commenting on these lines, you have written that "the modern possibility of the photograph joins, in a single system, death and the referent."³ Already in this commentary, you spoke of the "phantomatic effect," which Barthes himself had put forth.⁴ In the film, in which you play yourself, you say to Pascale Ogier, your partner: "To be haunted by a ghost is to remember what one has never lived in the present, to remember what, in essence, has never had the form of presence. Film is a 'phantomachia.' Let the ghosts come back. Film plus psychoanalysis equals a science of ghosts. Modern technology, contrary to appearances, although it is scientific, increases tenfold the power of ghosts. The future belongs to ghosts." Might you elaborate on this statement: "The future belongs to ghosts"?

JACQUES DERRIDA When Barthes grants such importance to touch in the photographic experience, it is insofar as the very thing one is deprived of, as much in spectrality as in the gaze which looks at images or watches film and television, is indeed tactile sensitivity. The desire to touch, the tactile effect or affect, is violently summoned by its very frustration, summoned to come back [*appelé à revenir*], like a ghost [*un revenant*], in the places haunted by its absence. In the series of more or less equivalent words that accurately designate haunting, *specter*, as distinct from ghost [*revenant*], speaks of the spectacle. The specter is first and foremost something visible. It is of the visible, but of the invisible visible, it is the visibility of a body which is not present in flesh and blood. It resists the intuition to which it presents itself, it is not tangible. *Phantom* preserves the same reference to *phainesthai*, to appearing for vision, to the brightness of day, to phenomenality. And what happens with spectrality, with phantomality – and not necessarily with coming-back [*revenance*] – is that something becomes almost visible which is visible only insofar as it is not visible in flesh and blood. It is a night visibility. As soon as there is a technology of the image, visibility brings night. It incarnates in a night body, it radiates a night light. At this moment, in this room, night is falling over us. Even if it weren't falling, we are already in night, as soon as we are captured by optical instruments which don't even need the light of day. We are already specters of a "televised." In the nocturnal space in which this image of us, this picture we are in the process of having "taken," is described, it is already night. Furthermore, because we know that, once it has been taken, captured, this image will be reproducible in our absence, because we know this *already*, we are already haunted by this future, which brings our death. Our disappearance is already here. We are already transfixed by a disappearance [*une disparition*] which promises and conceals in advance another magic "apparition," a ghostly "re-apparition" which is in truth properly *miraculous*, something to see, as admirable as it is incredible [*incroyable*], believable [*croyable*] only by the grace of an act of faith. Faith which is summoned by technics itself, by our relation of essential incompetence to technical operation. (For even if we know how something works, our knowledge is incommensurable with the immediate perception that attunes us to technical efficacy, to the fact that "it works": we see that "it works," but even if we *know* this, we don't *see* how "it works"; seeing and knowing are incommensurable here.) And this is what makes our experience so strange. We are spectralized by the shot, captured or possessed by spectrality in advance.

What has, dare I say, constantly haunted me in this logic of the specter is that it regularly exceeds all the oppositions between visible and invisible, sensible and insensible. A specter is both visible and invisible, both phenomenal and nonphenomenal: a trace that marks the present with its absence in advance. The spectral logic is de facto a deconstructive logic. It is in the element of haunting that deconstruction finds the place most hospitable to it, at the heart of the living present, in the quickest heartbeat of the philosophical. Like the work of mourning, in a sense, which produces spectrality, and like *all* work produces spectrality.

To come back to the *Ghostdance* experience, I regret the expression that came to me while improvising (the scene you cited was improvised) from start to finish. I remember it from this one sentence because it was a rather singular experience with Ken McMullen, the English filmmaker: we had studied that morning, in the bar of the Select, for an hour, a scene which lasted a minute, and which we repeated, repeated, repeated to the point of exhaustion. Then, that afternoon, in my office, conversely, we improvised from beginning to end a completely different scene, it was very long, which Ken McMullen kept almost in its entirety and in which the exchange you mentioned was shot. Thus I improvised this sentence, "Psychoanalysis plus film equals ... a science of ghosts." Of course, upon reflection, beyond the improvisation, I'm not sure I'd keep the word "science"; for at the same time, there is something which, as soon as one is dealing with ghosts, exceeds, if not scientificity in general, at least what, for a very long time, has modeled scientificity on the real, the objective, which is not or should not be, precisely, phantomatic. It is in the name of the scientificity of science that one conjures ghosts or condemns obscurantism, spiritualism, in short, everything that has to do with haunting and with specters. There would be much to say about this.

With regard to emanations and the very beautiful text by Barthes which you cited, rather than problematize what he says, I would like to tell you what happened with this film, *Ghostdance*. Having invented this scene with Pascale Ogier, who was sitting across from me, in my office, and who had taught me, in the intervals between shots, what in cinematic terms is called the *eye-line* [in English in the original], that is to say, the fact of looking eye to eye (we spent long minutes, if not hours, at the request of the filmmaker, looking into one another's eyes, which is an experience of strange and unreal intensity: you can imagine what this experience of the eye-line can be when it is prolonged and passionately repeated between two actors, even if it is only fictional and "professional"), and after she had taught me that, then, after I had said roughly what you repeated, I had to ask her: "And what about you, do you believe in ghosts?" This is the only thing the filmmaker dictated to me. At the end of my improvisation, I was to say to her: "And what about you, do you believe in ghosts?" And, repeating it over and over, at least thirty times, at the request of the filmmaker, she says this little sentence: "Yes, now I do, yes." And so, already during shooting, she repeated this sentence at least thirty times. Already this was a little strange, a little spectral, out of sync, outside itself; this was happening several times in one. But imagine the experience I had when, two or three years later, after Pascale Ogier had died, I watched the film again in the United States, at the request of students who wanted to discuss it with me. Suddenly I saw Pascale's face, which I knew was a dead woman's face, come onto the screen. She answered my question: "Do you believe in ghosts?" Practically looking me in the eye, she said to me again, on the big screen: "Yes, now I do, yes." Which now? Years later in Texas. I had the unnerving sense of the return of her specter, the specter of her specter coming back to say to me – to me here, now: "Now ... now ... now, that is to say, in this dark room on another continent, in another world, here, now, yes, believe me, I believe in ghosts."

But at the same time, I know that the first time Pascale said this, already, when she repeated this in my office, already, this spectrality was at work. It was already there, she was already saying this, and she knew, just as we know, that even if she hadn't died in the interval, one day, it would be a dead woman who said, "I am dead," or "I am dead, I know what I'm talking about from where I am, and I'm watching you," and this gaze remained dissymmetrical, exchanged beyond all possible exchange, eye-line without eye-line, the eye-line of a gaze that fixes and looks for the other, its other, its counterpart [vis-à-vis], the other gaze met, in an infinite night.

You will remember what Gradiva said: "For a long time now, I have been used to being dead."

This is what I meant to say a moment ago when I spoke of inheritance. In inheritance, there is always this experience which I dubbed, in the book on Marx, the "visor effect": the ghost looks at or watches us, the ghost concerns us.[5] The specter is not simply someone we see coming back, it is someone by whom we feel ourselves watched, observed, surveyed, as if by the law: we are "before the law," without any possible symmetry, without reciprocity, insofar as the other is watching only us, concerns only us, we who are observing it (in the same way that one observes and respects the law) without even being able to meet its gaze. Hence the dissymmetry and, consequently, the heteronomic figure of the law. The wholly other – and the dead person is the wholly other – watches me, concerns me, and concerns or watches me while addressing to me, without however answering me, a prayer or an injunction, an infinite demand, which becomes the law for me: it concerns me, it regards me, it addresses itself only to me at the same time that it exceeds me infinitely and universally, without my being able to exchange a glance with him or with her.

"The visor effect" in *Hamlet*, or what in any case I have called this, is that, up or down, the king's helmet, Hamlet's father's helmet, reminds us that his gaze can see without being seen. There is a moment where Hamlet is very anxious to know whether the witnesses who saw his father, Marcellus and Horatio, saw his eyes. Was his visor up? The answer is: "Yes, he wore his visor up," but it doesn't matter, he could have worn it down: the fact that there is a visor symbolizes the situation in which I can't see who is looking at me, I can't meet the gaze of the other, whereas I am in his sight. The specter is not simply this visible invisible that I can see, it is someone who watches or concerns me without any possible reciprocity, and who therefore makes the law when I am blind, blind by situation. The specter enjoys the right of absolute inspection. He is the right of inspection itself.

And this is why I am an inheritor: the other comes *before* me,[6] I who am before him, I who am because of him, owing to him [*l'autre est avant moi devant moi qui suis devant lui*], owing him obedience [*lui devant obéissance*], incapable of exchanging with him (not even a glance). The father comes before me, I who am "owing" or indebted [*avant moi qui suis "devant" ou redevable*]. The one who watches or concerns me is or comes before me. The predecessor has come before me [*est arrivé là avant moi devant moi*], I who am before him, I who am because of him, owing to him [*qui suis devant lui*], owing him everything [*lui devant tout*]. This is the law of the genealogy of the law, the irreducible difference of generation. From the moment that I cannot exchange or meet a glance, I am dealing with the other, who comes before me; an absolute autonomy is already no longer possible. And I cannot settle my debt, I can neither give back nor exchange because of this absence of the other, which I can't look in the eye. Even if I do it or think I do it, viewer and visible can only succeed one another, alternate, not be confused in the other's eye. I can't see the eye of the other as viewing and visible at the same time.

This is why I am in heteronomy. This does not mean that I am not free; on the contrary, it is a *condition of freedom*, so to speak: my freedom springs from the condition of this responsibility which is born of heteronomy in the eyes of the other, in the other's sight. This gaze is spectrality itself.

One has a tendency to treat what we've been talking about here under the names of image, teletechnology, television screen, archive, as if all these things were on display: a collection of objects, things we see, spectacles in front of us, devices we might use, much as we might use a "teleprompter" we had ourselves prewritten or prescribed. But wherever there are these specters, we are being watched, we sense or think we are being watched.

This dissymmetry complicates everything. The law, the injunction, the order, the performative wins out over the theoretical, the constative, knowledge, calculation, and the programmable.

It is in this way that I would be tempted to understand what Barthes calls "emanation." This flow of light which captures or possesses me, invests me, invades me, or envelops me is not a ray of light, but the source of a possible view: from the point of view of the other. If the "reality effect" is ineluctable, it is not simply because there is something real that is undecomposable, or not synthesizable, some "thing" that was there. It is because there is something other that watches or concerns me. This Thing is the other insofar as it was already there – before me – ahead of me, beating me to it, I who am before it, I who am because of owing to it [*avant moi, devant moi, me devançant, moi qui suis devant lui*]. My law. I have an even greater sense of the "real" when what is photographed is a face or a gaze, although in some ways a mountain can be at least as "real." The "reality effect" stems here from the irreducible alterity of another origin of the world. It is another origin of the world. What I call the gaze here, the gaze of the other, is not simply another machine for the perception of images. It is another world, another source of phenomenality, another degree zero of appearing.

A singularity.

Yes, and it is not simply a *point* of singularity. It is a singularity on the basis of which a world is opened. The other, who is dead, was someone for whom a world, that is to say, a possible infinity or a possible indefinity of experiences was open. It is an opening. Finite-infinite, infinitely finite. Pascale Ogier saw, she will have seen, she did see. There was a world for her. From this other origin, this one that I cannot reappropriate, from this infinitely other place, I am watched. Still, today, this thing looks at me and concerns me and asks me to respond or to be responsible. The word "real," in this context, signifies the irreducible singularity of the other insofar as she opens a world, and insofar as there will have always been a world for her.

To link this statement up with that of spectrality, let's say that our relation to another origin of the world or to another gaze, to the gaze of the other, implies a kind of spectrality. Respect for the alterity of the other dictates respect for the ghost [*le revenant*] and, therefore, for the non-living, for what it's possible is not alive. Not dead, but not living. This is where I try to begin in the book on "Marx's specters," when I ask myself how to "learn how to live" and what "learning how to live" might mean. There is no respect and, therefore, no justice possible without this relation of fidelity or of promise, as it were, to what is no longer living or not living yet, to what is not simply present. There would be no urgent demand for justice, or for responsibility, without this spectral oath. And there would be no oath, period. Someone pointed out to me that the word "specter" is the perfect anagram of "respect." I since discovered by chance that another word is also the perfect anagram of these two, which is "scepter." These three words, respect, specter, and scepter, form a configuration about which there would be much to say, but which goes without saying, too. Respect would be due the law of the other, who appears without appearing and watches or concerns me as a specter, but why would this unconditional authority, which commands duty without duty, without debt, even beyond the categorical imperative, still be figured by the spectral phallus of the king, by the paternal scepter, by an attribute which we would have to obey just as we would the finger and the eye? The scepter would be to the finger what the phallus is to the penis. Would its fetishistic spectrality be enough to unsettle the identity of the sex organ, the virility of the father? These are questions. In any case, for it is the case, as it happens, here is a very lucky thing: these three words are composed of the same letters. This chance can only arise, don't you think, thanks to alphabetic writing – and in a singular language.

Barthes mentions touch, you recalled this a moment ago. He certainly had a number of reasons for doing so, but it was probably first and foremost in order to insist on the technical character of this effect. He analyzes the way photography functions in its mechanical, chemical, and optical dimensions.

We have the impression, and it would be difficult to avoid this feeling, that a substitution can be made for all the senses except touch. What I see can be replaced. What I touch cannot, or in any case, we have the feeling, illusory or not, that touch guarantees irreplaceability: hence the thing itself in its uniqueness.

Barthes says that in order for the reality effect to take place when I see a photograph, it is actually necessary – if for example I am looking at a portrait of Baudelaire, photographed by Nadar – it is actually necessary for the rays emitted by Baudelaire's face as photographed by Nadar to have touched a photographic plate, for this plate to have been duplicated, and consequently, for luminances to have touched all the duplicates, and that there be a properly "material" chain ensuring that, ultimately, these luminous emanations will end up touching my eye, and so there is, in all this, a . . .

. . . a series of contiguities . . .

. . . of material contiguities, contiguities on the order of matter, which effectively ensures that this thing is looking at me, it is watching me, it concerns me, and it touches me, but I cannot touch Baudelaire's face.

It touches me, but I can't touch it, and there is, with what Barthes calls the spectrum (the photograph itself), this "visor effect" and spectrality in the sense you just described. I want to emphasize matter and technicity. Barthes's sudden and rather striking interest in technicity leads him to say that a camera is a "seeing clock," a magnificent expression. I emphasize this now because you mobilize this thematic in your Specters of Marx *(the subtitle of which we should also remember:* The State of the Debt, the Work of Mourning and the New International*), which you moreover announced in a way, without having planned it, at the time of* Ghostdance, *since you say: "It would be necessary to work through this question starting with Freud and Marx." That was over ten years ago. I am talking about matter here especially because everyone knows that Marx is the theorist of dialectical materialism and because you end up challenging Marx's philosophy as a definite figure of materialism – while at the same time doing justice to a certain materialism – on the basis of this question of the specter. You do this by showing the degree to which this question is at work in Marx, the degree to which it is thematized throughout his entire oeuvre, and to which it unsettles it and frightens him, by showing how he criticizes this mobilization of the specter in Stirner and how, at the same time, he is himself haunted by this question. And this leads you to disturb, on the basis of what you call a "hauntology," the distinction that Marx is able to make between exchange-value and use-value. It also brings us back to the questions we were just discussing with respect to the market. Doesn't the Marxian thought of justice stumble here, in the face of a structural difficulty that would essentially have to do with technics? Again, technics is at the heart of all this, and with it and its spectrality, time – it is not possible to dissociate, in this distinction, technics and time.*

On this point, as on many others, Marx's thought – I don't dare say Marx's philosophy – this thought which divides itself into a philosophy and something other than a philosophy, seems to me tormented by contradictory movements. Which, incidentally, obey a common law. On the one hand, no doubt better than anyone of his time, Marx understood, let's call it, so as to move quickly, the essence of technics or, in any case, the irreducibility of the technical, in science, in language, in politics, and even the irreducibility of the media. He paid constant, obsessive attention to the press, to the modern press, to what was developing between the press and politics at the time. Few thinkers of his time sharpened their analysis of the political stakes of the effects of the press to this degree. On the other hand, as you just reminded us, he paid attention, in a way that was almost compulsive, to the effects of spectrality – I have tried to show this in as precise a way as I could. But at the same time, he shares with all philosophers and perhaps with all scientists . . . dare I call it a belief? in any case, the axiom, at once naive and sensible, according to which there is no such thing, the phantom does not exist. It must not exist, *therefore* we have to get rid of it, *therefore* we have to be done with it. Here you have a "therefore" that would already be enough to rattle good sense from the inside. For if there is no such thing, why would we have to chase after the specter, to chase it out or hunt it down? Why would we have to let the dead bury their dead, as Marx says in the *Eighteenth Brumaire*, in the biblical tradition? Why would we have to analyze phantomality to the point of making it disappear? Marx reproached Stirner for not doing it properly, and he had, in his critique of Stirner, compelling arguments – we would have to look at it closely – for indicating the conditions on which phantomality could be critiqued, just as fetishism can be critiqued, to the point of making them *effectively disappear* (the question of fetishism, like that of ideology, is at the center of this debate about spectrality). All of this proceeds from a point where Marx reminds us that the ultimate foundation remains *living* experience, *living* production, which must efface every trace of spectrality. In the final analysis, one must refer to a zone where spectrality is nothing. This is why Marx seemed to me to contradict or to limit the movement that ought to have prompted him to take technicity, iterability, everything that makes spectrality irreducible, more seriously. And even the motif of justice – I don't dare say eschatology – a certain "messianicity," which is in my opinion irreducible (I am not talking about messianism), a messianicity irreducible in its revolutionary movement, ought to have made him more respectful of the spectral. (I try elsewhere to show why. I am not able to do it here.) He didn't make this gesture, he *couldn't* make it, he *had to not* make it; I don't know how or in what modalities to present this kind of necessity. But in any case, there is a classical movement in his text to deny all spectrality a scientific, philosophical, political, or technical dignity, or in any case a dignity of thinking or of the question, etc., and this seems to me to constitute an essential limitation of his work, its rootedness in a metaphysics of the effectivity of the living present . . .

As regards the 1848 Revolution, he demonstrates that a return of the dead tormented this revolution, like that of 1789, but he criticizes this revolution insofar as it didn't know how to bury its dead.

One would have to analyze closely this movement and this text of the *Eighteenth Brumaire*. In it, Marx consecrates admirable analyses to the return of the specters that made the revolutionary discourse, and even the revolutions, possible. There's a moment where he announces that the coming revolution, the social revolution, the one that failed in 1789 and in 1848, the coming revolution as social revolution, will have to put an end to this separation between form and content, to the inadequation between what he calls the "phrase" and the "content," and so will put an end to this need for dressing up in specters' clothing, in the costume of the past or of phantomatic mythologies, in order to bring the revolution off. What he announces is the end of specters. He announces that the ghost of communism, which, according to the *Manifesto*, was haunting the

European powers, this ghost will have to become, through the revolution, fully present, and so cease to be a ghost, and that this is what the powers of the old Europe, including the papacy, are as it were afraid of. For once the *social* revolution has taken place and this ghost of communism has *presented* itself, and presented itself in person, at this moment, for this very reason, there won't be any ghosts anymore. And so he believes in the disappearance of the phantom, in the disappearance of the dead.

This statement seems very grave to me. In its implications and in its consequences. That is why, even if I have saluted Marx in this book, what I say on this subject may be taken for a fundamental reticence with respect to what he said, and with respect to the politics and even to the idea of justice that this discourse carries within itself. As soon as one calls for the disappearance of ghosts, one deprives oneself of the very thing that constitutes the revolutionary movement itself, that is to say, the appeal to justice, what I call "messianicity" – which is a ghostly business, which must carry beyond the synchrony of living presents ... But I am not able to show this here ... I must refer you to *Specters of Marx* ...

History itself is an effect of spectrality. The return of the Romans in the French Revolution would belong to a mode of spectral transmission which overdetermines all historical events, and this in an irreducible way. Perhaps one should say, furthermore, that this spectrality belongs to what could be called a history in deferred time, a history in the play of writing, which has the structure, it seems to me, with the exception of a few very particular cases (such as signatures on contracts or events of the clearly performative type), of an irreducible distension between the event and its recording. It seems to me that, in an essential way, orthographic writing constitutes a deferred time. Today, we are living a number of events "live," "in real time." To what extent – this is yet another extremely complicated question – is the spectrality at work in this kind of transmission incommensurable with this spectrality in deferred time? In other words, what is the problematic of eventization [événementialisation] that is taking shape around this today?

In principle, every event is experienced or lived, as one says and as one believes, in "real time." What we are living "in real time," and what we find remarkable, is access precisely to what we are not living: we are "there" where we are not, in real time, through images or through technical relation. There happen to us, in real time, events that aren't happening to us, that is to say, that we aren't experiencing immediately around us. We are there, in real time, where bombs are exploding in Kuwait or in Iraq. We record and believe that we are perceiving in an immediate mode events at which we are not present. But the recording of an event, from the moment that there is a technical interposition, is always deferred, that is to say that this "différance" is inscribed in the very heart of supposed synchrony, in the living present. Past events, for example a sequence in Roman history such as it is mimicked, reconstituted in simulacrum during the 1789 Revolution, are clearly something else, but something else which tells us that what happened there, in Rome, is the object of new recordings. We record again, this happens to us again, and through historical reading, historical interpretation, even through mimicry, the mimetic, or simulation, we record what is past. The imprint, in essence, continues to be printed. The shortening of the intervals is only a shrinking in the space of this "différance" and of this temporality. As soon as we are able – this is an effect of modernity, an effect of the twentieth century – to see spectacles or hear voices that were recorded at the beginning of the century, the experience we have of them today is a form of presentification, which, although it was impossible and even unthinkable before, is nonetheless inscribed in the possibility of this delay or of this interval which ensures that there is historical experience in general, memory in general. Which means that there is never an absolutely real time. What we call real time, and it is easy to understand how it can be opposed to deferred time in everyday language, is in fact never pure. What we call real time is simply an extremely reduced "différance," but there is no purely real time because temporalization itself is structured by a play of retention or of protention and, consequently, of traces: the condition of possibility of the living, absolutely real present is already memory, anticipation, in other words, a play of traces. The real-time effect is itself a particular effect of "différance." This should not lead us to efface or minimize the extraordinary gulf separating what today we call real-time transmission from what had been impossible before. I do not want to try to reduce all of technical modernity to a condition of possibility that it shares with much more ancient times. However, if we are going to understand the originality and the specificity of this technical modernity, we must not forget that there is no such thing as purely real time, that this does not exist in a full and pure state. Only on this condition will we understand how technics alone can bring about the real-time "effect." Otherwise we wouldn't talk about real time. We don't talk about real time when we have the impression that there are no technical instruments.

It is also an opportunity [une chance], if what a moment ago I was calling reflexivity can only be conceived in deferral. And what you've just said calls into question the opposition, set forth by Paul Virilio and to which many people are referring at the moment, between television and text [l'écran et l'écrit].

These oppositions remain very useful and even productive, but even as one uses them and puts them to work, one has to be aware of their limitations. Their pertinence is restricted.

Everything we are saying about spectrality is tied to the question of inheritance – they are in fact the same question – which is very important

in the thematic you are developing at the moment, and very important in
the quotidian reality we are living. It is at the very core of Heideggerian
thought, in Being and Time, *particularly in paragraph 6, in which he writes*
– and this brings us back to a spectrological or "hauntological" analysis:
"The past does not follow Dasein *but has rather always already preceded*
it."[7] *A structure of coming-back [*revenance*] constitutes* Dasein. *And in*
some ways, one could say that Heidegger, well beyond Being and Time, *is*
one big spectrological analysis.

Yes ... I'd like to say something about this in a minute, yes ...

This being the case, one could also venture a critique of Heidegger for the
same reasons, and for reasons related to the critique you make of Marx,
insofar as, even if Heidegger, undoubtedly, has opened this question to a
much larger extent by inscribing the irreducibility of coming-back at the
very core of his thought – since it is nothing other than temporalization
– it nonetheless seems he is seeking, not to purify the event (what he calls
"resolution") of all spectrality (he shows that every event is rooted in this
kind of spectrality), but to purify this spectrality of its technicity.

As you know, the thought of technics in Heidegger is at least double; it
resists any univocal simplification. Before coming back to this, I would
like to highlight a difficulty. Doubtless Heidegger places this dimension of
inheritance at the heart of existence, and so at the heart of the existential
analytic of *Dasein* – and the theme appears very early, to be developed
especially at the end of *Being and Time*. Doubtless the concept of
Unheimlichkeit, of "uncanniness" – which may well define, in Heidegger
as in Freud, the element of haunting (the other at home, the reapparition
of specters, etc.) – is at the center of *Being and Time*. This could be shown,
but it hasn't been much remarked or analyzed until now. And yet, despite
this, Heidegger almost never speaks, it seems, of the phantom itself, of the
ghost [*le revenant*] itself, as if he were wary of what this concept naturally
implies of obscurantism, of spiritualism, of dubious credulity. As I have
noted elsewhere,[8] the word "phantom" appears only once, if I am not
mistaken, in a rather rhetorical form, in an argument about time and about
that which, in time, might seem not to be. This rhetoric moreover confirms
this wariness with respect to the very word phantom and to the credulity
that goes along with this indistinct mirage. So, in a way, at the very moment
where, in his analysis of temporality or of inheritance, he insists, as you
pointed out, on what ought to open the field of a kind of spectrology, he
guards against the spectral. One might say that, when he speaks of *Geist*
(I've tried to show this elsewhere), the specter (which also means *Geist*) is
never far off, and that, in texts such as those devoted to Trakl in *On the
Way to Language*,[9] the phantom is there. And yet, he doesn't talk about

it, he doesn't make it a theme, as we are trying to do right now. What particularly interests me in what he says about inheritance is notably the structure he designates by citing a phrase from Hölderlin. For Hölderlin, we are inheritors in our very being: language is as it were given to existence, to *Dasein*, to man as *Dasein*, so that he will be able to bear witness, not to this or that thing, but to bear witness to the fact that he is an inheritor in his very being. We inherit language in order to be able to bear witness to the fact that we are inheritors. That is to say, we inherit the possibility of inheriting. The fact that we inherit is not an attribute or an accident; it is our essence, and this essence, we inherit. We inherit the possibility of bearing witness to the fact that we inherit, and this is language. We receive as our share the possibility of sharing, and this is none other than the possibility of inheriting. This structure seems circular, clearly it is, but it becomes all the more striking as a result. We are drawn into this circle in advance. We inherit nothing, except the ability to inherit and to speak, to enter into a relation with a language, with a law, or with "something" that makes it possible for us to inherit, and by the same token, to bear witness to this fact by inheriting ... We are witnesses, by bearing witness to – and thus by inheriting – the possibility of bearing witness.

And the impossibility of inheriting too.

As well as the impossibility of the task of inheriting which is left to our responsibility. It is in this space, this home outside itself, that the specter comes. There is nothing; we inherit nothing. In fact, the dead are dead. And, as Marx reminds us by citing the Gospel, we let, we can always want to let the dead bury their dead. But this in no way changes the law of the return – I mean, here, of the return of the dead. Just because the dead no longer exist does not mean that we are done with specters. On the contrary. Mourning and haunting are unleashed at this moment. They are unleashed before death itself, out of the mere possibility of death, that is to say, of the trace, which comes into being as immediate sur-vival – and as "televised."

And then, the fact that there is no such thing, that this doesn't exist, in no way absolves us of the task. On the contrary, it assigns an infinite responsibility. Autonomy (we are left alone with duty and the law) as heteronomy (which has come from the place of the death of the other, as death and as other); the injunction can no longer be reappropriated. The law and mourning have the same birthplace, that is to say, death. It is always easy and tempting to abuse this by saying that something can be reduced to "nothing." And in effect, this objection and this abuse may always leave us without any response. This possibility (of abuse or of the "no response") is irreducible, it *must* remain irreducible, like the very *possibility* of evil, if responsibility is going to be possible and significant, along with decision, ethics, justice, etc.

Let's come back to the most difficult part of your question. Heidegger, a thinker who is very attentive to the great question of *tekhnē*, to the question of the relation between technics and philosophy, technics and metaphysics, technics and the West, perhaps remains, at a certain moment, tempted by a certain relegation of the technical to a secondary position in relation to a pretechnical originariness or a *physis*. Naturally, this *physis* is not what will later and in everyday usage be called "nature," but insofar as it *is*, insofar as it is being itself or the totality of being, *physis* would not yet be, or not in itself, *tekhnē*. Here, a presence, a present, or a presentifiable essence, a being as presence of *physis* would perhaps reconstitute itself, not simply before any technics in the modern sense, but before any *tekhnē*. Even if *tekhnē* belongs to the movement of truth, there would be, in *physis*, something like a truth that would not be *tekhnē*. I am only marking out here, in the conditional, a big problem in the reading of Heidegger who, on this point as on others, cannot be reduced to the simplicity of this or that proposition. But how can we overlook a Heideggerian "pathos" which, despite so many denials on this subject, remains antitechnological, originaristic, even ecologistic?

Earthy [Terrien].

Earthy. But we also have to take into account the distinction so insistent in Heidegger, between the "earth" and the "world." Still, even if we neutralize this "pathos" and these connotations, even if we confine ourselves to Heidegger's least ambiguous statements (when he reminds us that, in his eyes, technics is not evil, as he is often made to say), it remains the case that he tries to think a thought of technics that would not be technical (the thinking or essence of technicity is not a technicality). Isn't he tempted to subtract, in this way, the thinkable or thinking from the field of technics? Doesn't he suggest that there is a thinking pure of all technics? And in his eyes, that techni*city* is not technical, that the thinking of technics is not technical, this is the condition of thinking. He would not say that the thinking of essence is neither thinking nor essence. This gesture by which he incessantly reminds us that the scientificity of science is not scientific, this gesture in which one hopes to think [*pense penser*][10] the ontological difference, that is to say, the fact that the essence of this is not this, and that this is the condition of thinking, ensures that between thinking and technics, as between thinking and science, there is the abyss of which Heidegger wants to remind us. This is, for me in any case and if I understand it correctly, the title of an immense question – and of an immense reserve with respect to the ensemble not only of what Heidegger thinks, but of what he thinks of thinking in general. Even if I find it necessary or important not to reduce thinking to philosophy, or to science, or to technics, it seems to me that to try to make of thinking or of the thinkable something that is pure of all philosophical, scientific, or technical contamination (I don't confuse these three domains, but it is a question of determinations that stand in the same relationship here), it seems to me that this purification of the thinkable is not self-evident. Nor is the desire for purification in general, the desire for the safe and sound, for the intact or immune (*heilige*), the pure, purified, or purifying restraint (*Verhaltenheit*), this theme that is so insistent in the *Beiträge* ...

Notes

1 *Ghostdance*, dir. Ken McMullen, perf. Pascale Ogier and Jacques Derrida, Loose Yard LTD, Channel Four, ZDF, 1983.

2 See Roland Barthes, *La chambre claire. Note sur la photographie* (Paris: Cahiers du Cinema, Gallimard, Seuil, 1980), pp. 120, 126–7, or *Camera Lucida: Reflections on Photography*, trans. Richard Howard (New York: Hill and Wang, 1981), pp. 76, 80–1.

3 Jacques Derrida, "Les morts de Roland Barthes," in *Psyché, Inventions de l'autre* (Paris: Galilée, 1987), p. 291; see, in English, "The Deaths of Roland Barthes," trans. Pascale-Anne Brault and Michael Naas, in Hugh J. Silverman, ed., *Philosophy and Non-Philosophy since Merleau-Ponty* (Evanston, IL: Northwestern University Press, 1997), pp. 259–96.

4 A commentary on this commentary can be found in the first chapter of Bernard Stiegler, *La désorientation* (Paris: Galilée, 1996).

5 The verb *regarder* may mean either "to look at" or "watch" or "to regard," in the sense of "to concern" (as in "This does not concern you," etc.). In this and following sentences, I have (rather violently) expanded the original phrases in order to give both meanings. (Trans.)

6 Lost in English here is an extended play on the prepositions *avant* and *devant,* both of which mean "before" (*avant* generally in the temporal sense, *devant* generally in the spatial), as well as on the latter's homonym, the present participle of the verb *devoir,* "to owe." Again, I have expanded what in the original is a single word or phrase into multiple phrases in English. (Trans.)

7 Martin Heidegger, *Sein und Zeit*, 17th edn (Tübingen: Max Niemeyer, 1993), p. 20; see, in English, *Being and Time*, trans. John Macquarrie and Edward Robinson (New York: Harper, 1962), p. 41. I have modified Macquarrie and Robinson's translation to follow Stiegler's French. (Trans.)

8 See *Apories: Mourir – s'attendre aux "limites de la vérité"* (Paris: Galilée, 1996), p. 110, note 1. [This note does not appear in the English edition, which was published prior to the French. (Trans.)]

9 *Unterwegs zur Sprache* (Pfullingen: Günther Neske, 1959); see, in English, *On the Way to Language*, trans. Peter D. Hertz (New York: Harper and Row, 1971).

10 Or, in the more cynical reading: "this gesture in which one thinks one is thinking the ontological difference." (Trans.)

3

État Présent: Hauntology, Spectres and Phantoms

Colin Davis

Hauntology, as a trend in recent critical and psychoanalytical work, has two distinct, related, and to some extent incompatible sources. The word itself, in its French form *hantologie*, was coined by Jacques Derrida in his *Spectres de Marx* (1993), which has rapidly become one of the most controversial and influential works of his later period.[1] Marxist and leftleaning readers have been less than enthusiastic about Derrida's claim that deconstruction was all along a radicalization of Marx's legacy, their responses ranging, as Michael Sprinker puts it, 'from skepticism, to ire, to outright contempt'.[2] But in literary critical circles, Derrida's rehabilitation of ghosts as a respectable subject of enquiry has proved to be extraordinarily fertile. Hauntology supplants its near-homonym ontology, replacing the priority of being and presence with the figure of the ghost as that which is neither present nor absent, neither dead nor alive.

Attending to the ghost is an ethical injunction insofar as it occupies the place of the Levinasian Other: a wholly irrecuperable intrusion in our world, which is not comprehensible within our available intellectual frameworks, but whose otherness we are responsible for preserving. Hauntology is thus related to, and represents a new aspect of, the ethical turn of deconstruction which has been palpable for at least two decades. It has nothing to do with whether or not one believes in ghosts, as Fredric Jameson explains:

> Spectrality does not involve the conviction that ghosts exist or that the past (and maybe even the future they offer to prophesy) is still very much alive and at work, within the living present: all it says, if it can be

thought to speak, is that the living present is scarcely as self-sufficient as it claims to be; that we would do well not to count on its density and solidity, which might under exceptional circumstances betray us.[3]

The second, chronologically prior yet less acknowledged, source of hauntology is the work of psychoanalysts Nicolas Abraham and Maria Torok, especially in some of the essays collected in *L'Écorce et le noyau* and Torok's work subsequent to the death of Abraham.[4] In fact, Derrida played a key role in getting the work of Abraham and Torok known to a wider audience. In 1976, the year after Abraham's death, their radical re-working of Freud's Wolfman case study, *Le Verbier de l'homme aux loups*, appeared in the Flammarion 'Philosophie en effet' series of which Derrida was one of the co-directors, and it was preceded by a long and influential essay by Derrida entitled 'Fors'.[5] Derrida's essay suggests some of the similarities between his thought and that of Abraham and Torok, but he has next to nothing to say about their work on phantoms and the marked differences between their conception and his. Abraham and Torok had become interested in transgenerational communication, particularly the way in which the undisclosed traumas of previous generations might disturb the lives of their descendants even and especially if they know nothing about their distant causes. What they call a phantom is the presence of a dead ancestor in the living Ego, still intent on preventing its traumatic and usually shameful secrets from coming to light. One crucial consequence of this is that the phantom does not, as it does in some versions of the ghost story, return from the dead in order to reveal something hidden or forgotten, to right a wrong or to deliver a message that might otherwise have gone unheeded. On the contrary, the phantom is a liar; its effects are designed to mislead the haunted subject and to ensure that its secret remains shrouded in mystery. In this account, phantoms are not the spirits of the dead, but 'les lacunes laissées en nous par les secrets des autres' (*L'Écorce et le noyau*, p. 427). This insight offers a new explanation for ghost stories, which are described as the mediation in fiction of the encrypted, unspeakable secrets of past generations: 'Le fantôme des croyances populaires ne fait donc qu'objectiver une métaphore qui travaille dans l'inconscient: l'enterrement dans l'objet d'un fait inavouable' (*L'Écorce et le noyau*, p. 427).

The ideas of Abraham and Torok have renewed psychoanalytic theory and therapeutic practice dealing with transgenerational trauma and family secrets.[6] They have also appealed to some critics working on literature and popular culture.[7] A notable success in this domain was scored by the psychoanalyst Serge Tisseron in his book *Tintin chez le psychana-lyste* (1985). Analysing a sequence of Tintin albums in which Captain Haddock is haunted by the ghost of an ancestor, Tisseron speculated about a possible connection between the ghost's illegitimate origins and a drama of legitimacy in the family history of Tintin's creator Hergé. Subsequent biographical research undertaken after Hergé's death showed that Hergé's father was indeed the illegitimate child of an unknown father; and in subsequent publications Tisseron took credit for deducing this secret purely from the analysis of the fictional albums, even though he had in fact been mistaken in suggesting that the illegitimacy was most probably on Hergé's mother's side of the family.

Literary critical work drawing on the thought of Abraham and Torok most frequently revolves around the problem of secrets, even if it generally neither achieves nor seeks the biographical confirmation found by Tisseron. The work of Nicholas Rand, especially his book *Le Cryptage et la vie des oeuvres* (1989), deserves particular mention here. Rand was instrumental in demonstrating the relevance of Abraham and Torok for literary criticism, and he also helped extend their work through his later direct collaborations with Maria Torok.[8] The other major study that should be mentioned in this context is Esther Rashkin's *Family Secrets and the Psychoanalysis of Narrative* (1992). This book offers what is still the best short account of Abraham and Torok's concept of the phantom and an attempt to develop a critical approach on the basis of it through readings of Conrad, Villiers de l'Isle Adam, Balzac, James and Poe. Rashkin is keen not to set up a prescriptive model for interpretation, but to attend to the specificity of each individual text. The works she studies are 'in distress', harbouring secrets of which they are unaware, but which the reader or critic may be able to elicit. Her readings track down secrets and bring them to light. In her chapter on Balzac's 'Facino Cane', for example, she endeavours to make intelligible Cane's 'perplexing obsession' with gold (*Family Secrets*, p. 82). She finds a possible solution in what she suggests is the secret drama of his Jewish origins, and this in turn is reflected in the narrator's unconscious desire to know the story of his own origins. 'Facino Cane' is not explicitly a ghost story, but in Rashkin's reading it revolves around the transmission of phantoms and family secrets in the sense of Abraham and Torok.

Despite the intellectual vigour of works by Rand, Rashkin and others, the direct impact of Abraham and Torok on literary studies has in fact been limited, perhaps because the endeavour to find undisclosed secrets is likely to succeed in only a small number of cases. By contrast, Derrida's *Spectres de Marx* has spawned a minor academic industry.[9] His hauntology has virtually removed Abraham and Torok from the agenda of literary ghost studies; or, to be more precise, when Abraham and Torok are now discussed by deconstructive-minded critics, their work is most frequently given a distinctly Derridean inflection. It is to say the least striking that the only mention of Abraham and Torok in *Spectres de Marx* is in a footnote which refers the reader to Derrida's essay on them, 'Fors' (*Spectres de Marx*, p. 24). In fact, Derrida's *spectres* should be carefully distinguished from Abraham's and Torok's *phantoms* (which is why the title of the present article maintains the distinction between them, even if the authors themselves are not always consistent).[10] Derrida's spectre is a deconstructive figure hovering between life and death, presence and absence, and making established certainties vacillate. It does not belong to the order of knowledge:

> C'est quelque chose qu'on ne sait pas, justement, et on ne sait pas si précisément cela *est*, si ça existe, si ça répond à un nom et correspond à une essence. On ne le *sait* pas: non par ignorance, mais parce que ce non-objet, ce présent non-présent, cet être-là d'un absent ou d'un disparu ne relève pas du savoir. Du moins plus de ce qu'on croit savoir sous le nom de savoir. On ne sait pas si c'est vivant ou si c'est mort. (*Spectres de Marx*, pp. 25–26; emphasis in original)

Derrida calls on us to endeavour to speak and listen to the spectre, despite the reluctance inherited from our intellectual traditions and because of the challenge it may pose to them: 'Or ce qui paraît presque impossible, c'est toujours de parler du spectre, de parler au spectre, de parler avec lui, donc surtout de faire ou de laisser parler un esprit' (*Spectres de Marx*, p. 32; emphasis in original). Conversing with spectres is not undertaken in the expectation that they will reveal some secret, shameful or otherwise. Rather, it may open us up to the experience of secrecy as such: an essential unknowing which underlies and may undermine what we think we know. For Abraham and Torok, the phantom's secret can and should be revealed in order to achieve 'une petite victoire de l'Amour sur la Mort' (*L'Écorce et le noyau*, p. 452); for Derrida, on the contrary, the spectre's secret is a productive opening of meaning rather than a determinate content to be uncovered. Elsewhere, in a move of key importance for literary hauntology, Derrida associates this kind of essential secret with literature in general:

> La littérature garde un secret qui n'existe pas, en quelque sorte. Derrière un roman, ou un poème, derrière ce qui est en effet la richesse d'un sens à interpréter, il n'y a pas de sens secret à chercher. Le secret d'un personnage, par exemple, n'existe pas, il n'a aucune épaisseur en dehors du phénomène littéraire. Tout est secret dans la littérature et il n'y a pas de secret caché *derrière* elle, voilà le secret de cette étrange institution *au sujet* de laquelle, et *dans* laquelle je ne cesse de (me) débattre. [...] L'institution de la littérature reconnaît, en principe ou par essence le droit de tout dire ou de ne pas dire en disant, donc le droit au secret affiché.[11]

The attraction of hauntology for deconstructive-minded critics arises from the link between a theme (haunting, ghosts, the supernatural) and the processes of literature and textuality in general. In consequence, much of the most committed work in this area combines close reading with daring speculation. The significant difference between the approach inspired by Abraham and Torok and poststructuralist hauntology can already be seen in Nicholas Royle's response to Rashkin's *Family Secrets and the Psychoanalysis of Narrative*. In her conclusion, Rashkin conceded that uncovering textual secrets always brings to the fore other enigmas which might demand, but not be susceptible to, solution (*Family Secrets*, pp. 161–62). Royle marks the key difference between critics inspired by Abraham and Torok and those of a more Derridean and poststructuralist bent: in principle, he suggests, Rashkin argues that the process of meaning may be open-ended and infinite, but in practice she closes down that process by assigning determinate meanings to identifiable secrets. *Family Secrets and the Psychoanalysis of Narrative* is thus 'a more disruptive, housebreaking book than it seems prepared to admit' ('This is Not a Review', p. 34). Whereas Rashkin insists that 'Not all texts have phantoms' (*Family Secrets*, p. 12), Royle wonders whether 'every text, including a book review, has phantoms' ('This is Not a Review', p. 35). Jodey Castricano makes a similar point in her *Cryptomimesis: The Gothic and Jacques Derrida's Ghost Writing* (2001): 'I find [Rashkin's] assertion that "not all texts have phantoms" to be problematic because her assertion marks a division between texts which reveal "secrets" and those that do not (presumably those that do not harbour an unspeakable secret are transparent)' (*Cryptomimesis*, p. 142).

Royle's musing and Castricano's observation provide a clue to the theoretical ambitions of literary hauntologists. Ghosts are a privileged theme because they allow an insight into texts and textuality as such. Rashkin deliberately restricts the scope of her approach in the name of attentiveness to the secrets of individual texts. Whilst remaining eager to respect specificity, the hauntologists also aspire to extend the validity of their enquiry to embrace a greater level of generality. As Buse and Stott put it in the introduction to the essays collected in *Ghosts: Deconstruction, Psychoanalysis, History*, 'modern theory owes a debt to ghosts' (p. 6). Some critics have repaid this debt by dramatically escalating the claims made for the spectral, and by association for their own work. Julian Wolfreys' *Victorian Hauntings: Spectrality, Gothic, the Uncanny and Literature* (2002), for example, opens with a series of increasingly bold assertions about the importance of literary ghosts. Ghosts 'exceed any narrative modality, genre or textual manifestation'; the spectral 'makes possible reproduction even as it also fragments reproduction and ruins the very possibility of reproduction's apparent guarantee to represent that which is no longer there fully'; in consequence 'all forms of narrative are spectral to some extent', and 'the spectral is at the heart of any narrative of the modern'; moreover, 'to tell a story is always to invoke ghosts, to open a space through which something other returns', so that 'all stories are, more or less, ghost stories' (*Victorian Hauntings*, pp. 1–3). In this breathtaking display, ghosts progress rapidly from being one theme amongst others to being the ungrounded grounding of representation and a key to all forms of storytelling. They are both unthinkable and the only thing worth thinking about.

The crucial difference between the two strands of hauntology, deriving from Abraham and Torok and from Derrida respectively, is to be found in the status of the secret. The secrets of Abraham's and Torok's lying phantoms are unspeakable in the restricted sense of being a subject of shame and prohibition. It is not at all that they cannot be spoken; on the contrary, they can and should be put into words so that the phantom and its noxious effects on the living can be exorcized. For Derrida, the ghost and its secrets are unspeakable in a quite different sense. Abraham and Torok seek to return the ghost to the order of knowledge; Derrida wants to avoid any such restoration and to encounter what is strange, unheard, other, about the ghost. For Derrida, the ghost's secret is not a puzzle to be solved; it is the structural openness or address directed towards the living by the voices of the past or the not yet formulated possibilities of the future. The secret is not unspeakable because it is taboo, but because it cannot not (yet) be articulated in the languages available to us. The ghost pushes at the boundaries of language and thought. The interest here, then, is not in secrets, understood as puzzles to be resolved, but in secrecy, now elevated to what Castricano calls 'the structural enigma which inaugurates the scene of writing' (*Cryptomimesis*, p. 30).

Hauntology is part of an endeavour to keep raising the stakes of literary study, to make it a place where we can interrogate our relation to the dead, examine the elusive identities of the living, and explore the boundaries between the thought and the unthought. The ghost becomes a focus for competing epistemological and ethical positions. For Abraham and Torok, the phantom and its secrets should be uncovered so that it can be dispelled. For Derrida and those impressed by his work, the spectre's ethical injunction consists on the contrary in not reducing it prematurely to an object of knowledge. Derrida's reading of Abraham and Torok in 'Fors' emphasizes how their work involves attentiveness to disturbances of meaning, the hieroglyphs and secrets which engage the interpreter in a restless labour of deciphering. In the process, Derrida underplays the extent to which Abraham and Torok attempt to bring interpretation to an end by recovering occluded meanings, and his reading has had a significant impact on the more general understanding of their work. Their phantoms and his spectres, though, have little in common. Phantoms lie about the past whilst spectres gesture towards a still unformulated future. The difference between them poses in a new form the tension between the desire to understand and the openness to what exceeds knowledge; and the resulting critical practices vary between the endeavour to attend patiently to particular texts and exhilarating speculation. As far as I know, the ghost of a resolution is not yet haunting Europe, or anywhere else.

Notes

1   References are to Jacques Derrida, *Spectres de Marx* (Paris, Galilée, 1993).

2   'Introduction', in *Ghostly Demarcations: A Symposium on Jacques Derrida's 'Spectres de Marx'*, ed. by Michael Sprinker (London and New York: Verso, 1999), p. 2. For political responses to Derrida's *Spectres de Marx*, see the essays in this collection; see also Gayatri Chakravorty Spivak, 'Ghostwriting', *Diacritics*, 25 (1995), 65–84, and Ernesto Laclau, 'The Time is Out of Joint', *Diacritics*, 25 (1995), 86–96.

3   'Marx's Purloined Letter', in *Ghostly Demarcations*, pp. 26–67 (p. 39).

4   References are to Nicolas Abraham and Maria Torok, *L'Écorce et le noyau* (Paris: Flammarion, 1987; first published 1978). See also Abraham and Torok, *Cryptonymie: le verbier de l'homme aux loups* (Paris: Flammarion, 1976).

5   'Fors: les mots anglés de Nicolas Abraham et Maria Torok', in Abraham and Torok, *Cryptonymie: le verbier de l'homme aux loups*, pp. 7–73.

6   For a review of work in this area, see Claude Nachin, *Les Fantômes de l'âme: à propos des héritages psychiques* (Paris: L'Harmattan, 1993), pp. 175–202. See also Nachin, *Le Deuil d'amour* (Paris: Éditions universitaires, 1989); Didier Dumas, *L'Ange et le fantôme: introduction à la clinique de l'impensé généalogique* (Paris: Minuit, 1985); Serge Tisseron, *Secrets de famille: mode d'emploi* (Paris: Éditions Ramsay, 1996); Serge Tisseron et al., *Le Psychisme à l'épreuve des générations: clinique du fantôme* (Paris: Dunod, 1995, 2000).

7   For criticism drawing on the work of Abraham and Torok, see, for example, Esther Rashkin, *Family Secrets and the Psychoanalysis of Narrative* (Princeton University Press, 1992); Nicholas Rand, 'Invention poétique et psychanalyse du secret dans "Le Fantôme d'Hamlet" de Nicolas Abraham', in *Le Psychisme à l'épreuve des générations*, pp. 79–96; Nicholas Rand, *Le Cryptage et la vie des oeuvres: étude du secret dans les textes de Flaubert, Stendhal, Benjamin, Stefan George, Edgar Poe, Francis Ponge, Heidegger et Freud* (Paris: Aubier, 1989); Serge Tisseron, *Tintin chez le psychanalyste: essai sur la création graphique et la mise en scène de ses enjeux dans l'oeuvre d'Hergé* (Paris: Aubier Montaigne, 1985), and *Tintin et le secret d'Hergé* (Paris: Hors Collection—Presses de la Cité, 1993); Colin Davis, 'Charlotte Delbo's Ghosts', *FS*, LIX (2005), 9–15.

8   See in particular Maria Torok and Nicholas Rand, *Questions à Freud: du devenir de la psychanalyse* (Paris: Les Belles Lettres, 1995).

9   See, for example, *Ghosts: Deconstruction, Psychoanalysis, History*, ed. by Peter Buse and Andrew Stott (Basingstoke: Macmillan, 1999); Jodey Castricano, *Cryptomimesis: The Gothic and Jacques Derrida's Ghost Writing* (Montreal, Kingston—London and Ithaca: McGill-Queen's University Press, 2001); Nancy Holland, 'The Death of the Other/Father: A Feminist Reading of Derrida's Hauntology', *Hypatia*, 16 (2001), 64–71; Jean-Michel Rabaté, *The Ghosts of Modernity* (Gainesville: University Press of Florida, 1996); Nicholas Royle, *Telepathy and Literature: Essays on the Reading Mind*

(Oxford: Blackwell, 1991), *The Uncanny* (Manchester University Press, 2003), and 'This is Not a Book Review: Esther Rashkin, Family Secrets and the Psychoanalysis of Narrative', *Angelaki*, 2 (1995), 31–5; Emily Tomlinson, 'Assia Djebar: Speaking to the Living Dead', *Paragraph* 26:3 (2003), 34–50; Julian Wolfreys, *Victorian Hauntings: Spectrality, Gothic, the Uncanny and Literature* (Basingstoke: Palgrave, 2002). For critical discussion of Derrida's hauntology, see Slavoj Žižek, 'Introduction: The Spectre of Ideology', in *Mapping Ideology*, ed. by Slavoj Žižek (London and New York: Verso, 1994), pp. 1–33. It should be stressed that interesting work is being done on ghosts which does not draw explicitly or significantly on the work of Derrida or Abraham and Torok; see, for example, Avery F. Gordon, *Ghostly Matters: Haunting and the Sociological Imagination* (Minneapolis and London: University of Minnesota Press, 1997), and Kathleen Brogan, *Cultural Haunting: Ghosts and Ethnicity in Recent American Literature* (Charlottesville and London: University Press of Virginia, 1998).

10   Nicholas Royle also comments on Derrida's surprising lack of reference in *Spectres de Marx* to Abraham and Torok; see 'Phantom Text', in *The Uncanny*, pp. 279–80 and, on differences between Derrida's and Abraham and Torok's conception of the ghost, see pp. 281–83.

11   *Papier machine* (Paris: Galilée, 2001), p. 398; emphasis in original.

4

from Introduction: The Spectral Turn

Jeffrey Andrew Weinstock

I. Spectral America

Our contemporary moment is a haunted one. Having now slipped over the edge of the millennium into the twenty-first century, it seems that ghosts are everywhere in American popular and academic culture. Beginning in the 1980s with *Poltergeist* (1982)—directed by Tobe Hooper and produced by Steven Spielberg—and Bill Murray and Dan Aykroyd in *Ghostbusters* (1984), American cinema has witnessed a spate of big-budget ghostly features including *Ghost* (1990) starring Patrick Swayze and Demi Moore, *The Sixth Sense* (2000) starring Bruce Willis, *What Lies Beneath* (2000) starring Harrison Ford and Michelle Pfeiffer, and *The Others* (2001) starring Nicole Kidman.[1]

On television, late-twentieth- and early-twenty-first century programs such as *The X-Files*, *Buffy the Vampire Slayer*, *Ally McBeal*, and, more recently *Tru Calling*, *Dead Like Me*, *The West Wing*, and *NYPD Blue*, more or less regularly featured and continue to include ghosts and supernatural intervention. On cable, *Crossing Over with John Edwards*, a program that features a psychic who communes with the dead, has become one of the SciFi channel's most popular programs. In contemporary literature, Stephen King, an author of supernatural tales, remains one of America's—and the world's—most popular authors, while even such "high brow" authors as Toni Morrison, Louise Erdrich, Maxine Hong Kingston, and Gloria Naylor routinely imbricate the spectral realm with the world of profane reality

(Morrison's ghost story *Beloved* won the Pulitzer prize for literature in 1988). On the American stage, two 1990s productions featuring ghosts won Pulitzer prizes for drama: August Wilson's *The Piano Lesson* in 1990 and Tony Kushner's *Angels in America, Part One: Millennium Approaches* in 1993.

Contemporary academia has followed suit in this preoccupation with ghosts; while studies of the supernatural in literature and culture are not new to academia,[2] the late 1980s also marked the beginning of heightened interest in ghosts and hauntings in cultural and literary criticism. Concerned specifically with accounts of "real" ghosts, F. C. Finucane's *Ghosts: Appearances of the Dead and Cultural Transformation* was published in 1996; Jean-Claude Schmitt's *Ghosts in the Middle Ages: The Living and the Dead in Medieval Society*, originally published in French in 1994, was introduced in English in 1998; and Gillian Bennett's *Alas Poor Ghost! Traditions of Belief in Story and Discourse* followed in 1999. As concerns ghosts in American literature and film, one can look to the following monographs issued with increasing velocity over the last twenty years: Howard Kerr, John W. Crowley, and Charles L. Crow's edited collection *The Haunted Dusk: American Supernatural Fiction, 1820–1920* (1983); Lynette Carpenter and Wendy K. Kalmar's edited collection *Haunting the House of Fiction: Feminist Perspectives on Ghost Stories by American Women* (1991); Katherine A. Fowkes's *Giving Up the Ghost: Spirits, Ghosts, and Angels in Mainstream American Comedy Films* (1998); Kathleen Brogan's *Cultural Haunting: Ghosts and Ethnicity in Recent American Literature* (1998); Lee Kovacs's *The Haunted Screen: Ghosts in Literature and Film* (1999); Dale Bailey's *American Nightmares: The Haunted House Formula in American Popular Fiction* (1999); and Renée Bergland's *The National Uncanny: Indian Ghosts and American Subjects* (2000).

Perhaps even more intriguing is the "spectral turn" of contemporary literary theory. Because ghosts are unstable interstitial figures that problematize dichotomous thinking, it perhaps should come as no surprise that phantoms have become a privileged poststructuralist academic trope. Neither living nor dead, present nor absent, the ghost functions as the paradigmatic deconstructive gesture, the "shadowy third" or trace of an absence that undermines the fixedness of such binary oppositions. As an entity out of place in time, as something from the past that emerges into the present, the phantom calls into question the linearity of history. And as, in philosopher Jacques Derrida's words in his *Specters of Marx*, the "*plus d'un*," simultaneously the "no more one" and the "more than one," the ghost suggests the complex relationship between the constitution of individual subjectivity and the larger social collective.

Indeed, the figure of the specter in literary and cultural criticism has become so common that one may refer to contemporary academic discourse as, in some respects, "haunted." The end of the millennium witnessed a proliferation of publications focused specifically on specters and haunting, including Jacques Derrida's *Specters of Marx* (1994), Jean-Michel Rabaté's *The Ghosts of Modernity* (1996), Avery Gordon's *Ghostly Matters: Haunting and the Sociological Imagination* (1997), Peter Buse and Andrew Stotts's *Ghosts: Deconstruction, Psychoanalysis, History* (1999), and Peter Schwenger's *Fantasm and Fiction* (1999). And, if one begins to consider contemporary poststructuralist theory more generally—for instance, the recent preoccupation with "trauma" in which the presence of a symptom demonstrates the subject's failure to internalize a past event, in which something from the past emerges to disrupt the present—the ubiquity of "spectral discourse" becomes readily apparent.

The question of *why* American popular culture and academia finds itself in the midst of this spectral turn is complex and, in various ways, the essays included in this volume will each address different aspects of the needs and desires that ghosts fulfill. However, I will briefly suggest here that the current fascination with ghosts arises out of a general postmodern suspicion of meta-narratives accentuated by millennial anxiety.

As I have indicated above, the idea of the ghost, of that which disrupts both oppositional thinking and the linearity of historical chronology, has substantial affinities with poststructural thought in general. The ghost is that which interrupts the presentness of the present, and its haunting indicates that, beneath the surface of received history, there lurks another narrative, an untold story that calls into question the veracity of the authorized version of events. As such, the contemporary fascination with ghosts is reflective of an awareness of the narrativity of history. Hortense Spillers observes that "[Events] *do* occur, to be sure, but in part according to the conventions dictating how we receive, imagine, and pass them on" (176). This is to say that there are multiple perspectives on any given event and one perspective assumes prominence only at the expense of other, competing interpretations. To write from a perspective other than the authorized one and "to write stories concerning exclusions and invisibilities" is, to quote Avery Gordon, "to write ghost stories" (17). The usefulness of the ghost in the revisioning of history from alternate, competing perspectives is one reason why tales of the spectral have assumed such prominence in contemporary ethnic American literature.[3] The ubiquity of ghost stories in our particular cultural moment is connected to the recognition that history is always fragmented and perspectival and to contestations for control of the meaning of history as minority voices foreground the "exclusions and invisibilities" of American history.

It is also no coincidence that the contemporary American fascination with ghosts seems to have reached a high-water mark at the turn of the millennium and has yet to abate. Ghosts, as all the essays in this volume argue, reflect the ethos and anxieties of the eras of their production. In this respect, the spectral turn of American culture should be read as a mark of millennial anxiety. As a symptom of repressed knowledge, the ghost calls into question the possibilities of a future based on avoidance of the past. Millennial specters ask us to what extent we can move forward into a new millennium when we are still shackled to a past that haunts us and that we have yet to face and mourn fully. The millennial explosion of supernatural cultural production thus seems to suggest that what is as frightening as the unknown field of the future is the tenacious tendrils of a past we cannot shake.

And yet it needs to be acknowledged that our ghosts are also comforting to us. They represent our desires for truth and justice (not to mention the American way), and validate religious faith and the ideas of heaven and hell. They speak to our desire to be remembered and to our longing for a coherent and "correct" narrative of history. We value our ghosts, particularly during periods of cultural transition, because the alternative to their presence is even more frightening: If ghosts do not return to correct history, then privileged narratives of history are not open to contestation. If ghosts do not return to reveal crimes that have gone unpunished, then evil acts may in fact go unredressed. If ghosts do not appear to validate faith, then faith remains just that—faith rather than fact; and without ghosts to point to things that have been lost and overlooked, things may disappear forever. How can we get it right if we do not know that we have gotten it wrong?

That ghosts are particularly prominent in our cultural moment indicates that we are particularly vexed by these questions. The ghosts that we conjure speak to these timely, context-bound fears and desires—they can do nothing else.

II. America's spectral turn

To be spectral is to be ghostlike, which, in turn, is to be out of place and time. Ghosts, as noted above, violate conceptual thinking based on dichotomous oppositions. They are neither fully present nor absent, neither living nor dead. The ghost is the mark or trace of an absence. As Avery Gordon puts it, ghosts are "one form by which something lost, or barely visible, or seemingly not there to our supposedly well-trained eyes, makes itself known or apparent to us" (8). Phantoms *haunt*; their appearances signal epistemological uncertainty and the potential emergence of a different story and a competing history.

This volume foregrounds the growing interest in the importance of ghosts and hauntings—of spectrality—to American cultural configurations, and it aims to address a salient gap: the absence of any sustained diachronic attention to the role of the spectral in American culture. In the general body of criticism on American literature, attention has historically been paid to the supernatural writings of individual authors, such as Edgar Allan Poe and Henry James, and individual articles have appeared here and there noting spectral motifs in virtually every time, region, and ethnic group in the United States. Studies have also focused on American ghost stories during discrete blocks of time (Kerr), ghost stories written by specific populations (Brogan; Carpenter and Kolmar; Lundie; Neary; Patrick), ghost stories with particular thematic foci or political orientations (Bergland), and cinematic ghost stories (Fowkes, Kovacs).

However, despite the development of what I am tempted to term "spectrality studies" in the 1990s, and the pronounced contemporary interest in ghosts and hauntings, what is lacking in American studies, literary studies, and cultural studies is any sustained approach to the importance of phantoms to the general constitution of North American national identity and consciousness.[4] That is, while there are specific studies of particular authors and bodies of literature, what all these isolated studies point to the need for, and what precisely is missing, is an analysis of the general importance of phantoms and haunting to the constitution of the "American imagination." *Spectral America: Phantoms and the National Imagination* speaks to this gap by assembling scholars who focus on how phantoms and hauntings have exerted their influences in literary and popular discourses across the span of American history and have shaped the terrain of American consciousness. This is an immense topic, of course, and it is not one that any single volume can hope to exhaust. However, it is my hope that the essays contained within this volume will begin to outline broad parameters for future investigation.

Taken together, the essays included in *Spectral America* demonstrate the ways in which phantoms have been a part of American culture since its inception, and the manner in which the preoccupation with the supernatural has been a defining American obsession—but one that has persistently been appropriated and redeployed to accommodate changing American sociohistorical anxieties and emphases. *Spectral America* thus reveals the idea of the ghost as one that has remained consistently vital to American culture, but demonstrates the ways in which particular ghostly manifestations are always constructions embedded within specific historical contexts and invoked for more or less explicit political purposes. What the contributions to this volume confirm is that America has *always* been a land of ghosts, a nation obsessed with the spectral. Part of the American national heritage is a supernatural inheritance—but each generation puts this inheritance to use in different ways and with differing objectives. This is to say that ghosts do "cultural work," but that the work they perform changes according to the developing needs of the living. Phantoms participate in, reinforce, and exemplify various belief structures. To investigate the role of the spectral in American life, therefore, is to engage with changing parameters of religion and science and to explore the ongoing importance of the liminal in the constitution of American subjectivity. Examining our ghosts tells us quite a bit about America's hopes and desires, fears and regrets—and the extent to which the past governs our present and opens or forecloses possibilities for the future.

[...]

Notes

1   One could supplement this list with Michael Keaton in *Beetlejuice* (1984), Spielberg's *Always* (1989), Kevin Costner in *Field of Dreams* (1989), Brandon Lee in the cult hit *The Crow* (1994), Kevin Bacon in *Stir of Echoes* (1999), big-budget 1999 remakes of both *The Haunting* and *House on Haunted Hill*, the re-release of *The Exorcist*, Tim Burton's version of *Sleepy Hollow* (2000) and *The Ring* (2002), and, depending upon one's interpretation of the ghostly elements, one could include *The Blair Witch Project* (2000).

2   Older studies of the supernatural in literature include Dorothy Scarborough's seminal survey, *The Supernatural in Modern English Fiction* (1917); H. P. Lovecraft's increasingly cited *Supernatural Horror in Literature* (1945), and Julia Briggs's *Night Visitors: The Rise and Fall of the English Ghost Story* (1977). There are also, of course, studies of the use of supernatural conventions in individual authors such as Poe and Irving and a large body of information on the Gothic novel.

3   See Hayes in this volume, as well as Brogan and Gordon, for studies of contemporary ethnic American ghost stories as forms of political critique. For discussions of feminist ghost stories, see Carpeter and Kolmer, Lundie, Neary, Patrick and Salmonson.

4   Bergland comes closest to this objective in her study of the importance of Native Americans as spectral to the constitution of American cultural identity.

Works cited

Bailey, Dale. *American Nightmares: The Haunted House Formula in American Popular Fiction*. Bowling Green, OH: Bowling Green State University Popular Press, 1999.

Bennett, Gillian. *Alas, Poor Ghost! Traditions of Belief in Story and Discourse*. Logan: Utah State University Press, 1999.

Bergland, Renée L. *The National Uncanny: Indian Ghosts and American Subjects*. Hanover, NH: University Press of New England, 2000.

Briggs, Julia. *Night Visitors: The Rise and Fall of the English Ghost Story*. London: Faber, 1977.

Brogan, Kathleen. *Cultural Haunting: Ghosts and Ethnicity in Recent American Literature.* Charlottesville: University Press of Virginia, 1998.

Buse, Peter, and Andrew Scott, eds. *Ghosts: Deconstruction, Psychoanalysis, History.* New York: St. Martin's, 1999.

Carpenter, Lynette, and Wendy K. Kolmar, eds. *Haunting the House of Fiction: Ghost Stories by American Women.* Knoxville: University of Tennessee Press, 1991.

Crow, Charles L., ed. *American Gothic: An Anthology 1787–1916.* Malden, MA: Blackwell, 1999.

Derrida, Jacques. *Specters of Marx: The State of Debt, the Work of Mourning, and the New International.* Transl. Peggy Kamuf. New York: Routledge, 1994.

Finucane, R. C. *Ghosts: Appearances of the Dead & Cultural Transformation.* Amherst, NY: Prometheus, 1996.

Fowkes, Katherine A. *Giving Up the Ghost: Spirits, Ghosts, and Angels in Mainstream Comedy Films.* Detroit: Wayne State University Press, 1998.

Gordon, Avery. *Ghostly Matters: Haunting and the Sociological Imagination.* Minneapolis: University of Minnesota Press, 1997.

Higley, Sarah, and Jeffrey Andrew Weinstock. *The Nothing That Is: Millennial Cinema and the Blair Witch Controversies.* Detroit: Wayne State University Press, 2004.

Kerr, Howard, John W. Crowley, and Charles L. Crow, eds. *The Haunted Dusk: American Supernatural Fiction, 1820–1920.* Athens: University of Georgia Press, 1983.

Kovacs, Lee. *The Haunted Screen: Ghosts in Literature and Film.* Jefferson, NC: MacFarland, 1999.

Kushner, Tony. *Angels in America: A Gay Fantasia on National Themes. Part I: Millenium Approaches.* New York: Theatre Communications Group, 1992.

Lovecraft, Howard Phillips. *Supernatural Horror in Literature.* 1945. Reprint. New York: Dover, 1973.

Lundie, Catherine A. "Introduction." In *Restless Spirits: Ghost Stories by American Women 1872–1926.* Amherst: University of Massachusetts Press, 1996.

Morrison, Toni. *Beloved.* New York: Plume, 1988.

Neary, Gwen Patrick. "Disorderly Ghosts: Literary Spirits and the Social Agenda of American Women, 1870–1930." Ph.D. diss. University of California, Berkeley, 1994.

Patrick, Barbara Constance. "The Invisible Tradition: Freeman, Gilman, Spofford, Wharton, and American Women's Ghost Stories as Social Criticism, 1863–1937." Ph.D. diss. University of North Carolina, Chapel Hill, 1991.

Rabaté, Jean-Michel. *The Ghosts of Modernity.* Gainesville: University Press of Florida, 1996.

Salmonson, Jessica Amanda. "Preface." In *What Did Mrs. Darrington See? An Anthology of Feminist Supernatural Fiction.* New York: The Feminist Press, 1989.

Scarborough, Dorothy. *The Supernatural in Modern English Fiction.* 1917. Reprint. New York: Octagon, 1978.

Schmitt, Jean-Claude. *Ghosts in the Middle Ages: The Living and the Dead in*

Medieval Society. Translated by Teresa Lavender Fagan. Chicago: University of
Chicago Press, 1998.

Schwenger, Peter. *Fantasm and Fiction: On Textual Envisioning*. Stanford:
Stanford University Press, 1999.

Spillers, Hortense J. "Notes on an Alternative Model: Neither/Nor." In *The
Year Left 2: An American Socialist Yearbook*. Edited by Mike Davis, 176–94.
London: Verso, 1987.

Wilson, August. *The Piano Lesson*. New York: Plume, 1990.

Films referenced

Always. Dir. Steven Spielberg. Perf. Richard Dreyfuss, Holly Hunter. MCA/
Universal Pictures, 1989.

Beetlejuice. Dir. Tim Burton. Perfs. Michael Keaton, Geena Davis, Alec Baldwin,
Winona Ryder. Warner Bros., 1988.

The Blair Witch Project. Dirs. Daniel Myrick and Eduardo Sanchez. Artisan
Entertainment, 1999.

The Crow. Dir. Alex Proyas. Perf. Brandon Lee. Miramax/Dimension Films, 1994.

Field of Dreams. Dir. Phil Alden Robinson. Perfs. Kevin Costner, James Earl Jones.
Gordon Co., 1989.

Ghost. Dir. Jerry Zucker. Perfs. Patrick Swayze, Demi Moore, Whoopi Goldberg.
Paramount, 1990.

Ghostbusters. Dir. Ivan Reitman. Perfs. Bill Murray, Dan Aykroyd, Sigourney
Weaver. Columbia Pictures, 1984.

Haunting, The. Dir. Jan de Bont. Perf. Liam Neeson. Dream Works SKG, 1999.

House on Haunted Hill. Dir. William Malone. Perf. Geoffrey Rush. Dark Castle
Entertainment/ Warner Bros., 1999.

Poltergeist. Dir. Tobe Hooper. Perfs. JoBeth Williams, Craig T. Nelson. Prod.
Steven Spielberg. Metro-Goldwyn-Mayer, 1982.

Ring, The. Dir. Gore Verbinski. Perf. Naomi Watts. Amblin Entertainment, 2002.

Sixth Sense, The. Dir. M. Night Shyamalan. Perf. Bruce Willis. Hollywood Pictures
and Spyglass Entertainment, 2000.

Sleepy Hollow. Dir. Tim Burton. Perfs. Johnny Depp, Christina Ricci. Paramount
Pictures and Mandalay Pictures, 2000.

Stir of Echoes. Dir. David Koepp. Perf. Kevin Bacon. Artisan Entertainment, 1999.

Truly, Madly, Deeply. Dir. Anthony Minghella. Perf. Juliet Stevenson. Samuel
Goldwyn Company, 1991.

What Lies Beneath. Dir. Robert Zemeckis. Perfs. Harrison Ford, Michelle Pfeiffer.
Twentieth-Century Fox, 2000.

William Peter Blatty's The Exorcist. 1973. USA Reissue. Dir. William Freidkin.
Perf. Linda Blair. Warner Bros., 2000.

5

Preface: On Textual Haunting

Julian Wolfreys

Can we speak of 'ghosts' without transforming the whole world and ourselves, too, into phantoms?

JEAN-MICHEL RABATÉ, THE GHOSTS OF MODERNITY

... ni vivant ni mort. C'est spectral.

JACQUES DERRIDA, 'MARX, C'EST QUELQU'UN'

What does it mean to speak of spectrality and of textual haunting? What does it mean to address the text as haunted? How do the ideas of haunting and spectrality change our understanding of particular texts and the notion of the text in general? These questions shape this book. They return repeatedly even though you won't necessarily see them clearly, if at all. Perhaps though, before anything, it should be asked why, and with what legitimacy, one can claim to talk of the textual, of textuality generally, as haunted, as being articulated – and disrupted – by the spectral, the phantom, the phantasm, the uncanny, the ghostly? We can situate some tentative answers in the light of the work of Jacques Derrida, who, like the instituting questions of this volume, haunts these pages, occasionally as its subject, sometimes as the ghost in the machine. Derrida, as he himself admits, has interested himself for a long time in the matter of spectrality and its effects in various media, forms or discourses, whether one considers his publications on aesthetics, phenomenology, the literary, virtual and tele-technologies, politics or writing. Indeed, it is arguably because of Derrida's interest, particularly in the manifestation of what is felt to be his untimely intervention in the question of Marxism today and its problematic heritage in *Specters of Marx*, that critical attention has turned to the spectral.

However, while Derrida turns up frequently, and with a frequency that is positively spectral throughout these pages, this is not a sustained consideration of Derrida's concerns with matters of haunting. That remains as another project, to come. Nevertheless, as an opening to the question of haunting, I would like to draft some possible responses to the question of what constitutes the textual as being haunted through the example of certain remarks of Derrida's on the subject of the spectral, taken from a short essay, 'Marx, c'est quelqu'un'.[1]

The problem of defining the spectral, of addressing spectrality, is encountered immediately because, for Derrida, the spectral is a concept without concept (Mcq 23). It is a concept or, more accurately, a quasi-concept, which, as Derrida puts it with regard to the notion of iterability, 'marks both the possibility and the limit of all idealization and hence of all conceptualization'.[2] '[H]eterogeneous to the philosophical concept of the concept' (*LI* 118), spectrality resists conceptualization and one cannot form a coherent theory of the spectral without that which is spectral having always already exceeded any definition. Indeed, the problem is such – or, to put this another way, the condition of haunting and spectrality is such – that one cannot assume coherence of identification or determination. Epistemological modes of enquiry implicitly or explicitly dependent in their trajectories and procedures on the apparent finality and closure of identification cannot account for the idea of the spectral. Having said that though, consider what seems to be a definition and yet which articulates the experience of the undecidable within what Derrida names the classical or binary 'logic of all or nothing of yes or no' (*LI* 117): the second epigraph to this preface, where Derrida suggests that the spectral is that which is *neither* alive *nor* dead (Mcq 12; emphases added).

The identification of spectrality appears in a gap between the limits of two ontological categories. The definition escapes any positivist or constructivist logic by emerging between, and yet not as part of, two negations: *neither, nor*. A third term, the spectral, speaks of the limits of determination, while arriving beyond the terminal both in and of identification in either case (alive/dead) and not as an oppositional or dialectical term itself defined as part of some logical economy. As paradoxical as this might sound, Derrida pursues his exploration in these terms, in response to asking himself what a spectre might be, and what one might call by this strange name, spectre (Mcq 23). Of course, says Derrida, the spectre is something between life and death, though neither alive nor dead: 'La question des spectres est donc la question de la vie, de la limite entre le vivant et le mort, partout où elle se pose' [the question of spectres is therefore the question of life, of the limit between the living and the dead, everywhere where it presents itself] (Mcq 23).

Thus, to reiterate the point, the question of spectres is a question of speaking of that which presents itself or touches upon itself at and in excess of the limits of definition. To speak of the spectral, the ghostly, of haunting in general is to come face to face with that which plays on the very question of interpretation and identification, which appears, as it were, at the very limit to which interpretation can go. Moreover, the question is more radical than this, because it touches on the very question of the appropriateness of naming. Names, conventionally applied, fix the limits of an identity. Yet this 'strange name' – *spectre* – names nothing as such, and nothing which can be named as such, while also naming something which is neither something nor nothing; it names nothing which is neither nothing nor not nothing. The idea of the spectre, spectrality itself, escapes even as its apparitional instance arrives from some other place, as a figure of otherness which traverses and blurs any neat analytical distinction. The spectral as other in this case is not, then, simply a dialectical figure, that which returns from the dead for example to haunt life as simply the opposite of life. For, as Derrida's seemingly paradoxical formula makes clear, the spectral is, strictly speaking, neither alive nor dead, even though this condition that we name spectrality or haunting is intimately enfolded in our understanding of life and death.

What does this have to do with texts, though? We speak and write of texts in strange ways. We often place them in a heritage or tradition, much as we would our ancestors. We archive them, we keep them around, we revere them. As John Updike has recently commented of books, 'without their physical evidence my life would be more phantasmal'.[3] Books appear to have a material presence, without which anchoring that such materiality provides, our lives would assume a ghostly condition of impermanence; or, rather say, as does Updike, *more ghostly, more phantasmal*. Thus the book, as one finite identity for textuality, seems to keep us in the here and now by remaining with us from some past, from our pasts, from the past in general.

At the same time, books comprise texts extending beyond the borders of a particular publication or imprint, however bound, framed or produced. There is thus already at work here a certain troubling, a trembling, in the idea of text itself, something which can appear to be both real and phantasmic, and yet simultaneously neither. Textuality is a figure, to borrow a remark of Nicholas Royle's, 'irreducible to the psychical or the real'.[4] We announce in various ways the power of texts to survive, as though they could, in fact, live on, without our help, without our involvement as readers, researchers, archivists, librarians or bibliographers (and we all engage in these pursuits whether or not these are our professions). Shakespeare, it is said, is not for an age but for all time. So, in some kind of rhetorical legerdemain, we keep up the plot, the archival burial ground, saying all the while that the life or afterlife of texts is all their own, and not an effect of the embalming processes in which we engage. In such pursuits, and in the paradoxical dead-and-alive situation by which texts are maintained, we find ourselves forced to confront the fact that what we call texts, what we constitute as the identity of texts is, in the words of Jean-Michel Rabaté, 'systematically "haunted" by voices from the past ... this shows in an exemplary way the ineluctability of spectral returns'.[5] Such voices are the others of the very texts we read in any given moment. Texts are neither dead nor alive, yet they hover at the very limits between living and dying. The text thus partakes in its own haunting, it is traced by its own phantoms, and it is this condition which reading must confront.

That acts of reading anthropomorphize the text suggests how uncomfortable we are with ghosts. We want to bury the text, to entomb or encrypt it, in the name of tradition or heritage for example, and yet we cannot quite live with such *necrobibliography*. As with John Updike's wholly typical if not symptomatic example, we maintain the text so as to keep the ghosts at bay, as though keeping the haunted form with us were in some strange way a means of disregarding the frequency of the spectral. So we frequently reanimate the text. We speak of the text as 'saying something', we write that the text does things or makes things occur, as though it had a life or will of its own; or, what is even more uncanny when you come to consider it, we substitute the author's proper name in rhetorical formulae such as 'Dickens comments', 'Tennyson says that', 'George Eliot remarks', as though the text were merely a conduit, a spirit medium if you like, by which the author communicates. Thus, even while this return of the author appears a little ghostly, it is a gesture within an acceptable range of oscillations. In speaking of a voice we implicitly assume some presence, form or identity which was once present and which was once the origin of any given text. We thereby locate the potentially haunting effect in a once-live presence. This keeps the haunting at arm's length through the promise that the text can be subordinated or returned to the idea at least of a living form. We all do this; I have probably had recourse to such phrases as those above, along with others like them, countless times throughout *Victorian Hauntings: Spectrality, Gothic, the Uncanny and Literature*.

Such procedure is simultaneously the most commonplace thing in the world of criticism and yet the most irrational. We accord writing – that which, strictly speaking is neither alive nor dead, neither simply material nor immaterial – life and volition through a critical response which does not or cannot acknowledge fully its own complicity in acts of uncanny revivification – how gothic – and at the same time make believe that the writer continues to speak to us, as though we had no role. However, what reading does in effect is to bear witness to the existence of something other, which is neither 'read into' the text nor of the text itself in any simple fashion. The question of the text therefore, like the question of spectres, reconfigures the question of the limit between the living and the dead, which everywhere, in every textual encounter, presents itself. It is not that the text is haunted by its author, or simply by the historical moment of its production. Rather, it is the text itself which haunts and which is haunted by the traces which come together in this structure we call textual, which is phantomatic or phantasmatic in nature while, paradoxically, having an undeniably real or material effect, if not presence.

Whether one speaks of discourse in general, or of text in the particular sense of the web of words which make up and yet are irreducible to a book, one is forced to concede, from the perspective of considering the notions of haunting and the spectral, that the idea of text is radically unstable. What constitutes text, textuality, as an identity is, in the final analysis, undecidable and irreducible to any formal description. Our experience of reading relies on a blurring, which is also a suspension, of categories such as the real or the imaginary. Textuality brings back to us a supplement that has no origin, in the form of haunting figures – textual figures – which we misrecognize as images of 'real' people, their actions, and the contexts in which the events and lives to which we are witness take place. We 'believe' in the characters, assume their reality, without taking into account the extent to which those figures or characters are, themselves, textual projections, apparitions if you will, images or phantasms belonging to the phantasmatic dimension of fabulation. And it is because they are phantasmic, because they appear to signal a reality that has never existed, that they can be read as all the more spectral, all the more haunting. Such uncanny figures or characters can be comprehended as phantasmatic in fact because, as with the nature of the spectral, they are readable in their acts of textual oscillation as undecidable, suspended, to draw from the essay by Derrida already cited, 'between the real and the fictional, between that which is neither real nor fictional' (Mcq 24). We cannot resolve this problem, which is the problem of haunting itself, for even as the figures of the text remain and return as held in suspension, so they also suspend our ability to read them, finally. Here, once again, is the *experience of the undecidable*. And so we continue to bear witness to the signs of spectrality, seeking to read that which resists reading, that which haunts not only textuality, but also ourselves.

Notes

1   Jacques Derrida, 'Marx c'est quelqu'un', in Jacques Derrida, Marc Guillaume, and Jean-Pierre Vincent, *Marx en jeu* (Paris: Descartes & Cie, 1997), 9–28. Hereafter Mcq.

2   Jacques Derrida, *Limited Inc*. Trans. Samuel Weber et al. (Evanston, IL: Northwestern University Press, 1988), 118. Hereafter *LI*.

3   John Updike, 'Books Unbound, Life Unraveled', *New York Times*, 18 June 2000.

4   Nicholas Royle, *Déjà Vu* in Martin McQuillan et al. (eds), *Post-Theory: New Directions in Criticism* (Edinburgh: Edinburgh University Press, 1999), 3–20; 11.

5   Jean-Michel Rabaté, *The Ghosts of Modernity* (Gainesville: University Press of Florida, 1996), xvi.

6

from The Contemporary London Gothic and the Limits of the "Spectral Turn"

Roger Luckhurst

Rupert Davenport-Hines, in his suitably uncontrolled history *Gothic: 400 Years of Excess, Horror, Evil and Ruin*, enthusiastically asserts that 'in the 1990s, gothic has sustained a strong revival'. His eclectic texts range from Poppy Z. Brite, The Cure and David Lynch to Damien Hirst and that hellish duo Jake and Dinos Chapman. In the main, he suggests that it is contemporary America that 'has been profoundly reinfiltrated by goth ideas'.[1] Patrick McGrath and Bradford Morrow, in their Poe-worshipping introduction to *The New Gothic* in 1991, include more representatives of a British tradition; like Davenport-Hines they emphasize psychological extremity as the keynote of this contemporary Gothic revival.[2] In both books, such 'counter-reactions to the prevailing emotional environment' are protean enough to ensure that the Gothic persists in transgressing 'dominant cultural values' across different national contexts and aesthetic forms – a sort of principled derangement that refuses to be ensnared by history or locale.[3] In the same diffuse spirit, a certain strand of cultural theory in France, Britain and America embraced a language of ghosts and the uncanny – or rather of anachronic spectrality and hauntology – following the publication of Jacques Derrida's *Specters of Marx* in 1993 (translated into English in 1994). This text has proved extremely influential, prompting something of a 'spectral turn' in contemporary criticism. When Martin Jay wished to sum up recent directions in cultural theory he chose the title 'The Uncanny Nineties' in deference to *Specters*. 'Are you a scholar who deals with ghosts?' Martin McQuillan asked Derrida's translator, Peggy Kamuf. 'Yes ... although I'm not sure I would have said so with as much conviction before *Specters of Marx*', she replied. She was answering, as we shall see, for a sizeable band of cultural critics.[4]

This essay is partly a response to Martin Jay's questions 'Why ... has the uncanny become a master trope available for appropriation in a wide variety of contexts? What are the possible drawbacks of granting it so much explanatory force?'[5] These questions have been crystallized, for me, by trying to reflect on the notable revival over the past twenty years of a newly Gothicized apprehension of London. I want to argue that the critical language of spectral or haunted modernity that has become a cultural-critical shorthand in the wake of *Specters of Marx* can go only so far in elaborating the contexts for that specific topography of this London Gothic – that, indeed, the generalized structure of haunting is symptomatically blind to its generative loci.

What follows is in two parts. In the first, I want to suggest an oeuvre of texts that might be included in this new London Gothic, and to explore it in relation to the discourse of spectralized modernity. The second part launches itself from the limits of this account, offering a reading of the work of Iain Sinclair and Christopher Fowler.

I

W.G. Sebald's extraordinary novel *Austerlitz* hinges on a moment that has become typical – even stereotypical. Austerlitz tells the anonymous narrator of his attempts to fend off the collapse of his identity by trudging through the city of London at night. As he crosses Liverpool Street station, then undergoing modernization, Austerlitz becomes attuned to the successive erasures enacted on the site. The station is built on the site of the asylum, St Mary of Bethlehem: 'I kept almost obsessively trying to imagine – through the ever-changing maze of walls – the location in that huge space of the rooms where the asylum inmates were confined, and I often wondered whether the pain and suffering accumulated on this site over the centuries had ever really ebbed away.'[6] The Broad Street excavations have similarly uncovered the compacted bodies of old burial grounds, and such locations prompt Austerlitz to speculate: 'It does not seem to me ... that we under-stand the laws governing the return of the past, but I feel more and more as if time did not exist at all, only various spaces interlocking according to the rules of a higher form of stereometry, between which the living and the dead can move back and forth as they like.'[7] Given these Gothic reflections on inheritance, indebtedness and the returning dead, it is fitting that Austerlitz uncovers the encrypted memories of his own orphaned

Jewish origins in an abandoned waiting room scheduled for demolition in the station. This is London's psychic topography: traumatic memory is recovered on the ground of the city's buried history.

The site of Austerlitz's revelation comes at the end of twenty years of the elaboration of a newly Gothicized London. Consider: in Will Self 's version of the city, the dead have spilled over from Crouch End in his early tale 'The North London Book of the Dead' to occupy a variety of 'cystricts' from Dulston in the northeast to Dulburb in the south in *How the Dead Live*. In *Mother London*, Michael Moorcock suggests that redemption for the traumatized city lies in a gaggle of telepaths, psychotically open to the lost voices of metropolitan history. Ghosts are inhumed in a Victorian terraced house in Michèle Roberts' *In the Red Kitchen*. In M. John Harrison's novel *The Course of the Heart*, an occultist living above the Atlantis Bookshop in Museum Street engages in elaborate rituals in anonymous north London houses, hoping for access to the plenitude of the Gnostic 'pleroma'. His reluctant, psychically damaged circle of initiates suffers punitive decades of haunting for their uncomprehending participation in these rites – obscene protrusions of the psychotic Real into dreary urban spaces. The horror writers Christopher Fowler and Kim Newman have unleashed vampires, personal daemons, reanimated corpses, undead media executives and murderous secret societies on to the London streets. In Neil Gaiman's *Neverwhere* one can fall through the cracks of cruel London indifference to find oneself in the parallel space of the Underside, or London Below. China Miéville's *King Rat* also invokes a wholly other system of networks and rat-runs inches away from the human dominion of the city. In *Perdido Street Station*, Miéville reimagines London as New Crobuzon, a metropolis of alchemy and magic. Marcello Truzzi notes that an important strand in occult belief is 'the inference of strange causalities among otherwise ordinary events'.[8] The poet, novelist and essayist Iain Sinclair has generated a tangle of these occulted causalities, often marking out trajectories through the East End of London. With undecidable intent (he is a dead-pan mythographer), Sinclair claims to unearth hidden lines of force and meaning – most notoriously in his poem sequence on the secret significances of Hawksmoor's churches, *Lud Heat*, undoubtedly one of the ur-texts for this resurgence of London Gothic since its publication in 1975. This opaque text, published by Sinclair's own Albion Press, gained kudos from its programmatic re-functioning by Peter Ackroyd in *Hawksmoor* in 1985 (*Lud Heat* gained even more kudos from being impossible to get hold of until its mass market reissue in 1995 – it worked its effect as a rumour as much as an actually read text). Sinclair has continued to conduct investigations into the marginal and the vanished through the language of lost inheritance and ghostly debt. The novel *Downriver* repeatedly stages forms of séance communication with London's disappeared. Forgotten and despised areas, abandoned buildings or empty rooms work as conductors to revivify buried histories. Sinclair entwines his own project with a host of other psychogeographers of London's occlusions, from the poets Aidan Dun and Allen Fisher to the film-makers Chris Petit and Patrick Keiller and the avant-garde provocateur Stewart Home.[9]

Many of these contemporary texts engage in historical excavations that self-reflexively incorporate knowledge of the Gothic genre itself. Robinson, Keiller's eccentric urban detective in the film *London*, navigates the city by turning again and again to its eighteenth-century traces, bad-temperedly fantasizing the erasure of Victorian London other than for the precious residues of Poe, Stoker or Rimbaud. Ackroyd omnivorously roams the centuries, but readers of this genre soon note that it is the Gothic revival of the late Victorian era that turns up repeatedly, clearly because this was the moment when a distinctively urban Gothic was crystallized. The parallel explosion of Gothic scholarship in the 1990s (the International Gothic Association was founded in 1991) tracked the movement of the genre from the wild margins of Protestant Europe to the imperial metropolis of the Victorian fin de siècle – precisely the trajectory that brings Count Dracula from the Carpathian mountains to the populous streets of London, or Arthur Machen's corruptive Helen Vaughan from the Celtic fringes of England to the wealthiest streets of Piccadilly in *The Great God Pan*. Christopher Fowler's most impressive novel to date, *Darkest Day*, traces a sequence of modern-day killings back to events in the newly built Savoy Theatre in 1888. Alan Moore and Eddie Campbell's influential graphic novel about the 1889 Whitechapel 'Ripper' murders, *From Hell*, condensed every available conspiracy theory into a supernaturalized account that included lengthy disquisitions from the killer on the occult power of place (this meta-commentary was largely excised from the 2001 film version).[10] Sinclair wrote his own contribution to the Ripper mythology, *White Chapell, Scarlet Tracings*, but *Downriver* also picks up traces of the dead of the 1878 Princess Alice disaster (in which over 600 people drowned in the sinking of a Thames pleasure-cruiser). Another séance conjures the seventeen dead from theatre at the Whitechapel Hebrew Dramatic Club in 1887. 'Fire is the essence of voices,' we are told. 'It is what you cannot reduce to ash.'[11]

Is this Gothic revival and its fascination with its own generic past anything other than self-referential involution – a kind of return of the repressed 'return of the repressed' as empty postmodern pastiche? This is the thrust of Michael Moorcock's short satirical tale, 'London Bone', in which the rapacious demand for authentic London history begins to disinter the bones of the dead from London graveyards for escalating market prices. The collapsed economy and exhausted imaginary of contemporary London can only feed on its own dead.[12] Yet the pervasiveness of Gothic tropes on the imagining of London across a diversity of discursive modes seems to be undertaking far more cultural work than empty repetition might suggest.

Patrick Wright's *A Journey Through the Ruins: The Last Days of London* stitches together a jeremiad against the London of the 1980s in true Gothic fashion, by haunting places of inner-city ruin left to the vagaries of the market or hurriedly redesignated as 'heritage' sites. 'An interest in debris and human fallout is part of the New Baroque sensibility', he claims.[13] Peter Ackroyd's best-selling *London: A Biography* transposed his novelistic explorations of the strange rhythms of London time and space into a method for apprehending a city apparently resistant to the cognitive regimen of history. The temporal slippages at certain specific locales in London in *Hawksmoor* and *The House of Doctor Dee* (which are figured through the Gothic very precisely as visiting derangement on their inheritors) become the principal device for the historian of the city. London origins are lost in semi-mythical or visionary accounts, and historiography is further mocked by the patterns of disappearance and return that crumple linear time into repeating cycles or unpredictable arabesques. 'The nature of time in London is mysterious',

Ackroyd claims, pointing to the 'territorial imperative or *genius loci*' that ensures certain zones retain their function across the centuries – not just the clusters of trades, but the homeless of St Giles, or the occultists of Seven Dials.[14] There is, Ackroyd affirms, 'a Gothic *genius loci* of London fighting against the spirit of the classic' (p. 580) – understanding the Classical mode as that which always wants to order and regiment the life of the city. This spirit exists 'beyond the reach of any plan or survey': we have to understand that 'the city itself remains magical; it is a mysterious, chaotic and irrational place which can be organised and controlled only by means of private ritual or public superstition' (p. 216). The 'spirit' of London survives the apocalyptic fires that periodically revisit it, and it will certainly outlast any of the passing political interventions dreamt up by the Westminster village. 'It does not respond to policy committees or to centralised planning. It would be easier to control the elements themselves', Ackroyd states in his conclusion, thus essentially naturalizing (or rather supernaturalizing) London 'muddle' (p. 764).

We might begin to sense something more purposive in the contemporary London Gothic here. One of Ackroyd's most attentive readers, Julian Wolfreys, suggests that London has encouraged these tropes since the huge expansion of the metropolis in the nineteenth century. As the first megalopolis of the modern era, London becomes a sublime object that evokes awe and evades rational capture. The 'London-effect', for Wolfreys, is the sense that there is 'always a mysterious supplement that escapes signification'. Writers since Blake and Dickens have understood that London is not a city that can be encompassed by the panoptical ambitions of novelistic realism but requires a writing that evokes 'the ineffability and lack which is always at the heart of London'.[15] This 'crisis of representation' argument is regularly rehearsed in postmodern urban theory – although it is usually the sprawl of Los Angeles or the ribbon developments of Phoenix that are the

focus.[16] London is different, the argument proceeds, and is more amenable
to the disorderly mode of the Gothic, because the creative destruction of its
specific embodiment of modernity is peculiarly hidebound by the ancient
commands and ancestral inheritances that live on amidst the mirrored
glass and cantilevered concrete. These traces, Wolfreys argues in *Writing
London*, are 'spectral through and through: they are the marks of already
retreating ghosts who disturb any certain perception we may think we have
concerning the city's identity'.[17]

This theory of a spectralized modernity is shared by a number of urban
theorists. James Donald presents a more gestural notion of a 'haunted city',
with the ghost acting as a supplement that evades totalized planning.[18] 'We
need,' Christine Boyer concurs, 'to establish counter-memories, resisting
the dominant coding of images and representations. . . . We are compelled
to create new memory walks through the city, new maps that help us to
resist and subvert the all-too-programmed and enveloping messages of our
consumer culture.'[19] The more indifferent to history the ruthless transformation of city-space, the more likely it is, Anthony Vidler suggests, that
'the uncanny erupts in empty parking lots around abandoned or run-down
shopping malls ... in the wasted margins and surface appearances of
postindustrial culture'.[20] Never far away from contemporary urban theory
is Michel de Certeau's *The Practice of Everyday Life*, and sure enough de
Certeau neatly condenses all of these strands in the passing comment:

> Haunted places are the only ones people can live in – and this inverts
> the schema of the Panopticon. But like the gothic sculptures of kings and
> queens that once adorned Notre-Dame and have been buried for two
> centuries ... these 'spirits', themselves broken into pieces in like manner,
> do not speak any more than they see. This is a sort of knowledge that
> remains silent. Only hints of what is known but unrevealed are passed
> on 'just between you and me.'[21]

The buried Gothic fragment thus operates as the emblem of resistance to
the tyranny of planned space, but this resistance is necessarily occluded and
interstitial, passed on only between initiates. (Indeed, given the embrace
of obscurity and scarcity by a number of recent London 'visionaries', this
transaction 'just between you and me' seems uncannily apt.)

We have the beginnings of an explanation situating the use of Gothic
tropes within a larger critique of amnesiac modernity. Jean-François
Lyotard wrote of the ghosts that structurally haunted any total or total-
izing system, and of the commitment of thought to open to 'the anguish
... of a mind haunted by a familiar and unknown guest which is agitating
it'.[22] Jean-Michel Rabaté concurs: 'we might say that "modern" philosophy
has always attempted to bury [its] irrational Other in some neat crypt,
forgetting that it would thereby lead to further ghostly reappearations.'

For him, 'a whole history of our spectral delusions remains possible, even urgent and necessary.'[23] Any proclamation of self-possessed modernity induces a haunting. This becomes, for David Glover, a 'spectrality effect' by which the Gothic haunts modernity in general.[24] From a somewhat different context, the science theorist Bruno Latour also joins this conjuncture by arguing that 'modern temporality is the result of a retraining imposed on entities which would pertain to all sorts of times and possess all sorts of ontological statuses without this harsh disciplining'. Because this project was an imperious imposition on heterogeneity, 'symptoms of discord are multiplied': 'The past remains, therefore, and even returns. Now this resurgence is incomprehensible to the moderns. Thus they treat it as the return of the repressed.'[25] Perhaps the global time zone system, zeroed on Greenwich in 1884, makes London particularly subject to magical and superstitious beliefs, as Maureen Perkins has recently argued.[26] Within these contexts, Gothic tropes can be exemplary symptoms of the horrors that beset an uncomprehending modernity, or can act as devices that acknowledge London as (in Latour's term) a polytemporal assemblage. In this set-up the past 'is not surpassed but revisited, repeated, surrounded, protected, recombined, reinterpreted, and reshuffled'.[27] 'There are little bubbles of old time in London', one character in Gaiman's *Neverwhere* explains, 'where things and places stay the same, like bubbles in amber. . . . There's a lot of time in London, and it has to go somewhere – it doesn't all get used up at once.'[28] Critical discourse makes similar claims: as Lynda Nead puts it in her discussion of London modernity, 'the present remains permanently engaged in a phantasmatic dialogue with the past'.[29] The comments in *Austerlitz* on the spatial ordering of time, the localized temporalities of London in Ackroyd, or Patrick Wright's observation that 'On Dalston Lane time itself seems to lie around in broken fragments: you can drop in on previous decades with no more effort than it takes to open a shop-door', are thus given a common root.[30] They can all be countersigned by Derrida's assertions in *Specters of Marx* regarding the 'non-contemporaneity of the present time with itself (this radical untimeliness or this anachrony on the basis of which we are trying here to think the ghost)'.[31]

De Certeau's assertion that unearthing gothic fragments might contribute to an aesthetic of resistance also helps explain more avant-garde interest in Gothic topology. There has been a long association of the metropolitan avant-garde with occult investigation. The Surrealists adopted the methods of the spiritualist trance-medium to unleash the revolutionary delirium of the unconscious. The city was explored in the same way: in André Breton's *Nadja*, for instance, chance encounters and certain zones of Paris become charged with occult significance. Breton's subjectivity was doubled or ghosted as a consequence of this exercise in the urban uncanny.[32] The Situationist International, formed from the European postwar rump of Surrealism, also reinvented the city through the dérive, a delirious or drunken drifting that tore up the tyranny of abstract city-space.[33] Claiming direct descent, the London Psychogeographical Association was formed in the early 1990s. Stewart Home, associated with the Neoist avant-garde, eventually edited a collection of LPA texts, which evidenced a fascination with occult modes of explanation. In one communication, 'Nazi Occultists seize Omphalos', the election of a British National Party representative in the Isle of Dogs is attributed to the exercise of Enochian magic. The BNP have tapped into the ley-line that runs between the Greenwich Observatory and Queen Mary College in Mile End. This line of occult force, the conspiratorial text informs us, has powered the formation of the British Empire, at least since John Dee's alchemical service to Elizabeth I.[34] Jenny Turner has suggested that Home 'is fascinated by the way that official, admired, respectable forms of knowledge are structurally identical to their occult, reviled shades, and in his best work shakes hard at the barriers between them'.[35] In *The House of Nine Squares*, a set of letters and texts on Neoism, Home records his delight that the dead-pan missives of the London Psychogeographical Association have been mistaken as products of 'an occult group': 'This type of misunderstanding makes it much easier for us to realise our real aim of turning the bourgeoisie's weapons back against them.'[36] Elsewhere, in response to critical comment from other radical avant-garde groupings, the LPA declared: 'We offer no attempt to "justify" or "rationalize" the role of magic in the development of our theories. It is sufficient that it renders our theories completely unacceptable.'[37]

Mystification and unlikely counter-factual histories, it would seem, are dialectically motivated by the creeping uniformity of commodified London. The LPA, Iain Sinclair comments, is 'the revenge of the disenfranchised. Improvisations on history that are capable of making adjustments in present time. Prophecy as news. News as the purest form of fiction.'[38] Sinclair, now in a curiously anomalous position as a hegemonic counterculturalist, works the same line of ambivalence as Home. The fractured lyric persona in Sinclair's *Lud Heat* defends the discovery of 'the secret routines' in the East End through a method of 'high occulting' against the languages of '*the objective*', '*the scientific approach*' and 'scholarly baby talk'.[39] Sinclair dowses along ley-lines and conducts séances in *Downriver*, yet the same text rants against 'stinking heritage ghosts', myths sustained 'only to bleed the fund raisers' (p. 122). The character given narratorial authority for the conclusion of *Downriver* expresses contempt for 'necrovestism: impersonating the dead, spook-speaking' (p. 399). The mysterious Spitalfields figure David Rodinsky – whose room was allegedly left untouched on his disappearance in 1969 and 'rediscovered' in 1987 – is mockingly debunked as a conjuration of heritage hype in one text, then becomes the basis for full-scale mythologizing in another.[40] The ambiguity is deliberately nurtured, for if 'the occult logic of "market forces" dictated a new geography' of London, Sinclair implies that his project is a necessary counter-conjuration, a protective hex against the advancing armies of orthodoxy.[41]

The framework of spectralized modernity can thus integrate widely divergent instances of the London Gothic – it makes unlikely bedfellows of Peter Ackroyd and Stewart Home. Yet it is the very generalized economy of haunting that makes me suspicious of this spectral turn. Jodey Castricano's reading of 'familiar Gothic tropes and topoi ... in Derridean deconstruction' toys with calling the philosopher a 'Gothic novelist' – one that speaks with a decided affinity to a popular and distinctively American tradition of obsessive returns from the dead that stretches from Poe to Stephen King.[42] Transposed in space by Castricano, Jean-Michel Rabaté's *Ghosts of Modernity* uncovers the same spectral reiteration by tracking across temporal moments, from Spinoza in 1674 via Marx and Engels to Beckett in 1952.[43] In Julian Wolfreys' work spectrality exceeds the Gothic as merely 'one proper name for a process of spectral transformation', and becomes a generalized deconstructive lever discernible everywhere.[44] No concept, no self-identity, no text, no writing that is not haunted: 'the spectral is at the heart of any narrative of the modern', the latest addition to his oeuvre states.[45] This extension is clearly legitimated by Derrida's own view that 'it is necessary to introduce haunting into the very construction of a concept. Of every concept, beginning with the concepts of being and time. This is what we would be calling here a hauntology.'[46] What is proclaimed by this structure is, as Martin Jay observes, 'the power of haunting per se': 'in celebrating spectral returns as such,' he continues, 'the precise content of what is repeated may get lost.'[47] Unable to discriminate between instances and largely uninterested in historicity (beyond its ghostly disruption), the discourse of spectralized modernity risks investing in the compulsive repetitions of a structure of melancholic entrapment. In this mode, to suggest an inevitably historicized mourningwork that might actually seek to lay a ghost to rest would be the height of bad manners. And because the spectral infiltrates the hermeneutic act itself, critical work can only replicate tropes from textual sources, punning spiritedly around the central terms of the Gothic to produce a curious form of meta-Gothic that elides object and instrument. This has happened from the very beginning of this spectral turn: 'Impossible, at least for me,' Nicholas Royle comments, 'to review this book about apparitions, phantoms, spectres, without feeling a need to respond in kind.... A phantom book calls for a phantom review.'[48]

The way in which *Specters of Marx* has been received and mobilized by literary critics shows some marked differences from the Marxist and broader political-philosophical response. Respondents from the Marxist tradition tend to concentrate on Derrida's deferred readings of Marx and the proposals for a largely spectral 'New International' in the latter half of the book. Kate Soper is typical in excoriating the emptying out of any possibility of a political ontology by Derridean hauntology once *Specters* gets around to filling out the generalized structure of the spectro-political.[49] Literary critics, as we have seen, tend to elaborate on the figurations of ghosts and hauntings, principally developed in the opening section of *Specters*. The play with Hamlet's father's spirit here makes things suitably homely for literary types, even if, as John Fletcher has carefully noted, Derrida rather misreads the import of the ghost in *Hamlet*.[50] What Derrida himself makes of this literary-critical mobilization may be hinted at in his lengthy response to the Marxist critiques collected in *Ghostly Demarcations*. In an essay that barely mentions spectres at all, the most sustained discussion of the term is in response to Fredric Jameson's judgement of it as 'aesthetic': 'to all those – they are legion – who think they can "re-aestheticize" matters in this book, reducing its concepts (the concept of the "spectre", for instance) to figures of rhetoric, or my demonstrations to literary experiments and effects of style: none of what matters to me, and, above all, may matter to the discussion under way ... can be reduced to, or elucidated by, this "aesthetic" approach.'[51] Nevertheless, what Derrida's hauntology has spawned, at least in Gothicized literary criticism, is the punning search for a textual reading machine for variously termed cryptomimetics (Castricano), spectrography (Rabaté), Gothic spectro-poetics (Wolfreys) or phantomistics (Royle) that largely recirculates Gothic-aesthetic tropes. This certainly 'respects' texts, but it rarely goes beyond what Derrida has elsewhere termed 'doubling commentary'.[52]

In order to read something of the specificity of the contemporary London Gothic I want to aim at breaking through this meta-Gothic discourse. When Chris Baldick proposes that Gothic tales evoke 'a fear of historical reversion; that is, of the nagging possibility that the despotisms, buried by the modern age, may yet prove to be undead', this could be taken as another generalized conjuring of haunted modernity.[53] In fact, it is part of a counter-move to the spectralization of the Gothic that situates it rather more precisely as a grounded manifestation of communities in highly delimited locales subjected to cruel and unusual forms of political disempowerment. A geography of the genre thus observes clusters at the colonial edges of England – Anglo-Irish Gothic, or a Scottish Gothic that speaks to 'issues of suppression in a stateless national culture'.[54] And surely what the contemporary London Gothic most evidently articulates is not simply empty structural repetitions of polytemporal spookiness: these are themselves symptoms of that curious mix of tyranny and farce that constitutes London governance.

[...]

Notes

1   Rupert Davenport-Hines, *Gothic: 400 Years of Excess, Horror, Evil and Ruin* (London: Fourth Estate, 1998), pp. 9, 375.

2   Patrick McGrath and Bradford Morrow (eds), *The New Gothic: A Collection of Contemporary Gothic Fiction* (London: Picador, 1991), p. xii.

3   Davenport-Hines, *Gothic*, p. 346.

4   Peggy Kamuf, 'Translating specters: an interview with Peggy Kamuf ', *Parallax* 7:3 (2001), p. 45. I would include myself as a minor member of this band, having contributed to collections on ghosts, the Gothic and Derrida in the 1990s. I note this not as a narcissist, but as someone who can cast no stones: any critique undertaken by this essay is an auto-critique too.

5   Martin Jay, 'The uncanny nineties', in *Cultural Semantics: Keywords of our Time* (London: Athlone Press, 1998), p. 157.

6   W. G. Sebald, *Austerlitz*, trans. Anthea Bell (London: Hamish Hamilton, 2001), p. 183.

7   Ibid., p. 261.

8   Marcello Truzzi, 'Definition and dimensions of the occult: towards a sociological perspective', *Journal of Popular Culture* 5:2 (1971–2), p. 638.

9   For some commentary on these groupings, see Peter Barry, 'Revisionings of London in three contemporary poets: Iain Sinclair, Allen Fisher, and Aidan Dun', in Holger Klein (ed.), *Poetry Now: Contemporary British and Irish Poetry in the Making* (Tubingen: Stauffenberg Verlag, 1999), and Robert Sheppard's review of Sinclair's anthology *Conductors of Chaos* in 'Elsewhere and everywhere: other new (British) poetries', *Critical Survey* 10:1 (1998), pp. 17–32.

10 Alan Moore and Eddie Campbell, *From Hell, Being a Melodrama in Sixteen Parts* (London: Knockabout, 1999).

11 Iain Sinclair, *Downriver (Or, The Vessels of Wrath): A Narrative in Twelve Tales* (London: Paladin, 1991), p. 143. All further page references in parentheses in the text.

12 Michael Moorcock, *London Bone* (London: Scribner, 2001).

13 Patrick Wright, *A Journey through the Ruins: The Last Days of London* (London: Radius, 1991), p. 12.

14 Peter Ackroyd, *London: A Biography* (London: Chatto & Windus, 2000), pp. 661 and 141. All further page references in parentheses in the text.

15 Julian Wolfreys, *Writing London: The Trace of the Urban Text from Blake to Dickens* (Basingstoke: Palgrave, 1998), pp. 8, 25.

16 See e.g. William Sharpe and Leonard Wallock on the 'crisis of terminology' for the contemporary city in 'From "Great Town" to "Nonplace Urban Realm": reading the modern city', in Sharpe and Wallock (eds), *Visions of the Modern City* (Baltimore, MD: Johns Hopkins University Press, 1987), p. 1.

17 Wolfreys, *Writing London*, pp. 204–5.

18 James Donald, *Imagining the Modern City* (London: Athlone, 1999), pp. 17–18.

19 M. Christine Boyer, *The City of Collective Memory: Its Historical Imagery and Architectural Entertainments* (Cambridge, MA: The MIT Press, 1996), pp. 28–9.

20 Anthony Vidler, *The Architectural Uncanny* (Cambridge, MA: The MIT Press, 1992), p. 3.

21 Michel de Certeau, *The Practice of Everyday Life*, trans. Steven Rendall (Berkeley, LA: University of California Press, 1984), p. 108.

22 Jean-François Lyotard, 'About the human', in *The Inhuman: Reflections on Time*, trans. Geoffrey Bennington and Rachel Bowlby (Cambridge: Polity Press, 1991), p. 2.

23 Jean-Michel Rabaté, *The Ghosts of Modernity* (Gainesville: University Press of Florida, 1996), pp. xviii and xxi.

24 David Glover, 'The "spectrality effect" in early modernism', in Andrew Smith and Jeff Wallace (eds), *Gothic Modernisms* (Basingstoke: Palgrave, 2001), pp. 29–43.

25 Bruno Latour, *We Have Never Been Modern*, trans. Catherine Porter (Hemel Hempstead: Harvester, 1993), pp. 72, 69.

26 Maureen Perkins, *The Reform of Time: Magic and Modernity* (London: Pluto, 2001).

27 Latour, *We Have Never Been Modern*, pp. 74–5.

28 Neil Gaiman, *Neverwhere* (London: Headline Publishing, 2000), pp. 235–6.

29 Lynda Nead, *Victorian Babylon* (New Haven, CT: Yale University Press, 2000), p. 8.

30 Wright, *A Journey through the Ruins*, p. 12.

31 Jacques Derrida, *Specters of Marx: The State of the Debt, the Work of Mourning, and the New International*, trans. Peggy Kamuf (New York: Routledge, 1994), p. 24.

32 André Breton, *Nadja*, trans. Richard Howard (New York: Grove Press, 1960). For commentary on the 'ghosted' subject in Nadja, see Margaret Cohen, *Profane Illumination* (Berkeley, LA: University of California Press, 1993) and Jean-Michel Rabaté, *The Ghosts of Modernity*, 'André Breton's ghostly stance', pp. 42–66.

33 For original documents, see *The Situationist International: An Anthology*, ed. and trans. Ken Knabb (New York: The Bureau of Public Secrets, 1989).

34 Stewart Home, *Mind Invaders: A Reader in Psychic Warfare, Cultural Sabotage and Semiotic Terrorism* (London: Serpent's Tail, 1997), pp. 29–32.

35 Jenny Turner, 'Aberdeen Rocks' [Review of Stewart Home, *69 Things to do with a Dead Princess*], *London Review of Books* (9 May 2002), p. 38.

36 Stewart Home, *The House of Nine Squares: Letters on Neoism, Psychogeography and Epistemological Trepidation* (London: Nine Squares, 1997).

37 LPA document, cited in Simon Sadler, *The Situationist City* (Cambridge, MA: The MIT Press, 1999), p. 165. Home has extended these investigations into an overheated pulp fiction about sex magic and London topography in *Come Before Christ and Murder Love* (London: Serpent's Tail, 1997).

38 Iain Sinclair, *Lights Out for the Territory: 9 Excursions in the Secret History of London* (London: Granta, 1997), p. 26.

39 Iain Sinclair, *Lud Heat and Suicide Bridge* (London: Vintage, 1995), p. 113.

40 See Iain Sinclair, 'The mystery of the disappearing room', in *Downriver*, and Rachel Lichtenstein and Iain Sinclair, *Rodinsky's Room* (London: Granta, 1999), perhaps particularly '"Mobile invisibility": Golems, Dybbuks and unanchored presences', pp.171–200.

41 Sinclair, *Downriver*, p. 265.

42 Jodey Castricano, *Cryptomimesis: The Gothic and Jacques Derrida's Ghost Writing* (Montreal: McGill-Queen's University Press, 2001), pp. 6, 26.

43 Rabaté, *The Ghosts of Modernity*, 'The "moderns" and their ghosts', pp. 216–33.

44 Julian Wolfreys, *Victorian Hauntings: Spectrality, Gothic, the Uncanny and Literature* (Basingstoke: Palgrave, 2002), p. 7.

45 Ibid., p. 3 (emphasis added).

46 Derrida, *Specters of Marx*, p. 161.

47 Jay, 'The uncanny nineties', p. 162.

48 Nicholas Royle, 'Phantom Review' [Review of *Specters of Marx*], *Textual Practice* 11:2 (1997), p. 387.

49 Kate Soper, 'The limits of hauntology', in 'Spectres of Derrida: Symposium', *Radical Philosophy* 75 (January/February 1996). For other Marxist responses see Michael Sprinker (ed.), *Ghostly Demarcations: A Symposium on Jacques Derrida's Specters of Marx* (London: Verso, 1999), and the special issue of *Parallax* entitled 'A New International?' 7:3 (2001).

50 John Fletcher, 'Marx the uncanny: ghosts and their relation to the mode of production', *Radical Philosophy* 75 (1996). Fletcher concludes by arguing that 'the ghost in *Hamlet* is different from the tropes of spectrality in Marx, [and] this difference dramatizes issues of the epochal and the historical that are foreclosed and misrecognized by Derrida's transcendental "hauntology"' (p. 36). (One might disagree with the characterization of hauntology as 'transcendental' here, but Fletcher's point remains a powerful one.)

51 Jacques Derrida, 'Marx & Sons', in *Ghostly Demarcations*, p. 248.

52 Jacques Derrida, *Of Grammatology*, trans. Gayatri Spivak (Baltimore, MD: Johns Hopkins University Press, 1976), p. 158.

53 Chris Baldick, 'Introduction', in *Oxford Book of Gothic Tales* (Oxford: Oxford University Press, 1992), p. xxi.

54 See Robert Mighall, *A Geography of Victorian Gothic Fiction: Mapping History's Nightmares* (Oxford: Oxford University Press, 1999) and some of the contributions to Glennis Byron and David Punter (eds), *Spectral Readings:*

Towards a Geography of the Gothic (Basingstoke: Macmillan, 1999). See also Margot Backas, *The Gothic Family Romance: Heterosexuality, Child Sacrifice and the Anglo-Irish Colonial Order* (Durham, NC: Duke University Press, 1999). Citation from David Punter, 'Heart lands: contemporary Scottish Gothic', *Gothic Studies* 1:1 (1997), p. 101.

PART TWO

Spectropolitics: Ghosts of the Global Contemporary

7

Spectropolitics: Ghosts of the Global Contemporary / Introduction

María del Pilar Blanco and Esther Peeren

This part explores the reach of spectrality in a geographical and theoretical sense. How far has the spectral turn, emerging from the western nexus of France, Britain, and the United States, extended? And how has it, in being taken up in different contexts to address the quandaries of not merely the past and its persistence in the present but also contemporary life and its socio-political configurations, been positioned in relation to influential critical frameworks such as postmodernism, postcoloniality, materialism, nationalism, and, especially, globalization?

In many ways, spectrality appears as a global figure. Across the world, there exist imaginative and social traditions involving ghost-like beings and other elusive phenomena. These include humans returned from the dead or contactable in an afterlife, animistic entities hovering between the perceptible and the imperceptible that occupy particular sites or are able to possess people, as well as forms of telepathic communication, alternative healing, and divination. Called by a variety of names, capable of producing widely divergent acts and effects, and eliciting reactions covering the spectrum from extreme fear and paranoia to comfort or reverence, the one element conceivably uniting these beings and phenomena is their ambivalent multiplicity—the reference to the liminal form of being (and thinking) encompassing life and death, human and non-human, presence and absence, that spectrality has been taken to exemplify. However, this aspect of *both* ... *and*—which is equally one of *neither* ... *nor*—does not necessarily have identical implications, as not every society is structured according to the same binary oppositions or assigns them the same degree of fixity. As Benson Saler has shown, the category of the supernatural, to which ghosts are readily assigned, is itself not universal, but a western construct with a convoluted history.[1] Thus, what appears as shared spectrality is in fact diachronically and synchronically refracted, comprising a range of habits, customs, and traditions, all subject to change. The very use of the term "ghost" already entails turning one, essentially Judeo-Christian, mode into the paradigmatic one, just as the seemingly neutral "spectral" carries with it implications of ocularcentrism that mark it as a product of western modernity. In order to avoid overlooking crucial differentiations, a more reflective use of the available terminology has emerged that acknowledges the necessity of ongoing efforts of intercultural translation, also *within* the so-called West, where certain parts are more pervasively haunted than others and very different types of ghostly creatures may be discerned.[2]

At the same time, in recent decades, the ghost has become an increasingly *globalized* figure as it relentlessly crosses borders, in multiple directions, in practices and imaginations transported through travel, migration, and the global culture industries. This has caused various traditions to intersect and intermingle, for example in the tsunami of Asian "ghost" films remade by Hollywood (where "Asian" should itself be differentiated into Japanese, Korean, and Chinese, at the least) and ensuing co-productions.[3] As we have noted, on the academic stage, too, spectrality has experienced a rapid spread: the theories of Derrida and others have been taken up across continents, in both affirmative and reconstituting manners. The point of this part is not to present different "ghostly" traditions as incommensurable or to reject spectrality as a potentially useful heuristic instrument, but rather to insist on taking seriously the disarticulations that remain even as a spectral Esperanto seems to be emerging.

Spectrality has also emerged as a figure *of* globalization, past and present. "Some might argue," Ann Laura Stoler writes in her introduction to *Haunted by Empire*, "that being an effective empire has long been contingent on partial visibility – sustaining the ability to remain an affective and unaccountable one."[4] Empire is conceived as a haunting structure, both in the way it worked when it was in operation—acting simultaneously at a distance and through "strangely familiar 'uncanny' intimacies"—and in its legacy of "implicated histories in the disquieting present."[5] Similarly, the processes associated with the present-day spread of particular economic models (most prominently, neoliberal capitalism) and new (social) media, which reconfigure the world as one of inescapable interconnection, have been conceived as spectral (ungraspably complex, only partially material, accelerated to the point of disappearance, capable of occupying multiple spaces at once) and spectralizing (producing subjects that stand apart from the rest of society, either, at the top, as unaccountable or, at the bottom, as expendable). This is clear, for example, in Derrida's enumeration of the ten plagues of the "new world order," comprising unemployment produced by deregulation, the exclusion of the homeless and other undesirable subjects, economic war, the contradictions of free market capitalism, the proliferation of foreign debt, the arms industry and trade, nuclear weapons, inter-ethnic wars grounded in "a *primitive conceptual phantasm* of community," the "phantom-States" of the mafia and drug cartels, and the limits of international law.[6] All four texts gathered in this part engage in what may be called, in Derrida's wake, a "spectropolitics," an attempt to mobilize spectrality to more precisely designate the diffuse operations and effects of present-day globalization, as well as to critique the way its processes produce certain subjects as consistently disenfranchised or, in Judith Butler's terms, forced to live in extreme precarity as "would-be humans, the spectrally human."[7]

In accordance with the general ambivalence of the specter, a spectropolitics is never straightforward: Derrida uses it to refer to Marx's attempt to "separate out the good from the bad 'ghosts,'" which turns out to be "so difficult and risky, beyond any possible mastery."[8] A necessarily confused and confusing concept capable of evoking both nightmarish scenarios of dehumanization and dreams of revolution, spectropolitics reveals, first of all, the increasingly spectral nature of the political. As Andrew Hussey notes, politics "has become an empty cipher in a world where the possibility of systematic critical thought has evaporated and with it the potential for any ideology to challenge the phantasmatic multi-layered structures of the post-political world."[9] This renders traditional Marxist strategies reliant on countering "global falsification" impotent and may require instead a form of counterconjuration.[10] Here, spectropolitics emerges as the site of potential change, where ghosts, and especially the ability to haunt and the willingness to be haunted, to live *with* ghosts, can work, as Janice Radway argues in her foreword to Avery F. Gordon's *Ghostly Matters*, to "revivify our collective capacity to imagine a future radically other to the one ideologically charted out already by the militarized, patriarchal capitalism that has thrived heretofore on the practice of social erasure."[11]

It is with the first, introductory chapter of Gordon's book—which, first published in 1997 and reissued in 2008, remains one of the most widely read texts of the spectral turn—that this part opens. As a sociologist, Gordon is primarily interested in exploring everyday life in the present, under the conditions of what she calls "racial capitalism."[12] Her recourse to an idiom of haunting and ghosts is prompted by the desire "to understand modern forms of dispossession, exploitation, repression, and their concrete impacts on the people most affected by them and on our shared conditions of living."[13] Situations of disorientation in which these forms, normally unacknowledged, unexpectedly come to the fore are conceived as scenes of haunting, producing ghosts or specters that impose a demand for attention and, crucially, action (recognition *and* reparation). Gordon's selectivity with regard to the many possible implications of spectrality—"To see the something-to-be-done as characteristic of haunting was, on the one hand, no doubt to limit its scope"[14]—is motivated by her desire to inspire political change through a broadening of the epistemological framework. If it is to engage with the whole of the social realm, sociology cannot remain blind to the claims for participation and alternative forms of knowledge that emerge from the subjugated—of the past and the present.

Most chapters in *Ghostly Matters* focus on specific hauntings originating in situated historical injustices: Sabina Spielrein's elision from the early history of psychoanalysis, the *desaparecidos* of Argentina's Dirty War, and North-American slavery. These injustices inhabit the present, in ghostly form, not yet understood, not yet fully known; truly apprehending and addressing them requires a perspective combining a materialist with an affective, sensuous dimension. What Gordon proposes, in this respect, is an "other sociological imagination" that invokes Walter Benjamin's notion of profane illumination and "conjures, with all the affective command the world conveys, ... do[ing] so because it has a greatly expanded impression of the empirical that includes haunted people and houses and societies and their worldly and sometimes otherworldly contacts."[15] The chapter included here, entitled "her shape and his hand," sets out the parameters for this new sociological imagination in which ghosts and haunting can come to matter by contrasting it with the "antighost" stance seen to characterize postmodernism.[16] Rather than assuming that everything is illuminated on a plane of hypervisibility, Gordon accommodates ghosts in order to reveal precisely that which normally escapes notice—that which, in Jacques Rancière's terms, is excluded by the reigning *partage du sensible* or distribution of the sensible.[17] Fittingly, her method exceeds the limits of what sociology considers to make sense by mobilizing the ghost tales of Luisa Valenzuela and Toni Morrison; in literature, Gordon suggests, blind spots can be located and ways of re-illuminating them imagined.[18]

On the basis that every society will have oversights and disavowals that reverberate below the surface, Gordon refers to haunting as a "generalizable social phenomenon."[19] In contrast, the second (excerpted) text in this part, Achille Mbembe's "Life, Sovereignty, and Terror in the Fiction of Amos Tutuola," deals with spectrality in an explicitly non-western manner. Confronting a political present that, particularly in previously colonized parts of the world, establishes "*extreme forms of human life, death-worlds,* forms of social existence in which vast populations are subjected to conditions of life that confer upon them the status of living dead (ghosts)" is thought to require a departure from dualistic western modes of thought grounded in the separation of the rational and the irrational, and all the other oppositions tied to these binaries, including that of the real and the spectral.[20]

From the Nigerian author Amos Tutuola—whose *My Life in the Bush of Ghosts* and *The Palm-Wine Drinkard*, based on Yoruba folktales, invoke ghostly realms reaching into the human world—Mbembe takes the figure of the *wandering subject*, for whom there is no self-mastery, but who is instead forced into a continuous re-making of the self through the profoundly ambiguous and fraught dimensions of imagination, work, and remembrance. The wandering subject is ruled by ghostly terror, manifesting as the fearsome machinations of an illogical, ungraspable system that negates all singularity and security, and imposes a constant threat of dismemberment and death. This applies, beyond Tutuola's protagonists, to those human subjects condemned by the globalized, postcolonial world to desperate existences on the verge of death, considered so dispensable that even to haunt may lie outside of their power.[21]

Mbembe invokes a non-western realm in which ghostly beings—in the literal sense—are part of the ordinary and exorcism (in the sense of completely doing away with them) is not an option; in such a realm, spectrality, even when taken as metaphor or concept, occupies a different ontological and epistemological position and mobilizes other meanings, effects, and affects. Most importantly, unlike Derrida's *hauntology*, it does not serve as a counterweight or corrective to a stable, unitary sense of self, but exemplifies a pervasive lack of permanence and singularity that was never otherwise. Whereas Gordon and Derrida focus on the haunted and how they should handle ghosts, which are always other to them, Mbembe takes the perspective of those who (are made to) live *as* ghosts. At the same time, he stresses how the ghost may also conceptualize the way power (especially when manifesting as terror and violence) is itself spectral (unpredictable, unassailable, unaccountable), making it virtually impossible to challenge or escape.

Another non-western context featuring its own singular refraction of the nexus between spectrality and globalization is addressed by Arjun Appadurai. His "Spectral Housing and Urban Cleansing: Notes on Millennial Mumbai," the third text of this part, traces the post-1970 transition, under the combined influence of "predatory global capital" and the growing virulence of Hindu nationalism, from Bombay as a cosmopolitan industrial center and "civic model" to Mumbai as an ethnicized city in which those marked as not belonging become targets for violence and removal.[22]

Spectrality is operative in this transition in interconnected ways. It characterizes, first of all, the city's monetary system, which, on the symbolic level at least, is driven by displays of cash as the "mobile and material instantiation of forms of wealth that are known to be so large as to be immaterial."[23] Cash, in other words, gives body to the ungraspable flows

of capital generated by official and shadow economies alike, while, through
its transactional status as always being passed on, marking the way this
body can never fully incarnate. Second, there is the housing market as
"space of speculation and specularities," where many homes are insecure
(to the point of existing as no more than a spot on the pavement), frenzied
imaginations of possible new supplies abound, and people partake in a
"spectral domesticity" that uses household goods to make up for the actual
home's inadequacy or absence.[24] The third site of spectrality, where the
other two converge, is that of the re-imagination of Bombay as Mumbai,
which, more than a rejection of colonial legacies, constitutes a projection
of Hindu nationalism. This re-imagination—which turned hallucinatory in
the riots that followed, in 1992 and 1993, upon the destruction of the Babri
Masjid in Ayodhya—retains global aspirations, while seeking to eradicate
internal difference. In it, the lack of space that characterizes the system of
spectral housing and the pressures of the cash economy provide justifica-
tions for removing unwanted Muslim bodies and businesses. Noting that
"specters and utopias—as practices of the imagination—occupy the same
moral terrain," Appadurai emphasizes that there has also been a counter-
conjuration proceeding through "powerful images of a cosmopolitan,
secular, multicultural Bombay, and a Mumbai whose 43,000 hectares could
be reorganized to accommodate its 5 million poorly housed citizens."[25]
Spectrality, when read in a certain way in relation to a particular context,
may represent a dangerous deformation of the real that, precisely in its
unreality, is capable of producing actual violence, but it may also work,
in a utopian mode, to effectuate a return to what was—and could again
be—real. Thus, the specter's association with the imagination, with that
which exceeds knowledge and rationality, does not make it inherently
emancipatory or reactionary, but cuts both ways.[26]

The final text in this part, Peter Hitchcock's "(   ) of Ghosts" from
Oscillate Wildly: Space, Body, and Spirit of Millennial Materialism (1999),
reconfigures the relation between spectrality and materialism. As a whole,
the book centers on the concept of oscillation, which, implying both
"restless inquiry" and "vacillation — a moment of doubt, of hesitation, of
wavering," may itself be seen as spectral.[27] The turn to oscillation is designed
to find a way for materialism to (continue to) matter as a route to "more
just, egalitarian forms of society" in a world remade by globalization:

> [T]he double entendre of oscillation is what must be risked if materialism
> is to articulate a radical politics apposite with the tremendous disloca-
> tions of contemporary social orders. Oscillation means embracing the
> dynamic changes of the present, the specific intensities of globalization
> or the aftermath of imploding socialist states for instance, but with the
> attendant hazard of vacillation. At the conscious and unconscious levels
> of intellectual inquiry it now presents itself as a *determinate condition*

of materialism. This is precisely how the assuredness (and masculinism) of traditional forms of materialism are being shaken out of their ossified practices.[28]

One of the ways Hitchcock reforms materialism for the twenty-first century is by invoking the ghost or spirit as inherent to it: "It is not mindless metaphoricity or torpid tropism that puts these spirits into play, but the oscillations of materialist thought itself ... The specters of Marx are not just the workers who do not have a social form for their socialization or realization, but the philosophical ghosts that Marxism cannot simply put to rest within its critical framework without collapsing it."[29] This notion is elaborated in a reading of class that oscillates between Derrida's deconstruction and the Marxism of Etienne Balibar. While class is thought to enter a state of disappearance under the conditions of global capitalism, it is in effect already ephemeral in Marx's work. The proletariat, in particular, is "unrepresentable," appearing only as it is being superseded.[30] Rather than resolving this paradox, it can be taken up critically in what Hitchcock calls a "spectral empiricism" that emphasizes materialism's status as a theory not so much of being as becoming.[31] Within such a framework, the ghost ceases to be a figure only of unreality or illusion: "The reality of class as spectral does not mean it does not exist; it means merely that one grasps the immaterial as also and already constituent of material reality."[32] In a later consideration of the way the communist past inheres in the preserved corpses of Mao and Lenin, Hitchcock places the reverse emphasis, on the need to retain the materiality of spectrality by configuring the ghost (through the uncanny, the cyborg, and the work of Slavoj Žižek) as a figure of likeness, of replication.[33] Spectrality, from this perspective, cannot be simply opposed to materialism, but is intimately intertwined with it, in ways that differ according to the specific historico-political context.[34]

While all four texts in this part take different angles—especially in terms of the theoretical frameworks employed and/or challenged—they share a concern with analyzing the metaphor of the ghost as it operates in the contemporary realm, as capable, on the one hand, of illuminating certain aspects of the way global capitalism works and, on the other, of proposing a new politics that would counteract its dispossessing effects. Moreover, they foreground the need to carefully contextualize and historicize spectrality. In the end, there are no truly global ghosts. Spectrality may have global reach (and provide a way of grasping globalization), but it invariably requires careful contextualization and historicization.

Notes

1   Benson Saler, "Supernatural as a Western Category," *Ethos* 5, no. 1 (1977): 31–53.

2   Recent volumes emphasizing the existence of distinct traditions include Judith Misrahi-Barak and Melanie Joseph-Villain, eds., *Postcolonial Ghosts* (Montpellier: Presses universitaires de la Méditerranée, 2009) and María del Pilar Blanco and Esther Peeren, eds., *Popular Ghosts: The Haunted Spaces of Everyday Culture* (New York and London: Continuum, 2010).

3   See, for example, Pieter Aquilia, "Westernizing Southeast Asian Cinema: Co-productions for 'Transnational' Markets." *Continuum: Journal of Media & Cultural Studies* 20, no. 4 (2006): 433–45.

4   Ann Laura Stoler, "Intimidations of Empire: Predicaments of the Tactile and Unseen," in *Haunted by Empire: Geographies of Intimacy in North American History*, ed. Ann Laura Stoler (Durham and London: Duke University Press, 2006), 9.

5   Ibid., 14, 20.

6   Jacques Derrida, *Specters of Marx: The State of the Debt, the Work of Mourning, & the New International*, trans. Peggy Kamuf (1993; London and New York: Routledge, 1994), 81–3.

7   Judith Butler, *Precarious Life: The Powers of Mourning and Violence* (London and New York: Verso, 2006), 91. The "spectrally human" connects, through Butler's reframing of Foucault's notion of governmentality, to Giorgio Agamben's *homo sacer*, the Roman figure of exclusion that reappears under the biopolitical conditions of modern democracy and technology as "a new living dead man, a new sacred man." Agamben, *Homo Sacer: Sovereign Power and Bare Life*, trans. Daniel Heller-Roazen (1995; Stanford: Stanford University Press, 1998), 131.

8   Derrida, *Specters*, 107.

9   Andrew Hussey, "Spectacle, Simulation and Spectre: Debord, Baudrillard, and the Ghost of Marx," *Parallax* 7, no. 3 (2001): 67.

10 Ibid., 70.

11 Janice Radway, "Foreword," in *Ghostly Matters: Haunting and the Sociological Imagination*, Avery Gordon (Minneapolis: University of Minnesota Press, 2008), xiii.

12 Avery Gordon, "Introduction to the New Edition," in *Ghostly Matters: Haunting and the Sociological Imagination* (Minneapolis: University of Minnesota Press, 2008), xv.

13 Ibid.

14 Ibid., xvii.

15 Gordon, *Ghostly Matters*, 204.

16 Ibid., 13. Whether Don DeLillo's novel *White Noise*, which Gordon takes as exemplary of this postmodernist stance, unambiguously endorses a world

without secrets, gaps, or ghosts is debatable; the novel has also been read as precisely a critique of the disenchanted society of the spectacle. See, for example, Matthew J. Parker, "'At the Dead Center of Things' in Don DeLillo's White Noise: Mimesis, Violence, and Religious Awe," *Modern Fiction Studies* 51, no. 3 (2005): 648–66; Cornel Bonca, "Don DeLillo's White Noise: The Natural Language of the Species," *College Literature* 23, no. 2 (1996): 25–44.

17 See Jacques Rancière, *The Politics of Aesthetics*, trans. Gabriel Rockhill (2000; London and New York: Continuum, 2004).

18 Rancière, too, argues that politics and sociology require a phantasmagoric element: "the ordinary becomes a trace of the true if it is torn from its obviousness in order to become a hieroglyph, a mythological or phantasmagoric figure. This phantasmagoric dimension of the true, which belongs to the aesthetic regime of the arts, played an essential role in the formation of the critical paradigm of the human and social sciences.... . Scholarly history tried to separate out various features within the aesthetico-political configuration that gave it its object. It flattened this phantasmagoria of the true into the positivist sociological concepts of mentality/expression and belief/ignorance." *Politics of Aesthetics*, 34.

19 Gordon, *Ghostly Matters*, 7.

20 Achille Mbembe, "Life, Sovereignty, and Terror in the Fiction of Amos Tutuola," *Research in African Literatures* 34, no. 4 (2003): 1.

21 See also Mbembe's "Necropolitics," which expands his consideration of *death-worlds* and the problem of sovereignty as "the power and the capacity to dictate who may live and who must die" in direct reference to Foucault's biopolitics and Agamben's *homo sacer*, and in relation to real-world examples, historical (slavery, Nazism, colonialism) and contemporary (late-modern colonial occupation, high-tech warfare). *Public Culture* 15, no. 1 (2003): 11. For other considerations of spectrality and the postcolonial, see Misrahi-Barak and Joseph-Villain, *Postcolonial Ghosts*; Michael F. O'Riley, "Postcolonial Haunting: Anxiety, Affect, and the Situated Encounter," *Postcolonial Text* 3, no. 4 (2007): 1–15; Stephen Morton, "Postcolonialism and Spectrality: Political Deferral and Ethical Singularity in the Writing of Gayatri Chakravorty Spivak," *Interventions* 1, no. 4 (1999): 605–20.

22 Arjun Appadurai, "Spectral Housing and Urban Cleansing: Notes on Millennial Mumbai," *Public Culture* 12, no. 3 (2000): 627, 628.

23 Ibid., 634.

24 Ibid., 643.

25 Ibid., 650.

26 For a different reading of spectral nationalism in the context of postcoloniality and globalization, see Pheng Cheah, "Spectral Nationalism: The Living On [*sur-vie*] of the Postcolonial Nation in Neocolonial Globalization," *boundary 2* 26, no. 3 (1999): 225–52. Critiquing theorists of nationalism for invoking a vitalist ontology that pitches the life of the people against the dead (ideology of the) state, Cheah takes up Derrida's notion of

spectrality to argue for "the mutual haunting of the nation-people and the state" (245): "As long as we continue to think of 'the people' or 'the people-nation' in analogy with a living body or a source of ever present life, then the postcolonial state qua political and economic agent is always the necessary supplement of the revolutionary nation-people, the condition for its living on after decolonization. The nation-people can come into freedom only by attaching itself to the postcolonial bourgeois state. It can live on only through this kind of death. The state is an uncontrollable specter that the nation-people must welcome within itself, and direct, at once *for itself and against itself*, because this specter can possess the nation-people and bend it toward global capital interests" (247). Arguing this requires rejecting Derrida's association of nationalism with ontopology: "The decolonizing nation is not an archaic throwback to traditional forms of community based on the blind ties of blood and kinship but a new form of political community engendered by the spectrality of modern knowledge, techno-mediation, and modern organization" (250).

27 Peter Hitchcock, *Oscillate Wildly: Space, Body, and Spirit of Millennial Materialism* (Minneapolis: University of Minnesota Press, 1999), 3.

28 Ibid., 2, 3–4.

29 Ibid., 144–5.

30 Ibid., 151.

31 Ibid., 152. Further on, Hitchcock writes: "Materialism is not just a theory of materiality but also about processes of materialization and dematerialization ... It is a theory (philosophical and more) about 'becoming.' Marx makes the conjuring of ghosts a symptom of the materialization of theory. It is not some idle image but an active component of his explanatory critique. The point is not to collapse back this theorization into the discursive trope that is its possibility, but to understand the trope as an operative logic in the model proposed" (155).

32 Ibid., 159.

33 Peter Hitchcock, "Uncanny Marxism: Or, Do Androids Dream of Electric Lenin?" in Blanco and Peeren, *Popular Ghosts*, 35–49. For Žižek's use of spectrality, see especially his "Introduction: The Spectre of Ideology," in *Mapping Ideology*, Slavoj Žižek ed. (London and New York: Verso, 1994), 1–33 and *Welcome to the Desert of the Real* (London and New York: Verso, 2002). In the latter text, he writes, in reference to 9/11: "the dialectic of semblance and Real cannot be reduced to the rather elementary fact that the virtualization of our daily lives, the experience that we are living more and more in an artificially constructed universe, gives rise to an irresistible urge to 'return to the Real', to regain firm ground in some 'real reality'. The Real which returns has the status of a(nother) semblance: *precisely because it is real, that is, on account of its traumatic/excessive character, we are unable to integrate it into (what we experience as) our reality, and are therefore compelled to experience it as a nightmarish apparition....* Much more difficult than to denounce/unmask (what appears as) reality as fiction is to recognize the part of fiction in 'real' reality" (19).

34 Against generalizing uses of the spectral that turn it into a "paradoxically unbound relationality," Hitchcock argues: "Yes, the process of the spectral actualizes, but the verb and the concept are tainted by the wisps of history which is why this symptom must be engaged and radically particularized rather than inflated. Only then will we begin to fathom how the public sphere became so phantomatic and communicative action so fanciful." Hitchcock, "The Impossibly Intersubjective and the Logic of the Both," in *The Shock of the Other: Situating Alterities*, ed. Silke Horstkotte and Esther Peeren (Amsterdam and New York: Rodopi, 2007), 34–5.

8

from Her Shape and His Hand

Avery F. Gordon

That life is complicated is a fact of great analytic importance.

PATRICIA WILLIAMS, *THE ALCHEMY OF RACE AND RIGHTS*

That life is complicated may seem a banal expression of the obvious, but it is nonetheless a profound theoretical statement—perhaps the most important theoretical statement of our time. Yet despite the best intentions of sociologists and other social analysts, this theoretical statement has not been grasped in its widest significance. There are at least two dimensions to such a theoretical statement. The first is that the power relations that characterize any historically embedded society are never as transparently clear as the names we give to them imply. Power can be invisible, it can be fantastic, it can be dull and routine. It can be obvious, it can reach you by the baton of the police, it can speak the language of your thoughts and desires. It can feel like remote control, it can exhilarate like liberation, it can travel through time, and it can drown you in the present. It is dense and superficial, it can cause bodily injury, and it can harm you without seeming ever to touch you. It is systematic and it is particularistic and it is often both at the same time. It causes dreams to live and dreams to die. We can and must call it by recognizable names, but so too we need to remember that power arrives in forms that can range from blatant white supremacy and state terror to "furniture without memories."

One day, the students in my undergraduate course on American culture and I made a thorough list of every possible explanation Toni Morrison gives in *The Bluest Eye* (1970) for why dreams die. These ranged from explicit externally imposed and internalized white supremacist standards of value, *the nature of white man's work*, and the dialectics of violence and hatred to *disappointment*, to *folding up inside*, to *being put outdoors*, to *the weather*, to *deformed feet and lost teeth*, to *nobody pays attention*, to *it's too late*, to *total damage*, to *furniture without memories*, to the *unyielding soil*, and to what Morrison sometimes just calls *the thing*, the sedimented conditions that constitute what is in place in the first place. This turns out to be not a random list at all, but a way of conceptualizing the complicated workings of race, class, and gender, the names we give to the ensemble of social relations that create inequalities, situated interpretive codes, particular kinds of subjects, and the possible and impossible themselves. Such a conceptualization asks that we constantly move within and between *furniture without memories* and Racism and Capitalism. It asks us to move analytically between that sad and sunken couch that sags in just that place where an unrememberable past and an unimaginable future force us to sit day after day and the conceptual abstractions because everything of significance happens there among the inert furniture and the monumental social architecture.

But this list also reminds us that even those who live in the most dire circumstances possess a complex and oftentimes contradictory humanity and subjectivity that is never adequately glimpsed by viewing them as victims or, on the other hand, as superhuman agents. It has always baffled me why those most interested in understanding and changing the barbaric domination that characterizes our modernity often—not always— withhold from the very people they are most concerned with the right to complex personhood. Complex personhood is the second dimension of the theoretical statement that life is complicated. Complex personhood means that all people (albeit in specific forms whose specificity is sometimes everything) remember and forget, are beset by contradiction, and recognize and misrecognize themselves and others. Complex personhood means that people suffer graciously and selfishly too, get stuck in the symptoms of their troubles, and also transform themselves. Complex personhood means that even those called "Other" are never never that. Complex personhood means that the stories people tell about themselves, about their troubles, about their social worlds, and about their society's problems are entangled and weave between what is immediately available as a story and what their imaginations are reaching toward. Complex personhood means that people get tired and some are just plain lazy. Complex personhood means that groups of people will act together, that they will vehemently disagree with and sometimes harm each other, and that they will do both at the same time and expect the rest of us to figure it out for ourselves, intervening and withdrawing as the situation requires. Complex personhood means that even those who haunt our dominant institutions and their systems of value are haunted too by things they sometimes have names for and sometimes do not. At the very least, complex personhood is about conferring the respect on others that comes from presuming that life and people's lives are simultaneously straightforward and full of enormously subtle meaning.

That life is complicated is a theoretical statement that guides efforts to treat race, class, and gender dynamics and consciousness as more dense and delicate than those categorical terms often imply. It is a theoretical statement that might guide a critique of privately purchased rights, of various forms of blindness and sanctioned denial; that might guide an attempt to drive a wedge into lives and visions of freedom ruled by the nexus of market exchange. It is a theoretical statement that invites us to see with portentous clarity into the heart and soul of American life and culture, to track events, stories, anonymous and history-making actions to their density, to the point where we might catch a glimpse of what Patricia Williams calls the "vast networking of our society" and imagine otherwise. You could say this is a folk theoretical statement. We need to know where we live in order to imagine living elsewhere. We need to imagine living elsewhere before we can live there.

The Alchemy of Race and Rights by Patricia Williams (1991) is a book that captured my attention because, among other things, here is a woman who does not know if she is crazy or not, who sees ghosts and polar bears and has conversations with her sister about haunted houses and writes all of it down for us while she is sitting in her bathrobe with disheveled hair. Patricia Williams is a commercial lawyer and a professor of contract and property law. Her great-great grandmother was a slave, property. Her great-great grandmother's owner and the father of her children was Austin Miller, a well-known Tennessee lawyer and jurist. What is Patricia Williams looking for?

> I track meticulously the dimension of meaning in my great-great-grand-mother as chattel: the meaning of money; the power of consumerist world view, the deaths of those we label the unassertive and the inefficient. I try to imagine where and who she would be today. I am engaged in a long-term project of tracking his [Austin Miller's] words—through his letters and opinions—and those of his sons who were also lawyers and judges, of finding the shape described by her absence in all this.
>
> I see her shape and his hand in the vast networking of our society, and in the evils and oversights that plague our lives and laws. The control he had over her body. The force he was in her life, in the shape of my life today. The power he exercised in the choice to breed her or not. The choice to breed slaves in his image, to choose her mate and be that mate. In his attempt to own what no man can own, the habit of his power and the absence of her choice.
>
> I look for her shape and his hand. (19)

I look for her shape and his hand; this is a massive project, very treacherous, very fragile. This is a project in which haunting and phantoms play a central part. This is a project where *finding the shape described by her absence* captures perfectly the paradox of tracking through time and across all those forces that which makes its mark by being there and not there at the same time. Cajoling us to reconsider (if only to get some peace), and because cajoling is in the nature of the ghost, the very distinctions between there and not there, past and present, force and shape. From force to hand to her ghostly presence in the register of history and back again, this is a particular kind of social alchemy that eludes us as often as it makes us look for it. Patricia Williams is not alone in the search for the shape of force and lost hands; there is company for the keeping. Wahneema Lubiano (1992, 1993), too, is looking for the haunting presence of the state in the cultural zones where it seemingly excuses itself. Kimberlé Crenshaw (1991) is trying to raise the specter of the ghostly violence of law's regime of objects, its objectivity. Catherine Clément has for some time been trying to "remember *today*" the "zone" that "somewhere every culture has ... for what it excludes" (Cixous and Clément 1986). Norma Alarcón (1990) is following the barely visible tracks of the Native Woman across the U.S.-Mexico border, as she shadows the making of the liberal citizen-subject. Hortense Spillers (1987) is reconstructing the American grammatology that lost some subjects in one passage and found others in a phantasmatic family of bad mothers and absent fathers. Maxine Hong Kingston (1977) is mapping the trans-Pacific travel of ghostly ancestors and their incessant demands on the living. Gayatri Spivak (1987, 1989, 1993) keeps vigilant watch over the dialectic of presence and absence that characterizes "our" benevolent metropolitan relationship to the subaltern women "over there."[1] *I look for her shape and his hand.*

  Ghostly Matters is about haunting, a paradigmatic way in which life is more complicated than those of us who study it have usually granted. Haunting is a constituent element of modern social life. It is neither premodern superstition nor individual psychosis; it is a generalizable social phenomenon of great import. To study social life one must confront the ghostly aspects of it. This confrontation requires (or produces) a fundamental change in the way we know and make knowledge, in our mode of production. *Ghostly Matters* is a theoretical and conceptual book that I hope demonstrates the utter significance of well-placed (as opposed to misplaced) concreteness and conveys the relevance of ghostly matters to the sociological enterprise, an enterprise at once in sociology and eagerly willing to make it into something entirely different. *Ghostly Matters* is an interdisciplinary work and in this sense representative of our times and needs. It is Roland Barthes's notion of interdisciplinarity that it strives to instantiate: "Interdisciplinary work, so much discussed these days, is not about confronting already constituted disciplines (none of which, in fact, is willing to let itself go). To do something interdisciplinary it's not enough to choose a 'subject' (a theme) and gather around it two or three sciences. Interdisciplinarity consists in creating a new object that belongs to no one" (quoted in Clifford and Marcus 1986: 1). Not owned by anyone yet, this interdisciplinarity is in the public domain, which does not guarantee anything except that there is still some room to claim rather than discipline its meaning into existence. *Ghostly Matters* looks for a language for identifying hauntings and for writing with the ghosts any haunting inevitably throws up.

Ghosts are a somewhat unusual topic of inquiry for a social analyst (much less a degreed sociologist). It may seem foreign and alien, marginal to the field that conventionally counts as living social reality, the field we observe, measure, and interpret, the field that takes the measure of us as much as we take the measure of it.[2] And foreign and alien it is, for reasons that are both obvious and stubbornly oblique. There is a long story of how I came to write a book about ghostly matters, much of which is relevant to an engaged sociology of knowledge and some of which is even perhaps interesting, but a good deal of it is not what my colleague Harvey Molotch would call news.

I came to write about ghostly matters not because I was interested in the occult or in parapsychology, but because ghostly things kept cropping up and messing up other tasks I was trying to accomplish. Call it grounded theory: in one field another emerged to literally capture my attention and become the field work. The persistent and troubling ghosts in the house highlighted the limitations of many of our prevalent modes of inquiry and the assumptions they make about the social world, the people who inhabit these worlds, and what is required to study them. The available critical vocabularies were failing (me) to communicate the depth, density, and intricacies of the dialectic of subjection and subjectivity (or what in my business we call structure and agency), of domination and freedom, of critique and utopian longing. Of course, it is not simply the vocabularies themselves that are at fault, but the constellation of effects, historical and institutional, that make a vocabulary a social practice of producing knowledge.[3] A vocabulary and a practice were missing while demanding their due. Haunted and, I admit, sometimes desperate, sociology certainly—but also the human sciences at large—seemed to provide few tools for understanding how social institutions and people are haunted, for capturing enchantment in a disenchanted world.

If haunting describes how that which appears to be not there is often a seething presence, acting on and often meddling with taken-for-granted realities, the ghost is just the sign, or the empirical evidence if you like, that tells you a haunting is taking place. The ghost is not simply a dead or a missing person, but a social figure, and investigating it can lead to that dense site where history and subjectivity make social life. The ghost or the apparition is one form by which something lost, or barely visible, or seemingly not there to our supposedly well-trained eyes, makes itself known or apparent to us, in its own way, of course. The way of the ghost is haunting, and haunting is a very particular way of knowing what has happened or is happening. Being haunted draws us affectively, sometimes against our will and always a bit magically, into the structure of feeling of a reality we come to experience, not as cold knowledge, but as a transformative recognition.

How I came to write a book about ghostly matters is a long story, and some of that story has to do with postmodernism, its trail of associations, its often deafening white noise. In 1992 the president-elect of the Society for the Study of Social Problems called the members to the annual meeting to discuss a new postmodern world order "structured around the dense and high velocity technological rituals of image management, informational CAPITAL, [and] cybernetic-like mechanisms of social control" (Pfohl 1991: 9) without forgetting that "it's not that the ghosts don't exist" (Pfohl 1992b: 7). The invitation linked a certain terminology of postmodernity with the critique of the social sciences' empiricist grounds of knowing. This was not inappropriate since over the past ten to twenty years there has been a veritable assault on our traditional ways of conceptualizing, studying, and writing about the social world and the individuals and cultural artifacts that inhabit this world. Whether the post-1945 period is conceived as the loss of the West's eminent metanarratives of legitimation or as a series of signposts announcing the arrival of significant reconfigurations of our dominant Western organizational and theoretical frames—poststructuralism, postcolonialism, post-Marxism, postindustrialism, postmodernism, postfeminism—many scholars across various disciplinary fields now are grappling with the social, political, and epistemological confrontations that have increasingly come to characterize it.

The claims and summons poststructuralism, in particular, has made on our traditional notions of the human subject, meaning, truth, language, writing, desire, difference, power, and experience have more recently "been placed in a larger context, or 'condition,' of which they have been seen equally as a symptom and as a determining cause. This larger condition—postmodernism—addresses a whole range of material conditions that are no longer consonant with the dominant rationality of modernism and its technological commitment to finding *solutions* in every sphere of social and cultural life" (Ross 1988: x). Situating postmodernism thus locates what is often construed as strictly philosophical or epistemological questions on a decidedly sociological and political terrain. As the invitation elaborated, and as Ross states, "postmodernist culture is a real medium in which we all live to some extent, no matter how unevenly its effects are lived and felt across the jagged spectrum of color, sex, class, region, and nationality" (ibid.: viii).

For the discipline of sociology, postmodern conditions have made their impact felt most strongly in the resurgence of "the ancient problem of the relationship between what in everyday language we call 'experience' of 'reality' and what we then decide to call 'knowledge' about it" (Jardine 1985: 145) and in the attendant dilemmas created for an empirical social science (see Agger 1989a, 1989b, 1990, 1991, 1992, 1993; Bauman 1992, 1993; R. Brown 1987, 1989; Clough 1992; Denzin 1986, 1991; Lemert 1990; Pfohl 1992a; J. W. Scott 1992; Seidman 1991, 1994a, 1994b). At the core of the postmodern field or scene, then, is a crisis of representation, a fracture in the epistemological regime of modernity, a regime that rested on a faith in the reality effect of social science. Such a predicament has led to, among other consequences, an understanding that the practices of writing, analysis, and investigation, whether of social or cultural material, constitute less a scientifically positive project than a cultural practice that organizes particular rituals of storytelling told by situated investigators. The promise of this postpositivist and, in a limited sense, post- or antimodern rupture for sociology is that rather than leading away from an analysis of the social relations of power (which is the presumed drawback of a concern with representation), it will lead to a different agenda for asking how power operates. Such an agenda could deliver, albeit with necessary improvements, on the unfulfilled promissory note given to sociology by Horkheimer and Adorno: namely, to link a thoroughgoing epistemological critique of modernity as what is contemporaneously ours with an insurgent sociological critique of its forms of domination (Frankfurt Institute for Social Research [1956] 1973).

Questions of narrative structuring, constructedness, analytic standpoint, and historical provisionality of claims to knowledge direct sociology to the ways in which our stories can be understood as fictions of the real. The challenge to the monopolistic assumption that sociology can provide an unproblematic window onto a more rather than less secure reality is both necessary and desirable in order to understand how the real itself and its ethnographic or sociological representations are also fictions, albeit powerful ones that we do not experience as fictional, but as true. At the same time, the increasingly sophisticated understandings of representation and of how the social world is textually or discursively constructed still require an engagement with the social structuring practices that have long been the province of sociological inquiry. It is these that draw our attention to the multiple determinations and sites of power in which narratives of and about our culture and its artifacts are produced and disseminated.

Part of the widespread ambivalence toward postmodernism and postmodernity stems from the complicated relationship between reality and its modes of production, a relationship crucial to the primary investigation of exclusions and invisibilities: Neither postmodernism nor postmodernity resolve this relationship by any means. (And, indeed, the common tendency to distinguish between postmodernism as a kind of voluntary idealism—a style or choice of approach—and postmodernity as a kind of crushing, all-encompassing materialism does not help matters at all. In fact, it sends social theorists back to the drawing board needlessly.) What some feminists and critical theorists have sensibly insisted on retaining is precisely a double structure of thought that links the epistemological and the social (see Flax 1992; Lubiano 1991). Feminism's presumed (and putatively paradigmatic) relationship to postmodernism rests on its participation in the critique of the transparency of language, objective causality, transnational generalization, and so on, all of which are part and parcel of the so-called crisis in representation (see Nicholson 1990; Butler 1992). But the critique of representation does not solve the problem of the continuing crisis of domination—coercive and consensual—unless it is linked to issues of governmentality, broadly understood (see Hennessy 1993; Mouffe 1992). Coupling problems with representation to an ongoing and aggressive concern with representability, in the political sense, is what enables epistemology to be properly situated in the ensemble of social relations of power in which such epistemologies are ensconced.

To say that sociology or social analysis more broadly must retain a double structure of thought that links the epistemological and the social, or, in other words, to say that sociology has to respond *methodologically* and not only as if from an autonomous distance begs the question of what exactly the novel postmodern social conditions to which we ought to respond are. Difficult diagnostic issues are at stake here, exacerbated by "the effort to take the temperature of the age without instruments and in a situation in which we are not even sure there is so coherent a thing as an 'age,' or zeitgeist or 'system' or 'current situation' any longer" (Jameson 1991: xi). It is no doubt true that some of the central characteristics of the modern systems of capitalism, state and subject formation, and knowledge production are undergoing significant modifications, and many are working to describe these changes and their implications (see Bauman [1988] 1994; Haraway 1985; Harvey 1989; Jameson 1991; Lash 1990). An equally powerful argument could be made, as Derrick Bell (1992) does in one of the more moving examples of Antonio Gramsci's maxim—optimism of the will, pessimism of the intellect—that things have hardly changed at all. I am simply not in a position to adjudicate the degree of continuity or discontinuity at such a grand scale and am inclined to consider most conclusions premature at this point, and perhaps at any point. In my own limited view, therefore, we are not "post" modern yet, although it is arguably the case that the fundamental contradictions at the heart of modernity are more exposed and much is up for grabs in the way we conceive the possibilities for knowledge, for freedom, and for subjecthood in the wake of this exposure. It is also arguably the case that the strong sense of living in "a strange new landscape ... the sense that something has changed, that things are different, that we have gone through a transformation of the life world which is somehow decisive but incomparable with the older convulsions of modernization and industrialization" (Jameson 1991: xxi) so pervasive in many quarters is an influential and itself motivating social and cultural fact.[4]

Of one thing I am sure: *it's not that the ghosts don't exist*. The postmodern, late-capitalist, postcolonial world represses and projects its ghosts or phantoms in similar intensities, if not entirely in the same forms, as the older world did. Indeed, the concentration on haunting and ghosts is a way of maintaining the salience of social analysis as bounded by its social context, as in history, which is anything but dead and over, while avoiding simple reflectionism. Yet, in one particularly prominent framing of postmodernism, an overweening and overstated emphasis on new electronic technologies of communication, on consumerism, and on the spectacular world of commodities has, despite the rhetoric of exposing the new machinery, replaced conventional positivism with a postmodernist version that promotes the telecommunicative visibility—of all codings and decodings. Crudely put, when postmodernism means that everything is on view, that everything can be described, that all "tacitly present means ... [become] conscious object[s] of self-perfection" (Bauman [1988] 1994: 188), it displays an antighost side that resembles modernity's positivities more than it concedes.

Let me give you an example. Don DeLillo's 1985 best-selling novel *White Noise* is a paradigmatic postmodern text. Nothing much happens in it really. Jack Gladney, professor and inventor, in 1968, of Hitler studies, ruminates on American popular culture and family life while trying to learn German, which he doesn't speak. He has a hard time keeping his tongue in place, but does keep his competitive edge by refusing to really help his friend Murray set up a similar institutional program to promote Elvis studies. Jack loves his extended family, composed of children from various marriages, all of whom display a level of maturity Jack and Babette, his wife, lack. Babette is, like Jack, obsessed with a fear of dying, and all their shopping doesn't seem to help her, although it does "expand" her husband. Her fear leads her to covertly trade sex for drugs, which is all just fine until Jack and the children find her out. At this point, Babette becomes irrelevant and Jack plots to recover the drugs, his wife's sexual propriety, and his manhood. He never learns to speak German and the whole drama is interrupted by a toxic disaster that confuses the town, which had been simu-planning it for months. It is of no consolation to Jack that he might really die from postindustrial contamination, although the specter of "real" death provides him with enough justification to minimize his wife's "unreal" fears.

DeLillo's novel is a descriptively rich evocation of white suburban North America in the commodified landscape of late capitalism, full of clever insights and portable quotations. It conjures up some of the dominant and disturbing features of American life that are increasingly named postmodern: television-structured reality, the commodification of everyday life, the absence of meaning and the omnipresence of endless information, the relentless fascination with catastrophes, and the circulating advertisements for the death of author, referent, and objective reality set within image upon image of the electric connections among life, death, and sex.

Notwithstanding my docudrama rendering of the plot, the familiar and familial noise of *White Noise*, a fiction, reads like a sociological map of white postmodern America, like an ethnography of sorts. Significantly, this reading effect is precisely related to those social conditions that the text itself identifies as challenging the distinctions between the fictive and the factual, and between the imaginary and the real. This is *White Noise*'s great strength as a social science fiction: it attempts to link the sociological and the epistemological dimensions of postmodernism. At the level of everyday language and procedure, DeLillo captures the optimistic cynicism of imploded meanings, empty memory banks, and televisual screenings. He is neither critical nor celebratory. Abandoning the terrain of politics, the contestation about and over power, he opts instead for a kind of market media effect where *everything was on television last night*.

White Noise is, however, a ghost-busting text that refuses to confront what has been rendered spectral by the twin hands of the social and the writer. At the close of *White Noise*, the language of enthusiasm for an American culture mediated and saturated by commodities whose hieroglyphics and secret codes fascinate and offer entrance into a world full of abandoned meanings and momentary ecstatic experiences gives way to a "sense of wandering ... an aimless and haunted mood." *Smeared print, ghost images*. The members of DeLillo's television public find that the "supermarket shelves have been re-arranged ... one day without warning":

> The men scan for stamped dates, the women for ingredients. Many have trouble making out the words. Smeared print, ghost images. In the altered shelves, the ambient roar, in the plain and heartless fact of their decline, they try to work their way through confusion. But in the end it doesn't matter what they see or think they see. The terminals are equipped with holographic scanners, which decode the binary secret of every item, infallibly. This is the language of waves and radiation, or how the dead speak to the living. (325–6)

At the end of DeLillo's novel, his story of contemporary white suburban everyday life (which in this novel is the virtual history of post-World War II American culture) is figured by the rearrangement of the supermarket shelves. This is an apt metaphor for the social world *White Noise* articulates and orients around its protagonist, Jack Gladney: a commodified, post-Hiroshima landscape of late (night) capitalism where "everything was on television last night." Up until this point, Jack, who constantly interprets and theorizes (in perfectly encapsulated, spectacular one-sentence units) the popular culture that fascinates him, has been enthusiastic about the *waves and radiation* of an electronically simulated culture. *The myth being born right there in our living room* has its dark side, of course: *they believed something lived in the basement.* But neither the Airborne Toxic Event (Blacksmith's Bhopal), nor a world full of *abandoned meanings*, nor a wife fearful for her life for inexplicable reasons—can shatter the smooth switching of channels that gives us *Family Ties* and *Guiding Light(s)*. At the end all that remains is confusion, an inability to make out the words, and the postmodern surface sheen gone cynical and pessimistic. DeLillo's conclusion eerily encants: *But in the end it doesn't matter what they see or think they see.* The terminals can *decode the secret of every item.* No secrets, no gaps, no errant trajectories, only a passive scene of waiting and watching. From my point of view, and simply put, *But in the end it doesn't matter what they see or think they see* is the language of waves and radiation, a language in which the ghostly (or the living for that matter) cannot get a word in edgewise. *But in the end it doesn't matter what they see or think they see* is the postmodern positive language of power and indifference that is nothing more than the "second nature" of commodification speaking as our common culture (Jameson 1991: 314).

If the ghostly haunt gives notice that something is missing—that what appears to be invisible or in the shadows is announcing itself, however symptomatically—then in *White Noise* there are no ghostly haunts, or shadows, only the insistent visibility of fetishized commodity surveillance and that which masquerades as its absence. Indeed, one could argue that *White Noise* enacts a detour around just those issues of power it aggressively renders explicit. And it enacts that detour by its insistent emphasis, to the exclusion of a more dialectical way of seeing, on the hypervisibility of what could be called technological irrationality.

Visibility is a complex system of permission and prohibition, of presence and absence, punctuated alternately by apparitions and hysterical blindness (Kipnis 1988: 158). It is perhaps DeLillo's "hysterical blindness" to "apparitions" and to the "complex system of permission and prohibition, of presence and absence" that makes his book an example of postmodernist positivism, or hypervisibility. Hypervisibility is a kind of obscenity of accuracy that abolishes the distinctions between "permission and prohibition, presence and absence." No shadows, no ghosts. In a culture seemingly ruled by technologies of hypervisibility, we are led to believe not only that everything can be seen, but also that everything is available and accessible for our consumption. In a culture seemingly ruled by technologies of hypervisibility, we are led to believe that neither repression nor the return of the repressed, in the form of either improperly buried bodies or countervailing systems of value or difference, occurs with any meaningful result.

The representation of value or difference is indispensable for understanding the cleavages that power's divisive work accomplishes. To the extent that DeLillo's text performs some of the new ways in which difference, rather than simply being excluded or marginalized, is being staged or simulated, it tells an important story. For example, *White Noise* clearly puts the reader on notice that it will not (and then cannot) tell, with any sympathetic apprehension, the story of Jack's panicking wife, Babette, a powerful indicator of the way in which even silence and invisibility can be accessed. Such a narrative makes it difficult, if not impossible, however, to imagine her story as other than a kind of visible invisibility: *I see you are not there.* In other words, not much is left of Babette's value other than the fact that her absent life world can now be acknowledged, advertised, and consumed as background white noise. DeLillo's text may very well echo Jean Baudrillard's point that postmodern culture can increasingly bring within view (for consumption) that which previously remained at the margins, but it also reproduces the same features it describes. In so doing, it offers no place from which to challenge the ubiquity of that white noise and offer a countermemory. Indeed, the obsession with death in the novel is a substitute for dealing with the ghostly matter, the ghostly and haunting trouble. Rather, we are confronted with the morbidity of existence as a symptom of the inability to confront modernity's phantoms. Kept busy just surviving in the confusing supermarket of life, itself already having coded and decoded all exchanges, reification—the effacement of the traces of production—appears, in this milieu, to be the welcome relief one hopes for. Jameson (1991: 314–15) puts it well: "the point of having your own object world, and walls and muffled distance or relative silence all around you, is to forget about all those innumerable others for a while." To remember "would be like having voices inside your head" (315).[5] *It would be like having voices inside your head* because a postmodern social formation is still haunted by the symptomatic traces of its productions and exclusions. A different language than the one DeLillo offers is needed to even begin the work of writing a text that might have something more to say about *smeared print, ghost images.*

In a 1981 introduction to *Invisible Man*, Ralph Ellison wrote: "despite the bland assertions of sociologists, [the] 'high visibility' [of the African-American man] actually rendered one un-visible" (xii). Hypervisibility is a persistent alibi for the mechanisms that render one *un*visible. "His darkness ... glow[ing] ... within the American conscience with such intensity that most whites feigned moral blindness toward his predicament." The difficulty for us now, as it was for Ellison when he published *Invisible Man* in 1952, is the extent to which the mediums of public image making and visibility are inextricably wedded to the co-joined mechanisms that systematically render certain groups of people apparently *privately* poor, uneducated, ill, and disenfranchised.

Ellison's *Invisible Man* gives double reference both to the unvisibility of the hypervisible African-American man and to the invisibility of "the Man" who persistently needs an alibi for the blindness of his vision. As a strategy of analysis, Ellison's insight underscores the need to conceptualize visibility as a *complex system of permission and prohibition, punctuated alternately by apparitions and hysterical blindness.* If Ellison's argument encourages us to interrogate the mechanisms *by* which the highly visible can actually be a type of invisibility, Toni Morrison's (1989) argument that "invisible things are not necessarily not-there" encourages the complementary gesture of investigating how that which appears absent can indeed be a seething presence. Both these positions are about how to write ghost stories—about how to write about *permissions and prohibitions, presence and absence, about apparitions and hysterical blindness.* To write stories concerning exclusions and invisibilities is to write ghost stories. To write ghost stories implies that ghosts are real, that is to say, that they produce material effects. To impute a kind of objectivity to ghosts implies that, from certain standpoints, the dialectics of visibility and invisibility involve a constant negotiation between what can be seen and what is in the shadows. Why would we want to write such stories? Because unlike DeLillo's indifference, *in the end* and in the beginning *it* does *matter what they see or think they see.* It matters because although *the terminals are equipped with holographic scanners,* they cannot *decode the secret of every item, infallibly.* Indeed, what is at stake here is the political status and function of systematic hauntings.

If the ghost is a crucible for political mediation and historical memory, the ghost story has no other choice than to refuse the logic of the unreconstructed spectacle, whether of the modern or postmodern variety. *White Noise* might bring us to the brink of establishing the necessity of reckoning with the instrumentality of hauntings. But because it does not invite us to make contact with haunting, to engage the shadows and what is living there, it does not help us to develop a form of historical accounting distinct from the diagnostics of postmodern hypervisibility. The purpose of an alternative diagnostics is to link the politics of accounting, in all its intricate political-economic, institutional, and affective dimensions, to a potent imagination of what has been done and what is to be done otherwise.

How do we reckon with what modern history has rendered ghostly? How do we develop a critical language to describe and analyze the affective, historical, and mnemonic structures of such hauntings? These questions have guided my desire to articulate, however insufficiently, a sense of the ghostly and its social and political effects. I use the word *sense* here deliberately to evoke what Raymond Williams called a structure of feeling—perhaps the most appropriate description of how hauntings are transmitted and received. I have not endeavored to establish transhistorical or universal laws of haunting per se[6] but rather to represent the structure of feeling that is something akin to what it feels like to be the object of a social totality vexed by the phantoms of modernity's violence. What does this mean? It means following the insights that come to those who see all these forces operating at once. Such a way of seeing can make you a bit crazy and imprecise and wary of shorthands. While it may be true that the constellation of social forces all collide in various ways, that social life's complication is, to use an often overused phrase, overdetermined, the obvious task of the critic or analyst is to designate the precise contours of experience and causality in particular instances. It is not a matter of accepting or rejecting any of a range of notions of social totality, and, academic common sense to the contrary, Marxists do not have a lock on this concept (Gordon 1992). Rather, it is a matter of exploring here the particular mediation that is haunting. As a concept, mediation describes the process that links an institution and an individual, a social structure and a subject, and history and a biography. In haunting, organized forces and systemic structures that appear removed from us make their impact felt in everyday life in a way that confounds our analytic separations and confounds the social separations themselves. Paying attention to the disjuncture between identifying a social structure (or declaring its determinate existence) and its articulation in everyday life and thought, I have hoped that working at understanding these gaps, the kinds of visions they produce, and the afflictions they harbor would enable us not to eradicate the gap—it is inevitable—but to fill in the content differently. Could it be that analyzing hauntings might lead to a more complex understanding of the generative structures and moving parts of historically embedded social formations in a way that avoids the twin pitfalls of subjectivism and positivism? Perhaps. If so, the result will not be a more tidy world, but one that might be less damaging.

It was in such a spirit that Horkheimer and Adorno ([1944] 1987) wrote a two-page note, appended to *The Dialectic of Enlightenment*, entitled "On The Theory of Ghosts." Despairing at the loss of historical perspective, at our "disturbed relationship with the dead—forgotten and embalmed," they believed we needed some kind of theory of ghosts, or at least a way of both mourning modernity's "wound in civilization" (216) and eliminating the destructive forces that open it up over and over again: "Only the conscious horror of destruction creates the correct relationship with the dead: unity with them because we, like them, are the victims of the same condition and the same disappointed hope" (215). One wonders what a completed theory of ghosts would have looked like had Horkheimer and Adorno actually written more than the note.[7] I have not written the Theory of Ghosts, a far too singular proposal for my purposes, but *Ghostly Matters* does attempt to describe, in homage to the viability of a Marxist concept of haunting, the ghostly haunt as a form of social figuration that treats as a major problem the reduction of individuals "to a mere sequence of instantaneous experiences which leave no trace, or rather whose trace is hated as irrational, superfluous, and 'overtaken'" (216).

And a problem it remains despite all that we can claim now to understand in the wake of what are, without doubt, major changes in who is permitted to make public knowledge and in the assumptions that direct and underwrite much contemporary inquiry. We have taken the legs out from under that fateful and deceptive Archimedean standpoint, substituting the view from somewhere for the old view from nowhere. We have become adept at discovering the construction of social realities and deconstructing their architecture, confounding some of the distinctions between culture and science, the factual and the artificial. We have rethought the relationship between knowledge and power, between text and context, highlighting the relationship between authorization and modes of authority. And we have made considerable representational reparations for past exclusions and silencings, making the previously unknown known, telling new stories, correcting the official records. These are major accomplishments for work in universities, which change slowly and which, despite their ideology of invention, do not like too much of it. Yet I have wondered sometimes whether, for example, we have truly taken seriously that the intricate web of connections that characterizes any event or problem *is the story*. Warnings about relativism to the contrary, truth is still what most of us strive for. Partial and insecure surely, and something slightly different from "the facts," but truth nonetheless: the capacity to say "This is so." But truth is a subtle shifting entity not simply because philosophy says so or because evidentiary rules of validation are always inadequate, but because the very nature of the things whose truth is sought possesses these qualities. To tell the partial deconstructive truth of the thing that is the complex relation between subjection and subjectivity requires making common cause with the thing, requires what Michael Taussig calls sympathetic magic, that is, "granting . . . the representation the power of the represented" (1993: xviii). Particularly for those who believe in the progressive quality of modernity's secularity, this is a somewhat remarkable claim. But a kind of sympathetic magic is necessary because in the world and between us as analysts and the worlds we encounter to translate into world-making words are hauntings, ghosts and gaps, seething absences, and muted presences. The political and affective modalities by which we gain access to the facticity of constructed power either reckons with or displaces these ghostly matters and the matter of the ghost, with consequences either way.

Bloodless categories, narrow notions of the visible and the empirical, professional standards of indifference, institutional rules of distance and control, barely speakable fears of losing the footing that enables us to speak authoritatively and with greater value than anyone else who might . . . Our methods have thus far been less than satisfactory for addressing the very nature of the things and the problems it is our responsibility to address, leaving us not yet making something new enough out of what are arguably many new ideas and novel conditions. A different way of knowing and writing about the social world, an entirely different mode of production, still awaits our invention. Such a mode of production would not reject the value of empirical observation per se, but might, to use Taussig's words, be more "surprised" by social construction, the making and making up of social worlds, thereby giving it the "respect" it "deserves" (1993: xv-xvi). Indeed, we might expand the domain of the empirical considerably to include not only haunting and ghostly matters but also our own relations to social analysis. We might make common cause with our objects and subjects of analysis. Making common cause with our objects and subjects of analysis involves "understanding ... the representation as contiguous with that being represented and not as suspended above and distant from the represented" (Taussig 1992: 10). Making common cause with our objects and subjects of analysis, which *is* to take social determination quite seriously, means "that one has to see oneself and one's shared modes of understanding and communication included in that determining. To claim otherwise, to claim the rhetoric of systematicity's determinisms and yet except oneself, is an authoritarian deceit, a magical wonder" (ibid.). Making common cause means that our encounters must strive to go beyond the fundamental alienation of turning social relations into just the things we know and toward our own reckoning with how we are in these stories, with how they change us, with our own ghosts.

Doing so is not easy because, among other things, knowing ghosts often shows up not as professional success, but as failure: the one whose writing/ not writing only came together as she came together with the object, with the reality of fictions and the unrealities of the facts; the slightly mad one who kept saying, "There's something in the room with us," as those bloodless reified categories became animated through wonder and vexation. But it is also true that ghosts are never innocent: the unhallowed dead of the modern project drag in the pathos of their loss and the violence of the force that made them, their sheets and chains. To be haunted and to write from that location, to take on the condition of what you study, is not a methodology or a consciousness you can simply adopt or adapt as a set of rules or an identity; it produces its own insights and blindnesses. Following the ghosts is about making a contact that changes you and refashions the social relations in which you are located. It is about putting life back in where only a vague memory or a bare trace was visible to those who bothered to look. It is sometimes about writing ghost stories, stories that not only repair representational mistakes, but also strive to understand the conditions under which a memory was produced in the first place, toward a countermemory, for the future.

Sociology, in particular, has an extraordinary mandate as far as academic disciplines go: to conjure up social life. Conjuring is a particular form of calling up and calling out the forces that make things what they are in order to fix and transform a troubling situation. As a mode of apprehension and reformation, conjuring merges the analytical, the procedural, the imaginative, and the effervescent. But we have more to learn about how to conjure in an evocative and compelling way. If haunting is a constitutive feature of social life, then we will need to be able to describe, analyze, and bring to life that aspect of social life, to be less fearful of animation. We ought to do this not only because it is more exact, but also because to the extent that we want our writing to change minds, to convince others that what we know is important and ought to matter, we need to be more in touch with the nature of how "the pieces of a world ... littered all over a sociological landscape" (D. Smith 1987: 99) affect people. And we do not usually experience things, nor are affects produced, in the rational and objective ways our terms tend to portray them. The counterpart to reification, the conjuring trick, might be better captured by Walter Benjamin's profane illumination or Marx's sensuous knowledge. Of course, the tricky thing is that scholars too are subject to these same dynamics of haunting: ghosts get in our matters just as well. This means that we will have to learn to talk to and listen to ghosts, rather than banish them, as the precondition for establishing our scientific or humanistic knowledge.

Ghostly Matters is thus, on the one hand, a modest book and, on the other hand, quite ambitious. Its modesty lies in its very simple point. Ghostly matters are part of social life. If we want to study social life well, and if in addition we to want to contribute, in however small a measure, to changing it, we must learn how to identify hauntings and reckon with ghosts, must learn how to make contact with what is with without doubt often painful, difficult, and unsettling. The book's ambition lies in asserting that in order to do this, we will have to change the way we have been doing things.

I have many more questions than answers, a potentially disappointing feature of this book, but endemic to the enterprise. In the chapters that follow, I have tried to explore three broad questions. First, what are the alternative stories we ought to and can write about the relationship among power, knowledge, and experience? I have been particularly troubled by the contrast between conceptual or analytical descriptions of social systems and their far more diffused and delicate effects. Haunting occurs on the terrain situated between our ability to conclusively describe the logic of Capitalism or State Terror, for example, and the various experiences of this logic, experiences that are more often than not partial, coded, symptomatic, contradictory, ambiguous. What is it to identify haunting and follow its trajectory? Second, if the ghost's arrival notifies us of a haunting, how does the ghost interrupt or put into crisis the demand for ethnographic authenticity—what Jacqueline Rose (1986: 12) has called the "unequivocal accusation of the real"—that we expect from those who can legitimately claim to tell the truth? The intermingling of fact, fiction, and desire as it shapes personal and social memory situates us on the border of the social sciences and makes me wonder, What does the ghost say as it speaks, barely, in the interstices of the visible and the invisible? And, third, we are part of the story, for better or worse: the ghost must speak *to me* in some way sometimes similar to, sometimes distinct from how it may be speaking to the others. How then can our critical language display a reflexive concern not only with the objects of our investigations but also with the ones who investigate? What methods and forms of writing can foreground the conditions under which the facts and the real story are produced?

What is my method for answering these questions? The method here is everything and nothing much really. (The question of method has also gotten me into some trouble, as chapter 2 shows.) I do not devise procedures for the application of theories because one major goal of this book is to get us to consider a different way of seeing, one that is less mechnical, more willing to be surprised, to link imagination and critique, one that is more attuned to the task of "conjur[ing] up the appearances of something that [is] absent" (Berger 1972: 10). A way of seeing is not a rule book for operationalizing discrete explanatory theories. It is a way of negotiating the always unsettled relationship between what we see and what we know (ibid: 7). I suppose you could say that the method here involves producing case studies of haunting and adjudicating their consequences. What kind of case is a case of a ghost? It is a case of haunting, a story about what happens when we admit the ghost—that special instance of the merging of the visible and the invisible, the dead and the living, the past and the present—into the making of worldly relations and into the making of our accounts of the world. It is a case of the difference it makes to start with the marginal, with what we normally exclude or banish, or, more commonly, with what we never even notice. In Gayatri Spivak's formulation, it is a case of "what ... it [is] to learn, these lessons, otherwise" (1992: 775). It is not a case of dead or missing persons sui generis, but of the ghost as a social figure. It is often a case of inarticulate experiences, of symptoms and screen memories, of spiraling affects, of more than one story at a time, of the traffic in domains of experience that are anything but transparent and referential. It is a case of modernity's violence and wounds, and a case of the haunting reminder of the complex social relations in which we live. It is a case that teaches a lesson (or two) about how to write what can represent that haunting reminder, what can represent systematic injury and the remarkable lives made in the wake of the making of our social world.

Literary fictions play an important role in these cases for the simple reason that they enable other kinds of sociological information to emerge. In the twentieth century, literature has not been restrained by the norms of a professionalized social science, and thus it often teaches us, through imaginative design, what we need to know but cannot quite get access to with our given rules of method and modes of apprehension. Where else do we learn of the tremulous significance of *furniture without memories*, learning about it in the same moment as we are drawn in, hearts in hand, to a story told just so? In the broadest sense, sociology is concerned with both the production and the interpretation of stories of social and cultural life. Yet the division of the disciplines separates literature (story/ fiction) and social science (fact). This disciplinary segregation is an uneasy one, however; the border is not quite as secure as institutional mandates presume. Not only is the origin of sociology as a unique discipline bound up with its relationship to literature (see Lepenies 1988), but sociology's dominant disciplinary methods and theoretical assumptions constantly struggle against the fictive.[8] By the fictive I mean not simply literature but that complication with which I began: the ensemble of cultural imaginings, affective experiences, animated objects, marginal voices, narrative densities, and eccentric traces of power's presence. For sociology, the fictive is our constitutive horizon of error; it is what has been and must be exiled to ordain the authority of the discipline and the truthful knowledge sociology can claim to produce.

As a mode of storytelling, sociology distinguishes itself from literature by its now historical claim to find and report the facts expertly. The mainte- nance of a disciplinary object, social reality, that meets something akin to the juridical strict scrutiny test is predicated upon a clear distinction between what is (socially) real and what is fictional. As Michel de Certeau puts it, "At the level of analytic procedures ... as at the level of inter- pretations ... the technical discourse capable of determining the errors characteristic of fiction has come to be authorized to speak in the name of the 'real.' By distinguishing between the two discourses—the one scien- tific, the other fictive—according to its own criteria, [sociology] credits itself with having a special relationship to the 'real' because its contrary is posited as ... [fictive]" (1983: 128). To the extent that sociology is wedded to facticity as its special truth, it must continually police and expel its margin—the margin of error—which is the fictive. But these facts are always in imminent danger of being contaminated by what is seemingly on the other side of their boundaries, by fictions. Like a taboo that is always being approached in the act of avoidance, when sociology insists on finding only the facts, it has no other choice but to pursue the fictive, the mistake it seeks to eliminate. A marginal discourse, the story of how the real story has emerged, consistently shadows and threatens to subvert the very authority that establishes disciplinary order.

If "the margins of the story mark a border between the remembered and the forgotten" (Haug et al. 1987: 68), my use of fiction to designate this border intends to call attention to both the broader issues of invis- ibility, marginality, and exclusion, and also to the "twist[s] and turn[s], reinterpret[ations] and falsifi[cations], forget[tings] and repress[ings] [of] events" (ibid.: 40) that are part of the research and writing process. These are characteristically the elements an objective account attempts to minimize. But these are precisely what interest me. So, I have tried to make the fictional, the theoretical, and the factual speak to one another. In that conversation, if we can call it that, I have hoped to acknowledge and foreground as real and operative just those twists and turns, forgettings and rememberings, just those ghostly haunts that a normal social scientific account routinely attempts to minimize. I have hoped to find in writing that knows it is writing as such lessons for a mode of inscription that can critically question the limits of institutional discourse. More importantly, I have hoped to draw attention to a whole realm of experiences and social practices that can barely be approached without a method attentive to what is elusive, fantastic, contingent, and often barely there.

There is no question here of privileging Literature. Literature has its own problems or, rather, it has its own business. It has a history and a market that implicates it in the production of a highly ideological enterprise called Culture; part of its economy of literacy situates it within an academic discipline, literary criticism or now cultural studies, where particular struggles over value and access take precedence. My concern is unequivocally with social life, not with Literature as such (even if literature itself is, of course, riddled with the complications of the social life—my object of inquiry—it represents and sometimes influences). But fictions are what stand on the other side of the facts in our lingering Manichaean scheme, and so they have helped to highlight the problems with "logical and chronological frameworks" and "the simplicity of casual chains"; they have helped to show what "breaks through precisely where the [sociologist] assembles and joins" (Robin 1980: 234–35). It is precisely the relationship between what *assembles and joins* and what is gaping, detouring, and haunting that concerns me and is central to the cases I have analyzed. Fictionality and the inventiveness of social constructionism are not ends in themselves, however. They open the door to understanding haunting. Haunting is a part of our social world, and understanding it is essential to grasping the nature of our society and for changing it. Social life, especially when so fraught with ghosts, does not obey our rules of method and our disciplinary organization of it. We need not, however, find the loss of this deluding innocence so terribly frightening.

[...]

Notes

1   This list is not complete. Others who could be added include Felman and
     Laub (1992), Haraway (1989), Minh-ha (1989, 1991), and M. B. Pratt
     (1984). If we were to include Silko (1977, 1991) or Wideman's recent work
     (1994) or Baldwin (1985) or Du Bois ([1940] 1984, [1903] 1989) or Ellison
     ([1952] 1981, 1964) or ... well, then, a whole field begins to emerge whose
     broad expanse is cause for a serious analytic pause.

2   See Charles Lemert's recent book *Sociology after the Crisis* (1995), especially
     chapters 5 and 8, for a wonderfully thoughtful discussion of taking the
     measure of the social world.

3   My focus on social practices is written in the spirit of a crucially important
     point Harvey Molotch makes in his excellent article on the state of sociology,
     "Going Out" (1994: 222, 224): "One of the things wrong with sociology, in
     our country, is that we need a better country.... We really have to change
     America to change us."

4   There is a certain degree of repetition to this sentiment, even if one takes a
     fairly short historical perspective. Here is C. Wright Mills, in 1959: "We are
     at the ending of what is called The Modern Age ... so now The Modern
     Age is being succeeded by a post-modern period. Perhaps we may call it: The
     Fourth Epoch.
         The ending of one epoch and the beginning of another is, to be sure, a
     matter of definition. But definitions, like everything social, are historically
     specific. And now our basic definitions of society and of self are being
     overtaken by new realities. I do not mean merely that we *feel* we are in an
     epochal kind of transition. I mean that too many of our explanations are
     derived from the great historical transition from the Medieval to the Modern
     Age; and that when they are generalized for use today, they become unwieldy,
     irrelevant, not convincing" (236).
         That Mills's statement was written at the height of the New American
     Century is not without a certain significance since one persuasive
     periodization of postmodernity links it to the end of the century, most
     usually indicated by the OPEC oil crisis of 1973. Mills's statement should be
     read in the context of then current debates on postindustrialism, to which
     he contributed significantly with his seminal work on class, *White Collar*
     (1951), and that bear a striking resemblance to current attempts to define
     the contours of a late capitalism. It should also be read in the context of the
     1950s version of the politically motivated claim, most prominently made
     by Daniel Bell in *The End of Ideology* (1960) and repeated in the 1990s
     by Francis Fukuyama (1992), that history had ended and ideology become
     bankrupt, the proof being the preeminence of worldwide U.S. hegemony.
     Mills's most direct and pointedly acerbic response to Daniel Bell was "The
     New Left" (1960 [1963]).

5   Taussig (1993: 98–9) and Pietz (1993: 141–3) offer intriguing speculations
     on "communist fetishism" and postcapitalist animism that have
     potentially interesting implications for haunting's future. To quote Taussig,

"*Post*capitalist animism means that although the socioeconomic exploitative function of fetishism ... will supposedly disappear with the overcoming of capitalism, fetishism as an active social force inherent in objects will remain. Indeed, it must not disappear, for it is the animate quality of things in post-capitalist society without the 'banking' mode of perception that ensures what the young Marx envisaged as the humanization of the world" (1993: 99). See also T. Keenan (1993) on commodity fetishism and ghosts.

6   In this respect, *Ghostly Matters* differs from the important work by James C. Scott (1990) on domination and resistance. But his very potent notion of the "hidden transcript" that "helps us understand those rare moments of political electricity when, often for the first time in memory, the hidden transcript is spoken directly and publicly in the teeth of power" (xiii) is clearly necessary to understand haunting. Indeed, one could argue that the ghost mediates between the public and hidden transcripts, producing a particular kind of valence to the operation of and "study of power that uncovers contradictions, tensions, and immanent possibilities" (xii).

7   Jacques Derrida has now written a theory of the specter in direct engagement with Marx's texts in a moving and beautiful book about Marx's ambivalent yet obsessive relationship to ghosts. *Specters of Marx* (1994) is a very significant book of philosophy and a crucial political intervention by perhaps the most influential European philosopher living today. But it is not, I think, despite its similarly motivated distress at the claim of history's end, quite the theory of ghosts Horkheimer and Adorno would have written. See Jameson's (1995) generous and learned review essay of Derrida's book.

8   The history of the origins of American sociology (see Ross 1991; M. Smith 1994) could be reconceived such that what I am here calling the fictive would be more central to our historic mission. Acknowledging and incorporating the foundational role of W. E. B. Du Bois would be a first step (see the virtually unparalleled efforts of Lemert 1993, 1994, and 1995, especially chapters 6 and 8). Although this is not the place for an extended review of Du Bois, which in any event would have to account for the developments and refinements in his thought subsequent to his early and heavily emphasized work, *The Souls of Black Folk*, suffice it to say that the profession might have developed otherwise had Du Bois's notion of double consciousness become sociology's common sense, rather than its suppressed history. Double consciousness is a sociological imagination, in the most profound sense in which Mills deployed the term. It is an imagination bound to a dialectics of shadows and acts, approaching our gravest social problems from the "second sight" of "being" the problem itself and thereby confounding, in that very moment, the boundary between subject and object (see the especially astute conclusion to chapter 5, "The Concept of Race," in *Dusk of Dawn* [1940] 1984). Double consciousness is a sociological imagination that fixes its sight on that very remainder of the tangible or the factual that haunting signifies and that an attention to its sign-work captures: "But after all that has been said on these more tangible matters of human contact, there still remains a part essential to a proper description of the South which is difficult to describe or fix in terms easily understood by strangers. It is, in fine, the

atmosphere of the land, the thought and feeling, the thousand and one little actions which go to make up life. In any community or nation it is these little things which are most elusive to the grasp and yet most essential to any clear conception of the group life taken as a whole. What is thus true of all communities is peculiarly true of the South, where, outside of written history and outside of primed law, there has been going on for a generation as deep a storm and stress of human souls, as intense a ferment of feeling, as intricate a writhing of spirit, as ever a people experienced. Within and without the sombre veil of color vast social forces have been at work,—efforts for human betterment, movements toward disintegration and despair, tragedies and comedies in social and economic life, and a swaying and lifting and sinking of human hearts which have made this land a land of mingled sorrow and joy, of change and excitement and unrest.... But if he lingers long enough there comes the awakening: perhaps in a sudden whirl of passion which leaves him gasping at its bitter intensity; more likely in a gradually dawning sense of things he had not at first noticed. Slowly but surely his eyes begin to catch the shadows of the color line" ([1903] 1989: 127–8).

Bibliography

Agger, Ben. 1989a. *Reading Science: A Literary, Political, and Sociological Analysis*. Dix Hill, NY: General Hall.

—1989b. *Socio(onto)logy: A Disciplinary Reading*. Urbana: University of Illinois Press.

—1990. *The Decline of Discourse: Reading, Writing, and Resistance in Postmodern Capitalism*. New York: Falmer.

—1991. *A Critical Theory of Public Life: Knowledge, Discourse, and Politics in an Age of Decline*. New York: Falmer.

—1992. *Cultural Studies as Critical Theory*. Washington, DC: Falmer.

—1993. *Gender, Culture, and Power: Toward a Feminist Postmodern Critical Theory*. Westport, Co: Praeger.

Alarcón, Norma. 1990. "Chicana Feminism: In the Tracks of the Native Woman." *Cultural Studies* 4, 3:248–56.

Baldwin, James. 1985. *The Evidence of Things Not Seen*. New York: Holt, Rinehart & Winston.

Bauman, Zygmunt. [1988] 1994. "Is There a Postmodern Sociology?" In *The Postmodern Turn: New Perspectives on Social Theory*, Steven Seidman ed., 187–204. Cambridge: Cambridge University Press.

—1992. *Intimations of Postmodernity*. New York: Routledge.

—1993. *Postmodern Ethics*. Oxford: Basil Blackwell.

Bell, Daniel. 1960. *The End of Ideology: On the Exhaustion of Political Ideas in the Fifties*. Glencoe, IL: Free Press.

Bell, Derrick. 1992. *Faces at the Bottom of the Well: The Permanence of Racism*. New York: Basic Books.

Berger, John. 1972. *Ways of Seeing*. London: British Broadcasting Corporation and Penguin Books.

Brown, Richard Harvey. 1987. *Society as Text: Essays on Rhetoric, Reason, and Reality*. Chicago: University of Chicago Press.

—1989. *Social Science as Civic Discourse: Essays on the Invention, Legitimation, and Uses of Social Theory*. Chicago: University of Chicago Press.

Butler, Judith. 1992. "Contingent Foundations: Feminism and the Question of 'Postmodernism.'" In *Feminists Theorize the Political*, ed. Judith Butler and Joan W. Scott, 3–21. New York: Routledge.

Cixous, Hélène, and Catherine Clément. 1986. *The Newly Born Woman*. Trans. Betsy Wing. Minneapolis: University of Minnesota Press.

Clifford, James, and George E. Marcus, eds. 1986. *Writing Culture: The Poetics and Politics of Ethnography*. Berkeley: University of California Press.

Clough, Patricia T. 1992. *The End(s) of Ethnography: From Realism to Social Criticism*. Newbury Park, CA: Sage.

Crenshaw, Kimberlé. 1991. "Demarginalizing the Intersection of Race and Sex: A Black Feminist Critique of Antidiscrimination Doctrine, Feminist Theory and Antiracist Politics [1989]." In *Feminist Legal Theory: Readings in Law and Gender*, ed. Katherine Bartlett and Rosanne Kennedy, 57–80. Boulder, CO: Westview.

de Certeau, Michel. 1983. "History: Ethics, Science, and Fiction." In *Social Science as Moral Inquiry*, ed. Norma Haan et al., 125–52. New York: Columbia University Press.

DeLillo, Don. 1985. *White Noise*. New York: Viking.

Denzin, Norman. 1986. "Postmodern Social Theory." *Sociological Theory* 4 (Fall):194–204.

—1991. *Images of Postmodern Society: Social Theory and Contemporary Cinema*. Newbury Park, CA: Sage.

Derrida, Jacques. 1994. *Specters of Marx: The State of the Debt, the Work of Mourning, and the New International*. Trans. Peggy Kamuf. New York: Routledge.

Du Bois, W. E. B. [1903] 1989. *The Souls of Black Folk*. New York: Bantam.

—[1940] 1984. *Dusk of Dawn: An Essay toward an Autobiography of a Race Concept*. New Brunswick, NJ: Transaction.

Ellison, Ralph. [1952] 1981. *Invisible Man*. New York: Vintage.

—1964. *Shadow and Act*. New York: Random House.

Felman, Shoshana, and Dori Laub, M. D. 1992. *Testimony: Crises of Witnessing in Literature, Psychoanalysis, and History*. New York: Routledge.

Flax, Jane. 1992. "The End of Innocence." In *Feminists Theorize the Political*, ed. Judith Butler and Joan W. Scott, 445–63. New York: Routledge.

Frankfurt Institute for Social Research. [1956] 1973. *Aspects of Sociology*. Trans. John Viertel. Boston: Beacon.

Fukuyama, Francis. 1992. *The End of History and the Last Man*. New York: Free Press.

Gordon, Avery. 1992. "Marketing Differences: Feminism as Cultural Capital." *Mediations* 16, 2:37–41.

Haraway, Donna. 1985. "Manifesto for Cyborgs: Science, Technology, and Socialist Feminism in the 1980's." *Socialist Review* 80:65–108.

Harvey, David. 1989. *The Condition of Postmodernity: An Enquiry into the Origins of Cultural Exchange*. New York: Blackwell.

Haug, Frigga, et al. 1987. *Female Sexualization: A Collective Work of Memory.* Trans. Erica Carter. London: Verso.

Hennessy, Rosemary. 1993. *Materialist Feminism and the Politics of Discourse.* New York: Routledge.

Horkheimer, Max, and Theodor Adorno. [1944] 1987. *Dialectic of Enlightenment.* Trans. John Cumming. New York: Continuum.

Jameson, Fredric. 1991. *Postmodernism: or, the Cultural Logic of Late Capitalism.* Durham, NC: Duke University Press.

—1995. "Marx's Purloined Letter." *New Left Review* 209 (January/February): 75–101.

Jardine, Alice. 1985. *Gynesis: Configurations of Woman and Modernity.* Ithaca, NY: Cornell University Press.

Keenan, Thomas. 1993. "The Point Is to (Ex)Change It: Reading *Capital,* Rhetorically." In *Fetishism as Cultural Discourse,* ed. Emily Apter and William Pietz, 152–85. Ithaca, NY: Cornell University Press.

Kingston, Maxine Hong. 1977. *The Woman Warrior: Memoirs of a Girlhood Among Ghosts.* New York: Vintage.

Kipnis, Laura. 1988. "Feminism: The Political Conscience of Postmodernism?" In *Universal Abandon? The Politics of Postmodernism,* ed. Andrew Ross, 149–66. Minneapolis: University of Minnesota Press.

Lash, Scott. 1990. *Sociology of Postmodernism.* New York: Routledge.

Lemert, Charles. 1990. "The Uses of French Structuralisms in Sociology." In *Frontiers of Social Theory: The New Synthesis,* ed. George Ritzer, 230–54. New York: Columbia University Press.

—1994. "A Classic from the Other Side of the Veil: Du Bois's *Souls of Black Folk.*" *Sociological Quarterly* 35, 3:383–96.

—1995. *Sociology after the Crisis.* Boulder, Colo.: Westview.

Lemert, Charles, ed. 1993. *Social Theory: The Multicultural and Classic Readings.* Boulder, Colo.: Westview.

Lepenies, Wolf. 1988. *Between Literature and Science: The Rise of Sociology.* Trans. R. J. Hollingdale. Cambridge: Cambridge University Press.

Lubiano, Wahneema. 1991. "Shuckin' Off the African-American Native Other: What's 'Po-Mo' Got to Do with It?" *Cultural Critique* 18 (Spring): 149–86.

—1992. "Black Ladies, Welfare Queens, and State Minstrels: Ideological War by Narrative Means." In *Race-ing Justice, En-Gendering Power: Essays on Anita Hill, Clarence Thomas, and the Construction of Social Reality,* ed. Toni Morrison, 323–63. New York: Pantheon.

—1993. "Standing in for the State: Black Nationalism and 'Writing' the Black Subject." *Alphabet City* 3: 20–3.

Mills, C. Wright. [1959] 1963. "Culture and Politics." In *Power, Politics and People: The Collected Essays of C. Wright Mills,* ed. Irving Louis Horowitz, 236–46. New York: Oxford University Press.

—[1960] 1963. "The New Left." In *Power, Politics and People: The Collected Essays of C. Wright Mills,* ed. Irving Louis Horowitz, 247–59. New York: Oxford University Press.

Minh-ha, Trinh T. 1989. *Woman, Native, Other: Writing, Postcoloniality and Feminism.* Bloomington: Indiana University Press.

—1991. *When the Moon Waxes Red: Representation, Gender, and Cultural Politics*. New York: Routledge.

Molotch, Harvey. 1994. "Going Out." *Sociological Forum* 9, 2:221–39.

Morrison, Toni. 1970. *The Bluest Eye*. New York: Washington Square.

—1989. "Unspeakable Things Unspoken: The Afro-American Presence in American Literature." *Michigan Quarterly Review* 28, 1:1–34.

Mouffe, Chantal. 1992. "Feminism, Citizenship, and Radical Democratic Politics." In *Feminists Theorize the Political*, ed. Judith Butler and Joan W. Scott, 369–84. New York: Routledge.

Nicholson, Linda J., ed. 1990. *Feminism/Postmodernism*. New York: Routledge.

Pfohl, Stephen. 1991. "Postmodernity is a Social Problem: Race, Class, Gender and the 'New World Order.'" *Society for the Study of Social Problems Newsletter* 22, 3:9–14.

—1992a. *Death at the Parasite Café: Social Science (Fictions) and the Postmodern*. New York: St. Martin's.

—1992b. "Postmodern Pittsburgh: New World Disordered Conventions?" *Society for the Study of Social Problems Newsletter* 23, 2:4–8.

Pietz, William. 1993. "Fetishism and Materialism: The Limits of Theory in Marx." In *Fetishism as Cultural Discourse*, ed. Emily Apter and William Pietz, 119–51. Ithaca, NY: Cornell University Press.

Pratt, Minnie Bruce. 1984. "Identity: Skin Blood Heart." In *Yours in Struggle: Three Feminist Perspectives on Anti-Semitism and Racism*, ed. Elly Bulkin, Minnie Bruce Pratt, and Barbara Smith, 11–63. New York: Long Haul Press.

Robin, Régine. 1980. "Toward Fiction as Oblique Discourse." *Yale French Studies* 59:230–42.

Rose, Jacqueline. 1986. *Sexuality in the Field of Vision*. London: Verso.

Ross, Andrew. 1988. Introduction to *Universal Abandon? The Politics of Postmodernism*, ed. Andrew Ross, vii–xviii. Minneapolis: University of Minnesota Press.

Ross, Dorothy. 1991. *The Origins of American Social Science*. Cambridge: Cambridge University Press.

Scott, James C. 1990. *Domination and the Arts of Resistance: Hidden Transcripts*. New Haven, CO: Yale University Press.

Scott, Joan W. 1992. "'Experience.'" In *Feminists Theorize the Political*, ed. Judith Butler and Joan W. Scott, 22–40. New York: Routledge.

Seidman, Steve. 1991. "Postmodern Anxiety: The Politics of Epistemology." *Sociological Theory* 9, 2:180–90.

—1994a. *Contested Knowledge: Social Theory in the Postmodern Era*. Cambridge: Blackwell.

—1994b. "The End of Sociological Theory." In *The Postmodern Turn: New Perspectives on Social Theory*, ed. Steve Seidman, 119–39. Cambridge: Cambridge University Press.

Silko, Leslie Marmon. 1977. *Ceremony*. New York: Viking Penguin.

—1991. *Almanac of the Dead: A Novel*. New York: Simon & Schuster.

Smith, Dorothy E. 1987. *The Everyday World as Problematic: A Feminist Sociology*. Boston: Northeastern University Press.

Smith, Mark C. 1994. *Social Science in the Crucible: The American Debate over Objectivity and Purpose, 1918–1941*. Durham, NC: Duke University Press.

Spillers, Hortense. 1987. "Mama's Baby, Papa's Maybe: An American Grammar Book." *Diacritics* 17, 2:65–81.

Spivak, Gayatri Chakravorty. 1987. *In Other Worlds: Essays in Cultural Politics.* New York: Methuen.

—1989. "The Political Economy of Women as Seen by a Literary Critic." In *Coming to Terms: Feminism, Theory, Politics,* ed. Elizabeth Weed, 218–29. New York: Routledge.

—1992. "Acting Bits/Identity Talk." *Critical Inquiry* 18, 4:770–803.

—1993. *Outside in the Teaching Machine.* New York: Routledge.

Taussig, Michael. 1992. *The Nervous System.* New York: Routledge.

—1993. *Mimesis and Alterity: A Particular History of the Senses.* New York: Routledge.

Wideman, John Edgar. 1994. *Furtheralong: A Meditation on Fathers and Sons, Race and Society.* New York: Pantheon.

Williams, Patricia. 1991. *The Alchemy of Race and Rights.* Cambridge, MA: Harvard University Press.

9

from Life, Sovereignty, and Terror in the Fiction of Amos Tutuola

Achille Mbembe

The subject is a multiplicity.

NIETZSCHE

The remarks that follow bear upon the general question of life, sovereignty, and terror. To my mind, life does not exist in-and-of-itself. It does not reflect a generic property per se, but a mode of being-in-the-world, that is, a way of inhabiting the world; in short, a manner of confrontation and familiarity with the world and its full range of potentialities. The ultimate expression of sovereignty resides, to a large degree, in the power and the capacity to dictate who may live and who must die. To exercise sovereignty is to exercise control over mortality and to define life as the deployment and manifestation of power.

More precisely, I am interested in these manners of living and risking death that either are situated beyond the political as a vernacular (and socially obligatory) language of the social bond, or push its frontiers to the point of relegating the political to border zones; or, by simply ignoring it altogether, end up revealing its extraordinary vulnerability and weakening the authority and centrality that our era has wound up attributing to it. These forms of existence are born of singular experiences that I choose to call *threshold* or *specular experiences*. These are, essentially, *extreme forms*

of human life, death-worlds, forms of social existence in which vast populations are subjected to conditions of life that confer upon them the status of
living dead (ghosts). In the contemporary African context, these extreme
forms of human existence are experienced through the corruption of the
senses as well as through the horror that accompanies wars and outbreaks
of terror (see Mbembe, *On the Postcolony*).

To treat the question of the languages of life in their relationship with
sovereignty, specular violence, and terror, I will depart from what is
conventionally called Western thought. Forgetting for a moment its heterogeneity, I will demonstrate how (and implicitly critique the ways in which),
when it treats the languages of life, Western tradition—more than any
other—accords a critical role to the notions of self, truth, and time.[1] Using
the metaphor of the *mirror*, I will base my critique on a re-reading of two
African texts, *The Palm-Wine Drinkard* and *My Life in the Bush of Ghosts*.
This critique rests upon the notion—developed by Tutuola—of the ghost, or
better, of the *wandering subject*. The metaphor of the mirror, I will argue,
allows us to envisage ghostly power and sovereignty as aspects of the real
integral to a world of life and terror rather than tied to a world of appearances. Finally, I will show how Tutuola's fiction allows us to conceive of the
idea of life, sovereignty, and terror as fundamentally linked to that of the
imagination, *work*, and *remembrance*.

Dualisms

Five attributes have been decisive in the articulation of a certain idea of being,
time and truth in modern Western criticism. The first is the quasiontological
privilege granted to reason over all other forms of human understanding
(emotions, passions, and feelings). Whether the subject under consideration
is a knowing, an aesthetic, or a speaking subject, acting or producing and
manipulating tools, it is always a question of a self up against an object, in
an attitude that aims at the mastery of the said object by means of reason
and technique (see Hegel, *Phenomenology of Mind*; Heidegger, *Being and
Time*; Sartre, *Being and Nothingness*; Husserl, *Ideas*). A corollary of reason
is the emphasis placed upon self-possession, the desire for self-perfection,
and self-mastery (self-government) through the development of interiority
(see Foucault, *History of Sexuality*; Ricoeur, *Oneself as Another*; Charles
Taylor, *Sources of the Self*; Elias, *La civilization des moeurs*). To these
attributes, we must add two others: the differentiation between the human
being and other animals through work (Marx), and the importance of
desire and pleasure in the calculus of happiness (see Freud, *Civilization and
its Discontents*; see also Lacan, *Four Fundamental Concepts*, and Foucault,
History of Sexuality 3). Self-possession and freedom with respect to others

as well as happiness are experienced through the conscious mastery of the world, of one's own body and libido. In turn, mastery of the world is achieved essentially through knowledge and access to truth—the order of knowledge, the order of truth, and the will to power constituting the ultimate foundations of all subjectivity and every happy life.

Now, at the base of these postulates are found inherent dualisms. These dualisms have been the object of well-known critiques, even if it is not certain that we have drawn from them all the possible consequences: the opposition between the affective and the cognitive, the subject and the object, appearance and essence, reason and passion, the corporeal and the ideal, the human and the animal, reality and representation, the one and the multiple. By foregrounding these dichotomies, modern Western tradition has favored thinking on the self that privileges above all the ability to reason (*argumentation and deliberation*) and the will to power, giving short shrift to the ability to feel, to remember, and to imagine. The reason for this is the longstanding belief in Western metaphysics that the struggle for freedom and happiness, sovereignty, and self-rule is first and foremost a struggle against the libido and inner turmoil, the war within us that drives us to wage war upon one another. The world of the body, the passions, and the senses has been historically regarded as the realm of the false, the dream, and the mask (see Hume, *Treatise of the Passions*; Descartes, *The Passions of the Soul*; Hobbes, *Human Nature*). The senses in particular are seen as deceptive, and passions deemed ultimately unintelligible. The world of instincts and animality, Western tradition has long held, cannot be relied upon to produce truth, knowledge or a happy life.

According to this outlook, there can be no self except in the stability and permanence of the being. Identity being essentially incompatible with change, the self is said to always be identical to itself. It matters little what kind of being the self is, or even the singular matter of which the self is composed. The self is said to always distinguish itself from other selves of different species, and indeed from others of its own species. Because essence is said to embrace matter and form, there can be no thing but a particular thing. In other words, every life is singular. Implicit in modern Western thought is therefore the impossibility for a single and same thing, or a single and same being, to have several different origins or to exist simultaneously in different places and under different signs.[2]

Mirrorings

Nietzsche attempted to question these dead-ends in his criticism of the classical theory of knowledge and its corollaries, the notions—quite political—of "truth," of "being," and of "time." He did not oppose "being" and "truth" to "falsity." By "truth," Nietzsche had in mind the concept of life. In his view, in fact, all that can be thought—including life—is "fictive": "Nothing comes to our *consciousness* that has not been previously modified, simplified, schematized, interpreted." (Nietzsche 39). By thus insisting upon the "fictive" where others would emphasize the "rational," he in fact challenged the division between "likeness" and "presence," a "world of appearances" and a "true world." Appearance, he asserted, itself belongs to reality and is a form of its being. As for the world, it is essentially a world of multiplicity and proliferation—"seen from different points, it has just as many *different faces*; its being is essentially different at each point" (Nietzsche 89; emphasis in original).[3]

Another key way of imagining the relationship between self, life, and sovereignty comes from psychoanalysis. Psychoanalysis recognizes that something else that is not *I* speaks; that the self is split. By privileging the existence of a "nocturnal element" at the very core of what passes for the subject, psychoanalysis acknowledges the idea of an "otherness within," an unconscious that emerges from the phenomenal world of the psyche (see Vaysse). This "nocturnal element" is not the product of an accident. It is part of the subject just as it is part of the world of desire, dreams, and delirium. Recognition of the "nocturnal element" not only signals a break with conceptions of the corporeal being as a space of the negative: it is also an affirmation of the idea that "the ego is continued inwards, without any sharp delimitation, into an unconscious mental entity [...] for which it serves as a kind of façade" (Freud, *Civilization and Its Discontents* 253).

But if Nietzsche and psychoanalysis articulate the unsaid—that is, the fictitious character of reality and the "nocturnal side" of the subject—they do not always allow for an explanation of the radical processes that bring reality into being, processes that escape the dualisms fundamental to modern Western metaphysics. Now, one way of rendering such an explanation is to begin with the notion of *the mirror*—or, rather, the experience of ghostly sovereignty—in their dual relation with two key faculties: imagination and remembrance.

Considering the mirror, Lacan implicitly attributes to it two principal traits. First, the mirror is the site where the self is linked to its own image. The self that has identified with that image and has taken it on is inscribed in an irreducible line of fiction. The correspondences that unite the *I* to the image are projected as ghosts, in a completely ambiguous relationship of the subject with the world of its fabrication. On the other hand, the mirror is the place where "likeness" redoubles "presence." According to Lacan, "the specular image seems to be the threshold of the visible world, if we trust the disposition in the mirror presented in hallucination and in dream by the imago of the body itself [...] or if we notice the role of the instrument of the mirror in the apparitions of the *double* where psychic realities are manifested, realities that are moreover heterogeneous" ("Le stade du miroir" 93–101).

Following Lacan, three properties of the mirror are of interest to us in the interpretation of Tutuola's fiction. These three properties allow us to re-conceptualize the relationship between the ghost, terror, and life on the one hand, and, on the other, the function of the imagination and remembrance in this relationship. First of all there is the property of *the marvelous*. In his study of the mirror of Medusa, Jean-Pierre Vernant argues that "instead of reflecting appearances and returning the image of visible objects placed before it, the mirror opens a breach in the backdrop of 'phenomena,' displays the invisible [. . .] and lets it be seen in the brilliance of a mysterious epiphany" (*Mortals and Immortals* 141). This property derives from two types of powers belonging to the mirror: the power (experienced by the self looking at itself) first to project, create an appearance, and second to discover its own image.

In an operation that is as empirical as it is imaginative, the self becomes its own spectator. The self is present at the spectacle of its own division and duplication, acquiring, in the process, the ability to separate itself from itself. The self that views itself has a sharp awareness of the fact that what it sees beyond the material screen is indeed itself or, in any case, a reflection of itself. This power can be called the *power of reflection*. The same self can, after the act of looking at itself, remember more or less clearly its own reflection or shadow.

The power of the shadow originates from the possibility of escaping the constraints that structure perceptible and sensory reality, notably the sense of touch. One can see in the mirror, but cannot touch what is seen. For the double that is relayed by the mirror is a fleeting, fictive double. One can only *touch oneself*. And it is this *touching oneself* that is reflected in the mirror and which is returned to us through the mirror. And what the mirror sends back to us is, to a large extent, untouchable.

The divorce between seeing and touching, the flirtation between touching and the untouchable, the duality between that which reflects and that which is reflected is based on the double principle of immateriality and unreality, or, more precisely, on the spectralization of reality. In the mirror, being and identity are fugitive, intangible, but visible; they constitute that negative space which is the gap between the *I* and its shadow. The other law is that of luminosity. There is, in fact, no reflection in the mirror without a certain distribution of things in proximity and distance, a certain manner of playing light against darkness, and vice versa. Without such interplay, there can be no manifestation of the double.

The other property of the mirror is what could be called its *power of terror*. This power is born of the disquieting reality brought into being by this place that is not a place for it does not rest upon any terrain. Where, indeed, are the image and the self thus imaged by the mirror situated? What terrain, what ground supports them? Sabine Melchior-Bonnet provides this answer: "The self is both there and elsewhere, perceived in a troubling ubiquity and depth, at an uncertain distance: we see in a mirror, or rather the image seems to appear behind the material screen, so that the one who sees himself can question whether he sees the surface itself or across it," and adds, "The reflection causes the sensation of an immaterial underworld to rise up beyond the mirror and invites the gaze to a cross-over of appearances" (113–14).

Now strictly speaking, the crossing-over of appearances can be associated with a penetration into the heart of the "*psyché.*" Crossing through appearances is not only to go beyond the split between what one can see, what one can touch, and what is hidden, invisible. It also means running the risk of an autonomy of the *psyché* with respect to corporeality, expropriation of the body going hand-in-hand with the unsettling possibility of an emancipation of the fictive double. The latter acquires, in such a setting, a life of its own, a life given over to the dark work of the shadow—magic, dream, and delirium inherent to any confrontation between self and self.

The third property of the mirror is the *power of fantasy and imagination.* That such a power might be possible resides in the fact that every play of the mirror rests—as discussed above—upon the constitution of a gap between the self and its representation, a space of breaking and entering and of dissonance between the self and its fictive double reflected in the mirror. Because the self and its reflection are not superposable, duplication can never be easy. Dissemblance and duplicity are thus an integral part of the relationship with the mirror, that is, in the long run, in the confrontation between self and self.

Delirium

Let us break the mirror on Tutuola's writing. What do we see? The spectacle of a world in motion, ever reborn, made of fold upon fold, of landscapes and topographies, figures, circles, spirals and fractures, colors, sounds, and noises. A world of images, one could say. But above all, a world inhabited by beings and things that pass for what they are not. More than a geographical space, the ghostly realm is foremost a field of visions: fantasies, strange spaces, masks, surprises, and astonishment; in short, permanent commerce with families of signs that intersect, contradict, and nullify one another, set themselves back in motion, and go astray within their own boundaries. Perhaps that is the reason the ghostly realm escapes synthesis and geometry:

> [T]here were many images and our own too were in the centre of the hall. But our own images that we saw there resembled us too much and were also white colour, but we were very surprised to meet our images

there [...]. So we asked from Faithful-Mother what she was doing with all of the images. She replied that they were for remembrance and to know those she was helping from their difficulties and punishments. (248–49)

A world of hidden knowledge, no doubt. But, above all, as will be seen later, a world shaped by the remembrance of fragments of life, of the *work* that is the struggle for life.

It is also a world that one *experiences* and that one *creates*, in instability, in evanescence, in excess, in that inexhaustible depth that is generalized theatralization:

To my surprise, when I helped the lady to stand up from the frog on which she sat, the cowrie that was tied on her neck made a curious noise at once, and when the Skull who was watching her heard the noise, he woke up and blew the whistle to the rest, then the whole of them rushed to the place and surrounded the lady and me, but at the same time that they saw me there, one of them ran to a pit which was not so far from that spot, the pit was filled with cowries. He picked one cowrie out of the pit, after that he was running towards me, and the whole crowd wanted to tie the cowrie on my neck too. But before they could do that, I had changed myself into air [...]. (210)

We penetrate into the ghostly realm through its border, across the edges. From this perspective, the ghostly sphere is a lateral space. But it positions itself equally as a décor. It is found not at the periphery of life but on its edges. It constantly spills out over its assigned time and space. It is a scene where events continually take place that never seem to congeal to the point of consolidating into history. Life unfolds in the manner of a spectacle where past and future are reversed. Everything takes place in an *indefinite present*. Before and after are abolished, memory is destabilized, and multiplication reigns. There is no life but a life that is fractured and mutilated:

[A]ll the hero-ghosts who were fighting the enemies with us were killed and also many of the heads were cut away from their mother's body [...]. After we won the war the whole of us were gladly marching to the town. But as the "Invisible and Invincible Pawn" woke up all the dead soldiers and replaced their heads which were cut off by the enemies to their necks and as my own was cut off as well, so he mistakenly put a ghost's head on my neck instead of mine [...] so this head was always making various noises both day and night and also smelling badly. Whether I was talking or not it would be talking out the words which I did not mean in my mind and was telling out all my secret aims which I was planning in mind whether to escape from there to another town or to start to find the way to my home town [...]. (108–09)

The remembrance of the mutilated organ responds, as if in echo, to the violence of decapitation: the head—the visible seat of identity—passes into the void. It has fallen under the enemy's blow. Mutilation does not translate here as an open wound. Another bodily structure and another organization of the sensorial apparatus are added on to the trunk of the body. The head continues to speak, but in a disorderly manner. Every notion of the secret and of privacy is abolished. The subject lives with a sense of being perpetually spied upon. The joining of one's own body to a head that belongs to someone else renders the self a locus of uncontrollable speech. Words are spoken in place of a self that does not recognize the statements uttered as its own. Both the body and the self are enslaved to the conditions of the symbol.

Sent back across the edge, the self is projected into a moving horizon, at the core of a reality whose center is everywhere and nowhere. Events do not necessarily have recognizable origins. Some are pure memory-filters. Others crop up unexpectedly, without apparent cause, or have a beginning but not necessarily an end. Still others are stopped, then taken up again at a later time, and not necessarily by the same actors, in an indefinite declension of profiles and figures that are as ungraspable as they are unrepresentable, and through designs that are as complicated as they are ever liable to modification. The causes—never univocal—entwine, dis-entwine and entwine anew, willed into action by forces over which they have no control.

One does not enter into the ghostly realm out of curiosity or because one wants to. Ultimately, a tragedy, indeed a loss, is at the origin of everything. The fracture that ensues derives from the self's inability to control its desires and to bear the loss—the absence of enjoyment previously associated with the fulfillment of desire:

> I was a palm-wine drunkard since I was a boy often years of age. I had no other work more than to drink palm-wine in my life. [...]
> [W]hen my father noticed that I could not do any work more than to drink, he engaged an expert palm-wine tapster for me; he had no other work than to tap palm-wine every day.
> [...] So my friends were uncountable by that time and they were drinking palm-wine with me from morning till a late hour in the night. [...] when it was the 6th month after my father had died, the tapster went to the palm-tree farm on a Sunday evening to tap palm-wine for me. When he reached the farm, he climbed one of the tallest palm-trees in the farm to tap palm-wine but as he was tapping on, he fell down unexpectedly and died at the foot of the palm-tree as a result of injuries. (191–92)

Prior to the split, the subject's life was centered around a fixed object of desire. The effective realization of pleasure resulted almost exclusively from tapping (literally and otherwise) an inexhaustible flux, the encounter with the single object that could satisfy his urge: palm-wine. Once the pleasure was achieved, the subject could then attain a relative state of satiety and happiness, a certain sensual delight. In this exchange, the palm-wine tapster represented the living mediation without which there would be no satisfaction.

The brutal and premature death of the wine-gatherer is in many regards a fantastical castration: the coupling of seminal liquid and narcissistic power is abruptly brought to an end. A horrible plight: desire can no longer be consummated. Nor, on the other hand, can be it repressed. Thus everything is frozen, including the social connections made possible by the consummation. The pulsing of pleasure (represented by palm-wine) ceases to be the expression of life. The subject cannot tolerate any pain, any suffering caused by the absence of the seminal liquid, no matter how temporary:

> As I was waiting for him to bring the palm-wine, when I saw that he did not return in time, because he was not keeping me long like that before, then I called two of my friends to accompany me to the farm. When we reached the farm, we began to look at every palm-tree, after a while we found him under the palm-tree, where he fell down and died.
>
> But what I did first when we saw him dead there, was that I climbed another palm-tree which was near the spot, after that I tapped the palm-wine and drank it to my satisfaction before I came back to the spot. Then both my friends who accompanied me to the farm and I dug a pit under the palm-tree that he fell down as a grave and buried him there, after that we came back to the town. (192)

The "palm-wine drunkard" lives with the memory of an earlier ceremony that he is now incapable of re-enacting. The interruption of that ceremony gives rise to melancholy. What the subject mourns is the time during which the mastery of desires occurred not through continence, but through their immediate satisfaction. The seminal liquid is transformed in an inherent phantasm and drives the subject to leave his home:

> When it was early in the morning of the next day, I had no palm-wine to drink at all, and throughout the day I felt not so happy as before [...] when I completed a week in my house without palm-wine, then I went out and I saw one of [my friends] in town, so I saluted him, he answered but did not approach me at all, he hastily went away.
>
> Then I started to find out another expert palm-wine tapster, but I could not get me one who could tap the palm-wine to my requirement. [...]

When I saw that there was no palm-wine for me again, and nobody could tap it for me [. . .]! said that I would find out where my palm-wine tapster who had died was.

We thus penetrate into the world of ghosts by means of tragedy. The operation unfolds after a long walk, in search of a primitive meaning: a dead man. To emerge from oneself and enter into the order of itinerance is scarcely possible, however, without an exacerbation of sensorial perception:

[The old man] woke me up, and gave me a wide and strong net [. . .] He told me to go and bring "Death" from his house with the net. When I left his house or the town about a mile, there I saw a Junction of roads and I was doubtful when I reached the junction, I did not know which was Death's road among these roads [. . .] it was the market day [. . .] I lied down on the middle of the roads, I put my head to one of the roads, my left hand to one, right hand to another one, and my both feet to the rest, after that I pretended as I had slept there. (195)

Thus are the crossroads. They open, unbeknownst to us, onto the ghostly domain. We enter into it almost unwittingly, because it has no visible border. The crossroads constitute, in this regard, more than a simple point of passage. They are the gate that opens onto the process of *unwinding*. The unwinding centers its attack on the senses: the visual, the tactile, the auditory, the olfactory. We do not penetrate the ghostly theater without a certain bodily struggle. The head, the hands, and the feet are set there like inert traps in a game of chance in which there are many unwitting participants, including passers-by:

But when all the market goers were returning from the market, they saw me lied down there and shouted thus:—"Who was the mother of this fine boy, he slept on the roads and put his head towards Death's road." (195)

Knowledge of the path that leads to the ghost world is yielded by passers-by. The body, the road, and the market goers all come together with sleep to mimic death itself in order to better discover its paths. The ghost world is thus one of roads and crossroads, of simulation and resemblance. The crossroads are also the site of strange ceremonies:

At last I found myself where several roads meet together [. . .], but all these roads were foot paths. [. . .] It was an open place, except the bush which spread on it. There I remained till the morning without seeing a single creature. (69)
  [I]t was about eight o'clock in the morning all the ghosts and ghostesses with their children of that town came to me with two sheep and

two goats and also with some fowls. Having reached there the first thing they did was that the whole of them surrounded me, then all were singing, beating drums, clapping hands, ringing bells and dancing round me for a few minutes before they killed all the domestic animals which they brought before me and poured the blood of these animals on to my head which ran to the long neck and then into the pitcher in which the rest of my body was. (69)

In this nameless, early morning ceremony, the hole takes the place of the gallows. There is no high priest. The crowd, in its abstraction, presides over the ritual and performs the sacrifice. The victim's face is obliterated at the expense of his head and its natural extension, the neck. The remainder of the body, already buried, is nothing but an unnamable magma.

Here, ghostly terror finds its expression in the combined forces of song, dance, and immolation. In this linkage resides its *spiral* aspect, its singular violence, its effects of terror. The uniqueness of ghostly power is its encircling of the subject, surrounding it on all sides, investing it and tightening around it to the point that it cracks. From this perspective, ghostly terror is above all physico-anatomical, deriving in large part from the characteristic deformity of the ghost's body:

[M]any of them had no hands and some had no fingers, some had no feet and arms but jumped instead of walking. Some had heads without eyes and ears, but I was very surprised to see them walking about both day and night without missing their way and also it was this day I had ever seen ghosts without clothes on their bodies and they were not ashamed of their nakedness. (27)

Half-bodies that are cut every which way, made incomplete through mutilation and the resulting absence of symmetry, but nevertheless enjoying magnified acuity and force, and capable of limping along: such is the genius of these monsters and the source of their power (see de Heusch 125–55). The victim of ghostly terror is not sheltered from this symbolic of asymmetry. Where ghostly power undertakes to model its victim's bodies in its own image, terror can easily be transformed into a demiurgic surgery— crippled bodies, lost parts, scattered fragments, misshapings and wounds, the libidinal dance of hopeless wars, in short, generalized dismemberment:

[T]here were many kinds of African wars and some of them are as follows: general wars, tribal wars, burglary wars and the slave wars which were very common in every town and village and particularly in famous markets and on main roads of big towns at any time in the day or night. (17–18)

Everyone was fleeing, the living, the dead, the next-to-dead, the ain't-gonna-make-it, those who were whole, those who were halves, members, bits, that the blasts continued to pursue. (Sony Labou Tansi, *La vie et demie* 40–41).

There is another face of ghostly terror that ensues from the ghost's ugliness and wretchedness. Indeed, the ghost's body teems with a multiplicity of living species: bees, mosquitoes, snakes, centipedes, scorpions, flies. From it emanates a pestilential odor fed by never-ending feces, urine, blood—in short, the waste of victims that ghostly power endlessly crushes:

All kinds of snakes, centipedes and flies were living on every part of his body. Bees, wasps and uncountable mosquitoes were also flying round him and it was hard to see him plainly because of these flies and insects. [...] all his body was full of excreta, urine, and also wet with the rotten blood of all the animals that he was killing for his food. His mouth which was always opening, his nose and eyes were very hard to look at as they were very dirty and smelling. (29)

Together, the violence of deformity and the violence of ugliness allow ghostly power to acquire this ability to double and to divide into a multiplicity of opposites which, to paraphrase Nietzsche, in the end make of it "a reality that ceases its becoming at one moment, and then an instant later, is returned to its nothingness."

Ghostly violence is deployed under diverse shapes. At the base of all these figures there is nevertheless a common principle: the *desire to murder*:

To my surprise was that when it was about two o'clock in the midnight, there I saw somebody enter into the room cautiously with a heavy club in his hands, he came nearer to the bed on which he had told me to sleep, then he clubbed the bed with all his power, he clubbed the centre of the bed thrice and he returned cautiously, he thought that I slept on that bed and he thought also that he had killed me. (198)

Incidentally, in the ghostly realm, life and murder are one and the same thing. Ghostly terror operates also through *capture*. This too assumes diverse forms. The most ordinary of these is physical capture. It consists simply in binding the subject hand and foot and gagging him like a convict, beyond the bearable, to the point where he is reduced to immobility. From then on he can neither run, nor even move. He can barely stir: the spectator of his own powerlessness.

Other forms of capture occur through the projection of a light whose starkness, harshness, and brutality invest objects, erase them, recreate them, and then plunge the subject into a quasi-hallucinatory drama:

So as he lighted the flood of golden light on my body and when I looked at myself I thought that I became gold as it was shining on my body, so at this time I preferred most to go to him because of his golden light. But as I moved forward a little bit to go to him then the copperish-ghost lighted the flood of his own copperish light on my body too, which persuaded me again to go to the golden-ghost as my body was changing to every colour that copper has, and my body was then so bright so that I was unable to touch it. And again as I preferred this copperish light more than the golden-light then I started to go to him, but at this stage I was prevented again to go to him by the silverfish-light which shone on to my body at that moment unexpectedly. This silverfish-light was as bright as snow so that it transparented every part of my body and it was this day I knew the number of bones of my body. But immediately I started to count them these three ghosts shone the three kinds of light on my body at the same time in such a way that I could not move to and fro because of these lights. But as these three old ghosts shone their lights on me at the same time so I began to move round as a wheel at this junction, as I appreciated these lights as the same. (24–25)

The light reflects its brilliance and its radiance on the body that has become, under the circumstances, a luminous dust, a porous and translucent matter. This fluidification of the body results in the suspension of its prehensile and motor functions. Its component parts become legible. The light also causes new forms to emerge from the shadows. The startling combination of colors and splendor not only transfigures the subject; it plunges him into a whirlwind and transforms him into a whirligig: the plaything of antagonistic powers that tear at the subject so that he cries out in horror:

But as every one of these three old ghosts wanted me to be his servant [...] all of them held me tightly in such a way that I could not breathe in or out. But as they held me with argument for about three hours, so when I was nearly cut into three as they were pulling me about in the room I started to cry louder so that all the ghosts and ghostesses of that area came to their house [...] (26).

[...]

The wandering subject

But there is no body except in and through movement. That is why there is no subject but a wandering one. The *wandering subject* moves from one place to another. Journey as such does not need a precise destination: the wanderer can go about as he pleases. There can be predetermined stages for the journey. But the path does not always lead to the desired destination. What is important is where one ends up, the road traveled to get there, the series of experiences in which one is actor and witness, and above all, the role played by the unexpected and the unforeseen.

Along with motor functions, *work for life* rests upon olfactory functions. These are inseparable from the operation of other senses, for instance sight and taste. Such is notably the case when the subject experiences hunger or thirst. The status of odors and aromas is nevertheless complex; they also serve to locate the road that could lead to deliverance:

> [A]s I stood at the junction of these passages with confusion three kinds of sweet smells were rushing out to me from each of these three rooms, but as I was hungry and also starving before I entered into this hole, so I began to sniff the best smell so that I might enter the right room at once from which the best sweet smell was rushing out. Of course as I stood on this junction I noticed through my nose that the smell which was rushing out of the room which had golden surroundings was just as if the inhabitant of it was baking bread and roasting fowl, and when I sniffed again the smell of the room which had copperish surroundings was just as if the inhabitant of it was cooking rice, potatoes and other African food with very sweet soup [...]. (23)

The other ability required for this *work for life* is the ability to metamorphose. The subject can morph under any circumstances. This is notably the case in situations of conflict and adversity:

> Having left this village to a distance of a mile this ghost magician came to me on the way, he asked me to let both of us share the gifts, but when I refused he changed to a poisonous snake, he wanted to bite me to death, so I myself used my magical power and changed to a long stick at the same moment and started to beat him repeatedly. When he felt much pain and near to die, then he changed from the snake to a great fire and burnt this stick to ashes, after that he started to burn me too. Without hesitation I myself changed to rain, so I quenched him at once. Again he controlled the place that I stood to become a deep well in which I found myself unexpectedly and without any ado he controlled this rain to be raining into the well while I was inside. Within a second the well was full of water. But when he wanted to close the door of the well so that I might not be able to come out again or to die inside it, I myself changed to a big fish to swim out. But at the same moment he saw the fish he himself changed to a crocodile, he jumped into the well and came to swallow me, but before he could swallow me I changed to a bird and also changed the gifts to a single palm fruit, I held it with my beak and then flew out of the well straight to the 18th town. Without any ado he changed himself

again to a big hawk chasing me about in the sky to kill as his prey. But when I believed that no doubt he would kill me very soon, then I changed again to the air and blew within a second to a distance which a person could not travel on foot for thirty years. But when I changed to my former form at the end of this distance, to my surprise, there I met him already, he had reached there before me and was waiting for me a long time. Now we appeared personally to ourselves. Then he asked me to bring the gifts, but after both of us struggled for many hours, then I shared the gifts into two parts, I gave him a part, but he insisted to take the whole. However, I gave him all. (158–59)

The act *par excellence* of morphing consists in constantly exiting out of oneself, going beyond oneself in an agonizing, centripetal movement that is all the more terrifying as the possibility of returning to the center is never assured. In this context, where existence is tethered to very few things, identity can only live its life in a fleeting mode. Inhabiting a particular being can only be temporary. It is essential to know how to disguise this particular being, reproduce it, split it, retrieve it as necessary. Not to be ahead of oneself literally means running the risk of death.

[...]

The song of remembrance

Three conclusions emerge from this study. The first concerns time. In the ghostly paradigm, there is neither reversibility nor irreversibility of time. There is only *unfolding* and folding over anew [*déroulement/enroulement*] of experience. If stories and events have a beginning, they do not necessarily have an end, properly speaking. Indeed, they may be interrupted. But a story or an event may continue in another story or in another event, without there necessarily being a causal relationship between one and the other. Conflicts and struggles may be taken up again at the point they were stopped. But they can also be interrupted or resumed without the need for continuity. Furthermore, the same event can have more than one distinct beginning.

Throughout the process, one can pass from phases of loss to phases of enrichment for the subject—phases, moreover, which may occur simultaneously. Consequently, everything functions according to the principle of incompletion. As a result, there is no necessary continuity between the present, the past and the future. Strictly speaking, there is no genealogy. There is only an unfurling of temporal series that are virtually disjointed or linked together through a multiplicity of slender threads.

A second conclusion relates to the nature of ghostly terror. The terror that flows from this fractured temporality presents, if only metaphorically, a resemblance with the fluxes and organ-less bodies discussed by Deleuze and Guattari in *Anti-Oedipus*. In a context marked by ghostly violence and radical instability, a necessary condition of selfhood is the capacity, under all circumstances, to "faire entrer les fragments dans des fragmentations toujours nouvelles" (13) / "[the ability] to rearrange fragments continually in new and different patterns or configurations" (7). We then understand that in the ghostly realm, selfhood, subjecthood, and schizophrenia go hand in hand.

The schizophrenic, according to Deleuze and Guattari, passes from one code to another, blurs all codes, "dans un glissement rapide, suivant les questions qui lui sont posées, ne donnant pas d'un jour a l'autre la même explication, n'invoquant pas la même généalogie, n'enregistrant pas de la même manière le même événement, acceptant même, quand on le lui impose et qu'il n'est pas irrité, le code banal oedipien, quitte à la re-bourrer de toutes les disjonctions que ce code était fait pour exclure" (21–22) / "It might be said that the schizophrenic passes from one code to the other, that he deliberately *scrambles all the codes*, by quickly shifting from one to another, according to the questions asked him, never giving the same explanation from one day to the next, never invoking the same genealogy, never recording the same event in the same way. When he is more or less forced into it and is not in a touchy mood, he may even accept the banal Oedipal code, so long as he can stuff it full of all the disjunctions that his code was designed to eliminate" (15). Life, just as sovereignty in the framework at hand, is but a long series of accidents and incidents, events that could have happened but do not occur, while others that were not supposed to happen do, in effect, take place. Under these conditions where, according to the Nietzschean expression, "tout se divise, mais en soi-même, et où le même être est partout, de tous côtés, à tous les niveaux, *à la différence d'intensité près*" 'everything divides, but in itself, and where every being is everywhere, on all sides, at all levels, *except in terms of intensity*', the sole manner of life is in zigzags.

A third conclusion relates to the relationship between selfhood and remembrance. The wandering subject has neither a unique form nor a content that has been shaped definitively. Form and content change constantly, depending on life's events. But the deployment of existence can occur if the subject leans upon a reservoir of memories and images that are never fixed definitively. He leans upon them at the very moment that he transgresses them, forgets them, and places them in dependence upon something other than themselves. The work for life consists, consequently, in distancing oneself each time from memory and tradition at the very moment one is depending upon it to negotiate the twists and turns of life.

With life's contours barely sketched out, the wandering subject must escape from himself each time and allow himself to be carried away by the flux of time and accidents. He produces himself in the unknown, by means of a chain of effects that have been calculated beforehand, but never materialize exactly in the terms foreseen. It is thus in the unexpected and radical instability that he creates and invents himself. There is thus no sovereignty of the subject or life as such.

Perhaps that is why, in the middle of the night, the wandering subject can allow himself to yield to the song of remembrance. Quite often, this song is buried under the rubble of sorrow and thus prevented from investing existence with a mark of ecstasy and eternity. But liberated through tobacco, the wandering subject suddenly does away with everything limiting his horizon. He can henceforth project himself into the infinite sea of light that makes it possible to forget sorrow:

> After that he put a kind of smoking pipe which was about six feet long into my mouth. This smoking pipe could contain half a ton of tobacco at a time, then he chose one ghost to be loading this pipe with tobacco whenever it discharged fire. When he lit the pipe with fire then the whole of the ghosts and ghostesses were dancing round me set by set. They were singing, clapping hands, ringing bells and their ancestral drummers were beating the drums in such a way that all the dancers were jumping up with gladness. But whenever the smoke of the pipe was rushing out from my mouth as if smoke is rushing from a big boiler, then all of them would laugh at me so that a person two miles away would hear them clearly, and whenever the tobacco inside the pipe is near to finish then the ghost who was chosen to be loading it would load it again with fresh tobacco [...]
>
> After some hours that I was smoking this pipe I was intoxicated by the gas of the tobacco as if I drank much hard drink [...].
>
> So at this time I forgot all my sorrow and started to sing the earthly songs which sorrow prevented me from singing about since I entered this bush. But when all these ghosts were hearing the song, they were dancing from me to a distance of about five thousand feet and then dancing back to me again as they were much appreciating the song and also to hear my voice was curious to them. (74–75)
>
> —*trans. by R. H. Mitsch*

Notes

1   From this perspective my approach diverges from the thematics of "the unity of life" (Aristotle, Spinoza, Lamarck, and even Foucault), discussions concerning the "sciences of life" (Kant, Bergson, Canguilhem), or even

the relationships between "life and values." For a quick overview of these debates, see Hoquet. Some of these critiques can be found in, among others, Nietzsche, *Will to Power* 1; Merleau-Ponty, *Phénoménologie de la perception* and especially *Le visible et l'invisible*; Bataille, *L'érotisme*.

2   According to Hobbes: "[E]t tout d'abord, il est mianifesté qu'il n'existe pas deux corps qui sont le même; car voir qu'ils sont deux, c'est voir qu'il sont en deux lieux au même moment, puisque le fait d'être le même est le fait d'être au même moment en un seul et meme lieu." "And above all, it is clear that there cannot be two bodies that are the same; for to see that they are two is to see that they are in two places at the same time, since the fact of being the same is the fact of being at the same time in a single and same place." (*English Works 1*, ch. 11. See also Locke, *Essai concernant l'entendement humain 2*, 27: 1–3; Locke, *Identité et différence*. See also Hume, *Traité de la nature humaine* 284–6. For Locke as for Hume, the principle of individuation is inseparable from the principle of invariability.

3   Nietzsche questioned whether appearance belongs to reality and determined that it is a form of its being, that the world is essentially a world of relations—seen from diverse points of view, it has as many different faces, and its being is essentially different in each point. See *La volonté de puissance 1*: 89. He also added that the true being of things is an invention of the subject who represents them to himself and cannot represent things to himself without this fiction (259).

Works cited

Aristotle. *De la génération et de la corruption.* Trans. Julies Tricot. Paris: Vrin.

Bataille, Georges. *L'érotisme.* Paris: Les Editions de Minuit, 1957.

Cassirer, Ernst. *La philosophie des formes symboliques.* Paris: Editions de Minuit, 1981.

Deleuze, Gilles, et Félix Guattari. *Capitalisme et schizophrénie: L'Anti-Œdipe.* Paris: Editions de Minuit, 1972/73.

—*Anti-Oedipus: Capitalism and Schizophrenia.* Trans. from the French by Robert Hurley, Mark Seem, and Helen R. Lane. Pref. by Michel Foucault. Minneapolis: University of Minnesota Press, c1983.

Descartes, René. *Les passions de l'âme [Passions of the Soul].* Paris: Flammarion, 1996.

—*Discours de la méthode [Discourse on Method].* Paris: Editions de Minuit, 1981.

Elias, Norbert. *La civilisation des moeurs.* Paris: Calmann-Levy, 1973.

Foucault, Michel. *Histoire de la sexualité. Le souci de soi.* Paris: Gallimard, 1984. Trans. by Robert Hurley as *History of Sexuality.* New York: Pantheon, c1978.

Freud, Sigmund. "Dualisme des instincts, instinct de vie et instinct de mort." "Au-delà du principe de plaisir." *Essais de psychanalyse.* Paris: Payot, 1983.

Hegel, G. W. F. *Phénoménologie de l'Esprit [Phenomenology of Mind].* Trans. J. P. Lefebvre. Paris: Aubier, 1991.

Heidegger, Martin. *Être et Temps [Time and Being].* Trans. F. Vezin. Paris: Gallimard, 1986.

Héraclite. *Fragments*. Trans. M. Conche. Paris: Presses Universitaires de France, 1986.

de Heusch, Luc. *Le roi de Kongo et les monstres sacrés*. Paris: Gallimard, 2000.

Hobbes, Thomas. *La nature humaine [Human Nature]*. Trans. D'Holbach. Paris: Babel, 1997.

—*The English Works of Thomas Hobbes*. Vol. 1. Sir W. Molesworth ed. London: J. Bohn, 1839.

Hoquet, T. ed. *La vie*. Paris: Flammarion, 1999.

Hume, David. *Dissertation sur les passions. Traité de la nature humaine. Livre II [Human Nature]*. Paris: Flammarion, 1991.

—*Traité de la nature humaine. [Human Nature]*. Trans. P. Baranger et P. Saltel. Paris: Flammarion, 1995.

Husserl, Edmund. *Idées directrices pour une phénoménologie [Ideas: General Introduction to Pure Phenomenology]*. Paris: Gallimard, 1950.

Labou Tansi, Sony. *La vie et demie*. Paris: Seuil, 1979.

Lacan, Jacques. *Les quatre concepts fondamentaux de la psychanalyse. [The Four Fundamental Concepts of Psycho-Analysis]*. Paris: Seuil, 1973.

—"Le stade du miroir comme formateur de la fonction du Je." *Ecrits*. Paris: Seuil, 1966. 93–101.

Locke, J. *Identité et différence. L'invention de la conscience [Of Identity and Diversity]*. Trans. E. Balibar. Paris: Seuil, 1998.

—*Essai concernant l'entendement humain [An Essay Concerning Human Understanding]*. Trans. P. Coste. Paris: Vrin, 1983.

Mbembe, Achille. *On the Postcolony*. Berkeley: University of California Press, 2001.

—"Necropolitics". *Public Culture*. Vol. 15 (1), 2003.

Melchior-Bonnet, Sabine. *Histoire du miroir*. Paris: Imago, 1994

Merleau-Ponty, M. *Phénoménologie de la perception*. Paris: Gallimard, 1945.

—*Le visible et l'invisible*. Paris: Gallimard, 1964.

Nietzsche, Friedrich. *La volonté de puissance 1 [The Will to Power]*. Trans. G. Bianquis. Paris: Gallimard, 1995.

Platon. *Théétète-Parménide [Theaetetus/Parmenides]*. Trans. Emile Chambry. Paris: Flammarion, 1967.

Ricoeur, Paul. *Oneself as Another*. Trans. K. Blamey. Chicago: University of Chicago Press, 1992.

Sartre, Jean-Paul. *L'être, et le néant [Being and Nothingness]*. Paris: Gallimard, 1944.

Taylor, Charles. *Sources of the Self*. Cambridge: The MIT Press, 1989.

Tutuola, Amos. *The Palm-Wine Drinkard* and *My Life in the Bush of Ghosts*. 1954. New York: Grove, 1994.

Vaysse, J.-M. *L'inconscient des modernes. Essai sur l'origine métaphysique de la psychanalyse*. Paris: Gallimard, 1999.

Vernant, Jean-Pierre. *Mortals and Immortals. Collected Essays*. Princeton: Princeton University Press, 1991.

10

Spectral Housing and Urban Cleansing: Notes on Millennial Mumbai

Arjun Appadurai

Cities like Bombay—now Mumbai—have no clear place in the stories told so far that link late capitalism, globalization, post-Fordism, and the growing dematerialization of capital. Their history is uneven—in the sense made commonsensical by a certain critical tradition in Marxism. It is also characterized by disjunct, yet adjacent, histories and temporalities. In such cities, Fordist manufacture, craft and artisanal production, service economies involving law, leisure, finance, and banking, and virtual economies involving global finance capital and local stock markets live in an uneasy mix. Certainly, these cities are the loci of the practices of predatory global capital—here Mumbai belongs with Bangkok, Hong Kong, Saõ Paulo, Los Angeles, Mexico City, London, and Singapore. But these cities also produce the social black holes of the effort to embrace and seduce global capital in their own particular ways, which are tied to varied histories (colonial and otherwise), varied political cultures of citizenship and rule, and varied ecologies of production and finance. Such particularities appear as images of globalization that are cracked and refracted. They are also instances of the elusiveness of global flows at the beginning of the new millennium.

Typically, these cities are large (10–15 million people) and are currently shifting from economies of manufacture and industry to economies of trade, tourism, and finance. They usually attract more poor people than they can handle and more capital than they can absorb. They offer the magic of wealth, celebrity, glamour, and power through their mass media. But they often contain shadow economies that are difficult to measure in traditional terms.

Such cities, too, are the site of various uncertainties about citizenship. People come to them in large numbers from impoverished rural areas. Work is often difficult to obtain and retain. The rich in these cities seek to gate as much of their lives as possible, travelling from guarded homes to darkened cars to air- conditioned offices, moving always in an envelope of privilege through the heat of public poverty and the dust of dispossession. Frequently, these are cities where crime is an integral part of municipal order and where fear of the poor is steadily increasing. And these are cities where the circulation of wealth in the form of cash is ostentatious and immense, but the sources of cash are always restricted, mysterious, or unpredictable. Put another way, even for those who have secure salaries or wages, the search for cash in order to make ends meet is endless. Thus everyday life is shot through with socially mediated chains of debt—between friends, neighbors, and coworkers—stretched across the continuum between multinational banks and other organized lenders, on the one hand, and loan sharks and thugs, on the other.

Bombay is one such city. It has an interesting history as a set of fishing villages, many named after local goddesses, linked by bridges and causeways and turned into a seat of colonial government in western India. Later, in the second half of the nineteenth century, it blossomed as a site of commercially oriented bourgeois nationalism, and, until the 1950s, it retained the ethos of a well- managed, Fordist city, dominated by commerce, trade, and manufacture, especially in the realm of textiles. Well into the 1970s, in spite of phenomenal growth in its population and increasing strain on its infrastructure, Bombay remained a civic model for India. Most people with jobs had housing; most basic services (such as gas, electricity, water, and milk) reliably reached the salaried middle classes. The laboring classes had reasonably secure occupational niches. The truly destitute were always there, but even they fit into a complex subeconomy of pavement dwelling, rag picking, petty crime, and charity.

Until about 1960, the trains bringing in white- and blue-collar workers from the outer suburbs to the commercial and political core of the city (the Fort area in South Bombay) seemed to be able to move people around with some dignity and reliability and at relatively low cost. The same was true of the city's buses, bicycles, and trams. A three-mile bus ride in 1965 Bombay cost about 15 paise (roughly the equivalent of two U.S. cents at then-current rates). People actually observed the etiquette of queuing in most public contexts, and buses always stopped at bus stops rather than fifty feet before or after them (as in most of India today).

Sometime in the 1970s all this began to change and a malignant city began to emerge from beneath the surface of the cosmopolitan ethos of the prior period. The change was not sudden, and it was not equally visible in all spheres. But it was unmistakable. Jobs became harder to get. More rural arrivals in the city found themselves economic refugees. Slums and shacks began to proliferate. The wealthy began to get nervous. The middle classes had to wrestle with overcrowded streets and buses, skyrocketing prices, and maddening traffic. The places of leisure and pleasure—the great promenades along the shore of the Arabian Sea, the wonderful parks and *maidans* (open grass fields designed for sport and pastime in the colonial era), the cinema halls and tea stalls—began to show the wear and tear of hypermodernization.

As this process began to take its toll on all but the wealthiest of the city's population, the groundwork was laid for the birth of the most markedly xenophobic regional party in India—the Shiva Sena—which formed in 1966 as a pro-native, Marathi-centered, movement for ethnic control of Bombay. Today the Shiva Sena controls the city and the state and has a significant national profile as one of the many parties that form the Sangh Parivar (or coalition of Hindu chauvinist parties). Its platform combines language chauvinism (Marathi), regional primordialism (a cult of the regional state of Maharashtra), and a commitment to a Hinduized India (Hindutva, the land of Hinduness). The Shiva Sena's appeal goes back at least to 1956, shortly before Bombay was made the capital of the new linguistic state of Maharashtra and after intense rioting in Bombay over the competing claims of Gujaratis for Bombay to be in their own new linguistic state. In retrospect, 1956 marks a moment when Bombay became Mumbai, the name now insisted on by the official machineries of the city, all of which have been influenced by the Shiva Sena. Since this period, mostly through the active and coercive tactics of the Shiva Sena and its cadres, Bombay's Marathi speakers have been urged to see the city as theirs, and every few years a new enemy is found among the city's minorities: Tamil clerks, Hindi-speaking cabdrivers, Sikh businessmen, Malayali coconut vendors— each has provided the "allogenic" flavor of the month (or year).

A high point of this ethnicization of the city was reached in late 1992 and early 1993, when riots broke out throughout India after the destruction of the Babri Masjid in Ayodhya (in the state of Uttar Pradesh in north India) by Hindu vandals on 6 December 1992. Bombay's Hindu right managed in this period to join the national frenzy of anti-Muslim violence, but this violence, too, had a Bombay flavor. In keeping with more than two decades of the Shiva Sena's peculiar mix of regional chauvinism and nationalist hysterics, Bombay's Hindus managed to violently rewrite urban space as sacred, national, and Hindu space. The decades of this gradual ethnicizing of India's most cosmopolitan city (roughly the 1970s, 1980s, and into the 1990s) were also the decades when Bombay became a site of crucial changes in trade, finance, and industrial manufacture. This essay is in part an effort to capture this more than circumstantial link. I turn now to a series of ethnographic interventions whose purpose is to think through the complex causalities that mediate between the steady dematerialization of Bombay's economy and the relentless hypermaterialization of its citizens through ethnic mobilization and public violence.

I have suggested so far that Bombay belongs to a group of cities in which global wealth and local poverty articulate a growing contradiction. But this essay is not an effort to illuminate a general class of city or a global urban dilemma. It is an effort to recognize two specificities about Bombay that mark and produce its singularity. The first is to note the peculiar ambiguities that divide and connect cash and capital (two quite distinct forms of wealth) from one another. The second is to show that this disjuncture is part of what might let us understand the peculiar ways in which cosmopolitanism in Bombay has been violently compromised in its recent history. I do this by sketching a set of circumstances to make an argument about wealth, housing, and ethnic violence, that is, at this stage, circumstantial. Future work on Mumbai may allow me to be more precise about causalities and more definite about comparisons.

City of cash

In some ways, Bombay is as familiar with the history of capital as the most important cities of Europe and the United States. Long a site of seafaring commerce, imperial trade, and colonial power, Bombay's colonial elite— Parsis, Muslims, and Hindus (as well as Baghdadi Jews, Syrian Christians, Armenians, and other exotics)—helped shape industrial capitalism in the twilight of an earlier world economy built around the Indian Ocean. That earlier world economy (made vivid in Amitav Ghosh's *In An Antique Land*) can still be glimpsed in the traffic of dhows between the west coast of India and the states of the Persian Gulf, in the escalating illegal traffic in gold along this circuit, in the movement of thousands of migrants to the Gulf states from Kerala and elsewhere on the west coast, in the post-OPEC invasion of Arab tourists into Bombay seeking the pleasures of the monsoon, cheap medical care, the flesh trade, and the cheaper-than-Harrod's prices for many delicious goods. Bombay's citizens began to complain that they could no longer afford their favorite summer fruit—the Alphonso mango—because exports to the Middle East had shrunk local supplies and pushed mango prices beyond their reach.

Partly because of its huge film industry (still among the world's largest); partly because of its powerful role in trade, banking, and commerce; and partly because of its manufacturing sector, centered on textiles but extending to metalworks, automobile factories, chemical industries, and more—for all these reasons, Bombay after World War II was quintessentially a cosmopolis of commerce. People met in and through "business" (a word taken over from English and used to indicate professions, transactions, deals, and a whole ethos of commerce), and through "business" they forged and reproduced links across neighborhoods, ethnicities, and regional origins. No ethnicity in Bombay escaped stereotyping, and all stereotyping had its portfolio of jokes. What counted was the color of money.

And money leads a complex life in today's Mumbai. It is locked, hoarded, stored, and secreted in every possible way: in jewellery, in bank accounts, in household safes and mattresses, in land and housing and dowries, in boxes and purses and coffee tins, and behind shirts and blouses. It is frequently hidden money, made visible only in the fantastic forms of cars and mansions, sharp suits and expensive restaurants, huge flats and large numbers of servants. But even more, Mumbai is a city of visible money—of CASH—where wads, stacks, piles of rupees are openly and joyously transacted.

I remember a local street hood in my 1950s Bombay neighborhood who managed to become the local controller of the numbers racket. He wore a terylene shirt with semitransparent pockets in which there was always the glimmer and clink of a huge number of little coins, the currency of his trade. The numbers racket then was tied to the daily close of the New York Cotton Exchange (or so I was told), and this flashy fellow never tired of strolling around with a little jingle sounding from his chest. He would laugh as he bought *pan* (betel nut rolled in betel leaf) from the local *panwalla* "on credit"; and when the panwalla would grab for his transparent pocket, he would flit away, laughing, gently guarding the coins near his heart. Coins were still tokens of wealth then. Today, he would need paper money in order not to look silly.

And it was also widely felt that cash, chance, and wealth were linked. This same numbers racketeer, who happened to come from the Tamil south of India and thus could speak to me in my native Tamil, always grabbed me on the street to ask, with a half smile, for me to give him two numbers so that he could use them to place his own bets. At issue was some notion of small children as bearers of good luck, idiot savants of probability, and I, a Brahmin child from a respectable Tamil family, probably embodied bourgeois prudence as well. This flashy hood somehow fell out with his bosses, turned into a humiliated beggar over a period of a few years, and, spurned by those very street people he had used and perhaps cheated, died broke. He surely never moved out of the magic circle of cash into the hazy world of bank accounts, insurance policies, savings, or other prudential strategies. He represented the raw end of the cash economy. Today, the numbers trade, still a major part of Bombay's street economy, has shifted away from the proto-global link to U.S. commodity markets to—so the popular narrative goes—the play of pure chance: the pulling of cards out of a pot in a rumored-to-be real location in suburban Bombay every evening, with runners fanning out in minutes to report the results. This system is simply called *matka* (pot).

Yet there is a lot of interest in today's Bombay in such things as bank accounts, shares, and insurance policies—instruments all concerned with protecting money, providing against hazard, hedging risk, and enabling enterprise. Bombay's commercial economy includes a large part of its citizenry. Even poor wage-earners strive to have small savings accounts (with passbooks) and, more fascinating, no one is immune from the seduction of "whole-life" insurance. I have sometimes suspected that all of India is divided into two groups: those who sell insurance (an extremely popular trade for the less credentialed among the literate classes) and those who buy these policies. In Bombay, the Life Insurance Corporation of India is mainly housed in a building the size of a city block—a monumental vault that contains hundreds of thousands of small policies bought and sold most often from one individual to another. Starting as early as the 1960s, ordinary middle-class housewives began to see the benefits of various forms of corporate paper, including stocks, shares, and related instruments. These were bought mostly to be held—not sold—and their circulation through various financial markets was restricted and sluggish, until the last few years, when money markets have begun to get fast, volatile, high-volume, and speculative.

But back to cash. Much of Bombay's film industry runs on cash— so-called black money. This is a huge industry that produces more than three-hundred Hindi films a year for a worldwide market and reaps huge revenues at the box office. As a shrewd local analyst said to me, there is no real film *industry* in Bombay, since there is no money that is both made and invested within the world of film. Rather, film financing is a notoriously gray area of speculation, solicitation, risk, and violence, in which the key players are men who have made killings in other markets (such as the grain trade, textiles, or other commodities). Some of them seek to keep their money out of the hands of the government, to speculate on the chance of financing a hit film and to get the bonus of hanging out with the stars as well. This sounds similar to the Hollywood pattern, but it is an entirely arbitrary cast of characters who might finance a film, so much time is spent by "producers" in trolling for businessmen with serious cash on their hands. And since these bankrolls are very large, the industry pays blockbuster prices for stars, and the entire cultural economy of the film world revolves around large cash transactions in black money. Periodically big stars or producers are raided by income tax officials, and a media bloodletting about seized assets is offered to the public, before business as usual resumes.

This sort of cash is everywhere in Bombay's "business" world, in huge rumored payments to government officials or businessmen to get things done, and equally in the daily small-scale traffic in black market film tickets, smuggled foreign goods, numbers racket payments, police protection payments, wage payments to manual labor, and so on. It has been said that the "parallel" or "black" economy in India might be half again as large as the tax-generating, official economy. In Bombay, the ratio is probably higher.

Money is still considered real—in most circles—insofar as it is readily convertible to cash. Liquidity is the dominant criterion of prosperity, for both corporations and individuals, and new understandings of monetary phenomena such as credit, mortgages, and other technical or temporal "derivatives" are only now entering Bombay—and that, too, for its upper middle classes. Even the most sophisticated international and national financial strategists and czars, who are now responsible for putting Bombay permanently on the map of global investment, find it difficult to escape the sensuous appeals of cash. Wealth is understood to be an abstraction, but it is never seen as fully real in forms of paper that are not currency.

Bills and coins are not primarily what moves global wealth through Bombay's industrial houses, government offices, and corporate headquarters, but they are still the hallmarks of wealth and sociability, anchors of materiality in a world of invisible wealth. This is a shadow economy whose very shadows take on their density from the steady flow of real bills and coins through the lives of many kinds of transactors. Nor is this just money fleeing the tax collector. It is also money seeking immediate expenditure, racing from pocket to pocket without the logistical drag of conversion, storage, restriction, accounting, and dematerialization to slow the fuel of consumption. And this is true for the poor and for the rich. Whether you want 10 rupees to send to your mother in a postal money order or 4,000 rupees to have a bottle of Chivas Regal delivered to your door, cash is king. The rest is rumor.

Note that none of this has much to do with galloping inflation, any simple kind of fetishization, or the absence of immense local skills in money handling, credit, trade, and trust-based transactions that are truly global. It is entirely wrong to imagine that cash transactions imply limited trust. On the contrary, since parting with cash is decisively terminal, giving and taking cash requires larger amounts of trust than dealings in other sorts of monetary instruments. Cash handed over—even more than in other cases in the world—vanishes without a trace. The diamond industry, for example, which links cutters and polishers in coastal Surat (Gujarat) with caste-linked traders in Bombay, London, Antwerp, and beyond, is an exquisite case of global transfers that use every available form of credit (based on trust) but run on the fuel of hard cash at every critical switch point.

Nor is this corruption-at-large, where cash is best for extortion and fraud, though both exist in substantial measures. Rather, cash rules in Bombay as the mobile and material instantiation of forms of wealth that are known to be so large as to be immaterial. This is more nearly a commoditization of the fetish than a fetishization of the commodity, since currency here is itself treated as powerful in the extreme. What is invisible is not the currency behind the currency at hand but the WEALTH embedded in it. So moving currency around takes materialities that are themselves deeply powerful—fetishes if you will—and puts them into generalized circulation. Cash here, to borrow Fredric Jameson's phrase from a very different context, is a central "signature of the visible."

What we know about Bombay in the nineteenth century and—more hazily—before that time, certainly suggests that cash and its circulation through various kinds of commerce was a vital ingredient of sociality. It was the guarantee of cosmopolitanism because its sources were distant and varied, its local traffic crossed ethnic and regional lines, and its presence was both entrepreneurial and civic. The vital importance of Parsi philanthropists in the civic and public life of nineteenth- and twentieth-century Bombay is one of many examples of the cosmopolitanism of its public sphere.

What then is new today about cash in the city of cash? One answer is that cash and capital have come to relate in a new and contradictory manner in Bombay since the 1970s. While cash still does its circulatory work, guaranteeing a complex web of social and economic relations and indexing the fact that the business of Bombay is "business," capital in Bombay has become more anxious. This can be seen in two areas. The first is the flight of industrial capital away from the city, which is addressed later in this essay. The second is that financial capital in Bombay operates in several disjunct registers: as the basis for multinational corporations tempted by new market seductions in India, as speculative capital operating in illegal or black markets, and as entrepreneurial energy operating in a city where it is increasingly difficult to coordinate the factors of capitalist production. Yet a large cash economy still governs Bombay. This uneasy relationship between cash and capital can be seen in a variety of arenas, but housing is perhaps the best place to follow how this disjunct relationship helps create the conditions of possibility for ethnic violence.

Spectral housing

It is a banality to say that housing is scarce in Bombay. This is so widely known to be true that it is scarcely ever discussed abstractly. But it haunts many conversations about resources, plans, hopes, and desires among all of its citizens, ranging from those who live in multimillion-dollar penthouses to those who pay protection money for rights to six feet of sleeping space in an aqueduct. It is always at issue when jobs are mentioned (But where will you live?), when marriages are negotiated (Will you give my son part of your flat as part of his dowry?), when relatives are visited (Is cousin Ashok staying with you now?), or when neighbors speculate on the identities of people going in and out of each other's flats (Is X a subtenant or a relative, or both?).

To speak of spectrality in Bombay's housing scene moves us beyond the empirics of inequality into the experience of shortage, speculation, crowding, and public improvisation. It marks the space of speculation and specularities, empty scenes of dissolved industry, fantasies of urban planning, rumors of real estate transfers, consumption patterns that violate their spatial preconditions, and bodies that are their own housing. The absent, the ghostly, the speculative, the fantastic all have their part to play in the simultaneous excesses and lacks of Bombay's housing scene. It is these experienced absurdities that warrant my use of the term *spectral* in a setting where housing and its lack are grossly real. What are these swollen realities?

The social traffic on Bombay's extraordinary vital metropolitan train service is entirely premised on the fact that millions of people travel increasingly huge distances (two hours and fifty miles is not uncommon) to get from home to work and back. And many of them undergo complex transformations in transit, turning from oppressed dwellers in shantytowns, slums, and disposable housing into well-dressed clerks, nurses, postmen, bank tellers, and secretaries. Their "homes" are often unstable products—a bricolage of shoddy materials, insecure social relations, poor sanitation, and near-total lack of privacy. As they move into their places of work, this vast army of the middle and working classes usually moves into more secure spaces of recognition, comfort, and predictability than the "homes" they return to at night, even when their jobs are harsh, poorly paid, or dangerous.

And this does not speak of the truly destitute: beggars; homeless children; the maimed and the disfigured; the abandoned women with small children; and the aged who wander deaf, dumb, or blind through Bombay's streets. These are the truly "homeless," who wander like their counterparts in other world cities from Chicago and Johannesburg to Frankfurt and Bangkok. These are in some cases "street people," although this category must not be taken to be wholly generic across different cities and societies. And that is because the streets themselves constitute specific forms of public space and traffic.

Much could be said about Indian street life and the life of Bombay's streets in respect to housing. But a few observations must suffice. Bombay's "pavement dwellers" (like Calcutta's) have been made famous in both sociology and popular media. It is true that there is a vast and semiorganized part of Bombay's population that lives on pavements—or, more exactly, on particular spots, stretches, and areas that are neither building nor street. These pavement dwellers are often able to keep their personal belongings with others in shops or kiosks or even inside buildings (for some sort of price, of course). Some actually live on pavements, and others sleep in the gray spaces between buildings and streets. Yet others live on roofs and on parapets, above garages, and in a variety of interstitial spaces that are not fully controlled by either landlords or the state. As we shall see in the concluding section, "pavement dwellers" and "slum dwellers" are no longer external labels but have become self-organizing, empowering labels for large parts of the urban poor in Bombay.

The important point here is that there is a vast range of insecure housing, from a six-foot stretch of sleeping space to a poorly defined tenancy situation shared by three families "renting" one room. Pavements shade into *jopad-pattis* (complexes of shacks with few amenities), which shade into semipermanent illegal structures. Another continuum links these structures to *chawls* (tenement housing originally built for mill workers in Central Bombay) and to other forms of substandard housing. Above this tier are the owned or rented flats of the large middle class and finally the fancy flats and (in a tiny number of cases) houses owned by the rich and the super rich. These kinds of housing are not neatly segregated by neighborhood, for one simple reason: the insecurely housed poor are everywhere and are only partly concentrated in *bastis* (slums), jopad-pattis, and chawls. Almost every one of these kinds of housing for the poor, including roofs, parapets, compound walls, and overhangs, is subject to socially negotiated arrangements. Very often, control over these insecure spaces is in the hands of semiorganized crime, where rent and extortion shade into one another.

Even in the apartment buildings of the rich and upper middle class, especially in the commercial core of South Bombay and in the posh areas of Malabar Hill, Cuffe Parade, Worli, and Bandra, there is a constant pressure from the house poor. The poor set up house anywhere they can light a fire and stretch out a thin sheet to sleep on. As domestic servants, they often have small rooms in the large apartment buildings of the rich, and these servants (for whom such housing is a huge privilege) often bring friends and dependents, who spill out into the stairwells, the enclosed compounds, and the foyers. The official tenants, owners, and landlords wage a constant war against this colonization from below, but it is frequently lost because—as in all societies based on financial apartheid—one wants the poor near at hand as servants but far away as humans.

At the same time, small commercial enterprises sprout on every possible spot in every possible street, attached to buildings, to telephone poles, to electricity switching houses, or to anything else that does not move. These petty enterprises are by nature shelters, so many commercial stalls are, de facto, homes on the street for one or more people. The same is true of the kitchens of restaurants, parts of office buildings—indeed, any structure where a poor person has the smallest legitimate right to stay in or near a habitable structure, especially one that has water or a roof. Electricity and heat are rare luxuries, of course.

In this setting, for the very poor, home is anywhere you can sleep. And sleep is in fact the sole form of secure being. It is one of the few states in which—though usually entirely in public—there is respite from work, from harassment, and from eviction. Sleeping bodies are to be found everywhere in Bombay and indeed at all times. People walk over sleeping bodies as they cross streets and as they go into apartments, movie theaters, restaurants, and offices. Some of these people are sleeping in spaces to which they are legitimately connected through work or kinship. Others, as on park benches and street corners, are simply taking their housing on the hoof, renting sleep, in a manner of speaking. Public sleeping is the bottom of the hierarchy of spectral housing, housing that exists only by implication and by imputation. The sleeping body (which is almost always the laboring body or the indigent body) in its public, vulnerable, and inactive form is the most contained form of the spectral house. Public sleeping is a technique of necessity for those who can be at home only in their bodies.

Here we must resituate the sleeping, indigent, and exhausted body back in the specificities of Bombay's terrain of habitation, lest we slip into the generic sense of the urban poor as a global type. For the huge presence of the not-properly-housed is part of a bigger network of fears, pressures, and powers that surround housing for everyone in Bombay. Bombay has a shrinking but still large body of tenants, governed by an obsolete rent control act that has been the subject of enormous contention since the beginnings of economic liberalization in the early 1990s. Landlords, especially in South and Central Bombay, are at war with their "old" tenants, who pay tiny rents for real estate worth fortunes in these desirable parts of Bombay. In the mid-1990s, in spite of a dramatic drop in real estate prices across the country, prices per square foot for flats in the most desirable parts of Bombay were between 8,000 and 12,000 rupees. Thus, in U.S. dollars, a fifteen-hundred-square-foot apartment would be valued at between $300,000 and $350,000. Prices in less desirable areas were predictably lower, but consider such prices in a country where more than 40 percent of the population live below the poverty line.

Since about 1992 there have been wild swings in the real estate market, partly fuelled by financial speculators, both local and global. Since 1994 or so, when real estate prices hit their all-time high, there have been drops. There is a complex legal battle, involving the city of Bombay, the state of Maharashtra, and the union government (in Delhi) to reform the tenancy acts pertaining to urban real estate to give some semblance of market rationality to real estate prices. But the tenants are powerfully organized (though relatively small in number), and the landlords like the inflated prices when they sell but not when they have tenants who pay old rent. Homeowners, in cooperatives and condominium style arrangements, also help the upward spiral since they have to think of housing as their most precious possession, potentially convertible into all sorts of other privileges.

In this context, mythologies of housing run rife, and no one is immune from dreams and fantasies. Tenants dream of a day when they will be allowed—by state fiat—to buy their houses for, say, fifteen years' worth of the "old" rent, which, from the point of view of the market, is a pittance. Landlords dream of a free market where they can kick out their poor tenants and bring in wealthy multinationals (believed to be honest and evictable). In the meantime, they allow their buildings to decay, and the municipality has now imposed a forced program of repair and restoration since the façades of these buildings and their internal structures are falling apart, creating a few major collapses and lots of accidents. So South and Central Bombay are strewn with repair projects based on a forced levy on tenants and landlords. Meanwhile, many of these old rent buildings feel like mausoleums, as tenants die or move but hold onto their places by locking them up or having servants take care of them. The vista looking from one of these buildings to another is of ghostly spaces, shut windows, silent verandas—spaces of houses without occupants, often gazing at bodies without houses on the streets and pavements below.

The market in "rental" houses is brisk and illegal, involving vast sums of cash, transacted as so-called *pagri* (key money), which often amounts to more than the market value of the house. The pagri is paid by the new "tenant," who comes in on a much higher rent, and is shared by the landlord and the "selling" tenant who, in fact, is selling his right to stay on distorted rental terms. The landlord seeks the best black money deal, and the buyer pays whatever the market demands.

This black market in "rentals" is even more distorted because its upmarket end is occupied by the multinationals who (through their middlemen) are willing to pay huge down payments (equivalent sometimes to rent for twenty years), along with a high monthly rental. In addition, dealings with multinationals allow such transactions to be legally binding and relatively transparent, as well as, in some ways, prestigious. The growing presence of multinationals with needs for office and residential space has done much to keep real estate values very high in the best parts of Mumbai, in spite of the emergent drift to find headquarters outside the city. This upper end of the market is also the zone of indigenous speculators with large amounts of black money who wish to make big returns. Below this level is the universe of middle-class owners and renters who typically entertain dreams of the big kill when they are in a position to sell their property or their rental rights. And still further down the hierarchy are the varieties of rights in tenements, slums, pavements, and shantytowns, where the buying and selling of rights is decisively connected to local thugs, ward-level politicians, and other smalltime peddlers of influence.

Knitting together this complex edifice of housing-related hysteria is a huge disorganized army of brokers and dealers, whose subculture of solidarity, networking, and jealousy is notorious and resembles that of pimp sociologies in many big cities. These are the individuals who turn up like vultures in every context of viewing or potential sale or change of tenant, ever fearful that buyer and seller will cut them out or that they will lose their share of the deal to others in their own business. These are the individuals who constitute the fiber optics of rumor, price information, news about potential legal changes, and solutions to tricky problems of money transfer, security, and value. They are the foot soldiers of the spectral housing scene, themselves fuelled not by the volume of transactions but by the ideology of the big hit, when a single big transaction will make their fortunes. They are also critical parts of the "nervous system" of spectral housing in Mumbai, in which rumors of big sales, big fees, and "good" and "bad" landlords circulate. It is also these brokers who ruthlessly boycott tenants who "show" their flats just to check the market, but always back out at the last moment, just as certain buyers always back out after everything has been settled. Given the huge cash sums, the secrecy and fear, the greed and transient trust that is required for these deals to be consummated, a reputation for being a "tease" in this market can be fatal.

Beyond all this nervous greed and fluid dealing, in which few explorations actually lead to real changes of owner or occupant, and against the steady buzz of rumors about changes in the law that governs tenancy, ownership, sales, and rights, there is a larger picture of globalization, deindustrialization, and urban planning in which the nervous system of real estate deals meets the muscularity of long-term structural developments in Mumbai's economy. This story has several interactive parts.

Over the last thirty years or so, Bombay has been steadily deindustrialized, especially in its historically most important industrial sector, the production of textiles. An industry that represented the most clear case of a workable compact between state support, entrepreneurial skill, civic amenities, and productive union organization, the mill sector of Central Bombay was for decades the heart of the modernist geography of manufacture in Bombay, with the mills and their associated tenement houses occupying an area of several square miles in Central Bombay (and smaller areas elsewhere). These were solidly working-class neighborhoods, much as in the industrial cities of Europe and the United States at the height of the industrial revolution, and, like them, tied to the imperial-global economies of the nineteenth century. Over the last two decades, several forces have played havoc with this manufacturing core of Bombay. These include the growing obsolescence of equipment, as textile industries worldwide become high tech, and the reluctance of Bombay's indigenous capitalists to negotiate with the unions, stemming from their recognition that cheaper and less militant labor was available in the smaller towns of Maharashtra state (Nasik, Pune, Aurangabad, Nagpur, and many others). This process (as in many parts of the world) has been both a cause and an effect of the move towards flexible, part-time, and insecure forms of labor, the growth in which has steadily taken the fangs out of the union movement in Bombay. In recent years, a more disturbing global pull has reinforced this local process, as major multinationals also start to flee Bombay seeking lower rents, cleaner environments, more pliant labor, and simpler logistical systems.

This trend, in which national and transnational manufacturing is steadily leaving Bombay, is counterbalanced by the continued importance of Bombay's legal, political, and fiscal infrastructure, which cannot be fully outsourced to smaller towns and industrial centers. So the new geography of post-Fordism in Bombay has a set of abandoned factories (or unprofitable ones) at its heart, a growing service economy that has locational advantages not yet matched by smaller towns, a working class that is little more than a host of fragmented unions, and a workforce that has massively shifted to the service sector—with jobs in restaurants, small offices, the film industry, domestic service, computer cafes, "consulting" outfits, street vending, and the university system. In this regard, Bombay fits the broad global profile of swollen megacities that localize national/global speculative and service-oriented interests. In a sense, these are "octroi" economies that subsist by charging fees for intermediary services in transport, licenses, and the like, as industrial work fails to sustain a substantial proletariat.

Among the families that control large parts of these manufacturing enterprises that are being moved out to smaller towns, there is an effort to repackage their motives in the idiom of real estate, arguing that, as they vacate their erstwhile mills, large spaces will be opened up for the "homeless" with appropriate compensation for themselves through the state. Here is another major spectral narrative that dominates the upper ends of the nervous system of Mumbai's housing. A new imaginary is afloat, where thousands of acres of factory space are rumored to be lying idle behind the high walls that conceal the dying factories. Workers still live in the tenements of Parel, Worli, and Nagpada, and many of them listen to the sirens of the factories as they trudge towards this dying field of industrial dreams. But many of the buildings behind these high walls are silent, and, it is rumored, deals are being brokered between these industrialists, big developers, large corporations, and criminal syndicates to harvest these imagined thousands of acres in the very industrial heart of Mumbai. Rumors abound of major presentations by big developers in corporate boardrooms, displaying these lands with aerial shots and projecting the feast of hidden real estate just beyond the famine of the streets and buildings of visible Mumbai.

Here is the great imaginary of vast lands for Mumbai's poor and homeless, which might magically yield housing for those who, for a few decades, have had to go further and further out in order to find a space to live. This is the master specter of housing in Mumbai, a fantasy of huge tracts, some with very few structures on them, ready to be transformed, at the stroke of someone's pen, into Mumbai's paradise of habitation. Thus is the logic of deindustrialization and capital flight rewritten as the story of a chimerical landscape of trees, lakes, and open air waiting to be uncovered just behind the noise of the madding crowd of Central Mumbai. Yet global finance and its indigenous counterparts—as well as a host of other enterprises that rely on trade, speculation, and investment—still find Mumbai seductive, so that the pyramid of high prices and rampant inflation is kept alive and every square foot of housing is defended as personal patrimony.

From the point of view of street life, consumption is fuelled by the explosive growth in small-scale hucksters, vendors, and retailers that have flooded Mumbai's pavements, rendering them almost impassable. Many of these vendor-dominated streets peddle items having to do with the fantasy of a global, middle-class consumer, with the truly smuggled, the imitated pirates, and the homegrown simulacrum all joyously mixed with each other: bras and juicers, lamps and window shades, underwear and cutting knives, sandwich makers and clothespins, decorative kitsch and T-shirts, women's dressing gowns and men's Levis. There seems to be no real annoyance with these vendors, despite the fact that they put pedestrians in the awkward position of either walking on the road (nudged by cars that could kill them), falling into the sewage grates just next to the curb (which are sometimes open), or picking their way through carpets of T-shirts, sneakers, and drinking glasses. In this extraordinary efflorescence of street vending, we see again that cash is king, that money moves, and that some entrepreneurial energy in the greater Mumbai area has moved massively into this retail sector, its provisioning, and its marketing. This market in petty goods, itself fuelled by Mumbai's relatively high wages, has taken the place of other forms of income (for the sellers) and of expenditure (for the buyers).

This immense landscape of street-level traffic in the petty commodities of everyday life is often physically contiguous to permanent shops and glitzy stores where the "A" list versions of the street commodities are also on display. These street markets (a late industrial repetition of the sort of medieval European markets described by Fernand Braudel) allow Mumbai's poorer working people, whose money is scarce but who have bought into the object assemblages of Mumbai's cashocracy, to enter the world of consumption—a world deeply influenced by real or imagined foreign objects, their local incarnations and applications.

But there is more to this than a surfeit of cash among Bombay's middle and working classes (for the indigent can only gaze at these piles of cargo). The key elements of these street bazaars (though the full taxonomy of vendor's goods is as complex as anything Jorge Luis Borges might have imagined), are the materialities of modern domesticity: bras, children's underwear, women's dresses, men's T-shirts and jeans, perfume, cheap lipstick, talcum powder, decorative kitsch, sheets and pillows, mats and posters. The people who throng these places and succeed in negotiating their deals walk away with virtual households, or elements of the collection of goods that might constitute the bourgeois household in some abstract modernist dream. Among other things, there are hundreds of vendors in Mumbai who sell old magazines from the West, including such discrepancies as *Architectural Digest* and *Home and Garden*, ostensibly meant for the creative designer in Mumbai but actually looked at by humbler consumers living in one- or two-room shacks.

These public dramas of consumption revolving around the accoutrements of domesticity constitute an investment in the equipping of houses that may be small and overcrowded, where individual space and rights may be highly restricted, and where much in the way of modern amenities may be limited or absent. These humble objects of domestic life are thus proleptic tools of a domesticity without houses, houseless domesticity. In the purchase and assemblage of these objects, which imply a domestic plenitude that is surely exaggerated, Bombay's working poor and nonprofessional service classes produce their own spectral domesticity, which in its sensuous, cash-based, pleasurable social reality recognizes the shrinking horizon of the actual houses in which these objects might have a predictable life. Of course, all modern shopping (in Mumbai and beyond) has the anticipatory, the imagined, the auratic, and the possessive about its ethos. But street shopping in Mumbai, like public sleeping, is a form of claim to housing that no one can contest or subvert in the city of cash. This is where the specters of eviction meet the agencies of consumption.

We now turn to an explicit effort to engage the slippage between Bombay and Mumbai, in this essay and in the social usages of the city. If Bombay was a historical space of commerce and cosmopolitanism, through what project did Bombay become Mumbai, so that, today, all official dealings, from control-tower traffic at Sahar airport to addresses on letters mailed to the city, must refer to Mumbai? What killed Bombay?

In the section that follows, I try to answer this question by linking the problems of scarcity and spectrality in the housing market to another kind of shrinkage, which is produced by the repositioning of Bombay's streets, shops, and homes as a sacred national space, as an urban rendition of a Hindu national geography. As struggles over the space of housing, vending, and sleeping gradually intensified, so did the sense of Bombay as a site for traffic across ethnic boundaries become reduced. The explosive violence of 1992–93 translated the problem of scarce space into the imaginary of cleansed space, a space without Muslim bodies. In and through the violence of these riots, an urban nightmare was rescripted as a national dream.

Urban cleansing

In 1996 the Shiva Sena proclaimed that Bombay would henceforth be only known as Mumbai. Even prior to this date, Mumbai had been the name for the city preferred by many of the Marathi-speaking majority, and especially by those who identify with the Shiva Sena. In one sense, the decision to officialize the name "Mumbai" is part of a widespread Indian pattern of replacing names associated with colonial rule with names associated with local, national, and regional heroes. It is an indigenizing toponymic strategy worldwide in scope.

In the case of Bombay, the move looks backward and forward simultaneously. Looking backward, it imagines the deity Mumba Devi (a goddess of one of the shrines that was vital to the fishing islands that later became Bombay). It evokes the fishing folk of these islands, and, because it is the name that was always used by Marathi speakers, it privileges their everyday usage over those of many other vernacular renditions of the name (such as the "Bambai" favored by Hindi speakers and the "Bambaai" of Tamil speakers). Of course, it gains respectability as an erasure of the Anglophone name, Bombay, and thus carries the surface respectability of popular nationalism after 1947. But its subtext looks to the future, to a counter-Bombay or anti-Bombay, as imagined by the Shiva Sena, whose political fortunes in the city wax and wane (as of this writing) but whose hold on urban life no one has dared to write off.

This is a future in which Marathi and Maharashtrian heroes and practices dominate urban culture, and this purified regional city joins a renascent "Hindu" India; it is a future that envisions Mumbai as a point of translation and mediation between a renascent Maharashtra and a re-Hinduized India. This Mumbai of the future is sacred national space, ethnically pure but globally competitive. Balasaheb Thackeray, the vitriolic head of the Shiva Sena, was happy to welcome Michael Jackson to his home a few years ago and had no trouble facilitating a major deal for Enron, a Texas-based multinational that wanted a major set of concessions for a new energy enterprise in Maharashtra. So the transformation of Bombay into Mumbai is part of a contradictory utopia in which an ethnically cleansed city is still the gateway to the world.

When the Babri Masjid in Ayodhya was destroyed by Hindu vandals on 6 December 1992, a watershed was marked in the history of secularism in India, in the context of a big effort to Hinduize India and to link local ethnopolitics and national xenophobia. The events of December 1992 were themselves the product of an immensely complex process by which the major political parties of the Hindu right, most notably the BJP (Bharatiya Janata Party), managed to turn a series of recent political changes in the Hindi-speaking northern part of India to their advantage. These changes—most important among them the new political power of lower castes—were often results of violent confrontations between lower and upper castes over land tenure, government job quotas, and legal rights. In the late 1980s, building on a century of localized movements towards Hindu nationalism and nationalized Hinduism, the BJP and its allies had mobilized hitherto fragmented parties and movements under the single banner of Hindutva (Hinduness). Seizing on the failures of other national parties, they managed to launch a full-scale frontal attack on the ideals of secularism and inter-religious harmony enshrined in the constitution and to convince Hindus of all classes that their salvation lay in Hinduizing the state.

In the process, they focused particularly on a series of neoreligious strategies and practices, drawing on existing cultural repertoires, to construct the imaginary of a Hindu soil, a Hindu history, and Hindu sacred places that had been corrupted and obscured by many outside forces, none worse than the forces of Islam. Anti-Muslim sentiments, available in various earlier discourses and movements, were transformed into what Romila Thapar called "syndicated" Hinduism, and one form of this politicized Hinduism took as its major program the liberation of Hindu temples from what were argued to be their illegitimate Muslim superstructures. The Babri Masjid became the symbolic epicenter of this more general campaign to cleanse Hindu space and nationalize the polity through a politics of archaeology, historical revisionism, and vandalism. The story of the events surrounding the destruction of the Babri Masjid has been well told elsewhere, and many scholars have placed these events in the deep history of Hindu-Muslim relations on the subcontinent.

There were riots after 6 December 1992 throughout India, substantially amounting to a national pogrom against Muslims (though there was some Muslim violence against agents and sites of state power). But this was the first time there was a massive, nationwide campaign of violence against Muslims in which soil, space, and site came together in a politics of national sovereignty and integrity. Not only were Muslims seen as traitors (Pakistanis in disguise), but also their sacred sites were portrayed as a treacherous geography of vandalism and desecration, calculated to bury Hindu national geography at both its centers and its margins. In a sense, the political geography of sovereignty, focused on border wars with Pakistan, was brought into the same emotional space as the political geography of cultural purity, focused on the deep archaeology of religious monuments.

As it was the home of the Shiva Sena, Mumbai was drawn into this argument about national geography as Hindu geography in December 1992 in a special way. The story of the growth of the Shiva Sena from the 1960s to the present has been well told and analyzed elsewhere, so just a few points need be made here. The party has succeeded in identifying with the interests of Mumbai's growing Marathi-speaking lumpen proletariat while also actively destroying its left (communist) union culture. After starting mainly as a group of urban thugs, the Shiva Sena has managed to become a regional and national political force. It has hitched its regional nationalism (with deep roots in Maharashtra's ethnohistory and vernacular self-consciousness) to a broader national politics of Hindutva. It has created a relatively seamless link between its nativist, pro-Maharashtrian message and a national politics of confrontation with Pakistan. It has sutured a specific form of regional chauvinism with a national message about Hindu power through the deployment of the figure of the Muslim as the archetype of the invader, the stranger, and the traitor. The Shiva Sena has achieved this suture by a remarkably patient and powerful media campaign of hate, rumor, and mobilization, notably in the party newspaper *Saamna*, which has been the favorite reading of Mumbai's policemen for at least two decades. The Shiva Sena has done all this by systematically gutting the apparatus of city government, by criminalizing city politics at every level, and by working hand-in-glove with organized crime in many areas, notably in real estate, which brings us back to space and its politics in Mumbai.

Here we need to note certain important facts. According to several analysts, about 50 percent of Mumbai's 12 million citizens live in slums or other degraded forms of housing. Another 10 percent are estimated to be pavement dwellers. This amounts to more then 5 million people living in degraded (and degrading) forms of housing. Yet, according to one recent estimate, slum dwellers occupy only about 8 percent of the city's land, which totals about 43,000 hectares. The rest of the city's land is either industrial land, middle- and high-income housing, or vacant land in the control of the city, the state, or private commercial interests. Bottom line: 5 million poor people live in 8 percent of the land area of a city no bigger than Manhattan and its near boroughs. As some have observed, it is amazing that in these conditions of unbelievable crowding, lack of amenities, and outright struggle for daily survival, Mumbai's poor have not exploded more often.

But they did explode in the riots of 1992–93. During the several weeks of intense rioting after 6 December, there is no doubt that the worst damage was done among those who lived in the most crowded, unredeemable slums. The worst zones of violence were among the very poorest, in areas such as Behrampada, where Hindu and Muslim "toilers," in Sandeep Pendse's powerful usage, were pitted against each other by neighborhood thugs, Shiva Sena bosses, and indifferent police. Though the Indian Army was called in to impose order, the fabric of social relations among Mumbai's poor was deeply damaged by repeated episodes of arson, rape, murder, property damage, and eviction.

In these few weeks of December 1992 and January 1993, there was also a frenzied mobilization by the Shiva Sena of its sympathizers to create public terror and to confront Muslims with the message that there was no public space for them and that they would be hunted down and killed or evicted from their homes wherever possible. There was a marked increase in ethnocidal uses of a new ritual form—the *maha arati*[1]—which was a kind of guerrilla form of public worship organized by Hindu groups to push Muslims out of streets and public spaces in areas where the two groups lived cheek by jowl. These ritual acts of ethnic warfare were mostly conducted in the middle-class rental zones of Central Mumbai; but in the slums and jopad-pattis of the north and west there was firebombing and arson, street murders and beatings, and the main victims were the poorest of the Muslim poor—rag pickers, abattoir workers, manual laborers, indigents. Across the city, the Shiva Sena mobilized a national geography, spreading the rumor that the Pakistani navy was about to attack Mumbai from its shoreline on the Arabian Sea, and anxious Hindu residents turned searchlights onto the ocean to spot Pakistani warships.

Meanwhile, inside the city, Muslims were cornered in slums and middle-class areas, in their own crowded spaces, hunted down with lists of names in the hands of organized mobs, and Muslim businesses and properties were relentlessly put to the torch. There was a strange point of conjuncture between these violent efforts to create Hindu public spheres and spaces, to depopulate Muslim flats and neighborhoods, and to destroy Muslim bodies and properties, and an ongoing form of civic violence directed against Mumbai's street dwellers, which I discuss below.

In the weeks preceding 6 December, there had been a renewed effort by the Municipal Corporation to destroy the structures built by unlicensed street vendors and to destroy unauthorized residential dwellings that had sprouted throughout Mumbai. Here, municipal zeal (personified by G. Khairnar, an overzealous city official who was strangely not a Shiva Sena client) joined with political propaganda to create a tinderbox in the heavily Muslim areas of Central Bombay from Bhendi Bazaar to Byculla, especially along Mohammed Ali Road, the great Muslim thoroughfare of contemporary Mumbai. In this neighborhood, Muslim gangsters had worked with the connivance of shady financiers and corrupt city officials to build many unauthorized residential structures (through intimidation, forgery, and other subversions of the law) while terrorizing any potential resistors with armed force.

The Bombay municipality has had a tradition of chasing after street vendors for at least three decades in a constant public battle of cat-and-mouse that the vendors usually won. There was also a long and dark history of efforts to tear down slum dwellings, as in other cities in India. But in the late 1980s, this battle was intensified, as the nexus between real estate speculators, organized crime, and corrupt officialdom reached new heights. Although this nexus involved illegal housing and unlicensed vending throughout Mumbai, Khairnar's muncipal gendarmerie just happened to focus their civic violence on an area dominated by the Muslim underworld. Thus, tragically, just before the Babri Masjid was destroyed in Ayodhya,

Bombay's Muslim underworld was in a rage, and Mumbai's Muslim residents were convinced that there was, indeed, a civic effort to dismantle their dwellings and vending stalls. This is where the battle for space—a heated triangle involving organized mafias, corrupt local officials and politicians, and a completely predatory class of real estate speculators—met the radical politics of Hindutva in December 1992.

The story of this encounter is sufficiently complex as to require detailed treatment elsewhere. But the big picture is relevant here. The geography of violence in Mumbai during December 1992 and January 1993 is overwhelmingly coincident with the geography of urban crowding, street commerce, and housing nightmares in Mumbai. In this violence, two grisly specters came to haunt and animate one another in the world of Mumbai's poorest citizens, as well as its working classes: the specter of a zero-sum battle for residential space and street commerce, figured as a struggle between civic discipline and organized crime; and the specter of Mumbai's Muslims as a fifth column from Pakistan, ready to subvert Mumbai's sacred geography.

In this macabre conjuncture, the most horrendously poor, crowded, and degraded areas of the city were turned into battlegrounds of the poor against the poor, with the figure of the Muslim providing the link between scarce housing, illegal commerce, and national geography writ urban. In 1992–93, in a word, spectral housing met ethnic fear, and the Muslim body was the site of this terrifying negotiation. Of course, the middle and upper classes suffered as well, largely through the stoppage of commerce, movement, and production. But the overwhelming burden of violence—both its perpetration and its suffering—was borne by the bodies of Mumbai's toilers and the massive sense of having no place in Mumbai (reinscribed as India) was overwhelmingly borne by its Muslims.

Here we must return to consider the links between spectral housing, the decosmopolitanizing of Bombay, and the ethnic violence of 1992 and 1993. The deliberate effort to terrorize Bombay's Muslims, to attack their vending stalls, to burn their shops and homes, to Hinduize their public spaces through violent ritual innovations, and to burn and maim their bodies can hardly be seen as a public policy solution to Bombay's housing problems. Neither can it be laid at the door of a single agency or power, even one so powerful and central to these events as the Shiva Sena. But it does seem plausible to suggest that in a city where daily sociality involves the negotiations of immense spatial stress, the many spectralities that surround housing (from indigent bodies to fantasy housing schemes and empty flats) can create the conditions for a violent reinscription of public space as Hindu space. In a city of 12 million persons, many occupying no more space than their bodies, it is not hard to see that imagining a city without Muslims, a sacred and Hindu city, free of the traffic of cash and the promiscuity of "business" (think of all the burnt Muslim shops of 1992 and 1993), could appear—briefly—to be a bizarre utopia of urban renewal. This monstrous utopia cannot be imagined without the spectral economies of Bombay's housing. But it also needed a political vision—the Shiva Sena's vision of a Hindu Mumbai—to move it towards fire and death.

The rest was contingency—or conjuncture.

Arguments for the real

This is a grim story about one of the world's most dramatic scenes of urban inequality and spectral citizenship. But specters and utopias—as practices of the imagination—occupy the same moral terrain. And Bombay does not lack for a complex politics of the real. Throughout the twentieth century, and even in the nineteenth century, Bombay had powerful civic traditions of philanthropy, social work, political activism, and social justice. These traditions have stayed powerful in the last three decades of the twentieth century and at the beginning of the twenty-first century, where globalization, deindustrialization, and ethno-urbanism have become linked forces. Both before and after the 1992–93 riots, there have been extraordinary displays of courage and critical imagination in Mumbai. These have come from neighborhood groups (*mohulla* committees) committed to squelching rumors and defusing Hindu-Muslim tensions; from housing activists; from lawyers and social workers; and from journalists, architects, and trade union activists. All of these individuals and groups have held up powerful images of a cosmopolitan, secular, multicultural Bombay, and a Mumbai whose 43,000 hectares could be reorganized to accommodate its 5 million poorly housed citizens.

These activist organizations—among them some of the most creative and brilliant pro-poor and housing-related nongovernmental organizations (NGOs)—are making their own arguments about the political real in Mumbai. Their story, which, among other things, has forced the publication of an extraordinary judicial report on the 1992–93 riots (which the Shiva Sena government tried mightily to bury), will be fully told elsewhere. This story is also linked to the extraordinary courage of ordinary people in Mumbai, and often among the poorest of the poor, to shelter their friends and neighbors from ethnocidal mob violence. These utopian visions and critical practices are resolutely modernist in their visions of equity, justice, and cultural cosmopolitanism. In the spectral world that I have described, they are not naive or nostalgic. They are part of the ongoing struggle for that space where Mumbai's Real meets the real Bombay.

Note

1   The maha arati is widely conceded to be a ritual innovation by the Shiva Sena, first developed in December 1992, in which a domestic Hindu ritual, traditionally conducted indoors, was converted into a large-scale, public devotional offering to various Hindu gods and goddesses. It is marked by the centrality of sacred fires (as in most domestic worship among Hindus), and, in this new format, was also accompanied by elaborate and incendiary anti-Muslim speeches and exhortations by pro-Hindu politicians and public figures. By various reliable estimates, it appears that several hundred of these inciting rituals were staged in the period between 6 December 1992 and 15 January 1993 in major streets, intersections, parks, and neighborhoods in Bombay. The *Report of the Srikrishna Commission* notes the high correlation between these public rituals and the frenzied destruction of Muslim lives and property when the crowds dispersed after these high-intensity politico-ritual spectacles. A full account of this major new cultural form is yet to appear in print.

Bibliographical note

There is a large scholarly literature that constitutes the foundation for this ethnographic essay. In lieu of detailed citations, I offer some indications of a few major debts and scholarly engagements. This essay would have been unthinkable without the major two-volume collection of essays on Bombay edited by Sujata Patel and Alice Thorner—*Bombay: Mosaic of Modern Culture* and *Bombay: Metaphor for Modern India* (Bombay: Oxford University Press, 1995). See also *Bombay: The Cities Within* by Sharada Dwivedi and Rahul Mehrotra (Bombay: India Book House, 1995) and *Damning Verdict: Report of the Srikrishna Commission* (Mumbai: Sabrang Communications and Publishing, n.d.). My sense of the predicament of megacities in Asia and elsewhere has been deeply informed by the work of my friend and colleague Saskia Sassen. My understanding of Bombay's special housing dilemmas has been enriched by a series of case studies and reports produced by A. Jockin, Sundar Burra, Celine D'Cruz, and Sheela Patel. My debts in regard to the analysis of Hindu nationalism in Bombay are too many to list, but special mention must be made of the ongoing work of Thomas Blom Hansen—see, for instance, *The Saffron Wave: Democracy and Hindu Nationalism in Modern India* (Princeton, NJ: Princeton University Press, 1999) —Ranjit Hoskote, and Kalpana Sharma. See also Romila Thapar, "Syndicated Hinduism" in *Hinduism Reconsidered*, edited by Günther-Dietz Sontheimer and Hermann Kulke (New Delhi: Manohar Publications, 1989), and Sandeep Pendse, "Toil, Sweat, and the City" in Patel and Thorner's *Bombay: Metaphor for Modern India*. My recourse to the trope of the *spectral* is on an ongoing engagement with the work of Jacques Derrida, Fredric Jameson, and James Siegel, though they may well not recognize themselves in this text.

11

from ( ) of Ghosts

Peter Hitchcock

I do not believe I have ever spoken of "indeterminacy," whether in regard to "meaning" or anything else. Undecidability is something else again. While referring to what I have said above and elsewhere, I want to recall that undecidability is always a determinate *oscillation between possibilities (for example, of meaning but also of acts).*

JACQUES DERRIDA

Capitalism as a world system is haunted. One hundred and fifty years after Marx and Engels's celebrated invocation of the specter haunting Europe, it torments the world. Derrida opines that there is no *Dasein* of the specter, and this, he believes, is why a Marxism that eschews the eschatology and ontology of Being must always return — must remain, in spirit, to haunt the contradictions of capitalist rationality.[1] It is an intriguing proposition and one that will certainly lurk in the pages that follow. One wonders, however, whether the ghost that Derrida conjures — the spirit of a Marxism internally differentiated (or *différantiated*) by the equivocation of the "event" of revolution (deferred then, within a structure of oscillation) — is a compensatory mechanism. It is not a personal compensation (Derrida always has an easy answer for that) but a conjuring wrought by the stunning absence of the event interpellated by Marx and Engels. Where there is no communism, what is left but to inure the spirit of its absence? A millennial materialism begins with this fact (as startling as ice cold water on a face quick from slumber): the claims of "actual existence" (of socialism, of communism), the bulwark of a traditional ontology in Marxist thought, lie almost completely disgraced across the landscape of history. And this is why the spirit of Marxism, the specter that haunts, is a problem of philosophy, a philosophy that struggles to articulate a process of political practice without succumbing to the mystique of interpretation, the dead-end that the eleventh thesis on Feuerbach explicitly warns against. Marxism oscillates now most forcefully around and between the elements of a philosophy that must remain dubiously inchoate and incoherent. "Without doubt" this sounds like the worst politics of all — a quagmire as deep and muddy as the state bureaucracies of "actually existing socialism" had become. Yet it is precisely the reinscription of this philosophical problem (What is the philosophy of Marxism?) that traces the differential space of the political in millennial materialism. The vacillation of the moment is an index not of the teleology that must be but of a constellation that *is*, an architectonic of what structures contemporary reality. Thus, the ghost is manifest in the way the philosophical problem is posed, and not simply as a projection of spirit onto an otherwise foreboding political situation: the absence of "actual existence."[2]

Oscillation as a concept elaborates a philosophical trace in the forms of praxis meant to subtend it. The restlessness is the spirit that looks over the shoulder of the forms of the political now possible. This ambivalence, a philosophical compulsion, is more pronounced in moments of crisis or, as I would contend, in *interregna*. But it is not just philosophy that marks contingent possibilities. As I tried to emphasize with the chronotope of the shoe, the worker within the logic of transnationalism is confined to spectrality as never before — these billions of ghosts who live and breathe but who do not devolve into classes, and yet whose concrete individuality cannot corporealize except through abstract conjunction.[3] We will not sentimentalize the once-occurrent Being of the workers of the world, as if that injunction might realize the "Unite!" of the *Communist Manifesto* — which was only ever, and can only be, a provisor (no *Dasein* indeed). But "the time is out of joint," as Shakespeare/Hamlet/Derrida tell us, and philosophy speaks to the break in that continuum, to the specificity of the worker's unrepresentability now unhinged from the state's ardent and arrogant delegation — those phantom states, as Derrida terms them, that have "infiltrated and banalized themselves everywhere" (*SOM* 83).

Similarly, as my exegesis on the body has indicated, the incarnation of a body subject — one that disarticulates the decorporealization of capitalism, the empty flesh of value extraction — oscillates within the history of materialist theory as a conceptual shade of the historical agents it attempts to recorporealize.[4] It is not mindless metaphoricity or torpid tropism that puts these spirits into play, but the oscillations of materialist thought itself. When Balibar boldly declares, "There is no Marxist philosophy and there never will be,"[5] he draws attention not only to Marx's antagonistic relationship to traditional philosophy (the Hegelian dialectic, etc.) but also to the nature of Marxist critical faculties, its dynamism with respect to historical determination: it cannot resolve itself into a philosophical system qua philosophy. Indeed, with respect to philosophy within Marxism (as Balibar shows on the question of ideology), Marxism is beside itself. Its systematicity is bound, paradoxically, by a spiritual double, an other Being that constantly troubles or undermines the philosophical underpinnings of its social prescriptions. The specters of Marx are not just the workers who do not have a social form for their socialization or realization, but the philosophical ghosts that Marxism cannot simply put to rest within its critical framework without collapsing it.

What follows is a philosophical answer to the double entendre of the ever-more-prescient question, Whither Marxism? In the ghostly presence of philosophy in Marxism, Marxism itself opens out onto different plains of social explanation. The danger, or vacillation, comes with the tenor of philosophy (which is why Balibar's statement must be closely observed) whose very language mimes the floating signifier's metonymic dance. I do not wish to save materialism from a certain irreducible play in language (it is social praxis itself that exceeds the linguistic predilections of discourse), but I do want to outline some of the conceptual instabilities that sign back across philosophy's semiosis of the social. On one level, to acknowledge the ghosts of Marxism is to reincarnate the founding spirit of Marx and Engels's injunction; on another, to take seriously the spirit of the letter is to address the Being and the space of Marxism now. The question Whither Marxism? does not necessitate fatalism: it requires an exorcism.

Specters of Marx and *Whither Marxism?* are two volumes that came out of a conference conceived by Bernd Magnus and Stephen Cullenberg at the University of California, Riverside, in 1993, and, to be sure, Derrida's spectral philosophy in the first volume haunts the collection of essays that compose the second book.[6] These are not, however, "companion" volumes as the editors contend. Derrida's contribution is in the spirit of the question posed by the collection and the conference, but it is also "out of joint," to use the epigraph that Derrida borrows from Hamlet and interrogates within his text. In the haunting presence of the Derridean mode, *Specters of Marx* fulfills two practical aims: first, it "proves" (and there is always already a beyond a "reasonable" doubt) that Marx, like Derrida, was fascinated by the history of ghosts (*Gespenstergeschichte*), a penchant that begins and permeates the materialism in his prose; second, Derrida's interpretation functions as an ambivalent shadow of the arguments entertained in the collection of essays, something that is less a "companion" and more a principle of "nonidentification." That this is in step with the general trajectory of deconstruction is obvious; what is less clear is whether it is the logic of Marxism, the *philosophies* of Marx as Balibar puts it, that draws or conjures the spirit of deconstruction toward it. In a strange way, what keeps coming back is the tendency that Michael Ryan identified almost two decades ago: that the kind of Marxism that deconstruction disables is the kind that deserves to be disabled.[7] Nevertheless, this ghostly return, this *revenant*, does not make deconstruction the autocritical function of Marxism, as some might wish, for if poststructuralist theory has deservedly pounced on the more flagrant examples of essentialism within materialist theory, then Marxism (from Ryan's position of "critical articulation" to Spivak's, Jameson's, and Eagleton's various disarticulations) has passionately resisted the idealism of textuality and textualism. My point is that the relationship is not resolvable in the way that two "companions" might embrace one another after sustained disagreement. The impasse is intrinsic to the methodologies at issue. In this sense, the ghostly metaphors that animate the prose of Derrida and Marx are not stylistic trivialities: they mark the conceptual difficulties of the "*philosophies* of Marx."

Now, to the extent that Ryan has already demonstrated the undecidability written into the conceptual terrain of Marxism, the problems posed by Derrida in *Specters of Marx* are quite literally prescribed. Ryan's discussion of the law of value, for instance, preempts in a rigorous way Derrida's somewhat casual reading of *Capital* on the question of the table as an example of the commodity form.[8] But, as I hope the analysis of the aura of the shoe has confirmed, there remains a mystery in the commodity that the hyperreality of the present does not simply sublate. Derrida addresses new contingencies not just because the ghost is his primary touchstone (which nicely expresses the paradox of its deployment — it is immaterial and cannot be touched) but because the nature of the relation articulated has profoundly changed in light of the events of the late 1980s and early 1990s. What may have been read as a prediction in Ryan's uneasy rapprochement is now a condition of the present. The ghost of philosophy, of a certain spirit in philosophy, has become almost worldly in light of the collapse of communism's social mandate. The era is not necessarily one of philosophical reflexion, however (except to the extent that reflexion remains part of the problem — According to what logic?), but is one where philosophy may speak to the process of spiriting away that some Western ideologues seem to foster (and thus, fear a return in Poland, Russia, Hungary, etc.).

I will not focus on all of the implications of Derrida's text (precisely because they might conspire to conjure away a politics that must be rethought, not rejected), but I do want to consider in some detail how "thinking the ghost" might reanimate materialist critique. I will do this obliquely in a number of ways. First, I want to examine the status of "class" among the specters of Marx that Derrida invokes and read this, not into the "companion" volume of the conference, but into Balibar's essay "From Class Struggle to Classless Struggle?" (which, coincidentally, also begins with the question, "Whither Marxism?").[9] I will argue that, far from going away or disappearing, the dislocations of the present have *incarnated* the question of class in a historically specific manner. Second, if as a concept oscillation partakes of a deterritorialization of space (and is what Deleuze and Guattari describe as a geophilosophy in that regard),[10] what is its relationship to the worlding of the world as world system? I have already pressed the issue in terms of imagination, which makes class and class subjects like Sadisah less a cognitive fantasy; but what if the desire to imagine such a world is itself implicated in the philosophical systematization of subjection?[11] This is not simply a question about the specter of Marxism's roots in the Western Enlightenment, but addresses what the consequences of global integration are for a materialism that must learn from its conceptual oscillations. To think globally one must sense the world differently from the synaptic largesse of capital. Here, politically, what comes back to materialism is the ghostly apparition of "freedom" or "emancipation," which was an assumption that became dogmatic in some of its expressions, but now returns in the form of a different philosophical dilemma, as something that cannot yet be thought of except in ghostly fashion. Jean-Luc Nancy has suggested that this requires a revolution in thinking itself, but only if we free this call from the voluntarisms of yesteryear.[12] Finally, "thinking the ghost" will take me back to ideology, the oscillation with which I began. Here, however, the exorcism is on the order of production and will register a materialism caught between its thought and consequences. Lest this sound too much like the familiar theory/practice binary I should add that I will read this against the philosopher's tendency to hypostatize this moment as a discursive dead-end. In oscillation, all roads do not lead straight back to the signifier: reality keeps making detours and providing alternative intensities. This remains the trajectory if not the answer to the specters that haunt us.

Class is the most ghostly concept within Marxism, and I will not rehearse that history (history back in its hearse?) in order to justify its centrality. Class, of course, is not a thing but a concept of relation (something with enough tempera-spatial import to connect it with our chief conceptual tool), which has made it all the more easy, apparently, to spirit it away according to the dictates of hegemonies of various kinds. As Balibar notes, quoting from Spinoza: "There is more than one way to perish."[13] If we have indeed produced social orders that construct classes and class divisions, then those systems and their classes are condemned to expire at some point in history (that is to say, they are historical systems). But there lies the trick of the spirit of class, and one that resists the eschatology that seems synonymous with such statements. The death of a world system does not correspond to the hasty analogy of our fated selves. Class does not live in the same way as its breathing constituents. This is why we must separate class from its experience or identification. The lack of the visibility of class is quite widespread today, but that is different from the object of class for science, or for Marxism for science. But surely, this does not make class a ghost.

Indubitably so. Class cannot be thought as a ghost; it is an example, however, of how to think the ghost. For Derrida, the scrupulous philosopher, the thingness of the ghost is its relationship to the Thing, not its identity as a thing. The distinction is important, not least because it helps to separate identity from presence. The specter is a special kind of ghost, for it appears as a "stealthy and ungraspable visibility of the invisible" ("la visibilité furtive et insaisissable de l'invisible" [*SDM* 27]) — let us call it the spirit of the Thing. Thinking the ghost is precisely this coming to grips with the ungraspable. Deconstructive practice is founded (and founders) on this difficulty: it is a calculation without rules between the incalculable and the calculable. It seems to me that although Derrida once said that he had found no "satisfactory protocols for reading Marx,"[14] those protocols seem to have found him; they have come back; they keep coming back first as a dimly remembered utopianism and now as a fully fledged critical approach. The specters of Marx are the materialist injunction of iterability. But does class, like communism, return in this way?

Here Derrida is less useful. He tracks the Marxist invocation of the specter in the *Communist Manifesto*, *The Eighteenth Brumaire*, and *The German Ideology* in a variety of ways (he is particularly jubilant about the Stirner/Marx conjunction), but his critique is also a symptom of the "out-of-jointness" of our time eliding the importance of class to the spectrality he otherwise quite forcefully presents. Note, it is not the primacy of class that is at issue, but its constitutive role in modes of socialization. Nevertheless, the implications of Derrida's approach must be engaged and/or otherwise extended, not least of which because the theoretical question he addresses cannot be answered by Marxism alone (a protocol that says that a philosophy cannot adjudicate its own meaning). This much Balibar admits when he asks the question "Whither Marxism?" but this is also why he attends to Marxism's philosophical disposition in *The Philosophy of Marx* by using the following formula (between the calculable and the incalculable):

L'activité de Marx, ayant rompu avec une certaine forme de philosophe, ne l'a pas conduit vers un système unifié, mais vers une *pluralité* au moins virtuelle de doctrines, dans lesquelles ses lecteurs et ses successeurs se sont trouvés embarrassés. De même, elle ne l'a pas conduit vers un discours uniforme, mais vers une oscillation permanente entre l'en deçà et l'au-delà de la philosophie. Par en *deçà* de la philosophie, entendons ici l'énoncé de propositions comme des "conclusions sans prémisses," ainsi qu'auraient dit Spinoza et Althusser. (*PDM* 6)

[Having broken with a certain form of philosophy, Marx was not driven by his theoretical activity toward a unified system, but to a virtual *plurality* of doctrines that his readers and successors have found perplexing. In the same way, it did not lead him to a uniform discourse, but to a permanent oscillation between "falling short of" and "moving beyond" philosophy. By *falling short* of philosophy, I mean stating propositions as "conclusions without premisses," as Spinoza and Althusser would have said it. (*POM* 4)]

If it seems as though I am moving Marxism in and around deconstruction, it is only because the latter, in spirit, moves to and within it. As Ryan notes: "Marxism, as a historical mode of theory and practice is, from the outset undecidable, that is, open to extension according to what history offers" (21). But iterability has almost always given way to irritability where Marxism and deconstruction are concerned. Where the latter disagrees wherever it finds eschatology and positivism, the former deplores a vacuum of tropology where social theory should be. But Balibar, nevertheless, offers a vision not just of a Marxism beset by the weight of its contradictory theorizations, but of one whose ambivalent relationship to philosophy, "short of and beyond," calls it into question in such a way as to open out its concepts into the realm of the political. The oscillations of Marxism are therapeutic for philosophy in the sense that they are homeopathic. And this is as true for philosophy with respect to Marxism, as long as we keep in mind that in the Pharmakon of ideas the line between poison and cure is itself an undecidable ("an oscillation between possibilities").

I have written about Derrida's use of Hamlet's quip "The time is out of joint" elsewhere as a suitable if problematic description for the disjunctions and dislocations of the present.[15] Central to this out-of-jointness is the diminution of class within materialism. Within theory, much of this can be placed at the doorstep of cultural materialism (a doorstep that already has tripped up a good many residents on their way in). But, of course, it is the objective conditions of the world system that have been pivotal in this regard, and this is why class goes away and comes back as a ghost in Balibar's critique (this is what is so odd in Derrida's speculative and spectral investigation: class is the ghost who is precisely not addressed). Most of these factors are well known: the deindustrialization of large sectors of Western Europe and North America accompanied by the burgeoning of service industries, de-skilling, and "acceptable levels" of unemployment (which has often meant recalculating the figures until an acceptable level is found!); the transnationalism and flexible accumulation strategies of major corporations that have decentered (or obliterated) traditional communities of opposition (attributable both to location and to organized resistance — unions, for instance); the financialization of capital circulation aided and abetted by technological advances and outright speculation that has denatured traditional class discourse; the rise and fall of nation-states that have both nurtured and malnourished consciousness of social position (to think the ghost is already to imagine one's community otherwise); and the emergence of several competing political discourses that have, if not turned the world upside down, made it imperative and possible not to think in the same way about social change. These factors are only viable causes for the diminution of class as they are articulated simultaneously at the social, political, and economic levels of theoretical analysis. This is indeed part of Balibar's approach, but, as we have noted, the first line of reflection is focused on the conceptual ambivalence of class as it is developed in Marx's writing.

When Balibar notes that classes have lost their "*visible*" identity (his emphasis), we know that it is visibility itself that is in question. Marxist critique depends on "grasping" the visible of the invisible — that the illusion of classlessness is a reality of the concept of class, something *both* historically determined and intrinsic to its ambivalent formulation. On one level, thinking the ghost means understanding the incommensurableness of the concept with its instantiation (again, the space between the calculable and the incalculable); on another level, it means separating a theoretical invocation from a historical conjuration. At a séance one may be predisposed to receive the spirit one desires, but in history class comes and goes (as Derrida notes, the specter always "begins by coming back" ["il commence par revenir"] [*SDM* 32]) according to a more complex pathology.

Balibar approaches the problem in two ways, by examining the contradictory logic of proletarianization and by picking away at the structural identity of capitalist class formations. In both cases he roots the conceptual instability in a reading of Marx, but the problem then becomes whether the present conjuncture provides an exit to the various kinds of impasse he identifies or whether these ambiguities are intrinsic to the methodology at stake. As I have tried to indicate throughout this study, much depends on the interpretative gambit here, overdetermined as it is by the intense oscillations that characterize if not define contemporary existence. I will provide a couple of brief examples from Balibar, but in the main I am interested in pushing the implications of his critique a good deal further than the first circle of his inquiry. It is only in this way that the Marxism he elucidates might be seen to haunt even the unlikely discourses of contemporary philosophy.

Following my exposition of the different interpretive levels of oscillation, it is clear that the initial conditions for the theorization of class in Marx's works (and subsequently, therefore, in Marxian extrapolations) are riven by contingent fluctuations so that we see a stark difference in formulations between what Balibar calls the "historic-political" writings and *Capital* itself. In Balibar's view, the former "suffer indirectly from the circumstances of their writing. The pictures they paint are like an adaptation of a basic historical scheme to the peripeteia of empirical history (for the most part European history), and they oscillate constantly between a posteriori rectification and anticipation" ("Class," 159). In these documents, the immediate conditions of theory produce what Balibar describes as personification, which makes it strategically easier to array one class against another as a series of symmetrical agents. This means plugging in the theory to examples that tend to render the characteristics of class ambivalent (think of the personification of Louis Napoleon for instance). *Capital* never quite lets go of the strategy of personification (to this extent, it too partakes of the "peripeteia of empirical history") but, crucially, presents a class struggle in fundamental "dissymmetry." Whether bourgeois or capitalist (these terms themselves are in oscillation) the ruling orders in *Capital* do not constitute one social group. In contrast, argues Balibar, the proletariat or working class (as we have seen, another oscillatory scission) appear always already constituted in the valorization of capital and capital accumulation. In a sense, suggests Balibar, there is only one class in *Capital*, and that is the working class (indeed, Marx says as much in his postface to the second edition).[16]

Certainly, the large sections of *Capital* devoted to the processes of proletarianization (the appropriation of surplus value, the expropriation of working skills, and the production of insecurity through competition) support Balibar's contention regarding dissymmetry. But, in personifying the capitalists and depersonalizing the workers in order that the latter might be more properly recognized for their group characteristics, Marx presents this dissymmetry in a contradictory form, one that comes with a significant risk. In *Capital*, the processes of proletarianization are not identical with a subject of those processes. What the processes do is produce effects that provide the character of class without its subject. Ironically, the dissymmetry that Balibar identifies has an opposite implication: *Capital* is about one class that is unrepresentable.

That labor is indeed nonidentical with itself is a function of capital: that is what it does to workers. But Balibar attempts to explain this identity in difference (or the indifference toward an identity) by giving some order to the oscillation he has so deftly revealed. Thus, for instance, the ambivalence of class is predicated on "an oscillation between economism and politicism" ("Class," 165), but then the revolutionary proletariat comes in as "a unity of contraries": a correspondence between the "working class as an 'economic' class and the proletariat as a 'political subject.'" On the one hand, this is precisely the conceptual limit of the dialectic that says, as Balibar does, "this oscillation cannot be preserved"; on the other, it opens class identity to a range of presumptive discourses that ceaselessly announce then stand in for the unity that the dialectic desires. I would argue that there is another way to understand the ambivalence at issue and that is by using oscillation as an *operative concept* for the logic that Marx sketches out rather than viewing it as an aberration, that which is remedied by a form of willed stasis. Balibar suggests that "for the theory to be intelligible and applicable, it must be *fixed* at one point or another" ("Class," 165), but this could be done as a function of oscillation itself rather than as its dialectical sublation. I have already suggested that oscillation as a concept encompasses such a point, in Adorno's homeostasis for instance, but here it might relieve the tendency (epitomized in the incidence of "actual existence") to hypostatize a revolutionary subject as a handy agglomeration of a ceaseless equivocation. If the "last instance" arrives, it is internally structured by the ambivalence that provides its very possibility. This is why the proletariat "appears," but at the moment of its annihilation (in the sense that its self-identity is the moment of transformation from capitalism). That the dialectic necessitates a limit is not incompatible with the conceptual range of oscillation, but one must maintain a sense of dynamism in the model or risk deemphasizing the processes at its heart and the openness to new evidence, the eventness of events. In light of the "end" that readings of the Cold War now encourage, this is not an insignificant theoretical endeavor.[17]

Ultimately, this is what Balibar attempts in his formulation of class and class struggle as a "process of transformation without pre-established end" ("Class," 168), but only after granting the opposite inclination precedence. In essence, what he identifies as speculative empiricism necessitates the spectral empiricism I advocate here. Although Balibar's approach is at one with the general premises of oscillation as concept, he draws back at those moments when oscillation might seem to threaten the logical integrity of his materialism. This, I believe, is a methodological error. This is true both at the interpretative level, the search for theoretical symptoms of oscillation, and at the conceptual level — that oscillation constellates an array of strategies that do no resolve themselves into a closed system. To some extent, this is indeed a "Marx beyond Marx" (the term, that Balibar borrows from Negri's reading of *Grundrisse*), a materialism at or beyond the borders of its normative claims. It is, more specifically, a Marxism beyond Marxism because it suggests that some of the interpretative claims of the materialist tradition have themselves been overreached (although, for philosophical reasons, this is not a case of simple transcendence).[18] This is not only a basic reaction to the frenzied transformations of late capitalism (many of which are a mask for otherwise good old-fashioned plodding exploitation), but also a proactive theoretical strategy that haunts the dynamism of materialism itself. That this dynamism is part of the machinery of capitalism (as some examples from Marx below will emphasize) is undeniable, but one must keep the principle separate from its purpose. If, as Balibar contends, one of Marx's key discoveries is that societies are based not on general interests but "on the regulation of conflicts" (and thus form a history of class war), then materialism must not mimic capitalism's regulative desire but disrupt it (in terms of both its model and application). While the term is flamboyant, "oscillate wildly" is a condition of such disruption.

Marx certainly details the oscillatory compulsions of capital. What Balibar does is elucidate, symptomatically, the conceptual oscillations of Marx's approach, and, as I have maintained, this is a service to materialism

much greater (and usually more sincere) than the incarnations and volun-
tarist embrace of the "new" or non-Marxist in theory (on this point at least,
Ahmad's contribution undeniably recommends itself).[19] But the next step
is a more nuanced understanding of the underpinnings of such conceptual
sway, one that recognizes an integrity in oscillation that incoherence would
seem to deny. This reading, itself caught between the calculable and the
incalculable, is the space where ghosts return, the spectral becoming that
cannot be laid to rest by the regulatory oscillations of capitalist logic.

The reason class is absent from Derrida's proto-Marxist text and
entirely central to Balibar's symptomatic exegesis is because of the status of
philosophy in their approaches. It is a question not of choosing between the
two on this occasion (although there are significant political consequences
at that level) but of understanding the spectrality marking that difference
and, I will maintain, mutual imbrication. In part this is a function of the
texts deemed appropriate to the reincarnation of Marx and Marxism for
the next millennium. Derrida concentrates on the exchange with Stirner and
The Eighteenth Brumaire primarily because there the spectral is, as it were,
manifest in the content of the discussions (the latter is so chock-full of ghostly
references that it is a veritable founding text of *Gespenstergeschichte*). For
Balibar, the ghosting occurs at the conceptual level by reading Marxist
principles beside themselves, as part of a theoretical process that does not
quite congeal (as he notes, "[T]hat doctrine does not exist" [*POM* 117]).
Whether through representation or through implication, both share the
same unspoken creed: class is ethereal.

But in Derrida the ethereality of class does not take place just in the
representational paradox of the specter (the visibility of the invisible): it is
also produced in the form of his reading. The shadow of class in Derrida's
approach is manifest in both the texts he uses and the displacements he
enacts. When he foregrounds Marx's discussion of money, for instance,
Derrida is drawn to its apparitional status in capital's "movement of
idealization" (*SOM* 100). Paper is rendered as gold in a process of magical
simulacra that Marx insistently links to the logic of capital itself. This would
be enough indeed to take seriously the symbolic structures of capital, but of
course in Marx's argument (chiefly *Capital*, volume 1), he accentuates what
is crucial in money's "illusion" for capital: what it can purchase in terms of
labor power. In other words, the symbolic structure of the criterion returns
to the question of the worker and then to the process of proletarianization
itself. The magical conversion of paper into gold is an equivalent of money's
transformation into capital but with one key difference: the spectrality of
the latter has a direct, fleshly embodiment (e.g., "[L]abor power exists
only as a capacity of the living individual" [274]; or "[T]he owner of labor
power is mortal" [275]). The use value of labor power is its real manifestation (*Äusserung*), just as necromancy might profit from the tissue of the
living. Again, the importance of this step is not that humanity comes into

play (and therefore, by association, humanism), but that the possibility of class resides in this commodity exchange, money for labor. Thus, Marx is less fascinated by the symbolic exchange qua symbol — the visibility of the invisible — than by elaborating its implications for socioeconomic formations. And in that direction Derrida gives up the ghost.[20]

Similar displacements occur in Derrida's discussion of the party, the state, and revolution. In each instance, the agency and actualization of opposition remain appropriately specular but unspecified, ghostly but unalloyed. The specter haunting Europe takes shape in the party that embodies the precepts of the *Communist Manifesto*, but does that mean that the Communist Party itself is the most feared form of those principles? Tactically, of course, the time called for this alignment, but in subsequent prefaces to the document both Marx and Engels suggest that its original conjuncture does not exhaust the possible manifestations of the specter.[21] And this spectrality is a product of the nature of class struggle, not the name of the party that takes such struggle as a central issue. The *Manifesto* answers the "nursery tale of the Specter of Communism" with a revolutionary document, but it is class struggle, not the party, that constitutes the spirit of the specter, the spectral grounds of ruling-class fear. The same displacement occurs in Derrida's invocation of the state, which is read as a "correlative" of the party in this context. This is the bad side, or the bad ghost, of communism whose manifestations have often produced a malevolent instantiation of state practice. But once again, this is not a "correlative" of the specter that haunts. Parties and states will die, but how can the specter of communism according to Derrida's approach and indeed according to the reasons for Marx and Engels's characterization in the first place? Derrida is surely right to underline the "equivocation of the event" (*SOM* 104) that is revolution (and not just because this is a function of oscillation in the social), but why has he no place for class and class struggle in the elaboration of that event? The specter of unity that ends the *Manifesto* is not about parties or states: it is about a force of history that will keep coming back as long as certain forms of economic exploitation depend upon its suppression. This is the difference between a specter and an empty space.[22]

[...]

Here we should clarify the political permutations of ghosts and ghosting. Clearly for Marx, the specter is a political barb used to attack what he saw as a policy of demonizing communism, particularly within the states of Europe. Thus, when the pope, or the tsar, or Metternich, or Guizot invoke communism it is within a discourse of reactionary incitement. To exorcise the ghost in this sense is to eradicate its possibility. In *The Eighteenth Brumaire*, however, Marx gives the ghost a different strategic inflection. Here, the ghost is part of the spectral economy of revolution, but an "old revolution" that Louis Napoleon conjures to repeat a history that was lost. This ghost is malevolent in a troubling way, for the "old world of ghosts" seeks to impose itself on the present and replace a revolution of transformation with one of repetition (the infamous farce of history). "The ghost of the empire" haunts the present in the form of Louis Napoleon's politics, he who is "making its ghost walk again."[23] For Marx, this is a politics of despair, but one not without political potential for mass opposition. The "parody of imperialism" that the ghost represents is also an inspiration, for in the out-of-jointness of time (Derrida's Shakespearean touchstone) a reactionary spirit produces its counter, one that works to transform the reactionary force that seeks simply to spectralize the real.

This second impulse in Marx's interpretation casts a ghostly shadow on the first. As Derrida points out, the political consequences of the specter and spectrality produce a dilemma. If the "red specter" (as Marx calls it) of opposition is indeed a shadow without a body (Marx describes the people and events of the Eighteenth Brumaire as "inverted Schlemihls," from the story of a man who lost his shadow), is not this itself a function of conjuration — one that places doubt over the ghost's realization? Marx argues that when the "red specter" finally appears the political order has been stabilized, the revolution has been usurped. Now the "reds" do not represent themselves, since (like the peasants) they have always already been represented as ghosts, as specters, as a phantasmagoria. This is precisely what allows the "magician" (Louis Napoleon) to cast aside universal suffrage in the form of what Derrida terms "a perverse, diabolical, and non-apparent exorcism" (*SOM* 119). Clearly, what begins the *Communist Manifesto* in such stirring fashion is an entirely ambiguous rhetorical strategy in *The Eighteenth Brumaire*.

Yet for Marx, the logic of the specter remains a strong antidote to idealist assumptions. What he wants to do, at key moments of political and philosophical reflection, is play on the fear of the immaterial as a contingent foundation of materiality. In effect, he leaves idealism for his political opponents while exacerbating the suspicion that the fear is indeed "grounded." This is the positive meaning of the specter and one that informs the present argument where conjuration is a sign of unsettled spirits, or spirits that cannot be put to rest for historically specific reasons. As we have noted, the end of the Cold War and the collapse of "actual existence" have brought to light, once more, the spectrality of a communism to be, even as this risks (according to Marx's own deployments) the repetition of spirits of yore. The ambiguity cannot be simply exorcised, but what comes back from the future, which is also a new sense of the world and the specter, is a mode of thinking that might critically explain spectrality, the condition of ghosts for materialism.

The ambiguity is written into Marxism's relation to philosophy, and indeed to science (for history shows that certain "Marxist" claims to scientificity have themselves been forms of sorcery). But does spectrality answer the question with which we began, "Whither Marxism?" and the concept of oscillation written into it? Certainly not in any univocal way, for the logic of the spectral is also one of deferral and dialogic differentiation. It describes a principle of noncoherence rather than the hard-edged negativity of incoherence often trivialized by normative notions of the rational. The problem of the specter defies the cozy mimesis that sutures images to their objects. Hence, the aporia of class in Balibar's argument, for he shows the difficulty of socialist class and class struggle ideologies when confronted with the forms of the nation-state: a historical condition in which these state forms become introjected, mimetically, into socialist political structures. In this sense, the ghost of socialism looks over the shoulder of its state instantiation of nationalist ideologies. And this ghosting is itself a moment of oscillatory import:

> This is the uncertainty that faces us at present; namely, that to prevent the crisis of nationalism from ending in an excess of nationalism and its extended reproduction, what is needed is that the example of class struggle becomes visible in the representation of the social — but as its irreducible other. The ideology of class and class struggle, therefore, under whatever name is appropriate, must discover its autonomy while liberating itself from mimicry. To the question "whither Marxism?," the answer, then, is: nowhere, unless this paradox is confronted in all its implications. ("Class," 182)

From Bosnia to Serbia, from Georgia to Chechnya, from Rwanda to Liberia, from Quebec to Ireland, and from China to Taiwan, the paradox that Balibar identifies in 1987 has grown in importance. To be sure, in Balibar's interpretation the paradox comes with an Althusserian twist — that the mimetic fallacies of "actual existence" and other formations must give way to the autonomy of ideology in the name of class and class struggle. For my purposes, the other of the social is the ghost as ideology, a condition of "nowhere" that troubles nationalism in its contemporary constellations. The paradox is not necessarily the autonomy of ideology in this formulation: the uncertainty resides in the visibility of the invisible that class ideology represents. The familiar maneuver that the denial of class is itself a class ideology remains pertinent, yet the future of Marxism does not rest on the confirmation or reaccentuation of that paradox, but on a political openness to the instability written into Marxism's status as critique.

In his answer to the same question, "Whither Marxism?" Douglas Kellner picks up on this issue in a way that was possible in 1992 but perhaps was not in 1987. Here, the spirit of Marxism must be separated from its ghostly aberrations in "actual existence" (Kellner writes of the "spiritual ancestors of the modern totalitarian state").[24] This is the positive exorcism of the post-Soviet era. But it is important to maintain the spectral contours of what Kellner calls "a reconstructed Marxism" (26). When he suggests that Marxism will "disappear" when the "nightmare of capitalism" is over (or when an alternative means to a free and democratic society recommends itself), Kellner alludes to without naming the ambivalent Being of the specter that opens the *Communist Manifesto*. Capitalism wants to awake from a nightmare of history because it conjures the monstrosity of communism. Yet, ironically, the conjuring itself is seen as a means to dispose of or disavow the political and social alternative that this specter represents. A counterconjuration, therefore, is not concerned with Being as such: it seeks to elaborate why the conjuration itself cannot overcome the conditions of possibility it denies. A ghost of the past is always a troubling spirit, but a specter of the future is an aporetic apparition.

Gayatri Chakravorty Spivak's answer to "Whither Marxism?" reflects and refracts the general problematic posed by deconstruction, one where the end of *Capital*, volume 3, is itself a "blueprint of *différance*"[25] Because of socialism's imbrication in the forms of capital articulated by Marx, it "exists" as a pushing away, or deferral, of social productivity according to capital. This is a useful way of characterizing the inseparability implied in ghosting. If we agree that socialism is an "other Being" of capital, then it cannot be expunged without exploding the very ground of its existence, its substantiality. Again, as philosophy this is a suspicious mode of argumentation (the interpellation would read: "Heh, Marxism, socialism, communism — you're not there but the condition of your existence is not-thereness, so in a sense you're always there where capital 'is'"), but the point is to maintain such *différance* as a philosophy beside itself or, as Balibar would have it, as philosophies of Marx beside themselves. It is clearer now why some pundits, including those of a nominally Leftist persuasion, might read "Whither Marxism?" as a pun, and that what we are witnessing in millennial materialism is the withering away of Marxism with its states. Such defeatism and/or cynicism is entirely natural according to the dictates of a philosophy of Being, or "actual existence." But rather than succumb to the ingenious (or disingenuous) attractions of the homonym, let us maintain a spirit of "whither" that does not depend upon second-guessing history.

Scratch the surface of "whither" as an interrogative and one finds an adjective within the discourse of oscillation. Here "whither" (as noted in the *OED*) is "a violent or impetuous movement," "a smart blow or stroke" (a *Stöss* or "shock" for and within Marxism, to recall an earlier discussion of Vattimo), "a quivering movement, a tremble," and, remembering Marx's carbuncles, "the onset or attack of illness." These meanings stand before Marxism as its specters stand before capital. Thus, as the question arrives, so too must the condition. The condition or state of oscillation does not lose the question mark that "whither" precedes: in a spectral economy the question is always there, if only parenthetically (it lurks in the space of this essay title). "Whither" marks the oscillation of theory; it is the sign of a distinct multiplicity in Marxism, the "philosophies of Marx." It is a multiplicity as instability foregrounded in the historically concrete condition of Marxism today. Millennial materialism cannot be reduced to *a* Marx, *the* Marx. Spectrality demands it. Or, as Derrida puts it, to understand the specters of Marx one must address a phantasmal imperative: *Le plus d'un* — the more than one and the no more one.

But the last word of ghosts is not just philosophical, despite these incarnations. What the ghost (*revenant*) always also comes back to is the status of science. Here Marxism has strengths that oscillation does not. Oscillation is a concept for materialism, but Marxism does not devolve, ultimately, into its constituent concepts. Yet here one faces a sharp dilemma that even "whither's" palimpsest cannot significantly displace. If, as Deleuze and Guattari propose, "A scientific notion is defined not by concepts but by functions or propositions" (117), then can one separate the wheat of Marxist propositions from the chaff of its concepts? Historically, there have been moments where this has appeared more possible (the Second International remains a crucial example), but if one accepts the conjunctural reading of Marxist theoretical formations, the process if not the actuality of those differences may now be more difficult to discern. This does not mean that such attempts are idealist or illusionist. On the contrary, work like Roy Bhaskar's identifies how materialist principles themselves can become mired in "epistemic fallacies" (the reduction of ontology to epistemology) that only a sustained critical (and in Bhaskar's terminology, realist) investigation can disarticulate as a science in the social.[26] But the ghost is neither a simple categorical error nor the reincarnation of some Hegelian absolute spirit (although, given the predilections of French philosophy, the "appearance" would be understandable). The ghost remains for science, just as a ghost of science haunts the Marxist dialectic. Here is not the place to adjudicate the truth claims of Marxism as science; I do, however, wish to counter the impression that any focus on Marx's deployment of spectral metaphors is to abjure the rational kernel for its mystical shell. If history has taught us anything in recent years, it is that the de facto rejection of the spectral in Marxism is partly what allowed utopia to congeal, then disappear, in dogma.

On the one hand, Deleuze and Guattari claim that science "slows down" variability by the use of constants or limits. A measure, or a principle of measurement, can pull reality from chaos and "suspend," however briefly, the process of the infinite. The examples they provide (the speed of light, absolute zero, the quantum of action, the Big Bang) all attempt to coordinate, to provide a scale, to provide a reference for what must always exceed them. And, not surprisingly, the sheer variability of constants produces a determinate disciplinary fear: "science is haunted not by its own unity but by the plane of reference constituted by all the limits or borders through which it confronts chaos" (119). Philosophy, on the other hand, is less troubled by the infinite as long as it can be thought consistently (philosophy, they claim, gives "the virtual a consistency specific to it" [118]). In this, science and philosophy can be linked to art: they all "cast planes over the chaos" (202). But this, of course, is an intellectual, political, and social challenge. Artists, philosophers, and scientists confront chaos not just to impose an order on it (for this alone would amount to hubris), but because a certain affinity with chaos is necessary for the crises we call change. Again, the image of this confrontation is striking: "The philosopher, the scientist, and the artist seem to return from the land of the dead" (202). And which one of these ghosts is the real Marxist?

Marxism is a science to the extent that it has developed forms of measurement (laws of motion) for the infinite chaos of socialization (in this respect, the charge of "totalization" is often a nonscientist's reaction to scientificity). These measurements (ideology, class, value, commodity, etc.) are not fictions to the degree that they have often elaborated the real contradictions that stand within and between the social and forms of socialization. But philosophy (and indeed art) is not to blame for the distortion of these measurements, at least according to Deleuze and Guattari's interpretation: it is a function of the plethora of methodologies vis-à-vis chaos. Chaosophy, as Deleuze and Guattari call it, is not for me only because I still tend to think in terms of the collective rather than the nomads who wander off into the infinite. I do believe, however, that it provides a strong antidote to knee-jerk reactions about the status of science and philosophy for Marxism at a time when "post-ality" is all too quick to dig a grave for it.

Ghosts do not make history, people do, but not under conditions of their own choosing (a point where Marx and the Shakespeare of *Hamlet* most assuredly agree). This little history of ghosts is not about the agency of the specter, but about materialism's accountability to and for specters. Derrida's bold declaration that there will be "no future without Marx" ("Pas sans Marx, pas d'avenir sans Marx" [*SDM* 36]) only makes sense within a spectral economy of materialism, a materialism that is not beholden to monologic causality but one that seeks an understanding of a material reality caught between the calculable and the incalculable, the undecidability of "determinate oscillations." Marx is dead; only the spectral can critically explain how Marxism comes back from the future. Not content with the naming of an undecidable, I have sought to interpellate Marx within his own *Gespenstergeschichte*: that is, to trace the function of the ghost, and thinking the ghost, for his materialist methodology. Millennial materialism must use this heritage not to reincarnate Marx (in the manner of a quaint religious observance) but to resist an inclination to resolve conceptual aporias merely by dogmatic statements to the contrary. The science of materialism includes its respect for the criteria of judgment, not the assumption of a universal truth in the judgment. The vacillations of class and class struggle in Marx's formulations are examples of determinate instability within the concepts and their application. What spectrality does is keep this instability "alive" at a moment when "actual existence" cannot possibly confirm or deny it.

In 1883 Engels stood by Marx's grave and predicted that "the gap that has been left by this mighty spirit will soon enough make itself felt" (an absence as agency indeed!). Yet barely a hundred years later Hobsbawm could opine that "the shadow of Karl Marx presides over a third of the human race."[27] The shade of Marx is still here, but not in the form that either Engels or Hobsbawm suggests. It exists now as a condition of possibility in a sense of the world radically different from the specters of the past, however answerable it must be to them. The ambivalence of the specter is not its virtue, only its dependence on concrete determination. And that is why the experience of freedom before us is also the space of ghosts.

Notes

1 See Jacques Derrida, *Specters of Marx*, trans. Peggy Kamuf (New York: Routledge, 1994), 100; subsequent references will be given in the text as *SOM* followed by page number; references to the French text will be noted within the text as *SDM* followed by page number (*Spectres de Marx* [Paris: Galilée, 1993]).

2 This is a philosophical and political knot of some complexity that I will attempt to untangle below. The standard argument says that the actual existence of socialism was predicated on a promissory note on which the state could not deliver. But this is not just because of the contradictions of socialism in one country or the globalization of capitalist social and economic relations. It is also a function of the way "actual existence" was posed. Think, for a moment, of Althusser's appeals to determination "in the last instance." The advantage of this move is that it offers an analytical framework that remains open to the processes of material change. The disadvantage lies in the advantage: that is to say, the proposition tends to prescribe a material reality to which another "instance" may not be reducible. The relative autonomy of other "instances" (like ideology) becomes something of a magical key leaving Althusser to opine famously that "the lonely hour of the 'last instance' never comes." The first problem of "actual existence" is its contradictory philosophical proposition. Without a serious rethinking of the logic of becoming in materialism one is left with a neat but dystopian Althusserian gesture: the lonely hour of "actual existence" never comes.

3 [Editors' Note: Hitchcock is referring to Chapter Four of *Oscillate Wildly*, entitled "Fetishism (of Shoes)," which, using the Nike athletic shoe as a case

study, seeks to "map the 'metaphysical subtleties and theological niceties' of commodity culture as it currently confers aphanisis on the workers of the world." Hitchcock, *Oscillate Wildly: Space, Body, and Spirit of Millennial Materialism* (Minneapolis: University of Minnesota Press, 1999), 111.]

4   [Editors' Note: Hitchcock is referring to Chapter Two of *Oscillate Wildly*, entitled "Bodies (of Materialism," where he sees materialist feminism "accentuat[e] in a transformative way the constitutive impossibility of materialism's situatedness — that the body of material exceeds or superadequates bodies of knowledge." Hitchcock, *Oscillate Wildly*, 56.]

5   Etienne Balibar, *The Philosophy of Marx*, trans. Chris Turner (New York: Verso, 1995), 1. On occasion, I will also use the French version, *La philosophie de Marx* (Paris: Éditions La Découverte, 1993); different page numbers will be noted accordingly within the text preceded by *POM* or *PDM*.

6   Bernd Magnus and Stephen Cullenberg (eds), *Whither Marxism? Global Crises in International Perspective* (New York: Routledge, 1995).

7   I refer, of course, to Michael Ryan, *Marxism and Deconstruction: A Critical Articulation* (Baltimore: Johns Hopkins University Press, 1982). Most of the groundwork for Ryan's book was worked out, as he indicates in his preface, in the arguments of the 1970s — another moment when "Whither Marxism?" gained prescience, this time in the wake of the failures of '68 in France.

8   See, in particular, chapter 4 of Ryan's book, which focuses on *Capital*. The example of the table, with its "wooden brain" and "grotesque ideas," comes from the fetishism section of chapter 1 of *Capital* (volume 1) on "the commodity." The dancing table is Marx's metaphor for fetishism, and spiritualism in particular. For his part, Derrida usefully connects the "thingness" of the thing to the ghostliness of the "thing" in *Hamlet*, but he seems to lose track of the reality of the thing for the worker in capitalist relations of production. The ghost in the commodity form is always already the trace of the worker's embodied labor paradoxically revealed in the absence of that body.

9   Etienne Balibar, "From Class Struggle to Classless Struggle?" in Etienne Balibar and Immanuel Wallerstein, *Race, Nation, Class: Ambiguous Identities*, trans. Chris Turner (New York: Verso, 1991), 153–84.

10 See Gilles Deleuze and Félix Guattari, *What Is Philosophy?* trans. Hugh Tomlinson and Graham Burchell (New York: Columbia University Press, 1994), especially chapter 4. Deleuze and Guattari here link geophilosophy to their notion of deterritorialization; in other words, they align their philosophical concept with actual spatial coordinates — Why does philosophy develop in Greece? and so on. Becoming, as a concept, is geographical rather than historical according to this scheme, but a little more of the temporal could specify the spatiality at issue. Geophilosophy is also a trajectory of theory and might benefit from the details of its movement.

11 [Editors' Note: Sadisah, a woman making Nike shoes in Indonesia, is

discussed by Hitchcock in "Fetishism (of Shoes)." In 1992, her paltry pay slip ($37 net for a month's work) was published by Jeffrey Ballinger in *Harper's Magazine*.]

12   See Jean-Luc Nancy, *The Experience of Freedom*, trans. Bridget McDonald (Stanford, CA: Stanford University Press, 1993). Nancy reads experience back into the thought of the imagination while questioning its status as a dream of empiricism. Thinking the ghost may seem to replay Nancy's exposition of the impasse in thinking freedom, but it is also part of his solution in that the "ground" of the ghost cannot be thought except as a function of the imagination. This is the way that the uncanny, for instance, haunts what is known. But there is another version of "haunting" in Nancy's reading of Kant, which we may call the ghost of moral consciousness. What Kant's categorical imperative appears to do is disregard "fact" in the service of a consciousness that legislates itself. Facts, therefore, haunt the consciousness that would deny them. Obviously, Nancy's target remains the brutality of the ground itself, "the positivity of wickedness," rather than the logic of shifting grounds that is my main concern. The logical trap of positing grounds has a certain inevitability to it, but the critique of, say, positivism does not in itself secure the experience of freedom. If your freedom is insecure, then perhaps we are all free already to the extent that insecurity is a topos of the present — which is only to say that the revolution in thinking necessary for the experience of freedom is currently (determinately) almost unimaginable. And the "almost" is where materialism comes back.

13   Balibar, "Class," 154; subsequent references to this work will be given in the text as "Class," plus the page number.

14   See Jacques Derrida, *Positions*, trans. Alan Bass (London: Athlone Press, 1972).

15   This argument was originally presented at Cerisy-la-Salle as "Representation et les travailleurs" (August 1995), forthcoming in André Collinot and Clive Thomson, eds., *Mikhail Bakhtine et la pensée dialogique* (London, ON: Mestengo Press). The following month a conference on "ghosts" took place in Cardiff. Ernesto Laclau's keynote speech, "The Time Is Out of Joint," has since been published in *Diacritics* and his *Emanicpation(s)* (London: Verso, 1996). Although my effort here is not directly influenced by Laclau's, it may complement it in certain ways.

16   Karl Marx, *Capital*, vol. 1, trans. Ben Fowkes (London: Penguin, 1976), 98.

17   This is part of what Derrida challenges in *Specters of Marx*. His section on Fukuyama's "end of history" thesis is, however, a curiously hurried reading that yet manages to grant Fukuyama a perspicacity his central idea does not deserve.

18   For an idea of the critical difference between "Marx beyond Marx" and "Marxism beyond Marxism" the reader might usefully consult Negri's book *Marx beyond Marx* in relation to his contribution to the volume of collected essays, *Marxism beyond Marxism*. The former includes a close reading of the *Grundrisse* in which Negri considers the possibility of the subject and subjectivity in the path to communism as an integer of the crises in the law of

value with which Marx's notebooks seem to grapple. The autonomous subject is the subject of "Autonomia," the independent Leftist movement in Italy in the 1970s. By the 1950s, Negri has broken with the progressivist implication in the classical texts of historical materialism that reads a subsumption of labor under capital. The philosophy of Marx, according to this interpretation, is more properly periodized in the sense that the law of value for Marx was predicated on a critique of industrial capital. In essence, the ghosting of Marxism is achieved by the intervention of periodicity (given to Negri in the present by forms of Post-Fordism). And this, of course, animates the ghost of Marx recalled in Negri's "Twenty Theses." See Antonio Negri, *Marx beyond Marx*, trans. Harry Cleaver, Michael Ryan, and Maurizio Viano (South Hadley, MA: Bergin and Garvey, 1984); and idem, "Twenty Theses on Marx," in *Marxism beyond Marxism*, ed. Saree Makdisi, Cesare Casarino, and Rebecca Karl, 149–80 (New York: Routledge, 1996).

19 *In Theory* is the kind of book that precipitates discussion on so many levels that it is destined to provide grist for materialist critique for some time (its half-life as a whipping post will be considerably shorter). Although he provides a useful gloss on the predicaments of the world system today, Ahmad tends to limit the oscillatory range of the principles he deploys. This purism can be devastating where liberal humanism is concerned, but it is less patient with the problematic internal dynamics of Marxist theory itself. See Aijaz Ahmad, *In Theory* (New York: Verso, 1993).

20 In this respect, Magnus and Cullenberg are overly generous in their introduction to Derrida's text where they suggest four ways in which *Specters of Marx* speaks to (or is "in direct conversation with") the contributors to *Whither Marxism?* Whether the conversation exists in either direction is not the point, but whether Derrida's procedures "suspend" the conversation at the moment where their logic is challenged by the "conditions" of the Marx made possible.

21 It would be interesting to explore the number of times and under what conditions the various prefaces to the *Manifesto* were left out of its editions even when, as Marx does in 1872, the general principles are reaffirmed. The various translations of the *Manifesto* also make for informative (and entertaining) reading. The first English translation of the *Manifesto* appeared in a journal called the *Red Republican* in 1850 and began: "A frightful hobgoblin stalks through Europe"! Personally, I think this perfectly captures the spirit of Marx's caricature of the ruling orders' fear.

22 Paradoxically, the condition of the former — the specter — can be "represented" by the materiality of the latter — an empty space. The empty parentheses of my chapter title are meant to signify this philosophical and political conundrum. The difference, I would argue, is an example of an undecidable, or what Derrida terms "a determinate oscillation."

23 These phrases are taken from *The Eighteenth Brumaire*, in *Surveys from Exile*, ed. and introduced by David Fernbach, trans. Ben Fowkes et al. (London: Harmondsworth, 1973).

24 See Douglas Kellner, "The Obsolescence of Marxism?" in *Whither*, 3–27.

25 Gayatri Chakravorty Spivak, "Supplementing Marxism," in *Whither*, 109–19.

26 Bhaskar is easily the most difficult theorist of materialism currently available in English, but the following works are recommended, particularly the last: *A Realist Theory of Science* (Leeds: Leeds Books, 1975); *Scientific Realism and Human Emancipation* (London: Verso, 1986); *Reclaiming Reality* (London: Verso, 1989); and *Dialectic: The Pulse of Freedom* (London: Verso, 1993). For a review essay that places Bhaskar within a tradition of Marxist philosophies of science, see Michael Sprinker, "The Royal Road: Marxism and the Philosophy of Science," *New Left Review* 191 (January/February 1992): 122–44.

27 Eric Hobsbawm, *The Age of Empire* (New York: Pantheon, 1987), 336.

PART THREE

The Ghost in the Machine: Spectral Media

12

The Ghost in the Machine: Spectral Media / Introduction

María del Pilar Blanco and Esther Peeren

The history of science, and of the popularization of this body of knowledge, is also a story about the uses of the metaphor. Following on the work of Friedrich Kittler in *Discourse Networks 1800/1900*,[1] Laura Otis has explained that the use of metaphors to explain the processes of science has been a way to not only explain these complexities to a popular audience; it is also how scientists can assimilate and understand their own observations of how living and mechanical bodies work. But this use of the metaphor to explain complex biological, chemical, and technological processes has not gone unchallenged. As Otis also notes, in the mid-nineteenth century—a period in which the popularization of science was becoming ever more widespread—scientist Claude Bernard expressed his skepticism about working comparisons to explain what was really happening within the body (and, in particular, the human nervous system): "Priding himself on his empiricism, Bernard mistrusted analogy as a means of constructing knowledge. Does one know more or less about something, if one asserts that it is like something else? What exactly is the relationship between metaphor and knowledge?"[2]

The metaphor can thus be understood as a double agent, in the sense that it can bring us closer to scientific enlightenment, but its reliance on displacement and association can nevertheless move us into unforeseen territories. While the recurrence to metaphors in science can often reveal an obscurity, or mysterious impasse, between the signifier and the signified, it can also unearth an incompatibility between the specific machinations of bodies, organic and inorganic, and human comprehension.

Science and technology have long exhibited an unlikely metaphoric association with the spectral or occult. With this association always on the verge of turning literal, it is hard to decide whether ghosts and haunting elucidated new scientific processes and technologies or vice versa. Inventions in the nineteenth century and beyond, while based on the most specific of mechanical processes, became entangled in the webs of the supernatural, and often returned to questions of life and what came after it. The rise of popular science (and the addition of entertainment value to this field of knowledge) in the nineteenth century was contemporaneous with the birth of Spiritualism, a doctrine that actively sought to prove the presence of ghosts in the living world. Disenchantment was thus constantly threatened by the return of enchantment, often becoming two sides of the same coin. In *The Invention of Telepathy*, Roger Luckhurst explains how Spiritualism and its many avatars (such as the Society for Psychical Research) had serious scientific and positivistic aspirations, and how its practitioners insisted on the meticulousness of their methodology as they tried to communicate with the dead.[3] Seen this way, the network and communication theories that were blossoming with the advent of new technologies were echoed in the desire for contact with the afterlife. The tension between Enlightenment thinking and (re)enchantment could be perceived in many of the new technologies that appeared in the nineteenth century: improvements in optics yielded the phantasmagoria shows, while the development of photography in the mid-1800s, as Tom Gunning asserts in the essay contained in this part of the *Reader*, was immediately embroiled in ideas of hauntedness (most insistently through the invention and success of spirit photography[4]).

Ghostliness and death also hover over the invention of phonography, Jonathan Sterne argues in *The Audible Past*, as the possibility of hearing the dead became an enticing prospect: "Although it is perhaps most pronounced in phonography, death is everywhere among the living in early discussions of sound's reproducibility ... One *Washington Post* writer speculated during an interview with gramophone and microphone inventor Emile Berliner that radio would eventually allow for communication with the dead since it picks up vibrations in the ether and the dead 'simply vibrate at a slower rate' than the living."[5] Ghostliness and the fantasy of perceiving the mystery of the afterlife thus clung steadfastly to the new technologies that became available throughout the nineteenth and twentieth centuries.

The proliferation of new machines in the modern age reminds us of the body's limitations (and the need to overcome them), as it can also remind us of the borders of life itself. Ideas of technology's position in the liminal spaces between life and death continued to persist well into the twentieth century. In his influential *Camera Lucida*, Roland Barthes explains how the photograph augurs a new relationship to death. If death was central to pre-modern life, in modern life we exchange the space of death with our technologies of repetition. He writes:

> For death must be somewhere in society; if it is no longer (or less intensely) in religion, it must be elsewhere; perhaps in this image which produces Death while trying to preserve life. Contemporary with the withdrawal of rites, Photography may correspond to the intrusion, in our modern society, of an asymbolic Death, outside of religion, outside of ritual, a kind of abrupt dive into literal Death. *Life/Death*: the paradigm is reduced to a simple click, the one separating the initial pose from the final print.[6]

Photography, as well as other technologies that have become integral parts of our everyday existence, such as the cinema, the sound recorder, and the television, aims to commemorate persons, places, and events. But the very moment of commemoration (that "simple click" to which Barthes refers) reminds the collector of memories of the passing of time, and the entry of death into the world of the living.

The ghost, to borrow Gilbert Ryle's famous phrase we use in the title of this part, has always occupied an important place within the machine.[7] Barthes's *Camera Lucida* meditates on the still photograph's power to decenter the experience of the living. The essays in this part expand on Barthes's theorizations of the camera's uncanny abilities by offering detailed accounts of the different technologies that appeared in the nineteenth and twentieth centuries, among them X-rays, cinema, radio, and television, and their myriad occult dimensions. Written in the 1990s and 2000s, they appeared at a time in which the new dimension in virtuality to which we now have become so accustomed (through the internet and other digital technologies) has made us once again reflect on notions of presence, absence, and simultaneity.[8] The authors—Tom Gunning, Jeffrey Sconce, Akira Mizuta Lippit, Allen S. Weiss, and David Toop—share an interest in historicizing the revolutions of the senses (particularly the visual and the aural) that transpired during this time and before, which were simultaneously revolutions in science and introductions of the uncanny into the everyday realm. They are timely interventions that connect our relationship with different media to similar sites of innovation in the past.

Tom Gunning opens his essay "To Scan a Ghost: The Ontology of Mediated Vision" with a reflection on the anachronistic insertion of Romantic science (and its employment of metaphoric correspondences) into Friedrich Murnau's *Nosferatu* (1922). While, by the 1920s, *Naturphilosophie* was an outdated system of thought, its apparition within the relatively new cinematic medium offers a peek into this technology's ability to renew itself via modes of what Gunning calls the "untimely" conjugations between modern progress and a more ancient form of enchantment.[9] Cinema, according to Gunning, is capable of integrating the old and the new by reflecting on its very history—a history of vision and the persistence of the ambiguous dialectic between the visible and the invisible.

Moving deftly between aesthetic genres and technological media, Gunning reflects on this long history of the "phantom" in visuality studies, noting how the ghostly persists as a fascinating "crisis" of the senses, despite science's triumph over superstition and the very belief in ghosts and spirits.[10] Gunning's aim in this essay, as he says, is not to reactivate Barthes's or Bazin's ontological readings of the photographic image. Instead, he "explore[s] the ontology and phenomenology of modern media of reproduction ... through the metaphor of the ghostly and the phantasm."[11] For Gunning, the ghostly in the different manifestations of visuality (from the phantasmagoria show to Henry Dircks's "Pepper's Ghost," spirit photography, and early cinema[12]) does not simply represent the re-enchantment of the modern; it also reveals how old theories and beliefs can make it into what we consider the "new" media. Gunning's essay, then, is an impressively thorough exploration of how "the virtual image becomes the modern phantom."[13]

In his "Introduction" to *Haunted Media: Electronic Presence from Telegraphy to Television*, which we have reprinted here, Jeffrey Sconce relates the bizarre reports that emerged at the dawn of the television era in the mid-twentieth century, in which different members of the public reacted to the fantasy of "liveness" and "presence" embodied by this medium.[14] One of his examples, from 1953, concerns the strange and persistent appearance of a woman's face on a family's television set during the broadcast of a children's show. The indelibility of the image, its stubborn *there-ness*, was enough to spook the whole family, and the story made it into *The New York Times*. Sconce's project is to explore how electronic media "have compelled citizens of the media age to reconsider increasingly disassociative relationships among body, mind, space, and time."[15] Investigating the inception of the telegraph, wireless communication, network broadcasting, television, and digital media, Sconce reveals certain continuities (persistent stories of disembodiment, teleportation, and anthropomorphization), but his main focus is on the divergent ways in which each of these technologies and its reception speaks—using metaphors of currents, streams, and flows—about the historical moments and "actual social, cultural, and political" contexts in which they emerge.[16] Such contexts, in turn, take in "a culture's changing social relationship to a historical sequence of technologies."[17] Thus, while many technologies can be considered "haunted" or "haunting," their imbrication with the ghost takes on a historical and cultural specificity, as well as a distinctiveness derived from each particular technological format.[18]

While Gunning and Sconce focus on a mediated spectrality that lies outside the observing or listening subject, in "Modes of Avisuality: Psychoanalysis

– X-ray – Cinema" Akira Mizuta Lippit writes a microhistory of 1895, a year of scientific milestones: X-ray technology was developed by Wilhelm Röntgen, female psychoanalysis was revolutionized with the publication of Breuer and Freud's *Studies on Hysteria*, and the Lumière brothers patented the cinematograph. Lippit calls these three revolutions *"phenomenologies of the inside,"* for they represent modes of invasion of the internal world of the subject that fundamentally "changed the terms by which interiority was conceived, imagined, and viewed."[19] As he also notes, the terms used within each of these sciences of subjectivity begin to be used within the other, thus introducing a concept of the phantasmic interior (and a new form of spectrality) predicated on the notion of penetration, and even the deathly annihilation of the human mind and body. These technologies that seek to discover the hidden and previously unseen human features have a capacity of rendering subjects spectral: able to dissect even during life, they, like Barthes's photographs but in a more literal manner, offer up a modern *memento mori*, a reminder of death in life.

Similarly to Lippit's microhistory of 1895, Allen S. Weiss, in the "Preface" to his *Phantasmic Radio*, looks at different years in which aesthetic and radiophonic advancements transpired across Europe and the United States: 1877 (the year in which, among other things, Edison first spoke into a phonograph), 1913 (the date the first radio transmission became a reality and Luigi Russolo published his *Art of Noise* manifesto), and 1948 (when recording tape became available and Antonin Artaud's *Pour en finir avec le jugement de dieu* radio transmission was suppressed). These historical moments represent different episodes in the eradication of the modern body as referent. As the corporeal gives way to the incorporeal, the subject appears to become less grounded in reality, turning unspecific, liminal, and uncanny. Lacking the indexicality of the photographic image, the radio-transmitted voice appears to arrive from nowhere and can linger inexplicably in the imagination.[20] Radiophony is embedded in the very idea of modernity, as the body becomes disengaged from the voice, and interiority and exteriority become indistinguishable from one another. Weiss argues that "[t]here exists a point, unlocalizable and mysterious, where listener and radio are indistinguishable."[21] Phantasmic radio thus represents the possibility of the singular body becoming obsolete by giving way to the evanescence of the voice. Put differently, radio technology allows for a new conception of the human as spectral, displaced, and ultimately disquieting.

David Toop's "Chair Creaks, But No One Sits There" (from his book *Sinister Resonance*), which completes this part of *The Spectralities Reader*, offers reflections on a host of different episodes of the aural uncanny in music, literature, and film of the nineteenth and twentieth centuries, from Dickens's *The Haunted House* to accounts of Chinese lute music and John Cage's prepared piano adaptations. Positing that "sound is absence, beguiling; out of sight, out of reach," Toop offers the reader meditations on how the elsewhere of sound, the "perplexing, disturbing, yet danger-ously seductive" possibility that it is "nothing," is a powerful destabilizing agent in modern art.[22] As he notes, the "interpretation of sound as an unstable or provisional event, ambiguously situated somewhere between psychological delusion, verifiable scientific phenomenon, and a visitation of spectral forces" has continuously haunted art, and reminds us of sound's ability to cross borders between subjects, and between the subject and the surrounding world.[23]

The essays selected for this part of the *Reader* demonstrate contem-porary media theory's interest in connecting our modern technological moment with those that have transpired in past centuries. Such histories allow us to understand how dreams of progress have never quite let go of the destabilizing agency of the spectral or uncanny. Put together, the inter-ventions by Gunning, Sconce, Lippit, Weiss, and Toop provide fascinating insights into the different histories of haunting's survival in the scientific advancements that have revolutionized how we perceive our world. Yet at the same time, they warn us against taking for granted—or, if you will, for *real*— our current techno-imaginaries and their spectral metaphors. As Sconce notes on the final page of *Haunted Media*: "We would do well to remember, however, that 150 years from today, it is doubtful anyone will be discussing or even remember our current debates over simulation, hyper-reality, cyborgs, cyberspace, techno-bodies, or virtual subjectivity, except perhaps for a few baffled historians interesting in the peculiar mystifying power that a certain segment of the intelligentsia invested in their media systems."[24]

Notes

1   Friedrich Kittler, *Discourse Networks, 1800–1900*, trans. Michael Metteer, with Chris Cullens (1985; Stanford: Stanford University Press, 1990). David E. Wellbery's foreword to Kittler's book invokes spectrality in opposing Kittler's post-hermeneutic criticism to the way hermeneutics, against its true status as a historical and thus finite phenomenon, "stylize[s] itself ... as a resuscitation of the living spirit from the tomb of the letter" (x).

2   Laura Otis, "The Metaphoric Circuit: Organic and Technological Communication in the Nineteenth Century," *Journal of the History of Ideas* 63, no. 1 (2001): 105.

3   Roger Luckhurst, *The Invention of Telepathy: 1870–1901* (Oxford: Oxford University Press, 2002).

4   On spirit photography, see also John Harvey, *Photography and Spirit* (London: Reaktion Books, 2007).

5   Jonathan Sterne, *The Audible Past: Cultural Origins of Sound Reproduction*

(Durham, NC: Duke University Press, 2003), 289. See also Friedrich A. Kittler, *Gramophone, Film, Typewriter*, trans. Geoffrey Winthrop-Young and Michael Wutz (1986; Stanford: Stanford University Press, 1999), 21–114 and Jacques Derrida, "Ulysses Gramophone: Hear Say Yes in Joyce," in *Acts of Literature*, ed. Derek Attridge (New York and London: Routledge, 1992), 253–309.

6   Roland Barthes, *Camera Lucida* (New York: Hill and Wang, 1981), 92. For critical (re)considerations of this work's reading of photography, see Geoffrey Batchen, ed., *Photography Degree Zero: Reflections on Roland Barthes's Camera Lucida* (Boston: The MIT Press, 2009).

7   Gilbert Ryle, *The Concept of Mind* (Chicago: University of Chicago Press, 1984).

8   According to Geoffrey Batchen, "a new spectre is haunting Western culture— the spectre of Virtual Reality. Not here yet but already a force to be reckoned with, the apparition of VR is ghost-like indeed. Even the words have a certain phantom quality. Virtual Reality—a reality which is apparently true but not *truly* True, a reality which is apparently real but not *really* Real." Batchen, "Spectres of Cyberspace," in *The Visual Culture Reader: Second Edition*, ed. Nicholas Mirzoeff (London and New York: Routledge, 2005), 237.

9   Tom Gunning, "To Scan a Ghost: The Ontology of Mediated Vision," *Grey Room* 26 (Winter 2007), 102.

10 Ibid., 116.

11 Ibid., 100.

12 For a history of Dircks's "Ghost," see also Martin Harries's *Scare Quotes from Shakespeare: Marx, Keynes, and the Language of Reenchantment* (Palo Alto, CA: Stanford University Press, 2000).

13 Gunning, "To Scan a Ghost," 111.

14 For an account of the way television's relationship to "liveness" has been reinforced in the era of reality TV, see Karen Williams, "The Liveness of Ghosts: Haunting and Reality TV," in *Popular Ghosts: The Haunted Spaces of Everyday Culture*, ed. María del Pilar Blanco and Esther Peeren (New York: Continuum, 2010), 149–61.

15 Jeffrey Sconce, *Haunted Media: Electronic Presence from Telegraphy to Television* (Durham, NC: Duke University Press, 2000), 7.

16 Ibid., 10.

17 Ibid.

18 A similar emphasis on the specific intersections between the occult and emergent media is found in the work of Stefan Andriopoulos, who relates the invention of television to psychic research on clairvoyance in "Psychic Television," *Critical Inquiry* 31, no. 3 (2005): 618–37, and that of cinema to interest in hypnotism in *Possessed: Hypnotic Crimes, Corporate Fiction, and the Invention of Cinema* (Chicago: University of Chicago Press, 2008).

19 Akira Mizuta Lippit, *Atomic Light (Shadow Optics)* (Minneapolis: University of Minnesota Press, 2005), 58.

20 On the spectrality of sound, see also Kevin J. Donnelly, *The Spectre of Sound: Music in Film and Television* (London: BFI, 2005).

21 Allen S. Weiss, *Phantasmic Radio* (Durham, NC: Duke University Press, 1995), 7.

22 David Toop, *Sinister Resonance: The Mediumship of the Listener* (New York: Continuum, 2011), vii.

23 Ibid., 130.

24 Sconce, *Haunted Media*, 209.

13

To Scan a Ghost: The Ontology of Mediated Vision

Tom Gunning

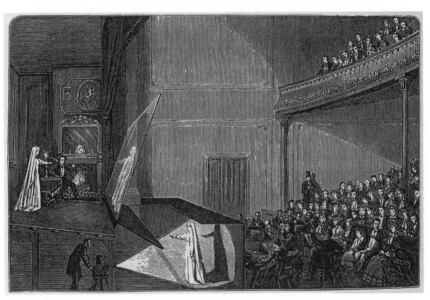

Figure 1 The Pepper's Ghost Illusion of 1862 created the impression of a transparent phantom by means of a reflection on a pane of glass.

1. Rendering the invisible world visible

Though in many of its aspects this visible world seems formed in love, the invisible spheres were formed in fright.

—Herman Melville, *Moby Dick* (1851)

Friedrich W. Murnau's 1922 "Symphony of Horror" *Nosferatu* cuts directly from a swarm of plague-bearing rats (one of which has just bitten a sailor on the foot) emerging from the hold of a ship in which the vampire lies in his coffin filled with earth, to Prof. Bulwer, "a Paracelsian," in a lecture room laboratory initiating his students into the night-side of Nature. Murnau intercuts Bulwer's lecture with shots a film historian (and likely a contemporary viewer) would recognize as taken from (or closely patterned on) the scientific films of the era, including a close-up of a Venus flytrap closing around its prey and a spider crawling along its web toward a trapped insect. Murnau uses complex and highly symbolic intercutting in this scene and throughout the film, less to arouse Griffithian suspense than to create a series of magically interlocking events carried by sinister correspondences and analogies.[1] Thus, although the cut to the spider web confirms Bulwer's demonstration to his students of the pervasive cruelty of nature, its vampire-like system of feeding on other species, this spider web does not cling to some untidy corner of Bulwer's lecture room. Rather, through editing's ability to juxtapose different spaces, this web hangs in the asylum cell of the vampire's minion, Knock, whom we have just seen devour insects, proclaiming, "Blood is life!" Just as Bulwer compares the carnivorous plant to the vampire, Murnau's editing compares the madman and the scientist, each the center of a dark system of deadly metaphors and hysterical imitations. Murnau cuts back from the asylum cell to Bulwer and his students bent over a water tank, as the scientist isolates another vampire of the natural world. A "polyp with tentacles" appears not merely enlarged by a close-up but obviously filmed through micro-cinematography, a frequent technique of scientific films since the invention of cinema.[2] As the microscopic monster's tentacles grasp another cellular creature and seem to devour it, this glimpse into an invisible world made possible by the conjunction of two emblematic modern optical devices (the microscope and the movie camera) still compels our wonder. In an intertitle Bulwer describes the creature: "transparent, almost ethereal ... but a phantom almost." (Indeed one can see, in this silent film, the actor's lips form the word *phantom*, evoking another phantom presence in silent cinema, the voice—eluded to, visualized, even translated into intertitles—but never heard directly[3]).

Murnau's intercutting gives Bulwer's analogies and metaphors a natural, if not a supernatural, demonstration. Cinema visualizes nature's sinister powers through the intercutting of predators across the various locales of the story (dockside, madman's cell, scientific lecture hall). The sequence also demonstrates the uncanny powers of the cinema. By supplying literal and disturbing images of nature's vampiric appetite through close-ups taken from (or closely imitating) scientific films, Murnau not only roots his horror tale in the seemingly objective world but aligns the medium of cinema with other optical devices of observation and display, such as the microscope. If we take this conjunction of the scientific and the supernatural merely as a motif of the horror genre, we miss Murnau's reference to German Romantic *Naturphilosophie*. Bulwer represents more than a horror film mad scientist, exceeding even the Victorian-era biologist Van Helsing from Bram Stoker's *Dracula* who provided the source for the film's scientist character in this free adaptation.[4] Murnau and his scriptwriter (the shadowy Henrik Galeen) backdated Stoker's tale from the end to the early nineteenth century, transforming Van Helsing into a Romantic scientist modeled on figures such as J.W. Ritter, Lorenz Oken, and Alexander von Humboldt.

These pioneers of Romantic life sciences took as their principle the unity of nature and the existence of archetypal forms (like Goethe's *Urpflanze*) throughout nature, uniting the vegetable and animal world (and even the organic and inorganic) in similar dynamic processes of growth, transformation, and decay. As Ritter put it, "Where then is the difference between the parts of an animal, of a plant, of a metal, and of a stone—Are they not all members of the *cosmic-animal*, of *Nature*?"[5] Describing plants as composing "the language of nature,"[6] Ritter, like most Romantic scientists influenced by the *Naturphilosophie* of Schelling, conceived of Nature not as inert material but as an organic entity shot through and enlivened by a system of correspondences and metaphors. By the end of the nineteenth century, however, the logic of such correspondences had been excluded from serious consideration by a positivist and empiricist current in science that had critiqued and replaced the Romantics. But in 1922 Murnau used editing to visualize such metaphors, reviving, through modern technology, an untimely system of thought. For Murnau the medium of cinema appears to demonstrate a system that science no longer endorsed.

In *Nosferatu* Murnau provided world cinema with one of the first masterpieces that systematically reflected on the artistic possibilities of the new medium of cinema. Far be it from me to underestimate the achievement of cinema during its previous two and a half decades (the works of Lumière, Méliès, Bauer, Griffith, and many others). Whereas Griffith aspired (rather disingenuously) to an appearance of transparency in his emulation of historical epic narrative in *The Birth of a Nation* and *Intolerance*,[7] Murnau synthesized the pictorial heritage of the cinema of the 1910s (Tourneur, Bauer, Hofer)[8] with Griffithian strategies of crosscutting, transforming both traditions in the process. *Nosferatu* explored the play between the visible and the invisible, reflections and shadow, on- and off-screen space that cinema made possible, forging a technological image of the uncanny. One senses throughout *Nosferatu* this excitement of innovation, of redefining a medium by testing and transforming its relation to its own history and to other media (the strong use Murnau makes of painting, literary texts, scientific discourse, and even musical rhythms). As such the film offers lessons not only in the nature of cinema as a visual medium but also in the question

Figure 2 *Nosferatu: A Symphony of Horror*. Dir. F.W. Murnau, 1922. Stills. Professor Bulwer, a Paracelsian, explores the vampires of the microscopic world.

of what a "new medium" can create by reflecting upon itself and its differences from and similarities to other media.

Not the least of my discomforts with the current term *new media* comes from the linear succession it inflicts on our still emerging understanding of media history—as if the prime modernist virtue of renewal followed automatically from technical innovation and commercial novelty. I want in this essay to explode the iron cage of historical succession to which this use of the term *new* unwittingly commits us. In its place, I want to celebrate the impact of untimely discovery (which often involves a recycling of the supposed "outmoded") that frequently motivates artistic renewal. But if the term *new* in "new media" seems to be easily critiqued, what about the term *media*? Too often the accent is placed exclusively on the first term with the assumption that the second goes without saying, a transparent channel of transmission, a technological conduit for communication. If the novelty of media is to be granted a purchase in aesthetic analysis, its historical lineage needs explication. What is it that mediates between the seen and the seer—what pathways do vision and the other senses take?—rather than being the mere vehicles of transmitting messages and meaning? As I want to explore and question in this essay the trope of vision and transparency, I also want to focus on the term *medium* itself, in all its polysemy and historical divagations, its very materiality and its paradoxical aspiration to immateriality.

This essay reflects on the occasionally untimely and potentially uncanny nature of modern media, visual and auditory, through a consideration of a pre-modern conceptualization of visual perception and the imagination in Western thought, guided by philosopher Giorgio Agamben's discussion of the "phantasm," and more literally by the untimely figure of the ghost or phantom, especially in visual form.[9] A "phantasm" denotes an image that wavers between the material and immaterial and was used by premodern philosophy and science to explain the workings of both sight and consciousness, especially the imagination (*phantasia*). Although a discredited and untimely concept in both philosophy and science, the phantasm provides a tool for thinking through modern— including "new"—media. I believe that in the new media environment based in the proliferation of virtual images, the concept of the phantasm gains a new valency as an element of the cultural imaginary. The ghost has emerged as a powerful metaphor in recent literary studies, cultural history, and even political theory. An examination of their history of representation, including the newly emerging visual devices can sharpen and renew these metaphors.

The polyp vampire projected by Murnau's microscopic cinema embodies a mediated, phantasmatic imagery whose visual appearance wavers ambiguously between the visible and the invisible. Bulwer's emphasis on the transparency of the predator polyp floating on the screen so highly magnified, its body almost as translucent as the water that bears it, offers not only a literal image of a phantasmatic body (visible, yet seen through); it also recalls for us the transparent nature of film itself, its status as a filter of light, a caster of shadows, a weaver of phantoms. "Transparent, almost a phantom." The act of seeing encounters a bizarre entity whose quasi-ethereal nature marks the limit (or contradiction) of visibility. By displaying the most primitive form of cellular life through the most modern of media, Murnau employs an untimely anachronism, suggesting the anticipation of cinema in this early-nineteenth-century lecture hall. Bulwer and his students are not shown peering into microscopes to see this creature. Instead, the image looms before us, oddly abstracted from any specified means of seeing it, a product of cinema not wholly absorbed back into the film's diegesis, a self-reflective moment that seems to float, in more ways than one, upon the movie screen. Bulwer's demonstration not only makes the drama of microscopic vampirism visible but also makes the medium of its presentation (whether thought of as microscope or cinema) seem to disappear, as the medium becomes transparent in the wake of its message. This elegant demonstration not only visualizes a gaze of scientific mastery but also explores an uncanny dialectic of the visible and the invisible introduced by technologically mediated images.

Bulwer's lesson, despite using scientific footage, occurs in a fictional film, but the attempt to establish an occult invisible world of phantoms through the modern devices of photography has historical foundation. The recent exhibition of spirit photography (originating in La Maison Européenne de la Photographie in Paris, then brought to the Metropolitan Museum of Art in New York City in September of 2005) focused unprecedented attention on nineteenth-century photographic images that were offered as evidence of the existence of spirits or ghosts.[10] While many reviewers treated this exhibition as a joke, it confronted alert viewers with more than a risible encounter with discredited beliefs or even an eccentric episode of photographic history. If these images continue to fascinate us, this may come less from what they indicate about a belief in ghosts than what they reveal of our beliefs about photographs. Rather than focusing on the claims made for such photographs as proof of the existence of a spirit world, I want to explore their formal, visual nature—what supposed photographs of ghosts or spirits *look like*—and their phenomenological aspect—how these images *affect us* as viewers. The convergence between phantoms and photography may prove more than fortuitous. In discussing these Spirit Photographs, the term *phantasmatic* denotes images that oscillate between visibility and invisibility, presence and absence, materiality and immateriality, often using transparency or some other manipulation of visual appearance to express this paradoxical ontological status. Beyond the literal sense of survival after death, ghosts, as phantasms revealing hidden assumptions about the nature of the visual image, still haunt our modern media landscape.

Ghosts or spirits appear in Spirit Photographs primarily as phantoms—bodies rendered optically strange, semitransparent or out of focus, dissolving into shrouds of gauze or simply incongruously "floating" in the space of the photograph. This iconography of phantoms not only draws on a widespread tradition in portraying the ghostly but mimes a visual experience that exceeds or contradicts normal conditions of sight and recognition. Most Spirit Photographs portray spirits alongside "normal" figures in familiar spaces (posed subjects in a studio or room), but the two sorts of bodies appear oddly superimposed upon each other or illogically juxtaposed. This collision of separate orientations betrays the technical means by which the photographs were produced (super-imposing two or more images photographed at separate times) and therefore undermines their claim to be evidence of a spirit world. Nonetheless, their incongruous juxtaposition yields an eerie image of the encounter of two ontologically separate worlds. Like the free-floating polyp of Bulwer's demonstration, Spirit Photographs portray a fissured space, one that allows visitors from another dimension to peek through, hovering within (or beyond), the space occupied by the "normal" figures.

Even if we did not take these unconventional images as rendering actual spirits, a clash of different representations of bodies confronts us (at least on a formal level), the one familiarly solid and positioned, the other somehow filtered by the process of transmission into a virtual body, weightless or permeable—a phantom. Spirit Photography juxtaposes physical presence with its contrary, a phantom-like transformation of the human body that does not remove it from our vision but does render it somehow unreal. Instead of simply being present, the phantom occupies the ontologically ambiguous status of "haunting"—enduring and troubling in its uncanny claim on our awareness and sense of presence yet also unfamiliar and difficult to integrate into everyday space and time. Such phantasms, with their haunting blend of presence/absence, not only formed the subject of Spirit Photography but cast a continued, if occluded, influence over our experience of mediated visual images and photographs in a contemporary culture increasingly dedicated to the virtual.

More than a decade ago I wrote a pioneering essay on Spirit Photography, whose research is now far surpassed by more recent work such as the essays included in the catalog for the Metropolitan Museum exhibition.[11] But the theoretical issues I raised in that earlier essay (and several other related essays dealing with the emergence of modern media recording both sound and images in the nineteenth century) remain crucial.[12] The modern media environment, the proliferation of virtual images and sounds that ever increasingly surround us, recalls earlier models of the relation between consciousness and the cosmos that drew on magical or supernatural analogies.[13] I am far from proposing here a project of reenchantment of technology. Rather I want to probe the unique cultural nature of modern media, which confront us with representations that are fundamentally different from conventional realist theories of mimesis based simply in resemblance. However, rather than offering yet another review of the ontology of the photographic image as proposed by André Bazin, Roland Barthes, and others, I want to explore the ontology and phenomenology of modern media of reproduction (the debates surrounding photography can be extended to both moving image and sound recording) through the metaphor of the ghostly and the phantasm. The ontological argument claims that photography not only portrays things but participates in, shares, or appropriates the very ontology of the things it portrays. In what way does the medium disappear in photography, abdicating in favor of the object portrayed? How does the photographic medium mediate? Spirit Photography opens one way of raising this question, with its ghostly conception of the medium as message.

2. Ghostly vision/ghostly images: Mediums and media

There would be as great an inconvenience in seeing spirits always with us, as in seeing the air that surrounds us, or the myriads of microscopic animals that flutter around us and on us.
—Allan Kardec, *The Book on Mediums* (1878)

Described in an intertitle as a "Paracelsian," Bulwer not only recalls the early-nineteenth-century Romantic scientist but also represents the heritage of "natural magic," an ancestor of experimental science, whose major authors, from Giambattista della Porta and Athanasius Kircher through to David Brewster, dealt with the wonders of nature more than its regularities and explored especially its visual illusions.[14] Scientific and occult beliefs, as well as a fascination with devices of wonder, mixed promiscuously in sixteenth- and seventeenth-century natural magic, creating a tangle that later scientists and philosophers tried hard to sort out. The optical effect of lenses, including microscopes and telescopes, even as they revealed new worlds of the infinitesimal or the seemingly infinitely distant, often got caught in this thicket.[15] Controversies and skepticism initially met images mediated by new optical devices, partly because the effects of mirrors and lenses were primarily associated with the catoptric illusions managed by conjurers and charlatans.[16] Natural magic remained associated with the world of illusions and entertainments, the display of curiosities and extraordinary devices, staging spectacular demonstrations of electricity, magnetism, and optical phenomenon, but often yoked to scientifically dubious explanatory systems.[17] Although accounts of the evolution of scientific thought and

Figure 3   *Nosferatu: A Symphony of Horror*. Dir. F.W. Murnau, 1922. Stills. The vampire's minion Krock eats flies, crying "Blood is life."

experiment privilege the dominant current of Enlightenment mechanistic investigation and explanation, the heritage of natural magic follows scientific thought and practice for centuries like a shadow. The Romantic scientists of the early nineteenth century wished to reform scientific thought by returning it to its roots in the correspondences and metaphors that made up the magical system of Paracelsus, the Renaissance occultist scientist and doctor, but they also endeavored to enrich this esoteric tradition through scientific observation, including employing new visual devices, as well as integrating new conceptions of electricity, magnetism, and the nature of life.[18]

Nineteenth-century American Spiritualism, a loose-knit ideology based on communication with spirits of the dead, primarily through "mediums" who conveyed messages while in a trance, in many ways continued this Romantic tradition.[19] Spiritualists embraced recent scientific devices, such as telegraphy and photography, both as tools for conveying or demonstrating their ideas and as central metaphors for their communication with the spirit world. In an ideology in which "mediumship" played the central role, a fascination with "new" media abounded, allowing a convergence of modern media of communication with occult systems.[20] As Jeffrey Sconce observes in his study *Haunted Media*, discussing the simultaneous development in the mid-nineteenth century of technological messages sent by telegraphy and supernatural messages conveyed by trance mediums, "the historical proximity and intertwined legacies of these founding 'mediums,' one material and the other spiritual, is hardly a coincidence."[21] Romantic *Naturphilosophie* and, in a more popular form, Spiritualism, each sought the dialectical reenchantment of science as well as the scientific foundation of supposed supernatural phenomenon. This quest to rediscover ancient knowledge and revelations implicit in new scientific discoveries encapsulates the untimeliness peculiar to the modern occult—torn between archaic and progressive energies. Bulwer's brief microscopic film, besides scientifically demonstrating the pervasive influence of the vampire throughout nature, also shows what the night side of nature looks like—displaying a devouring phantom, ethereal yet material, visible yet transparent. This convergence of modern media and the spirit world revolves, at least in its visual manifestation, around a phantasmatic body—visible yet insubstantial, an image, separated from its physical basis or somehow strangely rarified, become transparent—a phantom, almost.

What does a ghost look like? A ghost puts the nature of the human senses, vision especially, in crisis. A ghost, a spirit, or a phantom is something that is sensed without being seen. But this does not necessarily mean that ghosts are more easily heard, smelled, or felt (the sense of taste and ghosts seem to have rarely been paired, although orality plays a recurrent role in Spiritualism, as in the extrusion of ectoplasm from the mouths—and other orifices—of mediums). Ghostly presences may be betrayed by each of these senses, but the confluence of the senses that we think of as making up an ordinary reliable perception of reality seems somehow disaggregated in the case of ghosts. In fact, when encountering a ghost, the senses may contradict themselves rather than cohere. One of the earliest testimonies of an encounter with a ghost, given by Emperor Charles IV in the fourteenth century, describes the night the emperor and a companion endured in his castle in Prague during which they repeatedly heard the sound of a man walking and saw a chalice thrown across the room, but no specter ever became visible.[22] Likewise, ghosts frequently appear substantial but allow other bodies and objects to pass through them without resistance. The senses do not converge on ghosts: they can be heard without being seen, smelled without being touched, seen without registering a tactile presence, and so on. Further, the presence of a ghost is often sensed without generating a normal sensual experience. The ghost is there but is not really heard, smelled, felt, or seen.

The essential aspect of a ghost, its terrifying presence, comes from this uncertainty, this problematic relation to the senses and therefore to our sense of the world. One can, of course, discuss this uncertainty in terms of the ontology of the phantom itself, its mode of existence ambiguously perched between the living and the dead, the material and the incorporeal, rather than its mode of being perceived. From St. Augustine at the beginning of the Middle Ages, through the Protestant Reformation, to the polemics of orthodox Christians against the Spiritualists in the nineteenth century, the nature and even the possibility of ghosts have been hotly debated by theologians.[23] The uncertainty sowed by a ghost, then, would be metaphysical rather than phenomenological. But my focus precisely targets the phenomenological, how ghosts present themselves to the living, their mode of apprehension if not perception. The mode of appearing becomes crucial with ghosts and spirits because they are generally understood, by both believers and skeptics, to be apparitions rather than ordinary material objects. What does it mean for a ghost to be an appearance, to be an image? In the late nineteenth century, when people looked at Spirit Photographs, beyond the essential question of individual recognition—how did they know it was the late Uncle Harry?—lay a more basic question: How did they know it was a ghost? What does a ghost look like?

According to the admirable study by Jean-Claude Schmitt, the earliest attempts to give a visual representation of ghosts, illustrations included in medieval manuscripts, usually miniatures worked into the text itself, portrayed ghosts no differently than living people. Thus even ghosts in tales describing them as invisible were portrayed with conventional bodies (as in the illustration included in manuscripts of Charles IV's account of the Prague ghost). Sometimes their ghostly nature was indicted by macabre details, the wearing of a shroud, evidence of bodily decay, or outright portrayal as a cadaver. Toward the end of the thirteenth century ghosts first appear portrayed as phantoms. Schmitt describes an example from a Spanish manuscript: "he is lacking all color and material density; the description of his face and his clothing is reduced to a drawing that is uniformly diaphanous and scarcely visible."[24] As Schmitt puts it, this image "announces from afar those that, since the nineteenth century, have been imposed on us to the exclusion of all others."[25]

My interest in this question goes beyond the iconography of the ghostly; it circles back on the ghost as paradoxical figure of vision, the shadowy ontological status of the ghost as a virtual image, a visual experience that somehow differs from common perception and whose means of representation seek to convey that ontological waver. To fully explore this, I want to probe traditional understandings of visual perception and the role images play in the process as mediation between objects and human perception, a tradition gradually attenuated in the modern era of optics yet strangely re-emerged in the phenomena of photography and Spiritualism. In theories of human vision, the ghostly and the phantasmatic play a complex role, as sight has often been conceived as quasi-spiritual, somehow ethereal, as if the process of vision itself were almost phantom-like.

3. The ghostly medium of vision: The phantasm

These visible things come inside the eye—I do not say the things themselves, but their forms—through the diaphanous medium, not in reality but intentionally, almost as if through transparent glass.
—Dante Alighieri, *Convivio* III.9

Before Kepler and the rise of modern optics explained vision as a relation between light and lenses—that is, media that carried and shaped light, whether a lens precisely ground, a glass of water, or the human eye—the medium by which sight occurred was understood as consisting of images, *phantasmata*, that in effect worked as relays between objects seen and human vision. According to Aristotle, both perception and thinking rely on *phantasia* (usually translated as "images" or "imagination"), "for when the mind is actively aware of anything it is necessarily aware of it along with an image: for images are like sensuous contents except in that they contain no matter,"[26] adding, "the name *phantasia* (imagination) has been developed from *phaos* (light) because it is not possible to see without light."[27] In its sensual yet immaterial nature *phantasia* works through the virtual image, *phantasm*. The Stoics and Epicureans, while holding that these images possessed a more physical nature than Aristotle claimed (by which means they were able to impress their form on the soul in perception and thought) and disagreeing among themselves about their exact processes, still maintained the existence of such an imagistic intermediary.[28]

The premodern worldview, especially after the triumph of a Platonically tinged Christianity, constructed hierarchies and chains of being in which reality relied on a communication across gradations of distance from the divine. Across such distances intermediaries played essential roles. Thus St. Augustine described vision as threefold, corresponding to the triple nature of human being: intellectual vision (reason), physical vision (body), and spiritual vision (the soul). Human beings saw the physical world through corporeal vision, *sensus*, and recognized abstract ideas through intellectual vision, *mens*, which in its contemplation of God went beyond any image. But between these extremes, spiritual vision constituted a hybrid process, the realm of imagination; it experienced the images of things, but separate from their bodily being. Imagination included memory as well as fantasy and the realm of dreams. But all three realms of sight depended on intermediaries, whether the abstract ideas used by the intellectual vision, or the images that carried the imagination.[29] As Jean-Claude Schmitt summarizes this tradition in the Middle Ages, even physical sight involved the "concrete, physical interaction of the eye and the object through an external medium: *species* circulated and penetrated into the eye."[30]

This conception of sight pictured the eye's ability to form an image less as an optical process, as currently understood, than as a more material process as the human perceptive faculty became imprinted by an intermediary, the *phantasm* or *species* that already bore the nature of an image. While Greek authorities, followed by their Arabic translators and commentators, supplied numerous variations and modifications on this scheme, the extreme description provided by the Epicurean and atomist philosopher Lucretius remained both influential and typical.[31] Vision, Lucretius claimed, was carried by images (*simulacra*), which he described quite materially as *films*, "a sort of outer skin perpetually peeled off the surface of objects and flying about this way and through the air."[32] He explained their effect on human vision as one of direct contact: "while the individual films that strike upon the eye are invisible, the objects from which they emanate are perceived."[33] As David Lindberg summarizes this tradition, "films or *simulacra* ... communicate the shape and colour of the object to the soul of the observer; encountering the *simulacrum* of an object is, as far as the soul is concerned, equivalent to encountering the object itself."[34] Roger Bacon's thirteenth-century synthesis of theories of vision, aligned with an Aristotelian understanding of vision as involving a transformation of the medium of air (rather than the atomists' assumption of actual material, albeit rarefied, "films" that separated from visible objects), nonetheless depended upon intermediaries that ferried the image from object to observer moving through the medium of the air, explaining, "and this power is called 'likeness,' 'image' and 'species.'"[35]

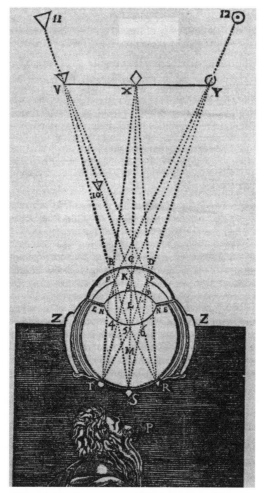

Figure 4   René Descartes. *Dioptrics*, 1637. Diagram of the retinal image.

To a modern eye, this explanation of the phenomenon of vision seems not only unduly complex and redundant but oddly ghostly. Lucretius's description of a universe in which "objects in general must correspondingly send off a great many images in a great many ways from every surface and in all directions simultaneously"[36] evokes a world thick with ghosts, a hall of reflecting mirrors (or perhaps a contemporary airport lounge stocked with successive monitors all broadcasting CNN). Among the terms that Bacon listed as synonyms for his *species—lumen, idolum, phantasma, simulacrum, forma, similtudo, umbra*[37]—are terms used then and now for ghosts. Indeed, before the nineteenth century the world of imagination and images, *phantasia* and *phantasmata*, constituted the medium not only of vision but also of psychology generally, as images were the means by which objects penetrated consciousness, dreams occurred, artists created works, lovers became obsessed, magical influences were conveyed, memories were preserved—and ghosts appeared. The Renaissance system of magical influence depended, as Iaon Couliano showed, on the manipulation and control of phantasms, powerful intermediaries that human action could direct, intensify, and control.[38] Giorgio Agamben describes this system of *phantasma* as "a kind of subtle body of the soul that, situated at the extreme point of the sensitive soul, receives the images of objects, forms the phantasms of dreams, and, in determinate circumstances, can separate itself from the body and establish supernatural contacts and visions."[39] Of course, different philosophical schools elaborated distinctions among these processes and debated various theories of their nature, but until relatively recently phantasms or similar intermediaries constituted a realm of images that determined contact between human beings and the world. Within such a worldview, filled with mobile insubstantial images, an atmosphere of virtuality, the experience of seeing ghosts seems almost natural, rather than supernatural.

Kepler's explication of vision as the interaction between light, the eye, and the retinal image can be considered to be as revolutionary as the almost simultaneous displacement of the earth-centered theory of the universe that he and Copernicus theorized.[40] Compared to Kepler's schema of vision, the unnecessary duplication created by the model of free-floating images posed a barrier to a true scientific understanding of perception.[41] This new optical understanding of the process of vision rendered the category of phantasms unnecessary for the understanding of vision and therefore made the medium that joined the mental and the physical (and by which ghosts were also experienced) no longer a necessary part of the explanation of ordinary experience. In the premodern system, insubstantial ghosts had shared the ontology of the phantasms that conveyed emotion, dreams, and artistic imagination. But in the modern era in which vision directly communicated with the world through the optical operation of the eye, ghosts' lack of clearly defined sensual properties placed them beyond the categories of scientific observation or consideration.

4. The apparatus of vision: Optical illusions and optical devices

Is it hard for you to accept such a mechanical and artificial system for the reproduction of life? It might help if you bear in mind that what changes the sleight-of-hand artist's movements into magic is our inability to see!
—Adolfo Bioy Casares, *The Invention of Morel* (1940)

After the Enlightenment, the question of what a ghost looked like bifurcated into issues of psychology (in which the concept of phantasia survived, albeit through a transformation of the understanding of psychic processes) and of optics. In contrast to traditional speculation on what ghosts might look like and how they were able to appear to the living, or theological arguments for or against the existence of spirits of the dead, optics or psychology primarily provided the means of explaining ghosts away, reducing them to mental delusions or visual illusions. Psychological explanation remains our major hermeneutic of the ghostly. As Terry Castle has put it, discussing the phantoms that haunt the Gothic novels of Ann Radcliffe, "Ghost and spectres retain their ambiguous grip on the imagination; they simply migrate into the space of the mind."[42] The optical explanation of ghosts primarily took the form of debunking ghosts as deliberately manufactured illusions, often by revealing the purely scientific means by which optical illusions that resemble ghosts or phantoms could be created. In this context ghosts no longer had any body, material, subtle or phantasmatic. They consisted simply of virtual images produced by optical devices. A new modern history of phantoms as optical phenomenon, images scientifically explainable and therefore natural, yet uncanny in their sensual effects, emerges once phantasms no longer explain the process of perception. Exiled from the realm of physical effects, phantasms (to paraphrase Castle) migrate to a new realm, that of the virtual image, whose uncanny sensual and psychological effects linger like the residue of a lost explanatory system, haunting new optical media such as the magic lantern, *camera obscura*, and, eventually, photography.

Much of this debunking discourse emerged as a Protestant critique of Catholicism and "popery mystifications."[43] Theologically, the Protestant denial of the existence of purgatory abolished a major argument for the existence of ghosts as visits from the souls of the dead (a possibility that had sometimes been controversial within Catholicism as well). If purgatory existed, souls there might visit the living to complain about their suffering and beseech the offering of alms or the saying of masses to ease their torments. But if Purgatory did not exist, or ghosts did not visit the living, how could one explain ongoing testimonies of such apparitions?[44] Keith Thomas cites seventeenth-century Protestant polemicists who claimed that Jesuits had faked apparitions in order to convert impressionable women to the Roman faith.[45]

Skepticism about the existence of ghosts was not new, but the new science of optics could explain away the ghost as a visual illusion created intentionally by means of an optical apparatus. This tradition began in the sixteenth century, partly cued by the Reformation. Scot's *Discoverie of Witches* from 1584 skeptically approached the issue of witchcraft, primarily attributing it to the magical illusion of juggling, sleight of hand, and fooling the eye and attempting to explain in this way the invocation of the ghost of Saul by the Witch of Endor described in the Old Testament (a source of controversy throughout Church history as one of the few places where spirits of the dead are mentioned in the Bible).[46] Charles Musser has pointed out that the key work on optical devices of illusion (and natural magic) from the seventeenth century, Jesuit Athanasius Kircher's *Ars magna lucis et umbra*, recommended a similar strategy of demystification, not only describing the scientific basis for optical devices such as catoptric lamps and mirrors (adding in the second edition [1671], the magic lantern) but urging that such devices be fully explained when displayed to the public.[47]

Creating optical phantoms became a form of entertainment in the eighteenth century and supplied a convention of the Gothic novel.[48] Schiller's 1784 novella, "The Ghost-Seer," described by the author as a contribution to the "history of deceit and artifice so often imposed upon mankind," revealed an apparent appearance of a ghost in its plot as the result of a concealed optical device, a magic lantern combined with mechanical effects of light and dark.[49] As if acting out Schiller's scenario, the phantasmagoria exhibitions staged in France in the late eighteenth century by Philipstahl and Robertson incorporated the demystification process into their elaborate magic lantern spectacles that claimed to present "phantasms of the dead or absent" to a paying public.[50] Thus when Philipstahl (using the name Philip Philidor) presented his phantasmagoria in Paris in 1793, he introduced his spectacle with this demystifying preamble:

> I will not show you ghosts, because there are no such things; but I will produce before you enactments and images, which are imagined to be ghosts, in the dreams of the imagination or in the falsehoods of charlatans.
> I am neither priest nor magician. I do not wish to deceive you; but I will astonish you.[51]

When Robertson presented an even more elaborate version of this ghost show in Paris a few years later he actually proclaimed his optical spectacle to be "a science which deals with all the physical methods which have been misused in all ages and by all peoples to create belief in the resurrection and apparition of the dead."[52] In the context of revolutionary Paris these optical demonstrations attacked religion as dependent on contrived illusions and claimed to reveal the optical means of deception that had been used by priests for centuries. Reproducing by optical devices the Old Testament account of the Witch of Endor's evocation of the ghost of Saul, Robertson attempted to demonstrate the long history of such deceptions and proclaimed his entertainment a sterling contribution to the revolutionary energy of the era.[53]

Likewise, Sir David Brewster's *Letters on Natural Magic* from 1832 defined his subject as the exposing of the means by which tyrants of all ages had enslaved mankind through superstitious belief in their supernatural power, claiming priests of ancient eras

> must have been familiar with the property of lenses and mirrors to form erect and inverted images of objects.... There is reason to believe that they employed them to effect the apparitions of their gods; and in some of the descriptions of the optical displays which hallowed their ancient temples, we recognize all the transformations of the modern phantasmagoria.[54]

Brewster's retrospective reading of supernatural beliefs or events as the product of optical conjuring reveals how firmly scientific explanation based in optics had replaced visual theories that blurred the line between object and phantasm in explaining supernatural effects. Premodern practices and beliefs were now reinterpreted from an optical point of view, with a typically modern hermeneutic of suspicion. Brewster devotes some time to discussing the physiology of the eye and claims that mental images, or phantasms, can in circumstances overwhelm normal sight and cause hallucinations. His explanation extends Kepler's model of the physiology of the eye with a claim that even in these psychological cases the retinal image is involved: "the 'mind's eye' is actually the body's eye, and ... the retina is the common tablet on which both classes of impressions are painted."[55]

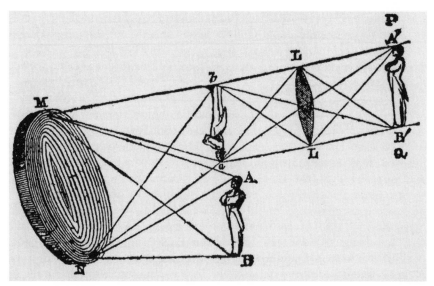

Figure 5   Sir David Brewster. *Letters on Natural Magic Addressed to Sir Walter Scott*, 1832. Illustration showing a catadioptrical phantasmagoria, whereby phantasm could be projected optically.

However, such a radical shift in models of explanation also produced untimely palimpsests in which older models remain legible beneath the inscription of new concepts, especially on the level of popular explanation or artistic metaphor, as if supernatural explanations still haunted the optically obtained virtual image. As ancient accounts of seeing ghosts were anachronistically redefined in terms of modern optical devices, advances in technology were often reinterpreted in an untimely fashion in terms of older, scientifically discredited, systems. Some initial receptions of photography exemplify this untimely persistence of older beliefs. In a well-known memoir, the great nineteenth-century photographer Nadar described a theory of the daguerreotype offered by novelist Honoré de Balzac to explain why he avoided being photographed:

> [A]ll physical bodies are made up entirely of layers of ghost-like images, an infinite number of leaflike skins laid one on top of the other. Since Balzac believed man was incapable of making something material from an apparition, from something impalpable—that is creating something from nothing—he concluded that every time someone had his photograph taken, one of the spectral layers was removed from the body, and transferred to the photograph. Repeated exposures entailed the unavoidable loss of subsequent ghostly layers, that is the very essence of life.[56]

In an era when a classical education still formed part of French culture, one wonders if Nadar failed to recognize Lucretius's theory of detached visual films emanating from objects as the source of Balzac's explanation (or perhaps assumed it was so evident he need not bother to mention it?). This description, which Nadar described as Balzac's resistance to the "purely scientific explanation of the Daguerreotype,"[57] added a macabre aspect to the phantasm. The photograph becomes not only the harbinger but a possible cause of death and decay, with an emphasis on the "ghostly" quality of the detaching films. Nadar's account of Balzac's theory was based on several personal discussions, but he added the author had developed it "in a little alcove somewhere in the immense edifice of work."[58] Balzac's discussion of this theory in *The Human Comedy* consists of a rather short passage in the novel *Cousin Pons* in which the narrator seems to be celebrating the novelty of the invention of Daguerre rather than resurrecting an aspect of ancient philosophy:

> If anyone had come and told Napoleon that a man or a building is incessantly and continuously represented by a picture in the atmosphere, that all existing objects project into it a kind of *spectre* which can be captured and perceived, he would have consigned him to Charenton as a lunatic ... and yet that is what Daguerre's discovery proved.[59]

However the untimeliness of this modern conception still plays a role in Balzac's conception of photography because this description occurs within a claim for the possibility of divination, albeit based on new discoveries within the occult sciences.

5. Phantasms of amusement and the modern everyday environment

Every fixture and every movement conjures up shadow plays on the wall—immaterial silhouettes that hover through the air and become mixed with the mirror-images from the glass room itself. The raising of this impalpable glassy ghost, which transforms itself like a kaleidoscope or light reflex, signifies that the new dwelling is not the last solution.
—Siegfried Kracauer, "Das neue Bauen" (1927)

For Balzac, the new optical device of photography, a direct application of Kepler's theory of the retinal image to a mechanical device, supplied proof of the existence of the visual phantasms that Kepler's optics had rendered redundant. This untimely revival of an ancient tradition is similar to Bulwer using micro-cinematography and biology to demonstrate the existence of vampires. In both these instances the appearance of the photographic image is so powerful, so unusual (in Balzac's case, partly because of the novelty of photography at the time he was writing), that it takes on an uncanny aspect even if fully scientific explanations are available. Uncanny aspects of the photographic image seem to outrun its more ordinary explanations because a photograph renders visible in objective form the immaterial phantasms that the optical revolution had exorcized. The virtual image becomes the modern phantom. Terry Castle has even described photography as "the ultimate ghost-producing technology of the nineteenth century," the true heir of the phantasmagoria.[60] Indicating that Balzac's uncanny sense of the photographic process still has resonance, Castle even claims that modern culture has felt impelled to find mechanical techniques for remaking the world itself in spectral form. Photography was the first great breakthrough—a way of possessing material objects in a strangely decorporealized yet also supernaturally vivid form. But still more bizarre forms of spectral representation have appeared in the twentieth century—the moving pictures of cinematography and television, and recently, the eerie, three dimensional phantasmata of holography and virtual reality.[61]

The fascination kindled by a decorporealized virtual body partly explains the uncanny experience we often have of Spirit Photographs, even when we know precisely the photographic means used to create them. As I described them earlier, the ghostly "extras" that appear in these images as either semitransparent superimpositions or oddly placed opaque interventions visualize a collision between the free-floating phantasm of Lucretius and a world of flesh and blood creatures. The disproportionate montage of these visually distinct realms makes a Spirit Photograph visually compelling— spooky, in fact. Ultimately, what emerges in these images may be less ocular evidence of another world (whether microscopic or ghostly) than the way photography itself, as a medium, becomes foregrounded. In these images, we no longer see *through* the photograph but become aware of the uncanny nature of the process of capturing an image itself. Our gaze is caught, suspended, stuck within the transparent film itself.

But perhaps the most extraordinary historical fact about Spirit Photographs lies in the fact that such images existed for years before any Spiritualist seemed to have claimed them.[62] Numerous amateur photographers had inadvertently produced them before, as when in 1856 Sir David Brewster, historian of science and magic, inventor of such optical devices as the kaleidoscope and one version of the stereoscope, described the effect of "ghostly" photographs. Brewster had observed (in this era which required long-lasting photographic exposures) that if someone moved out of the frame too soon she either did not appear on the final plate at all (like the passersby erased from Daguerre's famous 1839 photo of the Boulevard Temple), or, if she lingered a bit longer (but not long enough to be fully registered), left a semitransparent image of herself. These accidentally spoiled photographs amused Brewster, who pointed out that they could be composed intentionally to produce "ghost photographs."[63] In his earlier work on natural magic, Brewster had thoroughly explored the creation of optical illusions intended to create supernatural effects. The purpose of such manufactured photographic ghosts, he stressed, must be restricted to amusement and entertainment. For at least a decade such images were produced, domestically and commercially, before William Mumler famously proclaimed his photographs as images of actual ghosts or spirits. Although we don't know if such claims were made outside of the public sphere before Mumler, his images and *his claims* of their supernatural provenance caused such a stir that one has to assume that a shift in definition had taken place.[64] The supernatural explanation of such photographs ran contrary to readily available technical accounts (described in texts by Brewster and others) and the apparently fairly widespread practice of manufacturing similar superimpositions without any supernatural claim. Yet the photographic production of transparent superimposed bodies still offered an ocular experience of the image of ghosts or spirits (which were taken by some viewers as proof of their existence).

Around the same time as Mumler's claims, a theatrical device for the production of phantoms appeared whose visual acuity surpassed even the phantasmagoria and whose imagery and process closely resembles Spirit Photography: the famous Pepper's Ghost Illusion invented by Henry

Dircks and perfected and presented at London's Royal Polytechnic Institute in 1862 by John Henry Pepper.[65] Designed as stage machinery for the creation of transparent phantoms, the illusion used a pane of glass that emerged from slots in front of the stage and could be lowered as needed. The glass was angled so that it caught a reflection of a highly illuminated figure (usually an actor) posed in an area unseen by the audience. The glass also remained invisible to the audience, and only the reflection appeared, a transparent figure superimposed over the stage scene that was visible through the glass. Thus while the actors seen on stage would remain fully opaque and three dimensional, the reflections on the glass would seem virtual and transparent, as one could see scenery and actors through the glass in the foreground. Further, actors on the stage seemed to pass through the reflections. Used primarily to stage simple ghost stories of apparitions and hauntings, the Pepper's Ghost Illusion achieved an enormous success and became part of the stage machinery of the late Victorian spectacular theater. The device offered the optical experience of living, moving figures that nonetheless remained virtual and insubstantial within the space in which they seemed to appear. Alien visitors, the reflections appeared as detached images floating on air. A product of the science of optics (angles of reflection, the transparency of glass), the device superimposed flesh and blood bodies with phantoms in an uncanny and undeniable sensual experience.

Pepper's Ghost Illusion partly owed its success to the novelty of the large pane of glass without imperfections so necessary to the illusion. During the late nineteenth century the manufacture of large panes of glass became commercially and technically possible and enormously increased the visual attraction of the emerging commercial display culture, as reflective surfaces moved from being luxury items found only in palaces to mass-produced commodities adorning city streets. Instead of being restricted to multiplying the image of the king and his courtiers, store windows and mirrors greeted passersby on busy streets, endowing them with optical doubles, mixing passing crowds with their visual phantoms. Optical devices designed entirely as entertainment, such as the stereoscope and kaleidoscope that Brewster produced, joined scientific optical devices that had emerged in the seventeenth century and spawned a new realm of visual amusements ranging from the theater to the parlor to the nursery.[66] As the Renaissance phantasms faded from history, their optically manufactured doppelgangers appeared multiplied in a new daily environment of transparency and reflection.

Further, as glass windows became part of modern transportation systems, transparent and reflecting surfaces began to move, as one looked through (or looked at) windows on trains and trolleys. Yuri Tsivian has given me a rich description from the turn of the century of this new urban visual environment that mingled real and virtual images, visions transmitted or

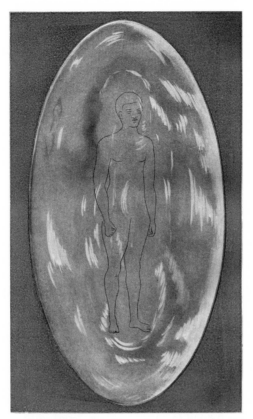

Figure 6   C. W. Ledbetter. *Man Visible and Invisible*, 1902. The astral bodies of the savage according to C.W. Ledbetter's Theosophical system.

reflected by glass, written in 1899 by a Dr. M.V. Pogorelsky for a Russian occult journal named *Rebus*. "The quality of multiple reflections that the modern city provides us with has turned it into the natural medium of haunting," Pogorelsky claimed, as he described a trolley trip through St. Petersburg:

> In the window opposite you see the real street; it also reflects the side of the street behind the observer's back. Reflections of the front and rear windows of the car fall on it as well; apart from that, the *double* reflection of the real part of the street under observation is imprinted on it. The fact that the car itself is in movement makes the whole picture especially complex. In clear air and bright sunlight both real objects and their mirages look particularly life-like, and what you get as a result is a magic picture, extremely complex and

mingled.... . Passing carriages are not one directional any more, they move in a chaos overtaking themselves or passing *through* each other. Some carriages and passersby look as if they were rushing forwards, but at the same time you are aware that, in fact, each step they make takes them backwards. If your attention wanders for a second you also lose the criterion that separates real objects from their equally life-like apparitions.[67]

Pogorelsky's visual experience of the new mobile modern city with its clash of reflective surfaces navigates through a perceptual space that would also inspire cubist and futurist painters about a decade later, painters often (as in the case of Severini, Kupka, or Duchamp) inspired by occult sources as well. For Pogorelsky, this novel visual environment produced a haunted space, the reflections capturing images he understood as ghostly.

In the modern environment the virtual visual image interpenetrates the everyday world of corporeality and solidity. For the Spiritualist, the spirit world intersects with the material world; perceiving it is simply a matter of the sensitivity of the medium. While a worldview based in scientific explanation may leave no room for the supernatural, modern spiritual movements, such as Spiritualism and Theosophy, strove to find resonance between their beliefs and the discoveries and devices of science, in effect reenchanting the disenchanted world but also fashioning a new synthesis between the occult and the technological.[68] The invisible world of modern science revealed by X-rays and radioscopes—beyond the immediate evidence of the senses, shot through with the vibration of invisible particles, interpenetrated by invisible rays or energy— provided the mystically inclined with a new vocabulary of occult forces drawn primarily from scientific metaphors rather than the scientific method.[69]

The convergence of the scientific dematerialization of the perceptual world with the possibility of its hypervisualization via optical devices could convert the whole of the cosmos and its history into a series of virtual images. Camille Flammarion, who popularized both recent scientific developments and Spiritualist beliefs to the French public in the nineteenth century (including a strong endorsement of Spirit Photography), composed such a vision of the cosmos and history in his science fiction fantasy *Lumen*. Flammarion's extraterrestrial narrator declares that all events "became incorporated into a ray of light; thus it will transmit itself eternally into the infinite."[70] Cosmic history appears as a succession of disembodied visual images projected into outer space and visible to an ideally placed observer aided by optical devices:

all the events accomplished upon the earth's surface, since its creations are visible in space at distances proportional to their remoteness in the past. The whole history of the globe and the life of every one of its inhabitants, could thus be seen at a glance by an eye capable of embracing that space.[71]

All of time can be conceived as a motion-picture beam projected into the infinite, envisioned by Flammarion decades before Edison's invention. Such purely optical images allow the possibility of witnessing all of past history as it streams through space.

The instruments of science gave birth to specters as scientific photography completed a circuit through avant-garde art and occult concepts. The chrono-photographic images Etienne-Jules Marey produced in the 1880s for the straightforwardly materialist purpose of the detailed observation of the physical human body in motion registered transparent specters as the bodies moved through the frame that Kupka (and perhaps Duchamp) reinterpreted in terms of the occult multiple bodies described by Theosophy.[72] The most complete synthesis of occult lore, combined with a highly creative interpretation of Hindu and Buddhist conceptions, in the late nineteenth century Theosophy devised a theory of bodies and perception that outdid the premodern system of correspondences and phantasms in complexity.[73] Human beings, according to Theosophy, have, even during life, a multiplicity of bodies—the physical, the astral, the mental, and the causal—all of which correspond to various types of extrasensory perception. A true clairvoyant can see each of these bodies and their variety of forms and colors, which indicate a person's stage of spiritual evolution. These bodies take the form of egglike auras surrounding the person, rippling with continually changing energies and flowing patterns of color.[74] For the Theosophist, the visual appearance of these occult bodies indicates a person's physical health, their dominant emotions, and their level of spiritual evolution.

Refusing to limit the total reality of the human body to the manifest physicality of the body examined by modern science, the occult devised a variety of visual forms to express a bodily existence that transcends ordinary sensual evidence. But the visual imagery of science in the twentieth century, while still determinately indexical and empirical, deviates sharply from the classical medical gaze of anatomy and has become increasingly abstract and technologically mediated, producing images often unrecognizable to the layperson, with appearances seemingly as fanciful in their deviation from ordinary vision as the most bizarre occultist imagery. As we move more and more into a world in which data takes on visual form, these forms seem to become less and less familiar. Modern scientific imaging, supplemented not only by complex lenses but by other forms of data collection often associated with the other senses (ultrasound, night vision's sensitivity to heat, the tactile bouncing of radar off objects) has produced new images of the body that reflect this constant transformation and defamiliarization. Looking at the rather naive superimpositions of transparent bodies in Spirit Photographs, we respond less to the images of the dearly departed than to the first impulse toward a new image of the body, captured by new technologies of vision and seemingly liberated from the constraints of mortal physiology. In comparison to the phantasms of modern medical imaging, they now seem quaintly pictorial.

6. Looking at death is dying: The virtual image and the aporia of vision

Alas, how is't with you,
That you do bend your eye on vacancy,
And with th'incorporal air do hold discourse?
              —Shakespeare, *Hamlet*, Act III, sc. iv.

We do not *believe* in ghosts, we are *haunted* by them. We do not see ghosts. Rather, our senses of vision and perception are brought to a crisis by them. As revenants of things past, ghosts make vivid to us the pairing of memory and forgetting. The ghostly returns even after being shown the door, even after death, just as the metaphors of the phantasmatic endure after scientific explanations seemingly triumph. As Jean-Claude Schmitt shows us, to forget the dead we must first remember them: traditionally, hauntings are the result of an inability to forget, due to an incomplete process of memorialization.[75] As harbingers of the future, ghosts show what we are to become in minatory mode: as they are now, so we shall be ...

The ghostly fascinates us as a complex of two fundamental fantasies. First, it envisions a phantasmatic body, fundamentally different from ordinary bodily experience, whose appearance seems to make us doubt or rethink the nature of our senses, our grasp on reality. Corporeality, the sign of the real and material becomes tricked out in the guise of the incorporeal. The fascination this paradox exerts reveals our discomfort with the original dichotomy of body and soul, material and spiritual. Second, the ghostly represents a fundamental untimeliness, a return of the past not in the form of memory or history but in a contradictory experience of presence, contained, as Derrida has shown us, in the term *haunting*.[76]

Technological bodies made of light, seizing and exceeding all the possibilities of physical movement, or an ability to overcome linear time, to navigate through, anticipate, or recycle past and future moments—such ghostly gifts also provide the substance of popular media fantasies. Yet if these modern media phantasms enact basic fantasies of release from limitations, they also carry, even if repressed, a warning of mortality and limitations, of the inevitable horizon of death. Roland Barthes has analyzed the deeply resonant association of still photography with death.[77] While

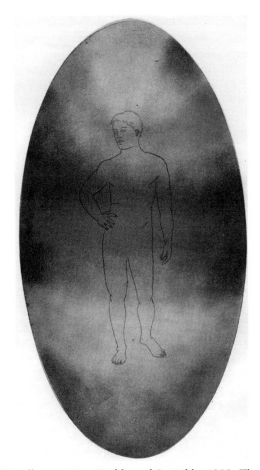

Figure 7   C.W. Ledbetter. *Man Visible and Invisible*, 1902. The astral bodies of the ordinary man according to C.W. Ledbetter's Theosophical system.

Barthes's discomfort with the moving image prevented him from extending this discussion to the cinema, all virtual images and recorded sound also invoke the ghostly ontology of phantasms rather than a simple triumph over death. As Garrett Stewart has brilliantly demonstrated, the still image haunts the cinema and emerges most frequently as a harbinger of death and the ghostly.[78] If the virtual escapes death, it is simply because, as a phantom, it also escapes life. It delights us because it shows us that which remains impossible for embodied human existence. It chills us because it crosses a barrier we cannot.

This essay takes its title from one of the most enigmatic poems by one of our most enigmatic poets, Emily Dickinson. I am not a Dickinson scholar, simply a devoted reader, but in closing I feel compelled to grapple with her text. Even more than most Dickinson poems, this one defies quick reading. Nearly every line ends with a dash, creating not so much a pattern of pauses, as a sequence of gasps, as if each sentence suspends itself in a sharp intake of breath, or perhaps a final choke. The poem seems to exist in fragments that refuse to cohere, replicating the frenzied yet halting viewing that a ghost might cause:

'Tis so appalling—it exhilarates—
So over Horror, it half Captivates—
The Soul stares after it, secure—
A Sepulchre, fears frost, no more

A subsequent stanza probes even more uncertain expression and syntax:

To scan a Ghost, is faint—
But grappling, conquers it—
How easy, Torment, now—
Suspense kept sawing so—

What does Dickinson mean by "to scan a ghost?" Whereas I chose it as my title partly due to its untimely pun on the most contemporary means of reproducing images, the computer scanner, what did Dickinson mean by scanning a ghost? "To scan" has two basic meanings that curiously combine in the modern use of a computer scanner: to analyze a poem in terms of metrics, line by line, and, according to the *Oxford English Dictionary* (*OED*), "to look at searchingly to examine with the eyes." Dickinson primarily intends the second meaning (i.e., it is difficult to examine a ghost closely), but as a poet writing a verse that in fact, scans quite unconventionally, she also intends at least an echo of the first meaning. To follow the patterns of stresses, the number of feet, would seem to characterize grappling with something, calculating its rhythm and weighing its meter, even more than a searching gaze. The unbalanced, unfinished syntax of these lines invokes the sawing of suspense, both the process of cutting in two and the up and down balancing of a seesaw.

The last stanzas increase this rhythm of suspended conclusions and unfinished statements left lingering in ambiguities and syntactical interruptions:

The Truth, is Bald, and Cold—
But that will hold—
If any are not sure—
We show them—prayer—
But we, who know,
Stop hoping, now—

Looking at Death, is Dying—
Just let go the Breath—
And not the pillow at your Cheek
So Slumbereth—

Others, Can wrestle—
Yours, is done—
And so of Woe, bleak dreaded—come,
It sets the Fright at liberty—
And Terror's free—
Gay, Ghastly, Holiday!

Depth of analysis is not needed to see this poem as driven by its ambivalence toward the sight of a ghost as the harbinger of death; it succinctly sums up what I have wanted to say in this essay about the challenge seeing a ghost offers to perception in its line "Looking at Death, is Dying—." Sight itself proceeds by phantoms, at least in reflection. While vision remains our prime image of presence, reflecting on sight also evokes the possibility of illusion, the delusion of bending the eye on vacancy. Dickenson's third and fourth stanzas maintain a struggle. Wrestling with hope and prayer contends with gestures of release, a stopping of hope, a letting go of breath, a slumbering. With this release the last stanza offers the proclamation that carries more finality than clarity: "Yours is done," and an invocation to "bleak dreaded" Woe to "come." This invocation releases things, fright at liberty, terror free, but the final uncertainty resides in the linguistic ambiguity of such release. What does it mean to set free Fright and Terror? That is, once freed, do they depart from us, leaving us alone? Or are they simply set unconfined, allowed to roam the earth? Almost humorous in its oxymoron, the final line seems to imagine the grim celebration found in traditional representations of the Dance of Death—"Gay, Ghastly Holiday."

To scan a ghost is faint. Like the medieval Spanish illustration of a phantom that Schmitt discusses, the image fades; it no longer seems to hold our gaze, which, instead, passes through it, transparently. But seeing through a phantom does not mean overlooking a ghost. Instead the transparency of vision terrifies the viewer. However, to liberate a ghost may also indicate a process of exorcism, "laying a ghost," as the traditional phrase puts it. Schmitt speculates that the faint appearance of the Spanish illustration may indicate a ghost that has been dead for some time; its connection with the physical cadaver has disappeared as the fleshly body has decayed.[79] In this view, ghosts would fade continuously. As Freud makes clear in his great essay, "Mourning and Melancholy," surviving the dead depends on our ability to slowly and purposefully forget them, to let them leave our world. But this work of mourning involves as well a task of remembrance, the conscious process that differentiates mourning from the disease of melancholia. Perhaps the ultimate power of Spirit Photographs lies in acting out our attempt to hold onto the dead, an attempt to retain them by capturing their image, balanced, however, with an uncanny visual image that, unlike, say, a snapshot of a loved one when still alive, expresses their alien nature, their bodies transformed even if recognizable, departed from our world. They appear to us, but they also elude us. They do not let us grasp them. Rather they may allow us to release them into the realm of pure imagery and virtuality—of mourning and untimeliness.

But surrounded by the plethora of virtual images that throng our modern media, do we simply witness that aspect of Spiritualism that most disturbed the symbolist (and occultist) J.K. Huysmans, its vulgar democratization of the supernatural, opening the sacred realm to the floodgates of the crowds of the dead?[80] Should we simply marvel with Eliot (and Dante) at the throngs of dead, unaware "death had undone so many"? The virtual often seems to offer less a mode of mourning and release than a Sisyphean process of endless proliferation and compulsive repetition and return, the mechanical reproduction of the image gone wild, with each person (to quote André Breton's marveling description of the climax of a silent American serial) "followed by himself, and by himself, and by himself, and by himself."[81] Understanding the virtual world that surrounds us as the legacy of long traditions of mediating images, of phantasms, allows us, however, to probe this confluence of presence and absence that both the phantasm and the virtual represent.

Freud understood the disease of melancholy as a regression from a world in which the loved one has died into an obsession with the introjected image of the lost loved one into the unconscious in order to preserve it from death and deny its loss "through the medium of a hallucinatory wishful psychosis."[82] As Agamben demonstrates in *Stanzas*, Freud's description of melancholia reproduces a long tradition of understanding this disease as springing from an obsession with the phantasm of the unattainable loved one. The dominant Western tradition of thought, especially after Christianity, eyes the phantasm with suspicion as the medium not only of imagination but also of lovesickness, madness, and magic.[83] But within some traditions of Western poetry and some schools of mystical contemplation, the phantasm exists as more than a path to melancholia understood pathologically. Agamben defines the peril of melancholia as taking the phantasm as an illusion of presence. Poetically understood, the phantasm mediates between presence and absence, possession and loss, reality and sign, opening up a realm not only of mourning and symbolic action but also of play and artistry: "the phantasm generates desire, desire is translated into words, and the word defines a space wherein the appropriation of what could otherwise not be appropriated or enjoyed is possible."[84]

Since the writing of her poem and her own death, the word Dickinson chose, *scan*, has continued to transform. This goes beyond naming a recent form of proliferation and reproduction of images via a computer scanner. More curious (and perhaps revealing), "to scan," which in the nineteenth century primarily meant "to examine closely," has taken on the meaning of its near opposite, defined in *Merriam-Webster's Collegiate Dictionary* as "to glance from point to point often hastily, casually, or in search of a particular item." In common parlance, "scan" seems now more frequently to indicate a rapid glance over a text (as several generations of students have "scanned" their reading assignments) than it indicates careful scrutiny. The earliest reference the *OED* gives for this newer meaning—to which it gives a slightly more strenuous sense than found in the *Merriam-Webster's* definition, or in student practice: "To search (literature, a text, a list, etc.) quickly or systematically for particular information or features"— comes from 1926 and seems to have emerged around the same time as the technical meaning of the term: "To cause (an area, object, or image) to

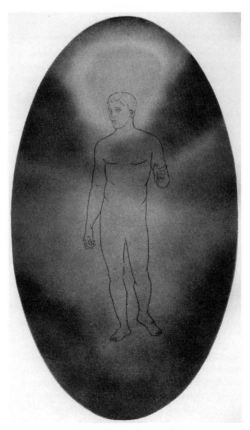

Figure 8   C.W. Ledbetter. *Man Visible and Invisible*, 1902. The Mental body of a developed man according to C.W. Ledbetter's Theosophical system.

be systematically traversed by a beam or detector; to convert (an image) into a linear sequence of signals in this way for purposes of transmission or processing" (whose first *OED* citation comes from 1928, in an early description of experimental television).

Dickinson could not have intended either meaning, but in the survival of her poem to the present day, in terms of an historical hermeneutics, it has become infected with these new meanings and holds its own in relation to them. We return to one of my key themes, the untimely nature not simply of phantoms but of our cultural interaction with media. If the more recent meaning of *scan* as a cursory glance seems beyond Dickinson's intention, nonetheless it seems to probe directly at the paradox of vision that seeing a ghost occasions, which she describes as "faint" (evoking both the visual vagueness and the syncope with which heroines since Ann Radcliffe traditionally greeted phantoms). Scanning a ghost is difficult because in some sense we cannot scrutinize them. They remain virtual, rather than embodied, images. As such phantoms make us reflect on the aporia of sight, the way the visible strives after the invisible, agonistically.

Photography represents the desire to capture an image of the real, that bald and cold Truth that Dickenson invokes—a faith that a scientifically designed visual apparatus can deliver us from our subjectivity. But as Dickenson says of Truth—oh so ambiguously—"that will hold—" Hold what? Hold the Truth? Hold us? Hold on? Put us on hold? To return to one of the enigmas contained in Dickenson's poem, what is it that we show those that "are not sure?" Will whatever it is that we show make them "stop hoping?" Believers in Spirit Photographs saw these images less as photographs conveying what spirits "looked like" than as media of communication with the other world, a token of recognition, a *symbolum* passed between realms of existence.[85] The faith they held in these odd photographs lay in their ability to speak to them, enigmatically to deliver oracles about the nature of death and loss. What a photograph gives us remains an image, peculiarly modern, uniquely technological, and strangely inhuman. Therein lies its fascination: a photograph seems to imprint directly the phantasm of reality. But phantasms also serve as the vehicle of our dreams or desires, our phantasies, and even our delusions. Likewise, the most powerful works of new media seem to evoke precisely the limits of our current environment of hypervisuality to make us again both soothed and frightened by the darkness.

It is up to us to keep these different roles seesawing in play, in a Gay, Ghastly Holiday.

Notes

1   For a fine discussion of Murnau's editing in this film, contrasting with
    Griffith, see Gilberto Perez, "The Deadly Space Between," *The Material
    Ghost: Films and Their Medium* (Baltimore: Johns Hopkins University Press,
    1989), 133–5. However, Griffith uses such metaphorical cutting, a likely
    inspiration for Murnau's use of scientific images, in his adaptation of Poe,
    The Avenging Conscience (1914).

2   Microscopic cinema appears as early as 1899. For a detailed discussion of
    early scientific cinema and of the integration of such images into nonscientific
    films such as Luis Buñuel's *L'age d'or* (1931), see Oliver Gaycken, "Devices
    of Curiosity: Cinema and the Scientific Vernacular" (Ph.D. diss., University
    of Chicago, 2005). A popular series of early scientific films specializing in
    microphotography offered by the Anglo-American filmmaker Charles Urban
    was known as "The Unseen World." Gaycken, 30–64.

3   Thanks to Karen Beckman for drawing my attention to this specter of the
    voice.

4   The best discussions of *Nosferatu* are M. Bouvier and J. L. Letraut, *Nosferatu*
    (Paris: Cahiers du Cinema, Gallimard, 1981); and Loy Arnold, Michael
    Farier, and Hans Schmid, *Nosferatu: Ein Symphonie des Grauen* (Munich:
    Belleville, 2000).

5   Walter D. Wetzels, "Johann Wilhelm Ritter and Romantic Physics in
    Germany," in *Romanticism and the Sciences*, ed. Andrew Cunningham and
    Nicholas Jardine (Cambridge: Cambridge University Press, 1990), 203. This
    excellent anthology provides a strong overview of Romantic science. See as
    well, Dietrich von Engelhardt, "Natural Science in the Age of Romanticism,"
    in *Modern Esoteric Spirituality*, ed. Antoine Faivre and Jacob Needleman
    (London: SCM Press, 1992), 101–31.

6   Johann Wilhelm Ritter, "Natural Philosophy of Femininity," in *Theory as
    Practice: A Critical Anthology of Early German Romantic Writings*, ed.
    Jochen Schulte-Sasse et al. (Minneapolis, MN: University of Minnesota Press,
    1997), 391.

7   See Griffith's description of film's objectivity as a medium of historical
    portrayal in "Five Dollar Movies Prophesied." Excerpted in Harry
    Geduld, ed. *Focus on D. W. Griffith* (Englewood Cliffs, NJ: Prentice Hall,
    1971), 35.

8   The classic account of the pictorial deep staging style of the 1910s is given
    by Yuri Tsivian, "The Voyeur at Wilhelm's Court: Franz Hofer," in *A Second
    Life: German Cinema's First Decades*, ed. Thomas Elsaesser (Amsterdam:
    Amsterdam University Press, 1996).

9   Giorgio Agamben, *Stanzas: Word and Phantasm in Western Culture*
    (Minneapolis, MN: University of Minnesota Press, 1993).

10 See the catalogue for this exhibition, *The Perfect Medium: Photography
    and the Occult*, exh. cat. (New Haven, CT: Yale University Press, 2005). An
    earlier exhibit was arranged by Alison Ferris at the Bowdoin College Museum

of Art. See *The Disembodied Spirit*, exh. cat. (Brunswick, ME: Bowdoin College, 2003).

11 See my "Phantom Images and Modern Manifestations: Spirit Photography, Magic Theater, Trick Films and Photography's Uncanny," in *Fugitive Images from Photography to Video*, ed. Patrice Petro (Bloomington, IN: Indiana University Press, 1995). See more recently, Tom Gunning, "Ghosts, Photography and the Modern Body," ed. Alison Ferris, in *The Disembodied Spirit*, 8–19. In addition to *The Perfect Medium*, recent scholarship on Spirit Photography includes Martyn Joly, *Faces of the Living Dead: The Belief in Spirit Photography* (London: British Library, 2005).

12 See my "Re-Newing Old Technologies: Astonishment, Second Nature, and the Uncanny in Technology from the Previous Turn-of-the-Century," in *Rethinking Media Change: The Aesthetics of Transition*, eds. David Thornburg and Henry Jenkins (Cambridge: The MIT Press, 2003), 39–59; "Doing for the Eye What the Phonograph Does for the Ear," in *The Sounds of Early Cinema*, ed. Rick Altman and Richard Abel (Bloomington, IN: University of Indiana Press: 2001), 13–31; "Re-Animation: The Invention of Cinema: Living Pictures or the Embalming of the Image of Death?" in *Untot/ Undead: Relations between the Living and the Lifeless*, ed. Peter Geimer (Preprint 250; Berlin: Max-Planck-Institut für Wissenschaftsgeschichte, n.d.), 19–30; "The Ghost in the Machine: Animated Pictures at the Haunted House of Early Cinema," *Living Pictures: The Journal of the Popular and Projected Images before 1914*, Issue 1 (Summer 2001), 3–17; and "Animated Pictures: Tales of Cinema's Forgotten Future," *Michigan Quarterly Review* 34, no. 4 (Fall 1995): 465–86.

13 "Modern media fire up magical or animist perceptions by technologically stretching and folding the boundaries of the self, these perceptions are then routinized, commercialized, exploited and swallowed up into business as usual." Erik Davis, *TechGnosis* (New York: Three Rivers Press, 1998), 68. (The pop style and New Age ideology of Davis's book should not cause serious readers to neglect its many insights.)

14 See John Baptista Porta (Giambattista della Porta), *Natural Magick* (1658) (New York: Basic Books, 1957); Athanasius Kircher, *Ars magna lucis et umbrae* (Amsterdam, 1671); David Brewster, *Letters on Natural Magic Addressed to Sir Walter Scott 1832* (New York: J.J. Harper, 1832).

15 See the discussion of such devices in Barbara Stafford and Frances Terpak, *Device of Wonder: From the World in a Box to Images on a Screen* (Los Angeles: Getty Research Institute Publications, 2001).

16 See the discussion of such controversies in Catherine Wilson, *The Invisible World: Early Modern Philosophy and the Invention of the Microscope* (Princeton, NJ: Princeton University Press, 1995), 215–18.

17 For a powerful account of the tradition of natural magic and its relation to scientific instruments, see Thomas Hankins and Robert Silverman, *Instruments and Imagination* (Princeton: Princeton University Press, 1995).

18 See Jochen Schulte-Sasse et al., eds., *Theory as Practice*; von Engelhardt,

"Natural Science"; and Andrew Cunningham and Nicholas Jardine, eds., *Romanticism and the Sciences*.

19   The best accounts of nineteenth-century Spiritualism are Ann Braude, *Radical Spirits: Spiritualism and Women's Rights in Nineteenth Century America* (Boston: Beacon Press, 1989); R. Laurence Moore, *In Search of White Crows* (New York: Oxford University Press, 1977); and Alex Owen, *The Darkened Room* (London: Virago Press, 1989).

20   See Davis, 63–8.

21   Jeffrey Sconce, *Haunted Media: Electronic Presence from Telegraphy to Television* (Durham, NC: Duke University Press, 2000), 24.

22   This account is described in Jean-Claude Schmitt, *Ghosts in the Middle Ages: The Living and the Dead in Medieval Society* (Chicago: University of Chicago Press, 1998), 39.

23   On the nature and existence of ghosts and spirits, see R. C. Finucane, *Ghosts: Appearances of the Dead and Cultural Transformation* (Amherst, NY: Prometheus Books, 1996); and Keith Thomas, *Religion and the Decline of Magic* (Oxford: University of Oxford Press, 1971), 589–606.

24   Schmitt, 211.

25   Schmitt, 212.

26   Aristotle, *On the Soul (De Anima)*, in *The Basic Works of Aristotle*, ed. Richard McKeon (New York: Random House, 1966), 595 (432a). See also the entry for *phantasía* in F. E. Peters, *Greek Philosophical Terms: A Historical Lexicon* (New York: New York University Press, 1967), 156.

27   Aristotle, 589 (429a).

28   See Julia E. Annas, *Hellenistic Philosophy of Mind* (Berkeley and Los Angeles: University of California Press, 1992), esp. 72–8, 81–3, 168–70. Annas translates *phantasia* as "appearance."

29   For a summary of Augustine's system, see Schmitt, 22–3.

30   Schmitt, 23.

31   The most useful summary of this tradition is David C. Lindberg, *Theories of Vision from Al Kindi to Kepler* (Chicago: University of Chicago Press, 1976).

32   Lucretius, *On the Nature of the Universe*, trans. Ronald Latham (London: Penguin, 1994), 95.

33   Lucretius, 101.

34   Lindberg, 58.

35   Lindberg, 113.

36   Lucretius, 99.

37   Schmitt, 23.

38   Ioan P. Couliano, *Eros and Magic in the Renaissance* (Chicago: University of Chicago, 1987).

39   Agamben, 23.

40   Couliano attributes what he calls the "abolition of the phantasmatic" to

the move by the Roman Catholic Church against the magical culture of the Renaissance as embodied in the persecution of Giordano Bruno, one of the great explicators of the system of erotic phantasms, and continued by the Reformation, with the Jesuits reveling in the phantasmatic culture "in all its power for the last time." Couliano, 192–5.

41 Kepler's theory of vision is discussed in Lindberg, 185–208.

42 Terry Castle, *The Female Thermometer: 18th Century Culture and the Invention of the Uncanny* (Oxford: Oxford University Press, 1995), esp. 135. Castle's important discussion of the role of the phantasmatic after the Enlightenment as not only explainable by psychological causes but a metaphor for psychological processes, a displacement of the supernatural into ordinary mental processes of memory, describes an important element of the survival of the phantasmatic tradition. However, she underestimates how much what she sees as a Romantic innovation maintains earlier, pre-Enlightenment attitudes. See Castle, 120–89.

43 Barbara Stafford, *Artful Science: Enlightenment Entertainment and the Eclipse of Visual Education* (Cambridge: The MIT Press, 1994), 5–6.

44 See Thomas; and Finucane, 49–114.

45 Thomas, 596.

46 Reginald Scot, *The Discoverie of Witches* (New York: Dover Publications, 1972).

47 Charles Musser, *The Emergence of Cinema: The American Screen to 1907* (New York: Charles Scribners and Sons, 1990), 17–27.

48 Castle's discussion of Ann Radcliffe emphasizes the interiorization or psychologization of the ghostly. Castle, 120–39.

49 J. F. von Schiller, "The Ghost-Seer or The Apparitionist," in *Gothic Tales of Terror*, Vol. 2, Peter Haining ed. (Baltimore: Penguin, 1973).

50 The literature on the phantasmagoria is extensive. I have discussed the phenomenon in "Phantasmagoria and the Manufacturing of Illusions and Wonder: Towards a Cultural Optics of the Cinematic Apparatus," in *The Cinema, A New Technology for the 20th Century*, ed. Andre Gaudreault, Catherine Russell, and Pierre Veronneau (Lausanne: Editions Payot, 2004), 31–44.

51 Laurent Mannoni, *The Great Art of Light and Shadow* (Exeter: University of Exeter Press, 2000), 144.

52 Mannoni, 148.

53 Castle offers a detailed discussion of the contradictory aspects of the phantasmagoria in *The Female Thermometer*, 140–55.

54 Brewster, *Letters on Natural Magic*, 17.

55 Brewster, *Letters on Natural Magic*, 53.

56 Nadar, "Balzac and the Daguerreotype," in *Literature and Photography Interactions 1840–1990*, ed. Jane M. Rabb (Albuquerque, NM: University of New Mexico Press, 1995), 8.

57 Nadar, 8.

58 Nadar, 8.

59 Honoré de Balzac, *Cousin Pons* (Harmondsworth: Penguin, 1968), 140–1.

60 Castle, 167.

61 Castle, 137–8.

62 See the excellent essay on this transformation by Clément Chéroux, "Ghost Dialectics: Spirit Photography in Entertainment and Belief," in *The Perfect Medium*, 45–71.

63 Sir David Brewster, *The Stereoscope: Its History, Theory, and Construction with Its Application to the Fine and Useful Arts and to Education* (London: John Murray, 1856), 204–10.

64 See the excellent account of Mumler by Crista Coutier, "Mumler's Ghost," in *The Perfect Medium*, 20–28.

65 The best account of the Pepper's Ghost Illusion is Jim Steinmeyer, *Hiding the Elephant* (New York: Carroll and Graf Publishers, 2003), 19–43. Martin Harries discusses the controversy over the "authorship" of the illusion and its dialectics of belief in *Scare Quotes from Shakespeare: Marx, Keynes and the Language of Reenchantment* (Stanford, CA: Stanford University Press, 2000), 23–53.

66 On display windows and the new commercial visual culture of nineteenth-century metropolises, see William Leach, *Land of Desire: Merchants, Power and the Rise of a New American Culture* (New York: Pantheon, 1993), esp. 39–70.

67 Dr. M. V. Pogorelsky, "Pisma o zhivontom magnetizme" (Letters on animal magnetism), *Rebus* (St. Petersburg), no. 20 (1899): 183–4; emphasis in original. Translation by Yuri Tsivian.

68 Alex Owen's important recent study of occult and magical systems in turn-of-the-century Britain makes a compelling case for the occult as a peculiarly modernist sensibility rather than a purely reactionary one. See Owen, *The Place of Enchantment* (Chicago: University of Chicago Press, 2004).

69 For a brilliant description of the blending of science and occult beliefs available to an avant-garde artist at the turn of the century, see Linda Dalrymple Henderson, *Duchamp in Context* (Princeton, NJ: Princeton University Press, 1998).

70 Camille Flammarion, *Lumen* (Middletown, CT: Wesleyan University Press, 2002), 66.

71 Flammarion, 69.

72 Marta Braun, *Picturing Time: The Work of Etienne-Jules Marey 1830–1904* (Chicago: University of Chicago Press, 1992), 264–318. See also Henderson.

73 For accounts of Theosophy, see Emily B. Sellon and Renée Weber, "Theosophy and the Theosophical Society," in *Modern Esoteric Spirituality*, ed. Faivre and Needleman, 311–29; and Bruce F. Campbell, *Ancient Wisdom*

Revived: A History of the Theosophical Movement (Berkeley and Los Angeles: University of California Press, 1980).

74 For a concise, illustrated account of these bodies, see C. W. Ledbetter, *Man Visible and Invisible* (Madras: Theosophical Publishing House, 1964).

75 Schmitt, 5–7.

76 Jacques Derrida, *Specters of Marx* (New York: Routledge, 1994).

77 Roland Barthes, *Camera Obscura* (New York: Hill and Wang, 1981).

78 Garrett Stewart, *Between Film and Screen: Modernism's Photo Synthesis* (Chicago: University of Chicago Press, 1999).

79 Schmitt, 211.

80 J. K. Huysmans, *La bas (Down There)*, trans. Keene Wallace (New York: Dover Publications, 1972), 132.

81 André Breton, *Nadja* (New York: Grove Press, 1960). He is describing the climax of the serial he knew as *The Grip of the Octopus*, which was originally released in the United States as *The Trail of the Octopus* (1919).

82 Sigmund Freud, "Mourning and Melancholia," *The Standard Edition of the Complete Psychological Works of Sigmund Freud*, Vol. XIV, ed. and trans. James Strachey (London: The Hogarth Press, 1957), 244.

83 See the description of the heroic malady in Couliano, 16–84.

84 Agamben, 129.

85 I discuss the often bizarre explanations by Spiritualists of what and how and Spirit Photograph represents in "Phantom Images and Modern Manifestations," 42–71. See also, *The Perfect Medium*, 50–2.

14

from Introduction to *Haunted Media*

Jeffrey Sconce

Amid daily newspaper coverage of national politics, foreign policy, and local crime, readers of the *New York Times* in the early fifties encountered three bizarre and seemingly unrelated stories concerning the then emerging medium of television. On the night of 20 October 1952, Frank Walsh went to bed in his Long Island home while his wife and children watched an episode of *Abbott and Costello* on the television set downstairs. Disturbed by the volume of the program and unable to sleep, Walsh got out of bed, found his handgun, and started down the staircase. Halfway down the steps, Walsh paused, aimed, and in the words of the *Times* reporter, "stilled the television with one shot from his .38 caliber revolver." After a few moments of stunned silence, Walsh's wife called the police to report the incident, but, as the paper observed, "Since there is no law against shooting television sets, the only charge against Mr. Walsh will be a substantial one from the repairman."[1] Walsh was able to avoid even this charge, however, by converting his newfound status as a television assassin ("They should give him back his gun; his work has barely started," quipped columnist Jack Gould) into an opportunity to appear on a quiz show. As a contestant on *Strike It Rich*, Walsh won a new television set.[2]

On 30 June 1953, Richard Gaughan, an unemployed shipping clerk who would later describe himself to police as a "professional justice man," rushed past the guards at CBS studios in New York with two newly purchased kitchen knives. Gaughan made his way onto a set where a rehearsal was taking place for the series *City Hospital*. In a scuffle with actors, technicians, and security personnel, Gaughan managed to stab a

CBS cameraman and smash a pitcher of water over an actor's head before finally being apprehended. Gaughan confessed at the police station that he had "purchased the knives for the specific purpose of killing someone connected with television." Later he told the police that he hated television because its shows were "scandalous." More important, he also felt he was being personally "slandered by the programs."[3]

Finally, on 11 December 1953, readers of the *Times* met a family from Long Island that had been forced to "punish" their TV set for scaring the children. As Jerome E. Travers and his three children were watching *Ding Dong School* one day, the face of an unknown woman mysteriously appeared on the screen and would not vanish, even when the set was turned off and unplugged. "The balky set," which "previously had behaved itself," according to the *Times*, "had its face turned to the wall ... for gross misbehavior in frightening little children."[4] The haunted television finally gave up the ghost, so to speak, a day later, but not before scores of newspapermen, magazine writers, and TV engineers had a chance to observe the phenomenon. Visitors to the Travers' home also included Francey Lane, a singer from the episode of the *Morey Amsterdam Show* that had preceded *Ding Dong School* on the day of the initial haunting. Lane was thought to be the face behind the image frozen on the screen, and her agent apparently thought it would make for good publicity to have the singer meet her ghostly cathode-ray double.[5]

Something less than newsworthy, these odd incidents from the early days of television are nevertheless of interest as diverse examples of a common convention in representing television and other electronic media. Each of these stories draws on a larger cultural mythology about the "living" quality of such technologies, suggesting, in this case, that television is *"alive* ... living, real, not dead"[6] (even if it sometimes serves as a medium *of* the dead). The "living" quality of television transcends the historically limited and now almost nonexistent practice of direct "live" broadcasting to describe a larger sense that all television programming is discursively "live" by virtue of its instantaneous transmission and reception. Central as well to the initial cultural fascination with telegraphy, telephony, and wireless, such liveness is at present the foundation for a whole new series of vivid fantasies involving cyberspace and virtual reality. At times this sense of liveness can imply that electronic media technologies are animate and perhaps even sentient. Although the various parties involved in the peculiar episodes detailed above may not have actually believed their TV sets were "alive," the reporters who needed to make sense of these assignments certainly wrote as if their readers would make, or at least understand, such an assumption. These stories are either amusing or alarming to the extent that the reader shares in a larger cultural understanding that television and its electronic cousins are, paradoxically, completely familiar in their seemingly fundamental uncanniness, so much so that we rarely question the often fantastic conventions through which we conceptualize and engage these media.

Perhaps initially only a product of Frank Walsh's insomnia, for example, shooting the TV set has become over the years a familiar gesture in the nation's hyperbolic loathing of television as an intruding house guest. Although it would be difficult to document exactly how many people really do shoot their sets in a given year, it is easy to gauge the symbolic importance of this act by how frequently it appears in films, books, and even in television programming itself. In this scenario, the television figures as an obnoxious, deceitful, cloying, banal, and/or boring visitor within the home who must be dispatched with extreme prejudice. The intrusive, imperious and, above all else, living presence of television is such that it cannot simply be turned off or unplugged – it must be violently murdered. The *Times* headline for Walsh's ballistic tirade reinforced the pseudo-sentience of the doomed set, justifying the act as "Obviously Self-Defense" (a sentiment that echoes in contemporary bumper stickers that implore surrounding drivers to "Kill Your Television"). Owners of personal computers make similar animating investments in their media, of course, but here the interactivity and intimacy of the computer more often transform the machine into a friend and confidant (albeit one with which we occasionally have a stormy relationship).[7]

Gaughan's paranoid attack on the TV studio, meanwhile, exemplifies another familiar theme involving the media's awesome powers of animated "living" presence: the delusional viewer who believes the media is speaking directly to him or her. A common symptom among schizophrenics,[8] this delusion also foregrounds in exaggerated but obviously compelling terms the powers of "liveness" and "immediacy" experienced by audiences of electronic media as a whole. With the delusional psychotic, the media assume a particularly sentient quality, figuring as a seemingly candid and intimate interlocutor engaged in direct contact with its (psychotic) audience (of one). The television industry, in particular, would no doubt like for its entire audience to consist of such schizophrenics (as long as they remained functional consumers), since it continually tries to maintain the illusion that it is indeed speaking directly to us. Some might argue that the home computer has allowed this long-latent psychosis to at last come true: the computer (and other operators) can now speak directly to us (and we to them) in an immediate electronic interface. Such interactivity, of course, has led to new stories of electropsychopathology, centering this time on "addicted" operators who find this living electronic connection so alluring as to shun the real world in favor of cyberspace. Here too "liveness" leads to a unique compulsion that ultimately dissolves boundaries between the real and the electronic.

The haunting of the Travers family, finally, highlights an uncanny and perhaps even sinister component in "living" electronic media. What exactly is the status of the worlds created by radio, television, and computers? Are there invisible entities adrift in the ether, entire other electronic realms coursing through the wired networks of the world? Sound and image without material substance, the electronically mediated worlds of telecommunications often evoke the supernatural by creating virtual beings that appear to have no physical form. By bringing this spectral world into the home, the TV set in particular can take on the appearance of a haunted apparatus. The concerns of the Travers family should be familiar to those who watched televisions with older model picture tubes in the fifties and sixties. Early viewers will always remember the eerie presence of the slowly fading dot of light appearing at the center of the screen once the set had been turned off, a blip that suggested something was still there in the cabinet even after the image itself had vanished. In media folklore past and present, telephones, radios, and computers have been similarly "possessed" by such "ghosts in the machine," the technologies serving as either uncanny electronic agents or as gateways to electronic otherworlds.

Tales of imperious, animate, sentient, virtual, haunted, possessed, and otherwise "living" media might seem at first no more than curious anecdotes at the fringes of American popular culture. And yet metaphors of living media also structure much academic thought on electronic telecommunications – albeit in a more specialized jargon. Perhaps the most visible scholar of the century, Marshall McLuhan, pronounced telecommunications media to be nothing less than an extension of humankind's "nervous system." Even those who stop short of such cybernetic propositions often operate from a similar assumption that electronic telecommunications have somehow forever and irretrievably altered human consciousness itself, if not as a prosthetic enhancement then as a form of narcotizing hypnosis. One could argue, for example, that a thin line divides the knife-wielding Richard Gaughan and his psychotic delusions from the hapless subjects posited by much social-scientific media effects research. Frequently portrayed as a public enmeshed in an immediate, interpersonal, patho-logical, and ultimately unmediated relationship with electronic media, these subjects, like Gaughan, are doomed to misapprehend the living artifice of television as the basis for their own social "reality" and personal behavior. Zombified cola drinkers, Bobo-punching kindergartners, and clueless Susan Lucci fans have thus, in their time, all been depicted by social scientists and journalists alike as slaves to a particularly persuasive electronic master, an almost malevolent entity whose powers of control are somehow believed to eclipse those of all previous nonelectronic media.

Other avenues of media theory, meanwhile, have taken the imagined powers of electronic simultaneity and "liveness" to increasingly apoca-lyptic heights through ever more complex improvisations on the concept of "simulation." In this postmodern vision of the media occult, the postwar period has represented the supernatural "dissolution of TV into life, the dissolution of life into TV."[9] From this perspective, the ubiquitous circulation and constant mediation of television imagery have contributed to an accelerated evaporation of reality into "hyperreality." For critics of postmodernity ranging in temperament from Jean Baudrillard to Fredric Jameson, television's constant transmission of instantaneous representations makes the medium both the prime catalyst and most pervasive symptom of an age marked by the increased dissolution of all referentiality. In the past decade or so, however, we have seen a major shift in these arguments. Whereas critics of television and postmodernity at first decried the electronic erosion of reality in harrowing parables of affective dissipation, more recent scholarship in the fields of cyberspace and virtual subjectivity frequently embraces these phantom landscapes and synthetic identities. Once the object of critical scrutiny and ideological debate, the "subject" of cybertheory now frequently reigns in academic discourse as a self-evident, emancipated entity free to reinvent itself in the new electronic frontier. Simulation, in turn, once a lamentable cultural condition, is now our beatific future, one so seductive that many current media theorists readily and routinely collapse previously meaningful distinctions between "subjectivity," "fantasy," and "identity" in order to forge the intrepid cybersubject – an autonomous being at last purged of annoying contact with history, the social order, and even the material world. For now and the foreseeable future, cyberspace and virtual subjectivity remain constructs more imaginary than technological, yet pop culture and pop academia often regard them as sovereign principalities somehow more "real" than the terrestrial geography and human subjectivity they are said to replace. Such are the conjuring powers of this seemingly most "live" of living technologies.

Variously described by critics as "presence," "simultaneity," "instantaneity," "immediacy," "now-ness," "present-ness," "intimacy," "the time of the now," or, as Mary Ann Doane has dubbed it, "a *'This-is-going-on'* rather than a *'That-has-been ...*,'"[10] this animating, at times occult, sense of "liveness" is clearly an important component in understanding electronic media's technological, textual, and critical histories. The sheer proliferation of such vague terminology around this phenomenon and the necessary imprecision with which it is often used, both in popular and academic circles, testifies to the need for a more sustained examination of this seemingly "inalienable" yet equally "ineffable" quality of electronic telecommunications and textuality. This book undertakes such a project by examining a variety of historical questions surrounding the issue of "presence" in electronic media, exploring how this basic quality of "liveness" has been conceptualized and creatively elaborated in American culture over the past century and a half.[11] Under what social and historical circumstances did electronic media come to be seen as "living" and "alive"? How have ideas of an animating sentience in electronic telecommunications changed across history and media? How have metaphors of living electronic technology impacted cultural debates over telecommunications technology? I will argue that electronic presence, seemingly an essential property of telecommunications media, is in fact a variable social construct, its forms, potentials, and perceived dangers having changed significantly across media history. This project, then, is a cultural history of electronic presence, an interpretive examination of the fields of electronic fiction socially generated around telecommunications technologies. I am interested here in the overall persistence of such expressive speculation over the past century and a half, as well as the sociohistorical specificity of individual articulations of media presence from telegraphy to virtual reality. In exploring the development of such media metaphysics, I wish to analyze the expressive functions of electronic presence, both as a historical phenomenon and as the foundation for our own era's continuing fascination with telecommunications media. Why is it, after 150 years of electronic communication, we still so often ascribe mystical powers to what are ultimately very material technologies?

Currents, streams, and flow

The elaboration of electronic media's capacity for "simultaneity" into a more expansive ideology of presence dates at least as far back as the advent of electromagnetic telegraphy in the mid-nineteenth century. The telegraph not only inaugurated a new family of technologies, of course, but also produced a new way of conceptualizing communications and consciousness. Whereas messages had previously been more or less grounded in the immediate space and time of those communicating, the wondrous exchanges of the telegraph presented a series of baffling paradoxes. The simultaneity of this new medium allowed for temporal immediacy amid spatial isolation and brought psychical connection in spite of physical separation. The central agent in these extraordinary exchanges was electricity. The focus of much popular scientific interest in the eighteenth and nineteenth centuries, electricity was for many a mystical and even divine substance that animated body and soul. When harnessed by the telegraph and the media that were to follow, this "life force" seemed to allow for a mechanical disassociation of consciousness and the body. Telegraph lines carried human messages from city to city and from continent to continent, but more important, they appeared to carry the animating "spark" of consciousness itself beyond the confines of the physical body. Electricity remains a somewhat uncanny agent in popular thought even today, making it a prime component in the continuing metaphysical presence attributed to contemporary media. From the initial electromagnetic dots and dashes of the telegraph to the digital landscapes of virtual reality, electronic telecommunications have compelled citizens of the media age to reconsider increasingly disassociative relationships among body, mind, space, and time.

Although the exact form that "presence" is imagined to take may vary greatly from medium to medium over the past 150 years, a consistent representational strategy spans these popular perceptions of electronic media. Grounded in the larger and more long-standing metaphysics of electricity, fantastic conceptions of media presence ranging from the telegraph to virtual reality have often evoked a series of interrelated metaphors of "flow," suggesting analogies between electricity, consciousness, and information that enable fantastic forms of electronic transmutation, substitution, and exchange. In the historical reception of each electronic telecommunications medium, be it a telephone or a television, popular culture has consistently imagined the convergence of three "flowing" agents conceptualized in terms of their apparent liquidity:

(1) the electricity that powers the technology
(2) the information that occupies the medium
(3) the consciousness of the viewer/listener

Electricity, for example, has for over two hundred years been conceived of as a "current," despite physicist Robert Maxwell's early admonitions as to the limited explanatory value of such a term.[12] Writing in the age of Victorian electrification, meanwhile, psychologist William James coined the now familiar phrase "stream of consciousness," arguing that "river" and "stream" are the metaphors that "most naturally describe" the human thought process.[13] Most recently, Raymond Williams provided media studies with the concept of *flow*, a term now in general critical circulation to describe the unending and often undifferentiated textual procession of electronic media and their reception in the home.[14] The cultural articulation of "presence" around electronic media thus depends in large part on how the public imagination of a given historical moment considers these flows of electricity, consciousness, and information to be homologous, interchangeable, and transmutable. In the more fantastic discourses of presence, these varieties of flow frequently appear as interrelated and interdependent, casting the media and audience as an interwoven and at times undifferentiated complex of electricity, consciousness, and textual data. This "flowing" imagination presents the possibility of analogous exchanges, electricity mediating the transfer and substitution of consciousness and information between the body and a host of electronic media technologies. Such electrical possibilities for fusion and confusion, of course, remain central in describing both the wonders and horrors of an emerging cyberculture.

As we will see in the following chapters, the shared electrical basis and apparent electrical transmutability of the body's flow of consciousness and flows of information in the media have produced a remarkably consistent series of cultural fantasies involving the telegraph, radio, television, and computer. Three recurring fictions are especially central to the development of telecommunications technology, familiar stories that appear in new incarnations with the advent of each new medium. In the first fiction, these media enable an uncanny form of disembodiment, allowing the communicating subject the ability, real or imagined, to leave the body and transport his or her consciousness to a distant destination. In more extreme versions of this technological fantasy, the entire body can be electronically dissolved and teleported through telecommunications technology, a convention at least as old as the imaginative adventures of Baron Munchausen in the mid-nineteenth century. Closely related to this fantasy of disembodiment is a second recurring fiction – the familiar premise of the sovereign electronic world. In this scenario, the subject emerges into an enclosed and self-sustaining "electronic elsewhere" that is in some way generated, or at least accessed, by a particular form of electronic telecommunications technology. Awestruck projections about the future splendor of virtual reality are perhaps the most familiar examples of this fiction today, but this fantasy of utopian electronic space also flourished as far back as the nineteenth century. Finally, a third common fiction based on the transmutable powers of electricity involves the anthropomorphizing of media technology. Perhaps most visible in the contemporary fascination with androids and cyborgs, this particular fiction is also more than a century old and, as the stories from the *Times* suggest, figured centrally in representing television during its earliest years.

Although the longevity of such fantastic accounts of the media may suggest an ahistorical "deep structure" to these tales, as if these stories were somehow the founding mythemes of the media age, I would argue that apparent continuity among these accounts is actually less important than the distinct discontinuities presented by the specific articulations of these electronic fictions in relation to individual media. In other words, although the process of elaborating electronic simultaneity into fantasies of disembodiment, teleportation, and anthropomorphization – all achieved through the common conceit of electronic transmutability – has remained constant over the last 150 years, there are tremendous differences in the actual social, cultural, and political "content" of these stories within differing historical and technological contexts. For this reason, the analysis of such fantastic media stories must recognize that the cultural construction of electronic presence is always inextricably bound to the social application of a technology within a given historical moment. Tales of paranormal media are important, then, not as timeless expressions of some undying electronic superstition, but as a permeable language in which to express a culture's changing social relationship to a historical sequence of technologies.

Through the analysis of five distinct moments in the popular history of electronic presence, I will argue that an early fascination in American culture with fantastic media technology has gradually given way to a fascination with forms of fantastic textuality. Whereas discourses of presence were once dominated by the varieties of contact and communion to be achieved through the discorporative powers of telecommunications, such discourse is now most often concerned with the extraordinary and seemingly sovereign powers of electronic textuality in and of itself. In the age of telegraphy and wireless, in other words, many believed telegraphs and crystal sets could be used to contact incredible and unseen yet equally "real" worlds, be they extrasensory or extraterrestrial. The ethereal "presence" of communications without bodies suggested the possibility of other similarly preternatural interlocutors, invisible entities who, like distant telegraph and wireless operators, could be reached through a most utilitarian application of the technology. As we shall see, the telegraph and early wireless held the tantalizing promises of contacting the dead in the afterlife and aliens of other planets. Fantastic accounts of media presence in this case emphasized the extraordinary powers of the technology itself and suggested that its rational application would eventually lead to crossing ever more incredible boundaries of time and space. The miracle of electronic simultaneity thus portended the possibility of "live" contact with distant frontiers, making early media presence an avenue of wonder bound to the exploratory social deployment of these early technologies.

The centralization of network radio and the subsequent hegemony of television broadcasting, on the other hand, led to a quite different account of electronic presence. In the gradual transition from point-to-point communication to mass broadcasting, presence became less a function of engaging an extraordinary yet fleeting entity across frontiers of time and space and instead assumed the form of an all-enveloping force occupying the ether. No longer a mere conduit for extraordinary exchange, electrical presence became instead an extraordinary world in and of itself. With the rise of the networks, "liveness" in radio and television meant joining a vast invisible audience as it occupied the shared, electronically generated worlds of national programming. The most fantastic accounts of such presence, both then and today, have gone so far as to grant this electronic shadow world a strangely tangible autonomy, where "reality" itself has in some mysterious manner been eroded by its electronically circulated analog. This is the strange virtual terrain that sustains both the high theories of hyperreality and the similar yet more prosaic notion of "televisionland." It is an electronic maelstrom where a ceaselessly mediated and ultimately phantom public sphere exists interwoven with the eternally unfolding diegesis of a thousand worlds in television's ever expanding universe of syndication.

In the playful and infinitely reversible binaries of television (or at least television theory), *The Brady Bunch* and CNN are equally real/unreal – each sealed in the common electronic space of televisionland's unending metadiegetic procession.

This book provides a historical preamble to this now familiar technologic, examining the articulation of electronic presence in five important cultural moments in telecommunication history: the advent of telegraphy in the nineteenth century, the arrival of wireless at the turn of the century, radio's transformation into network broadcasting in the twenties and thirties, television's colonization of the home in the early sixties, and contemporary debates over television and computers as virtual technologies. This series of technologies describes the gradual emergence of an expanding electronic sphere, one initially accessed at the other end of a distant wire but whose presence is now seemingly all pervasive. A historical analysis of this transformation, I believe, will answer why, in our contemporary fascination with television, cyberspace, and other worlds of digitized, mediated, and increasingly displaced consciousness, "presence" now exists as either the beatitude of an electronically liberated subject or as the incarcerating mirages of an encroaching electronic subjectivity.

[...]

Notes

1   "Obviously Self-Defense: Long Islander Puts Bullet into TV Set as 7 Watch," *New York Times*, 21 October 1952, 31.

2   See "An Irate Video Owner Has Come Up with an Unusual Solution to Your Chief TV Bete Noir," *New York Times*, 22 October 1952, 37; and "Quiz Shows," *New York Times*, 29 October 1952, 41.

3   "Crazed Knife-Wielder Invades a TV Studio, Stabs Cameraman, Fells Actor with Pitcher," *New York Times*, 1 July 1953, 39.

4   "Haunted TV Is Punished: Set with Face That Won't Go Away Must Stare at the Wall," *New York Times*, 11 December 1953, 33.

5   "Face on TV Set Goes, Mystery Lingers On," *New York Times*, 12 December 1953, 16. See also *Television Digest*, 12 December 1953, 11.

6   Jane Feuer, "The Concept of Live Television: Ontology as Ideology," in *Regarding Television*, edited by E. Ann Kaplan (Los Angeles: AFI, 1983), 14.

7   Sherry Turkle discusses such phenomena (termed the "Julia effect" and the "ELIZA effect") in her book *Life on the Screen: Identity in the Age of the Internet* (New York: Simon and Schuster, 1995), 101.

8   For a typical case study, see "A Note on the Meaning of Television to a Psychotic Woman," *Bulletin of the Menninger Clinic* 23 (1959): 202–3.

9   Jean Baudrillard, *Simulations* (New York: Semiotext(e), 1983), 55.

10 Mary Ann Doane, "Information, Crisis, Catastrophe," in *Logics of Television*, edited by Patricia Mellencamp (Bloomington: Indiana University Press, 1990), 222.

11 Of the various terms that might be used to describe this quality of the media, I will use *presence* most frequently because it seems the most inclusive term for describing the many versions of this phenomenon.

12 See W. E. Steavenson and Lewis Jones, *Medical Electricity: A Practical Handbook for Students and Practitioners* (London: H. K. Lewis, 1892), n.p.

13 William James, *Principles of Psychology* (New York: H. Holt, 1890), 239.

14 Raymond Williams, *Television: Technology and Cultural Form* (London: Wesleyan University Press, 1992), 80–112.

15

from Modes of Avisuality:
Psychoanalysis – X-ray – Cinema

Akira Mizuta Lippit

[...]

The Enlightenment project, which Ernst Cassirer characterizes as an epistemological movement acutely aware of and fascinated by the contours of the limit, reached a crucial threshold on 8 November 1895, when Wilhelm Conrad Röntgen discovered the X-ray.[1] Enlightenment reason mapped a psychogeography of limits, charting an economy of visuality and a subject seeking to see, expose, and appropriate—according to a presumed power of the gaze—the world around it. The "Enlightenment," write Max Horkheimer and Theodor Adorno, "is totalitarian."[2] Its ethos, what Horkheimer and Adorno refer to as "the mastery of nature," requires a seeing subject that stands outside the limit and frames the field of vision. An Apollonian view of the entire world from outside. From another world. Totality is defined by the limit that divides interiority from exteriority, achieved from without. The persistence of the limit, of the visible world, maintains the viability of such a subject, defined in its encounter with the limit of visuality as such. With the appearance of the X-ray, the subject was forced to concede the limits of the body. Erasing one limit against which it claimed to be outside, the X-ray image, with its simultaneous view of the inside and outside, turned the vantage point of the spectator-subject inside out. The point of view established by the X-ray image is both inside and out. Everything flat, interiority and exteriority rendered equally superficial, the liminal force of the surface has collapsed. Regarding the capacity of the surface to establish meaning in the world, Gilles Deleuze invokes Antonin

Artaud's surfaceless body and says: "In this collapse of the surface, the entire world loses its meaning."[3]

Against the field of X-ray vision, the Enlightenment subject lost its vantage point from the outside: the spectral subject now appeared inside the frame, to the extent that a frame remained at all, an aspect of the spectacle. In the X-ray image, everything—which is to say nothing—is visible. Describing Artaud's body as a "body-sieve ... no longer anything but depth," Deleuze invokes an inherent schizophrenia, one that might apply to the Enlightenment subject in the wake of the X-ray. Deleuze writes:

> As there is no surface, the inside and the outside, the container and the contained, no longer have a precise limit; they *plunge into a universal depth* or turn the circle of a present which gets to be more contracted as it is filled. Hence the schizophrenic manner of living the contradiction: either in the deep fissure which traverses the body, or in fragmented parts which encase one another and spin about.[4]

The erasure of the surface (which paradoxically renders the world and its depths and interiorities superficial), the disappearance of a discernible interiority, plunges the subject into a "universal depth." A total and irresistible depth, everywhere. The world is no longer only outside, but also within, inside and out. It moves within and without you. Catherine Waldby says of the X-ray:

> The surface of the body, its demarcation from the world, is dissolved and lost in the image, leaving only the faintest trace, while the relation between depth and surface is reversed. Skeletal structures, conventionally thought of as located at the most recessive depth of the body, appear in co-registration with the body's surface in the x-ray image. Hence skeletal structures are externalized in a double sense: the distinction between inside and outside is suspended in the image, and the trace of the interior is manifest in the exteriority of the radiograph, the artefact itself.[5]

In the X-ray image, the body and the world that surrounds it are lost. No longer inside nor out, within nor without, body and world form a heterogeneous one. (A one that is not one but together, side-by-side, a series of contiguous planes and surfaces, plateaus.) You are in the world, the world is in you. The X-ray can be seen as an image of you and the world, an image forged in the collapse of the surface that separates the two.

The crisis of X-ray visuality struck at the heart of the seeing subject, but also at the very conditions of the visual as such. According to Linda Dalrymple Henderson, Röntgen's discovery of the invisible rays "clearly established the inadequacy of human sense perception and raised fundamental questions about the nature of matter itself."[6] The X-ray forced a collapse of the Enlightenment figure. The metaphors of vision that constituted the Enlightenment were thrust into a literal semiology, which is to say, no semiology but a destruction of the semiological order itself. The absolute radiance unleashed by the X-ray absorbed the subject, enveloping it in a searing light. The Enlightenment subject had become the focus of its own penetrating look, susceptible to the "self-destructive" force that Horkheimer and Adorno identified as Enlightenment practice. One year before the atomic irradiation of Hiroshima and Nagasaki, they warned: "The fully enlightened earth *radiates* disaster triumphant."[7]

Like Freud, who discovered the "secret of dreams" in the dark, Röntgen discovered the new ray in a dark room, in a camera obscura of sorts. "At the time," says Richard Mould, "Röntgen was investigating the phenomena caused by the passage of an electrical discharge from an induction coil through a partially evacuated glass tube. The tube was covered with black paper and the whole room was in complete darkness, yet he observed that, elsewhere in the room, a paper screen covered with the fluorescent material barium platinocyanide became illuminated."[8] A mysterious form of radiation passed through solid objects, casting fluorescent light upon distant surfaces. A light that arrived elsewhere, displaced from its trajectory. "It did not take him long," Mould continues, "to discover that not only black paper, but other objects such as a wooden plank, a thick book and metal sheets, were also penetrated by these X-rays." And flesh. Like a dream, this form of light moved through objects, erased boundaries between solid objects, crossing their internal and external borders. Like a dream, avisual.[9] By fixing the penetrating fluorescence on a photographic plate, Röntgen both discovered and recorded a new type of ray that penetrated organic and inorganic matter and left a shadow of that object on the plate. Simultaneously a new type of ray and a new type of photography. The invisible electromagnetic ray, it would be learned later, consisted of a shorter wavelength (and thus a higher frequency) than visible light, which allowed it to penetrate and illuminate solid matter. Röntgen named the as yet unidentified rays "x." Unknown, secret, illicit.

From the beginning, Röntgen linked the X-ray to photography by fixing his discovery on photographic surfaces. Although Röntgen protested the association of the X-ray with photographic media, claiming that the use of photography had only been "the means to the end," the fusion, or confusion, had already taken hold of the public imagination. X-ray images came to be seen as photographic documents, indelibly marked by their relationship to the superficiality of photographs. They were images of a three-dimensional flatness. One of Röntgen's first published X-ray photographs is of his wife's left hand, which was taken in the final months of 1895, fifty years after his birth and fifty years before the atomic explosions in Japan. The image depicts Berthe's skeletal structure and the bones that constitute her hand, but also the wedding ring that hovers on the surface, infiltrating her hand from the outside. The trace of exteriority that Berthe's ring imposes on the interior dimension reveals the uncanny nature of the new medium. From Irma to Berthe, images of women's interiority appear to have increased after 1895. "The frequently published image of a woman's hand," writes Lisa Cartwright, "gained enormous popularity, becoming an icon of female sexuality and death."[10]

Cartwright explains, "In the public sphere as in medicine, the female hand X ray became a fetish object par excellence."[11] "Besides the many physicians who immediately repeated Roentgen's experiments," Cartwright says, "a woman's hand, sometimes captioned as 'a lady's hand,' or a 'living hand,' became a popular test object."[12] But the fascination with X-ray imagery exceeded the medical realms and became a fashion, which Cartwright describes: "The historian Stanley Reiser relates that 'New York women of fashion had X-rays taken of their hands covered with jewelry, to illustrate that beauty is of the bone and not altogether of the flesh' (or to use a more familiar turn of phrase, is not just skin deep), while married women gave X rays of their hands (presumably with wedding ring affixed, like Berthe Roentgen's hand) to their relatives."[13] The collapse of interiority and exteriority is marked in these images by the convergence of bones and jewelry, whose opacity renders them indistinguishable in the X-ray photograph. One wears one's skeletal structure, the architecture of the body, on the outside. Or rather, interiority and exteriority take place together on the surface. A depth rendered superficial.

On seeing her flesh transgressed, her interiority brought to the surface, Berthe is said to have shuddered at the "vague premonition of death" it evoked.[14] Visible in this image is "the true story of your death": an image of the future, a photography yet to come, your death. Berthe's vision emerges in the encounter with her body, its interiority, which returns to her as if from the outside, from the future. Like Borges's archive and Freud's discovery of formlessness inside Irma's body, Berthe may have glimpsed the avisuality of the fully illuminated self. In this moment of profound intimacy, Berthe peers into the depths of her own body and sees the future, sees her own death, an image of her absence at the center of her body. She is exposed. Interiority and futurity. Berthe recognizes the lethal anniversal force of the photograph. This architecture of the hand, of her hand, comes to Berthe as an alien touch from the irreducible distance of a secret body she carries within her. Of Freud's dream image of Irma,[15] Lacan says:

The phenomenology of the dream of Irma's injection … leads to the apparition of the terrifying anxiety-provoking image, to this real Medusa's head, to the revelation of this something which properly speaking is unnameable, the back of the throat, the complex, unlocatable form, which also makes it into the primitive object *par excellence*, the abyss of the feminine organ from which all life emerges, this gulf of the mouth, in which everything is swallowed up, and no less the image of death in which everything comes to an end.[16]

Medusa's head or acephalic hand. The woman's body—Irma's and Berthe's—comes to determine an archive in which your death is inscribed, formless and secret. In the encounter with radical exteriority, the looking subject disappears. Henderson makes explicit the line between X-rays and the iconography of death, claiming that Röntgen's discovery "triggered the most immediate and widespread reaction to any scientific discovery before the explosion of the first atomic bomb in 1945."[17] "The discovery of x-rays," Henderson concludes, "produced a sense that the world had changed irrevocably."[18]

One hundred years after the discovery of X-rays, the desire for total visibility returned in the form of the Visible Human Project (VHP) and its first embodied figures, the so-called Visible Human Man (Joseph Jernigan, convicted felon, 39, was executed in 1993) and Visible Human Woman (unnamed, "a Maryland housewife," 59, who died of a heart attack in 1995). Immediately after his execution, Jernigan's body was frozen, scanned, and then dissected into one-millimeter planes. Each plane was photographed and digitized over the course of nine months, after which a complete archive of the human body was born. "In this way," Waldby says, "the corpse was converted into a visual archive, a digital copy in the form of a series of planar images."[19] Human bodies transformed into planes of visibility, into thousands of unique visible surfaces, stored in a massive and virtual archive. An archive of the body, of the human body made totally visible in countless possible shapes and configurations. A paradoxical archive, according to Cartwright, at once universal and specific: "The projects share the paradox of seeking to create a universal archive through which to represent and to know human biology, while rendering their respective body models with a level of specificity that may ultimately confound goals such as the establishment of a norm."[20] Waldby likens the advent of the VHP to an inversion of H. G. Wells's "invisible man": "Every structure and organ in the interior of Jernigan's body was about to become an object of exhaustive and globally available visibility."[21] Global visibility: a universal archive, in which everything in the world is visible, and everything is visible to the world.

Even with 3–D and virtual reality techniques, one of the early challenges of the VHP involved reconciling the depth of the body, its volume, with the flatness of the image. It is a problem, according to Waldby, that exists already in the practice of anatomical representation. "The central problem of anatomy is the incommensurability between the opaque volume of the body and the flat, clean surface of the page."[22] The solution, says Waldby, lies in the analogical link between the body and the world, between their figures and modes, between anatomy and cartography. In the case of anatomy, Waldby writes:

> This problem was resolved to some extent through the creation of analogies between anatomical and cartographic space, analogies evident in the fact that the book of anatomy is known as an atlas. If the interior of the body could be thought of and treated as *space*, rather than as a self-enclosed and continuous solid volume, then it could be laid out in ways which are amenable to mapping.[23]

The body shares its figures and modes of spatial representation with the world. In anatomical and geographic maps, both are rendered "as an accretion of laminar 'surfaces,' as landscapes to be traversed by the eye, a volume composed of layers and systems of tissue which are laid one upon the other."[24] The world is a body, the body a world, both *exscribed* in flat space.

From anatomy to the VHP via the X-Ray, the problem of visual representation, of the visibility and visuality of the body, remains located on the surface, on the screen. The body and world, actual and virtual space are *exscribed* on a document, photographic surface, or screen. The VHP "enacts," says Waldby, "the proposition that the interface between virtual and actual space, the screen itself, is permeable, rather than an hygienic and absolute division."[25] A tissue, inside and out, inside out. Waldby traces one genealogy of the VHP to the X-ray, which transgressed the interior of the body, the very structure of the interior as such. She writes:

> The x-ray introduced a form of light which no longer glanced off an inner surface to make it accessible for medical vision but rather cut through the very distinction between inner and outer. Its spectral images rendered the body's interior as irradiable *space* and illuminated scene. . . . The light of the x-ray does not simply penetrate its object, it also projects it, moving through it until its force is interrupted by a screen. Hence the trace of anatomic structure can be both externalized and fixed as radiographs.[26]

The X-ray projects the body's interiority outward until it reaches a screen. The anatomic light of the X-ray *exscribes* the body, irradiates and projects it on an exterior surface. Its destination always a screen, the X-ray achieves a form of completion in the VHP. "The Visible Human figures," says Waldby, abolish "all distinction between surface and depth, demonstrating that all interior spaces are equally superficial, that all depth is only latent surface."[27]

At work from the X-ray to the VHP is also a form of destructive visuality, a visibility born from annihilation. The process of preparing the human body for the VHP archive also annihilated it. The method of dissecting the human body into minute planes "effectively obliterated the body's mass, each planed section dissolving into sawdust due to its extreme desiccation," says Waldby.[28] Like the X-ray, total visibility brought destruction, which is perhaps its condition of possibility. The body reduced to sawdust, to ashes, to cinders. An atomic body, avisual.

Röntgen, the X-ray, photographic media, and the atomic weapon circulate in a specular economy, bound—as are all *photographic* events— by the logic of anniversaries. By capturing single moments in time, all photographs suggest future anniversaries. Individual moments become monumental, arbitrary instants are fixed in the chronic time of anniversaries. Photographs constitute archives and archaeologies of the past but also initiate, like Borges's Library, a "minutely detailed history of the future": in the sense that made Roland Barthes shudder, each photograph inscribes "the true story of your death." It waits for you to arrive to the place of your anniversary, your apocalypse, "now, forever, whenever," as William Haver says.[29] Like the apocalypse that Haver describes, the logic of anniversaries, of photographs, is always accidental, imagined, invented, "unpredictable": anniversaries consist of projections that never adhere, as it were, to the present moment, but always to another time that has passed and will come again. Sometime. Of the apocalypse, an *arkhê*anniversary of sorts, of the temporality that marks the apocalyptic event of my death, Haver writes:

> We must think the apocalyptic as an infinite and indifferent *punctuality*. This punctuality would not be the punctuation that would mark either fate or destiny; neither would it be the punctuation that brings a narrative temporality to term. Punctuality would here indicate, precisely, a nondelay that is not presence, the indifference of the time of material singularity, that entropic "historical space" which would be radical atemporality.[30]

"An infinite and indifferent *punctuality*," like the *punctum*, perhaps, the photographic wound (prick) that Barthes imagines.[31] Punctuality, punctuation, and *punctum*: temporality, inscription, and corporeality. The anniversary can be said to cohere in this indifferent and infinite *punctuality*: inside and outside time, always written or yet to be written, always on the body's surface, either on its inside or outside. An event of writing, of inscription, on the body, there, always—at this precise moment—this or that moment (indifferent yet punctual), "now, forever, whenever." Circumscribed and circumspect. Your death, your apocalypse, your anniversary, always singular and indifferent, for you and whomever else.

Anniversaries are forged by suturing one indifferent moment to another, one *extemporality* to another (one improvised moment outside time to another), toward an infinite singularity; they are inexorably allusive, atemporal, and antihistorical. One moment suggests another, by association, through a secret logic of coincidence; each moment casts a shadow over the future. In the case of 1895, the advent of radiographic imagery permeated by allusion scientific and cultural practices, establishing a kind of spectral episteme that revolves around the representation of interiority. Moving forward and backward in history, 1895 haunts the anniversaries that precede and succeed it. The centennial of Röntgen's birth (1845–1923) and the semicentennial of his discovery, Victor Bouillion notes, coincide with the fiftieth anniversary of the advent of cinema and the annihilation of Hiroshima and Nagasaki.[32] Expanding the cycle of radiation and mnemic phenomena, the first successful daguerreotype of the sun was taken by Hippolyte Fizeau and J.-B. Leon Foucault on 2 April 1845, one week after the birth of Röntgen on 27 March. From solar to atomic radiation, the anniversaries, measured in fifty-year units, converged in 1995, bringing into sharp focus the thanatographic legacies of the twentieth (XX) century. Some of the events that marked the continuing dynamic of this anniversary included the global festivities commemorating the centennial of cinema; the controversy that erupted over the Smithsonian Institution's failed Enola Gay exhibit; and the awarding of the Nobel Prize for physics to two scientists who were said to have developed techniques that exceeded the capacity of the X-ray.[33]

The X-ray situates the spectacle in its context as a living document even when it depicts, actually and phantasmatically, an image of death or the deterioration of the body that leads to death. A living image of death and the deathly image of life are intertwined in the X-ray. Soon after its discovery, the destructive nature of the X-ray became visible on the human bodies that it pierced. As the euphoria of Röntgen's discovery began to settle, a series of symptoms began to appear on the bodies submitted to the X-ray. Sunburns, hair and nail loss, scaling of the skin, nausea, and an array of other pathogenic signs began to expose the X-ray's destructive capacities. To see and to burn. The two functions and effects are fused in the X-ray, which makes the body visible by burning it. The extravisibility of the X-ray is an effect of its inflammatory force. X visuality. It sees by burning and destroying. An extravisuality that *cinefies*. Under the glare of the X-ray, the body moved from a referent to a sign, from a figure to the primary site of inscription.

X-rays had turned the human body itself into a photographic surface, reproducing its function directly on the human skin. The legacy of photography already contained a version of this fantasy with regard to the human body. Felix Nadar recounts Honoré de Balzac's belief that the human essence comprises "a series of specters, infinitely superimposed layers of foliated film or skin [*pellicules*]."[34] In Balzac's fantasy, a layer of skin is removed and captured each time one poses before a camera. The X-ray amplifies the effects of an intrinsic *photophobia* already encrypted in photography.[35] The direct effects of radiation on the human surface would be reenacted exponentially fifty years later when the atomic explosions in Hiroshima and Nagasaki turned those cities, in the instant of a flash, into massive *cameras*; the victims grafted onto the geography by the radiation, *radiographed*.[36]

As sign, the X-ray assails the movements of visual signification: the referent of the X-ray photograph, for example, trembles between *what* is seen and the *process* by which it is seen. For the histories of optics, photography, and phenomenology, the impact of Röntgen's discovery of the X-ray remains immeasurable. Michel Frizot says: "The discovery of X-rays and its effects had considerable repercussions on modern thought. What had been demonstrated was that a completely invisible emanation could manifest its presence on a photographic plate ... and that this invisible emanation could be used to make the internal reality of the body which was also invisible—a kind of 'inner life'" (*une sorte d'"intériorité"*)."[37] One hears in this description the resonances of Freud's dream. The convergence of psychology and photography, Frizot suggests, altered the epistemology of the twentieth century, creating, in the process, an epistemology of the inside.

Although it developed primarily within medical and scientific institutions (Röntgen was a professor of physics at the University of Würzburg in Bavaria), the X-ray image has always hovered at the intersection of science and art, technique and fantasy. In the first years after its discovery, X-rays figured in a variety of commercial products and legal considerations: "In London a firm advertised in February 1896 the 'sale of x-ray proof underclothing,' and in the United States Assemblyman Reed of Somerset County, New Jersey, introduced a bill into the state legislature prohibiting the use of X-ray opera glasses in the theaters."[38] The idea of the X-ray, its imagined and imaginary properties, determined the response to its appearance. Still, "others thought," notes Röntgen biographer Otto Glasser, "that with the x-rays base metals could be changed into gold, vivisection outmoded, temperance promoted by showing drunkards the steady deterioration of their systems, and the human soul photographed."[39] The X-ray had become a fantastic repository, an extensive archive of unfulfilled wishes—an unconscious, of sorts. X-rays are "identified in the public mind," says Daniel Tiffany, "with the existence of a world of hidden energies or forms, with visual registrations of invisibility."[40] Many artists have turned to the alluring play of deep surface, or flat depth, in the X-ray: the Futurists, Marcel Duchamp, Frantisek Kupka, Man Ray, and László Moholy-Nagy in the early twentieth century, Jean-Michel Basquiat, Barbara Hammer, Gary Higgins, Alan Montgomery, and Ann Duncan Satterfield, among many others, in the latter half of the XX century. Throughout its history, science and art appear confused in the X-ray, provoking a fundamental problem with regard to its visuality: what does one see *there*, in the X-ray? What constitutes, defines, determines the *thereness* of the X-ray? What is *there* in the X-ray, depth or surface, inside or out? What is *there* to be seen? A *thereness*, perhaps, that is avisual: a secret surface between the inside and out, the place where you are, there, secret and invisible. A spectacle of invisibility, shining, shown, avisual. When technological advances facilitate the appearance of previously unknown phenomena, they often take on the semblance of an artwork. The legacy of the atomic bomb, particularly its spectacular form, attests to this effect.

* * *

In 1946, one year after two atomic explosions incinerated Hiroshima and Nagasaki, the Hungarian artist László Moholy-Nagy (1895–1946)— who also shares a birthday with the X-ray—discussed the impact of X-ray technology on the practice of art: "In x-ray photos," he writes, "structure becomes transparency and transparency manifests structure. The x-ray pictures, to which the futurist has consistently referred, are among the outstanding space-time renderings on the static plane. They give simultaneously the inside and outside, the view of an opaque solid, its outline, but also its inner structure."[41] Moholy-Nagy's description of the use of X-ray technologies in art exceeds mere technique. The ability to simultaneously expose the inside and outside of a thing, to retain the object's surface while probing its depths, describes a scientific fantasy as well as imperative. "Roentgen's initial report," says Cartwright, "was received in the popular press as a discovery of a new force in nature, and not of a new technique."[42] A force rather than a technique, a nature rather than a technology.

X-rays retain the contours of their object while rendering its inside, generating an impossible perspective. Figure and fact, an object's exterior and interior dimensions, are superimposed in the X-ray, simultaneously evoking and complicating the metaphysics of topology in which the exterior signifies deceptive surfaces and appearances while the interior situates truths and essences, what Francis Bacon calls "the brutality of fact."[43] The term *artefact* perhaps best describes the X-ray image, which is at once buried and revealed, invoking its archaeological nature as spectacle. The X-ray image determines a kind of living remnant, a phantom subject. "Art" and "fact," fused together like the sign and referent of Barthes's photograph, arrive as a superimposition in the X-ray, an *artefact*.[44]

Moholy-Nagy posits the fundamental obscurity of X-rays, suggesting a semiology of the image. X-ray images, he says, "have to be studied to reveal their meaning; but once the student has learned their language, he will find them indispensable."[45] A type of exegesis is thus required, a hermeneutics of the X-ray image that, not unlike dream analysis, extends, according to Moholy-Nagy, into the realm of language. A super- or extralanguage, indispensable. X-rays invoke an inherent grammatology. The term *X-ray*, its theatrical prefix, conjures a cultural semiology that includes pornography (X-rated or triple X-rated films), Christianity (Xmas), drugs (ecstasy, or "x"), algebra, signature ("X"), and erasure (crossing out, Malcolm X).

Even before the eruption of radioactive violence in 1945, the signifier "x" was in circulation and overdetermined. Within military circles, Japan's 7 December 1941 strike on Pearl Harbor was code-named "X-day" to signify both the unnameable information embedded within a military communication and the unnameable violence that marked the beginning of the Pacific War. Simultaneously known and unknown, "x" eludes the economy of signification, generating a phantasmatic signifier without signification or, conversely, a full signification with no signifier. "X" can be seen as the master signifier for no signification, for deferred or postponed, overinscribed and erased signification. An image of imagelessness, a figure for what Tiffany calls the "negativity of the modernist Image."[46] Both a letter of the Roman alphabet, a number, and a figure, a graphic symbol, "x" operates within various economies of signification and meaning at once, never reducible to one system or another, to language or image. A trace: an erasable sign and sign of erasure that erases as it signs and is in turn erased already. On the topographic economy of the trace, Derrida says:

> Since the trace is not a presence but the simulacrum of a presence that dislocates itself, displaces itself, refers itself, it properly has no site— erasure belongs to its structure. And not only the erasure which must always be able to overtake it (without which it would not be a trace but an indestructible and monumental substance), but also the erasure which constitutes it from the outset as a trace, *which situates it as the change of site*, and makes it disappear in its appearance, makes it emerge from itself in its production.[47]

As a residue of the sign, the trace of a sign that erases itself—constituted from the outset as the trace of erasure—"x" signals a "change of site," of the sign, of changing sights, which takes place behind but also on the surface "x." "X" marks or strikes the sign (a sign of the strike, a strike over and against the sign, and the strike itself), replacing the sign as a sign inscribed over the sign, the mark of an illusory or phantasmatic depth. Beneath the "x" opens a phantom depth, inscribed on and as a surface—"x" as the sign for an imaginary topography deep beneath the signifier. "X" signs what is not there, not yet there, or what lies beneath the sign—what was there before the mark "x." "X" marks a spatial and temporal displacement of the sign. A sign that functions like a signifier (like a photograph, according to Barthes's photosemiography). A sign of negative writing: a writing that overinscribes, inscribes itself over inscription, on its surface. "X" obscures what was there, it *xscribes*. An *xscript, xscription, exscription*. A mark on the outside, but also a mark that is no longer a mark, a former mark or *aftermark, ex-scription*.

The rhetoric of photography reveals a constant tension between nature (the signifier of the real) and the photographic referent. From its inception photography was endowed with an organic artifice, seen as a paradoxical form of natural technology. William Henry Fox Talbot describes photography as the "pencil of nature." The critical terminology that frames the photographic practice—"photogenic drawing" (Talbot) or "biogrammatology" (François Dagognet's description of Etienne-Jules Marey's chronophotography), for example—underscores the ambiguity between figure and fact in photography.[48] The X-ray expanded not only the limits of the empirical world and the human sensorium but also the trajectory of photography: it extended the graphic reach of the apparatus into the invisible spectrum of light. It introduced *exscriptive* writing, an inside-out writing that reverses the trajectory of Enlightenment writing from inscription to *exscription*. The mark is no longer made from the outside in nor, for that matter, from inside out: writing takes place outside, it remains irreducibly elsewhere, an *exscriptive* mark that never adheres to the interiority of a text or document—displaced, atopic, and atextual.

* * *

Several coincidences punctuate 1895, bound by a specular and ultimately phantasmatic historicity. During 1895, Freud, the Lumières, and Röntgen made significant advances in their respective fields, initiating a heterogeneous history of visuality that remains illegible, invisible, and ahistorical.[49] No historiography can produce an adequate narrative for the events of 1895, which are themselves secure only as momentary designations for events that, like most historical processes, take place over time. A phantasmatic history, then, imagined and imaginary. A coincidence of histories, a history of coincidences, bound only by a phantom chiasmus, "x."[50]

On 13 February of the year that Röntgen published his discovery of the X-ray, Louis Lumière patented the Cinématographe.[51] The Lumières' first public screenings were held at the Grand Café in Paris on 28 December, the *exact* date of Röntgen's publication.[52] Louis Lumière's idea to adapt the drive device of a sewing machine to the Cinématographe came to him "one night," says Emmanuelle Toulet, citing Lumière: "One night when I was unable to sleep, the solution came clearly to my mind."[53] Like Freud's dream, the secret of cinema, its solution was revealed to Lumière at night. The dream of cinema. The original configuration of the screening space included a translucent screen, hung in the middle of the chamber, which passed the image in reverse to the other side. Spectators could pay more to sit on the side of the projector or less to view the screenings from the other side. The contemporary organization of the theater, which limits the viewing surface to one side, developed later. In this sense, the original apparatus with its transverse flow of light more closely resembled the luminous economy of the X-ray. The first film screen was itself a kind of porous tissue.

One film presented by the Lumières on 28 December, *Leaving the Lumière Factory* (*Sortie d'usine*, no. 91, 1895), remains as an emblem of the early cinema. Shot in front of the Lumière factory, the version shown at the Grand Café was in fact its third remake.[54] The brief *actualité* opens onto a frontal view of the Lumière factory. The factory doors open and workers emerge from the back of the frame toward the front. They move toward the camera, before veering to either side. Two large doors toward the right of the frame open inward, and workers begin to stream outward from it and from a smaller door on the left of the frame. They emerge at different speeds, initially aiming toward the camera before breaking to the right or left. Among the women and men are a dog and several bicyclists. As the factory empties, and before the end of the film, one man rushes against the flow back into the nearly empty factory, reversing the outward, background-to-foreground trajectory. In the distance, a solitary figure remains visible inside the factory, in the distance, deep inside.

The very architecture of the film, the series of flat surfaces that moves from screen to wall to interior background, suggests that this cinema is an exploration of depth. An imaginary, impossible depth that extends into the screen, that opens behind it, revealing a virtual interiority and distance, far away. Noel Burch describes the sensation of depth this film produces:

> Although a wall occupies half the picture, the sense of space and depth which was to strike all the early spectators of Lumière's films is already present in the contrast between this wall blocking the background to the left and the movement of the crowd emerging from the dark interior on the right.[55]

This "sense of space and depth" is a general feature of all the Lumière films, establishing an axis along which objects (people, animals, and other animate things) move toward and away from the spectator. An extra space, an extra dimension that exists only as an effect of cinema projection. An abyss, *mise-en-abîme*, abyssal space. The deep space opens only there, in an avisual world, folded from the outside in and the inside out. It has no reference, indexical or otherwise, to any place outside the film, although, as a photograph, it originated somewhere. A space that is not really there. An archive where there is no space. Like the unconscious, like the X-rayed body, an abyss.

Figures 1 & 2   Auguste and Louis Lumière (*Sortie d'usine*, no. 91, 1895).

In May 1895 Josef Breuer and Sigmund Freud published *Studies on Hysteria*, after years of treating hysterics with hypnosis.[56] The *birth* of psychoanalysis in 1895 was followed by at least two significant after-births: the "dream of Irma's injection" in July and the birth of Anna, the last of Freud's children, in December. Using a term shared by film and psychoanalysis, Freud wrote in 1915, "A dream is, among other things, a *projection*: an externalization of an internal process."[57] To further overdetermine the shape of 1895—overdetermination being, among other things, a key feature of Freud's typology—Thomas Edison, according to Henderson, asserted confidently "that x rays would ultimately unveil the activity of the human brain."[58] Cartwright and Brian Goldfarb document Edison's and Louis Lumière's immediate efforts to explore X-ray imaging of the body and brain.[59] Brain, body, mind, and soul appear to orbit 1895 in a specular constellation that blurs the distinctions between each form of interiority. The material and immaterial, anatomical and spiritual, psychical and organic aspects of human interiority are confused by the rapid proliferation of imagining techniques and devices in 1895. Psychoanalysis, X-ray, cinema offer new possibilities for the organization of interiority, new designs, new organs. Moholy-Nagy describes the sense of confusion that erupted between scientific developments and desire in the late nineteenth century:

> In the 19th century telescopic and microscopic "miracles," x-ray and infrared penetrations were substituted for fantasy and emotional longing. These phenomena, motion and speed, electricity and wireless, seemed to give food enough to the imagination without introducing subconscious automatism. Photography was the golden key opening the door to the wonders of the external universe to everyone. The astonishing records of this period were *objective* representations, though they went in some cases beyond the observation capacity of our eyes as in the high speed, micro-macro, x-ray, infrared and similar types of photography. This was the period of "realism" in photography.[60]

Inside and outside are lost in the fantasies of realism and desire. For Moholy-Nagy, photography represents the visualization of desire in the nineteenth century, a realist exteriorization of "fantasy and emotional longing." It locates the topology of the unconscious prior to the advent of psychoanalysis, serving as the sign for an unconscious yet to be named.

Three *phenomenologies of the inside* haunt 1895: psychoanalysis, X-ray, and cinema seek to expose, respectively, the depths of the psyche, body, and movements of life. These three technologies introduced new signifiers of interiority, which changed the terms by which interiority was conceived, imagined, and viewed. They transformed the structure of visual perception, shifting the terms of vision from phenomenal to phantasmatic registers, from a perceived visuality to an imagined one. From visual to avisual.

Psychoanalysis, X-ray, and cinema appear fused to one another in a heterogenealogy of the inside—each seems to appropriate another's features, functions, and rhetorical modes. The capacity to see through the surface of the object, to penetrate its screen, emerged in 1895 as the unconscious of the Enlightenment, but also as an unimaginable light. Benjamin recognized the proximity of photography and film to psychoanalysis, as did Jean-Martin Charcot, Albert Londe, and Freud before him, finding in these two probes two passages toward the discovery of the unconscious. "Evidently," writes Benjamin in "The Work of Art in the Age of Mechanical Reproduction," in 1935–36, "a different nature opens itself to the camera than to the naked eye—if only because an *unconsciously penetrated space* is substituted for a space consciously explored by man... . The camera introduces us to unconscious optics as does psychoanalysis to unconscious impulses."[61] Another nature, different and displaced, emerges from an unconscious optics. In Benjamin's language, the movement from photography to the unconscious develops from the logic of penetration.[62] A penetration, like the one that pierces the surface of Irma's dream body, leads to a phantasmatic architectonics of the psyche and the secret body it *exscribes*.

Psychoanalysis, X-ray, and cinema introduce complex signs of interiority that resemble antisigns or traces of signs that signal the view of an impossible interiority. Each sign functions more as a trace than a signifier, each linked with the force of an irreducible exteriority. Derrida says of the trace, of *arkhê*writing: "This trace is the opening of the first exteriority in general, the enigmatic relationship of the living to its other and of an inside to an outside: spacing."[63] A sign of the outside. An ex-sign. Psychoanalysis, X-ray, and cinema: trace of exteriority and interior *design*. A design, both as an architectural imprint or sketch and as an ex-sign, a designation of interiority. A design of the inside, a designation of its contours, but also its appearance as a form of designification. An exemplary design.

Notes

1   Ernst Cassirer, *The Philosophy of the Enlightenment*, trans. Fritz C. A. Koelln and James P. Pettegrove (Princeton, NJ: Princeton University Press, 1951).

2   Max Horkheimer and Theodor Adorno, *Dialectic of Enlightenment*, trans. John Cumming (New York: Continuum, 1944), 6.

3   Gilles Deleuze, *The Logic of Sense*, ed. Constantin V. Boundas, trans. Mark Lester with Charles Stivale (New York: Columbia University Press, 1990), 87.

4   Ibid., 87 (emphasis added).

5   Catherine Waldby, *The Visible Human Project: Informatic Bodies and Posthuman Medicine* (London: Routledge, 2000), 91.

6   Linda Dalrymple Henderson, "X Rays and the Quest for Invisible Reality in the Art of Kupka, Duchamp, and the Cubists," *Art Journal* 47.4 (1988): 324. See also Linda Dalrymple Henderson, "A Note on Francis Picabia, Radiometers, and X Rays in 1913," *Art Bulletin* 71.1 (1989): 114–23; W. Robert Nitske, *The Life of Wilhelm Conrad Röntgen, Discoverer of the X Ray* (Tucson: University of Arizona Press, 1971).

7   Horkheimer and Adorno, *Dialectic of Enlightenment*, 3 (emphasis added).

8   Richard F. Mould, *A Century of X-Rays and Radioactivity in Medicine: With Emphasis on Photographic Records of the Early Years* (Bristol, PA: Institute of Physics Publishing, 1993), 1.

9   [Editors' Note: Lippit introduces avisuality earlier in his book as an extension of Derrida's notions of the visible in-visible and the absolute invisible: "Together, Derrida's excess visualities might point to a category of complex visuality, a system of visuality that shows nothing, shows in the very place of the visible, something else: *avisuality*. Avisuality not as a form of invisibility, in the sense of an absent or negated visibility: not as the antithesis of the visible but as a specific mode of impossible, unimaginable visuality. Presented to vision, there to be seen, the avisual image remains, in a profoundly irreducible manner, unseen. Or rather, it determines an experience of seeing, a sense of the visual, without ever offering an image." Lippit, *Atomic Light (Shadow Optics)* (Minneapolis: University of Minnesota Press, 2005), 32.]

10   Lisa Cartwright, "Women, X-rays, and the Public Culture of Prophylactic Imaging," *Camera Obscura* 29 (May 1992): 30. A revised version of Cartwright's essay appears in her study of medical imagery, *Screening the Body: Tracing Medicine's Visual Culture* (Minneapolis: University of Minnesota Press, 1995). Operating simultaneously in the fields of film history, medical rhetoric and culture, and feminist theory and criticism, Cartwright's searching analysis situates the X-ray at the crossroads of twentieth-century arts and sciences. She writes: "The X ray is the pivotal site of investigation for this book's exploration of medicine's technological/visual knowledge, desire, and power. It is also the most conflicted site, embodying multiple paradigms of visuality and multiple political agendas" (*Screening the Body*, 108).

11   Cartwright, *Screening the Body*, 115. Hands, says Mould, were also among the most vulnerable areas of the human body, where many of the earliest signs of X-ray injuries to pioneer physicians and technicians first appeared. Röntgen's own hands were unscathed. Alongside a photograph of a plaster cast made of Röntgen's hands "immediately after his death in 1923," Mould notes that "unlike the hands of other X-ray pioneers, it is seen that Röntgen's are undamaged" (*Century of X-Rays*, 5).

12   Cartwright, *Screening the Body*, 115.

13   Ibid.

14   Otto Glasser, *Wilhelm Conrad Röntgen and the Early History of the Roentgen Rays* (Springfield, IL: Thomas, 1934), 81. "Many people," according to Glasser, "reacted strongly to the ghost pictures. The editor of the *Grazer Tageblatt* had a roentgen picture taken of his head and upon seeing the picture 'absolutely refused to show it to anybody but a scientist. He had not closed an eye since he saw his own death's head'" (81).

15   [Editors' Note: Lippit discusses Freud's dream about his patient Irma, which centers on her oral cavity, in the first part of this chapter, which is not included here. "In the dream, Irma's interiority appears to obstruct Freud's view of the unconscious. Or rather, two competing forces are at work in the dream: one brings the image closer, by pushing deeper and further into the body, toward greater clarity, figuration, and materiality; the other follows the same route toward dissolution, disappearance and formlessness. By compressing Irma's interiority onto the surface of his psyche, Freud has invoked a spectral architecture, an architectonic of interiority that moves at once toward representation and abstraction." Lippit, *Atomic Light (Shadow Optics)*, 39.]

16   Jacques Lacan, "The Dream of Irma's Injection," in *The Seminar of Jacques Lacan, Book II: The Ego in Freud's Theory and in the Technique of Psychoanalysis, 1954–1955*, ed. Jacques-Alain Miller, trans. Sylvia Tomaselli (New York: Norton, 1988), 163–64.

17   Henderson, "X Rays and the Quest for Invisible Reality," 324.

18   Ibid., 336. A similar pattern of immersion in the fantastic properties of unknown fluids followed Marie Curie's discovery of radium in 1898, in the wake of Henri Becquerel's discovery of radioactivity in 1896. The same imaginary properties that were attributed to X-rays accrued to radium, which was seen as an elixir of life, as the source of life itself. A frantic effort to introduce radium into the body ensued, flooding the marketplace with radioactive commodities and services: toothpaste, cocktails, spas, as well as bug sprays, which also cleaned and polished furniture. In pure form, bottled *Agua Radium* allowed the fastest means of ingestion. After the initial euphoria began to fade, the toxic but also photographic effects of radioactivity began to appear, glowing. At watch factories where women painted the hands and dials of watches with radium, a practice known as "tipping" (licking the brushes to form a point at the tip) served as a method for transporting the radium into their bodies. Like a Cheshire cat, the image of a woman's mouth survives. Her teeth absorbed so much radium she could develop film in her mouth. Her radioactive mouth had become a camera lab, a *camera dentata*. Pierre Curie himself, says Mould, hoped that "radium might help restore eyesight to the blind" (*Century of X-Rays*, 21). See Claudia Clark, *Radium Girls: Women and Industrial Health Reform, 1910–1935* (Chapel Hill: University of North Carolina Press, 1997).

19   Waldby, *Visible Human Project*, 14. "The Visible Woman," Waldby notes, "represents a technical improvement on the Man: the body was planed into

much finer cross-sections (5,189 sections [as opposed to 1,878 sections of the Man]) which produced higher resolution in the resulting images, and a much larger data file" (15).

20 Lisa Cartwright, "A Cultural Anatomy of the Visible Human Project," in *The Visible Woman: Imagining Technologies, Gender, and Science*, ed. Paula A. Treichler, Lisa Cartwright, and Constance Penley (New York: New York University Press, 1998), 39.

21 Waldby, *Visible Human Project*, 13.

22 Ibid., 63.

23 Ibid., 63 (original emphasis).

24 Ibid., 64.

25 Ibid., 5.

26 Ibid., 92 (original emphasis).

27 Ibid., 159.

28 Ibid., 14.

29 William Haver, *The Body of This Death: Historicity and Sociality in the Time of AIDS* (Stanford, CA: Stanford University Press, 1996), 55. Haver is following the idiom and tone of Derrida's "NO APOCALYPSE, NOT NOW (full speed ahead, seven missiles, seven missives)," trans. Catherine Porter and Philip Lewis, *Diacritics* 14.2 (1984): 26.

30 Haver, *Body of This Death*, 55 (original emphasis). The apocalypse is framed, in Haver's discussion, by the atomic bombings of Hiroshima and Nagasaki and the AIDS pandemic, by "the force of an Outside that is not merely the outside of an inside, but the outside that is inside, the insidious inside" (53).

31 Roland Barthes, *Camera Lucida: Reflections on Photography*, trans. Richard Howard (New York: Hill and Wang, 1981). Barthes writes: "A photograph's *punctum* is *that accident* which pricks me (but also bruises me, is poignant to me)" (26–7, emphasis added).

32 Victor Bouillion, "War and Medicinema: The X-ray and Irradiation in Various Theaters of Operation," in *Incorporations*, ed. Jonathan Crary and Sanford Kwinter (New York: Zone, 1992), 253.

33 Concerning the partnership between the field of physics and X-ray technology during the twentieth century, the decision of the 1994 Nobel Prize committee may have signaled a critical moment. Among the recipients of the awards in science were two physicists, Clifford G. Shull and Bertram N. Brockhouse, who had succeeded in developing "neutron probes [that] gave scientists a set of tools more powerful than X-rays and other forms of radiation used for exploring the atomic structure of matter" (Malcolm W. Brown, "American Awarded Nobel Prize in Chemistry," *New York Times*, 13 October 1994). X-rays may have been superseded, even rendered obsolete, on the eve of the centennial of their discovery. Röntgen himself was the recipient of the first Nobel Prize for science in 1901.

34 Félix Nadar, *Nadar: Dessins et Écrits*, 2 vols. (Paris: Hubschmid, 1979), 2:978 (my translation). "Donc selon Balzac, chaque corps dans la nature

se trouve composé de séries de spectres, en couches superposées à l'infini, foliacées en pellicules infinitésimales, dans tous les sens où l'optique perçoit ce corps. L'homme à jamais ne pouvant créer,—c'est à dire d'une apparition, de l'impalpable, constituer une chose solide, ou de *rien* faire une *chose*,—chaque opération Daguerrienne venait donc surprendre, détachait et retenait en se l'appliquant une des couches du corps objecté."

35 A version of this phobia also existed in Meiji Japan (1868–1912). "During this time," writes Sakuma Rika, "numerous superstitions were associated with photography, including the beliefs that 'posing for a photograph drained one's shadow,' 'posing for a second shortened one's life,' and 'when three subjects posed for a photograph, the one in the middle would die'" (Sakuma Rika, "Shashin to josei – atarashî shikaku media no tôjô to 'miru/mirareru' jibun no shutsugen" ["Photography and Women: The Advent of New Visual Media and the Creation of a Self That Looks/Is Looked At"], in *Onna to atoko no jikû: semegiau onna to otoko* [*The Timespace of Women and Men: The Confrontation of Women and Men*], vol. 5 of *Nihon joseishi saikô* [*Redefining Japanese Women's History*], ed. Okuda Akiko [Tokyo: Fujihara Shoten, 1995], 200 (my translation). Regarding the photoiconography of hands and the image of Berthe Röntgen's left hand, many Japanese women at that time feared having their hands photographed. Small hands were considered a sign of feminine beauty, and, according to Sakuma, these women believed that their hands not only looked bigger in photographs but that the photographic process actually made their hands swell (228).

36 See Akira Mizuta Lippit, "Photographing Nagasaki: From Fact to *Artefact*," in *Nagasaki Journey: The Photographs of Yosuke Yamahata, August 10, 1945*, ed. Rupert Jenkins (San Francisco: Pomegranate, 1995), 25–9.

37 Michel Frizot, "The All-Powerful Eye: The Forms of the Invisible," in *A New History of Photography*, ed. Michel Frizot, trans. Susan Bennett, Liz Clegg, John Crook, and Caroline Higgitt (Cologne: Könemann, 1998), 281.

38 Glasser, *Wilhelm Conrad Röntgen*, 82.

39 Ibid., 83.

40 Daniel Tiffany, *Radio Corpse: Imagism and the Cryptaesthetic of Ezra Pound* (Cambridge, MA: Harvard University Press, 1995), 226. "On the one hand," says Tiffany of the relation between radium and the X-ray, "we have a substance whose radiant energy is invisible, whereas on the other we have a form of radiant energy that produces images of the unseen" (226).

41 Lázló Moholy-Nagy, *Vision in Motion* (Chicago: Theobald, 1947), 252.

42 Cartwright, *Screening the Body*, 113.

43 David Sylvester, *The Brutality of Fact: Interviews with Francis Bacon* (Oxford: Thames and Hudson, 1987). Of the photograph, Bacon, who claims to have been influenced by radiographic images, says: "I think it's the slight remove from fact, which returns me onto the fact more violently" (30).

44 In *Camera Lucida*, Barthes says: "A specific photograph, in effect, is never distinguished from its referent.... It is as if the Photograph always carries its referent with itself, both affected by the same amorous or funereal

immobility, at the very heart of the moving world. . . . The Photograph belongs to that class of laminated objects whose leaves cannot be separated without destroying them both" (5–6).

45 Moholy-Nagy, *Vision in Motion*, 252.

46 Tiffany cites "Pound's fascination with radium and radioactivity" as an example of the "negativity of the modernist Image—a negativity that is signaled by the Image's resistance to visuality" (*Radio Corpse*, 226).

47 Jacques Derrida, "Différance," in *Margins of Philosophy*, trans. Alan Bass (Chicago: University of Chicago Press, 1982), 24 (emphasis added).

48 François Dagognet, *Etienne-Jules Marey: A Passion for the Trace*, trans. Robert Galeta with Jeanine Herman (New York: Zone, 1992).

49 Richard Crangle says that in the British press, for example, excited discussions in 1896 about the "New Photography" referred not to the Cinématographe but to the X-ray. "The interest surrounding the New Photography in early 1896 seems, a century later, to have eclipsed the almost parallel launch in Britain of an optical sensation which became far more influential: the projected moving picture" (Richard Crangle, "Saturday Night at the X-rays—The Moving Picture and 'The New Photography' in Britain, 1896," in *Celebrating 1895: The Centenary of Cinema*, ed. John Fullerton [Sydney: Libbey, 1998], 138).

50 Paula Dragosh suggested the relationship between the logic of reversibility and anniversaries, "a chiasmus, after the Greek name for the letter 'x'" (letter to author, June 2005).

51 Wilhelm Conrad Röntgen, "On a New Kind of Rays (Preliminary Communication)," in Glasser, *Wilhelm Conrad Röntgen*, 41–52. The article was reprinted in the *Annual Report of the Smithsonian Institution* in 1897.

52 Other advances in film technology during 1895 include the introduction of R. W. Paul and Brit Acres's movie camera in March, the advent of the so-called Latham loop by Woodville Latham and his sons in April, and the debut of C. Francis Jenkins and Thomas Armat's Phantoscope in October. Thomas Alva Edison's "Kinetoscope" and "Vitascope" exhibitions straddled 1895, taking place in 1894 and 1896, respectively.

53 Emmanuelle Toulet, *Birth of the Motion Picture*, trans. Susan Emanuel (New York: Abrams, 1995), 40.

54 According to Bertrand Tavernier's narration on the Kino Video collection of the Lumières' films, *The Lumière Brothers' First Films* (1996).

55 Noel Burch, *Life to Those Shadows*, ed. and trans. Ben Brewster (Berkeley: University of California Press, 1990), 15.

56 Josef Breuer and Sigmund Freud, *Studies on Hysteria, in The Standard Edition of the Complete Psychological Works of Sigmund Freud*, ed. and trans. James Strachey (London: Hogarth, 1955), vol. 2.

57 Sigmund Freud, "The Metapsychological Supplement to the Theory of Dreams," in *The Standard Edition of the Complete Psychological Works of*

Sigmund Freud, ed. and trans. James Strachey (London: Hogarth, 1957), 14:223 (original emphasis). "A dream tells us," Freud writes, "that something was going on which tended to interrupt sleep, and it enables us to understand in what way it has been possible to fend off this interruption. The final outcome is that the sleeper has dreamt and is able to go on sleeping; the internal demand which was striving to occupy him has been replaced by an external experience, whose demand has been disposed of. A dream is therefore, among other things a *projection*: an externalization of an internal process."

58 Henderson, "X rays and the Quest for Invisible Reality," 325.

59 Lisa Cartwright and Brian Goldfarb, "Radiography, Cinematography and the Decline of the Lens," in *Incorporations* (New York: Zone, 1992), 190–201.

60 Moholy-Nagy, *Vision in Motion*, 210. See in this connection Thomas Mann, *The Magic Mountain*, trans. H. T. Lowe-Porter (New York: Knopf, 1951).

61 Walter Benjamin, "The Work of Art in the Age of Mechanical Reproduction," in *Illuminations*, ed. Hannah Arendt, trans. Harry Zohn (New York: Schocken, 1968), 236–7 (emphasis added).

62 Addendum to 1895: Albert de Rochas published in 1895 his collection of spectral and psychic images, *L'Exteriorisation de la sensibilité: Étude experimentale et historique in Paris*. Also in 1895, Hippolyte Baraduc began work on psychic photography—accomplished by inducing the subject to excrete "psycho-odo-fluidiques" that were then captured on the photographic plate. His *L'Âme humaine, ses mouvements, ses lumières et l'iconographie de l'invisible* appeared the following year (Paris: Carré, 1896). Baraduc, a gynecologist, believed that the human soul emitted a "subtle force" only perceptible to the camera. The specter of women's interiority is again invoked to provide a figure for the representation of the invisible. Regarding the popularity of spirit photography that erupted in the late nineteenth century, Tom Gunning writes: "The medium herself became a sort of camera, her spiritual negativity bodying forth a positive image, as the human body behaves like an uncanny photomat, dispensing images from its orifices" (Tom Gunning, "Phantom Images and Modern Manifestations: Spirit Photography, Magic Theater, Trick Films, and Photography's Uncanny," in *Fugitive Images: From Photography to Video*, ed. Patrice Petro [Bloomington: Indiana University Press, 1995], 58).

63 Jacques Derrida, *Of Grammatology*, trans. Gayatri Chakravorty Spivak (Baltimore, MD: Johns Hopkins University Press, 1976), 70.

16

Preface: Radio Phantasms, Phantasmic Radio

Allen S. Weiss

> ... *tra la la la la misère.*
>
> ANTONIN ARTAUD

In Western metaphysics, subjectivity has traditionally been conceived of as a paradox, a tension where interiority exists beneath the pressure of exteriority, and where technology develops as a metaphoric appendage of the body. The principal disjunction or aporia guiding this study is between *stream-of-consciousness* (dream logic, depth psychology, libidinal primary processes, fantasy, interiorization) and *stream-of-existence* (aleatory constructs, the concrete, montage, cut-up, structuralization). This work, polemical and passionate, is a study of transmission, circuits, disarticulation, metamorphosis, mutation – and *not* communication, closure, articulation, representation, simulacra.[1] There is no single entity that constitutes "radio"; rather, there exists a multitude of radios. Radiophony is a heterogeneous domain, on the levels of its apparatus, its practice, its forms, and its utopias. A brief, and necessarily incomplete, sketch of some possibilities of non-mainstream concepts of radio will give an idea of this diversity. F. T. Marinetti: "wireless imagination" and futurist radio; Velimir Khlebnikov: revolutionary utopia and the fusion of mankind; Leon Trotsky: revolutionaty radio; Dziga Vertoz: agitprop and the "Radio-Eye"; Bertolt Brecht: interactive radio and public communication; Rudolf Arnheim: radiophonic specificity and the critique of visual imagination; Upton

Sinclair: telepathy and mental radio; Glenn Gould: studio perfectionism and "contrapuntal radio"; William Burroughs: cut-ups and the destruction of communication; Marshall McLuhan: the primitive extension of the central nervous system; and also the labyrinthine radio narratives of Hörspiel; the diversity of community radios; free radio; guerilla radio; pirate radio; radical radio.[2]

To bring the problematic up to date, consideration of just a few radical experiments in radiophony, centered in underground Amsterdam radio, will give an idea of the broad potential of radio beyond the various stultifying "laws" that guide mainstream radio: the law of maximal inoffensiveness, the law of maximal indifference, the law of maximal financial return. A sort of perverse specialization – perhaps a manifestation of what Deleuze speaks of as a "logic of the particular" – reigns in these contemporary pirate Amsterdam radio stations, which determine the margins of aesthetic culture.[3] *Radio Romantique Urbain*: Live connections to different urban soundscapes around the world, changing cities every four hours. *Radio Privacy*: The broadcast of stolen private and intimate documents such as diaries, letters, tape-recordings, and video soundtracks. *Radio Open Ear*: Collages of different worldwide radio bands – longwave, middlewave, short- and ultrashortwave, as well as television soundtracks – from all continents. *Radio Random*: Broadcast of ten-second segments of randomly selected telephone conversations tapped from the Dutch phone network. *Radio Bug*: Investigative reporting via eavesdropping using directional microphones and bugs. *Radio Alfabet*: The reading of poems, stories, and novels from all cultures. *Radio Adventure*: Interactive listener role-playing on air, via telephone and computer linkup, partially guided by routines and scenarios suggested by the station.

Multiple (and contradictory) histories of radiophony could be consti-tuted, depending upon both the historical paradigms chosen to guide the research and the theoretical phantasms behind the investigation. This study does not purport to be a history of experimental radio, but rather an open-ended disclosure of several crucial paradigms which could articulate such a history. Several possibilities suggest themselves, yet for our purposes three dates are emblematic: 1877, 1913, 1948.[4] If the history of mainstream radio is a suppressed field, the history of experimental radio is utterly repressed.

6 December 1877: On this date, Thomas A. Edison made the first recording of the human voice onto a tinfoil roll, singing "Mary Had a Little Lamb." As never before, voice is separated from body and eternalized in a technological mechanism – breeding the first of sundry techno-phantasies, followed by those of Villiers de l'Isle-Adam, Raymond Roussel, Alfred Jarry, etc., where the fears, hopes, and phantasms of disembodiment are finally actualized. At the very moment that the invention of the typewriter and the practice of experimental psychophysics freed words from both their gestural significance and their meaning, and at the time that psychoanalysis dissociated meaning from consciousness, phonography transformed voice into object, marking an end to several millennia of pneumatological, ontotheological belief.[5]

This is the epoch in which new metaphors of transmission and reception, as well as novel modes of the imagination, were conceived. The "animal magnetism" of mesmerism was replaced in the nineteenth century by the spiritualist manipulation of electric waves in the ether, destined to merge with the psychic waves of the departed, such that electricity would permit contact with the afterworld. By 1855 Walt Whitman had already announced "I Sing the Body Electric" as one of the poems in *Leaves of Grass*; and the entry for the year 1900 of Henry Adams's autobiography, *The Education of Henry Adams*, was entitled "The Dynamo and the Virgin." Nothing better expresses the difference between ancient and modern paradigms of aesthetics and ontology, where the rapidity and excitation of electric power would serve as the new symbol of a body now ruled by technology, without divine interference. In this century, electricity would shock us out of depression and psychosis through the use of electroshock therapy; it would fry us to death on the electric chair, that hidden modern substitute for the more theatrical guillotine; it would provide numerous prostheses for lost organs and diminished capacities.

The dynamo-virgin opposition effectively expresses the different paradigms to be established nearly a quarter of a century later at the interior of radiophonic art. The theater is a stage of history, theology, and metaphysics, of the body given to God and the Virgin, to nature and culture – the body imbued with life-force. The dynamo is something quite other, creating a new current, flow, circulation, excitation – a force closely allied with the destructive powers of technology. Electricity transformed the very form of the imagination through which we discover our utopias and dystopias, offering us Villiers de l'Isle-Adam's *The Future Eve*, Marcel Duchamp's *The Bride Stripped Bare by Her Bachelors, Even*, Karel Capek's *R.U.R.*, the android of Fritz Lang's *Metropolis*, the erotic apparatus in Roger Vadim's *Barbarella*, as well as many other human machines, *célibataires*, and otherwise.[6] And with electricity operating in Europe today at fifty cycles – resonating at roughly G-sharp – it established a new, inexorable, unconscious tonal center which inhabits our every thought and underlies our every enunciation.

17 February 1913: This date has been inscribed as mythical in the history of modernism, marking the opening of *The International Exhibition of Modern Art*, commonly referred to as *The Armory Show*. The New York Armory Show brought modern art into public consciousness with the succès de scandale of Marcel Duchamp's *Nude Descending a Staircase*, likened by a vicious but prophetic critic to "an explosion in a shingle factory." (It is also the year Duchamp shattered musical composition with his aleatory *Musical Erratum*.) This visual explosion was echoed in the realm of sound that same year, in Luigi Russolo's futurist manifesto, *The Art of Noise*. In an epoch of increasing mechanization, and inspired by the winds of war, Russolo saw the evolution of music as progressing towards the incorporation of mechanized noise; indeed he demanded the replacement of music by noise. The limited tonal sphere of musical sound was to be broken, just as the futurist notion of the *parole in libertà* (words in freedom) freed the word from syntactic and lexical restraints. "We find far more enjoyment in the combination of the noises of trams, backfiring motors, carriages and bawling crowds than in rehearing, for example, the *Eroica* or the *Pastorale*." Beyond Wagner's chromaticism, beyond Schoenberg's atonality, Russolo expanded the extremely limited Western musical vocabulary by including the vast variety of noises. He established the following categories of sound for a futurist orchestra: (1) rumbles, roars, explosions, crashes, splashes, booms; (2) whistles, hisses, snorts; (3) whispers, murmurs, mumbles, grumbles, gurgles; (4) screeches, creaks, rustles, crackles, scrapes; (5) noises obtained by percussion on metal, wood, skin, stone, terracotta, and other materials; and (6) voices of animals and men: shouts, screams, groans, shrieks, howls, laughs, wheezes, sobs. These considerations were intended to change the very nature of auditory perception as well as sonic creativity. Russolo postulated that we can distinguish at least as many different noises as there are machines; as the number of machines increases, so does the quantity of discrete, perceptible noises. But, most crucially, he predicted machines built specifically to create new noises which at that moment could only be imagined – prefiguring Edgard Varèse's dream of a musical instrument with as broad a range as the musician's imagination.

But independent of these aesthetic innovations and expectations, 1913 was also the year of a momentous yet aesthetically unheralded event: the creation of the first feedback in electrical circuitry. On 31 January 1913, Edwin H. Armstrong had notarized his diagram of the first regenerative circuit, an invention which was to be the basis of radio transmission. His discovery was that the audion (vacuum tube) could be used not only as a detector of electrical waves but also, through regeneration or feedback, as a signal amplifier. Furthermore, as a generator of continuously oscillating electromagnetic waves, it could be used as a transmitter. The very first demonstration of audio amplification, by Lee de Forest in November 1913, created the "crashing sounds" of a handkerchief dropping. Radio was created – and with it, an unfortunate electronic side-effect was first heard, that of static.[7]

The confluence of these developments was of the utmost practical and symbolic import, as they provided auditory possibilities not even imagined up to that time: amplification of existing sounds, the broadcast of sound, and the creation of new sorts of noise. Though these new inventions perfectly matched the needs of the contemporary aesthetic avant-gardes, the artistic benefits were long in coming.

Audio feedback, as one example, consists of the accumulation of sound mass by establishing a continuous circuit of output and input; this is achieved by raising the sound level of the signal to such a degree that the amplified sound returns to the input, a sort of electrical or electronic solipsism. This continuous circuit feeds on itself, generating a vicious howling sound, ever increasing to a deafening shriek. The control of these effects created new musical possibilities exemplified by Jimi Hendrix's electric guitar feedback, as in his rock classic *Star Spangled Banner* solo recorded at the 1969 Woodstock festival. Yet the implications of feedback reach far beyond the strictly musical, as in the notion of a self-feeding system seeking its own catastrophe, its own sonic destruction – noise may be coaxed or pressured toward music or silence.

2 February 1948: This is the date of the non-event which inaugurates my study – the suppression of Antonin Artaud's scheduled radio broadcast of *To Have Done with the Judgment of God*. The year 1948 also marked the origin of modern radiophonic and electroacoustic research and creativity, for it was at this moment that magnetic recording tape was perfected and began to become available for artistic purposes. The confluence of these two events – Artaud's final attempt to void his interiority, to transform psyche and suffering and body into art, *and* the technical innovation of recording tape, which henceforth permitted the experimental aesthetic simulation and disarticulation of voice as pure exteriority – established a major epistemological-aesthetic shift in the history of art.

There are indeed creative possibilities that operate at the very interior of mainstream, government, military, or commercial radio, rare as they may be: parasites and viruses that determine other limits, functions, and pleasures of radiophonic art. Yet however sophisticated the montage, most works for radio never surpass the conditions of music, theater, poetry – radio rarely realizes its truly *radiophonic* potentials. For radiophony is not only a matter of audiophonic invention, but also of sound diffusion and listener circuits or feedback. Thus the paradox of radio: a universally public transmission is heard in the most private of circumstances; the thematic specificity of each individual broadcast, its imaginary scenario, is heard within an infinitely diverse set of nonspecific situations, different for each listener; the radio's putative shared solidarity of auditors in fact achieves their atomization as well as a reification of the imagination.

René Farabet, cofounder and director of the Atelier de Création Radiophonique of Radio France, suggests that memory itself is a sort of montage structure and that the temporal present creates the ultimate sound mix.[8] At any given moment, everything we hear is "mixed" in the ear and thematically organized by the mind. All modes of such passive "montage" must be confronted, organized, and transformed by the active gesture of the *cut*, activated on all levels of radiophonic art: project, transcript, recording, cutting, cleaning, overlaying, mixing, rerecording. Here, where one may "feel the shadow of the person who worked on the piece leaning over us," montage is creative, no longer merely a "cleansing" of sound. The implications of these suggestions open phonography and radiophony far beyond the corporeal limits of the imagination. There exists a point, unlocalizable and mysterious, where listener and radio are indistinguishable. We therefore seek that realm where the voice reaches beyond its body, beyond the shadow of its corporeal origins, to become a radically original sonic object.

Hence the theme of this book, which is not primarily concerned with radio theater, *bruitage* (sound effects), *poésie sonore* (sound poetry), *musique concrète* (concrete music), or electroacoustic music. Rather, I wish to investigate the effects of what Marinetti termed the "wireless imagination" in its most extreme form. This study attempts to show how radiophony transforms the very nature of the relation between signifier and signified, and how the practice of montage established the key modernist paradigm of consciousness. This task is informed by the *motivated, nonarbitrary* relationships between signifier and signified [S/s], where the mediating term is not the slash that delineates the topography of the unconscious [/], but rather the variegated, fragile, unrepresentable flesh of the lived body. As such, this work participates in the linguistic and epistemological polemic at the center of continental philosophy – between phenomenological, structuralist, and post-structuralist hermeneutics – concerning the ontological status of body, voice, expression, and phantasms. Antonin Artaud's "body without organs" establishes the closure of the flesh after the death of God and at the opening of the nuclear age; John Cage's "imaginary landscapes" proffer the indissociability of techne and psyche; Valère Novarina reinvents the body through the word in his "theater of the ears"; Gregory Whitehead disarticulates vocal and radio circuits according to a radiophonic "principia schizophonica," whereby the radio disembody takes its place at the margins of media existence; Louis Wolfson reveals the psychotic use of the radio as a quotidian menial prophylaxis; and Christof Migone leads us to the point where solipsistic expression and universal communication become indistinguishable through perpetual and ambiguous feedback.

Between voice and wavelength, between body and electricity, the future of radio resounds.

Notes

1   See also Allen S. Weiss, "Broken Voices, Lost Bodies: Experimental Radiophony," in *Perverse Desire and the Ambiguous Icon* (Albany: State University of New York Press, 1994).

2   Though there is no comprehensive history of radio, experimental or otherwise, the most useful sources to date are Douglas Kahn and Gregory Whitehead, eds., *Wireless Imagination: Sound, Radio, and the Avant-Garde*

(Cambridge: The MIT Press, 1992); Neil Strauss, ed., *Radiotext(e)*, a special issue of *Semiotext(e)*, no. 16 (1993); Daina Augaitis and Dan Lander, eds., *Radio Rethink: Art, Sound and Transmission* (Banff: Walter Phillips Gallery, 1994).

3   Geert Lovink, "The Theory of Mixing: An Inventory of Free Radio Techniques in Amsterdam," in *Mediamatic* 6, no. 4 (1992): 225.

4   The prehistory of radio and audio art is traced out in a detailed chronology established by Hugh Davis, "A History of Recorded Sound," in Henri Chopin, *Poésie sonore internationale* (Paris: Jean-Michel Place, 1979), pp. 13–40.

5   See Friedrich Kittler, *Discourse Networks, 1800–1900* (1985), translated from German by Michael Metteer with Chris Cullens (Stanford: Stanford University Press, 1990), pp. 177–264, passim.

6   See the catalog of the exhibition *Junggesellenmaschinen/Les machines célibataires*, inspired by the work of Michel Carrouges, Harald Szeemann ed. (Venice: Alfieri, 1976).

7   Lewis Tom, *Empire of the Air* (New York: HarperCollins, 1991), pp. 73–7.

8   Farabet's comments were set forth in a seminar on montage theory directed by Jacques Munier at the Collège International de Philosophie, in Paris, during the session of June 1992.

17

from Chair Creaks, But No One Sits There

David Toop

When the lights go out, hearing stays awake. *The Chimes: A Goblin Story*, was one of a series of Christmas books written by Charles Dickens in the 1840s. His tale opens with a hypothesis calculated to seduce, to lure in through its cold haunted design the reader who is settled in an opposite condition of warm secure comfort. Few people care to sleep in a church at night, alone, Dickens claims; the cause of this is not supernatural, nor even general discomfort, but the spooky noise of the night-wind as it encircles and penetrates the church. His anthropomorphic description of this night-wind is exhaustive. He gives it form and purpose, devious ingenuity and volatility of mood:

> For the night-wind has a dismal trick of wandering round and round a building of that sort, and moaning as it goes; and of trying, with its unseen hand, the windows and the doors; and seeking out some crevices by which to enter ... Anon, it comes up stealthily, and creeps along the walls: seeming to read, in whispers, the Inscriptions sacred to the Dead. At some of these, it breaks out shrilly, as with laughter; and at others, moans and cries as if it were lamenting. It has a ghostly sound too, lingering within the altar; where it seems to chaunt, in its wild way, of Wrong and Murder done, and false Gods worshipped ... Ugh! Heaven preserve us, sitting snugly round the fire! It has an awful voice, that wind at Midnight, singing in a church![1]

Charles Dickens returned to this theme of spectral noise in *The Haunted*

House, written in collaboration with five other authors in 1862. In the haunted house, the dog howls when the narrator strikes an accidental discord on the piano, again when the servant's bell rings incessantly, even though no living person is there to pull the cord, and no servant in attendance to hear it. 'Noises?' he wrote. 'With that contagion downstairs, I myself have sat in the dismal parlour, listening, until I have heard so many and such strange noises that they would have chilled my blood if I had not warmed it by dashing out to make discoveries. Try this in bed, in the dead of the night; try this at your own comfortable fireside, in the life of the night. You can fill any house with noises if you will, until you have a noise for every nerve in your nervous system.'[2]

Dickens suggests that noises, real and unreal, reveal themselves through conscious, intent acts of listening. The nervous body fills the vacuum of silence with phantom sounds generated by its own hyperacuity. If we believe that what we cannot see, we cannot know, then the possibility exists that inert and lifeless objects may have a secret life that only reveals itself when we look away or fall asleep. In Hans Anderson's story, 'The Sandman', the purpose of the Sandman is to create sufficient quiet for the imagination to be unleashed; unless they are quiet, or better still silently sleeping, children are unable to hear his stories. A little boy named Hialmar is the listener. One night when he is in bed, the Sandman touches all the pieces of furniture in his room with a magic wand: 'Thereupon they all began to chatter, and each piece talked only about itself, excepting the spittoon, who stood quite still, and was much vexed at their being so vain, all chattering about themselves, without ever thinking of him, who stood so modestly in the corner and suffered himself to be spat upon.'[3] Images are brought to life by the Sandman's wand. As he touches pictures that hang on the walls, the birds within them begin to sing; with this enlivening of silence, the Sandman (as if inventing the animated film) lifts Hialmar into the frame of the picture so that he can cross over into the world of images.

The propensity for sound to summon or accompany uncanny sensations and atmospheres has been noted only fitfully in the extensive literature devoted to Freud's essay, *The Uncanny*; invariably its significance is set aside for more ocular concerns. In his own version of *The Uncanny*, a book-length study of this subject, Nicholas Royle takes the trouble to locate and analyse the obscure story from the *Strand Magazine*, which Freud described only in précis: a young couple move into a flat and among the existing furnishings is a table carved with crocodiles. As darkness falls the flat is filled with an obnoxious stench, the tenants trip over things and see some inexplicable creature gliding over the stairs. As Royle discovers, this story, entitled 'Inexplicable', was written by a now forgotten author, Lucy Gertrude Moberly. Royle's reading uncovers material that Freud chose not to consider. The opening paragraph, for example, revisits a familiar trope: the fateful crossing of a threshold, just prior to entering an unfamiliar house. The gate's rusty hinges creak dismally, and when the latch clicks into its socket, 'with a sharp clang', the narrator is startled into thoughts of prison doors and turnkeys. Once again, sound serves as a presentiment of events to come.

'This sense of eeriness in the ear, the "eariness" of the uncanny, recurs throughout the story', writes Royle. Incidents of 'eary' phenomena include a 'far-away bellowing ... pregnant with evil' and the 'sliding and pattering' of crocodiles in the darkness. 'Once again, that is to say, this story provides striking examples of an auditory dimension that is crucial to a critical appreciation of "the uncanny".'[4] Crucial it may be, but Royle's exploration of the auditory dimension takes us no further than this provocative remark.

In his *The Uncanny*, Freud described E. T. A. Hoffmann as 'the unrivalled master of the uncanny in literature.'[5] Born in Königsburg in 1776, Hoffmann juggled a number of careers by using alcohol to obscure any incompatibilities that existed between them. He composed operas, stood as a member of the Commission for the Investigation of Treasonable Organizations and other Dangerous Activities, and in Berlin wrote the short stories and novels that made him famous. Freud's essay concentrates on 'The Sandman', a complex short story initially narrated by a young student, Nathaniel. He begins with a letter written to his foster brother, Lothario, but mistakenly addressed to his foster sister and fiancée, Clara. The letter relates a recent incident in which a seller of barometers has revived memories of a traumatic childhood experience. The narrative returns to this childhood, to memories of their father, and the evenings when their mother would hurry them to bed, telling them the sandman was coming. 'On these occasions,' wrote Hoffmann, 'I really did hear something come clumping up the stairs with slow, heavy tread, and knew it must be the sandman. Once these muffled footsteps seemed to me especially frightening, and I asked my mother as she led us out: "Mama, who is this sandman who always drives us away from Papa? What does he look like?"'[6] The mother reassures him with a white lie, telling him that there is no sandman, only the feeling of being sleepy, as if somebody had sprinkled sand in his eyes. Others have a more sinister explanation. The old woman who looks after his sister tells him that the sandman comes for children who won't go to bed, throws sand in their eyes so that they jump out of their heads, then tosses them into a sack and carries them to the crescent moon as food for his children. The children have crooked beaks, like owls (or harpies), and peck out the eyes of these naughty children.

From this point, Nathaniel is terrorised by sounds or their absence — his father's silence on the nights when the visitor is due, the invader's feet as he clumps up the stairs, the noise of him wrenching open the door of his father's study, then entering for some unknown purpose. Years pass, the sounds continue, the intensity of Nathaniel's terror persists. Finally, he is moved to a bedroom closer to his father's study. As usual, he hears the stranger open his father's door, but with the closer proximity, he senses something new, 'a subtle, strange-smelling vapour' spreading through the house. Finally reaching a point at which these combinatory signs of an invisible intruder impel him to see their perpetrator, he hides himself in a cupboard behind a curtain in his father's room. Again the sounds reach him in the darkness of his eavesdropper's cubbyhole: 'The footsteps thudded nearer and nearer, and there was a strange coughing, rasping and growling outside. My heart quaked with fear and anticipation. Close, close behind the door — a quick footstep, a violent blow on the latch and the door sprang open with a clatter!' With the crescendo of this noise symphony, the rupture of heimlich by unheimlich, Nathaniel looks out and sees a familiar but repugnant figure: the aged advocate, Coppelius. Whatever horrors were imagined through the agency of the nursery tale, the silence of his father, the noises, or the strange odour, had been replaced by unpalatable visible reality, 'a repellent spectral monster bringing misery, distress and earthly and eternal ruination wherever he went.'

From these 'lifelike' beginnings, sympathetic to universal memories of childhood anxiety, Hoffmann's story grows stranger, more convoluted, as if preparing for all that follows. Nathaniel watches in horror as his father and Coppelius perform a ghastly alchemical experiment in which eyeless faces float in an atmosphere of smoke and confusion. Screaming when Coppelius demands eyes, 'in a dull hollow voice', he is discovered, narrowly avoids losing his own eyes, and is subjected to bizarre manipulations of his hands and feet. In the escalating tension of those intervening years in which Nathaniel has eavesdropped upon the auditory double of the unseen intruder clumping up the stairs of the family home, we can imagine the multifarious bodies and faces he has fitted to the disembodied sounds, banal in themselves but terrifying for their implicit threat. The climactic impact of this first phase of Hoffmann's story — eyeless faces in the smoke, the scream, the unscrewing of Nathaniel's hands and feet, a huge explosion that kills his father, more screams, wailing and lamentation — is a necessary trauma to justify the suspense of this auditory prolongation. After the explosion — 'a fearful detonation, like the firing of a cannon' — Nathaniel hears 'a clattering and rushing' past the door of his room, then the front door of the house slamming with a crash. By this point, Nathaniel is intimately familiar with Coppelius and his auditory signs. As sound, he enters the home, materializes, wrenches open a door, destroys both the father and the space of the father, then as sound again, closes the door to the home and exits.

The psychoanalytic conclusions of Freud's analysis of 'The Sandman', particularly his assertion that the fear of being robbed of ones eyes is a substitute for castration anxiety, have been exhaustively picked apart, notably by Hélène Cixous in 'Fiction and Its Phantoms: A Reading of Freud's *Das Unheimliche* (The "uncanny")'.[7] All of these examinations of Freud and Hoffmann glide over the unsettling relationship between Nathaniel's initial 'blindness', in which the noises of the unseen sandman are an unreliable (and disbelieved) witness to events that later prove to be unimaginable, and the theme of enucleation that persists until Nathaniel's demise. In her sceptical reply to Nathaniel's letter, Clara tells him that almost everything in his story took place within his misdirected imagination. 'Perhaps there does exist a dark power which fastens on to us and leads us off along a dangerous and ruinous path which we would otherwise not have trodden,' she writes, 'but if so, this power must have assumed within us the form of ourself, indeed have become ourself, for otherwise we would not listen to it, otherwise there would be no space within us in which it could perform its secret work.' At the end of the story, when all seems settled, Nathaniel succumbs to the enucleating device planted by his nemesis. He roars, laughs hideously, screams and chants in a 'piercing cry', ending his own life by jumping from a high tower. The last paragraph of 'The Sandman' portrays Clara seated in a bliss of 'quiet domestic happiness', her space of repressed hearing a heimlich middle ground that Nathaniel, inhabiting a place of uncanny extremes, of forensic listening and unrestrained vocalisation, could never have supplied.

As a footnote to this complacent withdrawal from the sounding world, Metallica's 'Enter Sandman' draws out a further subtext of the story. Though the lyrics are a litany of all the familiar defences against darkness — quiet obedience (children should be seen but not heard), lullabies, prayer and vigilance — the domain of night and nightmare gains ascendance over these fragile consolations as the song reaches its conclusion. With Metallica's retrospective approval, the song proved extremely popular with US psyops troops as an instrument of so-called 'torture-lite', played repeatedly at overwhelming volume to prisoners in Guantanamo Bay and in a prison facility known only as 'the disco', located somewhere on the Iraqi-Syrian border. Searching for a theoretical base for this practice, retired US Air Force Lt-Col Dan Kuehl, an instructor in psychological operations at the time, drew upon the Biblical story of Joshua, whose army used ram's horns and voices as sonic weapons in their conquest of Jericho.

The haunting

This interpretation of sound as an unstable or provisional event, ambiguously situated somewhere between psychological delusion, verifiable scientific phenomenon, and a visitation of spectral forces, is a frequent trope of supernatural fiction. In Bram Stoker's *Dracula*, after all the whisperings and susurrations, howling wolves, bats flapping at windows, the 'low piteous howling of dogs', the 'churning sound of her tongue' when Jonathan Harker is seduced by three voluptuous vampires, and their silvery musical laughter, 'like the intolerable, tingling sweetness of water-glasses when played on by a cunning hand', one of the first signs of Count Dracula's imminent arrival in Whitby is auditory:

> Shortly before ten o'clock the stillness of the air grew quite oppressive, and the silence was so marked that the bleating of a sheep inland or the barking of a dog in the town was distinctly heard, and the band on the pier, with its lively French air, was like a discord in the great harmony of nature's silence. A little after midnight came a strange sound over the sea, and high over head the air began to carry a strange, faint, hollow booming.[8]

Whereas other omens are described as shared visual experiences — the erratic progress of the *Demeter*, the ship in which Dracula lies in his earth-filled box, and an unusually vivid sunset followed by a storm of spectacular violence — these notations of sound are given as a private occurrence. The hearing of anomalous sounds implies a degree of interiority that may border on hallucination or madness, yet through this ambiguity, the place of sound in the natural order is interrogated. A fictional archetype is established, in which the sudden and unnatural absence of sound opens up space in nature for supernatural sound, a sound that shares the characteristics of sound yet lacks its materiality.

Long John Silver, of all characters in fiction, challenges the false logic of supernatural sound in *Treasure Island*. As the last remnants of his pirate band search for treasure, they are taunted by the hidden voice of a marooned sailor. The more susceptible of the men assume it to be the ghost of the dreaded Flint, but Silver is unconvinced: '"Sperrit? Well, maybe," he said. "But there's one thing not clear to me. There was an echo. Now, no man ever seen a sperrit with a shadow; well, then, what's he doing with an echo to him, I should like to know? That ain't in natur', surely?"'[9] If the form of an apparition has no physical substance, then its voice must also be insubstantial, otherwise contradicting nineteenth-century science's explanations of sound as a wave or pulse that moves through air to make a physical impact on the tympanic membrane. As physicist John Tyndall pointed out in his pioneering study, *Sound*, first published in 1867, sailors must understand something of acoustics. The use of lights as fog signals often proved useless when visibility dropped to zero. 'No wonder, then,' he wrote, 'that earnest efforts should have been made to find a substitute for light in sound-signals, powerful enough to give warning and guidance to mariners while still at a safe distance from the shore.'[10] Victorian-era writers like Stevenson, Bram Stoker and Sir Arthur Conan Doyle shared a deep interest in the scientific discoveries of their time. Informed by this, Silver enacts a conflict between the sailor's pragmatic knowledge of natural phenomena and his tenacious superstition, engendered by the spectre of death haunting those whose occupation depends upon the sea.

This uncertain relationship between real and imagined shadows the fate of Eleanor, the central subject of Shirley Jackson's novel, *The Haunting of Hill House*. First published in 1959, the book was filmed as *The Haunting*, directed to unsettling, edgy effect by Robert Wise in 1963, then remade by Jan de Bont in 1999. The latter misses the point in its dependence on CGI effects, 'materializing' the haunting as a firework display of whizzing spooks, whereas Wise preserves the ambiguity and restraint of Jackson's story.

Eleanor has cared for her invalid, tyrannical mother all her life. One night her mother knocks on the wall, calling repeatedly for her medicine. For once, Eleanor sleeps through the noise. Subsequently, her mother dies, leaving thirty-two-year-old Eleanor with an ultimately fatal dose of guilt. A researcher in supernatural manifestations, Dr John Montague, is given the opportunity of investigating Hill House, notorious for its malign atmosphere. Searching through records of psychic phenomena for assistants who might be sensitive to presences in the house, he finds Eleanor. Shortly after her father died, Eleanor and her family were driven from their home by showers of stones falling from the sky for three days, 'rolling loudly down the walls, breaking windows and pattering maddeningly on the roof.'[11] In her vulnerable state, liberated from her mother's needs, she joins the ill-matched group who assemble at Hill House under the paternalistic direction of Dr Montague.

What transpires in the house is inconclusive yet mysteriously powerful. The horror, such as it is, might be described as 'mild threat' by those picturesque summaries now printed as warnings of what to expect in a film. More accurately, it is sonic menace. On arrival, Eleanor finds herself drawn into a silence, trying to put her suitcase down without making a sound, walking in stocking feet conscious that the housekeeper had moved soundlessly: 'When she stood still in the middle of the room the pressing silence of Hill House came back all around her. I am like a small creature swallowed whole by a monster, she thought and the monster feels my tiny little movements inside.'[12] There are intimations of this swallowing, as the house resists all attempts to understand its spatial logic, yet nothing happens until the feeling of nothing happening is firmly established. Significantly, though the reader is waiting for ghosts, the first manifestation is a loud knocking on the door of the bedrooms shared by Eleanor and Dr Montague's other female assistant Theodora. Shocked awake by this noise, Eleanor thinks she is back at home, her mother knocking on the wall. She and Theodora attempt to rationalize the noise and its physiological effects. 'Just a noise,' says Theodora; 'It sounded, Eleanor thought, like a hollow noise, a hollow bang, as though something were hitting the doors with an iron kettle, or an iron bar, or an iron glove.'[13] The sound moves with a similar anthropomorphized purpose (though a more specific intimation of domestic violence) to the wind that probes Charles Dickens's church, searching methodically, diminishing, thundering to a climax and falling ominously silent, then, with silence, a spreading of cold air: 'Little pattings came from around the doorframe, small seeking sounds, feeling the edges of the door, trying to sneak a way in.... . The little sticky sounds moved on around the doorframe and then, as though a fury caught whatever was outside, the crashing came again, and Eleanor and Theodora saw the wood of the door tremble and shake, and the door move against its hinges.'[14]

Though Hill House has little to recommend it as a home, Eleanor imagines herself within a family. Her delusion is fragile, yet it serves to enclose the isolated space of repressed memories, misanthropy and loneliness that has grown within like a cancer born of too much harsh reality, and so the invasive sound that manifests with every significant death in her life is an uncanny response to her brief moment of security. Predictably, the sound offers unreliable evidence to scientific rationalist, sceptic, medium or Eleanor herself, who doubts her own fear. Not everybody hears the sounds, so Eleanor begins to question their material reality, their 'outside' existence: 'Now we are going to have a new noise, Eleanor thought. listening to the inside of her head; it is changing.... . Am I doing it? she wondered quickly, is that me? And heard the tiny laughter beyond the door, mocking her.'[15] Jackson's subtle mockery of the clichés of supernatural and gothic fiction echoes this laughter, yet she refuses to supply a rational explanation, or confirm the psychological undercurrent. In its scenario of flawed and incompatible individuals forced to share enclosed space, *The Haunting of Hill House* resembles Jean Paul Sartre's play, *No Exit*, whose message was that hell is ourselves. Hill House is, after all, one vowel away from Hell House.

Myth enters the story as they move into the grounds of the house, when Theodora describes the third assistant, Luke, as Pan. Soon after this invocation by naming, Eleanor's senses sharpen, turn to paranoia. She hears distant murmurs of conversation, a brush of footsteps, a voice: '"Eleanor, Eleanor," and she heard it inside and outside her head; this was a call she had been listening for all her life. The footsteps stopped and she was caught in a movement of air so solid that she staggered and was held. "Eleanor, Eleanor," she heard through the rushing of air past her ears.'[16] Soon after this revelation, Eleanor sits and listens to the sounds of the house, her hearing capabilities expanded to animalistic sensitivity: a door swinging shut, a bird touching the tower and flying off, the stove settling and cooling, an animal moving through bushes by the summerhouse outside: 'She could even hear, with her new awareness of the house, the dust drifting gently in the attic, the wood aging.'[17] At this point of fusion between the extended space of Eleanor's hearing and the projected soundings of the house, there is little reason to expect a happy outcome. In the final line of the book, all noise is stilled: '. . . doors were sensibly shut; silence lay steadily against the wood and stone of Hill House, and whatever walked there, walked alone.'[18]

[...]

Instrument of death

In ancient Chinese literature, the motif of the abandoned musical instrument was used to symbolise a wider social decay, or the pathos of old customs in decline. Tang dynasty poet Po Chü-i's 'The Five-String' begins as rhapsody for the five-string lute and its player, 'The soft notes dying almost to nothing; / "Ch'ieh, ch'ieh," like the voice of ghosts talking.' The poem ends with a nostalgic coda:

> Alas, alas that the ears of common men
> Should love the modern and not love the old.
> Thus it is that the lute in the green window
> Day by day is covered deeper with dust.[19]

Sometimes an instrument claims a form of autonomy, aspiring to automatism by sounding itself (the rattling snare drum, or resonating grand piano), like a house in which a chair creaks, no one sitting there, as if no longer needing any entity other than itself, as if haunted by the sounds and players that have activated its body in the past. In *The Lore of the Chinese Lute*, Robert Hans van Gulik gave the example of a Chinese ghost story in which the lute, the guqin (or ch'in), sounds without human agency: 'Ch'ên Ch'iuyang fell ill and died. His father thought much of him, and placed his son's lute before his soul-tablet. Always after that in the middle of the night the tones of this lute would be heard; they could be heard even outside the house.'[20]

Of all instruments, the piano is most conducive to this ghostly activation, its keys either visibly undisturbed or lowering and rising by themselves. As a piece of furniture it harbours disturbing undertones of uncanny automata, of innate violence (those scenes in films in which the lid is slammed down on the fingers of the pianist), even coffins and caskets. In *Bruges-la-Morte*, by Georges Rodenbach, the grieving widower, Hugues Viane, has moved to Bruges for its melancholy atmosphere of quiet decay. Dedicating his life to mourning, he surrounds himself with mementoes of his dead wife, including the long locks of her hair:

> In order to be able to see them all the time, these locks that were still Her, he had placed them on the piano, silent from now on, in the large, never-changing drawing room. They simply lay there, a cut-off plait, a

broken chain, a rope saved from the shipwreck. And to protect the hair from contamination, from the moist atmosphere that could have taken the colour out of it or oxidized its metal, he had had the idea, naïve if it had not been touching, of putting it under glass, a transparent casket, a crystal box, the resting place of the bare locks to which he paid homage every day. For him, as for the silent objects living around, this plait of hair seemed bound up with their existence, seemed the very soul of the house.[21]

The piano never sounds during the novel but at the end, it is the hair that becomes (in English translation at least), 'the instrument of death'.[22] The idea that silent objects might be repositories of the soul of a house has great dramatic potential, since their auditory activation would suggest that the house itself has chosen to speak. Jack Clayton's 1961 film, *The Innocents*, based on *The Turn of the Screw* by Henry James, contains a key scene in which the governess, played by Deborah Kerr, experiences a ghostly visitation of sounds. She hears piano notes playing the music box melody of a tune that recurs throughout the film; the camera cuts away to the grand piano, but no one sits there. Voices whisper; laughter swirls around her. The scene shows nothing alarming — its elements are clichés of the genre — yet through effectively montaged sound design, a chilling sense of the uncanny is conveyed.

In the 1920s, the American composer Henry Cowell applied his overtone theories to a project that shifted the conceptualization of the grand piano into unknown territory. Extending Debussy's revolutionary notion of the piano as a sounding frame, he activated the instrument as if it were a resonant flat harp, an echo chamber of complex harmonic sensitivities (implicit in existing compositions by composers such as Scriabin and Schumann, perhaps, but otherwise left undisturbed as potentiality within the bowels of the instrument). In a number of Cowell's short works, the pianist sounds the strings by plucking, pressing, stroking, damping or rubbing them. Some of these 'string piano' pieces were given titles based on the atmospheres they evoke—*Aeolian Harp* or *Sinister Resonance*— while others drew on Cowell's Irish ancestry, or tales of Irish mythology interpreted by the mystic poet John Osborne Varian, then a member of a Californian Theosophical sect, The Temple of the People. One of Varian's obsessions was the importance of the harp in Irish mythology. For years he worked on developing a large harp with two sound chambers, loud enough to be used in outdoor settings. He hoped that Cowell would take over the responsibility of what seems to have been an impractical instrument. Instead, Cowell adapted the idea to his own music for piano interiors, composing pieces such as *The Banshee*, performed by two players, one holding down the damper pedal for maximum resonance and sustain, the other standing at the tail of the piano and either rubbing strings lengthwise or plucking them. Its eerie sound evokes the Irish spirit woman of myth, the messenger from the Otherworld who wails outside a house if an occupant is about to die, then flies away into the night. These ghostly properties housed within a piano proved to be seductive to American composers after Cowell: John Cage, whose adaptation of prepared piano inclined to more meditative atmospheres, and George Crumb, whose *Music of Shadows*, *Ghost Nocturne*, *The Phantom Gondolier*, and *Otherworldly Resonances* are unambiguous about such spectral associations. More recently, in his notes on Salvatore Sciarrino's *D'un Faune*, for alto flute and piano (1980), flautist Mario Caroli describes the transmogrification originally initiated by Cowell in terms that suggest an evolutionary process, a mutation from mechanical to organic and corporeal: 'The piano changes from an instrument with felt-covered hammers into an instrument with lungs with their particular characteristics of changeable dynamics and colour and light effects.'[23] An instrument breathes.

[...]

A phonographic ghost

To hear the noises of another, from concealment or some unseen place, is to be unnerved, at some level to feel shame and desire, to become a body cleaved, split between two places, to become a spy, a voyeur, or more accurately, an eavesdropper. In Sir Arthur Conan Doyle's short story of 1899, 'The Japanned Box', a private tutor named Frank Colmore gains employment at Thorpe Place, the old ancestral home of a melancholy widower named Sir John Bollamore. One night, while the tutor is walking with the governess of Bollamore's daughter, the sound of a voice breaks into their conversation: 'It was a voice — the voice undoubtedly of a woman. It was low — so low that it was only in the still night air that we could have heard it, but, hushed as it was, there was no mistaking its feminine timbre. It spoke hurriedly, gaspingly for a few sentences, and then was silent — a piteous, breathless, imploring sort of voice.'[24] Known as 'Devil' Bollamore for his reputation as a drunken debauchee, gambler and bruiser, Colmore's employer had been 'cured' of decadent intemperance by marriage to Little Beryl Clare, a woman who then devoted herself to bringing him back to 'manhood and decency'. The silence of this brooding man is now compromised by the disembodied voice, explicable only as an audible sign of his return to debauchery, a ghost, or something more sinister still, an imprisoned woman or some occult manifestation conjured in Bollamore's secret room in the high turret. Suspicion falls upon a black japanned box kept locked in the room.

The nature of the secret is uncovered, quite literally, when the sleepless tutor treats his neuralgia with a dose of chlorodyne (a patent medicine containing laudanum, cannabis and chloroform) while indexing Bollamore's library. Overcome by sleep, he wakes in moonlight to see Bollamore seated at his table, unaware of the tutor's presence. Confused by his drugged state, he watches and listens in horror: 'He bent as I watched him, and I heard the sharp turning of a key and the rasping of metal upon metal. As if in a dream I was vaguely conscious that this was the japanned box which stood in front of him, and that he had drawn something out of it, something squat and uncouth which now lay before him on the table ... And then, just as it rushed upon my horrified perceptions, and I had half risen to announce my presence, I heard a strange, crisp, metallic clicking, and then the voice.'[25] All elements of the scene are impressively gothic to the point of parody: the dim radiance of moonlight; chlorodyne visions; hints of devilry, séance and orientalism; harsh metallic noises; the squat shape that suggests the incubus of Fuseli's eighteenth-century painting, *The Nightmare*; a strange rhythmic clicking and then the eerie apparition of a female voice, sounding in space yet lacking any visible form. Out of this hallucinatory melodrama emerges an explanation that is both prosaically rational and remarkable. Within the japanned box is a phonograph, a machine whose uncanny clicking mechanism gives access to the invisible world of the dead; the source of the voice is a phonograph recording of Beryl Clare. While Bollamore's account of his wife gasping a deathbed message into the machine with her last breath is suitably maudlin, the implications are affecting, since the voice is both a haunting and an object of stability, a repeatable reminder that the speaker and hearer will join each other in the afterlife. 'The technology that had at first suggested to the narrator a secret life of vice', writes John M. Picker, in *Victorian Soundscapes*, 'instead ends up facilitating a monotonous pattern of solitary sobriety.'[26]

A silent room

This work may have begun in a room, sitting, thinking, listening, writing, reading, dozing, and if so, then the room may have been quiet, and if that were the case, then that quiet room was not just one room, because quiet rooms accumulate throughout life, rooms within rooms within rooms, fragmented rooms of childhood and dreams, sharply defined rooms, now virtual chat rooms and online sites for social networking, all enfolded within unfamiliar rooms barely remembered or selectively forgotten: those rooms of pleasure and dread, action and boredom, safety and danger. Their atmosphere collects as dust, standing in relation to the feeling of being in rooms when something important was at stake: classroom, exam room, bedroom, doctor's surgery interview room, hospital ward. Clocks once defined the feeling of otherwise silent rooms: clocks ticking, measuring time, slowly, quietly, a presence, an interior atmosphere, dividing time with their chimes, then resuming their steady plod through, what exactly? For those who grew up in the era of audible clocks, time has been measured out by the constancy of their ticking. 'Behind me, on the other side of where I'm lying down, the silence of the house touches infinity', wrote Fernando Pessoa in *The Book of Disquiet.* 'I hear time fall, drop by drop, and not one drop that falls can be heard.'[27] If the clock stopped then the feeling of a room would change, a drama of sudden absence. Virginia Woolf ends a beautiful passage from *Jacob's Room* — the dramatic transformation of a landscape as snow falls, colour, temperature, sound, the dead severity of frozen matter, then light banished as the day goes out — with interior sound, the burden of measuring duration, 'The worn voices of clocks repeated the fact of the hour all night long.'[28]

This occupation of a silent room, regulated and even articulated by a mechanical clock, was not silence at all of course. Tick and tock were paroxysms around which silence gathered, momentarily suspended in the pause of a pendulum at the top of its swing. Clocks, clock chimes and church bells granted people time, by glossing an auditory reality onto its constant but elusive existence. At the same time, time was sacrificed, every new sound subtracting from time remaining. The chimes of Big Ben strike out as a periodic structuring device in Virginia Woolf's *Mrs. Dalloway*: 'There! Out it boomed. First a warning, musical; then the hour, irrevocable. The leaden circles dissolved in the air.'[29] As the stability of its measuring decomposes, each chime joins other sounds of beating whose mark of time is more free, or carefree — cricket bats and the hooves of ponies — and all these sounds are shadowed by a more ominous beating of drums, 'a rustling, regular thudding sound', as young men in uniform marched to war. The novel was written between 1922 and 1924, when memories of the Great War were still vivid, its catastrophic effects apparent. 'The Empire is perishing', Woolf thought, 'the bands are playing; the exhibition is in ruins.'[30]

Even as time ran out, there was plenty of time to listen to all this time, the ticking, chiming and ringing; time's sounding acquired both pleasurable and sinister resonance, fluctuating from moment to moment. Time's immortal click will not stand still, whereas time's biological counterpart, the heartbeat, will eventually stop. As Woolf wrote in *Mrs Dalloway*:

> It is half-past eleven, she says, and the sound of St. Margaret's glides into the recesses of the heart and buries itself in ring after ring of sound, like something alive which wants to confide itself, to disperse itself, to be, with a tremor of delight, at rest ... It is Clarissa herself, he thought, with a deep emotion, and an extraordinarily clear, yet puzzling recollection of

her, as if this bell had come into the room years ago, where they sat at some moment of great intimacy, and had gone from one to the other and had left, like a bee with honey, laden with the moment.... Then, as the sound of St. Margaret's languished, he thought, she has been ill, and the sound expressed languor and suffering. It was her heart, he remembered; and the sudden loudness of the final stroke tolled for death that surprised in the midst of life ...[31]

Georges Rodenbach's late nineteenth-century novel, *Bruges-la-Morte*, was also punctuated by a constancy of bells, sounding out 'the death of the hours'. Rodenbach described the atmosphere of Bruges as an invasive dust — 'the dead ashes of time, the dust from the hourglass of the years' — or mist: 'Towns above all have a personality, a spirit of their own ... Each town is a state of mind, a mood which, after only a short stay, communicates itself, spreads to us in an effluvium which impregnates us, which we absorb with the very air.'[32] There are intimations of airborne disease here, and the solemn rhythms of bells from antiquity combine with rain, mists, granite and the veiled northern light 'to influence the colour of the air'. Sometimes the bell sounds are pale, far distant; sometimes their sound oozes like sludge: 'The sound of the bells also seems blackish. Muffled, blurred in the air, it arrives as a reverberation which, equally grey, moves along in sluggish, bobbing waves over the waters of the canals.'

Though this sound lives on as metaphor — the ticking of biological clocks and so on — we measure a more silent, precise, urgent version of time with digital clocks, small battery-operated clocks with a tick so fugitive that only paranoid listening in the middle of the night can search it out, and the visual noise but apparent audio silence of numerical displays on TVs, ovens, microwaves, computers and mobile phones. Quiet rooms and the people within them now float within a more continuous and subliminal form of air. All of these devices radiate electromagnetic emissions, so their silence is illusory. With the right inductive equipment, sound materializes, just like the things of the air, thronging H. P. Lovecraft's fiction.

Small sounds are too quick, too slight, to leave any sense of overcrowding air or imposing authority, yet they form wisps into solids, glue fragments into forms, keep people sane. or shield them from loneliness and the void. In *Life: A User's Manual*, Georges Perec wrote about Gaspard Winckler, the craftsman who in old age stared at nothing, his radio playing at such low volume that no one really knew if he could hear it, yet when Madame Nochere went to switch it off, he stopped her. He listened to the hit parade every night. That was his claim. In the Parisian apartment block imagined and meticulously described by Perec, Valène's bedroom is directly above Winckler's workshop, so for nearly forty years, 'his days had been accompanied by the thin noise of the craftsman's tiny files, the almost inaudible throb of his jigsaw, the creaking of his floorboards, the whistling of his kettle when he boiled water, not for making tea but for some glue or glaze he needed for his puzzles.'[33]

[...]

Sighs from the depths

Thomas De Quincey's *Suspiria de Profundis* (sighs from the depths), was first published in 1845 as a sequel to his more celebrated *Confessions of an English Opium-Eater*. Recounting feelings connected with the death of his sister, De Quincey describes the sound of a mournful wind: 'Mournful! That is saying nothing It was a wind that had swept the fields of mortality for a hundred centuries. Many times since, upon a summer day, when the sun is about the hottest, I have remarked the same wind arising and uttering the same hollow, solemn, Memnonian, but saintly swell: it is in this world the one sole audible symbol of eternity.'[34] A trance fell upon him, whenever he heard the sound he called 'this vast Aeolian intonation'. De Quincey alludes to the Colossi of Memnon, the two huge statues erected to guard the mortuary temple of Pharaoh Amenhotep III, sited on the West Bank at Luxor. Constructed in the fourteenth century BC, the temple's collapse in an earthquake in 27 BC ran a fissure through one of the statues. From this point until its repair, the statue would emit a sound every morning at dawn, a 'singing' that led to the myth of Memnonian oracular powers.

Such sounds — howling wind, ghostly echoes, the moaning, whistling and rumbling of meteorological phenomena and geological formations — reverberate through myth, religions and the arts, symbolising the inchoate beginnings of existence, a time before the evolution of our animal selves, before the massing of coherent forms. Like Pan's flute, their uncanny, edgeless tones insinuate themselves into otherwise ordered lives as omens, disruptions, reminders that despite sciences and social mores, some aspects of life remain unknowable. In 2008, a BBC television adaptation of Thomas Hardy's *Tess of the D'Urbervilles* demonstrated a contemporary inability to understand the significance of such auditory metaphors. In the televised version, Tess and Angel Clare wander into Stonehenge in broad daylight, Tess draping herself tragically on one of the stones shortly before the police arrive to arrest her for murder. In the book, they stumble into the stone circle at night, unaware of what they have found but overwhelmed by its sudden massive presence within the landscape:

'It hums,' said she. 'Hearken!'
He listened. The wind playing upon the edifice, produced a booming tune, like the note of some gigantic one-stringed harp ...
'A very Temple of the Winds,' he said.[35]

Sound matters in Thomas Hardy's novels because critical moments of narrative turn upon what is left unsaid: the repressions, evasions and missed opportunities for openness that so often prove excruciating to a modern reader. What should be spoken is left silent, cannot be voiced, or by accident, is overlooked. The misunderstandings that follow invariably blossom into grim tragedies. At the climax of *Tess of the D'Urbervilles*, Tess and Angel emerge out of darkness into the humming drone of Stonehenge. They stay and listen 'to the wind among the pillars', like two pagans momentarily isolated from the strictures of the world. As light comes with the dawn so society returns. The romantic idea of Stonehenge as a 'heathen temple', and the uncanny natural wildness of the sounds produced by aeolian harps combine to haunting effect, echoing Coleridge's poem of 1795, 'The Eolian Harp', in which the sound of the harp floats softly as a spell, 'a soft floating witchery of sound / As twilight Elfins make ...'[36] In a passage from one of his John Silence stories, 'Ancient Sorceries', Algernon Blackwood's narrator recounts a story of hearing bewitching music that makes him think of 'trees swept by the wind, of night breezes singing among wires and chimneystacks, or in the rigging of invisible ships.' Despite the odd intervals and discords of half-broken instruments, he is charmed. 'He recognized nothing that they played, and it sounded as though they were simply improvising without a conductor. No definitely marked time ran through the pieces, which ended and began oddly after the fashion of wind through an Aeolian harp.'[37] These were still powerful ideas in the late nineteenth and early twentieth century. To ignore them not only misses the drama of Hardy's scene, but loses the contrast between this eerie sounding of stones in the landscape and the disastrous calcifying silences of the past.

Disturbing a moment of silences and mutters, 'all lost in thought' in Chekhov's *The Cherry Orchard*, a distant sound is heard, 'as if from the sky: the sound of a breaking string — dying away, sad.' What was that? asks Ranyevskaya. 'I don't know', Lopakhin answers. 'Somewhere a long way off, in the mines, a winding cable has parted. But a long, long way off.' The others speculate; perhaps a heron or some kind of owl? Ranyevskaya shivers. 'Horrible', she says. 'I don't know why.'[38]

Shingo, the sixty-two-year-old man at the centre of Yasunari Kawabata's *The Sound of the Mountain*, listens to the rasping screech of locusts in his Kamakura garden, wonders if they are troubled with nightmares, thinks he can detect the dripping of dew from leaf to leaf, then hears the sound of the mountain, like wind, faraway, but with depth, like a rumbling of the earth. He questions his own perception: could it be the wind, the sea, or within himself, a ringing in his ears? No, it was the mountain: 'It was if a demon had passed, making the mountain sound out ... He did not wake his wife to tell her of the fear that had come over him on hearing the sound of the mountain.'[39] Later, Shingo is shocked to be reminded of a previous occasion when the mountain roared, shortly before the death of his sister-in-law.

Again, like the death-watch beetle, the calls of the little owl, or Lady Macbeth hearing the hoot of an owl that shrieked, 'the fatal bellman which gives the stern'st good night', these uncanny sounds are unsettling enough to portend impending death.[40]

In *A Passage To India*, E. M. Forster wrote about interiors, the way in which no Indian animal had any respect for an interior, as soon nesting inside a house as out. Later, during a visit to the Marabar Caves twenty miles from Chandrapore, two English women who wish to see 'the real India' are affected by the echo of the cave. One of them experiences the echo as 'terrifying', whereas Professor Godbole, a Hindu, hears only a monotonous 'boum': 'Hope, politeness, the blowing of a nose, the squeak of a boot, all produce "boum". Even the striking of a match starts a little worm coiling, which is too small to complete a circle, but is eternally watchful. And if several people talk at once an overlapping howling noise begins, echoes generate echoes, and the cave is stuffed with a snake composed of small snakes, which writhe independently.'[41] And yet, like the bat or wasp who builds a nest inside a house, the echo within the cave threatens to dissolve the fragile boundaries between the outwardly regulated, socialized, de-sexualized body and some deeper intuition of the self: '... the echo began in some indescribable way to undermine her hold on life.'[42] As the scandal of the story breaks, the possibility that a young Muslim doctor has in some way assaulted the younger of the two women, the echo is implicated as an accessory to the crime:

'There was an echo that appears to have frightened her. Did you go into those caves?'
'I saw one of them. There was an echo. Did it get on her nerves?'[43]

Whether writing critically of sexual repression, social conformity or the institutional racism of the British in India, Forster returned often to these mysterious sounds, their metaphorical power contrasting vividly with the fraught complacency of his subjects and their nerves. Sound performs upon the social and physiological body as a subversive element, a Janus-faced agent of invasive disruption and vital force. 'From the new campanile there burst a flood of sound to which the copper vessels vibrated responsively', he wrote in 'The Eternal Moment'. 'Miss Raby lifted her hands, not to her ears but to her eyes. In her enfeebled state, the throbbing note of the bell had the curious effect of blood returning into frozen veins.'[44] In *Chaos, Territory, Art*, Elizabeth Grosz builds upon a theme of Deleuze and Guattari: architecture and all arts that follow it are linked to birdsong and other territorial displays that define space in the natural world. Art is a practice of sensations, intensities and affects derived from chaos and framing chaos to become territory. The body shields itself from chaos, 'in habit, cliché and doxa', as a way of containing sensations to render them predictable. 'I hope to understand music as a becoming,' she writes, 'the becoming-other of cosmic chaotic forces that link the lived, sexually specific body to the forces of the earth.'[45]

Air in motion, resistant to containment and the architectural impulses of humans, epitomizes the human sense of what is unheimlich. As Charles Dickens suggested in *The Chimes*, ghost stories work their magic when the reader is settled by a fire within the security of home, a cold wind whistling in darkness outside as an audible reminder of unknown night. In the 1939 film of *The Wizard of Oz*, a deafening wind twists through the landscape, drowning out speech and destroying human dwellings. Dorothy and her dog Toto are hurled out of sepia Kansas into the Technicolor dream world of Oz. After a series of ordeals in which she defeats the forces of darkness (including strange flying monkeys whose flight is heard as an eerie Aeolian wail) she wakes up back in bed in Kansas. Her final words of the film are: 'There's no place like home.'

For author John Cowper Powys, the wind was an unknowable breath, playing upon trees as if they were instruments fixed into landscape for that purpose. In a passage of sustained power in *A Glastonbury Romance*, published in 1933, he described the sound as a 'portentous requiem', a choir whose orchestration is familiar enough to be connected to human music, yet vast and alien, the sound of mythic beings for whom Cowper Powys experienced the nostalgia of a passing world:

> And then Cordelia, gazing directly into the wide-flung branches of the biggest of the two giant trees, was aware of something else upon the wind. Those enormous branches seemed to have begun an orchestral monotone, composed of the notes of many instruments gathered up into one. It was a cumulative and rustling sigh that came to the woman's ears, as if a group of sorrowful Titans had lifted their united voices in one lamentable dirge over the downfall of their race.[46]

Notes

1   Charles Dickens, *The Chimes: A Goblin Story*, London: Chapman & Hall, 1845, pp. 2–3.

2   Charles Dickens, *The Haunted House*, London: Hesperus Press, 2002, p. 13.

3   Hans Anderson, 'The Sandman', in *Anderson's Fairy Tales*, Blackie & Son. London and Glasgow, p. 77.

4   Nicholas Royle, *The Uncanny*, Manchester: Manchester University Press, 2003, p. 136.

5   Sigmund Freud, *The Uncanny*, trans. David McLintock, London: Penguin Books, 2003, p. 141.

6   E. T. A. Hoffmann. *Tales of Hoffmann*, London: Penguin, 2004, pp. 85–125.

7   Hélène Cixous. 'Fiction and Its Phantoms: A Reading of Freud's *Das Unheimliche* (The "Uncanny")', *New Literary History*, vol. 7, no. 3 (Spring 1976), pp. 525–48, 619–45.

8   Bram Stoker, 'Dracula', in *The Annotated Dracula*, ed. Leonard Wolf, New London: English Library, 1975, p. 79.

9   Robert Louis Stevenson, *Treasure Island*, Oxford: Oxford University Press, 2008, p. 177.

10   John Tyndall, *Sound*, London and Bombay: Longmans, Green, and Co., 1898, p. 286.

11   Shirley Jackson, 'The Haunting of Hill House', in *The Masterpieces of Shirley Jackson*, London: Raven Books, 1996, p. 229.

12   Ibid., p. 253.

13   Ibid., p. 313.

14   Ibid., p. 315.

15   Ibid., p. 364.

16   Ibid., p. 373.

17   Ibid., p. 379.

18   Ibid., p. 395.

19   Po Chü-i, 'The Five-String', in *Chinese Poems*, trans. Arthur Waley, George Allen & Unwin. 1946, pp. 131–2.

20   R. H. van Gulik, *The Lore of the Chinese Lute*, Tokyo: Sophia University/ Tokyo: The Charles E. Tuttle Company, 1968. p. 158.

21   Georges Rodenbach, *Bruges-la-Morte*, trans. Mike Mitchell, Sawtry: Dedalus, 2007, pp. 27–8.

22   Ibid., p. 131.

23   Mario Caroli, notes to Salvatore Sciarrino, *Fauno che Fischia*, Italy: Attacca CD, 2007.

24   Sir Arthur Conan Doyle, 'The Japanned Box', in *Tales of Terror and Mystery*. London: Pan Books, 1978. p. 166.

25   Ibid., p. 170.

26   John M. Picker, *Victorian Soundscapes*, Oxford: Oxford University Press, 2003, p. 133.

27   Fernando Pessoa, *The Book of Disquiet*, trans. Richard Zenith, London: Penguin, 2002. p. 34.

28   Virginia Woolf, *Jacob's Room*, London: Penguin, 1992, p. 85.

29   Virginia Woolf, *Mrs. Dalloway*, London: Penguin, 1996, pp. 2–3.

30   Virginia Woolf. quoted in Hermione Lee, op. cit. p. 462.

31   Virginia Woolf, *Mrs. Dalloway*, op. cit., pp. 48–49.

32   Georges Rodenbach, op. cit., p. 61.

33 Georges Perec, *Life: A User's Manual*, trans. David Bellos, London: Vintage. 2003, p. 32.

34 Thomas De Quincey, *Suspiria de Profundis*, University of Michigan, University Library reprints, pp. 175–6.

35 Thomas Hardy, *Tess of the D'Urbervilles*, London: Macmillan. 1970, p. 440.

36 Samuel Taylor Coleridge, *The Major Works*, Oxford: Oxford University Press and New York, 1985, p. 27.

37 Algernon Blackwood, *Ancient Sorceries and Other Weird Stories*, London: Penguin, 1968, pp. 83–4.

38 Anton Chekhov, *The Cherry Orchard*, trans. Michael Frayn, London: Methuen Drama, 1990, p. 33.

39 Yasunari Kawabata, *The Sound of the Mountain*, trans. Edward M. Seidensticker, London: Penguin, 1974, pp. 10–12.

40 William Shakespeare, *Macbeth*, (II.2.3).

41 E. M. Forster, *A Passage To India*, London: Penguin, 2005, p. 137.

42 Ibid., p. 139.

43 Ibid., p. 157.

44 E. M Forster, 'The Eternal Moment', in *Collected Short Stories*, London: Penguin, p. 209.

45 Elizabeth Grosz, *Chaos, Territory, Art: Deleuze and the Framing of the Earth*, New York: Columbia University Press, 2008, p. 26.

46 John Cowper Powys, *A Glastonbury Romance*, London: Picador, 1975, p. 216.

PART FOUR

Spectral Subjectivities: Gender, Sexuality, Race

18

Spectral Subjectivities: Gender, Sexuality, Race / Introduction

María del Pilar Blanco and Esther Peeren

Spectrality is a differentiated phenomenon, not only in terms of the divergent cultural-historical traditions it can evoke (as explored in Part Two of this *Reader*), but also when it comes to the entities involved, which range from humans to animals to natural elements to man-made objects. On the one hand, this evokes the potential of thinking spectrality together with posthumanism.[1] On the other hand, it points to the need to consider the stratification present even *within* the dominant western tradition, where most ghosts are of the human kind. Taking up the latter cue, a number of critics have explored gender, sexuality, and race as non-limitative examples of how instantiations of ghosts and haunting are linked to the histories and social positions of specific subjects. As a multitude of ghost stories teaches, when a spectral presence is detected, the first, dual question asked tends to be: *who* haunts and *who* is being targeted? Even if a definitive identification often remains elusive, ghosts are not interchangeable and it matters greatly (in terms of the effects and affects produced) in what guise they appear and to whom.[2] Thus, subjectivity inflects both structural positions in the scenario of haunting: being haunted by one's father is not the same as being haunted by one's mother, one's child, or a stranger, and hauntings that cross instituted borders between forms of subjectivity will play out differently than those that stay within them.[3] This applies, this part suggests, not only to fictions of the supernatural, but also to situations where spectrality is used as a conceptual metaphor to effect revisions of history and/or reimaginations of the future in order to expose and address the way certain subjectivities have been marginalized and disavowed in order to establish and uphold a particular norm, as well as the way such subjectivities can never be completely erased but insist on reappearing to trouble the norm.

Significantly, categories of subjectification like gender, sexuality, and race can themselves be conceived as spectral. The boundaries between normative and non-normative subject positions, despite being heavily policed, are not necessarily immediately perceptible, producing a pervasive anxiety that things may not be as they seem, that there may be more to a subject than meets the eye. Furthermore, the normative position (of masculinity, heterosexuality, whiteness) is ghostly in that it remains un(re) marked, transparent in its self-evidentiality.[4] This imperceptibility of that which is manifestly there can be explained by the performative process of retroactive naturalization charted in Judith Butler's *Gender Trouble* and *Bodies That Matter*.[5] There, the subject's identity is disjointed as it becomes both *revenant* and *arrivant*: it returns from the past (citing a history without being anchored in a singular origin or essence), while at the same time constituting its own futurity, arriving, as it were, from and through iterative acts yet to occur. Butler's theory of performativity (which pertains to gender, race, and sexuality) also invokes a sense of spectrality in the way the constant reiterations of the norm required for its maintenance are never perfect reproductions; a slippage occurs with respect to the ideal-image, resulting in a doubling or self-haunting by which the subject is constantly chasing—yet never catches—a posited "proper" self. As confidence in the ability of identity to congeal around an essence has eroded, therefore, the subject itself has become *plus d'un*. This does not mean, however, that every subject (or group of subjects) is spectralized to the same degree or in the exact same manner; the social position occupied, particularly in terms of distance to the normative ideal, installs significant differences.

The aim of this part of *The Spectralities Reader* is twofold: it focuses on the way ghosts and haunting, even when used as conceptual metaphors, cannot be abstracted from specific formations of subjectivity, while also exposing the haunting that inhabits the process of subjectification itself, from the individual to the national level. The part opens with excerpts from Gayatri Chakravorty Spivak's "Ghostwriting," her 1995 response to *Specters of Marx*. Besides arguing that it is only because of errors in Derrida's reading of Marx that the latter can be presented as an ontological thinker inadequately sensitive to the ghostly, Spivak takes Derrida to task for writing a "how-to-mourn-your-father book" that configures haunting as a masculine economy and, in describing the new world order, overlooks how global capitalism particularly exploits the labor and reproductive power of subaltern women.[6] To establish a more just present and future, it is necessary, Spivak suggests, to be attentive to the dispossessions suffered by particular groups, which should not be compiled into an undifferentiated spectral mass, as Derrida does when referring to "the ghosts of those who are not yet born or who are already dead, be they victims of wars, political or other kinds of violence, nationalist, racist, colonialist, sexist, or other kinds of exterminations, victims of the oppressions of capitalist imperialism or any of the forms of totalitarianism."[7]

Instead of a universalizing *danse macabre*, indiscriminately joining all the dead and all the living, Spivak proposes the "ghost dance" (derived from James Mooney's 1896 description of this practice among the Sioux) as a strategic tool for a particular group "to establish the ethical relation with history as such, ancestors real and imagined."[8] This ghost dance, which should unfold in the provisional temporality of the future anterior, as possibility rather than determination, does not take up the past *as it was*, but conjures *other* pasts in order to imagine a different, better future. Shown at work in Algerian author Assia Djebar's novel *Far From Medina*, where it reinserts women into the history of Islam, the ghost dance emerges as a spectral instrument with the potential to redress the silencing exclusion that characterizes particular hegemonic histories and traditions.

Spivak's ghost dance—as an experimental, conjuring relationship to the past in service of the future—reappears in the second text of this part, Carla Freccero's "Queer Spectrality: Haunting the Past." Freccero is concerned not with recovering specific queer subjects in or from the past but with mobilizing the combination of queer thinking (with its emphasis on multiplying sites of affectivity and pleasure) and spectrality (as an anti-teleological and non-binary mode) to challenge "the implicit heteronormativity of historical continuity, the way historical succession is tied ... to heterosexual reproduction."[9] The queer spectrality she proposes is designed to enable a more ethical historiography that eschews burial (associated with melancholia) or mastery (colonization) of the past in favor of the permission to mourn (to be revisited by a demand) signified by the ghost. Serving as Freccero's case study is Jean de Léry, a sixteenth-century French minister who traveled to the Bay of Rio, was exiled and lived among the Tupinamba Indians, and returned to France to survive the 1572 massacre of St Barthélemy and write a retrospective account of his time in Brazil. Freccero shows how Léry's colonial experiences—which introduced a certain queerness into his subject position as, among the Tupinamba, he was often grouped with the women and assumed a receptive rather than invasive position—return to haunt him in France, remaining before his eyes to refract his perspective on the religious and political events of his homeland. The notion of haunting thus comes to mark a reciprocal relationship between past and present, here and there: "a textualization of France through Brazil as much as of Brazil through France."[10] Such reciprocity, Freccero suggests, results from a *being haunted* that implies a certain passivity or dynamic suspension, an openness to a demand coming from elsewhere that reconfigures agency as a willingness to *attend* (in the double sense of waiting for and caring for).

While Freccero explores queer spectrality as a methodology or attitude opening up new, more ethical pathways to and from the past (as well as between the Old and the New World), the spectralization of queerness—the propensity for gay and lesbian subjects to be culturally configured as ghosts—has also received considerable critical attention. As mentioned in our general introduction, a seminal text in this respect is Terry Castle's *The Apparitional Lesbian*, which sees ghostly metaphors facilitating a centuries-long disavowal of lesbian subjectivities. Portrayed in literature from the eighteenth century on "as an absence, as chimera or *amor impossibilia*—a kind of love that, by definition, cannot exist," lesbianism, and in particular its erotic physicality, is de-realized.[11] This vaporizing effect, however, is diluted by the way the ghost simultaneously insists on appearing with such vividness that "one feels unable to get away from it."[12] Besides making lesbian bodies disappear, then, the spectral metaphor "can also solidify," as Castle sees happening in twentieth-century lesbian fiction.[13] Thus, in its very ambivalence, the ghost exemplifies Freud's adage that what is repressed (in this case by patriarchal, heteronormative society) always returns to the surface.[14]

Castle's work remains an absent presence here, but a related discussion of the ghostliness of repressed subjectivities—including queer ones—appears in Sharon Patricia Holland's *Raising the Dead: Readings of Death and (Black) Subjectivity* (2000), of which this part contains the introduction. Conceiving Toni Morrison's ghost story *Beloved* as recuperating a black culture "as invisible to the dominant culture as were most of the nation's black subjects," Holland ventures into what anthropologist Michael Taussig calls "the space of death"—the imaginary space holding those subjects whose disavowal (and desubjectification) is necessary to shore up the integrity of the American nation – in order to raise these subjects and allow them "to tell the story of a death-in-life."[15] Besides showing how the resurrected dead may be mobilized, from the margin, to destabilize dichotomous thinking in relation to the hegemonic categories of whiteness and the nation, Holland also addresses how queer black subjects are disavowed within the black community, producing a compounded spectralization or double death. In this way, attention is drawn to the degrees of ghostliness associated with different subject categories within a particular society, and to the influence this may have on their ability to assert themselves as viable subjects and lay claim to the agency associated with the ghost's power to haunt.[16]

The final text in this part, Renée L. Bergland's "Indian Ghosts and American Subjects," taken from *The National Uncanny* (2000), outlines the consequences of spectrality's fundamental ambiguity in pointing simultaneously to a dispossessing disappearance or erasure and the powerful ability to rematerialize as a disturbing force. Drawing attention to the prevalence of Indian ghosts, first in the imagination of European Americans and later in that of Native Americans themselves, Bergland argues that this rhetorical reclaiming, rather than challenging Indian removal, rendered it—prematurely—a *fait accompli*: "When Native people called on their forebears as vengeful ghosts, they acknowledged that the battles had already been lost, that the voices that inspired them were among the dead."[17] At the same time, the American persistence in recalling Indian ghosts marks an unsuccessful repression that reveals a particular dependency of the national consciousness on the continued presence (albeit only internalized, phantasmatic) of Native Americans. On the basis of Benedict Anderson's "ghostly national imaginings" and Etienne Balibar's notion that subjectivity is predicated on the denial of the process of subjection, Bergland argues that, as a national subject, "you cannot be fully conscious unless you are haunted."[18] Ghosts, here, do not pose a challenge to the status quo but are what holds it together, complicating theorizations of spectrality as invariably disjointing.[19]

Taken together, the texts in this part argue for the differentiation of spectrality, seeking acknowledgement that, even within the same tradition, not all invocations of ghosts or haunting have the same meanings or effects. With regard to this, gender, sexuality, and race are only some of the possible stratifying factors that should be taken into consideration. Moreover, while every subjectivity, individual or collective, is characterized by repressions, erasures, and disavowals that can never be completely successful and always harbor the possibility (and sometimes, as in the case of the Indian ghost in the American imagination, the necessity) of return, the precise nature of *who* or *what* needs to be "ghosted" to found and maintain a particular subjectivity remains important. Mobilizing spectrality to address dispossessing histories and imagine more inclusive futures at the concrete level of, for example, the subaltern woman of a particular time and place rather than that of generalized victims of history or the new world order can only be effective if the figures of ghosts and haunting are subjected to a sustained effort of demarcation and specification.

Notes

1   See, for example, Joshua Gunn, "Review Essay: Mourning Humanism, or, the Idiom of Haunting," *Quarterly Journal of Speech* 92, no. 1 (2006): 77–102; Ted Hiebert, "Becoming Carnival: Performing a Postmodern Identity," *Performance Research* 8, no. 3 (2003): 113–29; Christopher Peterson, "The Posthumanism To Come," *Angelaki: Journal of the Theoretical Humanities* 16, no. 2 (2011): 127–41; Cary Wolfe, *What is Posthumanism?* (Minneapolis: University of Minnesota Press, 2010).

2   Peter Fenves, reading together Derrida, Marx, Leibniz, and Benjamin, distinguishes angels as figures of singularity from ghosts as "distinguished, if they can be distinguished at all, *solo numero*." Fenves, "Marx, Mourning, Messianicity," in *Violence, Identity, and Self-Determination*, ed. Hent de Vries (Stanford: Stanford University Press, 1997), 258. While this notion usefully conveys capitalism's spectralizing eradication of particularity—"In our world, or at this time, it is possible, and indeed even necessary, to distinguish things *solo numero*: money, for instance, or commodities of equal value, including labor as a commodity and workers in their capacity as merchants of their own labor power" (258)—it contradicts the popular conception of the ghost as a lingering trace of a particular personal history.

3   While Derrida's reading of *Hamlet* can be criticized for ignoring the specific historical and religious context of the play's apparition—detailed by Stephen Greenblatt in *Hamlet in Purgatory* (Princeton: Princeton University Press, 2001)—it does take seriously its appearance as a paternal, sovereign figure. Peggy Kamuf stresses that, for Derrida, "the ghost is both specified, it is a some*one*, and at the same time of uncertain location or provenance." Kamuf, "Violence, Identity, Self-Determination, and the Question of Justice: On *Specters of Marx*," in *Violence, Identity, and Self-Determination*, ed. Hent de Vries (Stanford: Stanford University Press, 1997), 276.

4   Richard Dyer's *White* (London and New York: Routledge, 2010), for example, exposes "the invisibility of whiteness as a racial position" in western society (3). Notably, this invisibility is traced to the Christian notion of "spirit" as the "idea—paradoxical, unfathomable, profoundly mysterious—of incarnation, of being that is in the body yet not of it" (14).

5   Judith Butler, *Gender Trouble: Feminism and the Subversion of Identity* (1990; New York and London: Routledge, 1999); Judith Butler, *Bodies That Matter: On the Discursive Limits of "Sex"* (New York and London: Routledge, 1993).

6   Gayatri Chakravorty Spivak, "Ghostwriting," *Diacritics* 25, no. 2 (1995): 66. Nancy J. Holland also presents a critique of Derrida's focus on haunting as a patriarchal structure by delineating how daughters inherit differently from sons and lack the option of exorcism in relation to the father and the father's ghost, which is the internalized vision of "the eternal, idealized Woman." "The Death of the Other/Father: A Feminist Reading of Derrida's Hauntology," *Hypatia* 16, no. 1 (2001): 67. She is, however, more charitable to Derrida than Spivak, seeing his elision of daughters and mothers as a necessary consequence of the inescapable patriarchal tradition: "at the very moment when Derrida attempts to say something, however partial and attenuated, about *the* ghost, he must at the same time recreate a tradition in which the Father/Ghost, and all that they represent, speak only to the Son" (69). Derrida's own defense consists of arguing that, in invoking this tradition, he is not recreating but critiquing it: "Expressly identifying itself as a book on inheritance, *Specters of Marx* also analyzes, questions and—let us say, to save time—'deconstructs' the law of filiation, particularly patrimonial filiation, the law of the father-son lineage." "Marx & Sons," in *Ghostly Demarcations: A Symposium on Jacques Derrida's Specters of Marx*, ed.

Michael Sprinker (London and New York: Verso, 1999), 231 (see also 232–3 and 258). For other attempts to gender the ghost and ghost-seeing beyond the Derridean framework, see Karin Beeler, *Seers, Witches and Psychics on Screen: An Analysis of Women Visionary Characters in Recent Television and Film* (Jefferson: McFarland, 2008); Mary Beth Mills, "Attack of the Widow Ghosts: Gender, Death, and Modernity in Northeast Thailand," in *Bewitching Women, Pious Men: Gender and Body Politics in Southeast Asia*, ed. Aihwa Ong and Michael G. Peletz (Berkeley and Los Angeles: University of California Press, 1995), 244–73; Esther Peeren, "The Ghost as a Gendered Chronotope," in *Ghosts, Stories, Histories: Ghost Stories and Alternative Histories*, ed. Sladja Blazan (Newcastle: Cambridge Scholars Publishing, 2007), 81–96.

7　Jacques Derrida, *Specters of Marx: The State of the Debt, the Work of Mourning, & the New International*, trans. Peggy Kamuf (1993; London and New York: Routledge, 1994), xix.

8　Spivak, "Ghostwriting," 70.

9　Carla Freccero, "Queer Spectrality: Haunting the Past," in *A Companion to Lesbian, Gay, Bisexual, Transgender and Queer Studies*, ed. George Haggerty and Molly McGarry (Oxford: Blackwell, 2007), 195.

10　Ibid., 206.

11　Terry Castle, *The Apparitional Lesbian: Female Homosexuality and Modern Culture* (New York: Columbia University Press, 1993), 30–1.

12　Ibid., 46.

13　Ibid., 47.

14　John Fletcher supplements Castle's theory with a rigorous historicization of the apparitionality of male homosexuality. Specifically, he elaborates on how the particular form of "homospectrality" that characterized the period after the Oscar Wilde trial pervades the ghost stories of Henry James. Fletcher, "The Haunted Closet: Henry James's Queer Spectrality," *Textual Practice* 14.1 (2000): 56. For other work focusing on the intersection of queer studies and spectrality, see Bobby Benedicto, "The Haunting of Gay Manila: Global Space-Time and the Specter of *Kabaklaan*," *GLQ* 14, no. 2 (2008): 317–38; Samuel A. Chambers, "Telepistemology of the Closet; or, The Queer Politics of *Six Feet Under*," *Journal of American Culture* 26, no. 1 (2003): 24–41; Diana Fuss, "Inside/Out," in *Inside/Out: Lesbian Theories, Gay Theories* (New York and London: Routledge, 1991), 1–10; Mair Rigby, "Uncanny Recognition: Queer Theory's Debt to the Gothic," *Gothic Studies* 11, no. 1 (2009): 46–57; Jeffrey Andrew Weinstock, "Queer Haunting Spaces: Madeline Yale Wynne's 'The Little Room' and Elia Wilkinson Peattie's 'The House That Was Not,'" *American Literature* 79, no. 3 (2007): 501–25.

15　Sharon Patricia Holland, "Introduction: Raising the Dead," in *Raising the Dead: Readings of Death and (Black) Subjectivity* (Durham: Duke University Press, 2000), 3, 4.

16　For other explorations of the intersection of spectrality, race, and ethnicity, see Kathleen Brogan, *Cultural Haunting: Ghosts and Ethnicity in Recent*

American Literature (Charlottesville: The University Press of Virginia, 1998); Kevin Cryderman, "Fire for a Ghost: Blind Spots and the Dissection of Race in John Edgar Wideman's *The Cattle Killing*," *Callaloo* 34, no. 4 (2011): 1047–67; Benjamin D'Harlingue, "Specters of the U.S. Prison Regime: Haunting Tourism and the Penal Gaze," in *Popular Ghosts: The Haunted Spaces of Everyday Culture*, ed. María del Pilar Blanco and Esther Peeren (New York and London: Continuum, 2010), 133–46; Atsuko Matsuoka and John Sorenson, *Ghosts and Shadows: Construction of Identity and Community in an African Diaspora* (Toronto: University of Toronto Press, 2001); David Tyrer and Salman Sayyid, "Governing Ghosts: Race, Incorporeality and Difference in Post-Political Times," *Current Sociology* 60, no. 3 (2012): 353–67.

17 Renée L. Bergland, "Indian Ghosts and American Subjects," in *The National Uncanny: Indian Ghosts and American Subjects* (Hanover: University Press of New England, 2000), 3–4.

18 Ibid., 6, 10.

19 For other explorations of indigenous spectrality, see Emilie Cameron, "Indigenous Spectrality and the Politics of Postcolonial Ghost Stories," *Cultural Geographies* 15, no. 3 (2008): 383–93; Ken Gelder and Jane M. Jacobs, "The Postcolonial Ghost Story," in *Ghosts: Deconstruction, Psychoanalysis, History*, ed. Peter Buse and Andrew Stott (Basingstoke: Macmillan, 1999), 179–99; Gerry Turcotte, "Spectrality in Indigenous Women's Cinema: Tracey Moffatt and Beck Cole," *The Journal of Commonwealth Literature* 43, no. 1 (2008): 7–21.

19

from Ghostwriting[1]

Gayatri Chakravorty Spivak

ভিনদেশী এক পাগল মরে না ম'লে

—*first line of song allegedly written by a member of the*
Communist Party of India for the centenary of Karl Marx's death

I first published a piece on Derrida for *Diacritics*—"*Glas*-Piece"—eighteen
years ago. It took me a year to write. It is a pleasure to write one again,
in such august company. I am writing it at speed, and not only because
life has become harder in the intervening years. My relationship to
"deconstruction," whatever that may be, has become more intimate, more
everyday, more of a giving—away, and in—habit of mind, a kind of tic that
comes in to warn in the thick of what is called activism, formulas that guide
in the midst of those who have little or nothing. It has become a bit of a
pouvoir-savoir for me, thus defeating its own purpose, as it should.

So, I thought, why not mime this happy state of affairs—"*Glas*-Piece"
was all about miming—and write at ease? For "serious" reviews, consult
Ahmad or Jameson—or Laclau, in this issue.[2]

1

I have always had trouble with Derrida on Marx. A friend said maybe that's
because I feel proprietorial about Marx. Who knows? Maybe. At any rate,
I have laid out my trouble in print [see "Limits and Openings of Marx in
Derrida," *Outside* 97–119]. My main problem has been Derrida's seeming
refusal to honor the difference between commercial and industrial capital.
Derrida writes of speculative interest as excess and surplus value: money

begets money. Therefore, in *Given Time* [158–61; the quoted bits are on 158n, 160–61] and in *Specters of Marx* [138–39; hereafter cited as *SM*] he can chart a certain continuity from Marx back to Aristotle and Plato ("[a] nd of course Marx ...," "[t]he genetic vocabulary ... could lead us back from Aristotle to Plato"). Marx, on the other hand, seems to have thought that to explain industrial capitalism through the money circuit is the absurd and interested caprice of the bourgeois [Marx, *Capital* 2: 109–43].[3] Is it just my proprietorial reaction to think that you can't catch at any specter of Marx if you don't attend to the ghost's signature? Who knows? Maybe.

And yet, it was good that Derrida wrote *Specters*. Deconstruction has been so long associated with political irresponsibility by those who practice criticism by hearsay that it was significant for its inventor to have given his imprimatur to rereading Marx. The liberal French press was in general unstinting in its praise of this gesture.[4] And, although Fukuyama has been noticed interestingly elsewhere on the Left, the pages exploding his position remain important [see Ahmad, "Reconciling" 90].[5] There are enough people around who share Fukuyama's broad point of view for Derrida's critique to be useful, although one is not sure that such people will read *Specters*.[6] The book is powerful as superior propaganda. There are many passages like the one where Derrida excoriates the "Polish bishop who boasts ... [of] a Christian Europe," and links him to "the Holy Alliance of the nineteenth century,' which Marx excoriated [*SM* 100].

It is also a how-to-mourn-your-father book. (We must remember that "mourn" is a rich word in psychoanalysis and deconstruction, and there is something like a relationship between the two uses.) *Glas* had seemed the same sort of book to me, and, of late, *Of Spirit*.[7] The reading of *Hamlet*—the visor-effect of history as the face of the ghostly father (an entire Derrida-Lévinasian cluster there), the irreducible "out-of-joint"-ness of time, the rehearsal of justice as relation to the other, and, above all, the peculiar predications of ghostliness—is perhaps the best part of the book. In *Glas*, thanks to Genet, the absent place of the Mother was at least invoked, and the question of woman played a part in the lefthand column of the book as well, in the discussion of Hegel, Kant, Freud. But it is already noticeable that in the few references to Marx in that book, woman is nowhere. (There may be no reference to woman in *Of Spirit*, which is largely "about" Heidegger's Nazism, but Derrida has questioned Heidegger's ignoring of sexual difference elsewhere [see Derrida, *Spurs* 81 ff., 109; "Geschlecht"]. And she is nowhere in *Specters of Marx*. If Derrida plays Hamlet to Marx's Ghost, there are no takers for Gertrude or Ophelia.

Indeed, the ghost of Marx that Derrida is most haunted by returns to the bosom of Abraham, shorn of all specificity, mark of a messianism without content, carrier of merely the structure of a promise which cancels the difference between democracy and Marxism [*SM* 65, 75]. (The last sections of the book show how Marx's vision of a communist future is messianic.

Derrida gets to this by way of a suggestion that the religious, seemingly the target of the argument from ideology, is indispensable to it.) And it is not possible to think woman as agent of sacrifice.

> *Would the logic of sacrificial responsibility within the implacable univer-*
> *sality of the law, of its law, be altered, inflected, attenuated, or displaced,*
> *if a woman were to intervene in some consequential manner? Is the*
> *system of this sacrificial responsibility at its deepest [*au plus profond de
> lui*] an exclusion or sacrifice of woman? Of the woman, by this or that*
> *genitive [*De la femme, selon tel ou tel génitif*]? Let us leave the question*
> *in suspense.* [Derrida, *Gift of Death* 76].

The double genitive followed by suspension is an important move, but it cannot happen in *Specters*. This too troubles me. For the peculiar corporeality of the ghost, about which Derrida writes well indeed, is not just *any* corpus. And in the current global conjuncture, woman is the dubiously felicitous out-of-joint subject of the strictly Marxian version, in a number of ways.

I would cite the following sentence from *The Communist Manifesto*: "The less the skill and exertion of strength implied in manual labour, in other words, the more modern industry becomes developed, the more is the labour of men superseded by that of women" [62]. Although this passage immediately follows a description of the *pre*-Fordist factory, I would point out that Marx's prescience is fulfilled in postfordism and the explosion of global homeworking. The subaltern woman is now to a rather large extent the support of production.[8]

To go beyond this descriptive gesture, I would offer a reading of Marx's reading of the commodity-form as the locus of the homeopathy that would monitor the *différance* of capitalism and socialism [see Spivak, "Supplementing Marxism" 111, 118n7]. That imperialism introduces mobility toward socialization has proved itself, I would suggest, in the cases of both international communism and international capitalism. And, in the new new international economic order after the dissolution of the Soviet Union, it is the labor of the patriarchally defined subaltern woman that has been most effectively socialized.

I would expand this, by way of a Marxist theorization of reproductive engineering and population control, as the socialization of reproductive labor-power, not "the feminization of labor." (The nonexhaustive taxonomy that such a theorization has allowed me, tentatively, to formalize in the classroom I offer here in shorthand, in the hope that Marxist-feminists active in global economic resistance will be able to reproduce the analysis. But will they be interested in *Specters of Marx*? At any rate, here is the shorthand taxonomy of the coded discursive management of the new socialization of the reproductive body: (1) reproductive rights (*metonymic* substitution of the abstract average subject of rights for woman's identity); (2) surrogacy (*metaphoric* substitution of the abstract average reproductive labor power as fulfilled female subject of motherhood); (3) transplant (displacement of eroticism and generalized presupposed subject of immediate affect); (4) population control (objectification of the female subject of exploitation to produce alibis for hypersize through demographic rationalization); (5) post-Fordist homeworking (classical coding of the spectrality of reason as empiricist individualism, complicated by gender ideology). It is only after a discussion of a possible taxonomy of the recoding of this socialization that I would describe the theatre of global resistance where these issues are now paramount.)[9]

According, then, to the strictest Marxian sense, the reproductive body of woman has now been "socialized"—computed into average abstract labor and thus released into what I call the spectrality of reason—a specter that haunts the merely empirical, dislocating it from itself. According to Marx, this is the specter that must haunt the daily life of the class-conscious worker, the future socialist, so that s/he can dislocate him/herself into the counterintuitive average part-subject (agent) of labor, recognize that, in the everyday, *es spukt*. It is only then that the fetish character of labor-power as commodity can be grasped and can become the pivot that wrenches capitalism into socialism [discussed at greater length in Spivak, *Outside* 107 ff.]. (It wasn't Freud alone—as *Glas* insists—who speculated with the fetish.)

Marx did indeed ignore something: that the differantial play between capital-ism and social-ism was a case of a more originary agon: between self and other; a differantiation perhaps necessary for the business of living, a differantiation that may be described as the *fort-da* of the gift of time in the temporizing of lives.[10] (For me, the genius of Derrida is that he leads me to think this as no one else can, even if he perhaps goofs a bit by putting Marx down as a closet idealist about "empirical" actuality, although canny about the idealism of idealism [*SM* 225].) That originary agon comes clearest in the coding—the figuration—of birth and childrearing. (Once I finish this piece, I must get on with a commentary on Melanie Klein's teasing out of this coding ["Melanie Klein".) Reproductive labor is being socialized and "freed." (*The Columbia Spectator* apparently ran an ad offering high prices for the unfertilized ova of students. Chickens have supplied this commodity without consent or remuneration for some time now. In Marxian terms, domesticated poultry is *instrumentum demi-vocale*, domesticated human females caught in feudal patterns of loyalty (elaborately coded by psychoanalysis as deep-structural) are *instrumenta vocale*, and the students are "free labor.")[11] As reproductive labor is socialized and "freed," it will be unable to ignore that agon, for the commodity in question is children. If this labor were to use the fetish-character of itself as (reproductive) labor-power (as commodity) pharmakonically to bring about gender-neutral socialism in its traffic, equitable by need and capacity, from a common fund, would that be just? The issue is not simply to weigh in the balance the painless donation of sperm for spermbanks as opposed to the possibly painful donation of eggs for the hatcheries, as television discussions invariably emphasize.[12]

Since *Specters of Marx* cannot bring in women, I will not pursue this further here.

If the reading of *Hamlet* is the best part of the book, the section around the New International is the most unimpeachable in the liberality of its sentiments. No fault can be found with the black-on-black list of ten to show what's out-of-joint with the world and "our" present present. But Derrida can't see the systemic connections between the ten plagues of the New World Order [*SM* 81] because he cannot know the connection between industrial capitalism, colonialism, so-called postindustrial capitalism, neocolonialism, electronified capitalism, and the current financialization of the globe, with the attendant phenomena of migrancy and ecological disaster. (For him hi-tech is all good, and only the media, albeit broadly defined, is "technologically invasive" [*SM* 39].) He offers us rather the best of the West—the auto-critical Enlightenment ("the Bloomsbury fraction," Raymond Williams might murmur), messianic affirmation; and ends the list with a parody of the end of "The Ends of Man" [Derrida, "The Ends of Man" 135–36]. Do what we must in the short run, question the concepts for the long run. We cannot and must not choose [*SM* 86 ff.]. Can one question concepts and protocols one has not entered and embraced deconstructively? One seems finally obliged to explain: *This particular experiment might have failed, but what a change Marx imagined, what a great guy!*

> [I]*n the whole history of the world and of the earth, in all that to which one can give the name of history in general, such an event (let us repeat, the event of a discourse in the philosophico-scientific form claiming to break with myth, religion, and the nationalist "mystique") has been bound, for the first time and inseparably, to worldwide forms of social organization (a party with a universal vocation, a labor movement, a confederation of states, and so forth.) All of this while proposing a new concept of the human, of society, economy, nation, several concepts of the State and its disappearance.* [*SM* 91]

I don't want to be tactless, but this bit of praise reminded me of the morning when, during the manic wooing of Gorbachev (I hate agreeing with Aijaz Ahmad—"But look at what happened to *perestroika!*" [Ahmad, "Reconciling Derrida" 101n11]), I saw on the *Today* show, while I was doing my exercises, a eulogistic life story of Marx—was it his birthday?— including his head in Highgate Cemetery. How is the mighty fallen, thought I. It is possible in the US now to patronize old Karl on national television.

To continue with the program (which is not a program, of course): We won't repoliticize [*SM* 87], we will be "an alliance without an institution" [*SM* 86], and we will "produce events, new effective forms of action, practice, organization, and so forth" [*SM* 89]. In a world where nonalignment is no longer possible as a collective position, what good is such anonymous internationality? and how will it come to pass? Never mind. We don't like totalitarianism, and we are unsympathetic with the labor movement.

The New International, if I understand it right, asks the international law and international human rights folks to be aware of the economic.[13] On pages 93–94 Derrida assures us that "these problems of the foreign Debt—and everything that is metonymized by this concept—will not be treated without at least the spirit of the Marxist critique, the critique of the market, of the multiple logics of capital, and of that which links the State and international law to this market." This fine suggestion would gain in strength if it took into account the vicissitudes suffered by the sustained organizational opposition to legalized economic exploitation (the collusion of international law and international capital, legiferant capital— the Group of Seven today—law "carrying the subjectivity of capital," in other words), in the interest if not always in the declared name of human rights, ever since Bretton Woods (the annulment of the gold standard would have worked in nicely with *Timon of Athens*), through Bandung and all the global summits, and the machinations of the GATT, and now the WTO. How, in other words, is the New International so new? Perhaps it is, to the European left liberal; but why should the South feel any degree of confidence in the project? A researched account would need at least to refer generally to the longstanding global struggles from below (one of the problems with Human Rights and International Law lobbies is that they are so irreproachably well-bred), which undo the opposition between economic resistance, cultural identity, and women's minded bodies, to which part of my taxonomy refers.[14] "The debt to Marx, I think, needs to be *paid* and *settled*, whereas the Third World debt ought to be simply *cancelled*," writes Ahmad ["Reconciling Derrida" 106]. If one attends to the struggles I am speaking of, where the specter of Marxism has been at work, molelike, although not always identified with Left parties in the impotent state, one would perhaps think of the debt to Marx as an unrepayable one with which we must speculate, to make and ask for Reparation (in the Kleinian sense) in the field of political economy [Klein 306–43].[15] How much making and how much asking will depend on who "we" are. As for the "debt" increasingly incurred by the South (no longer the *third* world surely, Ahmad's paper was first given in Lublijana!), given the dynamics of capital and its relationship to socialism, it can never remain cancelled. What "should" happen (*o tempora, o mores*) is a recognition that the South supports the North in the preservation of its resource-rich lifestyle. This at least is the sustained message of those struggles, a reworking of Marx's theme in *Capital*, that the worker is not a victim (no black on black there) but the agent of the wealth in societies. Marx regularly used the phrase "agent of production" rather than "worker." Was this simply politically correct language? And, what, without infrastructural effort, would this recognition bring, to whom?

Let us get to the ghost dance, Hamlet on the ramparts of the state of Denmark, or Derrida on the other headland of the New Europe.[16] In one way or another, the ghost has been with Derrida for a long time. It is a complicated companion and I, as is my wont, will simplify it, summarize it, efface it as I disclose. I should mention that although I learned, as usual, from Derrida's mediations on the subject in *Specters*, my inspiration, in this case, came also from elsewhere.

In my understanding, the ghost dance is an attempt to establish the ethical relation with history as such, ancestors real or imagined. The ethical is not a problem of knowledge but a problem of relation. It is singular yet generalizable, or already generalized in its singularity. You crave to let history haunt you as a ghost or ghosts, with the ungraspable incorporation of a ghostly body, and the uncontrollable, sporadic, and unanticipatable periodicity of haunting, in the impossible frame of the absolute chance of the gift of time, if there is any. It is not, then, a past that was necessarily once present that is sought. The main effort is to compute with the software of other pasts rather than reference one's own hallucinatory heritage for the sake of the politics of identitarian competition.

My clue to this came from reading James Mooney's compendious volume, first published in 1896, on the Ghost-Dance Religion and the Sioux Outbreak of 1890.[17] Those in the know will notice the strong influence of the Subaltern Studies group of historians in this. Marx and Shakespeare are magisterial texts, however the former might be beleaguered in the New World Order. It is the subalternists who taught me to follow the ghost in documentary texts from the other side.

The Sioux effort, to be haunted by the ancestors rather than treat them as objects of ritual worship, to get behind the ritual to make a common multinational figured past return through the ghostly agency of haunting so that a future can dictate action as if already there as a "before" ("the past as absolute future" [*SM* 35]), did not of course succeed. "[N]o one can be sure if by returning [the ghost] testifies to a living past or a living future" [*SM* 99]. I would venture to say that a ghost dance cannot succeed. It must be supplemented by inspired scholarship and a feeling for the limits of "identity." The relationship is somewhat like that between justice and the law, between ethics and politics.

Thus the "end" of the ghost dance—if one can speak of such a thing—is to make the past a future, as it were—the future anterior, not a future present, as is the case with the "end" of most narratives of social justice.

Now we can see that this is an alternative way of reading Marx—relating him to an ancestrality that can appear as a future. The ghost dance can never "work" as the guarantee of a future present. Yet it is the only way to go at moments of crisis; to surrender to undecidability (since the "agent" is the ancestral ghost, without guarantee) as the condition of possibility of responsible decision, to transform religion into militancy. (Is it at all possible to be so crude as to say that *Specters*, on the other hand, is a transformation of militancy into religion?) And, because it coordinates the future in the past, the ghost is not only a *revenant* (a returner, the French for "ghost"), but also an *arrivant*, one who arrives.

In *Aporias*, a text of the same period as *Specters*, Derrida writes, "The absolute *arrivant* does not yet have a name or an identity. It is not an invader or an occupier, nor is it a colonizer, though it can become one. This is why I call it simply the *arrivant*, and not someone or something that arrives, a subject, a person, an individual, a living thing, even less one of the migrants I just mentioned" [*Aporias* 34]. Yet since, in deconstruction, narrow and general senses have always bled into each other, concepts embraced metaphors and vice versa, Derrida has no difficulty comparing Marx at the end of his book to "a clandestine immigrant [whom o]ne should not rush to make ... an illegal alien or ... neutralize him through naturalization" [*SM* 267–77].

I am writing these words in Berkeley, California, and the students are agitating outside against Proposition 187, which in their view (and mine) legalizes injustice against so-called undocumented immigrants. (Another student group is publicizing Jesus's love; messianism and migrant activism—the specters of Marx? as, a generation ago, war protesters and Jesus freaks?) No liberal or radical person in North America, the EEC, Australia et cetera could therefore be against the metaphorization of Marx as a clandestine immigrant [see Walker]. Yet this privileging of the metaphorics (and axiomatics) of migrancy by well-placed migrants helps to occlude precisely the struggles of those who are forcibly displaced, or those who slowly perish in their place as a result of sustained exploitation: globality. Now we can see why the middle section of the book, speaking of international matters, is the least interesting. For Derrida's itinerary is elsewhere: the anterior is the messianic and the future is migration. The criticism of "ontopology" ("an axiomatics linking indissociably ontological value to being-present [*on*] to one's *situation*, to the stable and presentable determination of a locality, the *topos* of territory, native soil, city, body in general" [*SM* 137]—a word that will undoubtedly be picked up by postcolonial criticism—can only see the unexamined religious nationalism of the migrant or the national. It can certainly be used to understand the often meretricious resentment of elite national intellectuals against the diasporic. But it is to me more important to point out that to see absolute migrancy as the mark of an impossible deconstruction, and to see all activity attaching to the South as ontopologocentric, denies access to the news of subaltern struggles against the financialization of the globe. The subaltern are neither "nationally rooted" nor migrant; their intra-national displacement is managed by the exigencies of international capital [*SM* 83]. Their struggles reflect a continuity of insurgency which can only too easily be appropriated by the discourse of a come-lately *New* internationality in the most extravagantly publicized theoretical arenas of the world. Subalternity remains silenced there.[18]

I take my clue, however, from Klein on Freud. Whatever Derrida's "permissible narrative," it is good to pray to be haunted [Klein 317].[19]

[...]

I do not applaud Derrida because he has said hello to Marx but because, once again, there is a lesson in reading here. *Specters of Marx* lets me read *Far from Medina* as a ghost dance, a prayer to be haunted, a learning to live at the seam of the past and the present, a "heterodidactics between life and death" [*SM* xviii].[20]

2

I have often quoted Assia Djebar's wish in "Forbidden Gaze," found it in this or that text of hers:

> *If only one could cathect [*investir*] that single spectator body that remains, encircle it more and more tightly in order to forget the defeat! ... But every movement that might recall the collective fury [*la furia*] of the ancestors immediately freezes [*se fige*], redoubling the immobility that makes of woman a prisoner.* [141, trans. modified]

In *Far from Medina*, Djebar works at the "but" between the two sentences, prays to be haunted by the vengeful ancestors. If rereading Marx is important in post-Soviet Europe, rethinking woman in Islam is crucial in the context not only of Algeria but that internationality, called "Islamic," which does not have the convenient name of a continent.[21]

Djebar correctly insists that her book is not pro or contra. It is an opening up of a liminary time into a counterfactual possible world.[22] At the beginning of the book Muhammad is alive and dying. No one is yet born Muslim.

As always (and, incidentally, like all subalternists), Djebar haunts the pores of what a lesser imagination would think of as "the other side." One of the things that jar in *Specters* is Derrida's constant correcting and patronizing of a "silly" Marx. Djebar reads "some historians of the first two or three centuries of Islam (Ibn Hisham, Ibn Sa'd Tabari)," who write about the Prophet's lifetime, with unfailing respect and attention [FM xv]. She finds accounts of thirty-three women there and, attempting to make their ghosts dance, she imagines thirty-three possible worlds. Some of these women are indeed "spectators." I will cite one example to convey a sense of this, to convey also a sense of catching the negotiable futurity of that past by means of the uncertain subjunctive. Here is Nawar, wife of a Bedouin rebel, in the eleventh year of the Hegira (Muhammad's emigration from Mecca to Medina):

> It is permissible [il est loisible] to meditate upon [rêver à] this staging [mise-en-scène] deployed in the open air [déployée à l'air libre] by the rebel, back behind the excitement of battle; a caricatured comedy with, as in primitive plays, a dialogue with ironic variations exchanged between the leader and those who fight in his place. Above all this—a pencil sketch attempting the finished design—the presence of the flower-wife. Unknown Nawar ... And if Nawar, "the flower," were still waiting for Gabriel, there, a Bedouin woman surrounded in some Syrian city? [FM 21, 23]

But Fatima, Muhammad's youngest daughter, will not remain a spectator. She rises as a specter to perform the impossible deconstruction of the binary opposition between male and female Muslims.

(Of course this is only a rereading of a past for a future—a future anterior; this is not a formula for a future present. The ghost dance cannot succeed as a blueprint. Its uses, if there are any, are elsewhere.)

That Islam is riven by a road not taken is a shared theme. Abdelkébir Khatibi, sad that Freud did not deal well with the youngest People of the Book, complains that the institution of Islam was obliged to efface the fact that there is no signature at the origin of Muhammad's revelation, no covenant, only writing [see "Frontières; discussed at greater length in Spivak, "Psychoanalysis in Left Field"]. He diagnoses this originary writer-liness of Islam from Khadija's role in the revelation.

I am no scholar of Islam; no doubt many other reasons are given. I quote here an authoritative account rather close to Djebar's, to show how she will open it up and "assign possible agency" to ghostly women, welcome the undecidable as the condition of possibility for responsible action:

> In 2.256 the Qur'ān clearly formulates the principle of freedom of faith: "There can be no coercion in matters of faith—truth has become clear from falsehood." This is a good illustration of the conflict between the values and principles laid down by the Qur'ān and those deduced by the jurists on the basis of the logic of the Islamic Imperium, which

emerged by swift conquests shortly after the Prophet's death. Before the conquests, however, immediately on hearing the news of the Prophet's death, many Arab tribes rebelled against the political authority of Medina and reverted to their old tribal sovereignty.... [T]heirs was a political rebellion. The rebellion was put down by force of arms, but by a mistaken argument Muslim lawyers deduced from this that a person who leaves the faith of Islam deserves capital punishment.... Hence the source of the Islamic law on apostasy is not the Qur'ān but the logic of the Islamic Imperium. The science of Qur'ānic ethics will have to decide the relative place of both in the structure of Islam. [Rahman 15]

For Djebar it is gender difference that breaks Islam apart:

It was as if the body of Islam had to divide itself [se diviser], to give birth to civil strifes and quarrels, all this as a tribute paid to [payé à] polygamy.... . Fatima, daughter of the Prophet, moves to frontstage in the Islamic theatre [au premier plan du théâtre islamique], equally as [également comme] wife and mother of three martyrs—killed by Islamic hands: Ali, Hasan and Hussain. Her avenging shadow is spread over the entire body, however bifid [quoique bifide], of secular Islam. [FM 48–49][23]

No authority is claimed, but the curious theme of sexual dehiscence is pursued throughout the records, and all along *Far from Medina*: "Umm Temim ... the Bedouin noblewoman ... becomes the fragile hinge at the heart of this division which will be enlarged ..." [FM 89, 90]; and so on and on.

The chief occasion for my essay is *Specters of Marx*. I am so taken by these ghostwomen of Islam that I cannot end the piece without giving an account of my possession. (In fact, this entire piece is obsessed with the stakes that academics develop after years of work, peculiar "identifications" that drive their "life": Derrida, Marx, women [no capital, plural].) I will keep it brief, in the hope that readers will turn to *Far from Medina* to see how much more could have been said. I will speak of marriage, inheritance, doubt as the closed-off spaces of woman in Islam that Djebar attempts to open—and make an end.

Djebar's Muhammad, like the "real" one, is a woman's man, with no brothers and sons: "Four sons all dying prematurely; four daughters who will live [vivront], of whom the fourth is called Fatima" [FM 47]. He is an inveterate polygamist, yet he cannot think of his daughter as an object of polygamy. Or at least that is how Djebar wants to imagine his refusal to let Ali, his youngest daughter Fatima's husband, marry a second wife. But Muhammad, as reported in the chronicles Djebar studies, had expressed his objection doctrinally and in public. And Djebar questions thus:

To be sure, the fact of having four wives [le fait d'avoir quatre épouses] is legal for every believer. It is the people of Medina who are taken as witness of a truth of the private order [Or ce sont eux, les gens de Médine, qui sont pris à témoin de cette vérité d'ordre privé]: "What upsets [bouleverse] Fatima, upsets me!" To whom did Muhammad say "No" that day in Medina? To a part of himself? The father in him, thrilling till then with tenderness [vibrant jusque-là de douceur] and hope, is turned around, toward the Messenger resident [le Messager habité] in him, in order to enable himself to speak [oser dire] aloud his confusion as a mere mortal: "I fear lest Fatima should find her faith troubled. . . ." [FM 64]

Djebar does not locate—by way of the chronicles—this split in Muhammad (public/private, law/love, wives/daughter) in order merely to praise monogamy. The question of woman is here a figure for the impossible contradiction in the heart of history.

The power of the figuration becomes clear as she moves us into the question of inheritance and imagines androgyny as a last resort. You will forgive a longish quote, but this is how she struggles to reconfigure the past, to imagine the ancestors (daughter, father, historians) as ghosts. Particularly noticeable is the play of past and future:

[A]t the Prophet's final moment of consciousness . . . in order to inform them of his wishes for his temporal successor, to guide the fragile Muslim community which was beginning (only ten years since the Hegira), Muhammad asked all his wives who were present to send for a scribe . . . [t]he wives, future widows, brought mostly their fathers; in fact, one after the other, the Prophet's two fathers-in-law will succeed him, to be sure by virtue of personal merit. . . . Yes, if Fatima had been a son, the final scene of the transmission would have been otherwise [autre]: whichever wife was instructed by the dying man, she would not have failed to bring him "the" son, if not [sinon] her own. . . . With the mode of succession thus established by the Prophet himself, there would have been no dissension, no fitnas which, twenty-five years later, will bloody [ensanglanteront] the Community. The Prophet's Companions and sons of his Companions will kill each other [s'entretueront], because Fatima, being a daughter, was not the scribe at the moment when death was drawing near to Medina. . . . Dreaming of [rêver à] Fatima personally, outside of [en dehors de] her father, of her husband, of her sons, and to say to oneself [se dire] that perhaps (who has ever sensed this, written or transmitted this, daring thus a sin of lèse-majesté . . . yes, that perhaps Fatima, ever since nobility [nubilité; lit. marriageability] or during adolescence, wished herself a boy. Unconsciously. At once Daughter (for the tenderness) and Son (for the continuity) of her father. In fact, by marrying her father's cousin, above all because [surtout parce

que] he is the father's adoptive son: marrying almost herself [presque elle-même] to tell the truth, in order to draw closer to that desired and impossible heredity [hérédité désirée et impossible], to that model of the male successor through whom Muhammad would have perpetuated his lineage. [FM 47–49]

This is the context where the humility of the imagination also declares its risks:

Is this to form a far too free "idea" of Fatima? Is it to animate her with too much of a masculinity drive [l'animer d'une pulsion de masculinité] ... [so] that this fiction is torn apart [se déchire]? Risking the improbable [invraisemblable], at the very least the anachronistic, by emphasizing her supposed frustration.... [FM 49]

I long, of course, to read these rich passages, but must content myself with remarking that reminders to the limits of imagining are found all over this book. Djebar is scrupulous about this with regard to all the women she must *faire revenir* (bring back) as *revenant(e)s* or ghosts.

We cannot know if Fatima longed to be a boy, for the ghost named Fatima has no more than an unanticipatable "reality." "Are all the sources really silent? Why does Fatima not appear for the chroniclers until she is the mother of Hasan and Hussain?" [FM 51]. The records do tell us that the elders refused her the inheritance (the legal), by invoking the gift (the ethical): "'From us, the prophets,' Muhammad is said to have stated one day, 'one does not inherit! What is given to us is given as a gift!'" [FM 67–68]. Djebar recounts the received account again; that Fatima spoke at the mosque against this deliberate confusion.[24] "Fatima represents doubt"—and again that gender-deconstructive force of the desiring imagination: *"their* doubt" [FM 74, emphasis mine]—so that a fissure can open in what is merely "history," and the ghost can dance in the fault.

Mazhar and Khatibi concentrate on Khadija, Muhammad's older first wife, with whom he had only a monogamous relationship [for Mazhar, see Spivak, *Outside* 317n15]. But that is not the specter of Muhammad that Djebar prefers. It is rather the much-marrying Prophet after the death of the intimidating Khadija. And therefore, at the end of the book, it is a comradeship of the ghosts of Aïsha (the child-bride) and Fatima (the beloved daughter) that Djebar wishes to put in the future perfect: "If Aisha, one day, decided to leave Medina? Ah, far from Medina, to rediscover the wind, the exhilaration, the incorruptible youth of revolt!" [FM 275]. And, although this is not an auteurist book (Djebar is never an auteurist writer), there is an "assigned" space (as Hamlet/Horatio is for "Derrida") for her to wish this wish, in the words of Fatima's sister, chronicling her death: *"What Muslim woman of this city or elsewhere will perpetuate that*

*inflamed eloquence which burned us, which held us in a state of heightened
consciousness? ... No, I shall not take up the chain. I am not a woman
of words"* [FM 81, 80]. Then she introduces the figure of Habiba ("the
Friend"), the "second *rawiya*," the only "totally imaginary [*totalement
imaginaire*] figure "[a]mong the principal characters" [*FM* xi]. Speak to
them, Habiba, thou art a friend.[25]

If privileging the illegal immigrant in the New World Order may
unwittingly occlude the Southern subaltern, this exodus from Medina
relates to a much older world, when it was about to begin, so that it can
produce a counterfactual past future. This is not the messianic, but rather
a pluralized reversal of the Hegira itself into an open diaspora, replayed
for women, for a different history. There is no room for a discussion of
women's migrancy here. But it should be said that this is no exercise in
ontopology. This counter-Hegira is to leave behind "the transformation
into cold lead [of] the skin and nerves of the sublime passions of yesterday
..." [*FM* 274].

As for ontopology proper (so to speak), Djebar's latest book ends with
a violent effort to answer the question: "How shall I name you, Algeria?"
[see Djebar, *Vaste est la prison*]. For the specters of Marx to be able to ask
questions of that genre, the *Specters of Marx* must travel in terrains that it
seems not yet to know.

Notes

1   Derrida wrote a harsh response to this article in Michael Sprinker, *Ghostly
     Demarcations: A Symposium on Jacques Derrida's* Specters of Marx
     (London/New York: Verso, 1999), 213–69, which I never read. On the
     occasion of his seventieth birthday, we performed together in New York
     City. When I said I hadn't read his criticism of me regarding Marx for fear of
     being hurt, he said, "Gayatri, what to do with you? I publish a critique and
     you don't read it." This affectionate exchange should not be forgotten when
     my critique is read. [Note added by Gayatri Chakravorty Spivak on 30 April
     2012.]

2   I was amused by Ahmad's admission that the "identification of 'historicity'
     with opening up 'access' to 'the messianic' leaves me somewhat speechless"
     (101). I respect his admission, rather than the pompous verbiage on the
     occasion of fantasmatic Heideggers and Lévinases that one encounters in
     cultural criticism today.

3   The presupposition that capitalism can be explained away by the money
     circuit alone (although he mentions capital elaborately, of course, most
     noticeably in *The Other Heading*) legitimizes the "figur[ing] of economic
     value ... [by] typical measures like rations of price to earnings or price to
     book value," a popularized description of the method followed by William H.

Miller 3d of Legg Mason Special investment Trust, who calls himself a "value investor" [Gould]. A Marxian description of price would be the relative form of value expressed in the money form.

4   I am grateful to Bernd Magnus for making some early international reviews of Specters available to me. There were a couple of laudatory Italian reviews, and reviews in Russian and Arabic that I could not read.

5   Ahmad's major objection, that there are "political and philosophical adjacencies between Fukuyama's end-of-history arguments and the announcements of the end of all metanarratives that one finds routinely in the work of so many deconstructionists" [90], relates to the deconstructionists quoting Jean-François Lyotard's *Postmodern Condition*. Derrida's point, that there can be no adequate metalanguage, nothing extratextual in the sense of the weave of work, life, words, would in fact be a critique of Fukuyama.

6   I am thinking even of the point of view of, say, Bruce Ackerman's *The Future of Liberal Revolution*, where the "future" presages, however implicitly, a continuous present of "the end of history," or, in Jameson's smart phrase, "the beginning of a market universe, which is a perpetual present" [Jameson 108].

7   It may be worth mentioning that an apparent ignorance of the psychoanalytic and deconstructive senses of "mourning work" weakens the shrewdest bit of Ahmad's review.

8   Etienne Balibar said to Alys Weinbaum in conversation that he did not believe labor has been feminized. I am not, of course, speaking about the so-called "feminization of labor," that the regular labor force is largely female. Nonetheless, I will try to find out Balibar's reasons, for I respect his work greatly.

9   The last few paragraphs are a slightly modified version of a passage in the first chapter of my forthcoming *Return of the Native Informant*.

10   I am developing from Derrida, *Given Time* 6–20. If "socialism," annulling/remembering the gift (if there is any) as (institutionalized) responsibility, were possible, it would be the experience of the impossible. It is with an inchoate sense of this that I wrote, in 1988: "that socialism can never fully (adequately) succeed is what it has in common with everything. It is after that fact that one starts to make the choices" [Spivak, *Outside* 68].

11   For an elaboration of marriage as feudal relations of production, see Fraad.

12   The idea that money begets money covers over the possibility that labor-power makes value beget value and must therefore behave like money in order to be utilized socially. When the metaphor in "beget" is literalized, the full concept-metaphoricity of this project comes into view.

13   What is Derrida going to make of the "German Ideology" passage, in those very pages that he reads, where Marx most uncooperatively says: "As far as law is concerned, we with many others have stressed the opposition of communism to law, both political and private, as also in its most general form as the rights of man" [Marx and Engels 5: 209]? It is possible, I suppose,

to say that if law and human rights became "aware of the economic" these objections would vanish.

14 For a description of how well-bred economically minded internationalists foil third world efforts at economic justice, see Raghavan [63–5].

15 Such thinking would transform the ghost of Marx outside of organized labor and the parties not into an illegal immigrant head of the family but into a mother.

16 For the iceberg under the "illegal immigrant" see Derrida, *The Other Heading*, and the final section of Derrida, *Aporias*.

17 Cargo cults that relate to the ghost in loosely comparable ways figured in *Ghost Dance*, a film made in 1983 by Ken McMullen for Channel Four Television (UK), where Derrida played himself in a cameo appearance.

18 As indeed it does in Jameson's curious definition of subalternity as "the experience of inferiority" [95].

19 She is not writing about Freud there. My argument is that her analysis can be applied to Freud's peculiar gender thesis.

20 In the text I have followed normal usage and used the spelling *Medina*. I have likewise and silently changed other spellings of Islamic names when they seemed to follow an earlier usage. Hereafter cited in the text as *FM*. Translation modified where necessary.

21 I am able to see the problem of the division of the world into continents by way of Kirti Chaudhuri's *Asia before Europe*.

22 I have noticed a similar counterfactual rewriting of Engels on the occasion of woman in Mrinal Sen's *Genesis* [Scarabée Productions, 1986] [*Outside* 71–2].

23 For a comparable image of a woman's corpse (here shadow) spread across secular space to give the lie to its success, see Devi [93].

24 I am enabled to understand the representation of Maitreyi ('*Brhadāraṇyaka Upaniṣad*') and Draupadi ('*Mahābhārata*') better by this figuration of inheritance and male doubt.

25 A *rawiya* is a woman who transmits the oral tradition of the *hadith*, stories of the Prophet's life. Women played an important role as *rawiyat* in the early centuries of Islam. As usual, Djebar's novel is constructed in chapters invoking various musical and narrative forms.

Works cited

Ackerman, Bruce. *The Future of Liberal Revolution*. New Haven: Yale University Press, 1992.

Ahmad, Aijaz. "Reconciling Derrida: 'Specters of Marx' and Deconstructive Politics." *New Left Review* 208 (1994): 87–106.

Chaudhuri, Kirti. *Asia before Europe: Economy and Civilization of the Indian Ocean from the Rise of Islam to 1750*. Cambridge: Cambridge University Press, 1990.

Derrida, Jacques. *Aporias*. Trans. Thomas Dutoit. Stanford: Stanford University Press, 1993.

—"The Ends of Man." *Margins* 109–26.

—*Glas*. Trans. John P. Leavey, Jr., et al. Lincoln: University of Nebraska Press, 1986.

—"*Geschlecht*: Sexual Difference, Ontological Difference." *A Derrida Reader: Between the Blinds*. Ed. Peggy Kamuf. New York: Columbia University Press, 1991. 378–402.

—*Given Time. I. Counterfeit Money*. Trans. Peggy Kamuf. Chicago: University of Chicago Press, 1992.

—*Of Spirit: Heidegger and the Question*. Trans. Geoffrey Bennington and Rachel Bowlby. Chicago: University of Chicago Pres, 1989.

—*Specters of Marx: The State of the Debt, the Work of Mourning and the New International*. Trans. Peggy Kamuf. New York: Routledge, 1994. [SM]

—*Spurs: Nietzsche's Styles*. Trans. Barbara Harlow. Chicago: University of Chicago Press, 1979.

Devi, Mahasweta. "Douloti the Bountiful." *Imaginary Maps*. Trans. Gayatri Chakravorty Spivak. New York: Routledge, 1994. 19–93.

Djebar, Assia. *Far from Madina*. Trans. Dorothy Blair. London: Quartet, 1995. [FM]

—"Forbidden Gaze, Severed Sound." *Women of Algiers in Their Apartment*. Trans. Marjolijn de Jager. Charlottesville: University of Virginia Press, 1992.

—*Vaste est la prison*. Paris: Albin Michel, 1995.

Fraad, Harriet, et al., eds. *Bringing It All Back Home; Class, Gender, and Power in the Modern Household*. London: Pluto, 1994.

Gould, Carole. "Making a Case for Market Optimism." *New York Times* 28 August 1994: F12.

Jameson, Fredric. "Marx's Purloined Letter." *New Left Review* 209 (1994): 75–109.

Khatibi, Abdelkébir. "Frontières." "Entre psychanalyse et Islam." *Cahiers Intersignes* 1 (1990): 13–22.

Klein, Melanie. "Love, Guilt and Reparation." *Love, Guilt and Reparation and Other Works*. London: Hogarth, 1975.

Marx, Karl. *Capital: A Critique of Political Economy*. Vol. 1. Trans. Ben Fowkes. Vols. 2 and 3. Trans. David Fernbach. New York: Vintage, 1977, 1978, 1981.

—*The Communist Manifesto*. Ed. Frederic L. Bender. New York: Norton, 1988.

Mooney, James. *The Ghost-Dance Religion and the Sioux Outbreak of 1890*. Gloriata: Rio Grande, 1973.

Raghavan, Chakravarthi. *Recolonization: The Uruguay Round and the Third World*. London: Zed, 1991.

Rahman, Fazlur. "Law and Ethics in Islam." *Ethics in Islam*. Ed. Richard G. Hovannisian. Malibu: Undena, 1985.

Spivak, Gayatri Chakravorty. "*Glas*-piece: A *compte-rendu*." *Diacritics* 7 (1977): 22–43.

—"Melanie Klein." In *The Logic of the Gift*. Ed. Alan Schrift. Forthcoming.

—*Outside in the Teaching Machine*. New York: Routledge, 1994.

—"Psychoanalysis in Left Field." *Speculation after Freud*. Ed. Sonu Shamdasani and Michael Münchow. New York: Routledge, 1994. 54–60.

—"Supplementing Marxism." *Whither Marxism*. Ed. Bernd Magnus and Stephen Cullenberg. New York: Routledge, 1994. 109–19.

Walker, Richard. "California Rages against the Dying of the Light." *New Left Review* 209 (1995): 42–74.

20

Queer Spectrality: Haunting the Past

Carla Freccero

In *Premodern Sexualities*, Louise Fradenburg and I raised questions concerning the fantasmatic relationship that we, as scholars of the past and scholars working "queerly" in the history of sexuality, might affirm in relation to the past, "ours" or that of others, in the name of pleasure.[1] It was an effort, in part, to honor the complex pleasure-positivity of queer theory in its resistance to the heteronormatively disciplining discourses that came to the fore when AIDS in the US became associated with "homosexuals" and "promiscuity." It was also a way of examining how desires and identifications – queer theory's psychoanalytically inflected terminological legacies – are at work in historical scholars' investments in the differences and similarities between the past and the present. Finally, it was a way of noting historiography's (self-) disciplining force, its "repudiations of pleasure and fantasy" in spite – or because – of its queer wishes.[2] Thus we argued for a queer historiography that would devote itself to a critical re-valorization of the places and possibilities of pleasure within the serious and ascetic work of history.

Insofar as queer historicism registers the affective investments of the present in the past, however, it harbors within itself not only pleasure, but also pain, a traumatic pain whose ethical insistence is to "live to tell" through complex and circuitous processes of working through. Thus we concluded the introduction with an ethically impelled wish:

The past may not be the present, but it is sometimes in the present, haunting, even if only through our uncertain knowledges of it, our hopes of surviving and living well. The questions we are raising about the practice of history may help us understand better the living and dying of twentieth-century bodies and pleasures. And we hope that consideration of the ways in which historicisms are currently questioning sexuality, and sex studies questioning historicism, will work to affirm the pleasures of mortal creatures.[3]

The past is in the present in the form of a haunting. This is what, among other things, we imagined for queer history, since it involves openness to the possibility of being haunted, even inhabited, by ghosts. What is transmitted in the co-habitation of ghostly past and present is related to survival, to "living well," and to the "pleasures of mortal creatures," survivals and pleasures that have little to do with normative understandings of biological reproduction. Jonathan Goldberg explores the implications of queering history in his essay in the same volume.[4] A scene in Eduardo Galeano's *Memory of Fire* describes a moment in the European invasion of the Americas where the Spaniards are surrounded and victory for the Indians is imminent. Goldberg analyzes the exchange between the Araucanian chief and Bernal, where the chief predicts the extinction of the Spaniards on New World territory, whereas the Spaniard declares that reproduction will occur and that the resulting *mestizaje* will complete the task of conquest for the Spaniards against their indigenous parents and relatives. This is a moment when, Goldberg argues, the question of the future is at stake and the "history that will be" is suspended, opened up for multiple possibilities. For although from a position of retrospection one might argue for the prescience of the Spaniard's assertion, nevertheless the question of the "outcome" of the history that produces a *mestizo* Latin America is still open to an indeterminate futurity:

> To see that in this moment the history that will be is an open question, not the one foreclosed by the Spaniard and by those who have written as if he spoke with the voice of history, is to become engaged in a scene of revisionary reading made possible not simply by Galeano's text, but by its full imbrication in the multiples of history that enabled him to write in the first place. Any number of voices, now, could find themselves in the open space of implicit rejoinder.[5]

Goldberg combines a desire to un-write the retrospection of historical accounts of the conquest with a deconstruction of the implicit heteronormativity of historical continuity, the way historical succession is tied – in Galeano's fictional encounter as in second-order historical narratives – to heterosexual reproduction. In its radical disruption of normative temporal continuities, both for what happens and for how we tell what happens, this kind of historical practice that is also a queering of the notion of "succession" aims to open up sites of possibility effaced, if not foreclosed, by (hetero) normative historicisms.

Like Goldberg, I wish to explore the ways a queering of history and of historiography itself reworks teleological narratives of reproductive futurity that locate in a culminating endpoint the "truth" of the past and the present and thus may open up spaces of foreclosed possibility. At the same time, I want to think about the question of haunting – a mode of "precarious life" – as an alternative model for how queer history might proceed.[6] I thus want to explore the possibilities of spectrality for queer historiography, why it might describe a more ethical relation to the past than our current historicisms permit, and how it might counter the symptomatic fantasy of reproductive futurity (so scathingly interrogated by Lee Edelman in *No Future*) without necessarily adopting its binaristic representation of "death" as the only (compulsory) alternative.[7] Spectrality counters the teleological drive of heteroreproductive futurity on the level of form, a phenomenon of narration scrutinized by Madhavi Menon and Jonathan Goldberg, among others, and proposes an alternative mode of non-linear temporality that queries the melancholic attachments of some counternarratives of queer, on the one hand, and the illusion of a choice between "life" and "death," on the other.[8]

Jacques Derrida's *Specters of Marx* and its application in Avery Gordon's *Ghostly Matters* and Wendy Brown's *Politics out of History* propose a theory of spectrality – and haunting – as a kind of model for a historical attentiveness that the living might have to what is not present but somehow appears as a figure, a voice, or a (spectral) kind of materialization, as a being that is no longer or not yet "present."[9] How might the Derridean concept of spectrality reconfigure familial, nucleated, heteronormative temporalities even as it articulates alternatives to a historicism that respects sequential chronologies? Spectrality invokes collectivity, a collectivity of unknown or known, "uncanny" (both familiar and yet not) strangers who arrive to frequent us. To speak of ghosts is to speak of the social.[10] Spectrality also acknowledges fantasy's constitutive relation to experience. It suggests that fantasy is the mode of our experiential existence, that it mediates how we live our desire in the world. Further, haunting, ghostly apparition, reminds us that the past and the present are neither discrete nor sequential. The borderline between then and now wavers, wobbles, and does not hold still.

Ghosts demand. Although (as Fradenburg and Freccero argue) historicisms also respond to a demand, this is rarely acknowledged or theorized as an explicit motive for the historicist enterprise. To assume the perspective of the ghost – or to include haunting in a conceptualization of history's effects – foregrounds the imperative issuing from the other in the labor of the historian. Popular representations, testifying to widely distributed persistent populist acceptance of the ghostly as a domain of legitimacy, tell us that the ghost comes back because there is something unfinished:

The ghost is ... pregnant with unfulfilled possibility, with the something to be done that the wavering present is demanding. This something to be done is not a return to the past but a reckoning with its repression in the present, a reckoning with that which we have lost, but never had.[11]

The ghost's demand engenders a certain responsibility. Spectrality is, thus, also a way of thinking ethics in relation to the project of historiography.[12]

Ghosts permit us to mourn; they are, indeed, a sign of trauma and its mourning. This is, argues Derrida, not the mourning that opposes itself to organizing in a kind of passive despair. Rather, it is "a mourning in fact and by right interminable, without possible normality, without reliable limit, in its reality or in its concept, between introjection and incorporation."[13] The goal of spectral thinking is thus not to immure, but to allow to return, to be visited by a demand, a demand to mourn and a demand to organize. Mourning is, in an important way, the work of history.[14]

We might spend a few moments thinking about two other models of history by way of contrast. One is the idea of burial: we bury the dead, giving them monumental tombs. Michel de Certeau has commented on this aspect of historiography, arguing that the historian posits him/herself as the subject whose writing replaces, covers over, or displaces the other about whom his/her discourse is being elaborated. He writes:

> "The sole historical quest for 'meaning' remains indeed a quest for the Other," but, however contradictory it may be, this project aims at "understanding" and, through "meaning," at hiding the alterity of this foreigner; or, in what amounts to the same thing, it aims at calming the dead who still haunt the present, and at offering them scriptural tombs.[15]

Thus de Certeau points to the mastery involved in the project of historiography and to the concomitant entombment that accompanies the gesture. In *Heterologies*, he includes a warning that opens the way for the question of spectrality: "These voices – whose disappearance every historian posits, but which he replaces with his writing – 're-bite' [*re-mordent*] the space from which they were excluded; they continue to speak in the text/ tomb that erudition erects in their place."[16] De Certeau suggests that the historian's gesture is a melancholic one, an attempt to entomb within writing the lost other of the past. And, as he also suggests, those who are buried – perhaps buried alive – will return to haunt us. This melancholic model is also a response to trauma – the trauma of historicity[17] – yet it is a response that will not acknowledge the loss and seeks instead to hush the voices or to "understand" or master them with meaning and discourse.

Another model, which is a kind of corollary to this one, is more directly colonial, and involves outright mastery or appropriation. This is a model de Certeau links to Western practices of knowledge production:

A structure belonging to modern Western culture can doubtless be seen in this historiography: intelligibility is established through a relation with the other; it moves (or "progresses") by changing what it makes of its "other" – the Indian, the past, the people, the mad, the child, the Third World. Through these variants that are all heteronomous – ethnology, history, psychiatry, pedagogy, etc. – unfolds a problematic form basing its mastery of expression upon what the other keeps silent, and guarantees the interpretive work of a science (a "human" science) ...[18]

These models have come under scrutiny within US queer political and historical practices relative to an emergent category of being within queer movement politics, the trans-sexual/gendered person, and the rape and murder of "Brandon Teena," which became an emblem and rallying cry for trans-politics.[19] The traumatic event that goes by the proper name of Brandon Teena – itself marked by a kind of belatedness[20] – repeats the violent effacement of difference, usually racial, that constitutes a primary trauma in the US national imaginary and in the auto-constitution of queer movement.[21] Although all movements doubtless take up the dead and carry them into battle like a banner, the danger of so doing involves an ethical dimension that queer historians might want to honor. In "Brandon"'s case, there is the problematic appropriation of identity that consigned him variously to the annals of lesbian history or the fledgling library of the transsexual movement. In either case, precisely the problem of identity with which he was involved – and which turned out to be lethal – is a problem "solved" by activists and historians' taking up his life in the name of a given – and thus also meaningfully defined – category.[22] And while the queer appropriation of "Brandon Teena" was certainly melancholic – an attempt to deal with trauma by in a sense refusing it, turning it instead into knowledge, into productive organizing – it was also colonizing. Both gestures – the melancholic and the colonizing – have worked to foreclose how he, as ghost, recurs in ways that are not so clear, and demands of us not a definition, but the creation of spaces where categorical definitions so dependent on gender and desire might prove affirmingly impossible. Using spectrality as our hypothesis, then, we might wonder what we would see and hear were we to resist identitarian foreclosures and remain open to ghostly returns.

And so too with the more distant past. Like Goldberg, scholars of New World conquest or encounter studies have tried numerous strategies to confront ethically the "event" of the conquest and to do justice to the historical traumaticity of the event, both "for" then and for now.[23] Some, such as Beatriz Pastor, invoke Hayden White's study of the rhetorical modalities of historiography to note the inter-contamination of historical and fictional discourses and thus to read the documents of the conquest/ encounter for the way they narrate not only "events," but also desire.[24] Pastor writes:

> In the case of Latin America, to rewrite the history of its conquest ...
> implies retracing the lost steps, listening; to other voices that could have
> related the history of a discovery rooted in dreams and lies, of a New
> World that, through the very process of its conquest, was lost forever.[25]

Here, writing the history of those without one is a fantasmatic activity
that describes an impossible wish; it involves following traces that are lost,
listening to voices that "could have" spoken (but, it is implied, did not), all
toward the goal of describing a New World that was – and thus is – lost
forever. This impossible task of retracing and listening, of locating desire
in the (not quite total) silences of texts, articulates a complex interplay of
desire and identification that is also Pastor's own:

> Where are the eyes that could show us the women's side of the world
> of war and conquest, about which so many famous historians have
> written so much? And where are the words that could break the silence
> that covers the voices of all those women who, like Malintzin, struggled
> in a world created and controlled by men, without even leaving a tiny
> scratch on the yellowing pages of so many historical documents: words
> that could show us what they were like as people, as women, as voices,
> as eyes, as tongues?[26]

Echoing the slogan of anti-Columbian demonstrations, "Where are
the Arawaks?," Pastor invokes Doña Marina as the exemplary and
overdetermined sign of a silence. The multilingual indigenous interpreter
about whom so much has been written and whose body parts and signature
are continually re-appropriated in documents of the conquest (she is Cortes'
tongue and he in turn is often referred to by her name) is precisely one whose
voice may be said to have determined history without, as Pastor notes,
leaving "even a tiny scratch on the yellowing pages of so many historical
documents."[27] Like Echo's voice to Narcissus' embodiment, Malintzin is
the ventriloquized word of the conqueror, unable to show us the difference
of her "women's side of the world." And yet, something about this passage
strains to hear, even from within the mournful lament of a loss. Pastor
enacts a kind of automatic writing then, a practice of scratching the page
as an act of listening to lost voices. She is, we might say, inhabited by a
ghost, the ghost of Malintzin and "the voices of all those women who, like
Malintzin, struggled in a world created and controlled by men."

Tzvetan Todorov, who also experiences an ethical imperative in narrating
the conquest, likewise suggests that what presses upon his project – as upon
the Europeans who will emerge victorious from their encounter with the
Aztecs and Mayans – is a silence from the past. Todorov's work has been
criticized – most notably by Stephen Greenblatt – for an overemphasis on
the already civilizationally overdetermined opposition between "speech"

and "writing," and between "traditional" or "ritual" and "improvisational," the Europeans representing the latter example in each binary.[28] But for Todorov, these oppositions are radically unstable to the extent that his attempt to describe differing world views in the domain of communication does not serve the purpose of historical explanation. His is a cautionary tale, motivated by moral rather than historical exigencies aimed at the present rather than the past:

> The Spaniards win the war. They are incontestably superior to the Indians in the realm of interhuman communication. But their victory is problematic, for there is not just one form of communication, one dimension of symbolic activity ... this victory from which we all derive, Europeans and Americans both, delivers as well a terrible blow to our capacity to feel in harmony with the world, to belong to a preestablished order; its effect is to repress man's communication with the world, to produce the illusion that all communication is interhuman communication; the silence of the gods weighs upon the camp of the Europeans as much as on that of the Indians.[29]

Here, the "silence" of (divine) voices weighs upon not only the Europeans of the past, but those of the present as well. Voices that once spoke – in the past – withhold their speaking in the present. But what is repressed (*refoulé*) threatens to return; this withholding continues to haunt.[30]

For Goldberg, the queering of the English encounters that will come to be called the conquest produces a scene in which the failed conquerors at Roanoke reproduce themselves in the future through the "invisible bullets" of disease; he argues that "in this auto-erotic scene of conjuring up the desired future, is the body of the Indian, a strange specular double for these English shooters."[31] Goldberg's is a scene of homoerotic encounters between the present of the English invaders and their spectral descendants performed across the body of the Indian (man); for Pastor, the spectral body is the missing (Indian) woman in a homosocial scene of transaction; for Todorov, finally, it is the gods, or the Indian woman consumed by Spanish dogs to whom he dedicates his book. All three invoke ghosts in scenes where Indian, woman, and god mark the trace of a non-speaking yet persistent and insistent otherness caught in, effaced or consumed by, these queer colonial encounters. The recurrence of "indigenous" haunting articulated in their writing also signals the repetition of a prior haunting, a haunting that was both a memorial and a messianic invocation, the "ghost dance" of the North American Plains Indians during their radical displacement and destruction.[32] As Gayatri Spivak imagines it, this dance that conjured ancestors for a future to come was "an attempt to establish the ethical relation with history as such, with ancestors real or imagined."[33] What does it mean, then, for a certain narration of conquest to invoke the figure of a ghost, a ghost who clearly continues to haunt the moment of reading and writing in the present?

In "Archive Fever: A Freudian Impression," Derrida remarks that "a spectral messianicity is at work in the concept of the archive."[34] Further, in a passage that makes the notion of the archive constitutively spectral and links that spectrality to the "being" of a ghost, he writes: "the structure of the archive is spectral. It is spectral a priori: neither present nor absent 'in the flesh,' neither visible nor invisible, a trace always referring to another whose eyes can never be met ..."[35] Thus for these writers engaged in an ethical relation to a traumatic past event, the trace that is also a calling, a demand, a messianic wish or hope, takes the troubled form of a ghost – neither altogether present nor quite absent – conjured by the moment of writing. And it is no coincidence that the figures invoked in these archival memorials are racially and sexually marked, for just as ghostliness designates an ambiguous state of being, both present and not, past and not, so too in these accounts racial mixture and sexual – including sexuality – difference stand in fix, even as they mark the material place of, a critique of originary purity, simplicity, and unmixedness.[36]

If figures of ghostliness – one way to think spectrality – appear as a way to relate to the past, this past is not, nevertheless, an origin, however much these discourses about conquest and traumatic genocidal encounters might seem to suggest this. Brown writes:

> The specter begins by coming hack, by repeating itself, by recurring in the present. It is not traceable to an origin nor to a founding event, it does not have an objective or "comprehensive" history, yet it operates as a force ... We inherit not "what really happened" to the dead but what lives on from that happening, what is conjured from it, how past generations and events occupy the force fields of the present, how they claim us, and how they haunt, plague, and inspirit our imaginations and visions for the future.[37]

That force, what I have been calling in the work of conquest or encounter studies writers an ethical imperative, is a social force and as such places a demand upon the present. It is thus also collective, another way of thinking spectrality's specificity as "historical."

Haunting engages alterity; "what comes back to haunt," writes Nicolas Abraham "are the tombs of others," ancestors or affines, our own or those of others.[38] There is no "propriety," no "proprietariness" in ghostliness; the ghost does not, in other words, necessarily belong to those who are haunted by it. Rather, "ghosts figure the impossibility of mastering, through either knowledge or action, the past or the present." Instead "they figure the necessity of grasping certain implications of the past for the present only as traces or effects."[39] In the writings I have been discussing, the past in question can in some sense be said to be, in spite of Goldberg's salutary resistance in particular, definitively past, and the longing or loss that marks these discourses with a certain solemnity testifies to this impression. And yet, each project – feminist, multicultural, and queer – also allows itself to be haunted in the context of an articulation of political aspirations in the present.

In commenting on the place from which a ghost emerges in the "cryptography" of Abraham and Torok's theories of melancholia, Derrida remarks, "the crypt is the vault of a desire."[40] Abraham, referring to the refused and unknown secret that is the encrypted phantom inhabitation, says, "this other ... is a love object."[41] Pastor, Todorov, and Goldberg all show, in different ways, how secret mobilizations of desire and identification inspire both the ghosts in their texts and their own spectral endeavors. If desire for – and of – the other is part of what is hidden in the crypt, part of what arrives or comes back as insistent and persistent phantom, then a spectral approach can make room for, or leave itself open to, the materialization and voicing of that desire so that it might thereby appear and speak.

Thus far I have been attending to the ways ghosts, ghostliness, and haunting appear as tropes or figures (of loss, of mourning, and also of a "something to be done") in discourses about a particular (and partially imagined) traumatic past, and how those figures articulate a "hauntology," a spectral approach to an ethico-historical situation. What might it mean to take such an approach – "historiography as hauntology"[42] – at a moment when the ghost – which in some ways resembles the ghosts conjured by Pastor, Todorov, and Goldberg – seems, from our perspective, to appear proleptically in the conjurings of a "colonial" European subject such as Jean de Léry?[43] What pasts return to haunt this subject in its present and what historico-ethical demands follow from that haunting? And further – as I hope to highlight in pausing on the moments when *History of a Voyage to the Land of Brazil* allows itself to be inhabited by returning others – how does this haunting suggest a specifically queer spectrality, queer both in its uncanniness and in its engagement with desire?[44]

Jean de Léry, a Protestant minister who, in 1556 at the age of 22, went to the French colony commanded by Villegagnon near the Bay of Rio to preach Calvinist doctrine, found himself exiled by Villegagnon from the fortress and "at the mercy of" the Tupinamba Indians, with whom he stayed as a guest for almost a year. Upon his return to France in 1558, he began his ministry. Later Léry directly suffered the bloodiest decades of the French religious wars, including the 1572 massacre of St Barthélemy. He survived by escaping to Sancerre and, in 1574, published an account of the siege and famine of that town, a Protestant stronghold where he ministered.[45] In 1578, more than 20 years later, he published the first edition of his *History of a Voyage to the Land of Brazil*, claiming that it had been written in 1563 then lost, found, lost again and found again.[46] The gap between Léry's first encounter with Brazilian land and people and his retrospective account of it is thus marked, both by loss (the inability to hang on to or preserve the recorded traces of the event) and by a shattering national event, the Saint-Barthélemy, that to this day haunts the French nation as perhaps the first modern moment when internal religious division precipitated mass murder.

Léry's text describes a haunting that differs both from triumphant conquest narratives such as that of Cortés and from the fearful accounts of indigenous cannibalism that threatened and titillated European travelers and observers in the New World. Indeed, cannibalism is in some sense haunting's double, its evil twin. A literalization of melancholic incorporation through the ingestion of the other, cannibalism is the flipside of the excorporation that a ghost might be said to be.[47] But cannibalism participates in the fundamental "impossibility" of mourning, in that the desire to incorporate the other within the self fundamentally destroys its alterity and consequently negates the other. Cannibalism is an act of erotic aggression, however ambivalent, that effaces alterity; haunting is passive, not in the sense of a lack of activity, but rather in the sense of opening oneself up to inhabitation by the other, and it is thus attentive to alterity. In his account of Sancerre, Léry mentions cannibalism – exclusively in order to condemn it – in a gruesome story about starving parents who devour their daughter.[48] However evoked by Léry's New World memories, cannibalism is not a practice specifically tied to those places. On the contrary, when the question arises it is in the context of a comic account of miscommunication on the one hand and, on the other, a diatribe against the cannibalism exemplified by combatants in the wars of religion in France.[49] For Léry, the cannibalism that occasions horror is not Tupi, it is European and French. Cannibalism, as a crisis of identification and desire, becomes, for him, the double emblem of a barbarous Catholicism and a civil war.[50] Léry thus turns away from cannibalism as the distinctive mark of indigenous othering and allows himself to be haunted instead, to live with ghosts and to dream of another order, condemning the cannibalistic order of political revenge. And what haunts Léry is the other's ethical imperative, his demand.

Being haunted is also a profoundly erotic experience, one that ranges from an acute visual pleasure to ecstatic transcendence. Léry's description of Tupi warfare (chapter 14) lingers on their physical dexterity and bodily superiority to Europeans; it also privileges the efficaciousness and beauty of pre-industrial warfare, praising the archery skills of the Tupinamba over and against the use of horses on the one hand and artillery on the other.[51] Both in relation to warfare and with respect to the religious ceremony described two chapters later, Léry and the other Frenchmen are positioned with the women as distinct and separate from the men, thus effecting a racialized gendering apart from the economy "men, women, and children" that is the repeated refrain of the ethnographer's observations.[52] This positioning "elsewhere" seems to allow Léry to articulate an erotics in relation to the Tupi men that successfully distances itself from that notorious "New World" practice, sodomy, and that also cannot quite be described as "homo"-erotic, since sameness and difference here do not line up neatly into gender binaristic columns.[53]

The chapter, "What one might call religion among the savage [sic; wild] Americans," represents, in some respects, the heart of Léry's book, for it deals with the most vexed of early modern questions in relation to the indigenous Americans, whether or not they were possessed of religion; it is also the subject closest to Léry's own field of expertise as a Calvinist minister. At the beginning of the chapter, he declares in the strongest terms that the Tupinamba are utterly devoid of religion[54]; nevertheless, the chanting ceremony he witnesses – like a voyeur happening upon a sacred scene – has all the characteristics of a profound mystical experience and indeed haunts Léry in the present of writing, some 20 years after the event:

> At the beginning of this witches' sabbath, when I was in the women's house, I had been somewhat afraid; now I received in recompense such joy, hearing the measured harmonies of such a multitude, and especially in the cadence and refrain of this song, when at every verse all of them would let their voices trail, saying Heu, heuaure, heura, heuraure, heura, heura, oueh – I stood there transported with delight. Whenever I remember it, my heart trembles, and it seems their voices are still in my ears.[55]

The voices of the men, much like the (soundless) women's voices that haunt Pastor, still seem to inhabit Léry; they live in his ears, ravishing him and causing his heart to tremble, unlike the withdrawn gods of Todorov's Europeans, who haunt precisely through their (ominous) silence. While Pastor and Todorov, modern scholars of the conquest, struggle and strain to listen to silenced voices from the past – and are haunted precisely through this struggle to attend – Léry is so thoroughly penetrated by these voices that they remain with him in the present. These lines echo in an aural register an earlier passage that also uncannily describes a ghostly mode of appearance: "During that year or so when I lived in that country, I took such care in observing all of them, great and small, that even now it seems to me that I have them before my eyes, and I will forever have the idea and image of them in my mind."[56] The spectral images of the indigenous Americans seem to be superimposed upon the French people who Léry does, in fact, have before his eyes; they are with him in a quasi-material way, phenomenal but not fully present.

This haunting – and its relation to the present of Léry's French situation – culminates when, at the moment of departure, Léry describes his longing to remain in Brazil:

So that saying goodbye here to America, I confess for myself that although I have always loved my country and do even now, still, seeing the little – next to none at all – fidelity that is left here, and, what is worse, the disloyalties of people toward each other, I often regret that I am not among the savages, in whom (as I have amply shown in this narrative) I have known more frankness than in many over here, who, for their condemnation, bear the title of "Christian."[57]

What might otherwise be understood as a simple and exoticizing expression of nostalgia takes on added meaning when the term "Christian" is invoked, for Léry's original mission involved his calling as a minister, and his account, at least on the descriptive level, declares the Tupinamba to be without religion. Here, then, at the purported end of his voyage, the intervening years have relativized the once absolute difference between "heathen" and Christian to the shame, on the one hand, Léry implies, of the nation (he uses the political term *patrie* in the sentence describing his love for France), and the honor, on the other, of America and the Americans. Although in one respect the discourse deploys the topos of comparison in order to shame the addressees into virtuous action, in another, it refuses altogether the possibility of a better future "over here" and remains steadfast in its past and persistently present desire to return. In the choice between "them" and "us," he suggests that he would have chosen – and still chooses – them.

Léry's political and religious experience at the hands of his countrymen – a traumatic event to which he returns even after the account of Sancerre has been written and published – thus finds a haunting reminder in the displaced figure of the Tupi cannibal. But that haunting – the one performed by the Tupinamba on the person of Léry – enjoins Léry not to condemn the New World inhabitants who have become legendary in the imaginations of European travel narrative readers, but to urge upon the present a halt to the genocidal practices of warfare that decimate the homeland and – we might understand by implication – the New World as well. Thus we might discern in Léry's "complaint" the formulation of an ethical imperative that articulates itself in excess of – and in uncomfortable contrast to – his providential Calvinist polemics.

Although Léry's discourse also participates in the colonizing will to know that de Certeau describes and the exoticizing movement that makes of the indigenous American a pleasurable remainder in the discourse of scientific knowledge, he is not subject to the "displaced abjection" Goldberg analyzes in relation to the conqueror's project in the New World.[58] He does not only wish to penetrate a (perceptually) violated body; instead, he also gives himself over to penetration, enacting the becoming-object that Roland Greene describes as occurring elsewhere in his text.[59] Indeed, in the chapter where Léry recounts his participation in the ritual of the *caraïbes* (chapter 16), a curious reciprocity of penetration occurs.[60] At the beginning of the shaman ceremony, Léry and the other Frenchmen find themselves waiting in the women's house while the men chant in a nearby building; Léry is at first terrified by the inhuman sounds issuing from the men. Suddenly the chanting shifts, and Léry is instead drawn to the marvelous harmonies; the women and his interpreters hold him back, warning him of possible danger.[61] Nevertheless, he takes the risk:

> I drew near the place where I heard the chanting; the houses of the savages are very long and of a roundish shape ... Since they are covered with grasses right down to the ground, in order to see as well as I might wish, I made with my hands a little opening in the covering ... we all three entered the house. Seeing that our entering did not disturb the savages as the interpreter thought it would, but rather, maintaining admirably their ranks and order, they continued their chants, we quietly withdrew to a corner to drink in the scene ... I had been somewhat afraid; now I received in recompense such joy, hearing the measured harmonics of such a multitude, and especially in the cadence and refrain of the song ... I stood there transported with delight. Whenever I remember it, my heart trembles, and it seems their voices are still in my ears.[62]

Léry makes a small opening in the wall of the men's roundhouse and, beckoning his companions to follow, enters. What begins as a voyeuristic scene of conquest becomes instead the receptive witnessing of a marvelous spectacle, one that at first inspires fear but then produces ravishment. Like the primal scene Freud describes as the traumatic origin of sexuality, the event both terrifies and excites, precipitating a kind of crisis of identification and desire whereby the witness is both penetrator and penetrated.[63] Léry imagines penetrating the men's secret round space, only to find himself in turn penetrated through the ears by the sound of their voices.

This image of penetrative reciprocity thus delineates a different subjectivity from the one informing Goldberg's conquerors, and it suggests the "self-shattering" impulse or *jouissance* Leo Bersani describes as distinctive and resistive in male "homo-sexual" subjectivity.[64] Bersani, indeed, muses that "same"-sex desire might be what permits the possibility of a reciprocity that resists the annihilative effacement of the other. "Can a masochistic surrender," he asks, "operate as effective (even powerful) resistance to coercive designs?"[65] If identification with the indigenous other man is experienced by conquerors as threatening, in need of radical and thus violent obliteration for difference to be produced – and if this is, in the context of the European-New World encounter, a "normative response" – then we might say that Léry's text enacts instead a "sodomitical subjectivity," a perverse, "masochistic" identification with that other he has come – even in the eyes of the French commander Villegagnon – to resemble.[66]

In *The Melancholy of Race*, Anne Cheng argues that national identity in the US is characterized by racial melancholia. The dominant white citizen-subject is melancholic for having "ghosted," by consuming, the racial others of the nation; the incorporated object – racialized subjects – also internalizes an impossible (white) ideal.[67] Her work argues for a different relationship to a traumatic history of loss, one that does not simply get over it (which, in any case, fortifies the attachment to loss through the encrypting or consumption of the lost object in the self; thereby denying loss). What alternative approaches to melancholic subjectivity and its unarticulated grief, she asks, might better serve the goal of achieving social justice and allow a "working through" that addresses the interimplications of the psychic or subjective and the social?

Cheng begins with the question, "What is the subjectivity of the melancholic object? Is it also melancholic, and what will we uncover when we resuscitate it?"[68] The attribution of melancholic subjectivity to the racialized other is a familiar strategy of the victors to legitimize their future and also characterizes a certain melancholic discourse of modernity in the West that shores up and retains the centrality of that Western subject of modernity.[69] Yet Cheng's question takes seriously the status of the incorporated other as object in the dominant melancholic subject and proposes a far more unsettling situation:

> It is as if, for Freud, the "object" has, for all practical purposes, disappeared into the melancholic's psychical interiority. In short, one is led to ask, what happens if the object were to return – would the melancholic stop being melancholic? That scenario would seem to make sense except that, since Freud has posited melancholia as a constitutive element of the ego, the return of the object demanding to be a person of its own would surely now be devastating.[70]

"The return of the object demanding to be a person of its own" is one way to think about haunting, the object's return and its demand being what might be said to emerge when one is willing to be haunted, to be inhabited by ghosts. Further, the mutual recognition, entanglement, and disentanglement entailed by this event suggest a more complex relationship between difference and resemblance, alterity and identity (or "sameness"), than (heteronormative) discourses of identity normally allow. For, in order to enable the melancholic object-other to emerge and to demand from "within" the self, there must be identification, if not identity, between the subject and object. And yet, at the same time, for that object to demand, to become (a ghost), somehow to materialize, it must have a subjectivity of its own; it must, therefore, be other/different.[71]

This fantastic model of an otherness struggling to emerge within and sometimes against the self delineates an intrasubjectivity that is nevertheless not incompatible with or absolutely different from intersubjectivity. Thus it can be said that the ghost arrives both from within and from without as a part of the self that is also – and foremost – a part of the world. The ghost's return is, in other words, not quite material yet phenomenal nevertheless and, much like its primary modality, affect or feeling, its appearance is the "material and immaterial evidence" of grief.[72]

To demonstrate this, Judith Butler adapts Freud's melancholic model of subjectivity from *The Ego and the Id* – the same model from which Cheng derives her theory of racial melancholia – and describes how "the social" or "the world" enters into the subject and becomes a constitutive element of its being.[73] She argues that melancholia is precisely what establishes the distinction between the social and the psychic[74] and renders "fictional" or fantastic the workings of the world within the self.[75] Like Pastor and Todorov, Butler reminds us that "what remains unspeakably absent inhabits the psychic voice of the one who remains,"[76] while Cheng concludes with an ethical injunction to listen that also invokes the metaphor of the ghostly voices of the absent, speaking through the living:

> If we are willing to listen, the history of disarticulated grief is still speaking through the living, and the future of social transformation depends on how open we are to facing the intricacies and paradoxes of that grief and the passions it bequeaths.[77]

These cautionary or injunctive insistences point to the persistence, in the present, of a melancholia that is perhaps not finally capable of allowing the other to return. Yet Léry's queer subjectivity, characterized by a penetrative reciprocity, a becoming-object for an other subject and a resultant joy or ecstasy, suggests an alternate path to the Western melancholic's incorporation of the lost other and its permanent, if uneasy, entombment within the crypt of history.

Cheng and Butler's theories of a melancholic condition that constitutes the subject through racial and sexual norms explore the "disarticulated grief" and the foreclosures occasioned by violent repudiations. Léry's non-foreclosure of either resemblance/identification or difference permits, potentially, a non-melancholic relation to the other (and the world) such that "he" – the other – could indeed become "a person demanding a subjectivity of his own." We might, on the one hand, read the success of Léry's openness to being haunted in the work he does to denounce and put an end to civil war, the way that haunting turns him toward a reparative future. His disaffiliation from and "disidentification" with the nation – a result, in part, of his status as an already "minoritarian subject"[78] – position him elsewhere than as imperial avatar in the New World. At the same time, he does not "go native" (though there were certainly many such examples among the *truchements de Normandie*, some of whom served as Léry's interpreters), but rather returns as "other," with voices in his head and ghosts before his eyes. His text is thus not "salvage" ethnography, the one-way inscription and recording of a "disappearing object," but an enactment of its own difference from itself, a textualization of France through Brazil as much as of Brazil through France.[79]

We might also read the persistence of the ghostly demand to be heard and recognized in a story that surfaces a century later in France, when a French Tupi descendant of the sixteenth-century French-Brazilian encounters is sued for back taxes owed to the state.[80] Captain Binot Paulmier de Gonneville returned from his voyage to Brazil in 1505 with Essomeric, the son of "Lord Arosca," in tow, the *seigneur* having expressed a desire for his son to "go to Christendom."[81] Although Essomeric – subsequently baptized as Binot (Gonneville's baptismal name) – was to have returned after two years, Gonneville was unable to provide him with passage. Instead, he made him an heir and married him to one of Gonneville's relations. These are the descendants who are brought to court 150 years later:

> It came to pass, in 1658, that a proceeding was brought against the family issuing from the savage Essomeric for payment of certain *aubaine* obligations ... the defendants rejected this claim, objecting that Essomeric, their ancestor, had never been an *aubain* [a non-naturalized foreigner] who had established himself voluntarily in France, but rather had been forced to remain in violation of commitments that had been made, which should exempt his descendants from the taxes that were being demanded.[82]

One of the descendants, Paulmier, who pleaded the case, had also spent time trying to set up a Catholic mission among the Tupinamba in Brazil. Yet here he is unequivocal and wins the day: his ancestor was kept in France by force, in violation of Gonneville's promise to provide for his return, and thus the descendants ought to be exempted from taxation by the state. This is not reparation or restitution, at least not in any positive sense. It is a "voice" that "speaks" before the law with a demand for recognition. Nor is it the melancholic logic Brown discerns in the impulse to resolve historical trauma through the "discursive structure of wrong, debt, and payment."[83] It is rather a "politico-logic of trauma" that responds to a different – we might say haunting – demand. It does not, in other words, appeal to the law; rather it refuses the law and stages its case "beyond right or law."[84]

This anecdote, the new historicist gesture *par excellence*, illustrates neither subversion nor containment, pointing, as it does, only to the persistence of a demand that, like Léry's queer subjectivity, suspends the difference between difference and resemblance, even as it insists on both. Léry thus did have the Tupinamba before his eyes in France, though he probably did not see them.[85] The story also returns us to Goldberg's admonitions concerning "the history that will be" as a moment of suspension that resists the retrospectivity of *either* triumphant *or* melancholic modern narratives of the conquest, of a choice, that is, between the future and death. For the process of ethnic cleansing (through systematic miscegenating rape) that the conqueror of Goldberg's tale invokes produces a far less determinate future than the conqueror imagines. Essomeric/Binot Paulmier's family "talks back" in a voice neither wholly French nor wholly "cleansed," and their rejoinders (to the law, to France) continue through to the present. What we might perceive from this moment, then, is a France *métissée*, a country not of late twentieth-century diasporic arrivals, but one whose history of forced migrations has never ceased to speak and to demand a certain responsibility.

If this spectral approach to history and historiography is queer, it might also be objected that it counsels a kind of passivity, both in Bersani's sense of self-shattering and also potentially in the more mundane sense of the opposite of the political injunction to act. In this respect it is also queer, as only a passive politics could be said to be. And yet, the passivity – which is also a form of patience and passion – is not quite the same thing as quietism. Rather, it is a suspension, a waiting, an attending to the world's arrivals (through, in part, its returns), not as guarantee or security for action in the present, but as the very force from the past that moves us, perhaps not into the future, but somewhere else.

Can we (a "we" not given in advance) live on – survive – beyond categorical imperatives in such a state of dynamic suspension, and is there a certain responsibility – in the name of "queer" – to do so? And, with our rage and sadness, Derrida urges us to perform an exorcism, "not in order to chase away the ghosts, but this time to grant them the right, if it means making them come back alive, as *revenants* who would no longer be *revenants*, but as other *arrivants* to whom a hospitable memory or promise must offer welcome – without certainty, ever, that they present themselves as such. Not in order to grant them the right in this sense but out of a concern for justice."[86] In the concern for justice, spectrality may allow an opening up – or a remaining open to – the uncanny and the unknown but somehow strangely familiar, not to determine what is what – to know – but to be demanded of and to respond.

Notes

1   Louise Fradenburg and Carla Freccero, eds., *Premodern Sexualities* (New York: Routledge, 1996): vii–xxiv. This essay represents a more condensed and revised version of chapter 5 of my *Queer/Early/Modern* (Durham, NC: Duke University Press, 2005).

2   Ibid., xvii.

3   Ibid., xxi.

4   Jonathan Goldberg, "The History that Will Be," in Fradenburg and Freccero, *Premodern Sexualities*, 3–21.

5   Ibid., 4.

6   See Judith Butler, *Precarious Life: The Powers of Mourning and Violence* (London and New York: Verso, 2004).

7   Lee Edelman, *No Future: Queer Theory and the Death Drive* (Durham, NC: Duke University Press, 2004).

8   See Madhavi Menon, "Spurning Teleology in Venus and Adonis," *GLQ: A Journal of Lesbian and Gay Studies* 11:4 (Fall 2005): 491–519, for a critique of heteronormative teleologies through a reading of a text that articulates an alternative to the normative telos of reproductive futurity. See also Jonathan Goldberg and Madhavi Menon, "Queering History," *PMLA* 120:5 (2005): 1608–17. José Esteban Muñoz, among others, adopts the notion of melancholia as de-pathologized "structure of feeling" in part to counter the positivity of futurity's heteronormative injunctions; see *Disidentifications: Queers of Color and the Performance of Politics* (Minneapolis, MN: University of Minnesota Press, 1999): esp. p. 74. Slavoj Žižek has written a diagnostic critique of the recent critical privileging of melancholia over mourning in Freud's theory of loss as an error of political correctness. He asserts that "The melancholic link to the lost ethnic Object allows us to claim that we remain faithful to our ethnic roots while fully participating in the global capitalist game"; see "Melancholy and the Act," *Critical Inquiry* 26 (Summer 2000): 657–81, at p. 659.

9   Jacques Derrida, *Specters of Marx: The State of the Debt, the Work of Mourning, and the New International*, trans. Peggy Kamuf (New York: Routledge, 1994); Avery Gordon, *Ghostly Matters: Haunting and the Sociological Imagination* (Minneapolis, MN: University of Minnesota Press, 1997); and Wendy Brown, *Politics out of History* (Princeton, NJ: Princeton University Press, 2001).

10 For an extended discussion of the ways spectrality differs from liberal individualist notions of "private" haunting, including those who would read Hamlet as a narrative of social disruption in favor of individual "alienation" from the social, see my extended readings of Brown, Derrida, and Gordon in *Queer/ Early/ Modern* (Durham, NC: Duke University Press, 2005), chapter 5.

11 Gordon, *Ghostly Matters*, 183.

12 "No justice ... seems possible or thinkable without the principle of some responsibility, beyond all living present, within that which disjoins the living present, before the ghosts of those who are not yet born or who are already dead, be they victims of wars, political or other kinds of violence, nationalist, racist, colonialist, sexist, or other kinds of exterminations" (Derrida, *Specters of Marx*, xix).

13 Ibid., 97.

14 In *The Ego and the Id*, Freud extends the melancholic model he developed in "Mourning and Melancholia" to suggest that the ego itself is formed as the "precipitate" of all the attachments to objects loved and then lost, and to suggest that the ego sublimates its attachment to – and contains the history of – lost others, who are taken up as identifications (ego ideals, for example). He thus invokes the historicity of loss in his theory of melancholic attachments and scripts melancholic sublimation as an alternative to the melancholia/mourning binary. See Sigmund Freud, *The Ego and the Id*, trans. Joan Riviere, ed. James Strachey (New York: Norton, 1960, reprinted 1989). Loss occupies an important place in recent theorizations of historicity and activism, as this essay suggests. See also David Eng and David Kazanjian eds., *Loss: The Politics of Mourning* (Berkeley and Los Angeles, CA: University of California Press, 2003).

15 Michel de Certeau, *The Writing of History*, trans. Tom Conley (New York: Columbia University Press, 1988): 2.

16 Michel de Certeau, *Heterologies: Discourse on the Other*, trans. Brian Massumi (Minneapolis, MN: University of Minnesota Press, 1986): 8.

17 For the "trauma of historicity," see Judith Butler, "Burning Acts: Injurious Speech," in *Deconstruction Is/In America: A New Sense of the Political*, ed. Anselm Haverkamp (New York and London: New York University Press, 1995): 149–80.

18 De Certeau, *The Writing of History*, 3.

19 For debates regarding the distinction between transgender and transsexual, see Jay Prosser, *Second Skins: The Body Narratives of Transsexuality* (New York: Columbia University Press, 1998), especially chapter 1. For an overview of some of the issues and problems in trans-discussions, see Judith Halberstam, "Transgender Butch: Butch/FTM Border Wars and the Masculine Continuum," in Susan Stryker, ed., *The Transgender Issue*, special issue of *GLQ: A Journal of Lesbian and Gay Studies* 4:2 (1998): 287–310. Brandon Teena is in scare quotes because part of what is at stake in the story is the way the proper name is linked to gender; the person in question used several proper names, see C. Jacob Hale, "Consuming the Living, Dis(re)membering the Dead in the Butch/FTM Borderlands," *GLQ: A Journal of Lesbian and Gay Studies* 4:2 (1998): 311–49.

20 Brandon Teena's rape and murder occurred in December 1993; the films and much of the commentary did not occur until 1998, the same year that James Byrd and Matthew Shepard were killed.

21 My use of the term, "queer movement" follows bell hooks' argument for using the expression "feminist movement" without the definite article that defines it as one/a thing. See bell hooks, *Feminist Theory: From Margin to Center* (Boston, MA: South End Press, 1984).

22 Halberstam, "Telling Tales: Brandon Teena, Billy Tipton, and Transgender Biography," *a/b: Auto/Biography Studies* 15:1 (2000): 62–81. See also Hale, "Consuming the Living."

23 Tzvetan Todorov, for example, in *The Conquest of America: The Question*

of the Other, trans. Richard Howard (New York: Harper and Row, 1985, reprinted 1992), makes his project an explicitly ethical one: "my main interest is less a historian's than a moralist's" (4).

24 Beatriz Pastor, "Silence and Writing: The History of the Conquest," in *1492–1992: Re/Discovering Colonial Writing*, eds. René Jara and Nicholas Spadaccini, Hispanic Issues 4 (Minneapolis, MN: University of Minnesota Press, 1989, reprinted 1991): 121–63. Hayden White, *Metahistory: The Historical Imagination in Nineteenth-Century Europe* (Baltimore, MD: Johns Hopkins University Press, 1973); "Historical Text as Literary Artifact," in R. H. Canary, ed., *The Writing of History: Literary Form and Historical Understanding* (Madison, WI: University of Wisconsin Press, 1978): 41–62. For the narration of desire, see Teresa de Lauretis, *Alice Doesn't: Feminism, Semiotics, Cinema* (Bloomington, IN: Indiana University Press, 1984): 103–57.

25 Ibid., 147.

26 Ibid., 149.

27 Pastor cites Cortés' comment about "la lengua que yo tengo, que es una india de esta tierra" ("the tongue that I have, who is an Indian woman from this land" – my translation) (148); see also Hernán Cortés, *Cartas de relación* (Mexico: Porrúa, 1975): 44. Todorov cites Bernal Díaz as reporting that the nickname given to Cortes was that of Malinche; *The Conquest of America*, 101.

28 Stephen Greenblatt, *Marvelous Possessions: The Wonder of the New World* (Chicago, IL: University of Chicago Press, 1991): 11–12.

29 Ibid., 97.

30 Todorov, like Pastor, also invokes another figure of loss that is gendered: "A Mayan woman died, devoured by dogs ... I am writing this book to prevent this story and a thousand others like it from being forgotten" (246–7).

31 "The History That Will Be," 17. Goldberg is commenting on Greenblatt's "Invisible Bullets: Renaissance Authority and Its Subversion, Henry IV and Henry V," in *Political Shakespeare*, Jonathan Dollimore and Alan Sinfield (eds) (Ithaca, NY: Cornell University Press, 1985): 18–47.

32 For various accounts of the ghost dance, see, among others, Dee Brown, *Bury My Heart at Wounded Knee: An Indian History of the American West* (New York: Pocket Books, 1970, reprinted 1981); Angie Debo, *A History of the Indians of the United States* (Norman, OH: University of Oklahoma Press, 1970, reprinted 1988); and James Mooney, *The Ghost-Dance Religion and the Sioux Outbreak of 1890* (Gloriata: Rio Grande, 1973). See also Joseph Roach, *Cities of the Dead: Circum-Atlantic Performance* (New York: Columbia University Press, 1996): 202–11. Roach, however, considers the ghost dance a "rite of memory" (208), and it is unclear therefore whether he sees the dance as commemorative or performative. He also views it as an act of self-possession – and thus potentially identitarian in its aspirations – whereas in my argument and in Spivak's, the ghost dance would be rather an opening onto inhabitation by others.

33 Gayatri Chakravorty Spivak, "Ghostwriting," *diacritics* 25:2 (Summer 1995): 65–84, at p. 70.

34 Jacques Derrida, "Archive Fever: A Freudian Impression," *diacritics* 25:2 (Summer 1995): 9–63, at p. 27. See also the expanded version, *Archive Fever: A Freudian Impression*, trans. Eric Prenowitz (Chicago, IL: University of Chicago Press, 1996).

35 Derrida, "Archive Fever," 54.

36 In "Marx's Purloined Letter" (in *Ghostly Demarcations: A Symposium on Jacques Derrida's Specters of Marx*, ed. Michael Sprinker [London and New York: Verso, 1998]: 26–67), Fredric Jameson relates kinds of hybridity to the philosophical project of Derridean spectrality (44).

37 Brown, *Politics out of History*, 149–50.

38 Nicolas Abraham and Maria Torok, *The Shell and the Kernel, vol. 1*, ed. and trans. Nicholas Rand (Chicago, IL: University of Chicago Press, 1994): 172. In "Fors," the preface to Abraham and Torok's *The Wolf Man's Magic Word*, trans. Nicholas Rand (Minneapolis, MN: University of Minnesota Press, 1986), Derrida makes a distinction between the "foreigner incorporated in the crypt of the Self," as the psychic phenomenon that Abraham and Torok analyze in relation to mourning and melancholia, and the sense of haunting as a collective and historical effect (119, n. 21).

39 Brown, *Politics out of History*, 146.

40 Derrida, "Fors," xvii.

41 *The Shell and the Kernel*, 188.

42 "Historiography as hauntology is thus more than a new mode of figuring the presence of the past, the ineffable and unconquerable force of the past; it also opens the stage for battling with the past over possibilities for the future" (Brown, *Politics out of History*, 151).

43 I put the word "colonial" in quotation marks to signal the complex and ambiguous role Jean de Léry and France itself could be said to have played in relation to early modern colonialism in the New World. France did not have "colonies," strictly speaking, in Brazil, and Léry's religious mission did not explicitly include indigenous conversion.

44 Jean de Léry, *History of a Voyage to the Land of Brazil*, ed. and trans. Janet Whatley (Berkeley, CA: University of California Press, 1990).

45 Géralde Nakam, ed., *Au Lendemain de la Saint-Barthélemy, guerre civile et famine. "Histoire mémorable du siège de Sancerre" de Jean de Léry* (Paris: Editions Anthropos, 1975).

46 For the French editions, see Jean de Léry, *Histoire d'un voyage en terre de Brésil*, ed. Jean-Claude Morisot (Geneva: Droz, 1975), facsimile edition; also Jean de Léry, *Histoire d'un voyage en terre de Brésil* (1578), ed. Frank Lestringant (Paris: Le Livre de Poche, 1994).

47 Freccero, "Cannibalism, Homophobia, Women: Montaigne's 'Des Cannibales' and 'De L'Amitié,'" in *Women, 'Race,' and Writing in the Early Modern Period*, eds. Margo Hendricks and Patricia Parker (New York: Routledge,

1994): 73–83; also "Early Modern Psychoanalytics: Montaigne and the Melancholic Subject of Humanism," *Qui Parle* 11.2 (Winter 1999): 89–114.

48 Léry also discusses Sancerre in a chapter significantly enlarged in the 1599 edition of the *Histoire*, appended as chapter 15 *bis* in the Lestringant edition. The culmination of the diatribe targets France as most ferocious and extravagant in its cannibalistic excesses (571–95).

49 See chapter 18 for Léry's account of the first night he spends in a Tupi village where, during a drunken celebration, he is offered "a foot" to eat by one of the villagers. Not understanding the language, Léry fears that he will be eaten next; in the morning he learns his error through his interpreter and concludes the account thus: "When he recounted the whole business to the savages – who, rejoicing at my coming, and thinking to show me affection, had not budged from my side all night – they said that they had sensed that I had been somewhat frightened of them, for which they were very sorry. My one consolation was the hoot of laughter they sent up – for they are great jokers – at having [without meaning to] given me such a scare" (163–4).

50 For a discussion of Montaigne's use of the metaphor of cannibalism to describe the French wars of religion, see David Quint, "A Reconsideration of Montaigne's 'Des Cannibales,'" *Modern Language Quarterly* 51:4 (1990): 459–89. Many sixteenth-century Protestants also made the comparison between New World cannibalism and Catholicism; see Peter Hulme, *Colonial Encounters: Europe and the Native Caribbean 1492–1797* (London and NY: Routledge, 1986, reprinted 1992); Maggie Kilgour, *From Communion to Cannibalism: An Anatomy of Metaphors of Incorporation* (Princeton, NJ: Princeton University Press, 1990); and Francis Barker, Peter Hulme, and Margaret Iversen, eds., *Cannibalism and the Colonial World* (Cambridge: Cambridge University Press, 1998).

51 Léry, *History of a Voyage to the Land of Brasil*, 120.

52 Jonathan Goldberg, in *Sodometries: Renaissance Texts, Modern Sexualities* (Stanford, CA: Stanford University Press, 1992), observes a similar phenomenon of the destabilization of both racial and gender identity in relation to Cabeza de Vaca (213–14).

53 See also Freccero, "Heteroerotic Homoeroticism: Jean de Léry and the 'New World'" in *The Rhetoric of the Other: Lesbian and Gay Strategies of Resistance in French and Francophone Contexts.* eds. Martine Antle and Dominique Fisher (New Orleans, LA: University Press of the South, 2002): 101–14.

54 Léry, *History of a Voyage to the Land of Brasil*, 134.

55 Ibid., 144.

56 Ibid., 67.

57 Ibid., 197–8.

58 In *Sodometries*, Goldberg analyzes the "preposterous logic" of the conquerors that impels their attack on the indigenous Americans through accusations of sodomy. He suggests that what marks the indigenous man as sodomitical is in part the spectacle of a pierced and porous male body.

"As the Spaniards see them," he writes, "these violated bodies register a resistance to Spanish violation" (196), and thus offer to some extent "an uncanny mirror of Spanish desires, above all, the desire to violate" (197). Goldberg pauses on a moment of disavowed identification that might be said to precede the absolute opposition between "them" and "us" and argues that the annihilative energy aimed at the sodomitical male body tries to efface this identification. It is, thus, this threatening moment of identification that triggers both the extravagant accusation and the savage acts that are justified by and follow upon it. The term "displaced abjection" is Jonathan Dollimore's; see *Sexual Dissidence: Augustine to Wilde, Freud to Foucault* (Oxford: Clarendon Press, 1991, reprinted 1992).

59 Roland Greene, *Unrequited Conquests: Love and Empire in the Colonial Americas* (Chicago, IL: University of Chicago Press, 1999).

60 Greenblatt writes about this episode at length in *Marvelous Possessions*, 14–19. See also de Certeau, *The Writing of History*, 209–43.

61 Ibid., 141.

62 Ibid., 141–4.

63 Sigmund Freud, "Some Psychological Consequences of the Anatomical Distinction between the Sexes" (1925), in *Sexuality and the Psychology of Love*, ed. Philip Rieff (New York: Macmillan, 1963; reprinted Collier, 1993): 173–83. See also Freud's discussion of the case of the Wolf Man, "From the History of An Infantile Neurosis" (1918), in *Three Case Histories*, ed. Philip Rieff (New York: Macmillan, 1963, reprinted Collier, 1993): 161–280.

64 Bersani, *Homos* (Cambridge, MA: Harvard University Press, 1995): "I call *jouissance* 'self-shattering' in that it disrupts the ego's coherence and dissolves its boundaries ... self-shattering is intrinsic to the homo-ness in homosexuality. Homo-ness is an anti-identitarian identity" (101). In an argument that spans several essays and books, Bersani outlines his theory of the willingness to relinquish control for the sake of pleasure that he regards as one of the potentially distinctive features of male homoerotic subjectivity. See "Is the Rectum a Grave?" *October* 43 (1987): 197–222; *Homos*; and "Sociality and Sexuality," *Critical Inquiry* 26:4 (Summer 2000): 641–56. In *Homos*, Bersani also re-interprets the Wolf Man's dream to demonstrate Freud's investment in castration anxiety at the expense of what Bersani reads as "one genealogy of gay love" (112).

65 Bersani, *Homos*, 99.

66 Kaja Silverman, in *Male Subjectivity at the Margins* (New York and London: Routledge, 1992), defines the conjunction of masculine-masculine identification and desire in the primal scene as "sodomitical identification" (173).

67 Anne Anlin Cheng, *The Melancholy of Race: Psychoanalysis, Assimilation, and Hidden Grief* (New York: Oxford University Press, 2001): xi.

68 Ibid., 14.

69 Ibid.; see also Trevor Hope, "Melancholic Modernity: The Hom(m)osexual

Symptom and the Homosocial Corpse," *differences: A Journal of Feminist Cultural Studies* 6:2–3 (1994): 174–98.

70   Cheng, *The Melancholy of Race*, 200, n. 22.

71   Psychoanalytic theories of subjectivity argue that subjectivity – the experience of thinking feeling embodiment – is, first and foremost, intersubjectivity, a relation to an other. In "Mourning and Melancholia," the essay that most vividly evokes the figure of "the other inside," Freud describes melancholia – the continued and ambivalent attachment to an object perceived to be lost – as a kind of incorporation, the taking in of the lost object so that it persists within the self and is preserved. See "Mourning and Melancholia (1917)," in *General Psychological Theory: Papers on Metapsychology*, trans. Joan Riviere, ed. Philip Rieff (New York: Simon and Schuster, 1991, reprinted 1997): 164–79. Later, in *The Ego and the Id*, Freud extends the melancholic model to suggest that the ego itself is the "precipitate" of all the attachments to objects loved and then lost, and that it sublimates its attachment to – and contains the history of – lost others, who are then taken up as identifications. Further, for Freud the ego is always a bodily ego; there is a relay of sensation, felt to emanate both from without and from within. This relay maps a kind of psychic body that usually corresponds to the surface of the skin. See *The Ego and the Id*, esp. p. 20.

72   Cheng, *The Melancholy of Race*, 29.

73   Judith Butler, *The Psychic Life of Power: Theories in Subjection* (Stanford, CA: Stanford University Press, 1997): esp. p. 181.

74   Ibid., 171.

75   The use of the word "fictional" here derives from Lacan; see ibid., 196.

76   Ibid., 196.

77   Cheng, *The Melancholy of Race*, 29.

78   Muñoz, in *Disidentifications: Queers of Color and the Performance of Politics*, discusses the complexities of identification for minoritarian subjects.

79   The expression, "salvage ethnography," is from James Clifford, "On Ethnographic Allegory," in *Writing Culture: The Poetics and Politics of Ethnography*, eds. James Clifford and George E. Marcus (Berkeley, CA: University of California Press, 1986): 98–121, at p. 112.

80   Jody Greene, "New Historicism and Its New World Discoveries," *The Yale Journal of Criticism* 4:2 (1991): 163–98, at p. 193, n. 32. For the account of this court proceeding, see M. D'Avezac, ed., *Campagne du navire l'Espoir de Honfleur, 1503–1505: Relation authentique du voyage du Capitaine de Gonneville ès nouvelles terres des Indes* (Paris: Challamel, 1869): 12–13. D'Avezac tells the story to explain how Gonneville's travel narrative came to be discovered and subsequently published. It was submitted as evidence in the court case by the descendants of Gonneville and Essomeric, the Tupi boy who traveled from Brazil to France with Gonneville.

81   Greene, "New Historicism and Its New World Discoveries," 176; D'Avezac, *Campagne du navire l'Espoir de Honfleur*, 101–2.

82 D'Avezac, ed., *Campagne du navire l'Espoir de Honfleur*, 12 (my translation).

83 Brown, *Politics out of History*, 140.

84 Derrida, *Specters of Marx*, 97.

85 I am not suggesting that Léry was anywhere near where Essomeric and his family were to be found, but rather that his musing that he seems to have them before his eyes "even now" (20 years after the fact, and in France) does not describe a far-fetched impossibility.

86 Derrida, *Specters of Marx*, 175.

21

Introduction: Raising the Dead

Sharon Patricia Holland

Anything dead coming back to life hurts.

AMY DENVER, IN *BELOVED*

In the late fall of 1987 Toni Morrison published *Beloved*. It is a story not about slavery, Morrison asserts, but about an infanticide that refuses to remain in the past and imbues the present with a haunting so profound that memory is jolted from its moorings in forgetfulness. Much of the critical response to the novel involved the representation of Beloved, her rising from the dead and the plausibility of such a resurrection.[1] Reviewers and critics were enthralled by Morrison's "ghost story" but also were sometimes skeptical of her reversal of a trenchant Western paradigm: that those who die do not come back, that the line between "us" and "them" is finite and, therefore, never porous.[2] As Marilyn Atlas's review of the novel's critics found, "*Beloved* simply makes some reviewers extremely uncomfortable, forcing confrontations not usually required by literature. These critics do not want to reflect upon these particular human issues and they are unable to see how exploring these new details from new perspectives permanently expands the tradition of American literature, and allows valuable characters into the world, ones they can see no value in examining."[3] Moreover, critics claimed that Morrison's *Beloved* was an amazing departure for American literature.[4] What seemed like a departure for most, however, was actually a phenomenon deeply rooted in the novel of the Americas. Following an American tradition stemming from Alejo Carpentier's and Arturo Uslar Pietri's intellectual work in the late 1940s expounding on what has now erroneously been coined "magical realism," Morrison uses the "fantastic" to comment on the experience of "being" marginal to the historical record of a culture that refuses to recognize difference as its own creation.[5] Why did Morrison's *Beloved* seem so different from Hawthorne's or Poe's ghosts? Although *Beloved* appeared to follow a familiar trajectory in American literature, it also offered something more jolting to the American psyche—a BLACK FEMALE "ghost" with agency to possess and destroy both house and sense of home. Although *Beloved* is a work of fiction, its ghostly presence merged with America's worst nightmares of both past and self. To imagine Beloved, readers and even critics had to work with what was available to them—this imaginary palate was already imbued with its own little shop of horrors—people had to work around what Fanon has called "negrophobia." Morrison's *Beloved* confronted readers with a persistent sense of simultaneity until all fact, all knowledge about slavery, about history begins to exist as in-between, and therefore fragile, as "all the inhabitants ... at 124 Bluestone Road are suspended between the past and the present, the living and the dead."[6] More disturbing than the presence of a BLACK FEMALE ghost was the idea that the novel's structure so closely mirrored that of the American imaginary and its subconscious machinations to disremember a shared past.

On 7 October 1988, within less than a year of *Beloved*'s publication, Morrison delivered the 1988 Tanner Lecture on Human Value at the University of Michigan. Her lecture, "Unspeakable Things Unspoken: The Afro-American Presence in American Literature," called for a return to the meaning of the "Africanist" presence in American life and letters. Attempting to intervene in the ongoing "canon debates" that raged during the mid-1980s,[7] Morrison proclaimed that "Afro-American culture exists and though it its clear (and becoming clearer) how it has *responded* to Western culture, the instances where and means by which it has *shaped* Western culture are poorly recognized and understood."[8] Morrison, then well on her way to a Nobel Prize with the publication of *Beloved*, sought to use both African American "literature and the awareness of its culture" to "resuscitate the study of literature in the United States." Early in the essay Morrison employs the word *miscegenation* to describe contemporary fears about the canon's revision, indicating that "canon defense is national defense. Canon debate, whatever the terrain, nature and range ... is the clash of cultures" (8). Ultimately, Morrison signals the need for a "reinterpretation of the American canon, the founding nineteenth-century works,"[9] where "the impact of Afro-American presence on modernity becomes clear and is no longer a well-kept secret" (11).

Returning to Michael Ragin's 1983 study, *Subversive Genealogy: The Politics and Art of Herman Melville*, which argues that ideas like American freedom were just as important to Melville as the nation's struggle with and abolition of slavery, Morrison called on academics to recast the net—to extend Ragin's critical matrix even further. It was time for us to rethink the existing canon's grand metaphors—like self-reliance, home, and destiny—to include the presence of and what some would call the "problem" presented by African Americans moving toward becoming subjects *in* rather than subjects *of* an America in the making. What Morrison revised was the notion that black culture was as invisible to the dominant culture as were most of the nation's black subjects. More than any canonical debate, Morrison's ideas in the fall of 1988 changed the direction and energy of scholarship in both African American studies and American literary studies. This shift and subsequent connection between two "literatures" is still being contested and renunciated in departments across the country, where debates about African American studies occur as if such a moment of confluence—where the study of African American literature and culture *becomes* the rubric for the study of American literature—never took place.[10] For those in my cohort at graduate school, Morrison's directive read like a Bible, and we set about the task of making good on our promise to change the profession, to recast the connection between African American literature and culture and canonical literatures as imbricated rather than segregated.

Somewhere between *Beloved* and "Unspeakable Things Unspoken" the seeds of "Raising the Dead" germinated. In 1988 I began to take Morrison's notion of "resuscitation" literally, and returning to "Unspeakable," I read: "We can agree, I think, that invisible things are not necessarily 'not-there'; that a void may be empty, but is not a vacuum. In addition, certain absences are so stressed, so ornate, so planned, they call attention to themselves; arrest us with intentionality and purpose, like neighborhoods that are defined by the population held away from them" (11). The connection between *Beloved* and "Unspeakable Things Unspoken" lay in a seemingly inarticulate but populated place. Raising the dead became a figurative enterprise, as well as an intellectual and therefore concrete endeavor. The task was both to hear the dead speak in fiction and to discover in culture and its intellectual property opportunities for not only uncovering silences but also transforming inarticulate places into conversational territories. I was convinced that Morrison's use of the word *miscegenation* obliterated the segregation of peoples and bodies inherent in the belief that between the living and the dead exists a finite line. Perhaps the more interesting place of inquiry was on the other side of that finite line; perhaps once in this populated place the line would no longer represent a demarcation but a suturing, a connection in the flesh. Ultimately, Morrison called for critics to transgress boundaries, to undertake a type of travel that necessitated another kind of understanding: that retrieving both literatures and imaginary subjects from a space that is simultaneously "spiteful," "loud," and "quiet" is necessary and dangerous work.

In *Shamanism, Colonialism, and the Wild Man*, anthropologist Michael Taussig argues that "the space of death is important in the creation of meaning and consciousness, nowhere more so than in societies where torture is endemic and where the culture of terror flourishes. We may think of the space of death as a threshold that allows for illumination as well as extinction."[11] Although some would argue that the United States is now "a kinder, gentler nation," we cannot escape the raw fact that our boundary is filled with the blood from five hundred years of slavery, removal, and conquest and that our border is a constant space of death and terror. We have chosen to relegate these experiences to the calmer reaches of our national subconscious, and most Americans would tell a far different story about the founding of our fair republic and contemporary life among its peoples. We have left the horror to our imaginations. Discovering who resides in the nation's imaginary "space of death" and why we strive to keep such subjects there is the central inquiry of this book.

The writers, artists, and critics discussed here have discovered that the line is not so finite. They are raising the dead, allowing them to speak, and providing them with the agency of physical bodies in order to tell the story of a death-in-life. Perhaps the most revolutionary intervention into conversations at the margins of race, gender, and sexuality is to let the dead—those already denied a sustainable subjectivity—speak from the place that is familiar to them. Moreover, speaking from the site of familiarity, from the place reserved for the dead, disturbs the static categories of black/white, oppressor/oppressed, creating a plethora of tensions *within* and *without* existing cultures. Embracing the subjectivity of death allows marginalized peoples to speak about the unspoken—to name the places *within* and *without* their cultural milieu where, like Beloved, they have slipped between the cracks of language.

Like many cultural studies projects—with no comprehensive study of the dead in the literature discussed here available—this one searches in sometimes unusual territories for its fuel. The book embraces both popular and academic texts in the search for keys to understanding what is at stake when the critic ventures into conversations at the boundaries between worlds, what Taussig has described as the "space of death."

Even with the somewhat liberal, if not outrageous, borrowing from different (re)sources, the book grounds itself at several junctures. It relies heavily on recent developments in the fields of African American, Native American, feminist, and queer studies, and it seeks to intersect these discourses whenever possible. When theorists think of margins, they often conjure competing forces, a dominance without and a subordination within. Radical and cultural feminists have posited that the margin is not an area of danger or suspicion but of power. Seizing that power, however, always necessitates transferring dominance from the center to the outside. I am concerned with moving away from a model of the margin as an adequate vehicle for a critique of how "oppressed peoples" experience hegemonic power. In other words, I am occupied with two things here: first, placing this marginal space on the inside, not as an entity from without but as an entity from within—a nation within, if you will—and, second, formulating an understanding and theory of marginalized existence that more adequately describes the devastating experience of being "outside" this culture. It is quite often the nation within that disrupts our ordinary sense of who we are, that has the power to dismantle blackness and nativeness, hereness and thereness. With conversations at the boundary between the dead and the living in constant interplay, the book proceeds to map the imaginative environment where authors and sometimes critics attend to the vicissitudinous "space of death." This book does not promise a reading of death that always focuses on "the dead"; instead, it offers discontinuous readings of death—as a cultural and national phenomenon or discourse, as a figurative silencing or process of erasure, and as an embodied entity or subject capable of transgression. At the outset I should also note one thing that this book does *not* do: it does not indulge in a comprehensive look at gendered bodies. It is my understanding from the literature that death, its consort—the dead—and our irrational fear of its bleeding edges create a genderless space. Our worst nightmare is a truly shared space, which might be our only successful attempt at a "healthy" integration.

The book comprises two parts. The first, "Imaginative Places, White Spaces: If Only the Dead Could Speak," centers on an oppositional approach to the study of the literature. This first section wrestles with dichotomies—blackness/whiteness, life/death, and past/present—in an effort to demonstrate the mistake of relying on finite categories in any critical or creative venture. The three chapters of part 1 therefore contain more traditional textual explications, where the tendency is to look outward rather than inward for the tension between communities.

Chapter 1, "Death and the Nation's Subjects," has two sections and seeks to interrogate the place of black subjectivity in the popular imagination, ultimately contending that black subjects are not just marginal to the culture. Their presence in society is, like the subject of death, almost unspeakable, so black subjects share the space the dead inhabit. Arguing that residual subject relations from slavery are still active in the American imaginary, I begin with an examination of the Hughes brothers' film *Menace II Society*, using it as a model of the interface of the nation, the dead, and blackness. Because of its emphasis on nation formation, Benedict Anderson's *Imagined Communities* serves as a theoretical palimpsest for this opening discussion. I then trace briefly attitudes toward death (and the dying) in a medical context, with attention to works by Michel Foucault and Philippe Ariès.

The second chapter, "Bakulu Discourse: Bodies Made 'Flesh' in Toni Morrison's *Beloved*," turns to the work of Hortense Spillers to create a template for discussing Morrison's novel, placing Morrison in conversation with other black female critics about the relative status of black women, about their invisibility and their haunting of the American imagination.

I treat my observation of Beloved as both spirit and orisha (deity) as an entryway into a discussion about the always already "dead" position of African Americans in the United States. Believing that blackness is truly a category one cannot transcend *and* noticing that black women under the law of slavery never arrived at the status of "mother" (according to Spillers), and therefore never achieved the category of "woman," I then ask, how might a return from the dead, from silence, be viewed as a tragic empowerment for black women?

Chapter 3, "Telling the Story of Genocide in Leslie Marmon Silko's Almanac of the Dead," takes this query even further. I perform a reading of Silko's text based on both the shortcomings and the value of theories of the grotesque. Although many critics have called Silko's novel a postmodern text, it lacks the cynicism directed at the category of the "dead" that most postmodern texts exhibit. In Silko's complex and often unnerving portrait of the Americas, the dead drive the narrative and can both facilitate and hinder the best efforts of the living. Silko is ever aware not only of the presence of the dead but also of their location. She is concerned with the forces of death that bring about genocide and those that transform disaster into possibility. For Silko death is a double-edged sword.

The ending of this chapter provides a segue into the second part of the manuscript, "Dead Bodies, Queer Subjects," which focuses on the invisibility of black gay and lesbian subjects in relationship to *internal* communities rather than in opposition to *external* hegemonies like whiteness. Whether the "home" community is the "family" of African American literature or the progressive left, the same kind of silencing experienced in external communities can occur for queer subjects seeking to connect with and simultaneously challenge familiar spaces.

Chapter 4, "(Pro)Creating Imaginative Spaces and Other Queer Acts: Randell Kenan's *A Visitation of Spirits* and Its Revival of James Baldwin's Absent Black Gay Man in *Giovanni's Room*," situates two novels by black gay men in the context of critical endeavors to name *black* gay presence within African American literary discourse. What distinguishes this chapter from the preceding ones is its almost exclusive focus on one particular field's construction of an image, a home, and a canon. I envision Kenan's novel as a gentle rewriting of Baldwin's work. Whereas Baldwin's characters are white and "exiled" in Europe, Kenan's protagonist is a black gay youth—a relation in a southern Baptist family. Kenan brings the exiled Baldwin home on several levels, placing queerness and blackness in direct confrontation with one another. I read the hallucinations of Kenan's Horace and the paranoia of Baldwin's David as manifestations of discomfort with gay presence in the African American imagination. Moreover, the attention to ghosts/ghosting in each text points toward the particular subject position of black gay men in the pantheon of American literature. Relegated to the space of the dead, they occupy our imaginative terrain on a persistently marginal level, and they are a danger to themselves and to others.

Chapter 5, "'From This Moment Forth, We Are Black Lesbians': Querying Feminism and Killing the Self in Consolidated's *Business of Punishment*," critiques the lyrics of a trash/hip hop band to access the translation of feminist principles in the realm of the popular. Claiming both a feminist and radical identity, Consolidated (an all-white, male band) embodies the complicated politics of maneuvering between identities. Listening to Consolidated's music requires the attending critic to adjust the distances between speaking/nonspeaking and black/white subjectivities. Group members consistently take on the identities of the people they sing about, becoming women in the sex industry, people who are HIV positive, and, finally, black lesbians. My central query is whether their "becoming" black lesbians represents a killing of a white self or an exercise of white authority through an ability to reinscribe black lesbian subjects in the familiar space of the "unspeakable." Consolidated puts whiteness in the spotlight by forcing us to ask: Can whiteness be transcended? And if so, what are the politics of, or at least, how can we theorize about, this particular killing of the self? In their attempt to respond to the HIV / AIDS crisis, the far right, and neofascism, they explore the feminist concept "the personal is political" and attempt to divest themselves of their own white supremacy. This chapter investigates not only the subtle way that Consolidated kills the self as they flirt with the space of silence and death but also the cultural context that allows for such transgression.

In the final chapter, I attempt to place several critics in conversation with one another, demonstrating that critical maneuvers are often figuratively placed at the boundary between the living and the dead. The discussion here is informed by feminist theories of the margin, coupled with theories of liminality and pollution from the discourse of anthropology. The process of naming and unnaming a literary trajectory is almost always an act of silencing someone or something, and critical interventions come dangerously close to the liminal space of death—and the silence that accompanies it. I also move into popular new age and spiritual forms of discourse to demonstrate that there might be useful material in the new subjectivities that the dead bring to life.[12] This last chapter represents the myriad places in critical, historical, and anthropological texts where discussions of death and the dead have taken place. It is hoped that these parting words move the project's future in several directions.

Many of the novelists discussed here have talked about being literally haunted by the characters who inhabit the worlds they bring to the printed page. *Raising the Dead* attempts to fill the space left by critical inattention to manifestations of the dead. I hope that cultural critics will find new fodder for explorations into imaginative landscapes—seen and unseen. When I began this work in 1989, I had no idea that Joseph Roach was engaged in similar explorations. It was only on completion of the manuscript that a colleague suggested I read his book, *Cities of the Dead*. I would like to acknowledge Roach as a fellow traveler in the endeavor to harass the border between the living and the dead. Roach identifies the "new way of handling (and thinking about) the dead" as a vestige of modernity.[13] This work perceives the difference between the living and the dead as the beginning binary, as the model for creating other dichotomous systems such as black and white or straight and queer. *Raising the Dead* is a new lens for citing alternative ways of seeing and, perhaps, believing.

Notes

1   Several reviewers and literary critics remarked on the presence of Beloved. Reviewing the novel for the *New York Review of Books*, Thomas Edwards stated that "Morrison provides us no cozy corner from which to smile skeptically at the thrills we're enjoying. If you believe in Beloved at all you must accept the ghost in the same way you accept the other, solidly realistic figures in the story" (5 November 1987, 18). On the other hand, Paul Gray of *Time* concluded that "The flesh-and-blood presence of Beloved roils the novel's intense, realistic surface. . . . In the end, the implausibilies in *Beloved* may matter less than the fact that Sethe believes them" (21 September 1987, 75). And commenting for the *Nation*, Rosellen Brown observed that "We feel about this vulnerable girl [Beloved], at least at first, as we might about a benign extraterrestrial" (17 October 1987, 418). Critics also made much of Beloved's "ghostly" presence. See Bernard Bell, "*Beloved*: A Womanist Neo-Slave Narrative; or Multivocal Rememberances of Things Past," *African American Review* 26, no. 1 (spring 1992): 7–15; Emily Miller Budick, "Absence, Loss and the Space of History in Toni Morrison's *Beloved*," *Arizona Quarterly* 48, no. 2 (summer 1992): 117–38; Stephanie A. Demetrakopoulos, "Maternal Bonds as Devourers of Women's Individuation in Toni Morrison's *Beloved*," *African American Review* 26, no. 1 (winter 1992): 51–60; Gayle Greene, "Feminist Fiction and the Uses of Memory," *Signs* 16, no. 2 (winter 1991): 290–321; Deborah Horvitz, "Nameless Ghosts: Possession and Dispossession in *Beloved*," *Studies in American Fiction* 17, no. 2 (fall 1989): 157–67; Sally Keenan, "Four Hundred Years of Silence: Myth, History and Motherhood in Toni Morrison's *Beloved*," in *Recasting the World: Writing after Colonialism*, ed. Jonathan White (Baltimore: Johns Hopkins University Press, 1993), 45–81; Linda Krumholz, "The Ghosts of Slavery: Historical Recovery in Toni Morrison's *Beloved*," *African American Review* 26, no. 3 (fall 1992): 395–408; David Lawrence, "Fleshly Ghosts and Ghostly Flesh: The Word and the Body in *Beloved*," *Studies in American Fiction* 19, no. 2 (fall 1991): 189–201; Andrew Levy, "Telling Beloved," *Texas Studies in Literature and Language* 33, no. 1 (spring 1991): 114–23; Lorraine Liscio, "*Beloved*'s Narrative: Writing in Mother's Milk," *Tulsa Studies in Women's Literature* 11, no. 1 (spring 1992): 31–46; Philip Page,

"Circularity in Toni Morrison's *Beloved*," *African American Review* 26, no. 1 (spring 1992): 31–40; Barbara Hill Rigby, "'A Story to Pass On': Ghosts and the Significance of History in Toni Morisson's *Beloved*," in *Haunting the House of Fiction*, ed. Lynette Carpenter and Wendy K. Kolmar (Knoxville: University of Tennessee Press, 1991), 229–235; Ashraf, H. A. Rushdy, "Daughters Signifyin(g) History: The Example of Toni Morrison's *Beloved*," *American Literature* 64, no. 3 (September 1992): 567–97; Maggie Sale, "Call and Response as Critical Method: African American Oral Traditions and *Beloved*," *African American Review* 26 no. 1 (winter 1992): 41–50; Carol E. Schmudde, "The Haunting of 124," *African American Review* 26, no. 3 (fall 1992): 409–16; Deborah Ayer Sitter, "The Making of a Man: Dialogic Meaning in *Beloved*," *African American Review* 26, no. 1 (spring 1992): 17–30; Jacqueline Trace, "Dark Goddesses: Black Feminist Theology in Morrison's *Beloved*," *Obsidian II: Black Literature in Review* 6, no. 3 (winter 1991): 14–30; and Molly Abel Travis, "*Beloved* and *Middle Passage*: Race, Narrative and the Critic's Essentialism," *Narrative* 2, no. 3 (October 1994): 179–200.

2 See especially Jonathan Yardley's review of Toni Morrison's *Beloved*. Yardley comments: "These relationships are convincing enough as devices for thematic exposition, but rather less so as genuine human connections" (*Washington Post Book World*, 6 September 1987, 3). See also Margaret Atwood, "Haunted by Their Nightmares," *New York Times Book Review*, 13 September 1987; Connie Casey, "Pain is the Stuff of Toni Morrison's Novels," *Chicago Tribune*, 27 October 1987; Stanley Crouch, "Aunt Medea," *New Republic*, 19 October 1987; Marsha Darling, "Ties that Bind," *Women's Review of Books* 5, no. 6 (March 1988): 4–5; Helen Dudar, "Toni Morrison: Finally Just a Writer," *Wall Street Journal*, 30 September 1987; Michiko Kakutani, review of *Beloved*, Toni Morrison, *New York Times*, 2 September 1987; Elizabeth Kastor. "Toni Morrison's *Beloved* Country," *Washington Post*, 5 October 1987; John Leonard, review of *Beloved*, by Toni Morrison, *Los Angeles Times*, 30 August 1987; Elizabeth Mehren, "A Haunting Death Inspires *Beloved*," *Los Angeles Times*, 14 October 1987; Mervyn Rothstein, "Toni Morrison, In Her New Novel, Defends Women," *New York Times*, 26 August 1987; Nicholas Shakespeare, review of *Beloved*, by Toni Morrison, *London Times*, 15 October 1987; and Judith Thurman, "A House Divided," *New Yorker*, 2 November 1987.

3 Marilyn Judith Atlas, "Toni Morrison's *Beloved* and the Reviewers," *Midwestern Miscellany* 18 (1990): 51.

4 Reviewing *Beloved*, Rosellen Brown proclaimed that Beloved's "astonishing presence is unlike that of any character in American fiction" (*Nation*, 18 October, 1987, 418).

5 For a more in-depth discussion of Carpentier's and Pietri's influence on the American novel, see Jose David Saldivar's *The Dialectic of Our America: Genealogy, Cultural Critique, and Literary History* (Durham: Duke University Press, 1991): 90–6.

6 Sally Keenan, "'Four Hundred Years of Silence,'" *Recasting the World*, 47.

7   Even in contemporary reviews of *Beloved*, the canon debate often influenced critics' reactions to the novel. John Leonard concludes his review of *Beloved* for the *Los Angeles Times*: "*Beloved* belongs on the highest shelf of American literature, even if half a dozen canonized white boys have to be elbowed off" (12).

8   Toni Morrison, "Unspeakable Things Unspoken: The Afro-American Presence in American Literature," *Michigan Quarterly Review* 28, no. 1 (winter 1989): 3 (italics mine).

9   Morrison is less careful in her later publication, *Playing in the Dark*, to confine her examination of black influence on U.S. literatures to the nineteenth century. In *Playing* she tends to obscure the contribution of other peoples to a growing national literature.

10 I am thinking of the creation of whiteness studies, and the reexamination of nineteenth-century literature and its icons in the context of black agency. Eric Lott's *Love and Theft: Blackface Minstrelsy and the American Working Class* (New York: Oxford University Press, 1993) is representative of this kind of influence.

11 Michal Taussig, *Shamanism, Colonialism, and the Wild Man: A Study in Terror and Healing* (Chicago: University of Chicago Press, 1987), 4.

12 I have talked about the appropriation of American Indian cultural traditions in my earlier work. See "Humanity Is Not a Luxury: Some Thoughts on a Recent Passing," in *Tilting the Tower: Lesbians Teaching Queer Subjects*, ed. Linda Garber (New York: Routledge, 1994), 168–76.

13 Joseph Roach, *Cities of the Dead: Circum-Atlantic Performance* (New York: Columbia University Press, 1996), 52.

22

from Indian Ghosts and American Subjects

Renée L. Bergland

For more than three hundred years, American literature has been haunted by ghostly Indians. In the seventeenth century, Puritan writings described Native Americans as demonic manifestations of an internalized psychic struggle. Ever since, spectral Indians have continued to return to American letters. During the Enlightenment, European American writings invoked Indians as symbols of internal darkness and irrationality. Later, American citizens began to write histories and historical romances that were structured around representations of Indians as vanishing Americans and even as actual ghosts. Many of America's most prominent authors seized on the figure of the spectral Native as central to their attempts to develop a uniquely American national literature: during the first half of the nineteenth century, Charles Brockden Brown, Washington Irving, James Fenimore Cooper, Lydia Maria Child, Edgar Allan Poe, Nathaniel Hawthorne, and Herman Melville all wrote works that relied upon the discourse of the Indian ghost. The various meanings and structures of the discourse of spectralization are complicated and ambiguous. This book begins, however, with a phenomenon that is clear and consistent: When European Americans speak of Native Americans, they always use the language of ghostliness. They call Indians demons, apparitions, shapes, specters, phantoms, or ghosts. They insist that Indians are able to appear and disappear suddenly and mysteriously, and also that they are ultimately doomed to vanish. Most often, they describe Indians as absent or dead.

Native American writers and orators have often resorted to the language of ghostliness themselves, in their negotiations with European colonialism and United States hegemony. One of the earliest examples comes from 1620, the first year that the English spent at Plymouth. During their first few months there, the English plundered a number of Native American graves. Finally, the sachem of Passonagessit protested the violation of his mother's grave by making a speech in which he said that his mother's ghost had come to him as he slept, imploring him to fight "against this thievish people, who have newly intruded in our land." If he fails to drive the English away, she had threatened, "I shall not rest quiet."[1]

As it turned out, that ghost did not rest quiet. American writers invoked her again and again in the next two hundred years. The first publication of the sachem's speech was in William Hubbard's 1677 history, *A Narrative of the Troubles with the Indians in New England*. Subsequently, Washington Irving quoted the speech at length in "Traits of Indian Character," which was published in *Analectic Magazine* in 1813, and in *The Sketchbook of Sir Geoffrey Crayon* a few years later. In turn, the Pequot writer William Apess incorporated Irving's piece into his appendix to *A Son of the Forest*, which was published in 1829. Neither Irving nor Apess significantly altered Hubbard's words, but there is no way of knowing how Hubbard's written, English text relates to the sachem's actual speech, which he probably made in his own language. Hubbard, Irving, and even Apess at once acknowledge and appropriate the sachem's words. In *The Poetics of Imperialism*, Eric Cheyfitz describes this as the process of colonial translation. The sachem's words, like his mother's bones, were "wholly alienated" from him.[2]

Because the sachem's speech was translated into a colonialist text and then repeatedly invoked for different purposes, it serves as a striking example of the divergent meanings that Indian ghosts may have in different contexts. The Native American sachem who originally made the speech intended it as an assertion of political resistance to European domination. Fifty years later a Puritan minister rewrote the speech in English, in order to demonize Indians and justify war against them. More than a century passed before Irving used the speech as part of his attempt to inform Americans that Native Americans had not disappeared from New England, and to demand better treatment for Native people, both in New England and in Georgia, where federal removal policies were beginning to be enacted. But since his ghostwriters were a Puritan minister and a nascent literary nationalist, the effectiveness of his protest was limited. In later writings, Apess would eschew the words of others and refuse to call on Native American specters.

As the history of the revisions of the sachem of Passonagessit's speech shows us, the figure of the Indian ghost is profoundly ambiguous. Although the ghosts register dissatisfaction with the European conquest of the Americas, the fact that they are ghosts testifies to the success of that conquest. Starting in the 1600s, countless North American Indians were dispossessed of their homes, fields, languages, tribal cultures, families, and even their lives. But when we focus on Indian ghosts, we risk forgetting the fact that many survived. Most Native communities in the United States remained viable and even New England Indians retained title to some of their lands, as they do today. By focusing almost exclusively on those who perished, early American writing enacted a literary Indian removal that reinforced and at times even helped to construct the political Indian Removal. American poems, fictional narratives, histories, philosophical and scientific essays, and public documents denied Indian survival as they mourned (or occasionally celebrated) Indian dispossession and extinction.

Motifs of dispossession recur again and again in early American descriptions of Native Americans. Indians are figures of melancholy and loss, homelessness and death. European Americans' elegies for their Native cohabitants are equally unrepresentative of the brutality of Indian Removal and the tenacity of Indian survival, but in spite (or perhaps because) of their untruth, they have surprising power. Europeans take possession of Native American lands, to be sure, but at the same time, Native Americans take supernatural possession of their dispossessors. It is hard to know who counts as the victor in such a contest. Although Native Americans can be said to have taken possession of the American imagination, this means that they have vanished into the minds of those who have dispossessed them.

A number of critical studies have focused on the myth of the vanishing Indian. Brian Dippie's *The Vanishing American* provides a useful analysis of nineteenth-century tropes, while Walter Benn Michaels's *Our America* makes an important argument about the modernist's reliance on the trope of the vanishing American. Additionally, Klaus Lubbers offers an extensive catalogue of ethnic stereotypes of Native Americans in *Born for the Shade*. Lucy Maddox's *Removals* places the shadowy, vanishing figure of the Native American into a discursive context, and argues that Indians were removed from the literature of the early nineteenth century just as they were being physically removed from American territory.[3] Building on Maddox, this book examines one specific discursive technique of Indian removal—describing them as insubstantial, disembodied, and finally spectral beings.

In the following pages, I will concentrate almost exclusively on the figure of the Indian ghost. For the most part, as I have said, Indian ghosts are deployed for nationalist purposes. I will, however, offer many examples of works that try to resist narratives of nationalization, and to use Native American ghosts as figures of such resistance. Quite a few of these counter-nationalist uses of the ghost metaphor have been authored by Native Americans. But the closer we look, the clearer it becomes that when Native Americans figured themselves as ghostly, they gained rhetorical power at the cost of relinquishing everything else. When Native people called on their forebears as vengeful ghosts, they acknowledged that the battles had already been lost, that the voices that inspired them were among the dead.

It makes sense that such Native appeals to the dead would be preserved and emphasized within American nationalist literature.

Triumphant narratives of American nationalism swallow narratives of resistance over and over again. This may mean that resistance is futile, but it does not necessarily mean that it is unimportant. What interests me is the fact that nationalist narratives continue to be hungry for resistant ones; that the very texts that inscribe United States nationalism require the presence of ghostly Natives, even though these presences question the overarching narrative that invokes them.

Why must America write itself as haunted?

Although spectral Indians appear with startling frequency in the literary works of the United States, no one has yet investigated the implications of this figuration. This book intends to provide a theoretical context for and a thorough study of literary representations of Native Americans as ghosts. I will argue that the interior logic of the modern nation requires that citizens be haunted, and that American nationalism is sustained by writings that conjure forth spectral Native Americans. In American letters, and in the American imagination, Native American ghosts function both as representations of national guilt and as triumphant agents of Americanization.

First and foremost, the ghosting of Indians is a technique of removal. By writing about Indians as ghosts, white writers effectively remove them from American lands, and place them, instead, within the American Imagination. One result of the internalization of Indians is that the American individuals who "contain" Indians thereby constitute themselves as representative Americans, and even as representative Americas. Many scholars have written about Americans' obsession with mapping their own mental landscapes as American. In *American Incarnation*, Myra Jehlen asserts that, "by assuming the American land (not the landscape but the land), the American man acquired an individualist substance."[4] She is arguing here that Americans think of themselves as Americas. This sort of internalization of national space is one of the central characteristics of nationalism. Etienne Balibar traces the idea back to the eighteenth-century political theorist Johan Fichte, who explained that, for a nation to establish itself, "'the external frontiers of the state' have to become the 'internal frontiers' of the citizen." When the nation is internalized this way, Balibar argues, the individual becomes something new: an entity he describes as *homo nationalis*.[5] As Indians are made to vanish into the psychic spaces of America's citizens, the psychic space within each citizen is itself transformed into American territory, and each citizen comes to contain an America, to be *homo Americanus*.

The discursive removal of Indians from American physical territory and the Americanization of the imaginative territory into which Indians are removed are two good explanations for the ideological power of the figure of the Indian ghost. The image also draws ideological power from the sense of *fait accompli* (the Indians are already gone), and from reinforcing the intractable otherness of Indians (they are so other that they are otherworldly).

On the other hand, the ghosting of Indians presents us with a host of doubts about America and American ideology. The entire dynamic of ghosts and hauntings, as we understand it today, is a dynamic of unsuccessful repression. Ghosts are the things that we try to bury, but that refuse to stay buried. They are our fears and our horrors, disembodied, but made inescapable by their very bodilessness. Ghostly Indians present us with the possibility of vanishing ourselves, being swallowed up into another's discourse, another's imagination. When ghostly Indian figures haunt the white American imagination, they serve as constant reminders of the fragility of national identity (as Priscilla Wald argues in "Terms of Assimilation"). Further, ghosts are impossible to control or to evade. When Indians are understood as ghosts, they are also understood as powerful figures beyond American control.

Accordingly, the practice of representing Indians as ghosts works both to establish American nationhood and to call it into question. By discursively emptying physical territory of Indians and by removing those Indians into white imaginative spaces, spectralization claims the physical landscape as American territory and simultaneously transforms the interior landscape into American territory. The horrors of this discursive practice are clear: the Indians who are transformed into ghosts cannot be buried or evaded, and the specter of their forced disappearance haunts the American nation and the American imagination. But in spite of the national guilt and horror that Indian ghosts signify and inspire, American writing invokes them obsessively. In order to explain this, we must think carefully about the nature of ghosts, words, and nations.

The argument that I am making links ghosts with words (and hence with history and memory) and also with nationalism (and by analogy with race, class, and gender). Like ghosts, words are disembodied presences. Therefore, in some senses, talking about ghosts in literature is as hopeless (and perhaps also as important) as talking about words in literature, or ideas in literature. All stories are ghost stories, if only because each word, each random collection of syllables, is intended to conjure forth an unreal reality, to embody and to animate a strange imaginary entity that is both there and not there, actual and not actual. Writers try to capture ghosts out of their own experience, snaring them in print so as to release them into readers' minds, or better yet, into the dark corners of readers' bedrooms. This is not exactly a metaphor. Instead, it is the language we use to talk about consciousness, memory, and imagination. We use the concept of the ghost so frequently in our descriptions of thought itself, that it is hard to know what a ghost might be, how a ghost might be different from an idea or a memory.

Although all types of language and thought are linked to the spectral, our contemporary understandings of ghostliness usually proceed from the assumption that ghosts are bad things. We often use the concept of the ghost to denote ideas or memories that frighten us. Ghosts are thought to arise from repression and guilt. However, this tacitly Freudian understanding of the ghost does not adequately explain our own uses of the figure of the ghost. Nor does it explain the ghosts of past eras. In the pages that follow, I will argue that ghosts are sometimes as much desired as they are feared.

Further, I will argue that ghosts are often public figures. Although we imagine ghosts as internal, mental entities, we also write and speak of them as entities that haunt many of us simultaneously. Like ideas, ghosts can be communicated. As we share fears and pleasures, so we share ghosts. These shared ghosts are often figures of history and power. In *Specters of Marx*, Jacques Derrida asserts that, "Haunting belongs to the structure of every hegemony."[6] He is saying here that hegemonic power—the dominance of one group over another—is structured around ghosts.

Derrida is right. The hierarchies of power that structure our lives are themselves ghostly. Power is unreal, insubstantial, somehow imaginary. At the same time, of course, it is undeniably real. When we describe hegemonies as socially constructed, we mean that they are built on history, memory, fear, and desire. They are made from the same things that ghosts are made from. Because the politics of the national, the racial, the classed, and the gendered are the politics of memory and false memory, they are also, necessarily, the politics of spectrality.

Blithely postnational, we don't believe in nations anymore. Rather, most of us think of nations as Benedict Anderson has described them for us, as "imagined political communities."[7] This doesn't change the fact that nations have power over us. At the close of the twentieth century, nations and nationalisms look as imaginary as, and even more powerful than, ghosts. In the first chapter of *Imagined Communities*, Anderson explains "ghostly national imaginings" in terms of the "modern darkness" that accompanied Enlightenment secularism.[8] He argues that nationalism was a secular faith that developed in response to Enlightenment denials of faith. But in many respects, denying the primacy of faith amounted to declaring the primacy of doubt. Though we usually think of the late eighteenth century as the apex of the Enlightenment, it may be equally appropriate to describe it as a very dark time. In *Nation and Narration*, Homi Bhabha emphasizes the darkness, explaining Anderson's "sense of 'nationness'" as constructed in opposition to "the *unheimlich* (or uncanny) terror of the space or race of the Other."[9] I agree with Bhabha's contention that modern nations were constructed in opposition to the particular darkness of a ghostly Other conceived within an imaginary geography of race, class, and gender.

Like nation, race, class, and gender can all be understood as ghostly entities. They may be imaginary, but they structure our lives nonetheless.

Therefore, I want to argue here for the importance of the unreal. Rather than dismissing hegemonic power as "imagined," I want to explore the works of imagination that build and inform it. If hegemonic powers are, in fact, ghostly powers, then all of us must believe in ghosts, just as we believe in stories, in histories, or in memories.

In this model, ghosts are tied to language, and therefore they are tied to stories. They are also tied to political powers, and therefore they are tied to history. These things have been brought together before. In 1848, Karl Marx began *The Communist Manifesto* with the declaration, "A specter is haunting Europe."[10] This European ghost, the specter of Communism, is clearly a political entity, a disembodied figure that represents political and economic power relations within a context of emergent nationalism. In the mid-nineteenth century, Europe *was* haunted by the specter of Communism, a ghost who probably appeared in the form of an oppressed worker. At the same time, America was haunted by the ghosts of African American slaves and Indians as well as disenfranchised women and struggling workers. The people who were described and imagined as ghosts were those whose existence challenged developing structures of political and economic power. Ghostliness was closely related to oppression and to the hope of denying or repressing the memory of that oppression.

This model of ghosts as public, political entities may seem to conflict with prevailing assumptions that ghosts are private and internal. But any dichotomy between the political sphere and the mental sphere is a false one, because our understanding of the political has shifted just as our notion of the ghostly has. Modern consciousness internalizes the political just as it internalizes the spectral.

Consider, first, the internalization of ghosts. Before the Enlightenment changed our definitions, ghosts were seen as external phenomena. They may have denounced the guilty, but they were not simply manifestations of guilt. They were not mental or perceptual beings at all. Rather, they existed outside our heads, independently. When rationalists denied the reality of ghosts, they denied their independence, their exteriority.

By the early nineteenth century, most people believed (as they do now) that ghosts were internal phenomena, creatures that haunted private, mental spaces rather than actually walking abroad through public, physical space. In *The Female Thermometer*, Terry Castle explains that during the eighteenth century, belief in ghosts changed, rather than disappeared. "Ghosts were not exorcized—only internalized and reinterpreted as hallucinatory thoughts." Banishing ghosts from the world, into the mind, she argues, is not a simple rationalist victory. Instead, "by relocating the world of ghosts in the closed space of the imagination, one ended up by supernaturalizing the mind itself."[11] Once they are all in our heads, it is difficult to distinguish between ghosts, demons, and dream figures. In fact, as Castle asserts, it becomes difficult to distinguish between perception and possession, hard to know if any perceived other is in fact other, or is merely a projection of the haunted self. The epistemological uncertainty that Castle evokes is characteristic of many of the works I will examine, and her work will help emphasize the point that haunted imaginations and haunted works of imagination are not merely haunted by metaphors. Within this discourse of haunted rationalism, the ghosts within the mind are more powerful and more significant than many of the beings that walk abroad. Ghosts may have become subjective experiences, but they have not stopped being historical or political, and they certainly have not become insignificant.

Ghosts and ghost belief have always been linked to law and justice. In *Religion and the Decline of Magic*, Keith Thomas explains that before the Enlightenment ghosts were almost always reported as appearing in order to "denounce some specific injustice," or "to alter some particular relationship between living people." The most common apparitions at this time, Thomas tells us, signified murder, the disturbance of gravesites, or the distribution of property against the wills of the deceased.[12]

Murder, disturbed graves, and unlawful distribution of property—these are not private issues. To this, I would add that pre-Enlightenment ghosts often protest unlawful transfers of political power. Think of Shakespeare's ghosts in *Hamlet, Macbeth, Richard III*, and *Julius Caesar*. They decry their own murders to be sure, but they also decry the usurpation of sovereignty—stolen kingdoms.

Of course, all of these issues of public justice give significant clues to the representation of Native people as ghosts. The history of European relations with Native Americans is a history of murders, looted graves, illegal land transfers, and disruptions of sovereignty. Among these, land ownership may be the source of the nation's deepest guilt. Ownership itself—that is to say property—is a concept that haunts the American national mythos, repressed and erased in the Declaration of Independence in a manner that both denies and emphasizes its centrality to the republic. In the Declaration, Jefferson alluded to Locke, who had written of the fundamental rights of life, liberty, and property. But he changed the words to the more palatable formulation that we all know so well: life, liberty, and the pursuit of happiness. This erasure of the troublesome concept of property speaks volumes about the vexed relation that the United States has to its own territory. It also gestures toward one of the most basic reasons that American nationalism must be predicated on haunted grounds: the land is haunted because it is stolen.

Keith Thomas argues that belief in ghosts diminished because people moved away from their parents' graves and from their parents' houses, and abandoned their parents' beliefs and traditions. Castle argues that ghosts were merely relocated, that is, internalized. I suggest that ghost belief changed, fundamentally. Family ghosts became less important, while communal ghosts grew more significant. "Enlightened" people began to speak less about the ghosts of their ancestors and more about the specters that haunted their imagined national communities. In Europe, the ghost of Communism. In America, ghosts of slaves and Native Americans.

This shift in the character of our communal ghosts points up the connection between ghosts and nations, or, more particularly, between nationalism and hauntedness. It also points toward a related connection between nationalism and consciousness. At the same time that people began to internalize spectral entities, they began to internalize political entities. The internalization of the political is usually explained in terms of the concept of subjectivity.

Subjectivity, in the modern philosophical sense, is a product of the Enlightenment. In an essay called "Subjection and Subjectivation," Etienne Balibar defines subjectivity as "the essence of humanity, of being (a) human, which should be present both in the universality of the species and in the singularity of the individual, both as a reality and as a norm or a possibility."[13] According to Balibar, Immanuel Kant invented the subject in 1781 in the pages of *Critique of Pure Reason*. It is important that subjectivity can be located in a specific historical moment, and especially important that this moment is the second to last decade of the eighteenth century, at the height of the Enlightenment, between the American and the French revolutions. Balibar argues that the philosophical revolution started by the invention of subjectivity was intimately related to these political revolutions. When people began to define themselves as subjects, they embraced both their own individuality and their status as representatives of all humanity. At this specific historical moment, each subject internalized both the human collective and the transcendant laws that govern the human collective. As subjects, individuals see themselves both as the ones who know the law, and also as the ones who are accountable to the law. Therefore, Balibar explains, each subject "performs his own subjection." The great political freedom of the late eighteenth century is the freedom for each subject to rule over him or herself; that is to say, to internalize his or her own subjection. Balibar characterizes this as "a new degree of interiorization, or, if you like, repression."[14]

Balibar bases much of his argument on works by Michel Foucault, who described the modern subject as both "subject to someone else by control and dependence and tied to his own identity by conscience or self-knowledge." In *The Imaginary Puritan*, Nancy Armstrong and Leonard Tennenhouse point out that the "two meanings of the word subject" work together to place "rational man in a position of cultural authority."[15] Balibar's emphasis on interiorization makes it clear that this cultural authority is, primarily, authority over the self. The enlightened subject, then, is a self that rules itself. Further, it is a self that must constantly deny its own submissive subjectivity in order to assert its authoritative subjectivity. In Balibar's construct, subjectivity itself *requires* the denial or repression of subjection.

If modern subjectivity cannot be constructed without repression, then you cannot be fully conscious unless you are haunted. You cannot claim to be a citizen-subject without claiming to deny, repress, bury, and be haunted by the specter of your own subjection. That ghost is the proof that you have attained subjectivity, at least as the discourses of the eighteenth century define it.

Following Armstrong and Tennenhouse's lead, we must locate the subjective moment spatially, as well as temporally. The geography of subjectivity that I am describing here is clearly connected to the geographies of Europe and America; it is, therefore, a colonialist geography. But since its temporal location is the American separation from Europe at the close of the Revolutionary War, modern subjectivity must be understood as an internalization of the colonial relation. As they establish self-rule, modern subjects colonize themselves, and they also repress the knowledge of their own subjection to internal colonization.

The repression of subjection lies at the heart of *The National Uncanny*. This idea is fundamentally Freudian, and although many of Sigmund Freud's writings have played a part in its formation, I can best outline it by referring to two of his earlier works: *Totem and Taboo* (1913), and "The Uncanny" (1919). *Totem and Taboo* is subtitled "*Some Points of Agreement between the Mental Lives of Savages and Neurotics.*" In this book, Freud describes the "collective mind"[16] of modern, civilized humanity as built on repressed Oedipal desires. There is no question that this model relies on racial and political hierarchies: offhandedly, but with chilling clarity, Freud equates civilization with "the social system of the white peoples of Europe and America" (14). The book assumes that civilized white Americans and Europeans go through childhood phases that are analogous to the adulthoods of savage races. Neurotic—that is, mentally ill—white people, he explains, are those who have insufficiently repressed their links to their own childhood desires, and also, analogously, to the desires and actions of savages (132). (The main difference between savage adults and white neurotics, Freud tells us, is that "it may be safely assumed" [161] that savage adults actually enact their Oedipal desires.) *Totem and Taboo* implies that the mental health of white Americans and Europeans depends upon the successful repression of their intimate relations to other, less inhibited races, as much as on the repression of their own childhoods.

From repressions, Freud teaches us, come ghosts. In "The Uncanny," Freud returns, as he so often does, to the link between childhood and savagery. In German, the word that Freud uses is *unheimlich*, which can also be translated as un-home-y, or, more gracefully, as unsettling. The sense of unsettledness in the word *unheimlich* is important, because it evokes the colonialist paradigm that opposes civilization to the dark and mysterious world of the irrational and savage. Quite literally, the uncanny is the unsettled, the not-yet-colonized, the unsuccessfully colonized, or the decolonized.

Freud defines the uncanny as a feeling of "dread and creeping horror," and asserts that "an uncanny experience occurs either when infantile complexes which have been repressed are once more revived by some impression, or when primitive beliefs which have been surmounted seem to be confirmed" (249, 248). This is a dual model of haunting—we are haunted either by the revival of what we have repressed or by the (seeming) confirmation of what we have surmounted. The equal weight given to the repressed and the surmounted makes it clear that willful forgetting must be understood by metaphors of both burial and conquest. Civilized subjectivity, as Freud describes it, is predicated upon repressing childhood and surmounting primitivism. To avoid horror, civilized people must avoid being reminded of what has been buried, and, just as important, what has been conquered. But of course, they cannot. It is not even certain that Freud thinks they should.

By 1930, when he wrote *Civilization and Its Discontents*, Freud would verge on an anti-civilization stance, arguing that "civilization behaves toward sexuality as a people or stratum of its population does which has subjected another one to its exploitation" (57). Clearly, this is a model of the internalization of subjection and exploitation, and the discontented tenor of *Civilization and Its Discontents* suggests that internalizing exploitations might be problematic. Although it would be absurd to cast Freud as a crusader for social justice here, it is also a mistake to cast him as a villainous supporter of the racist/imperialist status quo. His descriptions of white, middle-class American and European men's minds are insightful and accurate. He equates their sanity with their ability to maintain their places at the top of an internalized racial, gendered, geographic, and economic hierarchy. But he seems ambivalent at best about mental health, and much fonder of the neurotics, who cannot get over their discomfort with repressions or oppressions.

There is indeed something quite ominous about the implied prescription for both the neuroses and the ghosts that afflict civilized individuals—which would be to do a better job of repression and internal colonization. But in fact, the cure that Freud offers is precisely the opposite of the cure that his work seems to imply. For the mentally ill, he recommends the talking cure, rather than silence—memory, rather than the continuing effort to forget. For the haunted, he makes no prescriptions at all; to the contrary, the long, bizarre catalogue of the weird that he presents to his readers in "The Uncanny" betrays a willingness more to entertain ghosts and horrors than to exorcize them. Freud strikes me as playfully perverse in this respect. Though he describes sanity as successful repression, he encourages his patients to remember. Likewise, he invokes the spooky, the spectral, and the weird with a pleasure that goes far beyond tolerance. If one message comes across clearly in "The Uncanny," it is that Freud really likes E. T. A. Hoffmann's story "The Sandman." Likewise, *Totem and Taboo* leaves us with the overwhelming impression that Freud enjoys the primitive. Throughout, Freud's works show us the pleasures of contemplating the forbidden, the sick, and the scary.

I am reading Freud against the grain here, first by emphasizing his reliance on colonialist hierarchies of race and power, and second by emphasizing pleasure over pathology when I focus on Freud's enjoyment of the disruptions of these hierarchies. My first reading is far more conventional than my second; many scholars have implicated Freud in hierarchies of race, class, and gender, while relatively few have given more weight to pleasure than to pathology.

One scholar who does share my fascination with the compelling pleasures of hauntedness is Julia Kristeva. In *Powers of Horror*, Kristeva draws on the Freudian arguments that I have outlined here to develop the concept of abjection. She defines the abject as that which is expelled from the self, and yet not discarded, but buried deep within the self. It is "something rejected from which one does not part."[17] Kristeva's model of abjection is quite similar to Balibar's model of subjection. In both models, the self is built upon repressed and conquered selves. The repressed and the conquered—the abject and the subjected—are the foundations of modern subjectivity.

According to these definitions of subjectivity, it may seem that only bourgeois white men who live in Europe or America can be subjects. But that is not how it works. Although the subjectivity that I am describing here is certainly universalizing, it is not exactly exclusive. Instead, modern subjectivity compels everyone to internalize the same hierarchies. Thus, women think as men, people of color think as white people, workers think as owners, and everyone maps themselves as metropolitan. At the same time, all of us, including middle-class white men who live in European or American cities, contain (and are haunted by and afraid of) the female, the dark skinned, the alienated worker, and the geographically marginal.

In recent years, scholars from feminists to postcolonialists have examined the ambivalences attendant upon subjectivity in relation to these various groups.[18] But, surprisingly, few of them really focus on the American subject. In fact, few address nationalized subjectivity in general. The being whom Balibar would style *homo nationalis* is mostly absent from their pages. Instead, most contemporary analyses of fractured subjectivity tend to give us *homo imperiens*—the imperial subject instead of the national subject. Of course, empires and nations are closely related, but there are important historical and geographical differences between imperialism and nationalism. Nationalism, as Anderson most notably tells us, is both an Enlightenment phenomenon and an American phenomenon.

American subjectivity is different from European. It is explicitly national rather than imperial. This is not to say that America is not imperialist, but rather to assert that ideas of nation are more central to Americans than those of empire. Of course, nations and empires are intimately related to each other through the discourse of colonialism. American nationalist subjectivity internalizes the colonial relation, but, since the nation was established by denying the validity of colonialism, American subjects repress this interiorized colonialism far more deeply than do Europeans. I think this is why contemporary scholars are so puzzled about how to use postcolonial approaches to study America. On the one hand, America is and always has been a colony of Europe; on the other, America is an imperial power. But both of these facts are somehow shameful in an American context, since American nationhood is built on the denial of colonialism.

The relation between the United States and the various Native American nations within the territory of the United States gives us one of the most concrete examples of this conflicted and internalized colonialism. In 1831, Supreme Court Justice John Marshall described tribal governments as "domestic dependent nations" in his decision in Cherokee Nation v. Georgia. Though no one seems to be certain of what this means, Marshall's ambiguous definition is still upheld. One thing is certain: by calling Indian tribes domestic and dependent, Marshall's definition points to the fact that they are inside America—they are internalized nations. At the same time, by according them the status of nations, the definition grants them some kind of independence, some kind of sovereignty. Of course it's a dependent independence—whatever that may be. The paradoxical status of Native American "domestic dependent nations" points, I think, to a continuing attempt to repress the colonial structure of America, without giving it up. Native American people are legally defined as geographically interior rather than exterior. They are the colonized subjects who dwell within America's borders.

Since Americans like to think of their own minds as American territory, it makes sense that they would think of Native Americans as integral entities whose oppression must be repressed, but must not be given up. This dynamic makes American subjectivity unique and particularly interesting. In fact, critics from Leslie Fiedler to Caroll Smith-Rosenberg have argued that it makes Americans particularly insane. In *Love and Death in the American Novel* and *The Return of the Vanishing Americans*, Fiedler describes the place that Native Americans hold within the American psyche. Using a myth-critical approach he delineates an Indian archetype that is an archetype for madness. *Love and Death in the American Novel* asserts that "the final horrors are ... intimate aspects of our own minds."[19] At the close of *The Return of the Vanishing Americans*, Fiedler has located these horrors in the figure of the Native American, and called for each reader to embrace the "madness" of his or her secret and internal Indian "comrade." In the end, Fiedler tells us, "all of us seem men possessed."[20]

While Fiedler describes Americans as men in love with their own madness (which takes the shape of an archetypal Native American), Carroll Smith-Rosenberg describes Americans who try to deny their madness by defining themselves in opposition to the madness of Native Americans. In the article "Subject Female," she describes Americans as "decentered and fragmented," "subjects without cohesion," who finally refuse "the illusion of coherent subjectivity."[21] Smith-Rosenberg describes Native Americans as "negative others" whom white Americans use in the ultimately unsuccessful attempt to "solidify the American subject."[22] For her, Native Americans work as figures of irrationality against whom Americans attempt to figure themselves as rational. Americans are insane, Smith-Rosenberg argues, and their only hope of fooling themselves into thinking that they are not is to hold up for themselves imaginary Indians who represent something even more insane.

Both Fiedler's language of possession and Smith-Rosenberg's language of incoherence appeal to me, and both seem to get it partly right. But I have significant differences with both as well. Fiedler believes in an American psyche, which he attempts to analyze by means of archetypal literary criticism. In this book, I want to avoid assuming that there is an American mind that can be psychoanalyzed. Instead, I use psychoanalytic and historical approaches to analyze the ways that individuals have tried to create an American mind, and, equally important, tried to make their own minds American. This strategy aligns more with Smith-Rosenberg's approach. Like Smith-Rosenberg, I use Balibar's model of national subjectivity as an important starting point for my analysis. I also agree that Native Americans work as "negative others" as she describes them. I differ from Smith-Rosenberg, however, in my final analysis. She sees the American subject as fractured and incoherent. I see the same subject as strong and durable, cemented together by contradictory but interlocking impulses. The tensions that Smith-Rosenberg accurately delineates within the American subject seem to me to be joined in a Foucauldian sort of synthesis. American madness, if you will, is the foundation upon which an almost unassailable sanity is constructed. This Foucauldian understanding of American madness and sanity is crucial to the ideas of *The National Uncanny*.

Perhaps the most important theoretical and methodological cornerstone for *The National Uncanny* is *Constituting Americans* by Priscilla Wald. My ideas have developed through engagement with Wald's. In *Constituting Americans*, Wald uses Balibar, and also Freud's essay on "The Uncanny" to analyze the cultural "anxiety surrounding the conceptualization of personhood" in America. She argues that "the uncanny structured writers' experiences of their authorship," and that in America "authorship ...

emerges consistently as a means of exploring the internalized frontiers that constituted them as Americans."[23] Wald also points out that race is central to the formation of American subjectivity, and, in the mid-nineteenth century, was also a determining factor in American citizenship. In such a context, the very thought of American Indians or African Americans might be experienced as the uncanny confirmation of the terrifying possibilities of powerlessness (or subjection) that American citizen-authors attempt to repress.

During the nineteenth century, Wald tells us, American national discourse insisted that Native Americans were extinct, that they did not exist, or that they existed as representative of the past, rather than as contemporaries in a shared present. The same discourse denied Indians political existence. In 1831, in the same decision that framed all Native American people as members of "domestic dependent nations," the Supreme Court opined that the Cherokee People could not be heard in court because, legally, they had no American civil identity. Wald characterizes the Marshall court's decision, which was founded on, and also established legally, Indian lack of identity, as enacting a policy of "erasure."

The erasure of Native Americans was more than legal; it was cultural. One well-known example of such cultural erasure is Chief Logan's speech, which was reprinted and recited hundreds of times throughout the eighteenth and nineteenth centuries, and which ended in the plaintive question, "Who is there to mourn for Logan? Not one."[24] The speech depicted an individual on the brink of total erasure, political, cultural, and familial. White Americans' belief that, like Logan, all the Indians had "disappeared," presented them with the specter of disappearance, the possibility of being erased, unmourned, and forgotten.[25]

Wald's explanation shows us why Native American people might be terrifying, or at least uncanny, figures. It offers one rationale for describing them as ghosts. This construct also moves toward explaining the link between ghosts and nationalisms. But while Wald focuses on anxieties of authorship, *The National Uncanny* will focus more insistently on the ambivalences of Americanness. Where Fiedler describes Americans as "men possessed," and Wald describes American authors as estranged and anxious, I will describe an American subject that is obsessed.

To be obsessed, Freud tells us, is to be in the grip of an ambivalent impulse that arises equally from a wish and a counter-wish.[26] I believe that Americans are obsessed with Native Americans. What I mean is that everyone, Czech to Chickasaw, who tries to imagine himself or herself as an American subject, must internalize both the colonization of Native Americans and the American stance against colonialism. He or she must simultaneously acknowledge the American horror and celebrate the American triumph. The potencies of both the wish and counter-wish— here the desire to continue colonizing Native people and the desire to escape from colonialist regimes—create an obsessional mindset, in which American subjects continually return to the Native American figures who haunt them.

For the most part, *The National Uncanny* focuses on ghosts of Native Americans. Of course, ghostly Native Americans are allied to the ghostly African Americans, women, resident aliens, and poor people who haunted the nineteenth-century American national imagination along with them. In fact, by all accounts, America's uncanny national others in the eighteenth and early nineteenth centuries outnumbered her citizens. Raymond Williams argues that the term *civilization*, coined in 1772, is intended to describe a society in which "the central property and agency was reason."[27] On the other hand, barbarism or savagery, and the human beings who are understood to be barbaric or savage are understood to be irrational as well as uncivilized. Such an understanding refuses citizenship as well as civility to "savage" people, such as Native Americans. More important to this argument, the link between the uncivilized and the irrational pushes all of America's noncitizens into ghostliness. Not only Native Americans, but also women, poor people, foreigners, and African Americans are cast as uncivil, irrational, and even spectral.

National ghosts threaten rationalist hegemony, and hence they threaten the nation. One of the best examples of the threat posed by these composite figures is Abigail and John Adams's well-known exchange about remembering "the Ladies." Their interchange is often cited as an example of John Adams's anxieties about the "discontented tribes" that threatened American nationhood. It also illustrates the way that such anxieties could be pleasurable as well as fearsome. John Adams wrote: "As to your extraordinary Code of Laws, I cannot but laugh. We have been told that our struggle has loosened the bands of government every where. That Children and Apprentices were disobedient—that schools and Colledges were grown turbulent—that Indians slighted their Guardians and Negroes grew insolent to their Masters. But your Letter was the first intimation that another Tribe more numerous and powerfull than all the rest were grown discontented."[28]

John Adams's laugh rings hollow, while his anxiety mounts as his list lengthens. The young, the poor, the unlettered, Indians, Negroes, and ladies are threats to government. Only adult, propertied, learned, white men who are ruled by reason can be represented under John Adams's ordinary code of laws. He derides the "extraordinary" republic that Abigail Adams envisions as a dangerous fantasy, and denies her request to be remembered. But this is not the only significance of the letters. Along with the fear of being overthrown, John Adams expresses the pleasure of domination. His laugh may be anxious, but it is also flirtatious; eros is in play as well as anxiety. The tribes of discontented beings that haunt John Adams's letter to his wife may signify terror, but they signify defeated, controlled terror— which is closely allied to pleasure. John Adams's refusal to remember the ladies—his willful amnesia—and the conjoined fear and pleasure that he expresses when he writes about it fit very well within Freudian models of repression and obsession. This is the dynamic that pushes America's noncitizens into uncanniness.

The legislative and cultural domination of women by men depended on a rhetoric of irrationality and even supernaturalism. Troy Boone points out that "rationalist discourse appropriates metaphors of sexual difference in order to assign the 'proper' values to civilization by figuring them as powerful, orderly, and masculine—and to barbarism and supernatural belief by figuring them as weak, subversive, and feminine."[29] Although white women were accorded citizenship, their civil identities were precarious because of the legal conventions of coverture. Many women experienced their civil erasure as spectralizing: At the Seneca Falls Convention of 1848, the Declaration of Sentiments claimed that women were, "if married, ... civilly dead."[30]

The exclusion of women from the realms of reason and citizenship was paralleled by the exclusion of the poor. Poll taxes effectively disenfranchised the poor, while discourses that constructed women as subversive and irrational constructed poor people in the same way. One of the best examples of such a construction is *The Anarchiad*. In 1786 and 1787, the Connecticut Wits (including Timothy Dwight, David Humphreys, and John Trumbull) published a literary hoax built on an unwritten, fragmentary poem, which they said was called *The Anarchiad: A Poem on the Restoration of Chaos and Substantial Night*. The satire equated the discontented farm workers of Shay's rebellion in Massachusetts with the forces of darkness and irrationality. If the workers won, the wits prophesied, chaos and substantial night would ensue.

American citizens also saw ghastly possibilities in America's resident noncitizens. In "Alien-Nation," Jared Gardner connects the "aliens" demonized by the Alien and Sedition Acts with the Indian figures that haunt the American imagination, writing that "To be American is to be almost an Indian, almost a European, and in this dilemma lies the solution: collapsing Indian and alien together and clearing both from the land."[31] Gardner's argument is closely related to Wald's thesis about the uncanny aspects of citizenship. Aliens and Indians are repressed within American subjectivity because they represent the fearsome possibility of noncitizenship. When they return to consciousness, they are uncanny figures, made ghostly by their oppression and their repression.

Like Native Americans and women, the poor and the alien, African Americans were invisible entities that haunt the Constitution and the courts. The *Dred Scott* decision of 1857, which denied citizenship and even Constitutional personhood to Americans of African descent, worked as a judicial spectralization parallel to that of Indian Removal. African Americans also haunt American letters. Toni Morrison uses ghosts in her own fiction, and in the critical essay "Unspeakable Things Unspoken" she proposes that African Americans function as "ghosts in the machine," of nineteenth-century American letters, describing them as "active, but unsummoned presences that can distort the workings of the machine and can also *make* it work."[32]

When America denied the civil existence of the disenfranchised without denying their actual existence, it constructed them as simultaneously there and not there, and it confined them to a spectral role in American politics. They could not vote or bring lawsuits. They could not speak for themselves. In some basic senses, their presence was denied. However, these figures were never absent from nineteenth-century American political discourse. To the contrary, they haunted the American polity. Although they were silenced, disenfranchised Americans defined the political discourse of the antebellum period.[33]

Phantasmic descriptions of African Americans, women, aliens, and the poor point out the strength of the ghost metaphor and its strong association with white American men's anxiety and guilt over their complicity in American hierarchies of race, class, and gender. However, there are some significant differences between Indian ghosts and other American ghosts. As David Roediger points out, Native Americans are often taken as "a model, rather than a negative reference point" in the development of white Americanness.[34] Being haunted by Indians usually signals the positive development of white consciousness, while being haunted by the others is often merely an acknowledgment of guilt. In *Beyond Ethnicity*, Werner Sollors explains this by arguing that Native Americans served as "substitute ancestor[s]" for white Americans. Therefore, Sollors asserts, their curses were as cherished as (and much more frequent than) their blessings. Indian curses, like Indian ghosts, "were part of a presumptuous reconstruction of American kinship."[35] Etienne Balibar describes such reconstructions of kinship as "fictive ethnicities," and he argues that fictive ethnicity is indispensable to nationhood.[36] When they constructed Indians as ghosts and joyfully acquiesced to their own hauntedness, white Americans replaced their ancestral specters with American specters. In so doing, they also constructed themselves as American. Because Native American ghosts could stand in for European ancestral ghosts, they could work to Americanize anyone who wished to become an American subject. In this, they differed from the ghosts of everyone else who was oppressed or disenfranchised.

And so, I focus on Native American ghosts both because they are the most consistently spectralized Americans, and because they are a clear example of both the positive and the negative aspects of spectralization— the wish and the counterwish. For many Americans, both European and Native, Native American ghosts signify hope as well as fear. Although they threaten the American national project, they also nationalize the imagination. Guilt over the dispossession of Indians and fear of their departed spirits sometimes function as perverse sources of pleasure and pride for white Americans because they signify a successful appropriation of the American spirit. In Europe, people were haunted by their own ancestors. In America, they have the opportunity to be haunted by the ghosts of Indians.

[...]

Notes

1   William Hubbard's translation, quoted in Apess, *Son of the Forest*, 63.

2   Cheyfitz, *Poetics*, 43.

3   Dippie, *Vanishing American*; Michaels, *Our America*; Maddox, *Removals*; Lubbers, *Born for the Shade*.

4   Jehlen, *American Incarnation*, 13.

5   Balibar, *Race, Nation, Class*, 95, 93.

6   Derrida, *Specters of Marx*, 37.

7   Anderson, *Imagined Communities*, 6.

8   Ibid., 9, 11.

9   Bhabha, *Nation and Narration*, 2.

10 Marx and Engels, *The Communist Manifesto*, 203.

11 Castle, *The Female Thermometer*, 131, 161.

12 Thomas, *Decline of Magic*, 597, 602.

13 Balibar, "Subjection," 4.

14 Ibid., 10, 13.

15 Armstrong and Tennenhouse, *Imaginary Puritans*, 8. The Foucault quotation can be found there as well.

16 Freud, *Totem and Taboo*, 157. Subsequent quotations of works by Freud will be included parenthetically in the text.

17 Kristeva, *Powers of Horror*, 9.

18 Studies of women's ambivalent subjectivity include Sandra Gilbert and Susan Gubar's *The Madwoman in the Attic*, Nina Auerbach's *The Woman and the Demon*, and Luce Irigaray's *This Sex Which Is Not One*. Black subjectivity is addressed by W. E. B. Du Bois's *The Souls of Black Folk*, Frantz Fanon's *Black Skin, White Masks*, and also by a number of Homi Bhabha's essays, including "Of Mimicry and Man." Both Fanon and Bhabha offer analyses of explicitly colonial black subjectivity, while Gayatri Spivak's work presents (or at least announces its inability to present) the subjectivity of the colonized woman.
    There are also quite a few recent books that focus on the ambivalences within dominant subjectivity. I would characterize Edward Said's *Culture and Imperialism*, for instance, as a book about the minds (and cultures) of colonizers. Fredric Jameson's *Political Unconscious* is a Marxist analysis

that posits a collective mind, rather than an analysis of individual workers' fractured subjectivities. Anne McClintock's *Imperial Leather* brings together gender, race, colonial, and class analyses, but focuses more on dominant subjectivity than on the minds of women, people of color, colonial subjects, or workers.

19 Fiedler, *Love and Death*, 38.

20 Fiedler, *Vanishing Americans*, 185, 11.

21 Smith-Rosenberg, "Subject Female," 485, 504.

22 Ibid., 485.

23 Wald, *Constituting Americans*, 11, 13.

24 The speech was first published in 1775. Notably, Thomas Jefferson included it in his *Notes on the State of Virginia*, first printed in 1785. His acceptance of the speech as genuine caused some partisan controversy, and in the 1800 edition of *Notes*, he included a lengthy appendix "Relative to the Murder of Logan's Family." See Peden, *Notes on the State of Virginia*, 62–3, 226–58, 298–301.

25 Wald, *Constituting Americans*, 22–40.

26 Freud, *Totem and Taboo*, 35–6.

27 Raymond Williams, *Marxism and Literature*, 16.

28 John Adams to Abigail Adams, 14 April 1776, in Schneir, ed., *Feminism: Essential Writings*, 4. Also cited in Wald, *Constituting Americans*, 18.

29 Troy Boone, "Narrating the Apparition," 177.

30 *Declaration of Sentiments and Resolutions, Seneca Falls, 1848*, in Schneir, ed., *Feminism: Essential Writings*, 79.

31 Gardner, "Alien Nation," 453.

32 Morrison, "Unspeakable Things," 13.

33 See Berlant, *National Fantasy*, 1–18; and Wald, "Terms of Assimilation."

34 Roediger, *Wages of Whiteness*, 23.

35 Sollors, *Beyond Ethnicity*, 124, 125.

36 Balibar, *Race, Nation, Class*, 96.

Bibliography

Anderson, Benedict. *Imagined Communities: Reflections on the Origin and Spread of Nationalism.* New York: Verso, 1991.

Apess, William. *A Son of the Forest.* In *On Our Own Ground: The Complete Writings of William Apess, A Pequot*, Barry O'Connell ed.. Amherst: University of Massachusetts Press, 1992.

Armstrong, Nancy and Leonard Tennenhouse. *The Imaginary Puritan: Literature, Intellectual Labor, and the Origins of Personal Life.* Berkeley: University of California Press, 1992.

Balibar, Etienne. "Subjection and Subjectivation." In *Supposing the Subject*, edited by Joan Copjec. New York: Verso, 1994.

Balibar, Etienne and Immanuel Wallerstein. *Race, Nation, Class: Ambiguous Identities*. New York: Verso, 1991.

Berlant, Lauren. *The Anatomy of National Fantasy: Hawthorne, Utopia, and Everyday Life*. Chicago: University of Chicago Press, 1991.

Bhabha, Homi K. "Introduction: Narrating the Nation." In *Nation and Narration*, edited by Homi K. Bhabha. New York: Routledge, 1990.

Boone, Troy. "Narrating the Apparition: Glanvill, Defoe, and the Rise of Gothic Fiction." *The Eighteenth Century* 35 (1994): 173–89.

Castle, Terry. *The Female Thermometer: Eighteenth-Century Culture and the Invention of the Uncanny*. New York: Oxford University Press, 1995.

Cheyfitz, Eric. *The Poetics of Imperialism: Translation and Colonization from The Tempest to Tarzan*. New York: Oxford University Press, 1991.

Derrida, Jacques. *Specters of Marx: The State of the Debt, the Work of Mourning, and the New International*, translated by Peggy Kamuf. New York: Routledge, 1994.

Dippie, Brian. *The Vanishing American: White Attitudes and U.S. Indian Policy*. Middletown, CT: Wesleyan University Press, 1982.

Fiedler, Leslie A. *Love and Death in the American Novel*. New York: Anchor Books, 1992.

—*The Return of the Vanishing American*. New York: Stein and Day, 1968.

Freud, Sigmund. *Totem and Taboo*, trans. James Strachey. New York: W. W. Norton, 1950.

Gardner, Jared. "Alien Nation: Edgar Huntly's Savage Awakening." *American Literature* 66 (1994): 429–61.

Jefferson, Thomas. *Notes on the State of Virginia by Thomas Jefferson*, edited by William Peden. New York: Norton, 1982.

Jehlen, Myra. *American Incarnation: The Individual, the Nation, and the Continent*. Cambridge, MA: Harvard University Press, 1986.

Kristeva, Julia. *Powers of Horror: An Essay on Abjection*, translated by Leon S. Roudiez. New York: Columbia University Press, 1982.

Lubbers, Klaus. *Born for the Shade: Stereotypes of the Native American in United States Literature and the Visual Arts, 1776–1894*. Amsterdam Monographs in American Studies, no. 3. Amsterdam: Rodopi, 1994.

Maddox, Lucy. *Removals: Nineteenth-Century American Literature and the Politics of Indian Affairs*. New York: Oxford University Press, 1991.

Marx, Karl and Friedrich Engels. *The Communist Manifesto*. In *The Portable Karl Marx*, edited by Eugene Kamenka. New York: Penguin, 1983.

Michaels, Walter Benn. *Our America: Nativism, Modernism and Pluralism*. Durham, NC: Duke University Press, 1995.

Morrison, Toni. "Unspeakable Things Unspoken: The Afro-American Presence in American Literature." *Michigan Quarterly Review* 28 (Winter 1989): 1–34.

Peden, William, ed. *Notes on the State of Virginia by Thomas Jefferson*. New York: W. W. Norton, 1982.

Roediger, David R. *The Wages of Whiteness: Race and the Making of the American Working Class*. New York: Verso, 1993.

Schneir, Miriam, ed. *Feminism: Essential Writings*. New York: Vintage, 1972.

Smith-Rosenberg, Carroll. "Subject Female: Authorizing American Identity." *American Literary History* 5, no. 3 (Fall 1993): 481–511.

Sollors, Werner. *Beyond Ethnicity: Consent and Descent in American Culture.* New York: Oxford University Press, 1986.

Thomas, Keith. *Religion and the Decline of Magic.* New York: Scribners, 1971.

Wald, Priscilla. *Constituting Americans: Cultural Anxiety and Narrative Form.* Durham, NC: Duke University Press, 1995.

——"Terms of Assimilation: Legislating Subjectivity in the Emerging Nation." In *Cultures of United States Imperialism*, edited by Amy Kaplan and Donald E. Pease. Durham, NC: Duke University Press, 1993.

PART FIVE

Possessions:
Spectral Places

23

Possessions: Spectral Places / Introduction

María del Pilar Blanco and Esther Peeren

The essays in this part of *The Spectralities Reader* describe haunting's attachment to place, from homes and buildings to expansive landscapes in which specific events—often cataclysmic—have transpired. Haunting has been classically conceived as attached to a *where*, from the proverbial haunted house to the ghost town. That this propensity to situate the ghost is still very much alive today is clear from the proliferation of popular books mapping haunted sites across particular countries, cities, or regions, as well as the availability of ghost tours in virtually every major western tourist destination. The return to—or even first arrival at—a specific place can, willingly or unwillingly, result in a recollection of or encounter with past experiences and perceptions, making the concept of location immensely powerful as well as layered. Whether within the discrete space of a house with its objects and furnishings or a desolate landscape that has apparently been all but forgotten, these sites are anything but empty. As Toni Morrison has former slave Sethe insist to her daughter Denver in *Beloved*, "places are still there": "Where I was before I came here, that place is real ... if you go there and stand in the place where it was, it will happen again; it will be there for you, waiting for you."[1] Similarly, the essays included in this part remind us that places are simultaneously living and spectral, containing the experience of the actual moment as well as the many times that have already transpired and become silent—though not necessarily imperceptible—to the present.

Place, as marked out from more general *space* by people's use of it,[2] also shares an important connection to the experience of the uncanny. In the second part of Freud's 1919 essay *Das Unheimliche*, the psychoanalyst writes himself into the narrative by relating a strange experience of repetition and return that befell him during a visit to Italy:

> As I was walking, one hot summer afternoon, through the deserted streets of a provincial town in Italy which was unknown to me, I found myself in a quarter of whose character I could not long remain in doubt. Nothing but painted women were to be seen at the windows of the small houses, and I hastened to leave the narrow street at the next turning. But after having wandered about for a time without enquiring my way, I suddenly found myself back in the same street, where my presence was now beginning to excite attention. I hurried away once more, only to arrive by another *detour* at the same place yet a third time. Now, however, a feeling overcame me which I can only describe as uncanny, and I was glad enough to find myself back at the piazza I had left a short while before, without any further voyages of discovery. Other situations which have in common with my adventure an unintended recurrence of the same situation, but which differ radically from it in other respects, also result in the same feeling of helplessness and of uncanniness.[3]

Repetition of events, images, and localities is one of the recurrent motifs of the uncanny. The "helplessness" that Freud describes in this anecdote, to which so many readers can probably relate, introduces the dreamlike, and more often nightmarish, event into the experience of everyday life. As such, the uncanny feeling—the *Unheimlich*, or un-homely—propels the subject into a sense of alienation and disorientation, as the familiar is no longer so, and repetition becomes anything but comforting. In this particular episode of Freud's explication of the uncanny, this phenomenon has much to do with the notion of moving through space, of traveling through a series of recognitions and (mis)perceptions. The correlation between movement and progress is broken and the subject succumbs to a feeling of ungroundedness and spatio-temporal disjointedness. Freud's Italian adventure is a story of the disquieting paradox at play in the act of coming upon alienation in the recognizable; it is an estrangement, which, although harmless enough, can nonetheless be considered a narrative of haunting.

Places, as Michel de Certeau explains in *The Practice of Everyday Life*, are closely linked to narrative and enunciation. Every place has its own story, or even a proliferation of stories, and every spatial practice constitutes a form of re-narrating or re-writing a place, over and against the "'geometrical' or 'geographical' space of visual, panoptic, or theoretical constructions": "Walking," he writes, "affirms, suspects, tries out, transgresses, respects, etc., the trajectories it 'speaks.'"[4] The ability to re-narrate place is, however, dependent on the stories that already occupy it, as, according to de Certeau, "haunted places are the only ones people can live in."[5] Spirits or ghosts, then, signify the shared memories that render space (structured, disciplined, overseen) habitable as place.

Such forms of experiencing and traversing space not only produce a story of the present (as in Freud's experience of recurrence); they have evolved into explorations of the multiple narratives that have taken place within a specific location. The unearthing of old histories of a place can often result in the revival of past narrative stylizations of the uncanny, which have left an indelible mark on the aesthetics of haunting. In the case of contemporary London literature, for example—and as Roger Luckhurst notes in his essay contained in Part One of this *Reader*—the psychogeographic projects of such writers as Peter Ackroyd and Iain Sinclair seek to "engage in historical excavations that self-reflexively incorporate knowledge of the Gothic genre itself."[6] However, according to Luckhurst, there is a propensity to stylize the place which the observer wishes to understand in all its pastness, rather than understand it in terms of the history of disenfranchisement that it harbors. As noted before, in his critique of contemporary critical theory dealing with the re-Gothicization of London landscapes, Luckhurst argues for a reading of ghosts and haunted places that, instead of being a "generalized" (and, we could say, *generic*) "'spectral process'" (542), strives for specificity.

Spanning the disciplines of literature, architecture, geography, and cultural history, the essays gathered in this part of the *Reader* work against the generic and the general. They are explorations of the complex layers that make up the past, present, and future of a variety of spaces: buried and living cities and regions, and the landscapes that in the past have witnessed unspeakable trauma. Each in their unique ways, Anthony Vidler, Ulrich Baer, David Matless, and Giorgio Agamben theorize spectral locations according to the uncanny, trauma, folklore, and historical philosophy. Their works cross the borders of ontology and phenomenology to arrive at incisive readings of the various ways in which haunting is inscribed in our experience of interior and exterior spaces. Importantly, these authors achieve this by reminding us of the history of a location's making and unmaking, in real life and its representation.

Anthony Vidler's "Buried Alive" from his book *The Architectural Uncanny* opens this part with a history of the nineteenth century's fascination with ruins, and specifically the remains of the ancient city of Pompeii. The rise of archaeology as a discipline in the nineteenth century mirrors the development of a theory of the uncanny, despite Freud's attempts to keep them separate. What should have remained buried and undisturbed is unearthed, revealing, according to Vidler, a fascination with suspended life. He explains: "If the uncanny stems, as Freud argues, from the recurrence of a previously repressed emotional affect, transformed by repression into anxiety, then the fear of live burial" should be a compelling example of this phenomenon.[7] For Romantic tourists like Théophile Gautier, the very experience of visiting Pompeii was one of contrasts that proliferated from the confrontation between full life and sudden death: "of the banal and the extraordinary, the trivial and the momentous, the sublime and the grotesque aspects" of this ancient town that had once been domestic, full of life, and suddenly became buried alive.[8] The unearthing of Pompeii inspired an erotics of the ruin, as the combined beauty of the fragmented living body, interrupted by death, became a source of inspiration. The fascination with this buried city, Vidler argues, was based on a historical appreciation of the disastrous event, but it also gave rise to what he calls a "metahistor[y]" of the left-over fragment, which (similarly to Walter Benjamin's angel of history) carries on into the future.[9]

Ulrich Baer's "To Give Memory a Place: Contemporary Holocaust Photography and the Landscape Tradition" (from his book *Spectral Evidence*) offers a different take on the ruin, dealing with the ostensibly empty landscapes on which Nazi concentration camps once stood. In his focused analysis of two contemporary photographs by German photographer Dirk Reinartz (1947–2004) and American Mikael Levin, Baer argues that, unlike other Holocaust remembrance photographs, which are inscribed with "the oversaturated referents of ruin," these two pictures instead confront us with an almost total absence, a "disclosure of *nothing*," that forces an altogether different kind of relationship with memory and remembrance.[10] Starkly different from the immersive romanticization by tourists of the Pompeiian ruin that Vidler describes, the inspection of Reinartz's and Levin's photographs "comes closer to a state of witnessing rather than to visual analysis."[11] As Baer importantly puts it, however, to view these landscape photographs is a "belated" witnessing that urges us to ponder how the act of recollection and mourning should be performed.[12] Rather than offering us historical context or a secure perspective, they are stark reminders, in their destabilization of the distinction between inclusive place and exclusive space, of the contemporary subject's responsibility—at a distance—to the traumatic events and locations of the Holocaust.

In his "A Geography of Ghosts: The Spectral Landscapes of Mary Butts," which continues this part of the *Reader*, David Matless opens with a scrutiny of the extent to which spectrality studies today elides the discipline of geography, while nevertheless using spatial metaphors.[13] Seeking a middle ground between the generalization of the ghostly, which Luckhurst critiques in his essay, and a more stringent sense of historically specific sites of haunting, Matless offers a detailed model for reading the "ghost-in-context" in the works of English modernist writer Mary Butts (1890–1937) that integrates understandings of nation, region, and locale. Butts was a historian of the ghostly in her own right. For one, her essay "Ghosties and Ghoulies: Uses of the Supernatural in English Fiction," serialized in *The*

Bookman in 1933, offers a classification of ghosts in literature, as well as a personalized geography of southwest England in which haunting reveals a persona's magical, and even religious, relation to place. Matless moves through different works by Butts in order to reveal the often-contradictory layers of this personalized coterie with ghosts, to demonstrate how the spectral, seen through a cultural geographic lens, proves to be a "carefully constructed and contrived field of pleasures and anxieties, with a range of investigative methodologies and techniques."[14]

Closing this part, Giorgio Agamben's short essay "On the Uses and Disadvantages of Living Among Specters" from *Nudities* is a provocative meditation on the contemporary state of Venice, and Europe. As Vidler argues elsewhere in *The Architectural Uncanny*, buildings and cities, like human bodies, "may fall ill" and even die.[15] Agamben's excursus on Venice echoes Vidler's sentiment when he posits the Italian city as a cadaver, much like a dead language, whose inhabitants are clueless as to how to love it "since loving the dead is difficult."[16] Rather than seeing this city as one that is full of a quiet spectrality that the living catch unawares, Venice's spectrality is what Agamben calls "larval," or "born from not accepting its own condition, from forgetting it so as to pretend at all costs that it still has bodily weight and flesh."[17] The larval specter, he notes, has futuristic pretensions, despite its deceased condition. Agamben transposes this form of spectrality to an amplified cartography of European institutions. His is a eulogy whose retrospective logic tips forward on its axis, invoking the specter to think proleptically.

These four explorations of the spectral and uncanny are models for looking at place (and space) in its historical profundity. As we move through them, we can come to understand, if only belatedly, the places we inhabit, unearth, and visit as being replete with the past. As *arrivants* contemplating a spectral landscape, we are responsible for reading the emptiness or, conversely, the apparent fullness of the absence of the past in these spaces through the complex and often violent dialectics between past and present. While this interaction with the past of a place can become the stuff of genre and generalization, the authors we have included in this part of *The Spectralities Reader* call for a slower and more detailed contemplation of historical locations. Through their own assessments of the possibilities and impossibilities of reading the past lives of places, of living *with* or among specters, they offer us lessons on how to explain them to the future.

Notes

1   Toni Morrison, *Beloved* (New York: Plume, 1998), 35.

2   This traditional distinction between place and space is invoked in Ulrich Baer, *Spectral Evidence: The Photography of Trauma* (Cambridge, MA: The MIT Press, 2002), 73.

3   Sigmund Freud, *The Uncanny* (New York: Penguin, 2003), 144.

4   Michel de Certeau, *The Practice of Everyday Life*, trans. Steven F. Rendall (Berkeley: University of California Press, 1984), 93, 99.

5   Ibid., 108.

6   Roger Luckhurst, "The Contemporary London Gothic and the Limits of the 'Spectral Turn,'" *Textual Practice* 16, no. 3 (2002): 529.

7   Anthony Vidler, *The Architectural Uncanny: Essays in the Modern Unhomely* (Cambridge, MA: The MIT Press, 1992), 55.

8   Ibid., 48.

9   Ibid., 50.

10   Ulrich Baer, *Spectral Evidence: The Photography of Trauma* (Cambridge, MA: The MIT Press, 2005), 66, 75. Dylan Trigg provides a complementary reading of the ruin as a haunting structure oscillating between place and site, also in the context of Holocaust memory. Proposing a "phenomenological investigation of the testimonial attributes of ruins," he argues that spectrality and trauma come together in their refusal of narrative continuity: "The spectre becomes visible as the scene establishes a portal between the past and the present. The result of this opening is the sense of the ruin – in both its natural and built environment – becoming possessed by a past that cannot be reconstructed in a conventional narrative. Instead, the place of trauma vibrates with an indirect language, blocked from interpretation and displacing the certainty of self, memory and place. In the midst of this altered dreamscape, the terms 'place' and 'site' lose their comparative bearings. Whereas the term 'place' attests to the desire to orient ourselves in an environment, the resultant emergence of 'site' disrupts that desire, leading to a hybrid between the two dimensions. Between place and site, we are nonetheless in the centre of a scene that serves to gather the past through rupturing a surrounding narrative. In this way, the ruins of trauma do not redeem time and experience from annihilation and rupture, but help us to understand the structure of 'unclaimed experience' by mirroring our own attempt at giving presence to a place that refuses all evidence of presence." Dylan Trigg, "The Place of Trauma: Memory, Hauntings, and the Termporality of Ruins," *Memory Studies* 2, no. 1 (2009): 87, 99–100.

11   Baer, *Spectral Evidence*, 67.

12   Ibid., 68.

13   Matless's essay was originally published in a 2008 special issue of *Cultural Geographies* entitled "Spectro-Geographies." In their introduction, editors Jo Frances Maddern and Peter Adey discern a dual use of spectrality for

geography: "Much of geography, Thrift and Dewsbury once lamented, has seemed 'to follow the logic of the corpse; a geography interested in the broken, the static and the already passed', in a way that makes the world 'play dead'. Studies of the spectro-geographical, the hidden politics that haunts spaces in intimate and complex ways, can continue to animate silenced agencies and forgotten voices and histories, while also attending to the political aspects of those voices and histories. But at the same time, spectro-geographies may help us not to move too far in arousing the world. We should be careful not to forget the lifeless geographies of 'the broken, the static and the already passed'." Jo Frances Maddern and Peter Adey, "Editorial: Spectro-Geographies," *Cultural Geographies* 15, no. 3 (2008): 293. See also Kate Shipley Coddington, "Spectral Geographies: Haunting and Everyday State Practices in Colonial and Present-Day Alaska," *Social & Cultural Geography* 12, no. 7 (2011): 743–56.

14 David Matless, "A Geography of Ghosts: The Spectral Landscapes of Mary Butts," *Cultural Geographies* 15, no. 3 (2008): 349.

15 Vidler, *The Architectural Uncanny*, 71.

16 Giorgio Agamben, "On the Uses and Disadvantages of Living among Specters," in *Nudities* (Palo Alto, CA: Stanford University Press, 2010), 39.

17 Ibid., 40.

24

Buried Alive

Anthony Vidler

What had formerly been the city of Pompeii assumed an entirely changed appearance, but not a living one; it now appeared rather to become completely petrified in dead immobility. Yet out of it stirred a feeling that death was beginning to talk.

WILHELM JENSEN, *GRADIVA*[1]

Bound to sit by his chimney until he died, Melville's narrator was, in a very real sense, buried alive—a condition intensified by the similarity of the chimney itself to an Egyptian pyramid.[2] Here Melville was rehearsing another familiar trope of the uncanny, one that nicely intersected with the archaeological interests of the nineteenth century, and whose literary exploration followed, almost chronologically, the successive "rediscoveries" and excavations of antique sites—Egypt, Pompeii, Troy. As Freud was later to note, the uncovering of what had been long buried not only offered a ready analogy to the procedures of psychoanalysis but exactly paralleled the movements of the uncanny itself: "To some people the idea of being buried alive by mistake is the most uncanny thing of all."[3] Of all sites, that of Pompeii seemed to many writers to exhibit the conditions of unhomeliness to the most extreme degree. This was a result of its literal "buried alive" and almost complete state of preservation, but also of its peculiarly distinct character as a "domestic" city of houses and shops. The circumstances of its burial had allowed the traces of everyday life to survive with startling immediacy. The pleasures of Pompeii, in comparison to those of Rome, were, all visitors agreed, dependent on its homely nature.

Its streets, shops, and houses seemed to the traveler from the north at once intimate and private. Chateaubriand, who passed through in 1802, was struck by the contrast between "the public monuments, built at great cost in granite and marble," typical of Rome, and the "domestic dwellings," built with "the resources of simple individuals," of Pompeii: "Rome is only a vast museum, *Pompeii is living antiquity*."[4] He even dreamed of a new form of nonmonumental museum, which would leave in place the tools, furniture, statues, and manuscripts found among the ruins (and normally displaced to the museum at Portici), with the roofs and walls of the houses rebuilt as a mise-en-scène of everyday life in ancient Rome. "One would learn more about the domestic history of the Roman people, the state of Roman civilization in a few restored promenades of Pompeii, than by the reading of all the works of antiquity," he observed, proposing in this way an anticipation of the folk museums of the twentieth century: "It would only need an little brick, tile, plaster, stone, wood, carpentry, and joinery ... a talented architect would follow the local style for the restorations, models for which he would find in the landscapes painted on the very walls of the houses of Pompeii." Thus, at little cost, "the most marvelous museum in the world" might be created, "a Roman town conserved in its entirety, as if its inhabitants had just left a quarter of an hour before."[5]

Other writers, from Winckelmann to Le Corbusier, have attested to this humble, workaday quality of the ruins: the so-called Villa of Diomedes, the House of the Faun, the House of Championnet, the House of the Baker were only a few of those dwellings painstakingly described and "restored" by generations of architectural students. The sense of having intruded on a domestic scene not long abandoned was increased by the plethora of household goods uncovered by the excavations, some of which were carefully left in place for the benefit of visitors, but also by the intimate glimpses into the customs, mores, and even sexual life afforded by the wall paintings. What had been shrouded for reasons of prudery in museums was displayed as part of a complete panorama, a veritable ethnographic study, on the walls. Pierre-Adrien Pâris carefully copied the priapic bas-relief on the wall of a small shop, while the young Flaubert found it the only memorable ornament of the town.[6]

And yet, despite the evident domesticity of the ruins, they were not by any account homely. For behind the quotidian semblance there lurked a horror, equally present to view: skeletons abounded. In the soldiers' quarters, as Creuzé de Lesser noted, "the judges perished with the accused," and the remains of the prisoners were still chained to the walls. As opposed to the death of Herculaneum, which according to popular myth was slow—"the lava filled up Herculaneum, as the molten lead fills up the cavities of a mold," wrote Chateaubriand—that of Pompeii was sudden. Gérard de Nerval recreated the terrifying vision of the fiery rain of ashes, suffocating and burning those in flight; hidden until the mid-eighteenth century, this hideous destruction was revealed side by side with its less disturbing and apparently more normal context. The archaeological gaze was pitiless: "in the middle of the last century the scholars began to excavate this enormous ruin. Oh! Incredible surprise; they found a city in the volcano, houses under the ash, skeletons in the houses, furniture and pictures next to the skeletons."[7] The town was evidently no common archaeological site, its ruins bleached by the sun and exorcised of social memories: history here seemed to be suspended in the gruesome juxtaposition of these grisly remains and their apparent homely surroundings. Chateaubriand's folksy museum was, in fact, still inhabited.

This dramatic confrontation of the homely and the unhomely made Pompeii a locus for the literary and artistic uncanny for much of the nineteenth century, whether in the mystical formulations of Nerval, the popular melodramas of Bulwer Lytton, the full-blown romanticism of Théophile Gautier, of the dream narratives of Wilhelm Jensen. *L'étrange, l'inquiétant, das Unheimliche*, all found their natural place in stories that centered on the idea of history suspended, the dream come to life, the past restored in the present. Pompeii, in contrast to the conventional settings of haunting and horror, possessed a level of archaeological verisimilitude matched by historical drama that made of it the perfect vehicle, in a century obsessed by the fugitive relations between past and future, for what Gautier variously called "l'idéal rétrospectif," "la chimère rétrospectif," "le désir rétrospectif," or, in relation to Pompeii, "l'amour rétrospectif."[8] The special characteristic of this retrospective vision was its unsettling merging of past and present, its insistence on the rights of the unburied dead, its pervasive force over the fate of its subjects. In Pompeii, it seemed, history, that solid realm of explanation and material fact, was taking a kind of revenge on its inventors.

In these terms, Pompeii evidently qualified as a textbook example of the uncanny on every level, from the implicit horror of the domestic to the revelations of mysteries, religious and otherwise, that, in Schelling's view, might better have remained unrevealed. Gautier's tale "Arria Marcella" insistently contrasted the banal and the extraordinary, the trivial and the momentous, the sublime and the grotesque aspects of the town: the brilliance of the light and the transparency of the air were opposed to the somber tint of the black volcanic sand, the clouds of black dust underfoot, and the omnipresent ashes. Vesuvius itself was depicted as benign as Montmartre, an old fellow like Melville's chimney owner, quietly "smoking his pipe" in defiance of his terrifying reputation. The juxtaposition of the modern railway station and antique city; the happiness of the tourists in the street of tombs; the "banal phrases" of the guide as he recited the terrible deaths of the citizens in front of their remains: all testified to the power of the place to reproduce, quite systematically, the structures of the uncanny.[9]

On a purely aesthetic level, too, Pompeii seemed to reflect precisely the struggle identified by Schelling between the dark mysteries of the first religions and the sublime transparency of the Homeric hymns, but in reverse, as if reenacting the battle in order to retrieve the uncanny. For what the first excavations of Pompeii had revealed was a version of antiquity entirely at odds with the sublime vision of Winckelmann and his followers. The paintings, sculptures, and religious artifacts in this city of Greek foundation were far from the Neoplatonic forms of neoclassical imagination. Fauns, cupids, satyrs, priapi, centaurs, and prostitutes of every sex replaced the Apollonian grace and Laocoönian strength of Winckelmann's aesthetics. The mysteries of Isis and a host of Egyptian cults took the place of high philosophy and acropolitan rituals. Archaeology, by revealing what should have remained invisible, had irredeemably confirmed the existence of a "dark side" of classicism, thus betraying not only the high sublime but a slowly and carefully constructed world of modern mythology. Schelling, with Goethe and Schiller a true believer in the "congealed music" of classical architecture, had already noted this undermining archaeology in his ambiguous assessment of the temple sculptures of Aegina, "perfected" as much as possible by Thorvaldsen but betraying all the distortions characteristic of a presublime art. Their masklike features, he proposed, embodied a "certain character of the uncanny," the product of an older mysterious religion showing through.[10]

Perhaps the least forgivable aspect of this archaeological treason was its blatant display of classical eroticism, a world hitherto circumlocuted and circumscribed but now open to the view of tourists and the interpretation of historians. Not only did such a scandalous unmasking support a literature of dubious quality, from d'Hancerville to de Sade, but it also, as the next generation of romatics demonstrated, dangerously unsettled the apparatus of classical aesthetics. For all of the disturbing fragments found in the city, it was the erotic traces that most exercised the imaginations of those who, from Chateaubriand to Gautier, were themselves concerned to undermine the high sublime.

One of the more fascinating remains of Pompeii, described in detail by many visitors, and with relish by every guide, was a fragment of scorched earth found beneath the portico of the House of Diomedes and kept in the museum at Portici. Chateaubriand noted:

> The portico that surrounds the garden of this house is made up of square pillars, grouped in threes. Under the first portico, there is a second; there it was that the young woman whose breast is impressed in the piece of earth I saw at Portici was suffocated.[11]

This simple but lugubrious "impression" became the focus of a series of meditations, each a reflection on its predecessor, the burden of which was the strange way in which nature in its own death throes had, so to speak, become its own artist: "Death, like a sculptor, has molded its victim" (Chateaubriand). The coincidence with the story of Pygmalion and Galatea was too close to avoid, and it was somehow satisfying, if depressing, to find the classical theory of imitation thus trumped by fate. The sculptor whose creation was so lifelike that she seemed to blush at his embrace, who fell in love with and "married" his ivory statuette, was now replaced by nature, or even better, history, which had molded its own work of art from the life, turning, in a reversal that caught the romantic imagination, living beauty into dead trace. And, following the hardly subdued erotic subtext of the buried city, this trace was not simply a mummified body or skeleton but the ghost of a breast, a fragment that, in an age preoccupied with the restoration and completion of broken statues, demanded to be reconstituted, in the imagination at least.

As a fragment, this negative petrified sign of *nature morte* easily took its place among other similar fragments in literature and art that at once signaled an irretrievable past and evoked an unbearable desire for future plenitude: the Belvedere Torso, the Elgin Marbles, the Venus de Milo. But unlike these, the Pompeiian *terre cuite* in its isolated anatomical specificity represented a far more brutal cutting of the body, and thus imposed a greater interpretative effort. Its status was more that of the lost arm of the Venus de Milo than of the statue itself. Its archaeological equivalent would perhaps be the posthole of a hut or the pattern of woven cloth retained in dried mud.

The cutting of the body into significant parts, each representative of the perfect beauty of the whole, was of course a commonplace of classical aesthetics. Zeuxis after all had assembled the type of beauty by the selection and combination of the best parts of his models. It was precisely against this kind of mechanical imitation that Winckelmann and his students had fought, proposing in its stead a kind of preromantic Neoplatonism, an enthusiastic idealism. But the romantics themselves, while agreeing with Winckelmann's dislike of the copy, nevertheless invested the fragment with more than fragmentary significance. Forced to reconcile the material existence of fragments—the increasing quantity of bits and pieces from the past piled up in the basements of the new museums—with their organicist metaphysics, they preferred to take the fragment as it was an cultivate it as an object of meditation.

In Schlegel's celebrated formulation, the fragment, "like a small work of art, should be totally detached from the surrounding world and closed in on itself like a hedgehog." This closure, turning the fragment in on itself like an aphorism, on one level monumentalized it and allowed it to be framed and stabilized in the context of its historical origins. On another level, however, it released a kind of metahistorical potentiality by virtue of its incompletion, forming part of an imaginary dialogue, "a chain or a crown of fragments." In this way the fragment might become a "project," the "subjective germ of an object in becoming," a "fragment of the future." As Schlegel concluded, "numerous works of the Ancients have become fragments. Numerous works by Moderns are fragments from their birth."[12]

If the status of Chateaubriand's "piece of earth" was enhanced in these terms, it was even more so by its role as an object of impossible love, a theme given full play in Gautier's "Arria Marcella." In this story of the buried city as uncanny habitat, the "hero," Octavien, loses himself in a "profound contemplation":

> What he looked at with so much attention was a piece of coagulated black ash bearing a hollowed imprint: one might have said that it was a fragment of a mold for a statue, broken in the casting; the trained eye of the artist had easily recognized the curve of a beautiful breast and a thigh as pure in style as that of a Greek statue. It was well known, and the least of guidebooks pointed it out, that this lava, cooled around the body of a woman, had retained its charming contour.[13]

Out of such contemplation was engendered the uncanny dream of Arria Marcella's feast, where Octavien, long an admirer of statues, who had been known to cry out at the Venus de Milo, soliciting an embrace from "her marble breast," was finally brought face to face with the original of the molded copy. She, true to his desires, "surrounded his body with her beautiful statuelike arms, cold, hard, and rigid as marble." The reversal is clear and pointed directly by Gautier: the living body, impressed in its mold of earth, when revived took on the attributes of the artistic imitation. Classical aesthetics was thereby rendered dead, in favor of the life of "natural" fragments, themselves destined to be completed only by the powerless form of dreamed desire.

According to this analogy, we might also interpret the dreamlike "restoration" of the fragmented buildings of Pompeii that, in Gautier's tale, preceded Octavien's meeting with his Galatea. In this already strange night, a "nocturnal day" where the bright moonlight seemed to disguise the fragmentation of the buildings, repairing "the fossil city for some representation of a fantasy life," Octavien noted a "strange restoration" that must have been undertaken since the afternoon at great speed by an unknown architect:

> This strange restoration, made between the afternoon and the evening by an unknown architect, was very troubling to Octavien, certain of having seen the house on the same day in a sorry state of ruin. The mysterious reconstructor had worked quickly enough, because the neighboring dwellings had the same recent and new aspect.[14]

Such a dream of the past restored, like some exact copy of an architectural student's *restitution* for the Ecole des Beaux-Arts, acted, like the vision of Arria Marcella, to return history not to life but to death: "All the historians had been tricked; the eruption had not taken place." Archaeology with its precise materialism had overcome temporality at least for a moment. It would be tempting to read into Gautier's narrative an implicit attack on restorers, Beaux-Arts and medievalist alike, as they searched desperately to make contemporary historical monuments out of the remains of the past.

But where, in the too-complete visions of a literal architect, whether restorer or conservator, the aesthetic effect verged on a touristic sublime, all too often a response to something that through endless rerepresentation and reproduction had become a copy of itself—Carcassonne, the Acropolis, and of course Pompeii itself would be examples—the effect of the uncanny in Gautier's treatment was less predictable. The sublime, as defined by Kant, stemmed primarily from a feeling of inadequacy in the face of superior powers; the mental state of the uncanny, tied to the death or frustration of desire, remained both sublime and a threat to its banalization. In the version described by Gautier, it was a harbinger of a living death in the face of which the historical fate of Pompeii's inhabitants seemed almost preferable. Thus Octavien, returning to the site of his dream, finding the remains of Arria, "resting obstinately in the dust," despaired and was suspended in the same state of coldness, distance, banality as the statue he desired. In the same manner, d'Aspremont, in another tale by Gautier, "Jettatura," having courted death in a duel only to slay his opponent in the ruins of Pompeii, leaves the city like "a walking statue," finally to die by his own hand, his body never to be found.[15] Those who courted the remains of the buried alive evidently risked sharing the same fate.

In an apparently strange reversal, however, the tombs in Pompeii, city of the dead, were, unlike the catacombs of Naples and Rome, rarely the subjects of necropolitan meditations. To Octavien's companions, indeed, they were positively pleasant: "This road lined with sepulchers which, according to our modern feelings, would be a lugubrious avenue in a town ... inspired none of that cold repulsion, none of those fantastic terrors that our own lugubrious tombs make us feel." Rather the visitors experienced "a light curiosity and a joyous fullness in existence" in this pagan cemetery. Like shepherds in Arcadia, they frolicked, conscious of the fact that in these tombs "in place of a horrible cadaver" were only ashes, "the abstract idea of death" and not the object itself.[16]

Such pleasure in the face of a ritualized death contrasted with the terror felt at untimely death of the inhabitants under the eruption; it seemed to exorcise, in some way, the uncanny effect of the guide's recital of the death of Arria Marcella: "'It was here,' said the Cicerone in his nonchalant voice, the tone of which hardly matched the sense of his words 'that they found, among seventeen skeletons, that of the woman whose imprint can be seen in the Museum at Naples.'"[17] The fear stimulated by *l'amour rétrospectif* was countered by the security, almost *heimlich*, to be found in tombs "embellished by art," as Goethe had it. Ritually placed ashes were part of a human plan; naturally created, they were a terrifying catastrophe.

Freud commented on this fear of being buried alive, which he linked to other uncanny tropes common in nineteenth-century literature such as the forces of animism, witchcraft, magic, the evil eye, and especially the "*Gettatore*, that uncanny figure of Roman superstition," that had, fifty years before, also inspired Gautier (U 365–366). His long analysis of Hoffmann's tale "The Sandman" persuaded him that on one level Schelling had been correct in ascribing the feeling of the uncanny to the return of "a hidden familiar thing that has undergone repression and emerged from it." In this way, the fragment—"dismembered limbs, a severed head, a hand cut off at the wrist" (U 366)—might be related to the castration complex, and superstition itself might be traced to the return of a primitive fear, long buried but always ready to be awakened in the psyche. In this sense, Freud reinterpreted Schelling's definition in terms of a recurrence of the repressed, the uncanny as a class of morbid anxiety that comes from something "repressed which *recurs*." Thus the phenomenon of haunting:

> Many people experience the feeling [of the uncanny] in the highest degree in relation to death and dead bodies, to the return of the dead, and to spirits and ghosts.... There is scarcely any other matter ... upon which our thoughts and feelings have changed so little since the very earliest times, and in which discarded forms have been so completely preserved under a thin disguise, as of our relation to death. (U 364)

Freud, himself an amateur archaeologist, was well aware of the uncanny effects of Pompeii: he had devoted a long essay to the analysis of Wilhelm Jensen's fantasy *Gradiva*, in which a young archaeologist found the original of his model—a bas-relief of a young girl "splendid in walking"—amidst the ruins of the city.[18] Jensen's Pompeiian fantasy was indeed a reworking of Gautier, with the addition of the archaeologist's dream content. But Freud, in this analysis, strangely refused any direct reference to the uncanny, or even to the buried discoveries of archaeology, preferring to enunciate the principles of the interpretation of dreams as represented in fiction. Perhaps this in turn was his own repression, for in *The Interpretation of Dreams* itself he had fully explored the question of the *unheimlich* with reference to one of his own dreams, one that incorporated both the fear of being buried alive and the desire for a fully restorative archaeology. It was also, as he noted, "strangely enough," an account of a dream that "related to a dissection of the lower part of his own body," a kind of self-fragmentation.[19]

In this dream, which he attributed to the reading of a popular melodramatic novel by Rider Haggard, *She*, Freud found himself, following the self-dissection scene, driving in a cab through the entrance of his own apartment house, thence to make his way over an Alpine landscape, and finally to arrive at a primitive "wooden house" within which were men lying on benches along the walls. His interpretation, refusing the more obvious reference to *She* as a dramatization of the return of the repressed, a figure of woman triumphant over history on the model of Arria Marcella, turned instead to his archaeological fantasies:

> The wooden house was also, no doubt, a coffin, that is to say, the grave.... . I had already been in a grave once but it was an excavated Etruscan grave near Orvieto, a narrow chamber with two stone benches along its walls, on which the skeletons of two grown men were lying... . The dream seems to be saying: "If you must rest in a grave let it be an Etruscan one." And, by making this replacement, it transformed the gloomiest of expectations into one that was highly desirable.[20]

Much later, in *The Future of an Illusion*, Freud was more explicit on this desire for archaeological fulfillment:

> The sleeper may be seized with a presentiment of death which threatens to place him in the grave. But the dream-work knows how to select a condition that will turn even that dreaded event into a wish-fulfillment: the dreamer sees himself in an ancient Etruscan grave which he has climbed down into, happy to find his archeological interests satisfied.[21]

If the uncanny stems, as Freud argues, from the recurrence of a previously repressed emotional affect, transformed by repression into anxiety, then fear of live burial would constitute a primary example of "this class of frightening things."

> To some people the idea of being buried alive by mistake is the most uncanny thing of all, and yet psychoanalysis has taught us that this terrifying fantasy is only a transformation of another fantasy which had originally nothing terrifying about it at all, but was qualified by a certain lasciviousness—the fantasy, I mean, of intra-uterine existence. (U 367)

Here the desire to return to the womb, displaced into the fear of being buried alive, would exemplify Freud's uncanny, as "in reality nothing new or alien, but something which is familiar and old established in the mind and which has become alienated from it only through the process of repression." In turn, the impossible desire to return to the womb, the ultimate goal represented by nostalgia, would constitute a true "homesickness":

> It often happens that neurotic men declare that they feel that there is something uncanny about the female genital organs. This *unheimlich* place, however, is the entrance to the former *Heim* [home] of all human beings, to the place where each one of us lived once upon a time and in

the beginning.... In this case too, then, the *unheimlich* is what was once *heimisch*, familiar; the prefix *un* is the token of repression. (U 368)

Perhaps it was out of homage to the power of an archaeology that refused to hide what it had laid bare that Freud hung on the walls of his consulting room, just above the famous couch, a large photograph of the rock temple of Ramses II at Abu Simbel, and this beside a bas-relief in plaster copied from the Museo Chiaramonti in the Vatican portraying one of the Horae, goddesses of vegetation, otherwise known as the "Gradiva" relief that inspired Jensen.

Notes

1   Wilhelm Jensen, *Gradiva: A Pompeiian Fancy* (1913), translated by Helen M. Downey, quoted in Sigmund Freud, *Delusion and Dream*, edited by Philip Rieff (Boston: The Beacon Press, 1956), pp. 175–6. Downey's translation of *Gradiva* was first published in 1917.

2   [Editors' Note: Vidler is referring to Melville's short story "I and my Chimney," discussed in the previous section of *The Architectural Uncanny* on "Unhomely Houses": "the narrator loved his chimney; it provided warmth and stability for the entire house, as structure and function; it did not, like his wife, "talk back," and it represented, symbolically enough, a last bastion of the good against the intrusions of a bad present. And yet the chimney, as he readily admitted, was something of a tyrant. Twelve feet square at the base, four feet wide at the top, it completely usurped the center of the house, permitting no passage from one side to another, forcing the inhabitants into continual peripheral movement.... Fear pervades this story: fear of being deprived of a "backbone" with the removal of the chimney; fear of losing the "one permanence" of the dwelling; fear of confrontation with the wife; fear, given the chimney's shape and vertical power, of loss of manhood" (42).]

3   Sigmund Freud, "The 'Uncanny'" (1919), in *The Standard Edition of the Complete Psychological Works of Sigmund Freud*, 24 vols. (London: Hogarth Press, 1955), vol. 17. All quotations from this essay will be taken from the corrected reprint of this edition in Sigmund Freud, *Art and Literature*, the Pelican Freud Library, vol. 14, edited by Albert Dickson (Harmondsworth: Penguin Books, 1985), p. 366, and will be cited in the text as "U."

4   Baron Taylor, letter to Charles Nodier, "Sur les villes de Pompéi et d'Herculanum," in François-René de Chateaubriand, *Oeuvres romanesques et voyages*, vol. 2 (Paris: Bibliothèque de la Pléiade, 1969), p. 1505.

5   Chateaubriand, *Oeuvres romanesques et voyages*, 2:1475.

6   Gustave Flaubert, *Correspondance, I, 1830–1851* (Paris: Gallimard, 1973), 773, letter to Louis Bouilhet: "Ah! poor chap, how I missed you in Pompeii! I send you flowers that I picked from a brothel over the door of which is set an erect phallus. There were in this house more flowers than in any other.

The sperm of ancient penises, fallen to the earth, have perhaps fertilized the earth."

7   Chateaubriand, *Oeuvres romanesques et voyages*, 2:1783, 1472; Gérard de Nerval, *Oeuvres*, 2 vols. (Paris: Bibliothèque de la Pléiade, 1952), 1:1175.

8   Théophile Gautier, "Arria Marcella, souvenir de Pompéi," in *Récits fantastiques* (Paris: Flammarion, 1981), p. 246.

9   Gautier, "Arria Marcella," pp. 240ff.

10 Friedrich Wilhelm Joseph Schelling, *Philosophie der Mythologie*, 2 vols. (Darmstadt: Wissenschaftliche Buchgesellschaft, 1966), 2:653. Translation by Eric Randolf Miller.

11 Chateaubriand, *Oeuvres romanesques et voyages*, 2:1474.

12 Friedrich Schlegel, *Athenaeum*, fragment 206, quoted in Philippe Lacoue-Labarthe and Jean-Luc Nancy, *L'absolu littéraire* (Paris: Seuil, 1978), pp. 126, 101.

13 Gautier, "Arria Marcella," pp. 237–8.

14 Gautier, "Arria Marcella," p. 253.

15 Gautier, "Jettatura," in *Récits fantastiques*, p. 379.

16 Gautier, "Arria Marcella," p. 243.

17 Gautier, "Arria Marcella," p. 245.

18 Freud, "Delusions and Dreams in Jensen's Gradiva," *Standard Edition* 9:1–95; corrected reprint in *Art and Literature*, pp. 33–118.

19 Freud, *The Interpretation of Dreams*, *Standard Edition* 5:452.

20 Freud, *The Interpretation of Dreams*, p. 454.

21 Freud, *The Future of an Illusion*, *Standard Edition* 21:17.

25

To Give Memory a Place: Contemporary Holocaust Photography and the Landscape Tradition

Ulrich Baer

When the morning light comes up
Who knows what suffering midnight was?
Proof is what I do not need.
BRENDAN KENNELLY, "PROOF"

The photograph shows a clearing hemmed in by short pines, more of an overgrown woodland than a forest (figure 1). The picture's elongated format invites us to scan the image horizontally to see whether the sky will open up as we advance hesitantly into the clearing. Because the space within the photograph is so powerfully centered by sharply focused tiers of grass and shrubs and trees, this stretched-out print offers us but a single-point perspective, while the sky, cropped off by the picture's unusually low framing, lends the image a palpable sense of heaviness. In the photographer's effort to capture each pine needle and stalk of grass with technical precision, he has overexposed the sky; only faint traces of clouds remain. The exactitude devoted to portraying this place betrays the photographer's interest and a familiarity that contrasts with the site's lack of conventional visual appeal and absence of identifiable markers. By using

Figure 1   "Sobibór." From Dirk Reinartz, *Deathly Still: Pictures of Former Concentration Camps*. New York: Scalo, 1995.

the large panorama format normally reserved for sweeping vistas to capture a rather confined space, Dirk Reinartz deepens our impression that at some time in the past this opening in the woods was cleared for a particular purpose.

But why does nothing grow in the sandy patches at the front? At first, we mistakenly assume that these bare spots lie at the picture's center, but they are in fact a good two-thirds of the way down from the upper margin of the print. If the perspective achieved in this image pulls us in, these patches keep us from fully entering the photograph. The pines on the margins of the visual field, which had first blended with the rather uniform and decidedly secondary background, now emerge as sentinels of a darker forest located just beyond the confines of the image. Trees at the left and right, which initially seemed to recede into space, are recognized upon prolonged inspection as uncomfortably close; the bristly pines nearly brush our eyes. These dwarfed trees signal to us that we have already been brought into the middle of the clearing while we were looking at it as if from the outside. The way their branches spill out beyond the print's sharply posited frame suggests that what we at first saw as a tightly organized visual field is really

a setting that has not been fully mastered and contained. Held back, as if by a premonition or a spell, we do not wish to project ourselves into the middle of the blotchy clump of trees. While we contemplate our own position in relation to the black-and-white print, a sense of trespass hovers near the bald patches in the grass. Although the picture positions us in the only possible point of reference, this sense that we don't belong here—that we are excluded, that we have arrived *après coup*, too late and perhaps in vain— feels undeniable. As if enlivened by a breeze, the silent print is animated by an aura or "spirit of place:" we sense that the grounds are haunted.

In Mikael Levin's image of Nordlager Ohrdruf (figure 2), we are faced with another study of space; but, unlike the first image, his print emphasizes the vastness of a site that today is not merely inaccessible but also virtually forgotten. The photograph shows a marshy meadow dotted with rushes and thistles and bordered by trees. A patch of stagnant water at the bottom of the print is cradled by the slightly rising meadow on both sides. The photograph draws this puddle toward us instead of allowing our gaze to center on it. Because the ground slants slightly downward a few inches to the left of the picture's lower right corner, only a clump of spiky grass seems to keep

Figure 2   Untitled. From Mikael Levin, *War Story*.

the water from spilling out of the image onto our feet. The bright spots in the foreground counterbalance the darkness of the trees in the background so that our gaze settles on the nondescript area lying in between. This photograph is even more brutally exposed than Reinartz's image: the water puddles barely reflect a sky utterly devoid of the consoling symbolic orders of cloud patterns or astral constellations. Only the shiny stalks of grass seem to spell out a cryptic message against the darker ground. The nearly black band of bushes separating this meadow from the entirely white sky at once prompts and limits the impression of spatial depth and perspective produced by the varied grays in the picture's bottom half; an actual survey of the area, it seems, would meet with an impenetrable limit at this line of shrubbery. What little sense of depth is present in these bushes vanishes into the flat white of the sky, and the groups of shrubs melt into abstract designs. Due to the photograph's overexposure or to darkroom work, it looks as if some of the leaves have come detached from the trees and are melting into the void above.

Levin places the viewer before a landscape whose spatial dimension is on the verge of collapsing into a flat abstraction. Solid trees dissolve into thin air; the stalks of grass beneath our eyes melt into the soggy ground. If this picture harbors a story, it is a story about the transformation of the depth of the *landscape* seen at the bottom of the print into the uninhabitable *terrain* and abstract whiteness near the top. Our eyes, trained by habit, infer the space and perspective of the image—and thus our own position in relation to the site—by translating the print's shades of gray into suggestions of proximity and distance. The landscape's imagined depth—where experience, imagination, and memory may be projected and contained—vanishes into abstracted and inhospitable terrain.[1] We are forced to enter a site that failed to accommodate human experience in the past and that will not allow itself, as a photographic sight, to be completely filled in by the present viewer's imagination.

The deliberately created tension between the print's landscape character as a setting for experience and memory and the abstracted depiction of inhospitable terrain puts the viewer into a peculiar position. We are allowed to enter a site that will not fully accommodate our view of it. The illusion of space in this picture does not engender, at all points, a sense of place; we are led into a site that, in the end, excludes us. Levin's way of structuring this image resembles Reinartz's organization of space into a landscape. Our nearly reflexive impulse to assume the intended point of view and share the photographer's line of sight is blocked, for the picture resists being fully conquered by means of visual projection. In both of these images, the invitation to relate to and to enter the site is fused with an equally strong message of exclusion.

The first image, of the former Nazi extermination camp at Sobibór in Poland, was published by the German photographer Dirk Reinartz in his book, *Deathly Still: Pictures of Former Concentration Camps* (1995).[2] All the images in his book are similarly aestheticized; but unlike this single photograph of Sobibór, the others show physical evidence—decaying buildings, rubble, or memorials—of the crimes committed there. The second image, of the former concentration camp of Ohrdruf in Germany, was taken in 1995 and published in *War Story* (1997) by the American photographer Mikael Levin. Although unaware of each other's work and pursuing different objectives—and quite dissimilar in background, national identity, and aesthetic beliefs—the photographers rely in these two images on the same artistic conventions of landscape art to find a place for absent memory.[3] The two photographs are unlike most other postwar images of Holocaust sites.[4] They contain no evidence of the sites' historical uses, and they rely explicitly on the aesthetic tradition of landscape art and, as I will explain, on the auratic "experience of place" to commemorate the destruction of experience and memory.[5] In most other images of former camps or killing fields, we are confronted with the oversaturated referents of ruin: crumbled buildings once built to kill and now maintained and "museumized" for purposes of commemoration; the scraps of barbed wire; the memorial stones.[6] Instead of showing such markers, Reinartz's and Levin's images refer to the Holocaust only through their titles and the accompanying texts that announce: "These are Holocaust sites."

Because they do not contain evidence of their importance, these photographs ask to be regarded on strictly modernist terms—as if their significance and merit derived not from our knowledge of context but from intrinsic formal criteria alone. By representing the Holocaust in such stringently formal terms, Reinartz and Levin force us to see that there is *nothing* to see there; and they show us that there is something in a catastrophe as vast as the Holocaust that remains inassimilable to historicist or contextual readings. Just when they posit the event as radically singular, and thus when they risk investing absence with spiritual meaning, Reinartz and Levin retract the promise that we can transcend the photographed void to reach some comprehensive, and thus consoling, meaning.

While rendering historicist analyses inadequate, these images also deconstruct the pictorial conventions that might be analyzed and disclosed in a formalist analysis. It is precisely by exposing as equally insufficient both the historicist and the formal approaches that these photographs require a new way of looking at the presumed photographic past. This new way of looking, as I will show in some detail, comes closer to a mode of witnessing than to visual analysis. It no longer regards the image as a depository or a mechanically archived slice of the past that is encrypted according to the codes of "realism." Rather, it recognizes how the image calls into question such processes of visual analysis, which aim at resurrecting the mechanically captured past. These photographs, I here argue, silently question the reliance on historical context as an explanatory framework. They situate us specifically in relation to something that remains off the map of historicist readings.

What is the dimension of the Holocaust that Reinartz and Levin seek to expose, and that cannot be fully accounted for by drawing on material or documentary evidence? The deliberate exclusion of historical markers in these pictures is not an irresponsible, vain, or ahistoricist gesture. Rather, Reinartz and Levin employ a classic aesthetic means of drawing attention to the difficulties of linking, on the one hand, philosophical efforts to understand and historicist attempts to explain with, on the other hand, the actual event of the exterminations. These photographs cannot *show* the abyss opened by the Nazis' crimes, which Hannah Arendt identified as "the crime against humanity—in the sense of a crime 'against the human status' ... an attack upon human diversity as such, that is, upon a characteristic of the 'human status' without which the very words 'mankind' or 'humanity' would be devoid of meaning."[7] But these photographs, like Arendt's work, do "not explain [the abyss], because that is not what one does with an abyss; instead, cutting through the restraint we have come to expect from serious writers on the Holocaust," these photographs place us in relation to it.[8] They also ask: How do we remember the Holocaust without inevitably forgetting that this event challenged both the individual and the collective capacity for memory and questioned the notion of survival in ways we are still struggling to comprehend?[9] Where is the proper position from which to face this stark truth, and how is this notion of a position related to the experience of place? Prior to all efforts at commemoration, explanation, or understanding, I would suggest, we—and this "we" is constituted precisely by the deconstitution of stable individual or group identities when facing the abyss of utter destruction—must find a place and position from which to gain access to the event. By casting the enormity of the Holocaust within the traditional genre of landscape photography, Reinartz and Levin emphasize that this question of the viewers' position, as belated witnesses to those originally on the scene of the crime, touches upon all efforts to explain the past, to judge, to mourn, to remember, to learn, to understand.

By drawing on the conventions of Romantic landscape art, these images create in us the feeling of being addressed and responsive to the depicted site and, crucially, of seeing the site not for its own sake but as a pointer back to our own position. The impulse they invoke—to locate ourselves within a space organized as landscape—is a response only recently acquired. With European Romanticism, the environment that had once been ground to build on, plow, defend, or conquer came to be seen as an aesthetic entity to be contemplated by an enraptured subject in a process of introspection and increasing self-awareness.[10] Looking at landscapes as we do today manifests a specifically modern sense of self-understanding, which may be described as the individual's ability to view the self within a larger, and thus potentially historical, context. Although this relation to the surroundings somewhat predates the Romantic era, it is the Romantic subject, who emerged roughly two hundred years ago as the prototype of the modern subject, who looks at a beautiful vista to see not the landscape but "an earlier instantiation of the self."[11] According to the Romantic sensibility that still organizes both our vision and these photographs, looking at a landscape means, as Joseph Koerner has argued, turning "the landscape back on the viewer, to locate *us* in our subjectivity as landscape [art's] true point of reference."[12] The two photographs I discuss here, however, rely on this aesthetic to place us in reference to experiences that resist integration into memory, historical narratives, or other mitigating contexts. While these images frame the sites in ways that force us to assume a viewing position, they also block these sights from being subsumed as "pleasing" vistas into our process of increasing self-awareness through identification or projection.[13]

By pulling the viewer into a setting that seems inhospitable and strangely placeless, these photographs point to a link between the "experience of place" and the enigmatic structure of traumatic memories. They also remind us that most extant Holocaust photographs—scenes of death and destruction but not necessarily of trauma—block access to the event instead of facilitating a self-aware, rather than rote, commemoration and witnessing. These highly deliberate images expose the limits of containing the catastrophe in historicist readings or documentary conventions while they challenge us to assess our own position in relation to it.

Positioning the viewer in reference to an event that resists full absorption into narrative memory changes a crucial methodological question about the status of all photographs of trauma. A constitutive question of both traditional and more recent art-historical inquiries concerns the extent to which the reading of an image may be inflected by (prior) knowledge of its historical context. I suggest reformulating this question by asking how to frame an image with references to a historical event that consisted in the lasting destruction of most, and possibly all, explanatory referential frames and contexts for understanding. This question about the limitations of contextual or historicist approaches to an entire genre of photography relates to a subtle but important shift in recent debates about representing the Holocaust. For several decades after the end of World War II these debates invoked tropes of the "unspeakable," the "ineffable," and the "limits of representation" of the Holocaust.[14] Currently, some of these problematically "ontotheological" concerns are being supplanted by the urgent question of whether the obligation to confront the Holocaust will diminish and finally disappear with the passing of the last survivors and witnesses. How can younger generations be taught that the Holocaust poses a problem for representation except by representing it? How can its senselessness be conveyed except by turning it into a (negative) lesson? And how can its shattering effects on all categories of thought and known modes of transmission be conveyed except by turning it into a circumscribed, and thus finally graspable, object of inquiry?[15] What, finally, compels individuals increasingly removed in time to continue facing the Holocaust as a watershed event of history?

Paradoxically, the scholarly, artistic, and media attention to the Holocaust occasionally obscures, and even blocks, understanding of its impact on all forms of cultural practice. Saturated by references to the catastrophe, many are no longer aware of any difficulty in imagining and mentally picturing an event that has been so effectively packaged and depicted in Hollywood creations, national and local museums, and on television. A further flood of Holocaust kitsch in popular literature and film—including works by critically acclaimed artists—heightens the impression that there is little difficulty in remembering, representing, and communicating the Holocaust and that, far from defeating the imagination, the Holocaust provides a useful screen for self-exploration.[16] The decades-long debates over the Holocaust's resistance to representation and understanding are no longer recognized as intrinsic to the catastrophe but are, increasingly and incorrectly, viewed as mere academic concerns.

The very word *Holocaust* triggers a surge of derivative and familiar mental images, most of which originate with a number of news photographs taken by the Western Allies in 1945 after the liberation of camps in Austria and Germany. Even when part of laudable efforts to document and commemorate, these once-shocking and now ubiquitous images may lead today to the "disappearance of memory in the act of commemoration."[17] They represent the past as fully retrievable (as simply a matter of searching the archive), instead of situating us vis-à-vis the intangible presence of an absence, which Jacques Derrida has called the "hell in our memory."[18] When they have not become mute clichés, on the other hand, these graphic images of death are likely to disable the viewer's capacity to remember or to respond, either critically or with empathy. In their irreversible finality, such pictures represent history as locked in the past. The two photographs discussed here forestall such reflexive responses or cognitive numbing without diminishing the magnitude of the disaster. But they provide no easy answers. Instead, these photographs raise urgent questions about the task of showing the nothing that nonetheless triggers a response: about the difficulties of representing trauma and about the poetics of witnessing.

The experience of place

Reinartz's and Levin's pictures reopen questions about the status and reliability of the image that date back to the first landscape photographs of the 1840s. In these early photographs, an aestheticizing vision of the surroundings is paired with the truth claims inherent in the medium of photography to draw the viewer's eyes and mind into unknown regions. Critics of such images have indicted the landscape tradition for "naturalizing," by means of the aesthetic, the nefarious approaches and appropriations of territory by particular groups; such landscapes, they argue, are the symbolic underpinnings of brutal campaigns of colonial expansion. Whatever bucolic innocence there might have been in such depictions certainly vanished with the Nazis' explicit appropriation of the landscape genre (along with the myths of "blood and soil" and *Lebensraum*) into an ideology that led to the murder of millions of people. Reinartz and Levin rely on the landscape tradition, not to point to the historical event or the genre's corruption but to position us in relation to the fact that that event consisted in the radical destruction and unavailability of explanatory contexts. It is the unavailability of referential markers, and not information that could be embedded in historical contexts, that is captured in these images as the truth of history.

I maintain that the modernist, arguably Eurocentric, and wholly "aesthetic" approach to the landscape photograph as autonomous image is particularly well-suited to addressing the Holocaust as the historical event that calls into question that entire tradition.[19] Our task today cannot be met by simply logging more data—precisely because a truly ungovernable mass of "hard facts" (often invoked in polemics against aesthetically oriented readings) blocks access to an event that, as Jean Baudrillard has pointed out, due to "continual scrutiny ... has [become] less and less comprehensible."[20] By historicizing or contextualizing the image, we avoid the task of finding our bearings in relation to the event that destroyed the possibility of having recourse to historical contexts. However, while historicist readings of landscape art consider the aesthetic to be little more than the veneer over imperialist or fascist ideology, exclusively formal readings of these images also miss their import.[21] These two landscape photographs continually shuttle the viewer between the historicist, contextual frames of viewing and a visual tracing of their formal composition. Yet neither approach exhausts them.

Reinartz's photograph of Sobibór shows that a favored directive of academics—"*Always historicize!*"—represses the fact that an event's historicity might consist in the destruction of any explanatory context. In the case of the Holocaust, the immeasurable loss comprised in many cases also the capacity to experience and, subsequently, to properly remember. Even when we are armed with archival knowledge, numbers, and facts, Reinartz's photograph of Sobibór confronts us head-on by ungrounding our desire to know. When such images are contextualized by drawing on historical explanations, or on the imagination's power to project oneself into an image, these explanations deny that in Sobibór's shockingly small area the possibilities of knowledge, of comprehension, and of viewing oneself in relation to the surroundings and to history were all but destroyed. In order to be recognized at all, however, this encounter with irremediable loss needs a frame within which the viewer is visually implicated in the nondistinct, empty, and easily overlooked setting. In the pictures analyzed here, the compositional conventions of landscape art provide this frame, which situates the viewer in reference to the place where historical knowledge has burned out.

Reinartz's photograph restores a sense of place to the historical event that appears both geographically and conceptually placeless to us. "The Holocaust seems to have no landscape—or at best one emptied of features and color, shrouded in night and fog,"[22] writes historian Simon Schama; and the eerie elusiveness of the geographic sites where ultimately nothing is found haunts most contemporary visitors to the former camps. This geographic placelessness in "the mythical territory 'farther to the East' where the documents of the Nazi administration situated the ultimate deportation of the Jews" has its conceptual equivalent, and what psychoanalyst Nadine Fresco terms its "definitive [symbolic] beyond," in a realm where even immense accumulations of knowledge do not attain closure.[23]

Although they seek to establish the conceptual grounding on which to raise a context for these images, most historians facing the Holocaust's "no-man's-land of understanding" feel "despair and doubt and [possibly] recognition ... but assuredly no understanding."[24] Even when immersed in footnotes to archival documents and counterdocuments, memoirs, testimonies, facts, and figures, we are aware of something confounding and inexplicable about the existence of a place like Sobibór. The accounts in history books fail to offer closure, to make sense; in the case of survivor testimonies, little allows individuals to appropriate experiences that are all too much their own.[25] Each detail adds to the overall impression of despair; a place like Sobibór fails to become "whole." Survivor accounts often recount the deportations as the destruction of a symbolic notion of a place that could hold experience together.[26] A visit to a former camp undermines our hope that the quest for knowledge is an inherently liberating process. Fundamentally, Reinartz's photograph is a single shot and captures a view without context. By artificially isolating it from its context of captions, texts, and titles, I merely register this fact.

The psychoanalyst Jean Laplanche considers trauma to be the failed translation of an unremembered experience. Yet trauma is more than a simple failure of translation; it is also the result of the perplexing condition of a missing original. Reinartz's photograph seeks to return us to this missing original, and to translate it into sight, without pretending that it could be either fully recovered or forgotten or that there exists a stable, originary place and experience that he can show us. His image dispels the mythic status of the Holocaust's unavailable location, at once inaccessible and yet profusely documented, by depicting the site as landscape.[27] The photograph does not leave the site "unstoried," to rely on an older, American term that distinguishes *place*, which refers to the "landscapes that display us as culture," from *space*, as "the environment [that] sustains us as creatures."[28] But the story offered in this image is not found in history books. It is the story of the loss of the experience of place—a story told silently through artistic conventions that situate us in reference to the actual and metaphoric destruction of experience, place, context, and belonging.

Reinartz's quasi-anamorphic image leaves little room for the viewer's eyes to roam. The picture points back to one viewing position and, in an invisible grid pattern, places all viewers in the same line of sight. Before this photograph, all share one perspective and one point of view: this is why I insist on using the collective *we* when discussing the site of an event that all but completely shattered the most basic human bonds.[29] Because the photograph's perspective is so strictly organized, it turns our attention not to the site's natural beauty or to the marks of culture on the land but to our position in reference to the site. The forest clearing appears to deserve our attention, not for its own sake but because of our position.[30] The task of finding our position as viewers consists in discovering our bearings in reference to a place that is absorbing yet unstable.

Picturing nothing

Il faut donner à voir.
They must be made to see.

—Charlotte Delbo, *Auschwitz and After*

Mikael Levin's photograph dates from 1995 and depicts the former concentration camp at Ohrdruf in Germany. The camp was discovered on April 9, 1945, by American soldiers—soon joined by war correspondents such as Mikael Levin's father, Meyer Levin—one day after the SS had abandoned it. (And thus before Allied forces reached Belsen or Buchenwald, and before the surrender of Nazi Germany).[31] The younger Levin's task consists not only in recapturing his father's original sense of shock at arriving at a place that exposed Americans for the first time to visual evidence of the German atrocities but also in conveying the distance that separates us from that sense of shock.

Yet Levin's photograph cannot be decoded according to a logic of deferred meaning, or *Nachträglichkeit*, as belatedly bestowing meaning to a sight too overwhelming to be grasped at first glance. Rather, his image creates a viewing position from which to address the knowledge that still proves excessive, destabilizing, and indeed blinding fifty years later. The younger Levin seeks to show that the original sense of destabilization and excess has not been overcome or diminished.[32]

In his war diary (which I discuss in detail in the next chapter), his father, Meyer Levin, describes a nerve-racking search for evidence of German crimes he and a fellow war correspondent conducted during the last days of the war. At Ohrdruf they were led to a "half-dug pit as large as a swimming pool, filled with ooze" from which a Polish survivor, serving as guide, pulled a partly decomposed human body (129). When discovery of their crimes by the Allies was imminent the SS had exhumed the bodies of thousands of their victims and tried unsuccessfully to burn them. But just one day after the SS had abandoned the camp, Levin was faced with the fact that at first nothing could be seen there.

> On top of the hill there was a rut that gave out, *and then nothing...*.
> We were going to turn back when the Pole suddenly got his bearings and motioned to a clump of trees. *We saw nothing.* We drove there and got out and still *we saw nothing special.* (129, emphasis added)

Although these lines immediately precede the description of finding the slimy pit, they already register the overwhelming experience of encountering *nothing* in the inhospitable terrain. This experience could not be undone by the evidence uncovered. In this testimonial tale the narrative moves from a first *nothing* of impatience and fear (of mines or "bitter-end SS who could pot us off") to the sight of nothing centered by the pit. Yet the fact that up to this point they had seen nothing creates not just narrative suspense. *Nothing* is already a reference to what the witnesses are about to see beyond the "nothing special": a pit "with a section of narrow-gauge track ... beside it, *reaching from nowhere to nowhere*" (129, emphasis added). Although the pit is the end point of their search and would presumably dispel the sense of nothingness, it contains an absence without proper frame or closure, a sinkhole that cannot be called a grave, an opening in the ground that will not offer rest to thousands of prisoners whose names and stories passed unrecorded and of whose physical remains there remains no trace. At the very moment of its discovery, the site is literally sinking into oblivion and symbolically drifting toward the periphery of a public memory that is yet to be created and that will monumentalize other Holocaust sites but leave Ohrdruf unstoried.

Meyer Levin's account of the visit ends: "Now we knew. Nothing afterward told us more. Buchenwald, Bergen Belsen, Dachau[:] we became specialists" (130). The camp at Ohrdruf remains unsurpassed in horror because it is not bordered by a "beyond"; and in 1945 Levin already realized that the encounter with a radically voided site, with the shockingly vacant "nothing" witnessed there, would be outdone by nothing else. Even today—when the Russian army that in the postwar period used the place for war games is long gone—the former camp of Ohrdruf remains a military zone—a nonplace closed to visitors and to memory.

Mikael Levin's photograph of the site marks a place from which we are made to see an unfathomable void that will not be dispelled. In what we recognize as a paradox—once we have grasped that "landscapes" are never found in nature but only in our culturally specific ways of seeing—Levin's print captures the site as *a landscape without us in it*.[33] As it happens, even Meyer Levin's testimony tells us that the site's significance consists in its disclosure of *nothing*.

Historical accounts break down in the effort to document what unrealized stories vanished in the Holocaust. Through the photographs, we enter into sites out of which only death was supposed to lead; we are confronted with spaces designed to destroy all memory of those who were brought there. The deliberate destruction of evidence that would reveal these sites' significance constitutes the event's historical truth and limits the possibility of its telling. For the *nothing* to be "translated" into sight, it must be shown as *nothing*, rather than as the absence of something we could know.

The photograph's reference

Reinartz and Levin lead available historical narratives of the Holocaust—
the conventionalized accounts that attempt to make sense of what remains
senseless—into the deathly stillness of a photograph. But they also instantly
curtail the landscape genre's power of absorption, its lure for viewers to
project themselves into an imaginary pictorial depth, by marshaling the
melancholic dimension of photography, which excludes the viewer from
the depicted site. In every photographic image, the viewers' *here and now*—
their ability to draw on different explanatory contexts—is read against
the photographed moment's *then and there*. Regardless of subject matter,
photographs show a moment of the past as inalterable, as something that
has been brought back against time's passage. Even in our postphoto-
graphic era, when sensory perception is being reformatted according to new
technological paradigms, we continue to view photographs as snippets of
an unreachable and yet real past.[34] This sight is here, immovably preserved
and printed, but you are elsewhere. Before yielding information, all photographs (and not only Holocaust images) signal that we have arrived after
the picture has been taken, and thus too late. In our responses to the
medium we are still—although we know better—hard-wired to perceive
what we see in photographs as real.

Although Reinartz's and Levin's images, like all landscape depictions,
absorb the viewer, they also maintain, like all photographs, this "irretrievable
otherness for the viewer in the present."[35] These photographs present us
with images that we know belong to the past, and this knowledge excludes
us from the sites as powerfully as the conventions of landscape art pull us
in. The sense of nonbelonging in these images, then, originates not only
from the particularity of the photographed scene or the pictures' framing
but also from the apparently melancholic, yet actually affectless, retention
of the referent found in all photographs. Because something of this retained
past has not been allowed to depart but is still there, where the present
should have swallowed it up, we who view the picture in the present feel
excluded. Because we are aware of the site's historical significance, it draws
our gaze. This auratic sense of place that I locate in these pictures, against
dominant readings of the history of photography, is here paired with the
medium's uncanny power to make us feel excluded from a place because it
looks as if it has not yielded to the passage of time. This pairing results in
pictures in which absence becomes the referent.[36]

These darkly auratic pictures by Reinartz and Levin—hovering on
the brink of our resilient faith in the evidentiary status of the photograph—are all but useless as documents.[37] Although they are bereft of
documentary information, however, these images nonetheless tell the truth.
They challenge our notion of what constitutes knowledge by calling on

our deepseated trust in photography's reality effect and, thus, showing us that really nothing is pictured there or, put differently, that nothing in this picture is real. Since this nothing of information is cast according to the aesthetic conventions of photographic landscape art (with its apparently unshakeable truth claims), we do not find spiritual, ontological, or existential Nothingness or "nothing" but the sense—the premonition or uncanny aura—that something has disappeared, that the place has not been changed and yet is somehow less than it was before. Photography's potent illusion of the real—the sense that "nothing in the image can be refused or transformed"[38]—is combined in these prints with a convention that absorbs us in the landscape. These images turn a radical voiding, an obliteration of memory itself, into the referent for an event that involved the effort to destroy all traces of its occurrence. While other, referentially more stable documentary photographs might shelter us from this devastating truth, these photographs vacate our understanding of reference itself.

The limits of allegory

Reinartz's and Levin's images could be faulted for unduly aestheticizing the sites of atrocities.[39] Yet both photographs avoid the derivative pathos of books often sold at memorial sites, which render us doubly helpless because, though clearly sincere, they trivialize the event by evoking clichés of prefabricated sentimentality. Reinartz and Levin resist a similar temptation to infuse the lightly wooded area with the markers of the terribly spectacular, or the mass-produced sublime.

Besides risking a lapse into triviality or kitsch, the two photographers' reliance on the landscape genre also raises the specter of the Nazis' appropriation of the trope of the landscape in their genocidal redefinitions of nation, home, and *Heimat* as categories to be administered by decree.[40] When Reinartz and Levin photograph former camps as forest clearings, they subvert the Nazis' ideological uses of the German soil and forest as anchors of a people's "destiny." Even so, the trees in these images cannot serve as symbols of the victims of Sobibór and Ohrdruf, for the artistic vision cannot fully transcend the Nazis' use of natural settings in the killing campaigns. In 1943 and 1944, the Nazis planted real trees at Sobibór, Treblinka, and Belzec for the express purpose of concealing all traces of their staggering crimes. Reinartz and Levin took their pictures more than five decades later, after nature had almost completely covered the sites. It has thus become Reinartz's and Levin's task to unmask the sylvan tranquility without denying the sites' "misleading air of normalcy" and without dramatizing the places where every sense of the tragic was surpassed.[41] Their photographs capture the trees as part of the Nazis' design and record this deceptive normalcy, without succumbing to it, to mark the scope of the destruction. On a symbolic level, the trees stand in for the vanished masses murdered here. But the trees are both more, and less, than symbols. In their literal, nonsymbolic presence the trees are evidence not of death and destruction but of the denial and concealment of its occurrence. By keeping in focus both the trees' literal status as part of the Nazi deceptions and their symbolic significance as silent witnesses and anthropomorphic placeholders for Europe's murdered Jews, these pictures reveal the inadequacy of relying solely on either an allegorical or a literal interpretation of the forest scene.[42]

Landscape and trauma

In these two images the forest clearing is centered and rendered particular by means of compositional laws that viewers have so thoroughly internalized that the scenes appear inevitable, and therefore natural, or self-evidently *factual*. The pictures' field of vision seems to originate from a point of view we would have chosen on our own; and something somewhere in the picture seems to return our gaze and to suggest that our placement at the picture's only point of reference may not be accidental. By casting an unknown place in the haunting light of déjà-vu, landscape photographs produce the mild shock of recovering what seems to be an unremembered— rather than a forgotten—experience.

The appeal of these two photographs derives largely from their refusal to disclose to us the specific place from which they address us. We are left with the impression that these scenes should concern us precisely because we never knew them. The sense of belonging produced by the images' perspective contrasts with the equally powerful sense of nonbelonging and trespass produced by the sense of pastness captured in them. This tension— between the landscape's simultaneous invitation to project ourselves into them and to the inalterable pastness of photography—finds a parallel in the difficulties of representing historical trauma.

Historical trauma also needs to be cast in ways that involve the observer without glossing over the event's essential inaccessibility. In the Romantic tradition of landscape art, artists often sought to create a disturbing impression that the viewer was being watched from an unidentifiable spot in the picture. This illusion of the returned gaze, established by organizing the painting according to a one-point perspective, might be compared to the uncanny feeling that results from traumatic memories, which seem to "possess" and haunt an individual, even though they are not properly remembered. Maurice Blanchot writes that such experiences "cannot be forgotten because [they have] always already fallen outside memory."[43] If we rely on the metaphor of the mind as spatially organized, the "inner landscape" of a traumatized individual might be said to harbor what Cathy Caruth has called "unclaimed experiences" that register as painfully real but are inaccessible to consciousness.[44] Strikingly, when such fragments of traumatic memory intrude upon common memory, they often emerge as memories of a particular *site*. Trauma survivors may recall a particular place or area in great detail without being able to associate it with the actual event.[45]

The tradition of landscape art likewise seems to situate viewers against their will, by imbuing a scene with auratic significance but without necessarily linking this sense of familiarity to any remembered past. In this tradition, then, a site's apparent meaningfulness only appears to emanate from the setting; in fact, that impression really results from the viewing subject's position in front of the painting—thus not from the setting but from the viewing self. A structural analogy exists, then, between depictions of landscapes that refer the viewer not to a specific spot but to a heightened sense of self and the puzzlingly exact encoding of spatial markers that signals the presence of traumatic memories outside of, and yet within, an individual's mind. The aura of the photographed landscape—the impression of proximity, familiarity, and relevance in a possibly quite-distant scene—seems to tap into a memory we did not know existed, a counterpart in ourselves we may have felt but did not know. Conceptually and visually, we are subjected to something we recognize as crucially important, though in the end it eludes us.

To be sure, Reinartz's and Levin's landscape photographs place us in reference to sites made significant by history, even if their meaning is exposed to us by means of conventions like perspectival centering. The pictures neither confirm nor add to our knowledge of history; we cannot deduce from them what distinguishes these sites from countless others. And yet, regardless of—and even in spite of—our knowledge of their historical import, these images pull us in. They try to "speak from within erasure," as Claude Lanzmann's decidedly topographical film *Shoah* also attempts to do; they seek to give to loss a topography by showing us that nothing—not knowledge, empathy, commemoration, indignation, rage, mourning, or shame—can fill these silent spaces.[46] Through this powerful attraction to a void, we are thus *exposed to* (in the sense of being involuntarily subjected to) the site of a destruction so extreme that it seems to swallow up the possibility of ascribing meaning to it, even though it is indisputably significant. The point is no longer to establish a context for the picture but to note that the photograph posits as its meaning the suspension of such a stabilizing context.

The difficulty of traumatic memory, however, is not limited to its unavailability and resistance to representation. Very much like a photograph, traumatic memory can be characterized by the excessive retention of details that cannot be integrated into a nontraumatic memory or comprehension of the past.[47] The recovery of traumatic memory—and the process of healing—consists often in making the event seem less unreal by draining it of its vividness, its persistence, its haunting details, its color. Reinartz's and Levin's photographs share with traumatic memories the exact and unforgiving insistence on the reality of places whose significance derives neither from anything shown nor from their context. The sites are brought into focus without being reduced to irrelevance or mere facticity. By means of the landscape convention, Reinartz and Levin at once shelter us from, and expose us to, the trauma that for decades silenced many of the survivors and witnesses, who nonetheless had no choice but to feel addressed.

The limits of documentary photographs

In representations of the Holocaust, the mode of abstraction—an indispensable ingredient for understanding and remembrance—risks repeating the original injustice by denying victims yet again the singularity of which they were systematically deprived, even in death. In order to dispel the anonymity inherent in cold statistics, many books, memorials, and museums use photograpic portraits of Holocaust victims.[48] Like the staggering heaps of personal belongings found in museums, such photographs are commonly shown without any captions or explanations: the often poster-sized prints are supposed to speak for themselves.

Every photograph, however, is as much an aide-mémoire as a testament to loss. Each one makes the implicit and melancholic claim that the depicted sight is preserved in spite of, and as if to underline, the disappearance of the actual referent. If these forest settings give a place from which to witness the voiding of context effected by the Holocaust, then the photographs frame a less readily discernible moral concern about the use of documentary materials. Since all photographs present the past as absolutely unalterable, every photographic image promises momentary relief from the obligation to comprehend and to remember. Here is the photograph, every image asserts: this is the truth. In the case of the Holocaust, the sense produced by a photograph—that we have reached a momentary end point to our inquiry—conflicts with our awareness that the wish for complete understanding of the event either cannot be fulfilled or is morally suspect.[49] The forest pictures resist this implicit claim of photography to end reflection.

Reinartz's and Levin's pictures were evidently taken after prolonged visits to these places, as if the scene might retract and vanish upon sudden contact with a viewer. Reinartz's image does not match the evidentiary force of pictures used in museums and textbooks; and Levin's work cannot rival the informational content of his father's war diaries, nor the photographs by Erich Schwab that originally accompanied that text (which I discuss in the next chapter). And yet their works challenge our understanding of the nature of proof by presenting a staged and self-conscious refusal of information—a framed emptiness—as evidence of the crime's enormity.[50] At a moment when the Holocaust is rapidly fading from lived memory and passing into recorded history, the landscape prints of Sobibór or Ohrdruf do not format the past according to the specifications of existing archives. In casting the finality of the photographic image within the experience of place, these images extend the sense that the viewer is being addressed or called upon in ways that may no longer seem self-evident.

The viewer as witness

The matter-of-factness of the photographs, their ostensible literalness or "reality effect," captures what historical narrativization and conceptualization cannot.[51] These images uncannily stage—without resolving—the tension between the senses of being drawn into the sites (of viewing them as places) and of being excluded from them (of regarding them as space). As we oscillate between fascination with the images and bewilderment as to the source of their attraction, we become conscious of our relationship to sights that appear significant but do not provide any conclusive knowledge of their meaning. Compelled by their strong perspective, we examine these prints to find the hidden source of their pull. But this visual inspection is continually frustrated, for the pictures' almost hypnotic appeal originates not in any visible evidence they might offer but in the illusion of distance and depth in the flat prints. Our thwarted effort to locate the pictures' hidden source of significance, then, leads to the realization that the absence of understanding is linked to our own position *as viewers*.

It has been suggested that a person's engagement with the historical event of the Holocaust will be fundamentally shaped by his or her "subject-position." The Holocaust, argues Dominick LaCapra, "presents the historian with *transference in the most traumatic form conceivable*—but with a transference that will vary with the difference in subject-position."[52] LaCapra therefore urges those who engage with any aspect of the Holocaust to become aware of how their own identities shape their responses. However, as virtually every survivor testimony attests, the comforts of an easily claimable subject-position—and the inherent sense of identity—are by no means available to everyone. Awareness of one's psychological reactions to the Holocaust (whether categorized problematically as "most traumatic" or, presumably, "merely" difficult) is undoubtedly important. I would suggest, however, that even *prior* to reflecting on his or her subject-position in relation to the Holocaust, an individual needs to recall that all conceptions of cultural transmission, identity, and subject-position are inflected by an event that exposed not only the dialectical nature of

Enlightenment culture but also the corruptibility and deadly instrumentalization of a politically distorted understanding of identity.[53] My argument about the two photographs is that those who find themselves in these pictures' line of sight are put in the position of (or are being interpellated as) outsiders, regardless of personal background or assumed or imposed identity. At any given moment, the contaminating force of the disaster may diminish for some, while for others it may increase. As anyone can attest who has attempted to teach—rather than simply convey information about—the Holocaust, encountering the catastrophe does not facilitate, but often fractures or derails, identification with any given subject-position.

By creating an experience of place for areas designed to destroy the very possibility of experience, Reinartz and Levin show that Holocaust commemoration is not site-specific and that acts of secondary witnessing depend less on geographic or cultural positions than on becoming aware of our position as observers of experiences no one ever wanted to know about.[54] These pictures show us that the Holocaust's empty sites are radically inhospitable and that attempts to inhabit them ex post facto, through empathic identification and imaginary projection via transferential bonds, is illusory at best. With the passage of time, the investigation of its history, once fueled by a sense of trauma, will have to be prompted by other motives for representing the event. Some former killing fields—sites such as Ohrdruf where thousands were murdered—were never marked on the itineraries of disaster tourism, are rarely mentioned in historical studies, and are likely to sink into complete oblivion once the last survivors have passed away.[55] When such sites are framed in terms of landscape art, we recognize the disappearance of the event as part of the intention of their Nazi creators, a recognition that might motivate us to halt the disappearance. The images of Reinartz and Levin compel *all* viewers to reflect on how they are called upon to respond in unforeseen ways to a catastrophe such as the Holocaust. These photographs give the largely "figurative experience" of Holocaust memory a more literal form and create a new place of memory for those who consider themselves geographically, historically, or culturally removed from the camps.[56]

Several writers have described as shocking the experience of matching the real contours of the camps with the devastating sense of emptiness in their minds.[57] Landscape photographs of the Holocaust do not mitigate that experience, and the forest clearings at Sobibór and Ohrdruf lose nothing of their bleak nondescriptiveness when immobilized in print. Yet they do link the need to fit placeless memories into an imagined or imaginary place with the search for moral bearings and a point of view. The photographs train our gaze on this linkage of visual and moral perspectives and help us realize that *what* we see is always a question of *how*, and *from where*, we see it.

The landscape genre, which is so closely linked to the Enlightenment ideal of the subject's dialectical process of increasing self-awareness, is in Reinartz's and Levin's photographs used to prevent a moment of self-positioning from yielding intellectual gain. They position us as secondary witnesses who are as much spectators as seekers of knowledge. The aesthetic imperative offered in these images remains contemplative: it does not serve as a measure of our actions, and it compels us to respond without teaching us what to do. It merely prolongs the sense of inevitability that had been felt by those growing up in the Holocaust's more direct shadows. The images are visually arresting dead ends, well-composed but frustrating enticements to know. In their black-and-white neutrality, they apparently refuse to judge a situation in which a neutral stance appears immoral. But unlike original photographs from the camps, which are often displayed to silently accuse, they force us to face something we may never know. The rush of moral indignation that often accompanies the encounter with other graphic pictures of atrocities may be narcissistically satisfying, but it may also free us from the responsibility of placing our own experiences in relation to something that remains, finally, incomprehensible.[58] These photographs show us that the devastation of this massive trauma consists not merely in the ensuing difficulties of commemoration and forgetting but also in the fact that the erasure was so complete that it never fully entered either memory or forgetting.

I do not dispute that we do and should view images of the past in the hope that such encounters will improve our chances of shaping the present and the future. Yet the expressive silence of Reinartz's and Levin's tightly framed shots preempts closure and instead beckons us—without hinting at redemption or restitution—toward thought and language with which to reach from within the Holocaust's imploded sites to a place beyond it. From other images we may avert our gaze (thus serving forgetting and denial); or we may endow the event they record with a sanctity unmerited by a human campaign of destruction. In my analysis of Reinartz's and Levin's images in terms of landscape art, I try to articulate what remains to be said in response to an absence that cannot be undone. They do not allow us the option of turning away or evading this radical vacatedness by leaving our position and point of view; we cannot alter or escape from the picture's perspective.

Reinartz highlights the catastrophe's reality by shooting in the documentary idiom. Levin conveys to us that the second generation inherits from their predecessors not something that has been learned but something that remains a loss. Both enlist photography's claim of realism—the illusion that the shutter stamps an experience with inalterable finality—to show that this absence is immune to belated rescue missions in the form of restitutive or redemptive thought. Their works emphasize that part of the reality of the Holocaust consists in the fact that it has not receded into the past. Their pictures show that self-awareness, or the effort to situate oneself spatially and temporally within a greater whole, does not inevitably lead to understanding. Their work asks how we can situate future generations in relation to an event that calls into question many of our beliefs in the promises inherent in pedagogy and knowledge and forces us to reexamine our understanding of identity and of culture at large.

Finally, these two photos show that proof, as Brendan Kennelly's painfully ambiguous phrase suggests, "is what we do not need."

Postscript

Dirk Reinartz's photograph of Sobibór does not exist as a tangible object. The image I have analyzed to expose Reinartz's deployment of pictorial conventions that situate the viewer in relation to a site of historical trauma was created out of two separate photographs of Sobibór combined on a computer. For the reproduction in this book, a photolaboratory digitally erased the faint line in the center of the image that was hidden in the fold where his book, *Deathly Still*, was stitched together. There is no total and complete way of representing the Holocaust. The impression of containment, the sense of place, the feeling that this place is inhabited by ghosts, as I have argued throughout, are technical effects. These impressions result from the interplay of pictorial conventions, the photographer's intentions, and, finally, the camera's program. Once a scene such as Reinartz's Sobibór is created by fingers on a keyboard moving pixels on a screen, the "senseless mush of possibilities that rests beneath [the programmer's] fingers is invested with sense."[59] The sense here is of being called to respond, to reflect on the voiding of the sense of place that resists its own framing and emplacement.

With the digital image-engineer's fingers on the keyboard, however, we also enter "the situation of the new imagination, the Democritean mood."[60] Reinartz's photograph, which is addressed to a historical event that breaks with known practices of historicization, owes its existence to this new imagination, this Democritean mood. For this reason, it would be incorrect to stress and lament the artificiality of the image—as if a natural, untouched representation of such a spectral scene were possible. It is precisely the *construction* and encoding of a meaning *that had never existed*, which takes place in every photograph, that links photography, at least on a phenomenological level, to trauma. Under the Democritean gaze, we recognize Reinartz's photograph as one that lets us view a trauma that exceeds the historical imagination. The computer-generated illusion of Sobibór as a place where the notion of place was destroyed is no reason for despair, no cause to mourn the disappearance of immediately visible reality. Rather, it signals the promise of our present moment: a standpoint from which "we can see everything (including ourselves) photographically, as a grainy field of possibilities."[61]

Notes

1   Walter Benjamin was among the first to note the historical shift from the
    perception of *landscape* as the setting for an individual's passage through time
    to *terrain*, where coherent experience may no longer be available. Benjamin
    diagnosed the destruction of the landscape as the setting for historical
    experience and its violent transformation into mere terrain [*Gelände*] in
    the 1920s, when Europe was confronted by the vast, scarred areas left all
    but uninhabitable by warfare. The enormous battlefields of World War I
    had ceased to serve as settings for historical experience and had been seen
    purely in terms of strategic usefulness and ability to conceal troops. For a
    discussion of Benjamin's postwar notion of landscape, see Cornelia Vismann,
    "Landscape in the First World War," *New Comparison* 18 (1995): 76–88;
    and Bernd Hüppauf, "Räume der Destruktion und Konstruktion von Raum:
    Landschaft Sehen Raum und der Erste Weltkrieg," *Krieg und Literatur/War
    and Literature* 3 (1991).

2   Dirk Reinartz and Christian Graf von Krakow, *Deathly Still: Pictures of
    Former German Concentration Camps*, tr. Ishbel Flett (New York: Scalo,
    1995).

3   Mikael Levin, *War Story*, text by Meyer Levin (Munich: Gina Kehayoff, 1997).

4   Here and throughout I use the term *Holocaust*. Its problematic religious
    connotations of "sacrifice" have been analyzed by Omer Bartov, who also
    discusses the problems with alternative terms in *Murder in Our Midst:
    The Holocaust, Industrial Killing, and Representation* (New York: Oxford
    University Press, 1996), 56. See also Michael André Bernstein, *Foregone
    Conclusions: Against Apocalyptic History* (Berkeley: University of California
    Press, 1994), 132n.2. Replacing the term *Holocaust* with such terms as
    Shoah, Churbn, Auschwitz, or *Final Solution* would not only result in further
    problems (some of which have been discussed by Jean-François Lyotard in
    The Differend: Phrases in Dispute, tr. Georges van den Abeele [Minneapolis:
    University of Minnesota Press, 1988]). It might also suggest that we have
    arrived at an improved understanding of the event that the term *Holocaust*
    had left obscured. Notwithstanding the important studies by historians, I
    want to avoid the suggestion of such an improved understanding.

5   For the sense in which I use the Benjaminian term *auratic*, see n. 36.

6   Erich Hartmann's flawed *In the Camps* (New York: Norton, 1997) contains
    highly stylized images of former camps and contemporary memorials.
    After rehearsing pervasive tropes of Holocaust imagery and relying on a
    questionable, quasi-metaphysical aesthetics of light and dark (some of which
    is also employed by Reinartz), Hartmann ends with images suffused with a
    clichéd sentimentality that relieves viewers of the obligation to consider their
    own placement, situation, and subject-position vis-à-vis these sites.

7   Hannah Arendt, *Eichmann in Jerusalem* (New York: Viking, 1964), 268.

8   Greil Marcus, *The Dustbin of History* (Cambridge, MA: Harvard University
    Press, 1995), 91.

9   See Lawrence L. Langer, *Holocaust Testimonies: The Ruins of Memory* (New Haven: Yale University Press, 1991).

10 See also Joachim Ritter, "Landschaft," in *Subjektivität* (Frankfurt: Suhrkamp, 1974), 141–65; and J. H. Van den Berg, "The Subject and his Landscape," in *Romanticism and Consciousness: Essays in Criticism*, ed. Harold Bloom (New York: Norton, 1970), 57–65.

11 See Geoffrey H. Hartman's "Romanticism and 'Anti-Self-Consciousness,'" in *Romanticism and Consciousness*, ed. Bloom, 46–57.

12 Joseph Koerner, *Caspar David Friedrich and the Subject of Landscape* (New Haven: Yale University Press, 1990), 20 (emphasis in original).

13 John Barrell's study of images of the poor in English landscape painting addresses a similar concern. Although he warns against the illusion of identification with the rural poor in these paintings, the canvases he analyzes permit viewers to project themselves into the sites in ways that, I show, are cut short in the work of Reinartz and Levin. See Barrell, *The Dark Side of the Landscape: The Rural Poor in English Painting, 1730–1840* (Cambridge: Cambridge University Press, 1980).

14 For a discussion of approaches to the Holocaust as an ineffable event that nonetheless has permitted interpreters to draw lessons from it, see Sidra DeKoven Ezrahi, "Representing Auschwitz," *History and Memory* 7 (1996): 121–54.

15 For discussions of the questions of cultural transmission of the Holocaust, see Kali Tal, *Worlds of Hurt: Reading the Literatures of Trauma* (Cambridge: Cambridge University Press, 1996); Geoffrey H. Hartman, *The Longest Shadow: In the Aftermath of the Holocaust* (Bloomington: Indiana University Press, 1996); and the discussion and notes in chapter 3.

16 See, e.g. Martin Amis, *Time's Arrow, or The Nature of the Offense* (London: Jonathan Cape, 1991); D. M. Thomas, *Pictures at an Exhibition* (London: Bloomsbury, 1993).

17 Reinhard Matz, *Die unsichtbaren Lager. Das Verschwinden der Vergangenheit im Gedenken* (Reinbeck: Rowohlt, 1993), 19f. See also Geoffrey H. Hartman, "Introduction: Darkness Visible," in *Holocaust Remembrance: The Shapes of Memory*, ed. Hartman (Cambridge: Basil Blackwell, 1994); Yael Zerubavel, "The Death of Memory and the Memory of Death: Masada and the Holocaust as Historical Metaphors," *Representations* 45 (1994): 72–100.

18 Jacques Derrida, "Shibboleth for Paul Celan," in *Word Traces: Readings of Paul Celan*, ed. Aris Fioretos (Baltimore: Johns Hopkins University Press, 1994), 50.

19 Important debates center on the Romantic and aesthetic representation of surroundings and focus on the claim that all landscape art, because it tries to make the real desirable by means of aesthetic conventions, amounts to the artistic equivalent of militaristic, colonial desire. New historicist critics expose the presumably aesthetic focus of influential formalist critics of landscape art such as John Ruskin, Kenneth Clark, and E. H. Gombrich as complicit with nefarious nationalistic tendencies. See Ruskin, *Lectures*

on *Landscape* (Orpington and London: George Allen, 1897); Gombrich, "The Renaissance Theory of Art and the Rise of Landscape," in *Norm and Form: Studies in the Art of the Renaissance* (London: Phaidon, 1966); Clark, *Landscape into Art* (London: Murray, 1949). New historicists draw on the "hard facts" and "social energies" of history and cite the social contexts of the production and reception of landscape art to expose the imperialist drive presumably obscured in traditional aesthetically oriented art criticism. For the most pertinent historicist criticism, see the essays in W. J. T. Mitchell, ed., *Landscape and Power* (Chicago: University of Chicago Press, 1994). The assertion is that the purely aesthetic, Ruskinian approach to landscape art carried out in terms of organization of space, illusion of depth, viewer's placement, and the "experience of place" remains willfully blind to, and indeed complicit with, the Enlightenment's dark underside and the tremendous human costs of Europe's industrial and cultural development. The complicity between artistic landscape depictions and colonialist expansion cannot be denied; as I show in this chapter, this complicity might be deconstructed from within the genre of landscape photography.

20 Jean Baudrillard, *The Transparency of Evil: Essays on Extreme Phenomena*, tr. James Benedict (London: Verso, 1993), 91.

21 For sophisticated readings of the landscape tradition and its relation to imperialist ambition, see the essays in Mitchell, ed., *Landscape and Power*.

22 Simon Schama, *Landscape and Memory* (New York: Knopf, 1995), 27.

23 Nadine Fresco, "Remembering the Unknown," *International Review of Psycho-Analysis* 11 (1984): 424.

24 Dan Diner, "Zwischen Aporie und Apologie: Über Grenzen der Historisierbarkeit der Massenvernichtung," *Babylon* 2 (1987): 33; Raul Hilberg, *Unerbetene Erinnerung: Der Weg eines Holocaust Forschers* (Frankfurt: Fischer, 1994), 174–5. See also Saul Friedlander, "'The Final Solution': On the Unease in Historical Interpretation," in his *Memory, History, and the Extermination of the Jews* (Bloomington: Indiana University Press, 1993).

25 Langer distinguishes between "common" and "deep memories" in *Holocaust Testimonies*, 1–39.

26 The term *concentrationary* universe hints at this unbridgeable gap between the notions of a "place" or "world," and the occurrences in these nonplaces; it was used first by David Rousset, *L'univers concentrationnaire* (Paris: Payot, 1946). See Michel Pollack, *L'expérience concentrationnaire: Essai sur le maintien de l'identité sociale* (Paris: Metailie, 1990). On the relations between the places of the Holocaust and the knowledge of these places, see also Claude Lanzmann, "Le lieu et la parole," in *Au sujet de Shoah*, ed. Michel Deguy (Paris: Belin, 1990), 294.

27 The tension between a landscape photograph's aesthetic appeal and its documentary dimensions has resulted in debates about the possibility of categorizing such photographs as either aesthetic *landscapes* organized in terms of flatness, illusion of depth, and "aesthetic signification [of] sublimity

and transcendence" or purely informational *views*, in which space is properly "grounded, coordinated, mapped ... not so much by perspective as by photographic grid" (Rosalind Krauss, *The Originality of the Avant-Garde and Other Myths* [Cambridge, MA: The MIT Press, 1985], 133–5). Krauss analyzes the difference between landscapes and views by discussing photographs meant to document terrain slated for industrial, civilian, or military exploitation. See also Alan Trachtenberg, *Reading American Photographs: Images as History* (New York: Hill and Wang, 1989).

28 The term *unstoried* in relation to a place was first used by Washington Irving, in the preface to his 1819 *Sketchbook*, to refer to the expanses of the American West before their colonization by European settlers.

29 For an illuminating discussion of the link between anamorphic perspective and modern subjectivity, see Tom Conley, "The Wit of the Letter: Holbein's Lacan," in *Vision in Context: Historical and Contemporary Perspectives on Sight*, ed. Teresa Brennan and Martin Jay (New York: Routledge, 1996), 45–63.

30 Koerner, *Caspar David Friedrich*, 15.

31 On the centrality of Ohrdruf in the U.S. press coverage of Nazi crimes at the end of the war, see Barbie Zelizer, *Remembering to Forget: Holocaust Memory through the Camera's Eye* (Chicago: University of Chicago Press, 1998), esp. 86–120.

32 Levin, *War Story*, 155. Page numbers for quotations from this work hereafter appear in text in parentheses.

33 Sidra DeKoven Ezrahi discusses the paradoxical notion of a "place without the self," which I discuss here from an art-historical point of view, in the relations between photographs and writing in the work of the poet Dan Pagis; Ezrahi, *Booking Passage: Exile and Homecoming in Modern Hebrew Literature* (Berkeley: University of California Press, 2000), 166.

34 William Mitchell, *The Reconfigured Eye: Visual Truth in the Post-Photographic Era* (Cambridge, MA: The MIT Press, 1992).

35 Allan Sekula, "Reading an Archive," in Brian Wallis, ed., *Blasted Allegories: An Anthology of Writings by Contemporary Artists* (Cambridge, MA: The MIT Press, 1987), 121.

36 In order to strip the term *aura* (and its adjective, *auratic*) of its aura, we might best describe it as a ghostly premonition or a spell (in its Victorian usage), rather than as the nostalgic glow of authentic presence, as it is often misconstrued. In *Agon* (New York: Oxford University Press, 1982), Harold Bloom usefully draws on Benjamin's definition of *aura* and earlier explanations to define aura as "an invisible breath or emanation ... a breeze, but most of all a sensation or shock, the sort of illusion of a breeze that precedes the start of a nervous breakdown or disorder" (230). Benjamin's notion of the disappearance or destruction of the aura through technical reproduction has become a commonplace of photography criticism. This notion—which Benjamin modified in "Small History of Photography"— is often imported from his later essay "The Work of Art in the Age of

Mechanical Reproduction," in *Illuminations*, tr. Harry Zohn (New York: Schocken 1968). Ariella Azoulay has shown Benjamin's essay to be a "eulogy … to the loss of place … a transition from a unique place in which one must be present to experience it to a place that can be experienced without necessarily being there, due to the various technologies of reproduction" (Azoulay, *Death's Showcase* [Cambridge, MA: The MIT Press, 2001], 21, 22). Theodor W. Adorno offers a critique of Benjamin's thesis about the disappearance of aura in all mass-produced works in *Aesthetic Theory* (New York: Continuum, 1984), 82.

37   See Michael Fried's work on absorption in *Realism, Writing, Disfiguration: On Thomas Eakins and Stephen Crane* (Chicago: University of Chicago Press, 1987). For a history of the camps and a preliminary bibliography of survivor testimonies on Sobibór, see Yitzhak Arad, *Belzec, Sobibór, Treblinka: The Operation Reinhard Death Camps* (Bloomington: University of Indiana Press, 1987).

38   Roland Barthes, *Camera Lucida: Reflections on Photography*, tr. Richard Howard (New York: Hill & Wang, 1981), 91.

39   On kitsch and sublimity in Holocaust representation, see Saul Friedlander, *Reflections of Nazism: An Essay on Kitsch and Death*, tr. Thomas Weyr (New York: Harper and Row, 1984); and Lyotard, *Heidegger and 'the jews,'* tr. Andreas Michel and Mark Roberts (Minneapolis: University of Minnesota Press, 1990).

40   Philippe Lacoue-Labarthe has analyzed the ideological reworking of the Romantic tradition into "National Aestheticism" in *Heidegger, Art, and Politics*, tr. Chris Turner (Cambridge: Basil Blackwell, 1989), 58.

41   Gitta Sereny, *Into That Darkness* (New York: McGraw-Hill, 1974), 145.

42   Robert Jan van Pelt analyzes the link between the Holocaust and Heidegger's thoughts on space and dwellings (to which the term *Lichtung*, for "clearing," alludes here). Van Pelt and Carroll William Westfall, eds., *Architectural Principles in the Age of Historicism* (New Haven: Yale University Press, 1991).

43   Maurice Blanchot, *The Writing of the Disaster* (Lincoln: University of Nebraska Press, 1986), 28.

44   Caruth, "Introduction," in Caruth, ed., *Trauma: Explorations in Memory* (Baltimore: Johns Hopkins University Press, 1995), 14. For other discussions of representations of the Holocaust informed by trauma theory, see esp. the essays in Geoffrey H. Hartman, ed., *Holocaust Remembrance*; Dominick LaCapra, *Representing the Holocaust: History, Theory, Trauma* (Ithaca: Cornell University Press, 1994); Shoshana Felman and Dori Laub, *Testimony: Crises of Witnessing in Literature, Psychoanalysis, and History* (London: Routledge, 1992); Tal, *Worlds that Hurt*.

45   See, for example, Lenore Terr et al., "Children's Responses to the Challenger Spacecraft Disaster," *American Journal of Psychiatry* 153 (1996): 624.

46   Lanzmann, "Le lieu et la parole," in *Au sujet de Shoah*, 294.

47   Among the vast theoretical writings on trauma, the following texts are of particular interest to discussions of the precision of traumatic memory: Pierre

Janet, *L'amnésie et la dissociation des souvenirs par l'émotion* (Paris: F. Alcan 1904; reprint, Marseille, 1983); Sigmund Freud and Joseph Breuer, *Studies in Hysteria*, vol. 2 of Freud, *Standard Edition*; Jacques Lacan, "Tuché et Automaton," in *Le Séminaire*, vol. 11, *Quatre concepts fundamentaux de la psychoanalyse*, ed. Jacques Alain-Miller (Paris: Seuil, 1973); Robert Jay Lifton, *The Broken Connection* (New York: Simon and Schuster, 1980); Bessel A. van der Kolk, *Psychological Trauma* (Washington, DC: American Psychiatric Press, 1987); Bessel van der Kolk, Alexander C. McFarlane, and Lars Weisath, eds., *Traumatic Stress: The Effects of Overwhelming Experience on Mind, Body, and Society* (New York: Guilford Press, 1996); J. L Singer, ed., *Repression and Dissociation* (Chicago: University of Chicago Press, 1990); and Judith Herman, *Trauma and Recovery* (New York: Basic Books, 1992). Ruth Leys is skeptical about the literalist notion of traumatic memory but acknowledges—and regardless of the differences between theoretical models, this is relevant for the present purposes—that this conception, which is as historically and culturally specific as others, "is deeply entrenched . . . in the cultural imagery of the West" (Leys, *Trauma: A Genealogy* [Chicago: University of Chicago Press, 2000], 263).

48 The best-known example of this use of documentary photographs may be the so-called Auschwitz Album, taken by an unknown Nazi photographer and discovered by the survivor Lili Meier at the Dora labor camp; see Peter Hellmann, ed., *The Auschwitz Album: A Book Based upon an Album Discovered by a Concentration Camp Survivor, Lili Meier* (New York: Random House, 1981). See also the articles by Cornelia Brink, Detlev Hoffmann, and Hanno Loewy on the use of photographs in postwar Holocaust education and memorialization, in *Auschwitz: Geschichte, Rezeption und Wirkung*, ed. Fritz Bauer Institut (Frankfurt: Campus, 1996). Marianne Hirsch offers an intriguing analysis of the role of family snapshots in Holocaust commemoration in *Family Frames: Photography, Narrative, and Postmemory* (Cambridge, Mass.: Harvard University Press, 1997).

49 On moral concerns about the desire for absolute understanding, see esp. Pierre Vidal-Naquet, *Assassins of Memory: Essays on the Denial of the Holocaust* (New York: Columbia University Press, 1992); and Lyotard, *The Differend*.

50 Manuel Köppen, ed., *Kunst und Literatur nach Auschwitz* (Berlin: Erich Schmidt, 1993), 166.

51 On the question of whether the "Final Solution" can be integrated into a historical narrative, see the debate between Hayden White, Martin Jay, and Carlo Ginzburg in Saul Friedlander, ed., *Probing the Limits of Representation: Nazism and the "Final Solution"* (Cambridge, MA: Harvard University Press, 1992).

52 LaCapra, *Representing the Holocaust*, 46 (emphasis added).

53 Adorno and Horkheimer's *Dialectic of Enlightenment* explores the violent aspect of the enlightened subject's subjugation of the outside world that is necessary for the subject's constitution.

54 The term *secondary witness* occurs in Terence Des Pres, *The Survivor* (New York: Oxford University Press, 1976); and in Langer, *Holocaust Testimonies*,

39. Geoffrey H. Hartman has elaborated on this concept in "Holocaust and Intellectual Witness," *Partisan Review* 65 (1998): 37–48.

55 On the work of Reinhard Matz, who tries to capture the nature of "memory-tourism," see James Young, "Das Erinnern und die Rhetorik des Fotos—Reinhard Matz," in *Die unsichtbaren Lager*, 15–19.

56 See James E. Young, *The Texture of Memory* (New Haven: Yale University Press, 1993), 53.

57 Peter Weiss, "Mein Ort," in *Rapporte* (Frankfurt: Suhrkamp, 1981); Sereny, *Into That Darkness*, 145–7, Young, *Texture of Memory*; Schama, *Landscape and Memory*.

58 Such total amnesia is rare in survivors of trauma but often determines the reality of those who come in contact with them. For an exceptionally effective and moving account of the dangerous sense of overwhelming mystery caused by the voiding of memory during the Holocaust, see David Grossman's novel, *See Under: Love* (New York: Farrar, Straus, Giroux, 1991).

59 Vilém Flusser, *Standpunkte: Texte zur Fotografie*, ed. Andreas Müller-Pohle (Göttingen: European Photography, 1998), 8: 157.

60 Ibid.

61 Ibid.

26

A Geography of Ghosts: The Spectral Landscapes of Mary Butts

David Matless

We have been careless lately what spiritual company we have kept;
in our choice of ghostly guests. The results are observable.

MARY BUTTS, 1933

I. Introduction

Through the writings of Mary Butts (1890–1937), this paper raises a geography of ghosts. Butts' novels, stories, essays and journals allow an elaboration of spectral landscapes, suggest political variations on the spectro-geographic theme, and indicate forms of cultural authority claimed by the spectrally attuned. Her work also indicates the importance of genre in spectro-geographies, the forms and conventions shaping the ghost and producing it as a character. Butts' phrase: 'our choice of ghostly guests', quoted above, is from an essay on the supernatural in fiction. Butts sought to shape such choices via interventions deploying a sense of the magical qualities of things, places, landscapes, writing in an inter-war Britain where attempts to define, claim and protect magical, sacred geographies were not uncommon. The paper proceeds through an episodic structure, with an introduction to Butts' life and work following discussion of the recent

critical currency of the spectral. Sections consider the ghost as literary
figure, Butts' own magic places, her tales of ghostly happenings, and
geographical claims to exclusive magic. We begin with some neglected items
from the geographical past, which will return to meet Butts in conclusion.

II. Our ghostly, magical, demonic past: Three curios

Connecting the languages of geography, the spectral and the magical is not
itself novel; Livingstone indeed indicates 'magical geography' as one of the
themes for his 'conversational conclusion' in *The geographical tradition*.[1]
The mystical, the magical and the spectral can be traced as warning signs,
boundary markers, temptations, for the academic discipline of geography, and
for popular and policy geographical discourse. Three curios from the twentieth
century indicate the geographical possibilities of figures of non-reason.

In 1941 Hans Speier, writing in the US journal *Social research* in
connection with the Research Project on Totalitarian Communication,
entitled an essay on propaganda maps 'Magic geography'. Speier, recognizing the capacity of maps to speak beyond a neutral 'representation of a
given state of affairs', noted wartime peril: 'Propagandists... rediscover...
symbolic values in maps, and by exploiting them, turn geography into a
kind of magic'.[2] This kind of magic is not something to wonder at, rather
geography as magical implies deceit, manipulation and the enchantment
of a gullible viewer. The scholar's task becomes one of demystification in
the service of a non-totalitarian scientific truth, which can be deployed
for liberal democratic political ends. For contemporary geographical
engagement with the magical, Speier offers an example of critique and
scepticism, asserting a hegemony of liberal reason.

In 1927 Montague Summers, literary scholar and Roman Catholic cleric
fascinated by the occult, produced a 600–page book on *The geography of
witchcraft*, supplementing his 1926 *The history of witchcraft and demonology* with an excursion through Greece and Rome, England, Scotland,
New England, France, Germany, Italy and Spain. Geography here denotes
national and local specificity, geographical variations on a general historical
theme. Summers enfolds Satanism, spiritualism and ghost beliefs into
witchcraft as a demonic category, and finishes his English chapter with
warnings. The Black Mass is 'said in London and Brighton – and I doubt
not in many other towns too', Hosts are stolen from London churches and
diabolic Eucharists conducted, 'societies of evil' work across the country,
'far-spread' and 'cunningly organized'. Witchcraft appears a kind of magic
at odds with civilization: 'To the ordinary man Satanism is incredible, or
at any rate a myth of the remote Dark Ages. He does not realize, and he

is happy in his ignorance, the evil fires that burn but just a very little way beneath the thin and crumbling crust of our boasted modern civilization'.[3] Summers was no devotee of rationalism, rather some supernatures carried truth while others led astray; Summers' 1938 history of the Gothic novel, *The gothic quest*, would end with a dismissal of Surrealism as an improper and atheistic sensibility: 'They are unmystical, unromantic. They deny the supernatural. Yet everything in the last analysis depends upon the supernatural, since as S. Augustine tells us, God is the only Reality'.[4] For contemporary geographical engagements with the magical, spectral or demonic, Summers illustrates the differential valuation of supernatures, and the consequent associations of fear, evil and burning (of souls, of witches).

In 1916 former Royal Geographical Society Map Curator and Instructor in Surveying E. A. Reeves published *The recollections of a geographer*, an account of a geographical career whose final chapter addressed 'Psychic experiences'. For Reeves this went beyond geography, although recent debates, of which the papers in this journal issue are a part, might gather the psychic back into Reeves' geographical life. Reeves recounts involvement in spiritualism following unexplained or apparently psychic happenings; knockings on doors, premonitions of the University Boat Race result, visions of Lord Kitchener on his bedroom wall, sightings of possible ghosts. One April Saturday, leaving the RGS at one o'clock and having 'a light lunch' at the A. B. C., Reeves met the ghost of Knightsbridge tube station, 'a tall man in a long old-fashioned black cloak and a round black hat', who he took for an artist or musician, and who walked straight through a white-tiled wall: 'I could not believe my eyes!... Was it possible that there was some hidden door?'. Scrutiny of the wall showed nothing: 'Could it be some hallucination?'[5] Reeves had only had a coffee at the A. B. C.. Later he hears of a tube station ghost. These defiantly sober recollections set up the psychic as a matter of true experience and reasoned enquiry, though one beyond strictly geographical business. The world of work could however shape psychic experience, as when Reeves encounters deceased explorers to whom he once taught surveying: 'on several occasions some of these have made their presence known at séances and given me messages that could only have come from themselves'.[6] Reeves' example of credulous reason may be borne in mind for any geographical engagement with the spectral, spiritual and psychic.

Speier, Summers and Reeves indicate practices and fields of thought which have grazed the language and discipline of geography. The term 'grazing' can here imply categories feeding off and nourishing one another, or scarring each other through unexpected encounters. If the spectral, the magical, the demonic, the psychic carry a family resemblance which can lead to their being lumped together from without on a common cultural ground, they are often furiously demarcated from within. Geographical movement into more-or-less occult domains, from whatever motivation, entails an appreciation of such commonalities and distinctions, and of the nuances of belief, mockery, deceit, terror, scepticism, credulity and incredulity, which move across the field.[7] With this in mind the paper now turns to the contemporary academic currency of the spectral.

III. The cultural geography of the spectral

The spectral, rather than the magical or spiritual or demonic, has gained recent scholarly currency. If Buse and Stott begin their collection *Ghosts: deconstruction, psychoanalysis, history* by suggesting that 'to be interested in ghosts these days is decidedly anachronistic',[8] their collection rides academic interest, prompted by Derrida's *Spectres of Marx*: 'Spectrality and haunting continue to enjoy a powerful currency in language and in thinking, even if they have been left behind by belief'.[9] Buse and Stott set up their project as moving beyond histories of a neglected 'outside of reason' (the occult, spiritualism etc.), instead seeking 'to inspect the inside of reason and see how it too is haunted by what it excludes'.[10] This moving beyond continues effectively to mark out properly sceptical scholarship from misguided credulity: 'even though it is now frivolous to believe in ghosts, they cannot shrug off the spectre of belief: it is simply that now they have been consigned to the task of representing whatever is not to be believed'.[11] Mary Butts played on similar cultural terrain, if for different ends, and, as discussed below, her stories of possession echo Buse and Stott's comment that 'where there are disputes over property, we find ghosts, or that where we find ghosts, there are bound to be anxieties about property'.[12]

What might be the geographical currency of the modern scholarly spectre as it grazes disciplinary borders? Byron and Punter's 1999 literary collection *Spectral readings*, subtitled *Towards a gothic geography*, circumscribes its ghost: 'By referring in the book's subtitle to a 'Gothic geography' we are, of course, speaking as always in a metaphor'.[13] The metaphor allows productive exploration of Gothic's limits of mappability, but the phrase 'of course' jars. Is this an embrace for the language of geography while anything smacking of the discipline is put to one side? Speaking 'as always' in a metaphor becomes speaking only in a metaphor, bypassing more complex possibilities of cultural geography. Such possibilities of the Gothic and spectral are more evident in Roger Luckhurst's essay on 'The contemporary London Gothic and the limits of the "spectral turn"'.[14] Asking what it means to place the spectre, Luckhurst pursues a scepticism concerning the 'generalized economy of haunting' informing the 'spectral turn'.[15] Considering the 'newly Gothicized apprehension of London' and the related 'discourse of spectralized modernity', Luckhurst argues that 'the generalized structure of haunting is symptomatically blind to its generative loci',[16] and counters in part via a 'geography of the genre'.[17] Deconstruction is turned on the general hauntology developed in the wake of *Spectres of Marx*, with singularity and the 'resistant residue of untranslatability' aligned with attention to the ghost as a specific symptom at a specific site. The ghost conjures a singular geography of unpredictable politics, rather than general rupturous possibility: 'The spectral turn reaches a limit if all it can describe is a repeated structure or generalized "spectral process" – perhaps most particularly when critics suggest the breaching of limits is itself somehow inherently political'. Luckhurst seeks geographical and historical purchase for spectrality, ending: 'we surely have to risk the violence of *reading* the ghost, of cracking open its absent presence to answer the demand of its specific symptomatology and its specific locale'.[18]

Luckhurst raises the ghost-in-context. Clive Barnett's caution over context as a device of secure framing, of return to spatio-temporal origin, and subsequent explanatory confinement, is pertinent here, though he echoes Luckhurst in scepticism concerning the politics of liminal freedom: 'One lesson of deconstruction is that the political value of either fixing meaning (of closure or of identity) or of maintaining instability (of ambivalence or of difference) is not open to prior, conceptual determination'.[19] Buse and Stott's comment that 'there may be no proper time for ghosts', that 'haunting, by its very structure, implies a deformation of linear temporality',[20] indicates that the ghost-in-context is nevertheless liable to break narrow frames, indeed the deconstructed ghost becomes a creature of precise if not necessarily linear geographies, histories, temporalities, spatialities, all contributing to its make up. Precision here can release as much as restrain.

In the narrowest subdisciplinary and broadest transdisciplinary sense, then, this article pursues, via the work of Mary Butts, a cultural geography of the spectral wary of either generalized models of haunting, or of ghosts trapped in contexts. Other geographical accounts pertinent to this approach and subject matter include Wylie's recent Derridean engagement with W. G. Sebald as exemplary practitioner of (and late haunting presence for) spectral geographies, and Nash's cultural-historical study of the 'Visionary geographies' of early twentieth century Irish poet and reformer George Russell.[21] Nash shows how, writing as 'AE', Russell aligned two senses of the visionary; a landscape transformed through rural reform, and a mystic vision of folklore, nature and nation. Butts performs parallel visionary geographies, and also echoes themes sketched in Lowerson's essay on 'The mystical geography of the English', moving through religion, folk religion, the parish church, pagan revivals, and the occult, the connection of all to senses of Englishness, and the cultural assumption that 'the countryside is full of places with permanent spiritual characteristics'.[22] From such work emerges a particular geoaesthetic of the spectral, embracing a geographical cultural politics at various scales. Ghosts work a cultural politics of nation, including versions of Englishness; of region, including in Butts' work areas such as west Cornwall and Dorset; and of locale, as something to be cherished, defended, retreated to. The combination of the spiritual, the ghostly and the intensely local leads Butts' spectral work to echo Freud's definition of the uncanny, 'that class of the frightening which leads back to what is known of old and long familiar'.[23] In Butts' work the ghost belongs in marvellous or horrible form to the place. If she could also forcefully write against alien presence or influence in her claimed country, her ghosts and spirits were familiars haunting home.

IV. Introducing Mary Butts

Mary Butts was born in 1890, growing up in the family home of Salterns, in Parkstone on the edge of Poole in Dorset, in southern England. Salterns as landscape of memory, myth, possession and dispossession shapes Butts' memoir *The crystal cabinet*, published posthumously in 1937.[24] Nathalie Blondel provides a comprehensive account of her complex life,[25] her studies in London, pacifism in World War One, lesbian relationships, 1918 marriage to John Rodker, an intermittent relationship with her daughter, born in 1920, her subsequent lovers and Bohemian life in 1920s Paris and southern France. Butts moved in high modernist circles, Cocteau illustrating her prose sequence *Imaginary letters* in 1928. Butts' first story collection, *Speed the plough*, was published in 1923, with her first novel, *Ashe of rings*, written during the war, issued in 1925. *Armed with madness* followed in 1928, *Death of Felicity Taverner* in 1932, with further historical narratives on Alexander the Great (*The Macedonian*, 1933) and Cleopatra (*Scenes from the life of Cleopatra*, 1935). Her many essays and reviews included '"Ghosties and Ghoulies"' (1933), on the supernatural in fiction, and the 1932 pamphlets *Warning to hikers* and *Traps for unbelievers*.[26] Butts married artist Gabriel Aitken in 1930, moving in January 1932 to Sennen Cove, near Land's End in Cornwall, living in a bungalow overlooking the Atlantic Ocean. The marriage broke up in 1934, Butts then converting to Anglo-Catholicism. She died suddenly in March 1937, and is buried in Sennen parish cemetery.

Butts' daughter Camilla Bagg describes the social milieu of her writings well, 'with their setting of taken-for-granted money, no necessity to find a job, cultivation of the mind, frequent assumptions that the reader was well up in French and the classics, and no interest whatever in ordinary people'.[27] Patrick Wright highlights her intimate connection of family and place; family 'a transcendent value threatened by its own historicity', and places of spiritual value threatened by materialism, suburbia, mass leisure, etc.[28] Butts' high literary modernism could resent modernity, with spiritual and class values merging in the evocation of landscapes of private meaning. Whether Salterns, the isle of Purbeck across Poole harbour, the Dorset earthworks of Badbury Rings a few miles inland, or Sennen and its environs in later life, Butts gave local topography literary form, vulnerable lands and strong coastlines dramatizing a conservative mythic modernism.

Butts claimed authentic measure of land against a supposedly false urban pastoralism driving contemporary country enthusiasms. Myth and magic serve for the critique of contemporary culture, marking out a select group of 'special people in special places'.[29] Butts' high European modernist style calls up an authentic green English world through myth and ritual, magic and ghosts, a modernism of ritual held to restore truth against an artificial modern culture. Butts, in common with modernists such as T. S. Eliot, drew on the classical anthropology of Jane Harrison and the Cambridge Ritualists, and Jessie Weston's 1920 *From ritual to romance*, an account of the Grail legends as rooted in primitive nature cults. Butts also explored formal magic though association with infamous occultist Aleister Crowley in the early 1920s, staying at his Sicilian abbey in summer 1921, though she later rejected his methods and views.[30] Psychoanalysis too offered resonant treatment of myth, though for Butts this was a symptom of modern problems rather than a means to their resolution; as Jane Garrity suggests, Butts is 'involved with scientific and psychoanalytical discourses even as she attempts to disavow them'.[31] Butts upheld Jane Harrison against Freud, with ritual presented as the basis of religious value. *Armed with madness* and *Death of Felicity Taverner* work around 'the female protagonist as a kind of living Grail, a genealogical signifier of England's cultural mythology', with ritual practice, cycles of nature and the female body mapping onto one another.[32] The dead Felicity achieves presence in the latter novel as 'a ghost who is the real link to an authentic England rooted in an idea of ancient and timeless continuity with the rural past'.[33]

As her life proceeded, Butts produced herself as a figure haunting England, a remnant of national essence and a sign of possible redemption. Moving to Sennen Cove, Butts haunts culture from the end of the land, a peripheral spirit set up as a true centre. Early death would help produce the ghost of a neglected modernism, her work later rediscovered as, variously, a lost female pioneer, a neglected seer, a skeleton in the modern cupboard.

V. Styles and thoughts of ghosts

There was never more curiosity than there is today about 'the uncanny' or 'strange things' – 'things' that even in our father's day it was improper to believe in at all.[34]

'"Ghosties and Ghoulies": uses of the supernatural in English fiction' was published in four instalments in *The bookman* between January and April 1933. Butts' essay developed from an unpublished article written in Paris in August 1928 on 'Use of the supernatural in fiction', and is signed as written 'Paris-Sennen 1928–1932'.[35] Various dimensions of the ghost appear.

Butts addresses the ghost as an object of thought, citing Weston and Harrison as setting out 'the *natural* history of so many of our beliefs, in bogy, ghost, daimon, demon, angel or god'.[36] Butts' is a particular kind of modernist ghost. *Traps for unbelievers* states: 'An old ghost accompanies the advances and speculation of man, inexorcisable, inexorable, materialising at will'.[37] Here are 'receipts which linked the phenomenal world to an eternal',[38] laid to one side in the modern world but never truly discarded. 'Ghosties and Ghoulies' draws from Harrison and Weston conceptions which might come round again, 'a great wheel turned and ground gained – to initiations which will really initiate; not by haphazard; not by fraud or hypnosis or superstition, but inevitably'.[39] Here are 'formulae that are very old', whose ritual origins may be traced and powers known, and from whose various demons and angels a careful choice should be made. The essay ends: 'We have been careless lately what spiritual company we have kept; in our choice of ghostly guests. The results are observable'.[40]

Butts also explores the ghost as literary form, having most time for the evocatory story, authors seeking 'only to produce horror and wonder; or at best, and without explanation, the consciousness of a universe enlarged'.[41] Butts deployed a chess analogy to indicate: 'the first law... of the interaction of other worlds with ours; that it can be somehow described by a parallel with the knight's move in chess. The other moves are comparable with ordinary activities. Only the knights move two squares and a diagonal, on and sideways and can jump'.[42] A clear grid reveals other capacities and dimensions. M. R. James is Butts' exemplary writer, and her own work sought parallel effect. While noting James' 'kind, sceptical disclaimers', Butts suggested 'some experience, apart from his immense scholarship, he must have had'.[43] Butts developed her discussion in a 1934 *London mercury* essay on 'The art of Montague James', emphasizing a 'matter-of-fact' style, not seeking to demonstrate any particular theory of the occult: 'the essence of his art is a sudden, appalling shock of visibility. The intangible become more than tangible, unspeakably real, solid, present'.[44] James' 'matter' is taken 'from his own surroundings and experience',[45] with 'an affection for some very plain, very subtle, very unambitious English landscapes it takes a long time to appreciate and understand'.[46] Butts then claims country affinity with ghostly magic:

Everyone who has lived much out of doors feels something of what he tells. Not by association with tradition, but by a direct kind of awareness, an impact on the senses – and something more than the senses. It can be a recurrent, almost an overwhelming, experience. Much ancient bogey-lore was a rationalisation of it. Today we talk of suggestion, exorcise with the magic word 'unscientific.' But I doubt if our ignorant scepticism is any nearer truth than our ancestors' ignorant credulity.[47]

Traps for unbelievers similarly defines magic through a geographically-shaped capacity to grasp 'relations between things of a different order: the moon and a stone, the sea and a piece of wood, women and fish', a 'very peculiar kind of awareness, an awareness modified and sometimes lost by people whose life has been passed in towns'.[48]

While applauding the evocatory ghost story, Butts has less sympathy for a second mode, that supporting a theory of life beyond perception, 'authors with a psychic axe to grind'.[49] Third, the 'lowest class',[50] comes 'the vulgar stuff, the sniggerers in the cheap magazines at stories of the appearance of the dead'.[51] Butts also notes purportedly non-fictional works, 'which profess to describe hauntings and disturbances', accounts so far written only by 'third- rate journalists'.[52] Marking out her ghosts of distinction, Butts wonders that the best authors continue to produce 'excellent work on the subjects they are not supposed to believe in at all'. And all this in 'an age when the accepted view is that anything may be true, "that anything may happen," while that none of the explanations – especially the religious explanations – we were once taught, *can* be the right one'. Taking aim at psychoanalysis, Butts suggests that such a perspective 'leads us to describe the beliefs and faiths of our ancestors as science misunderstood; or the visions of saint or artist, profound or fruitful, curious or bizarre, as nothing *more* than a way of externalizing the unconscious'.[53] Butts instead argues that the best ghost stories evoke a truth of experience, the residue left when other explanations fail: 'a question remains, more easy to feel than to ask'.[54] On what she regards as a transhistorical and transgeographical belief in gods and demons, Butts comments: 'all nonsense and misunderstanding of natural phenomena apart, when imaginative writing reaches a certain degree of precision, produces such an effect of reality, it is difficult to see how this is done if the observation implied in the writing is without *some* foundation in experience'.[55]

Transgeographical belief did not however imply a welcome for all geographically specific forms. Butts is dismissive of literary Celticism, chiding (with 'admirable exceptions' including Yeats, AE and Lady Gregory) 'shapelessness' and lack of realism:

Things happen as we know they do not happen, and as we do not want them to happen. The magic princesses – for this is just as explicit in their earliest epics – are too magic. Thirty invincible knights fight thirty invincible giants for thirty nights and days; without, as Professor Murray points out, any interval for meals. Not only do these things not happen; we do not care to pretend that they happen.

Butts presents such stories as potentially poisonous: 'an overdose of Celtic "magic" can give one a sense of something very like a special kind of evil'. Contrast is found in vernacular Celtic story: 'Very different are true countrymen's stories, of a small, green, strange, gay, earthy, child-stealing folk'.[56] Butts criticises the national use of the Celtic in Ireland:

> This essay is not the place to examine the Celtic field. Ancient or modern, there is too much of it. To-day it can be smug. Can assume, without so much as a polite gesture in the direction of evidence, that it is the mind of the debased Saxon, lost in materialism, which questions the stories of a supernaturally enlightened peasantry on the existence and nature of the Sidhe. Who exist in Ireland for the Irish; sole inspiration of the only art worth mentioning in Europe. ...
> It is cult that is fatal. And the Irish to-day seem to make of their folk-mythology a national asset.[57]

As a counter Butts upholds 'a supernatural story' from the Icelandic Grettir Saga, 'Glam's Ghost', reprinted in a recent ghost anthology, whose telling carries: 'a sober precision ... It might be a report written by an imaginative, simple and accurate person for the Society of Psychical Research'. Butts sums up her own everyday supernatural aesthetic as: '*If it happened at all, it happened like that*'.[58]

VI. Magic of person and place

Elsewhere in 'Ghosties and Ghoulies', Butts indicates that things may have happened to her.[59] The supernatural in fiction meets supernatural actuality, as Butts evokes enigmatic and mysterious sites and occurrences. So Butts encounters 'a tree, a scarred pine' in a French park, which may have exerted some agency in her loss of an earring and a subsequent sickness.[60] And, 'To quote again one's own experience: there is a part of Lincoln's Inn which does not always "stay put." Also Great Russell Street. But that, whatever it is, is something projected *out* of the British Museum'.[61] Butts includes sites outside 'the regular places where men went for initiation', beliefs and traditions 'that certain places exist, of themselves and quite unofficially, charged with mana and tabu'.[62] Butts notes a 'transition' observed 'when a place becomes another place; and you know what you have suspected before – that all the time it has been two places at once'.[63]

Half way through the essay Butts turns to the capacity of places to gather holiness: 'In the past certain holy spots, caves and "temenoi" were, at one and the same time, a place on this earth; a place where once a supernatural event had happened; and a place where, by luck or devotion or the quality of the initiate, it might happen again'.[64] Butts then makes 'a personal digression' to 'attempt to explain what is meant by the experience, so often used by writers on the supernatural, that a place can be more than its assembly of wood and leaf and stone visible to us; more than the atomic structure common to all things'.[65] Butts describes an unnamed Badbury Rings, a hill fort in south Dorset, with three rings of earthworks and a central grove of trees:

> Not always places you would expect. Explanation or theory apart, a good many sensitive persons have a list of their own. For instance there is a neolithic earthwork in the south of England. It is better not to say where. The fewer people who pollute that holy and delectable ground the better. No shepherd, no farmhand will go there after dark. In mediaeval romance, a place identified with it was a 'temenos' of Morgan le Fay. (The country people have forgotten her.) But there are other earthworks nearby, including Stonehenge, where they will camp out all night at lambing time. Not that one. It is, or was until lately, mana of high potency and, at the same time, strictly tabu. The writer of this essay discovered it when young; and it is no exaggeration to say that a great part of her imaginative life was elicited by it and rests there. Archaeology had begun to interest me, but I knew none of its stories then. It entered into me, 'accepted' me.[66]

Butts presents herself as drawn to the haunted, while the ordinary folk can sense the place but will not engage it. Garrity notes how part of the attraction of mana for Butts was its implication that things deemed foreign and contaminating should and might be expelled; Wright terms Butts' mana 'a secret rationality which discloses itself on occasion to the initiate'.[67] Contrary to Butts' opening statement, an ancient earthwork is perhaps exactly the place you would expect some such thing to happen, indeed the associations of magic and prehistory would again alight on 'the fort of Badbury Rings' in 1936 in artist Paul Nash's Shell Guide to Dorset:

> It is round rather than oval, and has the dread peculiarity of a crown of dense trees planted in concentric circles. I have read of enchanted places, and at rare times come upon them, but I remember nothing so beautifully haunted as the wood in Badbury Rings. Long afterwards I read of the tradition that King Arthur's soul inhabited a raven's body which nested there – indeed it is one of the last nesting-places of the wild raven in England – but I needed no artificial stimulus to be impressed. Beyond

the outer plateau the rings heave up and round in waves 40 feet high. A magic bird in a haunted wood, an ancient cliff washed by a sea changed into earth. There is scarcely anything lacking.[68]

Badbury had long been a key site for Butts, and *The crystal cabinet* gives a similar account of historical and legendary associations, magical qualities, initiation, dream, Butts glimpsing 'the makings of correspondence, a translation which should be ever valid, between the seen and the unseen'.[69] Butts plays on the ring motif to indicate her rescue from variants of modern thinking, contrasting ancient and eternal concentrated meaning with supposed repetitious circularities in modern thought: 'without the Rings, I know what would have happened to me – whirled away on the merry-go-round of the complex and the wish-fulfilment and the conditioned reflex, with Jung and Pavlov, Julian Huxley and Bertrand Russell, in all the consciousness of my group. On those rocking horses I might have pranced for ever, with the rest of us, in a ring we mounted with zest'. Butts then states a credo, with commentary alluding to the Rings and paralleling her warning on the results of ill-chosen ghostly guests:

> Without God there can be no man; without supernature there can be no nature; without philosophy there can be no psychology; without theology there can be no science; without mysticism there can be no commonsense.
>   This is truth, and our age has chosen, clause by clause, to reverse it, make the first of each term dependent on the second. With results we are beginning to appreciate, destroying piece by piece such natures as the war has spared. It is no part of this book to tell the secrets of Badbury Rings, yet it is no exaggeration to say that, in after years, it was because of them that I still remained, however uncertainly, critical of that reversal.[70]

VII. Spectral encounters

Butts termed one mode of story the '"plain ghost," the sober kind, fit for the ears of the Secretary of the Society for Psychical Research, and no less convincing for that'.[71] While Butts may not have shared the SPR's search for the reasoned explanation of supernatural phenomena, her straightforward aesthetic of 'If it happened at all, it happened like that' shapes her one formal ghost story, 'With and without buttons', written in 1932.[72]

Butts tells of a narrator and her sister in 'a remote village in Kent', seeking to unnerve their neighbour Trenchard's 'pseudo-rationalizations' via a trick with gloves, yet ending with something altogether more mysterious. Trenchard is presented as 'calling the bluff, in inaccurate language, of God, the arts, the imagination, the emotions'. They seek instead to 'suggest to him an experience – the worse the better – wholly incompatible with the incredulities of his faith'.[73] The supernatural is triggered by its denial: 'It was only because Trenchard said at lunch that the mass was a dramatized wish-fulfilment that what came after ever happened'.[74] The sisters use old kid gloves, with and without buttons, from a shoe box in the loft. For the narrator the phrase 'with and without buttons' immediately takes on the status of a 'rune'.[75] Hints of witchcraft and female power come through the story, with the sisters aligned with female powers of the earth and attuned to the mysteries of the stars. Their decision to 'haunt him', to 'try his simple faith', is in part an exercise of a female power – 'the pure, not erotic power' – over men.[76]

The loft in their 'very old cottages' extends over Trenchard's dwelling, though his loft access door is bricked up. They rent their cottage from a friend who 'bought it as it stood from a local family which had died out, and of which very little seemed known'. Trenchard also rents, having returned to 'his own part of England to rest, after a long time spent looking after something in East Africa'.[77] The sisters leave gloves around the house in ways confounding explanation, inviting Trenchard to believe in 'a ridiculous superstition in the village that there is Something Wrong with the house'.[78] Before they begin their trick, however, a separate glove appears, as if their thinking of the scheme has triggered some other presence. The narrator asks in the village about the previous resident, Miss Blacken, and is told of her leaving gloves about, and of a petticoat dropped on the green which blew to the sky on a windless day and never came to earth, hanging torn in the trees. As gloves continue to appear, the sisters and Trenchard combine against them, putting the gloves back in the box and locking the loft door. Trenchard knows a smell in the loft from his travels: 'smelt it in Africa in a damp place. Bad skins'.[79] The haunting continues.

Gloves appear on stairs, on clothes, on the food laid out for Trenchard's birthday party. White buttons are sprinkled onto sweet bowls, and a glove ruins a centrepiece:

> We went down together into the dining-room, and there my sister screamed. On the top of the centre strawberry pyramid, hanging over the berries like a cluster of slugs, was a glove, yellow-orange kid-skin, still and fat. A colour we had not seen in the box. The wrist and the fingers open and swollen. No buttons.
>
> 'What witches' trick is this?' he cried, and stared at us, for we were women. And like a wave moving towards us, rearing its head, came the knowledge that we were responsible for this; that our greed and vanity in devising this had evoked this: that we would now have to show courage, courage and intelligence to put an end to this, to lay this. And we had no idea how.
>
> 'The fire must burn,' I said. 'A great fire.'[80]

The sisters are as disturbed as Trenchard. The narrator's perfume turns to a scent of old kid gloves. The sisters burn the haunted material in Trenchard's fireplace; the strawberries and glove are thrown on together, the precious perfume emptied onto flame, the glove box explodes in the fire. The sisters consider they 'came off lightly'; Trenchard cannot shake off the experience: 'Now he cannot think what he used to think, and he does not know what else there is that he might think'.[81] The supernatural, through everyday objects, pulls the rug from the accepted world.

In *The crystal cabinet* Butts outlines parallel ghostly happenings which have happened to her, moving from the speculative to things truer than one could possibly credit. Butts had wanted a ghost at Salterns, something to show the other girls: 'not the tree and wind and leaf and garden potencies I knew, but a Real Ghost. A Grey Man or a White Lady, with a proper story, who put in regular appearances'.[82] Once, aged about 16, she thought she saw one: 'Left with the memory of a sudden transit of a swift, soundless figure, a small woman in a dark mantle. In the scattered gold of sunset, in a wood, a figure that crossed my path for a second and was gone'.[83] At school in Fife, however, coastal walking aged 18, Butts walked across sand 'into a ghost':

Half-way across the next cove I was stopped short. The sun blazed palely above, but on the dry sand I had walked into a pool. An air-pool, it was grey and whirling ... In dead, spinning cold I turned, not faint, but blind. With an immense effort, *wrenched* myself out of it. Torn on and sank on to a rock on the further side. What had I struck? It looked all right – or perhaps (I know more about it now) as if a patch of air in the mid-beach had gone dead.

Butts' enquiries found 'no story about that beach, no evil meeting that took place and left its mark there'. Of her stepping 'into a *focus*, a column of energy, cold and vile and hateful, spinning there', she never found 'what it was doing on a Fifeshire beach'.[84] This encounter in everyday space, a site which more than Badbury may fit her category of 'not always places you would expect', further claims attunement to and initiation in the supernatural; indicates that her ghost stories and grail renderings might just, for someone like her, qualify as realism.[85]

VIII. Magic out the ordinary

Butts moved to Sennen Cove in January 1932, from May 1932 occupying a bungalow bought by her trustees. This small modern detached bungalow, 1 Marine View, was renamed Tebel Vos, Cornish for 'House of Magic'. Butts' life in Sennen offers an example of everyday surroundings transfigured, and

daily life haunted, by past wonders and present anxieties. The naming of
Tebel Vos indicates a dual movement, making the ordinary magical, while
marking out a space from the ordinary around. Renaming helps magic out
the ordinary, while making something out of the ordinary. Butts' journal
entries from May 1932 suggest what Blondel terms a 'transubstantiation'
of an ordinary bungalow into 'an extraordinary sanctuary, a kind of
shrine';[86] the interior furnished, objects accumulated, the garden lovingly
tended as, in Butts' phrase, a 'nature sacrament',[87] the Atlantic viewed from
the window. Turning 1 Marine View to a House of Magic, the everyday
becomes of value if blessed with a capacity to be transformed, although in
The crystal cabinet, referring to the 'Tide' of suburban villas and bungalows
approaching Salterns in her youth, Butts indicates that Tebel Vos may not
entirely have shaken off 1 Marine View: 'Under the scurf of bungalows, like
the one on the Cornish cliffs I am at present inhabiting, as utterly, but not
as blessedly, as if the sea flowed over it'.[88]

The commonplace Cornish life and landscape around Sennen Cove could
also work magic. In part Butts follows a conventional English embrace of
the Cornish as exotic and mystical, within but not of England.[89] Butts'
comment in a letter to Hugh Ross Williamson on the renaming follows
such a formula, with Tebel Vos, this 'good cornish' name, being 'a translation for what we wanted to call it, which in English would have sounded
pretentious'.[90] Butts played on Cornwall, and West Penwith in particular,
as a place of mystery, furthering the Grail preoccupations most evident
in *Armed with madness*. In the winter of 1932–3 Butts considers that
the church at nearby Sancreed might witness something: 'I think that the
Grail might be seen here this winter'/'And I believe the Grail is stirring at
Sancreed'.[91] Butts' move to Anglo-Catholicism followed the influence of
Father Bernard Walke at the church of St Hilary, near Penzance, 16 miles
from Sennen but where she attended Sunday service when possible between
1934 and 1936, drawn by Walke's ritualism and his devotion to the place
of art in worship; St Hilary was decorated with the work of contemporary
Cornish Newlyn School artists.[92] Blondel notes that in her stories from
1932 'the Cornish landscape reverberates',[93] and her journals too give a
series of rapturous and reverent engagements with the place. Butts conveys
an ecstatic immediacy in her encounters with sea, moon and landscape, and
meets magic on the beach at night:

> Returning I met a stone, a rock, about 3 foot high, round, standing on
> end, the shape and the marks of the face of a little old goddess, an idol,
> a Notre dame de Sous Mer, this time. Perched on her haunches, not
> unfriendly but most strongly charged. Not so long ago we would have
> brought her up from the beaches, wreathed her in weed and shells and
> been very very careful in our tendance. As it was I saluted her with some
> reverence.[94]

In December 1933 Butts reviewed nine books for *The Bookman* under the title 'Magic of person and place', editor Hugh Ross Williamson noting Butts' own attention to 'the simple "magics" of place': 'Her books are, in a real sense, a self-revelation. Dominating everything is a passion for the actual land of England, not in the "happy country-side" sense, but as a concrete expression of mystical and spiritual forces'. To critics' suggestions that Butts was culturally a Left Bank Parisian, Williamson stated: 'The real Mary Butts is living quietly in a Cornish village'.[95] 'Magic of person and place' includes praise of two books on Cornwall, novelist and Sennen neighbour Ruth Manning Sanders' *The crochet woman*, and archaeologist Hugh O'Neil Hencken's *West Cornwall*:

> If it is not their native place, people have need of certain books to elucidate the piece of earth on which they live. For to know it, one must have a private map of one's own in mind. A magic map. Made on foot and by the senses that is usually in no more than two colours, of places which are 'mana' and places which are 'taboo'. They can overlap; and in West Cornwall you are living in a land where culture is overlaid on culture. This year two books have brought out its contours.[96]

Butts hails Sanders' 'exquisite imagination, the complex of stone, water, plants, air and human character on the moor the Ordnance calls Selene, the Moon-Moor'.[97] Hencken's 'scientific precision' equally sparks Butts, showing that 'one is walking among the bones of the First Men.' Butts lays myth onto Hencken's archaeology of megalithic culture: 'A land whose after-history seems nothing but an anti-climax, whose beginning itself may have been an end, supposing Atlantis to be true record; and that what was essential Cornwall perished with it, leaving the place empty for wandering tribes to settle, the tenants of its ghosts.' Hencken's work also helped 'enhance the isolation dwellers here feel from the rest of England. Nowhere else is one so sure that one is in a foreign land, whose significant history was over before what we call England began'.[98] In her House of Magic, Butts was the latest English-in-Cornwall appreciative tenant of these ancient ghosts, but her view of the contemporary native Cornish could be more jaundiced. Early 1932 journal entries note: 'The people of the Cove are all cousins and watchful and hate foreigners'/'There is a brutal, bull-necked, full bodied blooded type about here... Morals, one hears, to match'.[99] The Cornish place carries more magic than its people, though the place is itself threatened by new kinds of prosaic life. Thus Butts opposes further bungalow development in Sennen Cove on the part of businessman Mr Barton, who had earlier constructed her own bungalow.[100] A journal entry for 9 January 1937 projects subjects for unwritten stories, including 'On Barton (blowing up his houses)'.[101]

The sense of claiming a special place while pulling up the drawbridge to keep others out is echoed in Butts' novels, notably *Death of Felicity Taverner*, published in November 1932. Scylla Taverner, and her friends and relations, resist the plans of socialist Russian Jew Kralin to develop their beloved land with bungalows and leisure facilities: 'he would then build a hotel and a row of bungalows along the low cliff, light the sea lane and drain it. One of the least-known places in England, he would then advertise it'.[102] Scylla defends 'the flawless, clean and blessed, mana and tabu earth; strictly of their flesh, whose birds and beasts and eggs and fish, and fruit and leaf and air and water had nourished their bodies, "composed their beauties"; whose pattern was repeated in them, the stuff of a country made into man'.[103] The Taverners defend their England against multiple forms of the alien; Kralin stands for modernity, Left politics, racial otherness. Kralin is the widower of Felicity, Scylla's sister, and complicit in her death in an unspecified way. Felicity's ghost has a narrative presence, shaping relations between characters via hidden influence, present on the hill as Scylla describes to her friend Boris the ways in which Kralin's plans would transform the land: 'A breeze shivered in the grass beside them, the short grass of the high places that springs out of the earth upright, with a kind of sturdy passion, as the ghost of Felicity Taverner trod their light crest, looking down into the sea-valley over her cousin's head'.[104] Kralin approaches and 'The ghost left them',[105] not staying to hear Scylla damn Kralin to her betraying cousin Adrian as 'the blackmailer, your sister's murderer, the man who would sell the body of our land to the Jews'.[106] Felicity as ghost spirit of the land is addressed at the climax as Boris, an exiled White Russian and Taverner ally, murders Kralin in an island sea-cave, Felicity's own 'precious place'.[107] Kralin's body is left to the sea, though with the delicious possibility that his corpse might shoot from an island blowhole: 'that could only happen if there was a great storm, and the blow-hole worked in a jet with the strength of the Atlantic behind it'.[108]

Wright notes of *Death of Felicity Taverner* that this is not simply an 'innocent pastoral..., drifting into unfortunate but occasional contact with unsavoury attitudes',[109] rather 'the Jew is actively given a meaning which is culturally *necessary* to the valued England which he contaminates'.[110] Commentators have variously diagnosed Butts' work as manifesting and/ or dramatizing anti-semitism; her work proceeds through stark categories of race, as of class. Wright places such judgments as central rather than tangential: 'Exclusion and anathema are principles active at the foundation of Mary Butts' sacred geography, and in the writings they take two primary forms: one political, the other racial'.[111] The commonplace, everyday elements of Butts' aesthetic are far from any egalitarian social principle. This is a sensibility of a select few, who places like Badbury can accept and who might transubstantiate an ordinary bungalow. The everyday, the private, the elite and the numinous intermingle, and Butts' writings on the magic of place work alongside a publication such as *Warning to hikers*, where the kind of magic which would disturb those unfamiliar acts as cultural deterrent to the ordinary urban visitor. Butts ends that pamphlet by evoking a green deeper than the pleasantly pastoral:

> For once they have taken one step across the line of protection, the belt of urban needs and values each of them carry strapped tight about them, they will find themselves in a world as tricky and uncertain, as full of strangeness, as any wood near Athens. No friendly greenwood, fixed by poets; no wise gnome-tapped mountain; no gracious sea. *The dragon-green, the luminous, the dark, serpent-haunted.* Will they face it? When the Sirens are back at their business, sisters of the Harpies, the Snatchers? When the tripper-steamer – her bows to the sun – turns into the boat called Millions-of-Years?
>
> Quiet in the woods. They can be very quiet when a wind from nowhere lifts in the tree-tops and through the pine-needles clashing the noise of a harp runs down the trunks into the earth. *And no birds sing.*[112]

Butts here ends with a quotation from Keats' 'La belle dame sans merci', calling up a stern female nature spirit. If both dragon green and classical allusion are, by implication, unknown to hikers, nature knowledge and classical learning might yet combine to repel them, creating, in the divine sense, Panic.

IX. Conclusion

Mary Butts draws out cultural consequences of ghosts, the magics which might be worked, the claims to authority which might be made, the effects of one spectral aesthetic over another, the conventions through which ghosts perform, the thought which they might enlist. Alerting us to such matters, Butts can serve, in a time of academic fascination for the spectral, to direct us beyond the obvious dead (obvious for their anticipation of contemporary concerns or their clear theoretical antecedence), opening up the choice of ghostly guests who might fill any geographical ghost box. If ghosts notionally manifest at will, uncannily beyond the control of the haunted, there are evidently various strategies which invite their appearance, devices making haunting likely. The cultural history of ghosts shows the spectral as a carefully constructed and contrived field of pleasures and anxieties, with a range of investigative methodologies and techniques. Sensibilities of spectral retrieval include: genial folkloric gathering, the scavenging of found objects, delight in arcane scholarship, the tracing of lines of influence and descent, the identification and registering of things out of time (presupposing the ability to diagnose and juxtapose temporalities), connoisseurship of the strange antique, the pursuit of effects from terror to whimsy. The episodic structure of this paper has in part sought to echo Wylie's call that 'spectral geographies should themselves be spectral',[113] setting dimensions of ghostly work alongside one another, laying out material carrying resonance for the contemporary if without clear lessons to be learned or instruction to be imbibed, presenting in Mary Butts a person fit to haunt a contemporary geography of ghosts. To conclude, the paper returns to the geographical curios which opened the account. Introducing Mary Butts to Hans Speier, Montague Summers and E. A. Reeves indicates further possibilities.

Butts and Speier take their magic for different ends; Butts to search for select knowledge, Speier to deposit the magic of Nazi propaganda maps into a trash can, a gesture unsurprising for a refugee from Germany finding haven in the USA. Butts might also have put propaganda maps alongside official Celticism as a myth constructed narrowly for state power, yet seeks throughout her work to give belief foundation, reserving scepticism for what she might have regarded as a cult of reason. While her work shows fascination for a potential 'science of mysticism',[114] the latter is a term implying not sceptical explanation but the elevation of mystery. Psychoanalysis could for Butts sit as a practice drawing on myth and mimicking science yet ending as a symptom of rather than solution for modern dilemmas. Suspicion towards the claims of reason leads Butts towards an embrace of a truth defined as in essence supernatural. Magic ultimately points the way.

Not all magic though. Summers' Catholic discrimination is matched in Butts' rejection of the once-admired Crowley, whose magic is rejected as misguided or even charlatanry. Butts can pursue a comparative religion via Frazer, can suppose insights proceed from the mythic mutuality of different traditions, yet is always ready to dismiss myths deemed of lower order. Present in the very high modernist circles anathema to Summers, and with rather more sympathy for witchcraft, Butts nevertheless echoes his desire for foundation, her experiments in artistic life leading in the end to an embrace of Anglo-Catholicism. Butts' March 1935 description of her Sennen Cove garden as a nature sacrament is no pagan evocation: 'Yet today I praised God and Our Lady from my soul for this afternoon's gardening. A nature sacrament with the flowers and the earth and the quickening sun'.[115] Butts works across supernatures to end in orthodoxy.

It is doubtful that Butts ever haunted the RGS, though she might have unknowingly shared an underground carriage with E. A. Reeves. To approach ghosts and the occult via psychic research carries in Butts' work an aura of worthy yet futile scientism, a respect for the supernatural expressed through a misguided desire to search it out and pin it down. The consolations of spiritualism, of conversations with grandmother via ectoplasm over the suburban table, miss the wonders of mana and tabu. The sensibility which takes Butts to Badbury rather than the séance, which entertains the possibility that an approach to the Grail might be discerned, signals another distinction between Butts and Reeves. Studies of spiritualism indicate the ways in which magic circles draw from particular social circles, with the psychic pursuits appealing to Reeves via séances or domestic experiments in his Surrey home being associated with the middle or upper working classes.[116] Butts and Reeves show in their different ways how magic as social practice works through cultural distinction. Pursuing the occult with Crowley during her six weeks at his Abbey of Thelema at Cefalu in Sicily in the summer of 1921 was one thing; one doubts Butts would have been seen dead at a suburban séance. The supernatural for Butts acts as the supersocial, a device to mark out an elite, elect crowd.

Remarkable writings follow. Butts retains a presence through her novels, stories, essays and journals, works worthy of remark if not, for everyone, things to delight in. Labelling Butts as an 'acquired taste' would however be to exhibit precisely those judgments of aesthetic value which she sought and lived through; the assumption being that most people would neither wish nor be able to acquire such taste. Butts' rarefied modernism of high style, like her essay on 'Ghosties and Ghoulies' – whose title, gesturing to the popular and amusing, simply gives it house room while seeking to go much further – helps highlight her aesthetic of the ghost, always a geoaesthetic of haunted sites, spatial encounters and arcane claims to places deemed special. We should not however thereby assume that such self-evidently magical style exhausts a ghostly geoaesthetic. To use Butts' own already-cited phrase, 'it is cult that is fatal', and questions of aesthetic value do not only pertain through Butts' claimed aesthetic values. If Butts' work is distinctive and remarkable, it carries no unique capacity. Any person calling up ghosts, through whatever modes of expression and experience, might receive similar treatment to that given in this essay, whether 'third-rate journalists', 'the vulgar stuff', 'authors with a psychic axe to grind', fatal cultists. Speier, Summers and Reeves play out their own geographical aesthetic of the spectral, the magical, the demonic, the religious, whether through an aesthetic of clearly supreme reason, discriminating veneration, or credulous enquiry concerning visions of Lord Kitchener on a Surrey bedroom wall. A world of geographic possibility becomes apparent. Mary Butts' choice of ghostly guests can, in its distinctive elective manner, help alert us to a geography of ghosts beyond anything she might have imagined.

Notes

1   D. Livingstone, *The geographical tradition* (Oxford, Blackwell, 1992), pp. 349–50.

2   H. Speier, 'Magic geography', *Social research* 8 (1941), pp. 310–30, quotation p. 313; Speier was a Jewish émigré political sociologist who left Germany

to join the Graduate faculty of the New School for Social Research in New York. Between 1942 and 1948 Speier carried out US government service, including for the State Department, before joining the Rand Corporation as head of their Social Science Division.

3   M. Summers, *The geography of witchcraft* (London, Routledge and Kegan Paul, 1927), pp. 184–5; M. Summers, *The history of witchcraft and demonology* (London, Routledge and Kegan Paul, 1926). For a more consciously sober enquiry into witchcraft in a specific geographical historical context (sixteenth century Essex), carefully mapping events and prosecutions, see A. Macfarlane, *Witchcraft in Tudor and Stuart England: a regional and comparative study* (London, Routledge and Kegan Paul, 1970).

4   M. Summers, *The gothic quest* (London, The Fortune Press, 1968), p. 412; first published 1938.

5   E. A. Reeves, The recollections of a geographer (London, Seeley, Service and Co., 1916), pp. 190–1.

6   *Ibid.*, p. 208.

7   Relevant cultural histories include: J. Hazelgrove, *Spiritualism and British society between the wars* (Manchester, Manchester University Press, 2000); A. Owen, *The place of enchantment: British occultism and the culture of the modern* (Chicago, University of Chicago Press, 2004); A. Owen, *The darkened room: women, power and spiritualism in late nineteenth century Britain* (London, Virago, 1989); A. Owen, 'Occultism and the "modern" self in fin-de-siecle Britain', in M. Daunton and B. Rieger, eds, *Meanings of modernity* (Oxford, Berg, 2001), pp. 71–96; R. Luckhurst, *The invention of telepathy* (Oxford, Oxford University Press, 2002); W. de Blecourt, R. Hutton and J. La Fontaine, *Witchcraft and magic in Europe: the twentieth century* (London, Athlone, 1999); M. Warner, *Phantasmagoria: spirit visions, metaphors, and media into the twenty-first century* (Oxford, Oxford University Press, 2006).

8   P. Buse and A. Stott, 'Introduction: a future for haunting', in P. Buse and A. Stott, eds, *Ghosts: deconstruction, psychoanalysis, history* (London, Macmillan, 1999), pp. 1–20, quotation p. 1.

9   *Ibid.*, p. 3; J. Derrida, *Specters of Marx* (London, Routledge, 1994); S. Freud, 'The "uncanny"', in S. Freud, *Art and literature: the Pelican Freud library volume 14* (Harmondsworth, Penguin, 1985), pp. 339–76. For a fine reflection on spectrality in recent music, through the work of the Ghost Box label and others, see S. Reynolds, 'Haunted audio', *The Wire* 273 (November 2006), pp. 26–33.

10   Buse and Stott, 'Introduction', p. 5.

11   *Ibid.*, p. 3.

12   *Ibid.*, p. 9.

13   D. Punter, 'Introduction: of apparitions', in G. Byron and D. Punter, eds, *Spectral readings: towards a Gothic geography* (London, Macmillan, 1999), pp. 1–10, quotation p. 4.

14   R. Luckhurst, 'The contemporary London Gothic and the limits of the
     "spectral turn"', *Textual practice* 16 (2002), pp. 527–46.

15   Luckhurst, 'The contemporary London Gothic', p. 534.

16   *Ibid.*, p. 528.

17   *Ibid.*, p. 536; cf D. Pinder, 'Ghostly footsteps: voices, memories and walks in
     the city', *Cultural geographies* 8 (2001), pp. 1–19.

18   Luckhurst, 'The contemporary London Gothic', p. 542. See also R. Luckhurst,
     '"Something tremendous, something elemental": on the ghostly origins
     of psychoanalysis', in P. Buse and A. Stott, eds, *Ghosts: deconstruction,
     psychoanalysis, history* (London, Macmillan, 1999), pp. 50–71. Here
     Luckhurst explores the 'ghostly origins of psychoanalysis', suggesting that
     'what haunts Freud is haunting itself, both in its transgressive structure
     and in the many contemporaneous psychologies fully imbricated in ghosts,
     ghost-hunting and other communications outside recognized channels' (p.
     52). Luckhurst discusses Freud's own anxious writings on the occult, noting
     Derrida's discussion of the occult as 'an exemplary instance of liminal anxiety'
     for psychoanalysis (p. 56), but suggests this may have been less about fear of
     association with pseudo-science than worry that occult thinkers, especially in
     England the Society for Psychical Research (for whom Freud wrote a paper
     in 1912), may have been more orthodox and rigorously close to dominant
     orthodox psychology, from which Freud was being marginalized. Luckhurst
     argues that Freud sensed something about the ghostly which could add to
     psychoanalysis: 'In this, Freud is like many of his fin-de-siécle contemporaries,
     who underwent the strange experience of working with a demystificatory
     positivism that actually helped produce a disturbing, remystified and occulted
     supplement that exceeded "rational" science' (p. 65). Mary Butts' writing
     sought in part to offer contemporaneous dramatizations of such argument.

19   C. Barnett, 'Deconstructing context: exposing Derrida', *Transactions of the
     institute of British geographers* 24 (1999), pp. 277–94, quotation p. 285.
     Kneale notes Barnett's arguments in his essay on the horror writing of H. P.
     Lovecraft, suggesting that while 'contextual, historicist readings of Lovecraft'
     are not 'worthless', we might instead 'read his work as literature – rather
     than as biography or history, once removed'; J. Kneale, 'From beyond: H.
     P. Lovecraft and the place of horror', *Cultural geographies* 13 (2006), pp.
     106–26, quotation p. 108. Rather than deconstructing context, however,
     Kneale seems here only to reinstate a crude opposition of the historical/
     biographical and the literary. Barnett himself similarly ends falling back into
     distinction when concluding that 'a geography of texts must be premised
     upon movement, spacing and difference, rather than upon place, identity and
     containment', 'Deconstructing context', p. 290.

20   Buse and Stott, 'Introduction', p. 1.

21   J. Wylie, 'The spectral geographies of W. G. Sebald', *Cultural geographies* 14
     (2007), pp. 171–88; C. Nash, 'Visionary geographies: designs for developing
     Ireland', *History workshop journal* 45 (1998), pp. 49–78. Also see D. Dixon,
     'A benevolent and sceptical enquiry: exploring 'Fortean Geographies' with the
     Mothman', *Cultural geographies* 14 (2007), pp. 189–210.

22 J. Lowerson, 'The mystical geography of the English', in B. Short, ed., *The English rural community* (Cambridge, Cambridge University Press, 1992), pp. 152–74, quotation p. 171.

23 Freud, 'The "uncanny"', p. 340.

24 Freud, 'The "uncanny"', p. 340.

25 N. Blondel, *Mary Butts: scenes from the life* (New York, McPherson, 1998); see also N. Blondel, 'Mary Butts', *Oxford Dictionary of National Biography*. A selection of Butts' journals appears in N. Blondel, ed., *The journals of Mary Butts* (New Haven, Yale University Press, 2002). On Butts' writings see also C. Wagstaff, ed., *A sacred quest: the life and writings of Mary Butts* (New York, McPherson, 1995); R. R. Foy, *Ritual, myth, and mysticism in the work of Mary Butts* (Fayetteville, University of Arkansas Press, 2000); P. Wright, 'Coming back to the shores of Albion: the secret England of Mary Butts (1890–1937)', in P. Wright, *On living in an old country* (London, Verso, 1985), pp. 93–134; P. Wright, *The village that died for England* (London, Faber and Faber, 2002), pp. 95–108; J. Garrity, *Step-daughters of England: British women modernists and the national imaginary* (Manchester, Manchester University Press, 2003), esp. chapter 4, 'Mary Butts' England'; M. Hamer, 'Mary Butts, mothers, and war', in S. Raitt and T. Tate, eds, *Women's fiction and the great war* (Oxford, Clarendon, 1997), pp. 219–40; J. Rose, 'Bizarre objects: Mary Butts and Elizabeth Bowen', *Critical quarterly* 42 (2000), pp. 75–85.

26 Editions of key works by Mary Butts discussed in this essay are as follows: *Ashe of Rings*, in M. Butts, *Ashe of Rings and other writings* (New York, McPherson, 1998), pp. 1–232; *Armed with madness* (London, Penguin, 2001); *Death of Felicity Taverner*, in M. Butts, *The Taverner novels* (New York, McPherson, 1992 – edition also includes *Armed with madness*); *Warning to hikers*, in M. Butts, *Ashe of Rings and other writings* (New York, McPherson, 1998), pp. 267–96; *Traps for unbelievers*, in M. Butts, *Ashe of Rings and other writings* (New York, McPherson, 1998), pp. 297–332; '"Ghosties and Ghoulies": uses of the supernatural in English fiction', in M. Butts, *Ashe of Rings and other writings* (New York, McPherson, 1998), pp. 331–64. *The Macedonian* and *Scenes from the life of Cleopatra* are collected in M. Butts, *The classical novels* (New York, McPherson, 1994).

27 C. Bagg, 'Foreword', in M. Butts, *Crystal cabinet*, p. v.

28 Wright, 'Coming back', p. 96.

29 *Ibid.*, p. 104.

30 J. Weston, *From ritual to romance* (New York, Doubleday, 1957). On the influence of Harrison and Weston on Butts see Foy, *Ritual*, pp. 51–8. On Harrison see M. Beard, *The invention of Jane Harrison* (Cambridge, Harvard University Press, 2000). For an excellent essay on Butts' relation to such material in her 'adventure of the sacred', and the ways in which this connected to 1920s modernism, see R. Blaser, '"Here lies the woodpecker who was Zeus"', in Wagstaff, *Sacred quest*, pp. 159–224, quotation p. 165. Of Butts' complex engagement with the Grail in *Armed with madness*, Blaser

explores how she 'tests the symbol' through its various uses and properties (p. 171), and presents Butts as pursuing, along with writers such as William Carlos Williams, a 'relational imagination' of place (p. 162). On Butts and Crowley see Blondel, *Mary Butts*, pp. 102–6, Foy, Ritual, pp. 96–7, and Butts' own descriptions in Blondel, *Journals*, pp. 184–7. Crowley is the subject of A. Owen, 'The sorcerer and his apprentice: Aleister Crowley and the magical exploration of Edwardian subjectivity', *Journal of British studies* 36 (1997), pp. 99–133.

31 Garrity, *Step-daughters*, p. 189, also pp. 221–4; also Blondel, *Mary Butts*, pp. 83–4.

32 Garrity, *Step-daughters*, p. 189. See also A. Radford, 'Defending nature's holy shrine: Mary Butts, Englishness, and the Persephone myth', *Journal of modern literature* 29 (2006), pp. 126–49.

33 Garrity, *Step-daughters*, p. 219; also Blondel, *Mary Butts*, pp. 308–11. Felicity is discussed in the context of Butts' wider approach to the supernatural in B. O'Brien Wagstaff, 'The effectual angel in *Death of Felicity Taverner*', in Wagstaff, *Sacred quest*, pp. 224–42.

34 Butts, 'Ghosties and Ghoulies', p. 363.

35 Butts would also send out a questionnaire to various writers on their supernatural experiences in January 1935, a project for a possible collection, which came to nothing; see Blondel, *Journals*, p. 442.

36 Butts, 'Ghosties and Ghoulies', p. 363.

37 *Ibid.*, p. 305.

38 *Ibid.*, p. 306.

39 *Ibid.*, p. 363.

40 *Ibid.*, p. 364.

41 *Ibid.*, p. 337.

42 *Ibid.*, p. 345.

43 *Ibid.*, p. 338. Butts' one formal ghost story, 'With and without buttons', is discussed below. Of contemporary writers Butts also praises E. M. Forster, 'whose special sensibility, curiosity and faith makes him indifferent to any ultimate distinction between pagan and Christian supernatural values' (p. 361), and May Sinclair's *Uncanny tales*, then recently reissued. The latter (billed as *Uncanny stories*) are the starting point of Glover's essay 'The "spectrality" effect in early modernism', in A. Smith and J. Wallace, eds, *Gothic modernisms* (Basingstoke, Palgrave, 2001), pp. 29–43, and are the subject of Seed's essay in same volume, '"Psychical" cases: transformations of the supernatural in Virginia Woolf and May Sinclair', pp. 44–61.

44 M. Butts, 'The art of Montague James', *The London mercury* 29(172), February 1934, pp. 306–17. Extracts are collected in S. K. Hall, ed., *Twentieth-century literary criticism*, volume 6 (Detroit: Gale Research Company, 1982), pp. 206–8. Quotations here are given page references for the latter collection first, and then Butts' original article; pp. 207, 307.

45 Butts, 'Art of Montague James', pp. 207, 307–8.

46 *Ibid.*, pp. 207, 312.

47 *Ibid.*, pp. 208, 317.

48 Butts, *Traps for unbelievers*, p. 312; Blaser, 'Here lies …', p. 187.

49 Butts, 'Ghosties and Ghoulies', p. 337.

50 *Ibid.*, p. 337.

51 *Ibid.*, p. 336.

52 *Ibid.*, p. 358.

53 *Ibid.*, p. 333–4.

54 *Ibid.*, p. 339.

55 *Ibid.*, p. 338–9.

56 *Ibid.*, p. 354; as with Harrison, Butts was influenced by Gilbert Murray's work on Greek religion. For recent geographical discussion of the Celtic see D. C. Harvey, R. Jones, N. McInroy and C. Milligan, eds, *Celtic geographies* (London, Routledge, 2002).

57 Butts, 'Ghosties and Ghoulies', p. 353.

58 *Ibid.*, p. 354–5.

59 In December 1933 Butts reviewed nine books in *The Bookman* under the title 'Magic of person and place'; see below.

60 Butts, 'Ghosties and Ghoulies', p. 335; see also Blondel, *Journals*, pp. 370–3 for Butts' October 1931 account of her 'Personal experiences of supernormal perception'.

61 Butts, 'Ghosties and Ghoulies', pp. 350–1.

62 *Ibid.*, p. 349.

63 *Ibid.*, p. 342. Butts is here praising Scottish and Border poems and Thomas the Rhymer.

64 Butts, 'Ghosties and Ghoulies', p. 349.

65 *Ibid.*, p. 350.

66 *Ibid.*, p. 349–50.

67 Garrity, *Step-daughters*, p. 229; Wright, 'Coming Back', p. 117.

68 P. Nash, *Dorset: a shell guide* (London: Architectural Press, 1936), p. 10; Nash's book includes a watercolour of Badbury Rings, p. 20.

69 Butts, *Crystal cabinet*, p. 266; Blondel, *Mary Butts*, pp. 113–4, notes a poem written in her early twenties, 'On Badbury Rings', and a magical 1922 visit there with friends.

70 Butts, *Crystal cabinet*, p. 265.

71 Butts, 'Ghosties and Ghoulies', p. 357.

72 Page references here are given to the story's appearance in the collection M. Butts, *With and without buttons* (Manchester: Carcanet, 1991), pp. 85–99. The story also appears in M. Butts, *From altar to chimney-piece: selected*

stories (New York, McPherson, 1992), pp. 22–38. 'With and without buttons' was first published posthumously in 1938 in *Last Stories*. From a journal entry on 23 October 1932 discussing the draft of an essay on 'Use of the supernatural', it would appear that the story was completed before the essay, but the two evidently developed together; Blondel, *Journals*, p. 403. Butts sought to dedicate the story to M. R. James (with whom she had correspondence in 1922), and her journal for 21 September 1932 included a draft of a letter to James: 'I've at last managed to write a ghost story myself which should come out soon – in *The Adelphi* or something like that – anyhow in a book – and given any quality it may have it owes to your influence, I want to be allowed to dedicate it to you'. Butts says that if she does not hear from James she will assume a dedication is in order; Blondel notes that the journal does not mention any response from James. The story was eventually published without a dedication; Blondel, *Journals*, p. 401.

73   Butts, 'With and without buttons', p. 86–7.

74   *Ibid.*, p. 85.

75   *Ibid.*, p. 88.

76   *Ibid.*, pp. 86–7. The narrator states that the point of this power is 'that it shall have nothing to do with sex. We could have made him make love, to either or both of us, any day of the week', p. 87.

77   Butts, 'With and without buttons', p. 88.

78   *Ibid.*, p. 87.

79   *Ibid.*, p. 93.

80   *Ibid.*, p. 96.

81   *Ibid.*, p. 85.

82   Butts, *Crystal cabinet*, p. 150.

83   *Ibid.*, p. 152; allusions to ghosts also come when a ghost of a suicide girl who saw her lover hang is said to walk the sand-hills, p. 161, or when the dining room, the last room untouched after her father's death, is described: 'at any time one might meet one's father's ghost', p. 159.

84   Butts, *Crystal cabinet*, p. 192.

85   See also Butts' description of an encounter with a male 'full size figure I wish I could forget' at Sennen in March 1935: 'I had, I think, been repeating a psalm, and there was a protection round me'; Blondel, *Journals*, p. 445.

86   Blondel, *Mary Butts*, p. 288. For a reverent appreciation of Butts in Sennen, see D. Hope, 'Mary Butts, fire-bearer', in Wagstaff, *Sacred quest*, pp. 21–4. Hope's essay was first published in 1937, after Butts' death, as number 1 in a 'Sennen Pamphlet Series'; this would seem to have been the first and last pamphlet. See also Harcourt Wesson Bull's memoir, 'Truth is the heart's desire', in the same volume, pp. 53–88, including a possible meeting with Butts' ghost at Sennen soon after her death, p. 80.

87   Blondel, *Journals*, p. 444, also quoted in Blondel, *Mary Butts*, p. 290.

88   Butts, *Crystal cabinet*, p. 251.

89 Butts writes in her journal on 12 March 1933 of the strength of the sun in a Cornish early spring: 'No longer can one say "England" here'; Blondel, *Journals*, p. 420. On the imaginative geographies of Cornwall see E. Westland, ed., *Cornwall: the cultural construction of place* (Penzance, Patten Press, 1997); P. Payton, *Cornwall – a history* (Fowey, Cornwall Editions, 2004), A. Hale, 'Whose Celtic Cornwall? The ethnic Cornish meet Celtic spirituality', in D. C. Harvey et al., eds, *Celtic geographies*, pp. 157–70; E. Westland, 'D. H. Lawrence in Cornwall: dwelling in a precarious age', *Cultural geographies* 9 (2002), pp. 266–85.

90 Quoted in Blondel, *Mary Butts*, p. 287.

91 Blondel, *Journals*, entries for 11 December 1932, p. 407, and 7 January 1933, p. 410.

92 See Blondel, *Mary Butts*, pp. 365–7, pp. 407–10. The reputation of St Hilary and Walke was furthered when the church was the object of physical attack by a Protestant sect in August 1932. On Walke see D. Allchin, *Bernard Walke: a good man who could never be dull* (Abergavenny: Three Peaks Press, 2000); C. Phillips, 'Mystical geographies of Cornwall', University of Nottingham PhD thesis, 2006.

93 Blondel, *Mary Butts*, p. 291.

94 Blondel, *Journals*, p. 468, entry for 29 January 1937.

95 Williamson, editorial note at the beginning of M. Butts, 'The magic of person and place', *The Bookman*, vol. 85, December 1933, pp. 141–3, quotation p. 141.

96 Butts, 'Magic of person and place', p. 141.

97 *Ibid.*, pp. 141–2.

98 *Ibid.*, p. 142; Hencken was an American archaeologist who moved to live in Cornwall; his *The archaeology of Cornwall and Scilly* (London: Methuen, 1932) was the first major orthodox professional archaeological work on the subject.

99 Blondel, *Journals*, entries for 29 January 1932, p. 379, and 1 February 1932, p. 380. Notwithstanding Butts' own unconventional 'morals', the latter would seem a straightforwardly negative comment.

100 Blondel, *Mary Butts*, pp. 394–5.

101 Blondel, *Journals*, p. 467, entry for 9 January 1937.

102 Butts, *Death of Felicity Taverner*, p. 249.

103 *Ibid.*, p. 259. In *The crystal cabinet* a parallel narrative of the magic of dwelling place liable to erosion shapes Butts' story of Salterns and its subsequent 1923 sale and break up for development into 'the maggot-knot of dwellings that was once my home' (p. 16): 'Place I shall never see again, now they have violated it, now that body has been put to vile use, such uses as men from cities do to such places as these; such uses as its own people do not know how to prevent' (p. 15).

104 Butts, *Death of Felicity Taverner*, p. 343.

105 *Ibid.*, p. 344.

106 *Ibid.*, p. 346.

107 *Ibid.*, p. 356; Boris addresses Felicity's ghost on p. 358.

108 Butts, *Death of Felicity Taverner*, p. 364.

109 Wright, 'Coming back', p. 124.

110 *Ibid.*, p. 122.

111 *Ibid.*, p. 119; see also Wright, *Village*; Radford, 'Defending'. Garrity, *Step-daughters*, pp. 196–201 discusses *Warning to hikers*, including Butts presenting the country as a feminized landscape violated and prostituted by modernity.

112 Butts, *Warning to hikers*, pp. 294–5. On Butts' evocation of green see Wright, 'Coming back', p. 109. On forms of green see P. Bishop, *The greening of psychology* (Dallas, Spring Publications, 1990). Foy, p. 93, would seem to misread this passage on lack of bird-song as an anticipation of Rachel Carson. The motif of harp sounds from wind in trees also accompanies the terror of a mock-sacrificial scene at a thinly disguised Badbury Rings in *Ashe of Rings*, helping to protect heroine Vanna from her attacker Peter as she lies on the stone in the centre of the ring, Butts, *Ashe*, p. 189. The phrase 'The dragon-green, the luminous, the dark, serpent-haunted sea' appears in James Elroy Flecker's 1913 poem 'The Gates of Damascus'. Butts also quotes this in her journal for 12 September 1918; Blondel, *Journals*, p. 104. Other parts of the poem are quoted in her journal for 26 October 1917; Blondel, *Journals*, pp. 89–90.

113 Wylie, 'Spectral geographies', p. 184.

114 See for example Butts' journal for 1 February 1930, where she writes at length on the possible components of a 'science of mysticism'; Blondel, *Journals*, pp. 341–3.

115 Blondel, *Journals*, p. 444; entry for 2 March 1935; the same entry records acquiring an ashtray with her sign of the zodiac, and an encounter with a ghost at Sennen; Christianity had not entirely taken over her mythic imagination. For a parallel case of Christian nature theology by a strikingly parallel figure see D. Matless and L. Cameron, 'Devotional landscape: ecology and orthodoxy in the work of Marietta Pallis', in M. Conan, ed., *Sacred gardens and landscapes: ritual and agency* (Washington, DC: Dumbarton Oaks, 2007, pp. 263–94).

116 Hazelgrove, *Spiritualism*; Owen, *The darkened room*.

27

On the Uses and Disadvantages of Living among Specters

Giorgio Agamben

In the inaugural address at the University Institute of Architecture in Venice, delivered in February 1993, Manfredo Tafuri evoked the "cadaver" of Venice in no uncertain terms. Recalling the battle waged against those who proposed to host the World's Fair in the city, he concluded, not without a note of sadness: "The problem was not whether it was better to put makeup and lipstick on the cadaver, thus making it look so ridiculous that even children would have mocked it; nor was it what we—the powerless defenders, the disarmed prophets— ended up with, that is, a cadaver liquefying before our very eyes."[1]

Almost two decades have passed since this implacable diagnosis, penned by a person with ample authority and competence, whose accuracy no one could possibly challenge in good faith (not even the mayors, architects, ministers, and the rest who, then as today, had and have, in Tafuri's words, the "indecency" to continue to doll up and undersell the cadaver). To the careful observer this actually means, however, that Venice is no longer a cadaver, that if it somehow still exists, it is only because it has managed to move beyond the state that follows death and the consequent decomposition of the corpse. This new state is that of the specter, of the dead who appears without warning, preferably in the middle of the night, creaking and sending signals, sometimes even speaking, though in a way that is not always intelligible. "Venice is whispering," Tafuri writes, though he adds that such whispers are an unbearable sound to the modern ear.

Those who live in Venice attain a certain familiarity with this specter. It suddenly appears during a nocturnal stroll when, crossing a bridge, one's gaze turns a corner alongside a canal immersed in shadows, as a glimmer of orange light is switched on in a distant window, and an observing passerby on another bridge holds out a fogged-up mirror. Or when the Giudecca Island almost seems to gurgle as it drains rotten algae and plastic bottles onto the Zattere promenade. And it was yet again the same specter that—thanks to the invisible echo of a final ray of light, indefinitely lingering over the canals—Marcel saw enshrouded within the reflections of the palazzos in their ever-darkening obscurity. And prior still, this specter appears at the very origins of this city, which was not born, like almost every other city in Italy, as a result of the encounter between late antiquity in its decline and new barbarian forces but rather as a result of exhausted refugees who, abandoning their riches behind them in Rome, carried its phantasm in their minds, to then dissolve it into the city's waters, streaks, and colors.

What is a specter made of? Of signs, or more precisely of signatures, that is to say, those signs, ciphers, or monograms that are etched onto things by time. A specter always carries with it a date wherever it goes; it is, in other words, an intimately historical entity. This is why old cities are the quintessential place of signatures, which the flaneur in turn reads, somewhat absentmindedly, in the course of his drifting and strolling down the streets. This is why the tasteless restorations that sugarcoat and homogenize European cities also erase their signatures; they render them illegible. And this is why cities—and especially Venice—tend to look like dreams. In dreams the eyes of the dreaming person seize on each and every thing; each and every creature exhibits a signature that signifies more than its traits, gestures, and words could ever express. Nonetheless, those who stubbornly try to interpret their dreams are still at least partly convinced that they are meaningless. Similarly, in the city, everything that has happened in some lane, in some piazza, in some street, on some sidewalk along a canal, in some back alley is suddenly condensed and crystallized into a figure that is at once labile and exigent, mute and winking, resentful and distant. Such figure is the specter or genius of the place.

What do we owe to the dead? "The work of love in recollecting the one who is dead," Kierkegaard writes, "is the work of the most disinterested, free, and faithful love."[2] But it is certainly not the easiest. The dead, after all, not only ask nothing from us, but they also seem to do everything possible in order to be forgotten. This, however, is precisely why the dead are perhaps the most demanding objects of love. We are defenseless and delinquent with respect to the dead; we flee from and neglect them.

Only in this way can one explain the Venetians' lack of love for their city. They do not know how to love it, nor are they capable of loving it, since loving the dead is difficult. It is much easier to pretend that it is alive, to cover its delicate and bloodless members with some makeup and rouge in order to exhibit it to the tourists who pay an admission price. In Venice the merchants are to be found not in the temple but in the tombs, where they offend not only the living but even more so the cadaver (or rather what they believe to be a cadaver, though without being able to confess it). But this cadaver is actually a specter? that is to say (if the merchants are aware of its existence), the most nebulous and subtle entity, and thus as distant from a cadaver as one can imagine.

Spectrality is a form of life, a posthumous or complementary life that begins only when everything is finished. Spectrality thus has, with respect to life, the incomparable grace and astuteness of that which is completed, the courtesy and precision of those who no longer have anything ahead of them. It is creatures of this kind that Henry James learned to perceive in Venice (in his ghost stories he compares them to sylphs and elves). These specters are so discrete and so elusive, that it is always the living who invade their homes and strain their reticence.

But there is also another type of spectrality that we may call larval, which is born from not accepting its own condition, from forgetting it so as to pretend at all costs that it still has bodily weight and flesh. Such larval specters do not live alone but rather obstinately look for people who generated them through their bad conscience. They live in them as nightmares, as incubi or succubi, internally moving their lifeless members with strings made of lies. While the first type of spectrality is perfect, since it no longer has anything to add to what it has said or done, the larval specters must pretend to have a future in order to clear a space for some torment from their own past, for their own incapacity to comprehend that they have, indeed, reached completion.

Ingeborg Bachmann once compared language to a city, with its ancient center, its more recent and peripheral boroughs, and finally the encircling beltway and its gas stations, which are also an integral part of the city. The same utopia and the same ruin are contained in our city and in our language, and we have dreamt and lost ourselves in both; indeed, they are merely the form that this dream and this loss take. If we compare Venice to a language, then living in Venice is like studying Latin, like trying to pronounce every word, syllable by syllable, in a dead language; learning how to lose and rediscover our way in the bottlenecks of declensions and unexpected openings of supines and future infinitives. It must be remembered, though, that one should never declare a language dead provided that it still somehow speaks and is read; it is only impossible—or nearly impossible—to assume the position of a subject in such a language, of the one who says "I." The truth is that dead language, just like Venice, is a spectral language that we cannot speak but that still quivers and hums and whispers in its own special way, so we can eventually come to understand and decipher it, albeit with some effort and the help of a dictionary. But to whom does a dead language speak? To whom does the specter of language turn? Not to us, certainly, but not even to its addressees from another time, of whom it no longer has any recollection. And yet, precisely for this reason, it is as if only now, for the first time, that this language speaks, a language the philosopher refers to (though without realizing that he has thus bestowed it with a spectral consistency) by saying that *it* speaks – not we.

Venice is therefore the true emblem of modernity, even if in a completely different sense from the one evoked by Tafuri at the end of his inaugural address. Our time is not new [*nuovo*] but last [*novissimo*], that is to say, final and larval. This is what we usually understand as posthistory or postmodernity, without suspecting that this condition necessarily means being consigned to a posthumous and spectral life, without imagining that the life of the specter is the most liturgical and impervious condition, that it imposes the observance of uncompromising rules of conduct and ferocious litanies, with all their special prayers for dawn, dusk, night, and the rest of the canonical hours.

Hence the lack of rigor and decency of the larval specters who live among us. All peoples and all languages, all orders and all institutions, all parliaments and all sovereigns, the churches and the synagogues, the ermines and the gowns, have slipped one after another, inexorably, into a larval condition, though they are unprepared for and unconscious of it. And so writers write badly, since they need to pretend that their language is alive; parliaments legislate in vain because they need to simulate a political life for their larval nations; religions are deprived of piety because they no longer know how to bless the tombs and feel at home among them. This is the reason why we see skeletons and mannequins marching stiffly and mummies pretending to cheerfully conduct their own exhumation, without realizing that their decomposed members are leaving them in shambles and tatters, that their words have become glossolalic and unintelligible.

But the specter of Venice knows nothing of any of this. It no longer appears to the Venetians or, of course, to the tourists. Perhaps it appears to beggars who are chased away by brazen administrators, or to rats who anxiously cross from lane to lane with their muzzles to the ground, or to those rare people who, like exiles, try to lucubrate on this often avoided lesson. Since what the specter argues, with its choirboy-like voice, is that if all the cities and all the languages of Europe now survive only as phantasms, then only those who have understood these most intimate and most familiar deeds, only those who recite and record the discarnate words and stones, will perhaps be able one day to reopen that breach in which history—in which life—suddenly fulfills its promise.

Notes

1   Manfredo Tafuri, "Le forme del tempo: Venezia e la modernità," in
     Università IUAV di Venezia, Inaugurazioni accademiche, 1991–2006 (Venice:
     IAUV, 2006).

2   Søren Kierkegaard, *Works of Love*, trans. H. V. Long (Princeton, NJ:
     Princeton University Press, 1995), 358.

PART SIX

Haunted Historiographies

28

Haunted Historiographies / Introduction

María del Pilar Blanco and Esther Peeren

In his fifth thesis on the philosophy of history, Walter Benjamin highlights the problems faced by the twentieth-century historical-materialist investigator. "The past," he writes, "can be seized only as an image which flashes up at the instant when it can be recognized and is never seen again."[1] This assertion highlights the precariousness of the historian's task. It constitutes a hunt for a sign from the past that can in turn respond to a question posed by the present. However, it is difficult to know whether this sign will ever actually manifest itself in the search and re-search. How does the historian know what to look for? What does she prioritize in her search for a past that may revitalize the present and future? For Wendy Brown, who reads Benjamin's angel of history and Derrida's specters as sharing a "rejection of historical totalization in favor of a fragmented and fragmentary historiography," it is a question of finding ways, through an effort of conjuration, to cultivate the ghostly images of the past as *incitations* in the present."[2] Benjamin's warning about such a deliberate process of retrieval and mobilization is that "every image of the past that is not recognized by the present as one of its own concerns threatens to disappear irretrievably."[3] According to Benjamin, the way we see the past—what we see *of* it— is predicated on our relationship to the present; the quest for the past is activated by the questions we put to it in our now-moment. What, then, is our responsibility, and how do we formulate that responsibility toward the past, its lost subjects and objects, in the process of writing history in the twenty-first century?

Our relationship to the past, and to the process of writing history, has changed dramatically. During the mid-twentieth century, as Hayden White argues in *Metahistory*, the certainty and supposed objectivity and autonomy of the previous century's "'historical knowledge'" was put into serious doubt. As he explains, questions of what it meant to "think historically" became overshadowed by "an apprehension that definitive answers to them may not be possible."[4] This position against the truth-bearing power of history, White explains, succeeded in producing a new interpretation of the historical narrative as contingent on the ideological context that produced it. White's own position is a formalist one: history for him is a "verbal structure in the form of a narrative prose discourse that purports to be a model, or icon, of past structures and processes"—a form of explanation by way of representation, or demonstration.[5] The re-evaluations of the historiographical process that transpired in the last decades of the twentieth century return us again to that precariousness that Benjamin identifies in his "Theses." The past is difficult to recover; if we do encounter fragments of it, they may be difficult, or even impossible, to unpack. What is more, our recent perception of the historiographical can reveal the datedness of the historical narrative. This is because each generation represents a set of priorities in how it establishes a relationship with the past, what it preserves or archives, what it recounts, and how it tells it.[6] These conundrums put forth the question of how our histories can avoid eliding the present while speaking of the past, for we should recognize our position with respect to the past and acknowledge the limitations that we face within this complex temporal relationship.

More recently, the loss of assuredness about what the historical narrative can translate about and from the past has resulted in an admission that historiography is in fact a form of haunting—of the past haunting the present, as much as it is the present's haunting of the past. The future, too, is implicated by this spectral vision, as what Brown calls Derrida's "hauntology as historiography" is seen to "indicat[e] the way in which the future is always already populated with certain possibilities derived from the past; the way in which it is constrained, circumscribed, inscribed by the past; the way in which it is haunted before we make and enter it."[7] For Brown, this pervasive sense of haunting, through its corollary of conjuration, can install a form of political agency that uses history (reconfigured as inherently contestable) strategically. Yet at the same time she admits that it is never fully controllable and may also appear as a "failure of memory."[8] The ungraspable quality of what came before and what can be retained of it, which White alludes to in *Metahistory*—the uncertainty of how to handle what is absent to the historian's present—is echoed in our contemporary admission of hauntedness as a state of being in the world. This does not mean that our decoding of the past has become submissive to powerful ghosts. Rather, it has made historiographers perceive their relationship to the past through a kind of active questioning that Colin Davis has related to the notion of skepticism. Following on from Levinas's conceptualization of this mode of understanding the world as if in a suspended mode of disbelief, Davis explains skepticism as "speak[ing] for non-coincidence and fractured temporalities rather than a stable, unified plane of intelligibility to which everything can be reduced."[9] The difficulty of historiography lies in its potential discovery of that which does not make sense, or may seem impossible to the present subject. This questioning of the past is thus an admission that certain things must remain unintelligible, or else that the smooth narrative that the historian might have envisioned is taken over by the recognition of a thickness of detail (to recall Clifford Geertz's phrase), or a multiplicity of versions that are full of unquiet ghosts.

This final part of *The Spectralities Reader* explores that ethical and political play that the writer/teller of both place and event must engage with in order to produce a responsible account of what has transpired. The works included—by Judith Richardson, Jesse Alemán, and Alexander Nemerov—are three important reflections on how the process of writing history is in fact a haunted (and haunting) practice.

We must not disengage the relationship to a past event from our relationship to a location's past. As demonstrated in the essays in the previous part of this *Reader*, the spectral turn has reaffirmed the idea that places have history; more than that, they contain layers of history that, although seemingly erased by time, can be recalled (though not necessarily fully separated) through processes of active remembrance as re-membering, re-composing. The methodologies of history and geography are connected in how the scholar of a given time and place is indeed a recollector and reshaper of (fictional or nonfictional) stories about events that have slipped into the realms of memory and forgetting. This way of perceiving space entails a gathering of stories around a location; the producer of a spectrography is therefore responsible for the creation of an ethics that can tell the stories of that location, as well as the relations between subjects and these particular narratives, without claiming to tell in full. In other words, she has the responsibility of relating subjects' relationships to that place, as well as the events that, having transpired there, transform both location and subjects forever.

In "A History of Unrest," excerpted from her book *Possessions*, Richardson compellingly tackles the issue of why so many ghost stories have emerged within the specific region of the Hudson River Valley—a region that has seen intense transformation since the era of colonization. Moving from the 1600s to the twentieth century, and researching an extensive archive comprised of literature (such as the works of Washington Irving and James Fenimore Cooper's *Deerslayer*), tourist guides, and regional written and oral histories, Richardson argues that it is precisely because of the instability of the region's history, which fostered a potent sense of the unknown even within communities, that it has proven so hospitable to a myriad of haunting: "while historical demands made ghosts useful and desirable, it was ironically the *lack* of historical continuity and understanding that made the past mysterious and ghostly."[10] As she explains elsewhere in her book, "[g]hosts operate as a particular, and peculiar, kind of social memory, an alternate form of history-making in which things usually forgotten discarded, or repressed become foregrounded, whether as items of fear, regret, explanation, or desire."[11] Throughout the ages, the ghost stories of the Hudson River Valley have responded to the evolving social, ethnic, and cultural circumstances of this location. They have done so, however, in a distinct manner, privileging silent, unidentifiable or transient ghosts that can be seen as symptomatic of a disjointed and fractured local history. These ghosts are an integral part of the transformations the regions and the varied concerns that each generation brings to its environment. They demonstrate the ways in which societies look to the past—even or especially when this past is muddled—to understand their present, and to claim their own position within a given territory.

Jesse Alemán's essay "The Other Country: Mexico, the United States, and the Gothic History of Conquest" widens the focus of haunted historiography to include the American hemisphere, and particularly the nineteenth-century US romanticization of the Mexican Conquest. Alemán's is a timely intervention in the disciplinary field of hemispheric studies, as he interrogates how US narratives have situated themselves with respect to its American "Others," and, subsequently, how current scholarship deals with this inter-national relationship.[12] In his readings of nineteenth-century romances such as the anonymously written *Xicoténcatl* (1826), Robert Montgomery Bird's *Calavar, or the Knight of the Conquest* (1834), and William Prescott's *History of the Conquest of Mexico* (1843), Alemán explores how Mexico becomes the "uncanny imperial other" of the recently independent United States, where subjects from the north play out fantasies of a glorious, ancient past in a country that is near and familiar, but outside of its own borders.[13] This reimagination of the national past is a form of activating what Eric Sundquist calls "romantic primitivism," of seeking roots away from Europe and within the continent.[14] As Alemán argues, however, in this case it "generated an alternative literary and national narrative that placed the legacy of the Spanish conquest of Mexico strangely at the heart of the US's own historical emergence."[15] This leads him to reconceptualize US-Mexico relations as "inter-American" in a haunted, or what he addresses as "gothic," sense. Instead of thinking it in terms of a diagonal, even relation between the two national entities, "inter" here refers to the "burial" of cultural and national others within another: "'In-ter' Americanism understands that the nations of the western hemisphere already contain *within* ('intra') their borders national others whose formative presence is subsequently buried (interred) but nonetheless felt and often expressed through gothic discourse."[16] Alemán's essay is a vivid account of how a disciplinary field informed by questions of transnationalism can be read in haunted terms, and how national stories unearth neighboring, hemispheric ghosts that reveal social and ethnic anxieties brewing at home.

If reading a US romance can disinter a whole history of hemispheric relations, reading a ghost story in its original context can produce interesting, if fleeting, articulations between the narrative and the historical moment that engulfed its production and publication. In "Seeing Ghosts: *The Turn of the Screw* and Art History," Alexander Nemerov turns to the classic and arguably unrivaled ghost story by Henry James about a governess who believes she sees ghosts haunting, and even possessing, her two young charges. Nemerov provocatively suggests that James's governess is a "model" for the (art) historian, and what she does. He writes: "Historical revelation, as her experience defines it, takes some form like that of [the ghost] Quint on the tower. It is the sudden presence of something unlooked-for right there where we can never quite see it—not today, not tomorrow, not ever—that's yet perceptible all the same."[17] The governess, like the historian, searches for something that may or may not reveal itself. Nemerov attempts such a search in his reading of the first run of *The Turn of the Screw* (published in *Collier's Weekly* magazine from January to April 1898), which is found to have shared the page with the ongoing reportage of the explosion of the *Maine* in Havana Harbor on 15 February of that year. What does the historian do with such striking simultaneity between a work of fiction and its illustrations, and the visual and textual reportage of a historical event, on the pages of the same magazine? What associations should she draw, if any? Rather than look for rational answers or revelations about these coincidences, Nemerov's essay transports us through the very process of the historian's search through the past, focusing our attention on that first "instant when we come to see the past in the shape of something odd."[18] This marks the place where the present and the past collide in that indelible moment when we become haunted by something that we want within our grasp, but cannot pin down.

Richardson, Alemán, and Nemerov relate to history and historiography in distinct ways. Reading through fictions and a variety of archive material, each author contemplates details about the past that in turn open larger lines of inquiry—about a given place, or event, or about a history of transnational relations. They also remind us of how genres such as the romance or the ghost story are embedded in histories of cultural, social, and racial anxieties. The revelation of the spectrally strange and implausible within such narratives and their contexts is an important moment for the historiographer, for they may be seen as Benjaminian flashes that illuminate our relationship with the past, and remind us of our responsibility to carry it into the future.

Notes

1   Walter Benjamin, "Theses on the Philosophy of History," in *Illuminations*, ed. Hannah Arendt, trans. Henry Zohn (New York: Schocken Books, 1968), 255.

2   Wendy Brown, "Futures: Specters and Angels: Benjamin and Derrida," in *Politics out of History* (Princeton: Princeton University Press, 2001), 167, 168.

3   Ibid.

4   Hayden White, *Metahistory: The Historical Imagination in Nineteenth-Century Europe* (Baltimore: Johns Hopkins University Press, 1975), 1.

5   Ibid., 2.

6   In *Archive Fever*, Derrida exposes the traditional archive (and the determinate history it seeks to produce through its acts of *commencement* and *commandment*) as always already spectralized, destabilized: "the structure of the archive is *spectral*. It is spectral *a priori*: neither present nor absent 'in the flesh,' neither visible nor invisible, a trace always referring to another whose eyes can never be met, no more than those of Hamlet's father, thanks to the possibility of a visor. Also, the spectral motif stages this disseminating fissure from which the archontic principle, and the concept of archive, and the concept in general suffer, from the principle on." Jacques Derrida, *Archive Fever: A Freudian Impression*, trans. Eric Prenowitz (1995; Chicago: University of Chicago Press, 1996), 84–5.

7   Brown, "Futures," 153, 150.

8   Ibid., 153.

9   Colin Davis, "The Skeptical Ghost: Alejandro Amenábar's *The Others* and the Return of the Dead" in *Popular Ghosts: The Haunted Spaces of Everyday Culture*, ed. María del Pilar Blanco and Esther Peeren (New York: Continuum, 2010), 66.

10   Judith Richardson, *Possessions: The History and Uses of Haunting in the Hudson Valley* (Cambridge, MA: Harvard University Press, 2003), 25.

11   Ibid., 3.

12   For another investigation of hemispheric haunting, focusing on how ghosts in literature and film function "as experiments in a prolonged evocation of future anxieties and extended disquiet in multiple locations of the Americas," see María del Pilar Blanco, *Ghost-Watching American Modernity: Haunting, Landscape, and the Hemispheric Imagination* (New York: Fordham University Press, 2012), 7.

13   Jesse Alemán, "The Other Country: Mexico, the United States, and the Gothic History of Conquest," *American Literary History* 18.3 (Autumn 2006), 409.

14   Ibid., 408.

15   Ibid.

16 Ibid., 409–10.

17 Alexander Nemerov, "Seeing Ghosts: *The Turn of the Screw* and Art History," in *What is Research in the Visual Arts?: Obsession, Archive, Encounter*, ed. Michael Ann Holly and Marquard Smith (Williamstown, MA: Clark Art Institute, 2009), 14.

18 Ibid., 28.

29

A History of Unrest

Judith Richardson

The character of Hudson Valley history goes another long step toward explaining how the region came by its strange heritage of hauntedness. Despite tourbook images of the region as sleepy and timeless, the history of the Hudson Valley has largely been one of unrest, colored by territorial conflicts, social diversity and dissensus, and multiple, contending colonizations; it has taken shape from the movements of various populations through the region, from the rapid rate of change, and from an ambivalent hinterland relationship to what became in the early nineteenth century the nation's most populous city. This was a perpetually uncertain ground, a crossroads where no clear lines could be drawn between insiders and outsiders. Rather than dispelling ghosts, this history of unrest has been crucial in the production of hauntings.

The germinal moment of Hudson Valley history to which, like most, Maud Wilder Goodwin points is that of Dutch exploration and settlement. And there *is* something to this focus on the Dutch. Although settlement of New Netherland, beginning in 1624, was slow compared with contemporary growth of English colonies, the Dutch maintained a presence and influence in regional society and culture long after the English made New Netherland into New York, without battle, in 1664.[1] The Dutch presence set New York apart in its colonial milieu, and afterward gave the region a unique social and historical layer. The Dutch, though, were never alone in New York, nor was their possession of the territory ever secure. To begin with, there were those "strange aboriginal savages."[2] At the time of Dutch settlement, the river valley was inhabited by Lenape (Delaware), Wappinger, and Mahican tribes, with the Mohawks just to the northeast.[3] Although Dutch-Indian relations were not always violent, numerous incidents of misunderstanding, as well as a more broadcast uneasiness, are reflected in colonial accounts, and tension did on several occasions turn to outright warfare involving atrocities on both sides, as in the Indian Wars of 1643–1645 and the Esopus Wars of 1659–60 and 1663–64.[4] The Dutch colony also had to contend with other colonial powers—the French to the north, and especially the English to the east and south. A state of perpetual border warfare existed between New Netherland and the New England colonies, which continued even after the English took over New York (and indeed into the nineteenth and twentieth centuries).[5]

A sense of instability in colonial New Netherland/New York was further exacerbated by the extraordinary diversity and discord *within* the colony. Because the colony had difficulty attracting settlers from the Netherlands, it was forced to have an open-door policy, and almost half of the traceable immigrants to New Netherland during the seventeenth century came from places outside the Netherlands. The early colonial population included Germans, French Huguenots, Danes, Swedes, Belgians, and Norwegians, as well a significant number of African slaves; and when the region passed under English control, Scottish, English, and Irish elements and an increasing number of New Englanders joined the already uneasy mix.[6] The tensions and animosities caused by this ethnic heterogeneity constitute a major theme in contemporary and historical accounts of the region.[7] There were also unique class antagonisms created in New York by the manorial land system, begun by the Dutch and expanded by the English—antagonisms that led to armed uprisings by tenant farmers in the eighteenth and nineteenth centuries. "In a colony as complex as this one," writes historian Patricia Bonomi, "the materials for contention, of all sorts, were everywhere at hand."[8] A broad lack of social cohesion in the colonial period is evidenced by the fact that colonial New York had a significantly higher rate of crime and violence than the more homogeneous colonies of New England.[9]

From these shaky foundations, regional unrest and instability carried forward into the postcolonial period and beyond. First there was the Revolutionary War, which made the Hudson Valley the site of a disproportionate number of battles and produced intense in-fighting with long-lasting resonances in regional memory.[10] By removing most of the Native American population of upstate New York and a number of landholding loyalists, the war also paved the way for a massive in-migration of New Englanders in the late eighteenth and early nineteenth centuries.[11] The nineteenth century brought transportation developments that vastly increased accessibility and traffic along the river. With the invention of the steamboat, which made its debut run from New York to Albany in 1807, and the opening in 1825 of the Erie Canal, which linked the Hudson to the country's interior, the river became one of the busiest thoroughfares in the country.[12] By the 1850s the Hudson River Railroad was running the length of the east shore from New

York to Rensselaer, and by the mid-1880s railroads flanked both sides of the river and crisscrossed the adjacent counties.[13]

These developments fostered tremendous social and economic changes. Agriculture, the most prevalent activity in the Hudson Valley into the nineteenth century, was increasingly conducted with an eye to markets, and ultimately lost ground to western competition.[14] More strikingly, the region underwent a rapid and prolonged industrialization, peaking in the late nineteenth century, which added quarries, brickworks, tanneries, ironworks, and factories to the landscape.[15] Adjacent to the immigrant gateway of New York City, this industrial development also promoted demographic transformations in the region. At midcentury there was what one historian, speaking of Albany, has called the "Irish invasion," along with a large German immigration;[16] later in the century, the region's workforce and population drew in southern and eastern European immigrants, as well as African-American migrants from the South. These movements and migrations affected all the riverside counties, especially areas close to New York City: by the mid-1890s one-third of the population of Yonkers was foreign born, and another third was first-generation American, while the state census of 1925 reported that railroad workers living in Croton came from fifteen different countries.[17]

Improvements in transportation also aligned with the spread of romantic sentiment and aesthetics to produce another type of "invasion" in the nineteenth century: an enormous tourist interest in the river, which gave rise to a burgeoning number of resort hotels and recreational facilities along the Palisades, in the Highlands, and in the Catskills.[18] In the 1880s, with six trains a day arriving from New York City alone, between 60,000 and 70,000 tourists and summer boarders traveled to the Catskills every summer; by 1907 the number of annual visitors climbed to about 300,000.[19] The region was subject to more permanent urban extrusions as well. Wealthy New Yorkers and industrialists—including Rockefellers, Goulds, Vanderbilts, and Morgans—as well as artists and writers, lined the river's shores with summer homes and estates, and suburbs began growing up along rail lines, while the needs of the growing metropolis further encroached on the landscape in the form of massive reservoir projects.[20] The placid image these reservoirs now present masks the often bitter resentments that accompanied their development, as whole towns had to be moved or abandoned for their creation.

In the twentieth century, the social, economic, and physical character of the region continued to undergo radical transformations, and contests over territory and place continued to be predominant features of regional life. Suffering from southern and western competition, and in many cases terminally damaged by the Great Depression, a good deal of Hudson Valley industry fell to ruin in the early twentieth century.[21] As industry ebbed, automobile travel and spates of highway and bridge construction accelerated suburbanization, sometimes in explosive proportions: for instance, from 1955, when the Tappan Zee Bridge opened, to 1970, the population of Rockland County went from 89,000 to 230,000.[22] Such suburban development both paralleled and contended with a rise in conservation and park movements in the region, championed by such agencies as the Palisades Interstate Park Commission (created in 1900), which secured large parcels of land in the valley as recreational and scenic preserves. None of these changes came without battles. The construction of new highways, both because they displaced older routes, bypassing older towns, and because they were perceived to threaten local character and quality of life, often caused heated arguments.[23] Whereas industrial growth or reservoir building had caused outrage in the nineteenth century, in the twentieth century the erection of power plants became a perennial issue.[24] Not even the creation of parks has gone without opposition. These issues, the internal dividing lines they expose within the regional population, and the fact that some of the staunchest despoilers and defenders of the region were often far from "local," show how difficult it is, and has always been, to designate insiders and outsiders, how the ground is, and has always been, layered with contending desires and claims.

This restless and contentious history, replete with acts of dispossession, marginalization, and violence, was ripe for the development of regional haunting, not least because it left a considerable supply of potential ghosts. Along "no other river," the author of the 1868 *Legends and Poetry of the Hudson* asserts, have the "waves of different civilizations ... left so many *waifs* upon the banks."[25] The rapid rate of development, and thus of obsolescence, and the frequent social shifts bestowed on the region a large number of "pasts" in a relatively brief period, providing a plethora of raw materials from which hauntings could emerge, while also effectively foreshortening historical time, so that even recent events seemed remote. As James Fenimore Cooper theorizes in the opening to *The Deerslayer* (1841), "On the human imagination, events produce the effects of time," and thus the shallow histories of America and of New York could seem ancient simply as a result of "an accumulation of changes."[26] Along with bolstering supply, historical developments in the region created a variety of social, economic, and cultural demands for ghosts, whether as emblems of guilt and protest or as icons of nostalgia and tradition. Hauntings proliferated, for instance, in conjunction with the nineteenth-century tourist industry's need to attract romantic-minded travelers, or from efforts to establish moorings in times of upheaval, as was clearly the case in Westchester in the late nineteenth century.

The specifics of historical supply and demand are important, and I return to them throughout subsequent chapters. But there is a particular underlying factor, deriving from the overarching tendencies of Hudson Valley history, which I want to explore in greater depth here. Most significant in the restless history of the region is that it created a sense of social and historical tenuousness that was crucial to producing ghosts. The uncanny, writes Renée Bergland, is literally "the unsettled, the not-yet-colonized, the unsuccessfully colonized, or the decolonized."[27] Despite some longstanding settlements, and inhabitants who could trace their lineage back to the early colonists, the Hudson Valley has been, by and large, a place inhabited and crossed by strangers. The convergences of unfamiliar people, the uncertainty of place created by frequent influxes and movements, created a sense of troubling uncanniness and unfathomable otherness that could lend itself to a sense of hauntedness—something suggested by the frequent conflation or confusion of ostensibly living others with ghosts. Early descriptions and place-names suggest that the Dutch found Native Americans spooky; the Dutch in turn were cast as ghostly in the nineteenth and twentieth centuries.[28] One late-twentieth-century writer has attributed the proliferation of hauntings in the region to the fact that the later-arriving English "found the indigenous culture [of the Dutch and Germans] uncomfortably alien and thus inscrutable."[29] Ghostliness in part served to articulate and contain anxieties about strange places and people. Wondering why a cave in Dutchess County was called the "Spook Hole," a newspaper reporter in 1870 was told that it had once been occupied "by an old man of foreign aspect [with] a negress and their son."[30] In another instance, a man from Milton, in Ulster County, told the following story to a folklore student in 1945: "One night when I was a young man, I was walking home along the river road toward the station, when I suddenly heard footsteps following me.... I glanced back and saw a big black figure following me. I thought maybe it was a tramp or a nigger, so I pulled out my knife and snapped it like a gun. I turned around fast to scare whoever it was, but it was gone." Unable to identify this apparition, the man conjectures: "maybe it was the Black Lady," a ghost said to haunt the town.[31]

This uncertainty about who or what was out there had a historical correlative–an uncertainty about what had gone on here. In a country that, as Tuan writes, had "its face to the future," historical amnesia and a sense of pastlessness were common maladies.[32] In the Hudson Valley the disintegration of connection to the past could seem a chronic condition. From Irving's recurrent allusions to the history-erasing Yankee flood of the post-Revolutionary period, through the nineteenth and twentieth centuries, a troubled perception that history was being washed away under the myriad "waves of civilization" repeats as a leitmotif in regional writings. "We are drifting along with scarcely an effort to preserve from fast approaching oblivion the thousands of interesting facts, recollections, and reminiscences of the past, relating to our county," writes the editor of an 1874 Dutchess County book, *Local Tales and Historical Sketches*.[33] In the mind of Catskill historian Henry Brace, writing in 1884, it was already far too late. Had his work been undertaken seventy years earlier, he argues, "the annalist could have drawn a lively picture" from the reminiscences of now-dead townsmen. "Now ... all that one, even with the utmost diligence of research and inquiry, can do is to sketch in meager and almost colorless outline the history of a secluded community."[34] Such laments over the lost past abound in local accounts. And if relatively long-settled residents were shaky on the historical facts, new arrivals and visitors sometimes sensed an unbridgeable gap between themselves and local history. In *The Old Mine Road*, even the inveterately curious C. G. Hine writes of passing "several stone houses ... that suggest a possibility of stories and things, but if there are such they are a sealed book."[35]

This much-bemoaned sense of historical loss or obscurity has been central to the haunting of the region. While particular events, figures, and circumstances provided the potential substance for hauntings, and while historical demands made ghosts useful and desirable, it was ironically the *lack* of historical continuity and understanding that made the past mysterious and ghostly. This is a key point, one that goes to the very heart of my argument. Before discussing the historical reference points contained in various hauntings, as I do in later chapters, it is worth pausing here to notice how thoroughly regional ghostlore reflects disorientation, uncertainty, discontinuity, and unrootedness.

Recent scholarship has emphasized relationships between ghosts and language, ghosts and memory, ghosts and history. Renée Bergland writes explicitly: "Like ghosts, words are disembodied presences."[36] Although Bergland correctly suggests an expressive affinity between words and ghosts, the parity is not absolute. Rather, ghosts often represent the things that words have not expressed or cannot express. They emanate from and embody the blank spaces between words in historical narratives, the erasures and oversights—the "noisy silences and seething absences" described by sociologist Avery Gordon.[37] It is worth noting the correspondence between Henry Brace's lament at being able to present only a "meager and almost colorless outline" of local history, and the description offered when a folklore student in the 1940s asked her grandfather what ghosts looked like: "a ghost ... has [the] shape and outline of the person ... but they are not colored—merely a black and white outline. The whole figure looks light and wispy as if it could blow away any minute."[38] The common understanding of ghostliness articulated in this description is the very image of historical insubstantiality and fragmentariness.

Throughout the literature and folklore of the valley, ghosts are habitually discerned and described in terms of vagueness, colorlessness, wispiness, incompleteness; they are most often recognized and defined precisely by their lack of definition or identifiers. A "formless gray shadow" is reported to "whisk by in the neighborhood of the swamp," in Edgar Mayhew Bacon's *Chronicles of Tarrytown and Sleepy Hollow* (1897).[39] A "dark shapeless object ... [a] mysterious mass" is seen to move "silently across the road," in Charles Pryer's *Reminiscences of an Old Westchester Homestead* (1897).[40] In folklore collected in the mid-twentieth century, vague ghosts are everywhere: a "figure in black" at a Rensselaer house; "a white figure" at a Kerhonkson house; "something white" that appeared "around a tree" in Cohoes, "first on one side . . . then on the other . . . [then] a gust of wind" and it was gone; a figure "visible though transparent," with a "white cloudy appearance" in a Mount Airy home; a "white form" in an abandoned house in Middletown.[41] There are hosts of shadowy, unidentifiable women; there are numerous ghosts without heads.[42]

These types and images are not unique to the Hudson Valley: they echo larger traditions and iconographies. Yet the fact that so many of the ghosts of the region are so inchoate or faded, so incapable of being identified, has aesthetic and historical implications. Embedded in these depictions of ghosts is a problem of communication, a loss of essential information, an inability to articulate something reflected further in the general silence of the Hudson Valley's ghostly population. European ghosts often speak; New York area ghosts rarely do.[43] Like the ghosts that Rip Van Winkle encounters in the Catskill recesses, who disturb him most by the fact that "they maintained the gravest faces, the most mysterious silence," Hudson Valley ghosts are often either dead silent or, when they do try to communicate, are heard as muffled or otherwise incomprehensible.[44] And in many cases ghosts rob witnesses of the power of speech as well, defying description and eroding verbal expression.[45] The undescribable, unspeakable aspects of ghosts may simply stem from crises of abysmal horror or mourning. Yet the inarticulacy that defines so many instances of haunting in the Hudson Valley also shadows problems of historical continuity, of perennial change as repeatedly and cumulatively obscuring the regional past and undermining historical understanding. It is telling that whereas Irving describes the ghostly crew of "The Storm-Ship" as chanting, a late-nineteenth-century retelling says they chant "words devoid of meaning to the listeners."[46] The fault, of course, lies not with the ghosts, but with the observers. That is, if traces of the past presented themselves, if waves of settlers and visitors suspected that things had happened here, they were largely at a loss to identify them or to understand their implications.

Although my suggestion here—that the vagueness and incommunicativeness endemic to regional ghostliness is intertwined with a sense of historical uncertainty—is speculative, more concrete evidence of a link between regional ghostliness and a sense of rootlessness lies in the multiple ways that regional hauntings make reference to transience itself. There are, first of all, the wandering, transgressive habits of ghosts themselves, which seem to relate to senses of vulnerability, trespass, homelessness, and alienation. In the story of "The Spirit Lady," in *Reminiscences of an Old Westchester Homestead*, Charles Pryer writes that she "seemed to mind fences no more than grass-blades, and instead of climbing over seemed to glide through them."[47] Describing a ghost that passed her along the road, a Dutchess County woman said that he "seemed to come toward us out of nowhere. He seemed to glide past us like a streak."[48] That the author of *Legends and Poetry of the Hudson* chose to write of "so many *waifs*" along the river's bank is revealing in this regard, as the word *waif* connotes both fleeting wispiness and homelessness or abandonment.[49] Other accounts point to the transience of the living as the cause of ghostly restlessness; for instance, in *Myths and Legends of Our Own Land* (1896), Charles Skinner writes that "the walking sachems of Teller's Point" were awakened by "the tramping of white men over their graves."[50]

A link between regional haunting and a concern with transience is perhaps more profoundly reflected in the frequent haunting of sites of transition, such as roads, bridges, and taverns; and in the significant presence in regional lore of the ghosts of *transients*—hitchhikers, gypsies, tramps, itinerant musicians, pirates, and most prominently peddlers.[51] Peddlers tend to be coded as Yankee in American imaginations, and indeed such codings color early-nineteenth-century references to peddler ghosts in the region–something that in itself reflects a link between the Yankee invasion and the production of hauntings.[52] However, later stories of peddler ghosts seem to lose entirely such regionally or historically specific characteristics, as these ghosts come to epitomize more generally the intersection of shaky historical knowledge, transiency, and ghostliness. In *Local Tales and Historical Sketches* (1874), for instance, Henry D. B. Bailey presents a long tale about "The Haunted Tavern" in East Fishkill, which "was located some distance from the nearest settler, remote from any village, surrounded with forests dark and dense."[53] At length, "startling stories . . . were circulated throughout the settlement . . . that [a] peddler never left the tavern," and the tavern gets a reputation for being haunted.[54] An entirely possible, yet fleeting and identityless presence, the peddler makes for an easy ghost story. Notably, the tale itself invokes historical vagueness, as Bailey leaves the reader to judge the truth of the reported events, while the book's editor cannot contain his concern that "those who are not well acquainted with the early history of the County may take fiction for fact, and so be unconsciously led astray."[55]

This trend toward vagueness continues in folklore collected in the twentieth century, where peddlers frequently feature as default explanations for otherwise unexplained hauntings and unidentified remains. Perhaps the most revealing of these instances is a reference from Ulster County, in which the collector writes:

Up the pond road on the way to Glenford, there is a small bridge, crossing a little mountain stream. This little bridge in the Vly [swamp] is called the Spook Bridge. I've always wondered why it was called the Spook Bridge. . . . This is how one of the neighbors living on this road told it to me:

"That bridge you see there now is not the original Spook Bridge. The old bridge was a little below the bridge now standing. It seems that there were some workmen up near that stream and they had a little cabin there where they stayed. They were building the bridge at this time. One day, the workmen left and they had not finished the bridge. Someone went in the cabin and there they found a pack-peddler's pack and belongings behind an old trunk. I don't know jest [sic] why they did this, but they looked under the old Spook Bridge and there they found the body of the peddler. Well, they buried him there, and they say that when you go over that bridge at night, you can see ghosts and spooks moving around there, and they are all dressed in white. Yes, I reckon that old pack peddler must have been murdered. It's funny how those men disappeared so sudden like."[56]

Everything here is vagueness and transiency: a "spook" place whose name suggests but does not specify some sort of haunting; the presence not only of a wandering peddler but also of unfamiliar and nonlocal workmen (who also disappear like ghosts); ghosts and spooks "moving around" and "all dressed in white"; a historically uninformed interviewer; and, finally, language that emphasizes the speculative nature of the whole account.

Louis Jones argues that peddlers recur so frequently in regional folklore "because so many of them were murdered for the money they carried with them."[57] Jones's rationale, although it may have basis in fact, seems to miss something. Peddlers, along with gypsies and other transient figures, historically represented what might be referred to as common strangers. They were both historical facts and abstract symbols of community disruption.[58] An American version of the "Wandering Jew," they were uncanny presences, unsettling and unsettled, and in this held a certain kinship with ghosts.[59] Peddler ghosts served as a two-sided symbol of a troubled rootlessness, representing mysterious and disruptive presences within the familiar landscape of more-settled communities, while also emblematizing the potential perilousness of unfamiliar territories to strangers of all sorts. Along with the wider group of vague, incommunicative, and transient ghosts in regional lore, these peddlers were closely intertwined with anxieties over transiency, mutability, and historical uncertainty, and the proliferation of their ghosts suggests recourse to speculation and stereotype where historical substance was lacking.

The horror writer Stephen King has written that the basis of all human fear is not an entirely closed door, but a door slightly ajar.[60] Ultimately, Hudson Valley history was propitious for haunting in both its accretion of pasts and its tenuousness of historical continuity—a dual accumulation of substances and absences. History became, in essence, a matter of suspicion and conjecture. Of course, the historical crises represented in ghostly vagueness presented opportunities as well—something suggested in the worries of the editor of *Local Tales and Historical Sketches* that "those not so well acquainted" with local history could be "led astray" by ghost tales. As Hine writes of a mysterious house in Orange County, which was presented to him "with the vague statement that many historic memories cling about it": "Possibly the literary lights prefer it so, as each can then clothe it with his own imagination."[61]

Notes

1   According to Van Zandt, "Although Plymouth, New Amsterdam, and Jamestown were all founded within a few years of each other with approximately the same number of people, Massachusetts had 16,000 by 1643, Virginia had 15,000 by 1649, but as late as 1653 New Netherland still had only 2,000 inhabitants. In 1664 when England acquired New Netherland by force of arms, Virginia had 40,000, New England had 50,000, and the conquered Dutch province had about 10,000. By 1698, Virginia and Massachusetts each had 58 to 60,000, whereas New York still languished with less than 20,000"; Roland Van Zandt, *Chronicles of the Hudson: Three Centuries of Travelers' Accounts (New Brunswick: Rutgers University Press, 1971)*, p. 3. On Dutch culture and language in the Hudson Valley, see Alice P. Kenney, *Stubborn for Liberty: The Dutch in New York* (Syracuse: Syracuse University Press, 1975); and Van Cleaf Bachman, Alice P. Kenney, and Lawrence G. Van Loon, "'Het Poelmeisie': An Introduction to the Hudson Valley Dutch Dialect," *New York History* 61 (April 1980): 161–85, which reports that Dutch was still spoken in enclaves of the valley into the twentieth century.

2   Maud Wilder Goodwin, *Dutch and English on the Hudson: A Chronicle of Colonial New York* (New Haven: Yale University Press, 1919), p. 121.

3   For a detailed discussion of Native American tribes in the region, see E. M. Ruttenber, *History of the Indian Tribes of Hudson's River* (Albany: J. Munsell, 1872). According to Patricia Edwards Clyne in *Hudson Valley Tales and Trials* (Woodstock, NY: Overlook Press, 1990), Native American settlement in the region can be traced back at least nine thousand years, and from 1500 to 1700 the Native population in the region was composed of four major groups: "west of the Hudson, the Delawares (also called the Lenni-Lenape or Munsee) extended north to the land of the Mohawks, while east of the Hudson the Wappingers occupied the region roughly from Manhattan island into Dutchess, and north of them were the Mohicans (also spelled Mahicans or Mohegans)" (pp. 28–30). In *The Hudson River* (New York: Norton, 1969), Robert H. Boyle cites estimates that that in 1600 there were about 3,000 Mahicans, 4,750 Wappingers, including those in Connecticut, and 8,000 Delawares (p. 42).

4   For a detailed history of relations between colonists and Native Americans in the region, see Ruttenber, *Indian Tribes of Hudson's River*, pp. 99–157.

5   For New York–New England border disputes, see Dixon Ryan Fox, *Yankees and Yorkers* (New York: New York University Press, 1940). According to Fox, "between New England and New York the 'warfare,' with pen and sword, lasted actively from the sixteen twenties to seventeen ninety, the counterclaims were not entirely subdued until the eighteen seventies, and ... the Supreme Court of the United States was pronouncing on the issues as late as 1932" (p. ix).

6   See David Steven Cohen, "How Dutch Were the Dutch of New Netherland?" *New York History* 62 (January 1981): 49–60. The first record of African slaves in the region appears in 1626. The African slave population in New York was 2,170 in 1698 and 21,329 in 1790; Edgar J. McManus, *A History of Negro Slavery in New York* (Syracuse: Syracuse University Press, 1966), pp. 4, 197, 200. According to historian Oliver A. Rink, New Netherland was "the most culturally heterogeneous European colony in North American"; Rink, "The People of New Netherland: Notes on Non-English Immigration to New York in the Seventeenth Century," *New York History* 62 (January 1981): 34.

7   Colonial observers noted the particular animosities between the Dutch and the English. For instance, the Swedish botanist Peter Kalm, visiting in 1749–1750, wrote: "The hatred which the English bear against the people of Albany is very great, but that of the Albanians against the English is carried to a ten times higher degree.... They are so to speak permeated with hatred toward the English"; quoted in David M. Ellis, "Yankee Dutch Confrontation in the Albany Area," *New England Quarterly* 45 (June 1972): 264. For scholarly accounts emphasizing the discord of colonial New York, see especially Patricia Bonomi, *A Factious People: Politics and Society in Colonial New York* (New York: Columbia University Press, 1971).

8   Bonomi, *A Factious People*, p. 15.

9   Douglas Greenberg, *Crime and Law Enforcement in the Colony of New York, 1691–1776* (Ithaca, NY: Cornell University Press, 1974), p. 135. Greenberg argues that the high crime rate in New York as compared to New England reflects the fact that "neither New York City nor the rural counties were composed of 'consensual communities' where aggressiveness was limited by social structure" (pp. 55–6).

10 "Statistically," writes Roland Van Zandt, "the State of New York had borne a disproportionate share of the burdens and suffering of the war. Though it ranked only seventh in population, one-third of the total battles and engagements of the Revolution (an estimated 92 out of 308) had been fought on or near the banks of the Hudson"; *Chronicles of the Hudson*, p. 39. See Chapter 4 for a discussion of the Revolutionary War in regional memory.

11 Fox, *Yankees and Yorkers*, p. 197.

12 Raymond J. O'Brien, *American Sublime: Landscape and Scenery of the Lower Hudson Valley* (New York: Columbia University Press, 1981), p. 131.

13 For details of railroad development, see Greene, *History of the Valley of the Hudson*, 2: 691–700. At one time there were six railroad lines

running through Westchester (Laura L. Vookles, "Westchester: County of Railroads," in *Next Stop Westchester!: People and the Railroad* [Yonkers, N.Y.: Hudson Valley Museum of Westchester, 1996], p. 11). Putnam County had at least four railroads running through it by the end of the nineteenth century ("Chronology of Putnam County," compiled by the Putnam County Historical Society Workshop, 1957, PCHS). Rockland County was crossed by five railroads (O'Brien, *American Sublime*, p. 195). There were railroads running through the Catskills by the 1880s (see Roland van Zandt, *The Catskill Mountain House* [New Brunswick, NJ: Rutgers University Press, 1966], pp. 225–41). Albany, meanwhile was a major railroad hub.

14   For discussions of social and economic changes in the region in the nineteenth century, see Thomas S. Wermuth, *Rip Van Winkle's Neighbors: The Transformation of Rural Society in the Hudson River Valley, 1720–1850* (Albany: State University of New York Press, 2011); Martin Bruegel, "The Rise of a Market Society in the Rural Hudson Valley, 1780–1860" (Ph.D. diss., Cornell University, 1994).

15   *The Guidebook of the Hudson River with Notes of Interest to the Summer Tourist* (Albany, 1889) notes "extensive brickyards" as well as factories and ironworks. The author of the 1884 *History of Rockland County* writes of the "thousand wheels of extractive factories" along the Minisceongo creek (quoted in O'Brien, *American Sublime*, p. 234). Between 1860 and 1880 the number of manufacturing establishments more than doubled in Albany; Brian Greenberg, *Worker and Community: Response to Industrialization in a Nineteenth-Century American City, Albany, New York, 1850–1884* (Albany: State University of New York Press, 1985), p. 17. For a broad discussion of industrial developments in the lower Hudson Valley, see O'Brien, *American Sublime*. For individual industries, see James M. Ransom, *Vanishing Ironworks of the Ramapos* (New Brunswick, NJ: Rutgers University Press, 1966); Daniel DeNoyelles, *Within These Gates* (Thiells, NY: privately published, 1982), on the Haverstraw brickyards; and Lucius F. Ellsworth, *Craft to National Industry in the Nineteenth Century: A Case Study of the Transformation of the New York State Tanning Industry* (New York: Arno, 1975). County and town histories also offer accounts of local industrial development.

16   David M. Ellis, "Yankee-Dutch Confrontation in the Albany Area," *The New England Quarterly* 45 (June 1972): 269. Ellis writes that this "Irish invasion . . . reached a floodtide in the 1840s and 1850," accounting for 40 percent of Albany's population by the Civil War (p. 269). According to federal census date from 1880, every county along the river had a sizable Irish immigrant population, as well as immigrants from England, Scotland, Wales, Germany, France, and Scandinavian countries.

17   Vookles, "Westchester," pp. 18, 13 (caption).

18   For a discussion of American tourism in the nineteenth century, see John F. Sears, *Sacred Places: American Tourist Attractions in the Nineteenth Century* (New York: Oxford University Press, 1989). Regarding the Hudson Valley,

see also Van Zandt, *The Catskill Mountain House*; and Kenneth Myers, *The Catskills: Painters, Writers, and Tourists in the Mountains, 1820–1895* (Yonkers, N.Y.: Hudson River Museum of Westchester; Hanover, N.H.: University Press of New England, 1988).

19   Van Zandt, *The Catskill Mountain House*, p. 223.

20   These included the Croton reservoir system, begun in 1842, and enlarged several times thereafter, and the Ashokan Reservoir in the Catskills, built between 1906 and 1915. For histories of the reservoirs and aqueducts, see Frederick Shonnard and W. W. Spooner, *The History of Westchester County* (1900; reprint, Harrison, NY: Harbor Hill, 1974), pp. 610–14; Mary Josephine D'Alvia, *The History of the New Croton Dam* (N.p.: privately published, 1976); and Alf Evers, *The Catskills: From Wilderness to Woodstock* (Garden City, NY: Doubleday, 1972), pp. 590–7.

21   In Haverstraw, for instance, there were thirty-eight brickworks operating at the turn of the century; by 1942 there were none; see DeNoyelles, *Within These Gates*. Similarly, Putnam County had experienced an industrial boom between the Civil War and the 1880s, but then from 1891 to 1938 the historical record marks closing after closing; "Chronology of Putnam County," PCHS.

22   O'Brien, *American Sublime*, p. 25. The 1920s and 1930s saw the inception or completion of the Palisades Parkway, the Storm King Highway, the George Washington Bridge, the Bear Mountain Bridge, the Mid-Hudson Bridge, and the Rip Van Winkle Bridge. Another wave of highway and bridge building in the post-World War II period added the New York State Thruway and Tappan Zee Bridge.

23   For one instance, see documents and letters regarding the building of interstate highway 684 in Westchester in the 1960s, at the Westchester County Archives and Record Center, Elmsford, NY.

24   See, for instance, the foreword to Beatrice Hasbrouck Wadlin, *Times and Tales of Town of Lloyd* (Highland, NY: privately published, 1974): "At the point in time when this book is going to print, the Township of Lloyd is in a dilemma about … the proposed atomic energy plant which might locate in the north end of the town." Between health and environmental concerns, and the need for new energy sources and the promise of a significant reduction in local taxes, the foreword states, "Personal feelings are running high on both sides." Such battles are not limited to the local level. In the foreword to Frances F. Dunwell's *The Hudson River Highlands* (New York: Columbia University Press, 1991), Robert F. Kennedy Jr. writes: "Since the early 1960s an uncompromising collection of environmental associations … have fought to maintain the river's biological and aesthetic integrity…. During the past decade and a half, Hudson River environmentalists have succeeded in stopping the construction of two major Hudson River highways, two nuclear power plants, and the proposed pumped storage facility on Storm King Mountain" (pp. ix–x).

25   *Legends and Poetry of the Hudson* (New York: P. S. Wynkoop and Sons, 1868), p. 22.

26 James Fenimore Cooper, *The Deerslayer, or, The First War-Path* (1841), ed. James Franklin Beard et al. (Albany: State University of New York Press, 1987), p. 15.

27 Renée Bergland, *The National Uncanny: Indian Ghosts and American Subjects* (Hanover, NH: Dartmouth College, University Press of New England, 2000), p. ii.

28 In sorting out how the Danskammer (the "Devil's Dance-chamber"), a site along the river near Newbough, came to be so named, various sources suggest that the Dutch here observed Indians engaged in religious ceremonies, and thought them either to be demons or to be worshiping the devil; see Dirck St. Remy, *Stories of the Hudson*, 3d ed. (New York: G.P. Putnam and Sons, 1871), p. 46; Ruttenber, *Indian Tribes of Hudson's River* p. 28; and Paul Wilstach, *Hudson River Landings* (PortWashington: I. J. Friedman, 1969), p. 258. It was not only the Dutch who read Native Americans as uncanny. In the 1840s Lydia Maria Child, visiting the Hudson Valley, wrote of Native Americans she met there as "ghosts of the Past"; L. Maria Child, *Letters from New-York* (New York: Charles S. Francis; Boston: John Munroe, 1843), p. 18. There are several twentieth-century accounts of indecision as to whether a figure is a living Native American person or a ghost. See, for instance, E. E. Gardner, *Folklore of the Schoharie Hills* (Ann Arbor: University of Michigan Press, 1937), p. 87. Renée Bergland explores depictions of Native Americans as ghostly in *The National Uncanny*. Chapter 4 further examines Indian and Dutch associations with regional ghostliness.

29 H. A. Von Behr, *Ghosts in Residence* (Utica: North Country Brooks, 1986), p. vii.

30 "The Spook Hole, or Haunted Cave, Clinton Point-(Barnegat)-On-The-Hudson," *Poughkeepsie Telegraph*, September 24, 1870, p. i. Alternate explanations presented in this article also point to a suspicion of strange others: one story has to do with the pirate Captain Kidd; another says that the cave was the hiding place of a "negro murderer."

31 JFA, entry 32.30.

32 Yi Fun Tuan, *Landscapes of Fear* (Minneapolis: University of Minnesota Press, 1979), p. 127. See Lewis Perry, *Boats against the Current: Revolution and Modernity, 1820–1860* (New York: Oxford University Press, 1993), for a discussion of the contending pulls of memory and "anti-history" in the antebellum period.

33 Introduction to Henry D. B. Bailey, *Local Tales and Historical Sketches* (Fishkill Landing, NY: John W. Spaight, Fishkill Standard Office, 1874), p. 9.

34 Henry Brace, "Old Catskill," in *The History of Greene County* (New York: J. B. Beers, 1884), p. 86.

35 C. G. Hine, *The Old Mine Road* (1908; New Brunswick, NJ: Rutgers University Press, 1963), p. 148.

36 Bergland, *The National Uncanny*, p. 5. Similarly, the editors of *Ghosts: Deconstruction, Psychoanalysis, History* write that ghosts and literature share "simulacral qualities; like writing, ghosts are associated with a certain

secondariness or belatedness"; Peter Buse and Andrew Stott (eds), *Ghosts: Deconstruction, Psychoanalysis, History* (Hampshire: MacMillan; New York: St. Martin's 1999), p. 8.

37 Avery F. Gordon, *Ghostly Matters: Haunting and the Sociological Imagination* (Minneapolis: University of Minnesota Press, 1997), p. 200

38 JFA, entry 32.89.

39 E. M. Bacon, *Chronicles of Tarrytown and Sleepy Hollow* (New York: G. P. Putnam's Sons, Knickerbocker Press, 1897), p. 103.

40 Charles Pryer, *Reminiscences of an Old Westchester Homestead* (New York: G. P. Putnam's Sons, Knickerbocker Press, 1897), pp. 21–2.

41 Charles Wilde, "Ghost Legends of the Hudson Valley" (Master's thesis, New York State College for Teachers, 1937), p. 12; JFA, entries 32.26, 32.82, 32.48, and 53. See Louis C. Jones, "The Ghosts of New York: An Analytical Study," *Journal of American Folklore* 57 (October–December 1944): 237–54, for a discussion of trends in the ghostlore collected by his students in New York State.

42 A number of women in white, or sometimes in black or gray, appear throughout the region. Some of these will be discussed in Chapter 3. Other examples appear near the gatehouse at Lindenwald, in Kinderhook; at Forbes Manor, near Albany; in a graveyard in Dover Plains; at a mansion in Dobbs Ferry; and along Call Hollow Road in Rockland County (Wilde, "Ghost Legends of the Hudson Valley," pp. 24–5 and 10; JFA, entry 19; *Legends and Poetry of the Hudson*, p. 57; Andrew Smith, "Forgotten and Overlooked History of the Hudson Valley and Highlands" [Master's thesis, Columbia Pacific University, n.d.]). In addition to Irving's headless horseman (discussed in chapter 2), there are tales of a headless man who rides on passing wagons, a headless woman who rummages in cellars, and "the Headless Parson," in Columbia County; and "a white thing, headless, floating in the air" near an Albany church (Mayme O. Thompson, "Witchcraft! Halloween Ghosts Roam Year-Round over Taghkanic Hillsides," *Chatham Courier*, October 30, 1969, p. B1; W. V. Miller, "Folklore Tales of Columbia County: What Mission Sent the Headless Parson Coursing across a Moonlit Sky?" *Chatham Courier*, March 20, 1958, Folklore file, CCHS; Wilde, "Ghost Legends of the Hudson Valley," p. 14). The Jones collection contains references to a "headless Negro riding on a white horse" in Albany County, a procession of silent headless men in Rensselaer County, headless horsemen in Pine Plains, a headless man driving a wagon led by headless horses in Crescent, and a ghost from Ulster County whose head is replaced at times by a "ball of fire" and at other times by a "white floaty mass" (JFA, entries 143, 14, 146, 175.19, and 147.3). More headless ghosts appear in Yonkers, Kinderhook, Yorktown, Warwick and Hurley (Charles Elmer Allison, *The History of Yonkers* [1896; reprint, Harrison, NY: Harbor Hill, 1984], p. 109); "Yankee Visits Sleepy Hollow" *Yankee*, July 1953, p. 34; JFA, entries 147.2 and 61.51; C. G. Hine, *West Bank of the Hudson: Albany to Tappan* [1906; reprint, Astoria, NY: J. C. and A. L. Fawcett, n.d.], pp. 105–6).

43 According to Louis Jones, only 10 percent of the ghost stories in his collection

contain speaking ghosts, "while every third ghost makes one of a wide variety of noises. European stories tend to contain the element of discourse more frequently than American stories"; "The Ghosts of New York." p. 250.

44 Washington Irving, *The Sketch Book of Geoffrey Crayon, Gent.* (1819–20), ed. Haskell Springer (Boston: Twayne, 1978), p. 34. Any number of examples of ghostly silence or incomprehensibility might be cited here. A ghost in Coxsackie would not respond to questions in either English or Dutch, and vanished when the disconcerted questioner threw a rock to try to provoke a response (JFA, entry 32). A Dutchess Country man came to believe that his hay barn was haunted because he "heard noises and people talkin'." He found that "I could never understand what they said. The words weren't clear enough" (JFA, entry 32.66). At a mansion in Livingston, witnesses hear "all the sounds of guests for a gay evening ... save those of human voices"; Eileen Thomas, "Tales of Old Columbia," October 25, 1946, Folklore file, CCHS.

45 A man from Berne, New York, encountered a spook in the woods there that he "feared to describe" (JFA, entry 32.16). A man from Pine Plains, who one night followed the local headless horseman to the cemetery became "completely unnerved and [would] shake violently" whenever he tried to tell what he had seen there (JFA, entry 146). Ice-cutters who told of a Columbia County "Woman in Black" recalled feeling as if she had "cast a bad spell over them. Not a word was spoken"; "Folk Lore of Columbia County: Who Was the Woman in Black on a Lonely Poolesburg Road?" *Chatham Courier*, 1954, Folklore file, CCHS.

46 Washington Irving, "The Storm-Ship," in *Bracebridge Hall; or, The Humourists* (1822), Herbert F. Smith ed. (Boston: Twayne, 1977), p. 283; Charles M. Skinner, *Myths and Legends of Our Own Land*, vol 1 (Philadelphia: J. B. Lippincott, 1896), p. 50.

47 Pryer, *Reminiscences of an Old Westchester Homestead*, p. 25.

48 JFA, entry 32.65.

49 *The New Shorter Oxford English Dictionary* (1993 ed.) offers as definitions of *waif*: "a homeless and helpless person, *esp.* a neglected or abandoned child," and "a thing carried or driven by the wind; a puff of smoke, a streak of cloud."

50 Skinner, *Myths and Legends of Our Own Land*, p. 57. Skinner and others also attribute the wandering habits of regional ghosts to the wealth of "lost" graves, a mark of historical neglectfulness and abandonment. See Skinner's story about Thomas Paine, whose remains were moved from their original burial place and whose ghost thus hovers "between the two burial-places, or flitting back and forth ... lamenting the forgetfulness of men"; ibid. pp. 103–4.

51 According to Louis Jones in "The Ghosts of New York," bridges are as likely as cemeteries to be considered haunted (p. 248). Haunted bridges appear in Kinderhook, Wittenberg, Rosendale, Glenford, Centerville, and Kerhonkson (JFA, entries 78b, 170, 32.43, 61.54, 32.60; Hine, *The Old Mine Road*, p. 67). Two haunted taverns appear in Ghent, and others are

found in Germantown, Fishkill and Albany. See "Gone with the Wind: The Mystery of Mammy Doodle's Wayside Inn Deepens," *Chatham Courier*, December 13, 1946; "The Old Gray Ghost of Ghent," *Knickerbocker News Union-Star*, July 24, 1972; W. V. Miller, "Folklore of Columbia County," *Chatham Courier*, March 13, 1958, Folklore file, CCHS; Bailey, *Local Tales and Historical Sketches*, p. 119; and JFA, entry 32.34. On ghostly fiddlers haunting bridges in Dutchess County, see "Fiddling Ghosts at Frosts Mills," *Poughkeepsie Daily Eagle*, September 10, 1908, p. 8; JFA, entries 142.4 and 97.91. Ghosts of gypsies are reported in the towns of Highland and Clarksville (JFA, entries 86 and 32.71). Of ghostly hitchhikers, Louis Jones recorded more than 75 occurrences in the region; Alex Silberman, "A Handful of Hauntings," *Hudson Valley*, October 1996, p. 36.

52 William Leete Stone includes a tale titled "The Murdered Tinman" in his *Tales and Sketches, Such as They Are* (New York: Harper and brothers, 1834). In the story, which takes place in Ulster County, a local resident reports seeing the apparition of a peddler which leads the community to believe that the peddler was murdered by the new tavernkeeper. The apprehensions in the story derive in large part from cultural misunderstanding: the Dutch locals do not understand that a Yankee peddler is subject to wandering. (They also distrust the new Yankee tavern owner.)

53 Bailey, *Local Tales and Historical Sketches*, pp. 121–2. In Bailey's story the ghost of the tavern owner figures more prominently than that of the peddler. However, other versions of this story focus on the peddler's ghost—including a version in the *New-York Tribune* of May 18, 1902, and one given by a local man to a Poughkeepsie newspaper (Helen Myers, "Countian Recalls Tales of Restless Ghosts That Haunted Famous East Fishkill Tavern," *Poughkeepsie Sunday New Yorker*, July 11, 1954, p. C1).

54 Bailey, *Local Tales and Historical Sketches*, pp. 123, 8.

55 JFA, entry 61.54. Similar accounts of peddler-related hauntings occur in Crescent, Warwick, Hyde Park, and Ballston, and at "Packpeddler's Hill" in Columbia County (JFA, entries 50, 61.53, 127.5 and 127.21; Thompson, "Witchcraft!"). See Hine, *West Bank of the Hudson*, p. 10, for an analogous story from Coeymans, in Greene County, centering on mysterious strangers, an unidentified skeleton, and the subsequent proliferation of ghost stories.

56 Jones, "The Ghosts of New York," p. 242.

57 For a discussion of peddlers as historical agents of change, see David Jaffee, "Peddlers of Progress and the Transformation of the Rural North, 1760–1860," *Journal of American History* 78 (September 1991): 511–35. Regional sources suggest how transient figures aroused anxiety and fear. One story tells of gypsies kidnapping children (JFA, entry 32.71), while a woman in Putnam County, who lived along the Albany Post Road, told C. G. Hine that in the period after the Civil War she spent a considerable part of her day feeding tramps who came to the door: "she, being afraid of them, never refused" (C. G. Hine, *The New York and Albany Post Road* [New York: privately published, 1905], p. 45). E. B. Hornby similarly recalls, in *Under Old Rooftrees* (Jersey City, NJ : privately published, 1908): "Ere the county

poorhouse was built, Warwick Township literally swarmed with what is now called the 'tramp.'" (p. 181).

58 According to *The New Shorter Oxford English Dictionary* (1993 ed.), The Wandering Jew is "in medieval legend, a man who insulted Jesus on the day of the Crucifixion and was condemned eternally to roam the world until the Day of Judgement."

59 Stephen King, *'Salem's Lot* (1975), quoted in Manuel Aguirre, *The Closed Space: Horror Literature and Western Symbolism* (Manchester: Manchester University Press, 1990), p. 187.

60 Hine, *West Bank of the Hudson*, p. 135.

61 In addition to Irving and Maud Wilder Goodwin, numerous writers and historians point to the Dutch as the source of regional hauntings. An 1876 travel narrative, for instance, flatly asserts: "The old Dutch colonists were very much given to ghostly fears" (Daniel Wise, *Summer Days on the Hudson: The Story of a Pleasure Tour from Sandy Hook to the Saranac Lakes* [New York: Nelson and Phillips, 1876], p. 24). Maud Wilder Goodwin, while highlighting the Dutch, also names "the *wilden*" (i.e., Native Americans) and African slaves as co-conspirators in generating the region's supernatural sensibilities (Goodwin, *Dutch and English on the Hudson*, p. 120). For other attributions to African slaves, see Hine, *West Bank of the Hudson*, p. 70; and Wilfred Blanch Talman, *How Things Began in Rockland County and Places Nearby* (New City, NY: Historical Society of Rockland County, 1977), p. 276. For a discussion of the treatment of folk sources in Irving, Cooper, and James Kirke Paulding, see Donald A. Ringe, *American Gothic: Imagination and Reason in Nineteenth-Century Fiction* (Lexington: University of Kentucky Press, 1982).

30

The Other Country: Mexico, the United States, and the Gothic History of Conquest

Jesse Alemán

The idea of the "Western Hemisphere" ... establishes an ambiguous position. America simultaneously constitutes difference and sameness. It is the other hemisphere, but it is Western. It is distinct from Europe (of course, it is not the Orient), but it is bound to Europe. It is different, however, from Asia and Africa, continents and cultures that do not form part of the Western hemisphere. But who defines such a hemisphere?

WALTER MIGNOLO, "COLONIALITY AT LARGE"

In the introduction to Robert Montgomery Bird's 1834 *Calavar, or, The Knight of the Conquest*, an American wandering through Mexico sits on Chapultepec hill and muses on Mexico's pre-conquest history. The Toltecs first populated Mexico, the American imagines, and were "the most civilized of which Mexican hieroglyphics ... have preserved in memory" (v–vi). Other tribes followed, but none brought civilization until the Aztecs. "[F]rom this herd of barbarians," the American thinks, "grew ... the magnificent empire of the Montezumas, ... heaving again with the impulses of nascent civilization" (vi). Finally, the "voice of the Old World" rolls over the eastern mountains, but instead of fully civilizing the

Aztecs, the "shout of conquest and glory was answered by the groan of a
dying nation" (vii). So goes Mexico's romantic history of conquest for the
dreamy American. Spanish colonialism killed the "incipient greatness," the
potential for new-world civilization, in the Aztec empire and left Mexico
in the hands of "civilized savages and Christian pagans" (viii). Mexico
must "rekindle the torches of knowledge" (viii), the American thinks out
loud, and he is not alone in his idea. A Mexican curate has overheard the
American's musings and agrees that Mexico must regenerate itself from its
post-revolutionary "Pandemonium" of ambitious rulers and servile citizens
to reassert its past, indigenous potential as a civilized new-world nation
(xii). Until then, Mexico is a "gust of anarchy," the curate explains, that
will "disease thy imagination, until thou comest to be disgusted with the
yet untainted excellence of thine own institutions, because thou perceivest
the evils of their perversion" (xiii).

The curate presses the American to leave Mexico and to take with him
to translate and publish several volumes of Mexican history "which will
teach thee to appreciate and preserve ... the pure and admirable frame of
government, which a beneficent power has suffered you to enjoy" (xiv). A
historian and descendent of Montezuma, the curate has penned a history
that finds no favor in Mexico because Mexicans are too benighted to appreciate the nascent civilization of their indigenous past. "Your own people,"
the priest explains, "are, perhaps, not so backward" (xix). Written as an
Aztec palimpsest, the volumes span pre-conquest to the 1821 revolution
and assert that "reason reprobates, human happiness denounces, and
God abhors, the splendour of contention" (xix). The American accepts
the volumes—with rights to the profits accrued from their republication,
of course—and returns to the US where he unsuccessfully attempts to
crack the palimpsests until he reads of the curate's death in a Mexican
newspaper. The padre, it turns out, is a genius historian whose manuscript
pages were "arranged like those in the form of a printer" (xxv). Once the
American unfolds the volumes, "he beheld the chaos of history reduced to
order" (xxv). He transcribes the hieroglyphic text and discovers among the
volumes a story about the cavaliers of the conquest, which he translates,
edits, and republishes, after deleting much of the curate's philosophy and
changing the title to fit the "intellectual dyspepsia" of American readers.
The result is *Calavar, or, The Knight of the Conquest*, which the American
calls a *Historia Verdadera* (à la Bernal Diaz del Castillo), a fitting subtitle,
the introduction insists, because "the history of Mexico, under all aspects
but that of fiction, is itself—a romance" (xxviii).

Calavar's opening scene invokes a common frame for historical romances
in which the ghostly voices of bygone times inhabit a locale and impress
themselves on the mind of a romantic wayfarer, and Chapultepec in
particular is a significant site for hemispheric musings. Linked by a
causeway to Tenochtitlán, Chapultepec hill served as a fortified retreat

and burial ground for Aztec emperors, but during the nineteenth century, it became a contested symbolic space that embodied the living history of Mexico's indigenous past.[1] Cuban poet José María Heredia's 1820s poem "Las sombras," for instance, features a nineteenth-century democrat on a pilgrimage to Chapultepec, where he encounters the shades of past "indigenous rulers of the Americas," who debate and denounce tyranny and empire in a series of monologues (Gruesz 57–8). Frances Calderón de la Barca's 1839 visit to Chapultepec likewise conjured the sublime continuity between Mexico's indigenous past and its post-independence present: "Could these hoary cypresses speak," Calderón de la Barca muses on the hill's trees, "what tales might they not disclose, standing there with their long gray beards, and outstretched venerable arms, century after century: already old when Montezuma was a boy, and still vigorous in the days of Bustamante!" (80). The link between Montezuma and President Anastasio Bustamante is an apt juxtaposition, for while Calderón de la Barca fancies that "the last of the Aztec Emperors wandered with his dark-eyed harem" (80) at Chapultepec, Bustamante's presidential reign is rapidly collapsing: he will be pushed out of office in 1840, exiled by 1841, and succeeded by Antonio López de Santa Anna the same year. And Montezuma and Bustamante are not the only troubled spirits of Chapultepec: "the shade of the conqueror's Indian love, the far-famed Doña Marina," roams the area too (81). For Calderón de la Barca, Mexico's pre-conquest tranquility and post-independence instability converge on the ghost of La Malinche, who haunts the caves and woods of Chapultepec and functions as a reminder of the damning, subversive space women occupy when they literally and symbolically traverse two cultures and languages.[2]

Calavar's introduction thus marks the cultural moment when Mexico's antiquity becomes the US's hemispheric history following its revolutionary break from England. As Eric Sundquist explains, the "romantic primitivism that permeated much American literature in the antebellum period ... provoked echoes of revolutionary rhetoric about breaking the constraints of British and European custom" (132). Yet, even as the US turned away from Europe and the mother country, it turned to another country, Mexico, to stage its romantic primitivism and, in the process, generated an alternative literary and national narrative that placed the legacy of the Spanish conquest of Mexico strangely at the heart of the US's own historical emergence. As *Calavar*'s introduction makes clear, the US and Mexico share the same revolutionary spirit and hemispheric, republican ideals. Yet, the *translatio studii* assimilates Mexico's past and rearticulates it as Anglo-America's hemispheric story in a literary act that sets the stage for the US's continental colonization of the Americas. In this sense, Mexico functions as the US's "*imago*," to recall María DeGuzmán's argument about the US's relationship to the image of Spain, but where DeGuzmán sees Spain as a "virtual or mirror image in front of which, in a libidinal dynamic of identification and disavowal, Anglo American culture, despite its fragmentation and initial fragility, ascends toward a seemingly unified and coherent imperial identity" (xvii), Mexico more appropriately stands in as the US's uncanny imperial other because the continental proximity of the two countries and their shared revolutionary histories make them estranged national neighbors.[3]

"The 'uncanny' is that class of the terrifying which leads back to something long known to us, once very familiar," writes Freud (369–70). I maintain that Mexico is a strangely familiar place that troubles the US's trans-American imaginary. Freud's definition of the uncanny as *unheimlich*—the "unhomely"—is especially apt here because the fluidity of national borders collapses the otherwise clear distinctions between native and foreigner, domestic and international, and America and América. As Freud explains, the German word for "home" embodies two contradictory meanings: "that which is familiar and congenial" and "that which is concealed and kept out of sight" (375). The uncanny occurs when that which was concealed emerges as a familiar object that has been repressed (394). *Heimlich* also means "native," however, so that the notion of "home" can be extended to the idea of nation, as when Juan Seguín characterized his position in Texas after the 1848 signing of the Treaty of Guadalupe Hidalgo as being a "foreigner in my own land" (De la Teja 73). Seguín was emphasizing the haunting unhomeliness of colonial displacement that continues to trouble Mexican Americans. It is a dispossession, to be sure, but not strictly in the sense of being without a home; rather, it is an estrangement from the home, a momentary recognition that the foreign rests at the center of the familiar, leading to "the discovery that 'home' is not what or where we think it is," Priscilla Wald explains, "and that we, by extension, are not who or what we think we are" (7).[4]

My understanding of early-nineteenth-century narratives such as Bird's *Calavar*, William Prescott's *History of the Conquest of Mexico*, and the anonymously published *Xicoténcatl* runs the risk of reproducing a hemispheric paradigm that centers the US in relation to national "Others." Claudia Sandowski-Smith and Claire F. Fox put the problem this way: "we fear that an Americanist-led hemispherism will only promote a vision of the Americas in which all academic disciplinary configurations are subordinate to those of the United States and in which every region outside the United States is collapsed into a monolithic other" (23). But, I want to encourage an approach to "inter-American" studies that considers *inter* not as the prefix "across" but as the word for "burial" to emphasize the idea that the presence of the other in the nation is "that which is concealed and kept out of sight" but always felt as a haunting history that must be excavated. "In-ter" Americanism understands that the nations of the western hemisphere already contain *within* ("intra") their borders national others whose formative presence is subsequently buried (interred) but nonetheless felt and often expressed through gothic discourse. While liberal Mexican leaders fashioned Mexico's 1821 independent system of governance loosely on the US, for instance, *Calavar*'s opening reminds us that the US likewise imagined its place in the hemisphere by way of Mexico's antiquity. The US and Mexico thus share a familial relation that vexes citizenship as much as it troubles their national literary histories, for their confluences indicate how one country is already embedded within the history of the other, perhaps because the borders across the Americas are so porous.

As the hills of Chapultepec remind us, this hemispheric *unheimlich* is a trans-American gothic space haunted by the specters of empire, and narratives about the Spanish conquest of the Aztecs are particularly uncanny because the sixteenth-century conquest seemed strangely familiar to the US, especially after the Monroe Doctrine imagined hemispheric solidarity against Europe in the form of US imperialism throughout the Americas. Often characterized as historical romances, *Calavar, The History of the Conquest of Mexico*, and *Xicoténcatl* become gothic in the context of "inter-Americanism" because each work exhumes the legacy of conquest and racial rebellion that haunts the US's hemispheric presence. Rebellious Moors, republican Indians, and heroic Aztecs become horrifying in US conquest narratives written in the context of the Indian removal, the annexation of Texas, and black slavery—the home becomes unhomely as *Calavar* and *Conquest* link the Spanish empire in the Americas to US imperialism. Yet, both of the US narratives are related to another "inter-American" text, the anonymously published *Xicoténcatl*, which was only recently disinterred from literary history to express what *Calavar* and *Conquest* would rather keep buried: that the trans-American gothic emerged in the first place because republicanism became empire in the Americas.

1. Specters of empire

Robert Montgomery Bird, a physician interested in abnormal psychology, is often celebrated as the first successful US playwright, though mostly by default considering the dearth of early Anglo-American dramatists, and is best known for his 1837 *Nick of the Woods*, a gothic narrative about a seemingly inoffensive Quaker, Nathan Slaughter, who doubles as a demonic Indian killer. But between the years of his plays and his frontier novels, Bird imagined a native US literary history rooted in Spanish America. His last two popular plays, *Oralloosa, Son of the Incas* (1832) and *The Broker of Bogota* (1833), signaled Bird's growing interest in the Americas, and although the Philadelphian only got as far as New Orleans during his 1833 planned trip to Mexico, he was already imagining its landscape, political history, and potential for romance in his first historical novel, *Calavar, or, the Knight of the Conquest*. Written mostly in 1833, *Calavar* was published in Philadelphia by Carey, Lea, and Company in 1834 and was meant to be the first of at least eight historical romances about Mexico, spanning its conquest to its 1821 revolution for independence (Dahl 73). As with his trek south, however, Bird's literary plans fell short: he followed *Calavar* with its two-volume sequel, *The Infidel, or, The Fall of Mexico* (1835), but never returned again to Mexico's antiquity.

Although *The Infidel* is more recognizable as a gothic thriller, with its doublings, incest, and homicidal monks (Dahl 81), *Calavar* particularly interests me here, for it expresses the repressed histories of conquest the US inherits from the Old World and reproduces across the New World. Don Amador, a novice knight, enters the New World in 1520 to find Calavar, his father-knight, who, following his participation in the conquest of Granada, has fled to Mexico to help defeat the Aztecs. Calavar, however, is a skeleton of his former self, a ghostly relic who embodies the demise of Spain's old-world codes of chivalry in the New World: "He was in full armour, but the iron plates were rusted on his body, and in many places shattered. The plumes were broken and disordered on his helmet; the spear lay at the feet of his steed; his buckler was in the hands of his attendant; and instead of the red tabard which was worn in a season of war by the brothers of his order, the black mantle of peace, with its great white cross, hung or drooped heavily from his shoulders.... [H]e presented the appearance of a ruin majestic in decay" (1: 173). Alienated from himself and his fellow Spaniards, the knight suffers from the guilt of bloodlust, for he believes he killed Alharef-ben-Ismail, a Moorish noble, and his lover Zayda in a jealous rage during the conquest of Granada. His apprentice knight, Don Amador, fares no better. He too battled at Granada, where he fell in love with Leila, a Christianized Moor whom the knight believes to have been captured by infidels at the end of Granada's fall. Already unsettled by the conquest of Granada, Calavar and Amador find further estrangement in the New World when Amador arrives in Mexico, and the first battle the novice knight joins in Mexico is not between Spanish Christians and Aztec barbarians but between Cortés and Navarez, two Spaniards warring against each other for the right to conquer Mexico.

Specters of empire thus haunt the narrative as the Spanish colonization of Granada and the Moors mirrors the conquest of Mexico and the Aztecs. Roughly thirty years after Spain's 1492 Reconquista of Granada led to the large-scale persecution of Moriscos under the Inquisition, Abdalla the Moor and his son Jacinto are reminders, especially to Calavar and his novice knight, that the Spanish crusade in the New World is a legacy of a crusade waged for centuries in the Old World.[5] This legacy of empire, however, troubles Calavar and Amador to the point that they see ghosts of their Moorish princesses in Aztec temples leading pagan rituals of human sacrifice. As Amador explains to Jacinto of these ghostly sightings:

I am almost quite convinced, that she is a spectre, and an inhabitant of hell, sent forth upon earth to punish me with much affliction, and, perhaps, with madness. For I think she is the spirit of Leila; and her appearance in the guise of a pagan goddess, or pagan priestess,—the one or the other,—shows me, that she whom I loved, dwells not with angels, but with devils. (2: 141)

The conquest of Mexico literally conjures the Moorish dead, bringing them back to life in the form of strangely familiar Aztecs, but in this case, Amador's pale specter is nothing more than the return of the repressed. As it turns out, the pagan priestess is none other than Jacinto, who, it turns out, is none other than Leila. Amador finds his lost Morisco lover in Mexico in drag as Calavar's page boy cross-dresses as a pagan Aztec priestess as part of a plot devised by Abdalla to "inflame the [Mexican] people with fresh devotion and fury against the Spaniards" (2: 142). The transvestite terror Leila/Jacinto inspires in Amador is both sexual and transnational. That is, Leila's drag performance fosters queer desire that shores up the adage that conquest works under the logic of fear and desire. "But, father," Amador confesses to a priest:

here is another circumstance that greatly troubled me; and, in good sooth, it troubles me yet. It is known to thee that my kinsman had, until yesterday night, a little page,—a Moorish boy, greatly beloved by us both. As for myself, I loved him because he was of the race of Leila; and I protest to thee, unnatural as it may seem, I bore not for my young brother a greater affection than for this most unlucky urchin. A foolish fellow charged him to be an enchanter; and sometimes I bethink me of the accusation, and suppose he has given me magical love-potions. (2: 85)

Eventually, the narrative forecloses the subversive element of Leila's transvestism, for in the end, she embraces her Christian identity at the expense of her Moorish background and marries Don Amador, and the lovers, as his name suggests, relocate to Spain. Nevertheless, the event shores up the "inter-American" *unheimlich* as the buried history of Spain's conquest of Granada emerges from beneath the conquest of the Aztecs as a specter of empire that haunts the US's literary appropriation of Mexico's history and literal acquisition of Mexican territory, first by way of Texas and later through the US–Mexico War.

And Leila is not the only crossdressed Moor. Her father Abdalla is none other than Alharef-ben-Ismail, the Morisco prince Calavar believed he killed in Granada. In love with Zayda, Calavar "slew! slew! slew!" her when he learned she slept with Alharef-ben-Ismail, although Calavar did not know that Alharf-ben-Ismail and Zayda were betrothed at the time (1: 271). The guilt of bloodlust that Calavar attempts to escape in Mexico returns in the form of Abdalla *cum* Alharef-ben-Ismail, who betrays the Spaniards by siding with the Aztecs to seek revenge for the fall of Granada. The "black legend" takes on a whole new meaning in the text as Abdalla and several other Moors escape from their Spanish masters and teach the Aztecs modes of European warfare that help them expel the Spaniards from Tenochtitlán during *la noche triste*. Theirs is a racial rebellion that traverses histories of conquest as the Moors revenge the fall of Granada and help the Aztecs in the process take back their capitol city in an anti-imperial war for freedom that echoes the US's revolutionary rhetoric even as it expresses the threat of slave rebellion: "This is not a war of heaven against hell," says Abdalla, "but of tyranny against freedom" (2: 169). It is thus fitting that Abdalla and Calavar meet at the battle of Otumba, where the conquest of Mexico becomes a strangely familiar reenactment of the conquest of Granada that leaves Abdalla dead on the field and Calavar mortally wounded as the Spaniards rout the Aztecs in the background:

> [F]uriously descending the slope of the hill on the left hand ... seemed a Christian cavalier in black armour, mounted on a noble bay horse, and couching a lance like a trained soldier, only that, behind him, there followed, with savage yells, a band of several thousand Indians, bearing the well-known colours of Tenochtitlan itself.... . [At] the opposite mountain ... an armed and mounted cavalier descend[ed] with lance in rest, and with the speed of thunder, as if rushing to a tournay with him of the black armour, but without being followed by any one, excepting a single youth, who staggered far behind. (2: 265)

Abdalla is all the more terrifying because his radical republican rhetoric echoes the revolutionary spirit that fueled the US's break from England, but this time, a black subject of Spanish colonialism uses the rhetoric of republicanism to lead the Aztecs in collective racial resistance against the Spaniards in a gesture that speaks to early-nineteenth-century fears that blacks and Indians would unite in a war against Anglo America. The terror of slavery and slave revolt the narrative imagines raises the threat the US stands to inherit if it follows Spain's hemispheric legacy. In the wake of Nat Turner's rebellion, the Cherokee Trail of Tears, and the Seminole Wars, Bird's narrative situates blacks and Indians between anticolonial insurgents and semibarbaric infidels. Their anti-imperial resistance echoes Anglo-American revolutionary rhetoric, but their racialized protorepublicanism generates a race war that, as with Melville's "Benito Cereno," sees the gothic threat of racial rebellion as the legacy of colonialism in the Americas. The cross-dressed Moors, in other words, link the Aztecs to the Moors and Mexico to Granada and disclose a history of empire that, by Bird's preface to the 1847 edition of *Calavar*, the US stands to reproduce. "There is, indeed, a remarkable parallel between the invasions of the two great captains," Bird says of Cortés and General Winfield Scott:

> There is the same route up the same difficult and lofty mountains; the same city, in the same most magnificent of valleys, as the object of attack; the same petty forces, and the same daring intrepidity leading them against millions of enemies, fighting in the heart of their own country; and, finally, the same desperate fury of unequal armies contending in mortal combat on the causeways and in the streets of Mexico. We might say, perhaps, that there is the same purpose of conquest: but we do not believe that the American people aim at, or desire, the subjugation of Mexico. (iv)

At the height of the US–Mexico War, Bird returns to his narrative about the Spanish conquest of Mexico in an ambivalent recognition that the US is both following and not following in Spain's footsteps. While on the Congressional floor in 1847, Lewis Cass articulated a similar ambivalence to the stipulations of the Treaty of Guadalupe Hidalgo:

> It would be a deplorable amalgamation [uniting the US and Mexico]. No such evil will happen to us in our day. We do not want the people of Mexico, either as citizens or subjects. All we want is a portion of territory, which they nominally hold, generally uninhabited, or, where inhabited at all, sparsely so, and with a population which would soon receded, or identify itself with ours. (5–6)

Cass's contradictory stance balances the US's desire for Mexican territory and its fear of racial miscegenation through a gothic discourse that has its roots in *Calavar*'s mestizo nation, where blacks and Indians unite and scare the hell out of white people until they end up dead, like Calavar, or exiled back to the home, like Amador, whose domestic bliss with Leila and their mixed-blood child back in Spain concludes with the news that "Mexico has become a Spanish city" (2: 295). The home is not home after all.

2. Gothic history

It is literary commonplace to assert that romance characterizes William H. Prescott's *History of the Conquest of Mexico*. It is less commonplace to argue that Prescott's three volumes move from romanticism to the gothic as his narrative progresses through the history of Mexico's conquest, and the shift is probably indicative of Prescott's post- and neo-colonial "discovery" of empire in the Americas. Of course, as John Eipper notes, Prescott scholars usually view his history as pro-imperialist and often conflate his life with his works to come to the following conclusion: "namely, Prescott demonstrates how Christian (West) triumphed over Pagan (non-West) because History destined it to be that way, in both the sixteenth century and the now romantic, now 'scientific' nineteenth" (419). Every US navy ship library carried Prescott's volumes during the US–Mexico War, and, undoubtedly, his historical narrative fanned the romantic flames of US army volunteers in Mexico; his narrative also acted as travel guide and ethnography during the invasion, although Prescott never set foot in Mexico. Yet as a Bostonian Whig, Prescott opposed the annexation of Texas—for fear that it would extend slavery—and found the pro-war expansionist spirit fueling the US–Mexico War distasteful. He even refused to write a history of the war, despite General Scott's request and offer to open his war papers to Prescott (Johannsen 248). Prescott's *Conquest* suffers from the same ambivalence: it sees much to admire in the Spanish conquest of Mexico and much to abhor about it in the same way that the narrative wavers between recognizing the Aztecs as a civilized, indigenous empire and characterizing them as savage barbarians.

This racial "equivocation," to recall Vera M. Kutzinski's phrase (58), haunts Conquest in the form of competing racialized body politics whose battle over Mexico becomes a gothic, if not grotesque, event that seems strangely familiar to Prescott's 1840s historical moment. "The gothic's connection to American history," Teresa Goddu explains, "is difficult to identify precisely because of the national and critical myths that America and its literature *have* no history" (9). Ironically, *Conquest* may prove this to be the case as Mexico's history stands in for the history of the US and in the process invokes the quintessentially gothic terror, race, but places it within an "inter-American" context that, as with *Calavar*, is unsettling because one national identity is buried within another. In much the same way that the "Africanist presence" accounts for the US gothic (Morrison 5), the inter-American gothic emerges when the hemispheric horrors of the Spanish conquest of Mexico return in narratives, such as Prescott's, that sense how the US stands to inherit the monstrous race war hidden beneath the romantic veneer of Mexico's history. This process is all the more disturbing, I maintain, because it transforms Prescott's native country into an other country that anxiously exposes the historical presence of racial rebellion that should otherwise remain hidden.

The three-volume history does not begin gothic, but it becomes it as the Aztecs under Guatemozin fight to keep the Spaniards out of Tenochtitlán after expelling them during *la noche triste*. To be sure, before then, the specter of Aztec religion spooks the Spaniards, as when Cortés and the Spaniards first visit the Aztec temples and find the walls "stained with human gore," while "the frantic forms of priests, with their dark robes clotted with blood ... seemed to the Spaniards to be those of the very ministers of Satan" (2: 137). As if to match gore with gore, the Aztecs gather in an annual festival that celebrates Huitzilopochtli, the war god, but while Cortés is away from the capitol, the Spaniard in charge, Alvarado, orchestrates an Indian massacre that leaves the "pavement" covered with "streams of blood, like water in a heavy shower" (2: 243). The "massacre by Alvarado," as Prescott calls it, leads directly to the revolt of the Aztecs as they unite to expel the Spaniards from the city in what is known as *la noche triste*, or the "sad night" Cortés, his fellow Spaniards, and their Indian allies suffered their greatest loss during the conquest of Mexico. But even this night, which has all the potential of the grotesque, keeps the gothic at bay as "many an unfortunate victim" during the night-long Spanish retreat "was dragged half-stunned on board [Aztec] canoes, to be reserved for a protracted but more dreadful death" in the form of human sacrifice (2: 308).

The narrative thus buries much of the potentially gothic elements that might portray the Spaniards too sharply within the black legend or the Aztecs as too barbaric to be an example of an indigenous American civilization.[6] Cannibalism, sacrifice, and Spanish bloodlust are all mentioned, of course, but in measured language that frames the historical narrative within the purview of genteel romance—until the Spanish return to retake Tenochtitlán. Fortified with Spanish troops and Indian allies, the soldiers set out on a *reconquista* of the Aztec empire, and the narrative slides into the gothic. During the second siege of the city, for instance, Alvarado and Sandoval find themselves separated from Cortés and the main field of battle but within earshot of its tide against the Spaniards:

> The two captains now understood that the day must have gone hard with their countrymen. They soon had proof of it, when the victorious Aztecs, returning from the pursuit of Cortés, joined their forces to those engaged with Sandoval and Alvarado, and fell on them with redoubled fury. At the same time they rolled on the ground two or three of the bloody heads of the Spaniards, shouting the name "Malinche." The captains, struck with horror at the spectacle ... instantly ordered a retreat. (3: 134)

Heads abound during the fight, for, while the Aztecs toss three Spanish heads down in front of Alvarado and Sandoval, claiming that one of the heads belongs to Cortés ("Malinche," as they call him), two more heads tumble before Cortés as the Aztecs lob at him "the heads of several Spaniards, shouting at the same time, 'Sandoval,' 'Tonatiuh,' the well-known epithet of Alvarado. At the sight of the deadly trophies, [Cortés] grew deadly pale" (3: 136).

Undoubtedly, the Aztecs understand that decapitation functions as a symbolic act that severs from the body the part most associated with power, ideas, and leadership, but while Indian dismemberment occurs occasionally in the previous parts of the history, Spanish heads are not thrown about so amply and easily as they are in *Conquest*'s last volume. Even horses lose their heads in what is a blatant display of Aztec power: "Guatemozin sent several heads of the Spaniards, as well as of the horses, round the country, calling on his old vassals to forsake the banners of the white men, unless they would share the doom of the enemies of Mexico" (3: 141). With the Aztecs united in a fierce indigenous resistance against the Spanish conquest, the narrative gapes at the terror of human sacrifice:

> On its convex surface, [the captive's] breasts were heaved up conveniently for the diabolical purpose of the priestly executioner, who cut asunder the ribs ... and tore away the heart, which, hot and reeking, was deposited on the golden censer before the idol. The body of the slaughtered victim was then hurled down the steep stairs of the pyramid ... and the mutilated remains were gathered up by the savages beneath, who soon prepared with them the cannibal repast which completed the work of abomination! (3: 138–39)

What was previously concealed about human sacrifice is now revealed in gory detail as the greatest horror of the conquest—collective racial resistance by the Aztecs—is visited on the Spaniards in full force.

This explains why *Conquest* becomes gothic. Before the second siege of Tenochtitlán, the story of the Spanish conquest of Mexico is romantic because Mexico's Indians, save for the Tlascalans, an ostensibly independent republican nation, cannot muster an effective resistance to Spanish wile and warfare. Prescott's debt to the black legend at first favors the Aztecs, for as Anna Brickhouse explains, the legend "cast the Spanish conquistadores as bloodthirsty, Catholic villains who preyed mercilessly upon the hemisphere's indigenous races, who were simultaneously characterized as gentle and culturally advanced to an extent that ostensibly set them apart from the indigenous races of the United States" (75). But, when the Aztecs unite under Guatemozin, whose bellicosity is a far cry from Montezuma's "pusillanimity" (Prescott 2: 296), the romance of indigenous adversaries darkens as their terrifying resistance inspires the gothic in the romantic historian whose greatest fear in the 1840s may very well be collective racial rebellion to Anglo imperialism. Perhaps, then, the three volumes of *Conquest* can be considered as a narrative of disinterment whereby the genteel historian is shocked to find mutilated white corpses beneath the romantic history of Mexico's fall; equally disturbing is that the US stands to inherit such a gothic genealogy on the eve of its own conquest of Mexico.

3. Similia similibus curantur

In a scene recounted in Bernal Diaz del Castillo's 1632 narrative, an Aztec governor and ambassador under Montezuma arrives at the Spanish camp near the port of San Juan de Ulúa to greet the Spaniards, exchange gifts, and reconnoiter the invaders. Tendile brings with him "some clever painters" who "make pictures true to nature of the face and body of Cortés and all his captains" (121). Aware of the power of symbol, Cortés orders the cannons fired and the horses galloped across the sand to spook the Aztec ambassadors, but a week later, Montezuma responds with his own trick:

> Then one morning, Tendile arrived with more than one hundred laden Indians, accompanied by a great Mexican Cacique, who in his face, features, and appearance bore a strong likeness to our Captain Cortés and the great Montezuma had sent him purposely, for it is said that when Tendile brought the portrait of Cortés all the chiefs who were in Montezuma's company said that a great chief named Quintalbor looked exactly like Cortés and that was the name of the Cacique, who now arrived with Tendile; and as he was so like Cortés, we called them in camp "our Cortés" and "the other Cortés." (124)[7]

This encounter is a small reminder that the conquest of Mexico involved two empires—the Spanish and the Aztec—that mirrored each other in their determination to dominate Mexico's indigenous people. They are strangely familiar enemies more alike than different, haunting reflections of conquest that, as the Cortés *cuates* imply, collapse the difference between old- and new-world imperialisms, for if the Spanish find an "other" Cortés in Mexico, the Aztecs recognize their Quintalbor among the foreigners.

The scene is also an apt way of returning to the *unheimlich*, especially in relation to Mignolo's opening question: "Who defines such a hemisphere" situated ambiguously between "difference and sameness" (31)? For Mignolo, Saxon and Iberian colonial Creoles defined the hemisphere in the early nineteenth century through a "double consciousness" that was "geo-political" insofar as the Creoles imagined the hemisphere in opposition to Europe (England and Spain, respectively) and racial insofar as the Creoles consolidated their whiteness against indigenous groups, African Americans and black Creoles (34–5). This double logic works through a process that in effect renders the hemisphere unhomely, for, on the one hand, it characterizes the hemisphere by what it is geo-politically not (Europe) and, on the other, represses the presence of what the hemisphere geo-racially is (indigenous and mestizo). Estranged from itself, the western hemisphere is doubled—European but not Europe, native but not indigenous. The doubling itself is uncanny, but what I have been emphasizing with *Calavar* and *Conquest* is how this doubling becomes especially haunting when it manifests itself in sameness rather than difference, to reverse Mignolo's phrase. That is, difference maintains the borders across the Americas that distinguish one nation from the other, but sameness produces an inter-American gothic hemisphere that emerges when native nationalist writings uncover as their origin the history of another country.

Paula Moya and Ramón Saldívar explain this dichotomy in their discussion of the "trans-American imaginary": "it is first necessary ... to recognize the influence on literature of competing nationalisms ... *within* the borders of the nation. But it is also the case that much American literature responds to ideological pressures from *outside* the geopolitical borders of the sovereign United States" (4). But if the presence of the other is already buried within the nation, the distinction between "within" and "outside" collapses into a hemispheric *unheimlich* that vexes the definition of a national literature based on geo-political borders. Instead, as Moya and Saldívar remind us, the trans-American imaginary recognizes the "shared fates" of the Americas (17), which I understand as a history of conquest and resistance that troubles the difference between one nation and the other within the Americas. Take, for example, *Xicoténcatl*. The narrative was published in Philadelphia in 1826, nearly a decade before Bird's *Calavar*. It was written in Spanish and certainly penned by a Creole, although the exact authorship remains a toss-up between an unknown Mexican author, the Cuban priest Félix Varela, the Cuban poet José María Heredia or even Vincente Rocafuerte, a political exile of dubious hemispheric origins who, if he did not write the text, may have helped to complete it (Brickhouse 53–4). Its political stance about the fall of the Tlaxcalan republic is applicable equally to the past and early-nineteenth-century present of Cuba, Mexico, and the US, insofar as they all share a history of radical republicanism threatened by empire. The narrative is thus an "inter-American" text in more ways than one. The anonymity of its authorship is a standing reminder that the presence of the other is not always fully exhumed from history. The narrative itself has only recently been recovered and republished in Spanish and English editions. And perhaps, most importantly, *Xicoténcatl* collapses the distinctions of national histories to imagine a trans-American republican hemisphere made unhomely by conquest.

Of course, *Xicoténcatl* generates a critique against the Spanish conquest by viewing it as a force outside the Americas that has ostensibly corrupted the indigenous republicans within the Americas. Thus, the narrative reproduces much of the black legend in its description of Cortés and his conquistadors. They are, quite literally and liberally throughout the text, "monsters" (13), "inhuman" (34), "evil" (50), "treacherous" (83), "tyrants" (140), and, in a string of invectives reserved for Cortés in particular, "the most abominable of monsters ever aborted by the abyss!" (142). Their monstrosity encompasses their sexual desire, as when Teutila rebuffs Cortés' advances with "Monster! ... You are more inhuman than a tiger and more vile and treacherous than a snake. How can you not be horrified by your impudence?" (34); their duplicity, as when Teutila again rebukes Cortés: "In what kind of hell have you learned such hypocrisy and such evil?" (50); and their actions, as when Cortés cuts off the ears, noses, fingers, and toes of captured Tlaxcalan soldiers and then sends them back to terrify the indigenous republic (44). The gothic monstrosity of Cortés and his fellow Spaniards even extends to their system of governance:

> "But a king is a man," Xicoténcatl explains; "he has passions and can get to be a monster. Look at what is happening to that great Mexican empire. Moctezuma was virtuous, with an honest heart and with great generosity, and this same man ... now has become a haughty tyrant; he has forgotten that he is a man.... Those who are bad join him; the good become corrupted and evil is irreparable, and if it not, it exacts incredible convulsions, blood, and horrors." (57)

Oddly enough, Moctezuma and the Mexican empire appear at the center of Xicoténcatl's republican critique of the Spanish crown, suggesting that the conquest of Mexico occurred because empire was already within the hemisphere. In fact, *Xicoténcatl* is only nominally about the Spanish conquest of the Aztecs; it is more clearly about Tlaxcala's fall, which, the narrative reveals, has very little to do with forces outside of the republic. "When internal divisions destroy the unity of a people," the narrator explains, "they inevitably become the victims of their enemies, and more so if the practitioners of political shrewdness and craftiness are able to take advantage of that discord" (79). Recall that, even before the Spaniards arrive, Tlaxcala and the Aztec empire are at warring odds, and personal revenge divides the Tlaxcalan senate between Xicoténcatl the elder's ideal republicanism, the military republicanism of his son, and the political machinations of Magiscatzin, whose corruption culminates with his conversion to Christianity and subsequent tormented death. "Passions presided in the nation's council, and the Tlaxcalans at the end became the victims of their discord" (9).

Tlaxcala's internal fissures explain the narrative's double consciousness and its haunting sense of sameness instead of difference between republicanism and empire. Teutila's loyalty to republicanism and love for Xicoténcatl, for instance, lead her to betray both inadvertently, when, during her first interview with Cortés, she reveals Tlaxcala's instability to him: "As a good politician, he especially turned his attention to a great project that the division and discord in the Tlaxcalan senate suggested to him and, all the while, with his eyes he devoured the young American's attributes" (29). With the information he hears from Teutila, Cortés flatters Magiscatzin into treason, and he keeps Xicoténcatl in check by holding Teutila hostage. The narrative stages an even more telling event that externalizes the republic's internal, colonial double-ness. Fray Bartolomé de Olmedo and Diego de Ordaz first met Teutila at the entrance of a "grotto," where she often waits for Xicoténcatl (18); the site alone literally invokes the grotesque, if we can trust the English translation of the Spanish original to trace accurately "grotto" as the Latin root of "grotesque." Yet, when Teutila returns to the cave near the end of the narrative, she finds it covered with brush and stones and hears "a sad lament that seemed to be coming from the grotto" (132). She uncovers the cave's entrance, clambers in, and "What she saw before her shocked her modesty and filled her with compassion at the same time. It was a man, entirely naked and so tightly bound that it was impossible for him to move. The wretch was a Spaniard" (133).

He is not just any Spaniard either: he stood guard over Teutila when she was imprisoned in the Spanish camp, but he now finds himself a captive because he has raped a Tlaxcalan woman. Teutila orders him unbound and released, but his presence there in the first place is what is important, for he serves as a symbolic reminder that empire was already buried beneath the indigenous Americas before Spain's arrival. The fact that he is there because of rape is equally important. Throughout the narrative, the Spaniards rape or attempt to rape indigenous women, but instead of framing the fall of Tlaxcala as a sexual violation, which would be consistent with the Spaniards' behavior, the narrator explains the republic's demise because of sexual solicitation:

> From that moment on, the Republic of Tlaxcala ceased to exist as a nation. The sovereignty of states is like a woman's honor: when people maintain it intact, they are respected and esteemed ... but when self interest, corruption, weakness, or any other cause make them yield their appreciable jewel, neither one nor the other is more than the object of contempt.... Nevertheless, the wretched Republic of Tlaxcala was condemned, for the time, to suffer for a long while the worthy punishment of its vile act of prostitution. (118)

The narrator's misogyny articulates the hemispheric *unheimlich* that troubles *Xicoténcatl*, for the indigenous Americans are not what they seem. The Tlaxcalans, those "enem[ies] of effeminacy" (8), turn out feminized; Teutile, the "beautiful Indian maiden" (18), finds a double in the form of a Spanish conquistador; and Xicoténcatl, the narrative's republican hero, turns malinche by letting his passion divide him between Teutile and doña Marina: "In one word: without ceasing to love his Teutila, he fell in love with the graces with which doña Marina had beautified herself in her dealings with the Europeans, and speaking with one about the other, he spread his passion toward the two of them" (59). Ironically, La Malinche proper, doña Marina, who is at first figured as an indigenous traitor, has a change of heart after motherhood, rejects Cortés, and, with her two mestizo children, stands as a symbol of a hybrid American hemisphere that, as Debra Castillo puts it, gives "a new twist" to the "old historical narrative" of the Spanish conquest (48).[8]

It is true, then, when Xicoténcatl the elder tells his son, "Your homeland is no longer Tlaxcala" (84), but perhaps it never was, and it took the conquest to unearth the fact that indigenous republicanism and European empire are more similar than different in the Americas. This is a tragic realization for the novel's indigenous republicans, but for the Spaniards, it invokes a chiaroscuro gothic terror embodied best in Cortés's response to Teutila's death scene: "As pale as a corpse, his hair standing on end, his mouth agape, his eyes wide open, his arms half raised, not daring to either move backward or forward, his whole body trembling, Cortés was left stupefied, his external self well depicting the mortal anguish inside his black soul" (154). *Xicoténcatl*'s Cortés experiences the same anxiety that haunts Bird's *Calavar* and Prescott's *Conquest*—a fear that the republic is an unhomely empire after all. In this sense, the trans-American gothic that the anonymous novel exhumes has its origins in another familial narrative, the Monroe Doctrine, which distinguished the US from Europe by situating the new republic within the western hemisphere but also made the hemisphere subject to the US's new-world imperialism. That is, while Monroe's message ostensibly articulated the US as an anti-imperial republic, it also established the US's hemispheric neo-colonialism through a double logic that situated the US *within* the Américas by figuring the US *as* America. "Cortés acá, Cortés acullá" (our Cortés, the other Cortés, as Bernal Diaz del Castillo put it) thus returns in the duplicitous doctrine that turns the logic of homeopathy, *Similia Similibus Curantur*, into the cause of rather than cure for colonial disease, because one Cortés is the same as the other in the hemisphere's haunting history of conquest.

Notes

1 Here and throughout the use of misnomers, such as Aztec for the more historically accurate *Mexica* or *Montezuma* rather than *Moctezuma*, slights historical accuracy for the convenience of following the usage consistent with each text under consideration.

2 Nigel Leask notes that Calderón de la Barca haunts Prescott's *Conquest* in much the same way that Doña Marina haunts Chapultepec, for the historian's three-volume history filched Calderón de la Barca's ghostly description of Chapultepec (206). Compare Calderón de la Barca's passage above, for instance, with Prescott's "and the grounds are still shaded by gigantic cypresses, more than fifty feet in circumference, which were centuries old at the time of the Conquest.... Surely, there is no spot better suited to awaken meditation on the past; none, where the traveller [sic], as he sits under those stately cypresses grey [sic] with the moss of ages, can so fitly ponder on the sad destinies of the Indian races and the monarch who once held his courtly revels under the shadow of their branches" (2: 114).

3 DeGuzmán's otherwise compelling argument about the US's anxious imperial relationship with Spain almost entirely elides the significance of Mexico's

proximity to the US and how the continental presence of Mexico formed the US's image of Spain and Spaniards. DeGuzmán is not alone in this elision of Mexico. Richard Kagan's "Prescott's paradigm" views Spain as the US's "antithesis": "America was the future—republican, enterprising, rational; while Spain—monarchical, indolent, fanatic—represented the past," Kagan explains (430). Yet, the argument that Spain is the US's "antithesis" overlooks how Mexico functions as the synthesis of both countries. Eric Wertheimer's study remains the most convincing articulation of the imaginary relation between the US and the Americas in this regard. As Wertheimer explains, early nationalist American literature that viewed Columbus, Aztecs, and Incas as indigenous ancestors of American national identity created "an identitarian crisis of Anglo nativism—of claiming a native proto-republican Other as the anchor of national destiny" (5). This identity crisis, I maintain, manifests itself in the gothic.

4　　Homi Bhabha similarly writes that "the unhomely emerges when the borders between home and world become confused; and, uncannily, the private and the public become part of each other, forcing upon us a vision that is as divided as it is disorienting" (13). I would extend Bhabha's notion of the domestic to suggest that the unhomely emerges when the borders between one nation and another collapse.

5　　Benjamin Keen explains that the relation between Moors and Aztecs was not uncommon in Spanish conquistador writings: "The conquistadors were acquainted with one infidel civilization that offered a clue to the posture they should assume towards the Aztecs. This was the advanced Moslem culture, known to the Spaniards through centuries of contact in war and peace.... Occasionally [conquistadors] compare Moslem and Aztec cultural achievements, to the advantage of the latter, in order to demonstrate the high level of civilization attained by the Aztecs" (55–6).

6　　It is worth noting that gothic discourses certainly shaped the black legend the US inherited from England, especially as England's Hispanophobia corresponds chronologically with the rise of its gothic novel. Consider, for instance, how David J. Weber explains the black legend: "From their English forebears and other non-Spanish Europeans, Anglo Americans had inherited the view that Spaniards were unusually cruel, avaricious, treacherous, fanatical, superstitious, cowardly, corrupt, decadent, indolent, and authoritarian" (336).

7　　In the Spanish original, Diaz del Castillo invokes a spatial difference between the doppelgängers: "Cortés acá, Cortés acullá," which I translate literally as "Cortés from here, Cortés from there" (105). Prescott renders it nationally as the "Mexican Cortés" (1: 294). Both translations shore up the uncanny event and suggest the idea that Aztec culture understood and even deployed the duplicity of signs in much the same way that Cortés handled signification, as in his firing of the cannons.

8　　The "new twist" is that Doña Marina escapes her otherwise pejorative historical name. Known as "La Malinche," Doña Marina served as translator between the Aztecs and the Spaniards; she was also Cortés's mistress and thus earned the reputation as a cultural and sexual "traitor." In *Xicoténcatl*, however, Doña Marina rejects her pejorative history by denouncing Cortés and the Spanish while Xicoténcatl becomes "malinche" by betraying his wife and his republican ideals. In effect, the reversal mirrors the narrative's feminization of the Tlaxcalan republic.

Works cited

Anonymous. *Xicoténcatl* [an anonymous historical novel about the events leading up to the conquest of the Aztec Empire]. Trans. Guillermo I. Castillo-Feliú. 1826. Austin: University of Texas Press, 1999.

Bhabha, Homi. *The Location of Culture*. New York: Routledge, 2004.

Bird, Robert Montgomery. *Calavar, or, The Knight of the Conquest: A Romance of Mexico*. 2 vols. Philadelphia: Carey, Lea, and Blanchard, 1834.

—*The Infidel, or, The Fall of Mexico*. 2 vols. Philadelphia: Carey, Lea, & Blanchard, 1835.

Brickhouse, Anna. *Transamerican Literary Relations and the Nineteenth-Century Public Sphere*. Cambridge: Cambridge University Press, 2004.

Calderón de la Barca, Frances. *Life in Mexico*. 1843. Berkeley: University of California Press, 1982.

Cass, Lewis. "The Mexican War." *Senate of the US*. 10 Feb. 1847.

Castillo, Debra A. *Redreaming America: Toward a Bilingual American Culture*. Albany: State University of New York Press, 2005.

Dahl, Curtis. *Robert Montgomery Bird*. New York: Twayne, 1963.

De la Teja, Jesús F. *A Revolution Remembered: The Memoirs and Selected Correspondences of Juan N. Seguín*. Austin: State House Press, 1991.

DeGuzmán, María. *Spain's Long Shadow: The Black Legend, Off-Whiteness, and Anglo-American Empire*. Minneapolis: University of Minnesota Press, 2005.

Díaz del Castillo, Bernal. *The Discovery and Conquest of Mexico, 1517–1521*. Trans. A. P. Maudslay. Ed. Genaro Garcia. London: George Routledge, 1928.

—*Historia verdadera de la conquista de la Nueva España*. Ed. Ramon Iglesia Mexico City: Nuevo Mundo, 1943.

Eipper, John. "The Canonizer De-Canonized: The Case of William H. Prescott." *Hispania* 83 (2000): 418–27.

Freud, Sigmund. "The 'Uncanny.'" *Collected Papers*. Ed. Ernest Jones Vol. 10. London: Hogarth Press, 1948. 368–407.

Goddu, Teresa A. *Gothic America: Narrative, History, and Nation*. New York: Columbia University Press, 1997.

Gruesz, Kirsten Silva. *Ambassadors of Culture: The Transamerican Origins of Latino Writing*. Princeton: Princeton University Press, 2002.

Johannsen, Robert W. *To the Halls of the Montezumas: The Mexican War in the American Imagination*. New York: Oxford University Press, 1985.

Kagan, Richard L. "Prescott's Paradigm: American Historical Scholarship and the Decline of Spain." *American Historical Review* 101 (1996): 423–46.

Keen, Benjamin. *The Aztec Image in Western Thought*. New Jersey: Rutgers University Press, 1971.

Kutzinski, Vera M. "Borders and Bodies: The United States, America, and the Caribbean." *New Centennial Review* 1.2 (2001): 55–85.

Leask, Nigel. "'The Ghost in Chapoltepec': Fanny Calderón de la Barca, William Prescott and Ninteenth-Century Mexican Travel Accounts." *Voyages and Visions: Towards a Cultural History of Travel.* Ed. Jas Elsner and Joan-Pau Rubiés. London: Reaktion Books, 1999. 184–209.

Mignolo, Walter D. "Coloniality at Large: The Western Hemisphere in the Colonial Horizon of Modernity." *New Centennial Review* 1.2 (2001): 19–54.

Morrison, Toni. *Playing in the Dark: Whiteness and the Literary Imagination.* New York: Vintage, 1993.

Moya, Paula M. L. and Ramón Saldívar. "Fictions of the Trans-American Imaginary." *Modern Fiction Studies* 49.1 (2003): 1–18.

Prescott, William H. *History of the Conquest of Mexico, with a Preliminary View of the Ancient Mexican Civilization, and the Life of the Conqueror, Hernando Cortés.* 1843. 3 vols. Philadelphia: David McKay, 1892.

Sadowski-Smith, Claudia and Claire F. Fox. "Theorizing the Hemisphere: Inter-Americas Work at the Intersection of American, Canadian, and Latin American Studies." *Comparative American Studies* 21.1 (2005): 5–38.

Sundquist, Eric J. "Exploration and Empire." *The Cambridge History of American Literature.* Vol. 2. Ed. Sacvan Bercovitch. Cambridge: Cambridge University Press, 1994. 127–74.

Wald, Priscilla. *Constituting Americans: Cultural Anxiety and Narrative Form.* Durham: Duke University Press, 1995.

Weber, David J. *The Spanish Frontier in North America.* New Haven: Yale University Press, 1992.

Wertheimer, Eric. *Imagined Empires: Incas, Aztecs, and the New World of American Literature, 1771–1876.* Cambridge: Cambridge University Press, 1999.

31

Seeing Ghosts: *The Turn of the Screw* and Art History

Alexander Nemerov

Can a historical claim be based on a scarcely credible vision? Can an unprofessional method born of intuition and sentiment (hardly a method at all) somehow yield a valid insight about the past? If so, what would that visionary intensity look like? This essay, exploring these questions, is a defense of the governess in Henry James's tale *The Turn of the Screw*—a young woman who is a model of the historian's powers of sudden, revelatory awareness of the past.

This will immediately seem an odd thing to claim. The governess is not a likely figure to identify with a historian, for any reason at all. She sees ghosts, or claims to. She has an overactive imagination, an "infernal imagination," as she calls it.[1] The most famous of her sightings, the first—the appearance of the dead servant Peter Quint atop one of the crenellated towers of the house at Bly, a vision shown in one of Eric Pape's illustrations for James's story as it originally appeared in 1898 in the American periodical *Collier's Weekly* (fig. 1)—may be shocking, but it is also a fantasy. "He did stand there!" the governess exclaims, but James is careful to show that she is an unreliable guide to what is really out there.[2]

Consider the longer list of her failings. She is an impressionable reader of books such as Henry Fielding's *Amelia* and Ann Radcliffe's *The Mysteries of Udolpho*.[3] She is driven by dreams of noble purpose—of protecting her two young charges Miles and Flora from danger, even if she should perversely have to envision the danger she saves them from. She imagines that the ghosts of Quint and the other dead servant, Miss Jessel, reappear plain as day to lure the children across dangerous spaces, and even that the children

Figure 1   Eric Pape (American, 1870–1938), *"He Did Stand There!—But High Up, Beyond the Lawn and at the Very Top of the Tower."* Published in *Collier's Weekly*, 12 February 1898, 21. Beinecke Rare Book and Manuscript Library, Yale University, New Haven, Connecticut

are in league with the ghosts. Combating Quint and Jessel, she wants to save the day for her dashing employer, the children's uncle, a man she has met with only briefly but long enough to fall in love. The governess, in short, is a "fluttered anxious girl out of a Hampshire vicarage," as James's narrator Douglas describes her, without any knowledge of her drives and motivations.[4] She is a concocter of fantasies made straight from her susceptible, repressed mind: a Freudian hysteric, wrote the distinguished literary critic Edmund Wilson in 1934.[5] Still worse (not to hold anything back), she is a murderer, since her belief in the malevolence lurking around Bly eventually grows so strong that she terrifies the children and causes the heart of poor little Miles to stop.

Yet still I defend the governess as a model for what we do in one specific way: she sees with extraordinary vividness what is not exactly there. She receives a glimmer of the past that comes to her unbidden and all but unbelievably. She sees it take a form so strange that she despairs of ever being able to convey it to others, even as she knows from that moment on that she must do nothing but set her mind to describe and investigate it. Her failings, true, are just those as have been ascribed to her. But if we take away her tale-telling, her rush to conviction—the whole tissue of dire plausibilities she concocts so irresponsibly *about* her visions, and which, together, make up a list of *don'ts* for the historian—there yet remains this intensely admirable core to her method. Historical revelation, as her experience defines it, takes some form like that of Quint on the tower. It is the sudden presence of something unlooked-for right there where we can never quite see it—not today, not tomorrow, not ever—that's yet perceptible all the same.

Much about this way of seeing is not reputable, not professional. It takes the form of an insight destined for the perceiver alone. It does so not necessarily because of a historian's training but likely because of a more naïve set of motivations and backgrounds not easily separable from a fluttery, anxious susceptibility of mind, a morbid attunement, I guess, to the presence of the past: a belief not in ghosts but in the permeability of past and present, intermingling like the jigsaw interpenetration of thin air and solid stone in Bly's crenellated towers, which gather down and hold within their slots the invisibilities of the sky. It all sounds superstitious, yes. If the governess perceives "little difference" between the two towers, which are called respectively the "new" and the "old," she may represent a historian's disastrous confusion of present and past: there is always, many feel, a huge difference between what we claim to see now and what happened then.[6]

Yet her vision still partakes of historical insight. Partly this is because James himself linked her to the practice of history. For this writer whose work was in constant dialogue with the discipline of history—who thought of the novelist as a kind of historian and the novel as a history—the governess was one of many characters morbidly sensitive to the past.[7]

The narrator-researcher of *The Aspern Papers* (1888) stops at nothing to find the poet's letters he believes sequestered in the Venetian palace of the ancient Juliana Bordereau. Ralph Pendrel, the hero of the unfinished novel *The Sense of the Past*, "wanted the unimaginable accidents, the little notes of truth for which the common lens of history, however the scowling muse might bury her nose, was not sufficiently fine." More supernaturally inclined than his Aspern counterpart, "He wanted evidence of a sort for which there had never been documents enough or for which documents mainly, however multiplied, would never *be* enough"[8]—a pursuit that leads him magically through an Edwardian door and back into the world of 1820. The governess, whose tale James paired with *The Aspern Papers* in the New York Edition of his works, matches the archivist's obsession to get back into the past, even as she adumbrates Pendrel's more supernatural access.[9]

The best way to demonstrate the governess's historical powers, however, is to examine the original publication of *The Turn of the Screw* in *Collier's Weekly*. That original publication is haunted by something deeply odd, maybe even shocking. This haunting presence is not rationally to be believed, yet it is there all the same. I will need the governess's own way of envisioning to discern it—for this haunted presence is my own Quint-atop-the-tower—but I will also need to tell a more convincing story than her, to be more persuasive as a historian, so that you also can see and even understand what is not quite there to be seen.

A world-political event haunts the *Collier's* version of James's tale. *The Turn of the Screw* ran weekly in installments from 27 January to 16 April 1898. On 15 February, the United States battleship *Maine* blew up in Havana's harbor, killing some 266 sailors. The *Collier's* center spread of 26 February, illustrated by William L. Sonntag, shows the devastating explosion. Starting with that issue, *The Turn of the Screw* ran coinciden-tally with updates about the *Maine*—the explosion, the investigation, and the political and military aftermath. The two stories appeared together in eight issues overall until the mid-April conclusion of James's serial. Against probability, the recent events in Cuba somehow appear in *The Turn of the Screw* and the accompanying illustrations. They do so not because James was somehow reacting to world-political events in his tale. Even had he been inclined to do such a thing, which he was not, he had completed the story in December 1897, well before the events in Havana's harbor.

They do so instead through the sheer and suggestive juxtaposition of James's serialized tale and the Cuban coverage. This juxtaposition takes us out of our assumptions that a novel is always a discrete entity, enclosed in the format of a book, and into the strange experience of reading it as just one topic, one voice amid an echoing clatter of topics and voices, issues and opinions about widely different things that yet all seem strangely to speak to one another across the forced proximity of a periodical's bundled

Figure 2   John La Farge (American, 1835–1910), *Untitled*. Title piece for *The Turn of the Screw*. Published in *Collier's Weekly*, 2 April 1898, 17. Beinecke Rare Book and Manuscript Library, Yale University, New Haven, Connecticut

pages. This is the "powerful experience of heteroglossia" that literary historian William Todd describes in his work on the serialized nineteenth-century Russian novel—the experience that disrupts the modern reader's "sense of the difference between imaginative literature and journalism." Encountering Dostoevsky's *The Brothers Karamazov* in its original serialized form in *The Russian Herald*, Todd finds also "essays on biological science, ecology, technology, pedagogy, jurisprudence, prison organization, politics, philosophy, history, literature, and music"—all of them pressing the question of the novel's relation to these disparate topics.[10] This is the "hum and buzz of implication" that Todd, quoting Lionel Trilling, regards as a poetics and politics of serialization. That same hum and buzz—here the events in Havana—is there (and not there) in the serialized words and pictures of James's tale in *Collier's*.[11]

How is this so? Think first of John La Farge's recurring tide piece for *The Turn of the Screw* (fig. 2). Introducing all but one of the tale's twelve installments starting with the 27 January issue, the illustration shows the governess hovering over little Miles. The two of them huddle in a smoke of darkness flanked by mysterious ectoplasmic insignia evoking the ghosts of Quint and Miss Jessel. This is a picture about more than protection and care. It is about a deep, smothering, gothic concern—the concern of a woman who sees and feels death all around her and tries hard to shield the young man from it. This same concern unfolded in the *Collier's* coverage of the post-*Maine* buildup to war. A poem called "One Woman's Voice

Against War," written by Edith M. Thomas, appeared directly adjacent to
La Farge's title piece in the 19 March issue. "They see not, as I can see,"
Thomas's narrator says, talking about other women who gladly send their
sons and husbands to Cuba.

> They see not, as I can see, men biting the dust, in the fray
> They see not, as I can see, men pouring the blood of the brave—

And she goes on:

> Awake, or asleep, I should see the dark stream, with the life
> taking flight—
> The damp of the death-dew beading—the eye without vision or
> light!
> My sisters—they see not the sight . . .[12]

On the adjacent page, the governess also speaks of special sight—of her
"first sight of Quint," of the "ugly glimpse." She describes her own eyes
being just at that moment sealed, thank goodness, to further terrible sights
but still maintains her own conviction, as a moral principle, that she never
does wish to lose this faculty of terrible envisioning, of seeing what no one
else can or will see—this readiness, she says, "to know the very worst that
was to be known" so that she may save the children from a terrible fate.[13]
In this light, La Farge's picture epitomized the protective cry of the war
mother—her premonition of battlefield deaths, her sense that even as she
clasps the cherished boy, another hand (on his shoulder) also holds him
close. That she wears the clothing of the late nineteenth century—La Farge,
like Pape, chooses not to show her in the costume of the 1840s, the era
in which the recollected action unfolds—makes her seem all the more as
though she responds to contemporary events.

La Farge's picture also strangely matches and even criticizes the mother-
and-child iconography of the *Maine* disaster itself. The 2 April cover of
Collier's features the central group of George Julian Zolnay's proposed
monument to the battleship (fig. 3). Zolnay shows Columbia holding the
sword of justice, glowering outward with an air of immanent retribution.
Flanking her are a widow clutching her baby and an orphan boy whose
miniature fist-clenching mimics Columbia's vengeful rigor. Zolnay registers
the official view of the disaster in the right angles and sharpened clarity
of moral righteousness and indignation. The figures take their places as
decisively as other motifs in the overall memorial design not pictured here:
a coffin below and a broken obelisk above. There is no mistaking their
purpose.[14]

La Farge and James, by contrast, depicted a far more fraught war
emotion. La Farge's figures bond in a claustrophobic proximity that

Figure 3   George Julian Zolnay (American, 1863–1949), Detail of *Proposed "Maine" Memorial.* Cover of *Collier's Weekly*, 2 April 1898. Beinecke Rare Book and Manuscript Library, Yale University, New Haven, Connecticut

bespeaks both love and violence, protection and murder. The governess shields Miles from danger, yes—like the speaker in Thomas's poem, she fights for his soul against the demon of the smoky hand and staring eye— but her protection somehow also abets those forces. Maybe it is even the same as those forces. The governess's hand on the boy's head doubles the ghostly hand on his shoulder.[15] La Farge, evidently an astute reader of James's tale, makes the governess inseparable from the ghosts who claim and kill Miles, her caress and theirs each a spectral clutch. Her bodice is mysteriously like the ghostly forms flanking her, the tendrils of these strange calligraphic jellyfish having taken root as the frill upon her chest, making it still clearer that for La Farge, as for James, what is alien and disturbing is actually within the governess: the call, as they say in the horror movies, is coming from inside the house. All of this is appropriate, since the governess does kill Miles. Translated to a wartime context, La Farge suggests that the protector is also the killer. The national mother Columbia shielding the boy sends him to his death.

Another *Turn of the Screw* illustration shows sorrow and grief, now not just foretold (as in Thomas's poem) but happening before our eyes (fig. 4). Pape's center spread for the 19 March issue of *Collier's* depicts

Figures 4 & 5   Left: Eric Pape, *"He Presently Produced Something that Made Me Drop Straight Down on the Stone Slab."* Published in *Collier's Weekly*, 19 March 1898, 12–13. Right: Cover of same issue, photographer unknown, *Memorial Service at Graves of "Maine's" Dead, Havana, March 4*. Beinecke Rare Book and Manuscript Library, Yale University, New Haven, Connecticut

the governess and Miles in a churchyard, tombstones dimly visible behind them. The governess sits on "a low oblong table-like tomb," reduced to that position—dropped "straight down on the stone slab," the caption reads—by one of Miles's disarming statements.[16] Pape's illustration, for all its direct relation to James's tale, evokes the funerary imagery and ceremonies following the *Maine* explosion. It not only anticipates the Zolnay group meant to be poised above its sculpted coffin in the 2 April issue, it also echoes the cover of the 19 March issue itself, which features a photograph of mourners in Havana, their heads bowed, at a memorial service for some of the *Maine*'s dead (fig. 5). The resonance between these two pictures—the cover and the center spread of the same issue, the two largest images in the publication—makes all but unavoidable the Cuban significance of Pape's illustration and James's story as they first appeared. "We were, for the minute, alone among the old thick graves," says the governess,[17] describing the old English burials. Though those tombs differ from the tombs of those newly interred in Havana, the image of her with her head lowered, like the Havana mourners, makes it seem that she too grieves for the sailors just then on everyone's mind.

Coming upon the dead: this is another Cuban meaning of the *Collier's Turn of the Screw*. Pape's illustration for the 5 March issue shows the governess descending the stairs at night and seeing for the third time the ghost of Quint (fig. 6). Candle in hand, she glimpses the specter as he appears on the landing beneath a tall window in a wash of slanting "cold faint twilight," the two of them "fac[ing] each other in our common intensity."[18] During the preceding weeks, ever since 15 February, the American public had focused on something similarly macabre—the entombment of so many sailors in the underwater wreckage and the possible retrieval of those bodies. A photograph from the 12 March *Collier's* shows one of the bell-helmeted divers sent down to assess the wreck for clues, look for important artifacts, and examine the possibility of disinterring some of the dead. Latter-day descriptions of the process sound as gothic as the experience must have been: "Slowly, carefully shepherding his air hose," reads one of these accounts, "[the diver] groped down the passageway [of the ship] through the opaque, debris-filled water and entered the captain's quarters.... By the flickering light of his lamp he made a painstaking search" for missing keys and signal books.[19]

James's governess, with her own flickering light, travels through a similar murkiness. What she encounters, moreover, is a terrifying dead man akin to the legions awaiting the divers as they moved cautiously through the *Maine*'s corridors. Consider this quotation from one of these men, published in *Frank Leslie's Popular Monthly* in December 1898, when interest in these terrifying encounters evidently still ran strong:

HOLDING MY CANDLE HIGH, TILL I CAME WITHIN SIGHT OF THE TALL WINDOW

Figure 6　Eric Pape, *"Holding My Candle High, till I Came within Sight of the Tall Window."* Published in *Collier's Weekly*, 5 March 1898, 17. Beinecke Rare Book and Manuscript Library, Yale University, New Haven, Connecticut

As I descended into the death-ship, the dead rose up to meet me. They floated toward me with outstretched arms.... . Here and there the light of my lamp flashed upon a stony face I knew, which when I last saw it had smiled a merry greeting, but now returned my gaze with staring eyes and fallen jaw.... . They brushed against my helmet and touched my shoulders with rigid hands, as if they sought to tell me the tale of the disaster.... . From every part of the ship came sighs and groans. I knew it was the gurgling of the water through the shattered beams ... but it made me shudder.... . The water swayed the bodies to and fro, and kept them constantly moving with a hideous semblance of life.[20]

James's governess in that illustration of 5 March is in a world far removed from that of the *Maine*. But she too descends in the dark with light in hand and comes upon a ghost, a strangely "living detestable dangerous presence," a thing "human and hideous ... hideous just because it was human."[21] In those weeks immediately following the explosion, her experience resonated with and even expressed the horrors of the ship.

Not just these macabre sightings but the ideological justification for war also fantastically appears in *The Turn of the Screw*'s original publication. The 2 April *Collier's* includes a Pape illustration showing the governess prostrate in the foreground, having flung herself down, giving way, she writes, to "a wildness of grief" (fig. 7).[22] In the distance, standing on the far shore of the lake at Bly—a lake the governess and her charges have taken to calling the Sea of Azof, after part of the Black Sea they have learned about in geography lessons—is the ghost of Miss Jessel. The governess, crying because she feels that no one else confesses to seeing what she so plainly sees, might be read in a war context as yet another grieving mother. Devastated by a deathliness from across a far shore, even an ocean shore, she is a more abject version of the grief-wracked mother that appeared on the cover of this same issue in Zolnay's proposed memorial. War, it implies, is worth fighting to avenge grief.

Surveying the whole 2 April issue, however, one finds a still more direct rhetoric of military justification in Pape's image. Eight pages before his picture is a full-page spread of photographs from Cuba including two separate ones of peasants starving at the hands of their Spanish colonial lords. One of these photographs is especially striking (fig. 8). Such peasants were the very persons, numbering in the many thousands, in whose name William Randolph Hearst and Theodore Roosevelt had been clamoring for a war in Cuba since well before the *Maine* blew up. The appearance in *Collier's* of these *reconcentrados*, as they were called, was part of the meticulous ideological build-up for war that permeated the genteel press such as *Collier's* as much as it did Hearst's publications in the first half of 1898. If the gauntness of the figure is somewhat doctored, it did not alter

Figure 7   Eric Pape, *"I Must Have Thrown Myself, on My Face, on the Ground."*
Published in *Collier's Weekly*, 2 April 1898, 16. Beinecke Rare Book and Manuscript
Library, Yale University, New Haven, Connecticut

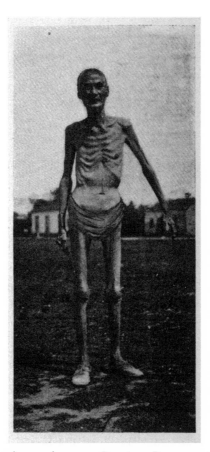

Figure 8 Photographer unknown, *Starving Renconcentrado*. Published in *Collier's Weekly*, 2 April 1898, 8. Beinecke Rare Book and Manuscript Library, Yale University, New Haven, Connecticut

the fact that the man was truly emaciated and making a plaintive appeal out of the pages of *Collier's* to those who might save him.

This same appeal strangely marks Pape's illustration of the grief-stricken governess. If we scan back and forth between the starving peasant on page eight and the illustration of James's story on page sixteen, the peasant comes to seem remarkably like the ghost silhouetted on the far bank of the lake at Bly. The resonance makes the governess appear to weep, wracked with emotion, at the plight of the skeletally living who confront her, beseeching her aid. The tree to the governess's left, which Pape includes to suggest her standing posture before her fall to the ground, connotes the willowy frenzy of her emotion as it branches to the subject of her sorrow. In those weeks of ideological justification, the governess was a type of emotional citizen—for example, a reader of *Collier's*—for whom the horror of the living dead on a faraway shore could no longer be ignored.

The governess judges here and elsewhere hastily and emotionally, and this trait is another of her *Maine* resonances. She is certain she sees ghosts and sure who they are, despite having only a few clues and never having seen Quint or Jessel alive. She is certain of the dark purposes of these ghosts and sure what she must do to save the children. She dreams of the accolades she will receive for having so bravely faced the villains. Week by week in early 1898, this rash reasoning made a strange counterpoint to the national press's own inexorable deliberations and conclusions, including those of *Collier's* itself. "We have but little patience," said a representative *Collier's* editorial of 5 March, " ... with those who, on alleged ethical or legal grounds ... attribute the loss of the *Maine* to accident, and ... assume that the Spaniards [must be] innocent of a dastardly crime until they have been proven guilty."[23] In those weeks the governess' storytelling ran strangely parallel to the nation's political-journalistic certitude, casting it implicitly as either stirring bravery or hysterical overreaction.

The horror that started her hasty line of reasoning also weirdly evokes the *Maine*. For the governess, it was the sight of Quint atop the tower. For the nation, it was the explosion of the battleship. Each caused sudden emotional devastation. The governess's shock is an explosion for Pape, who shows her sheer surprise, as she spots Quint, in that burst of spike-edged vegetation beside her (see fig. 1). This is Pape's conventional illustrator's way of signaling the jolt of agitation that shows, too, in the similar spiky lines marking the bunched fabric of her dress. Although this picture appeared in the 12 February issue, just before the *Maine* blew up and two weeks before Sonntag's center spread of the Havana explosion, the two pictures align in retrospect as twin signs of a month of disconcerting terrible impossibility—it simply could not happen but it has—eliciting a bold and emotional response.

If the *Maine* explosion and war buildup find their way into James's serialized tale, the ghost story in turn informs one of the most well-known paintings of the war. Winslow Homer's *Searchlight on Harbor Entrance, Santiago de Cuba*, painted in 1901, casts the scene of battle in haunted terms (fig. 9). The painting shows the foreground ramparts of the old Morro Castle at the mouth of Havana's harbor, a fort built by Philip II in the late sixteenth century to defend part of his empire. In the distance, searchlight beams play across the sky. The picture may show the outdated majesty of Spain versus the technological might of the United States, as the art historian Randall Griffin contends,[24] but it is still more preoccupied with a ghostliness transcending national affiliation: the moonlit night, the strange searchlight beams, the mysterious emptiness, and the castle setting—the essential scene of the ghost story, "the entire stock-in-trade of horror romanticism."[25] Fixating on this castle, Homer implies that his

Figure 9   Winslow Homer (American, 1836–1910), *Searchlight on Harbor Entrance, Santiago de Cuba*, 1901. Oil on canvas, 30½ x 50½ in. (77.5 x 128.3 cm). The Metropolitan Museum of Art, New York. Gift of George A. Hearn, 1906

picture has itself a ghostly tale to tell. Perhaps the tale is that of the *Maine* itself, which sailed directly past Morro Castle as it entered the harbor on 25 January 1898—a photograph in *Collier's* shows the two, fort and battleship, bristling with facing guns as they peacefully opposed each other that day.[26] No matter how we read it, Homer's painting seems a meditation on the spectral shadows and strange glows alleged so thick at places of war.

The ghostliness of the picture is more exact. It seems likely to both Griffin and me that Homer had in mind an earlier picture when he painted *Searchlight on Harbor Entrance*, a Civil War image made by the American artist James Henry Beard in 1865 called *The Night before the Battle* (fig. 10).[27] Beard's painting shows Union soldiers asleep on their ramparts while solitary Death vigilantly mans one of the cannons.[28] Homer worked as an illustrator for much of the Civil War and made many notable paintings of the conflict, some in 1865. Likely he knew of Beard's painting, especially since *The Night before the Battle* was exhibited at the National Academy of Design in New York, where Homer also exhibited, and in April of the very year, 1865, when he became an Academician. The fort, the ramparts, the moonlit night (with the moon appearing at upper left)—everything is there in Homer's picture except of course the sleeping men, the sentry to the right, and the skeleton. These have been excised in his understandable later-life wish to make a war scene where there is no crudity of clanking chains and scuttling bones, no sentiment of portentous allegory, but yet a

Figure 10 James Henry Beard (American, 1814–1893), *The Night before the Battle*, 1865. Oil on canvas, 30½ x 44½ in. (77.5 x 113 cm). Memorial Art Gallery of the University of Rochester. Gift of Dr Ronald M. Lawrence

haunted mood all the same, "so subtly and yet so poignantly observed," as a period critic wrote, not of this painting but of *The Turn of the Screw*, "that all the usual paraphernalia of ghostliness recede in to the background as irrelevant."[29]

Homer's picture is Jamesian. It is all implication and indirection, its darkness a kind of light and its very cloudiness a lucidity. In it, as in James, mid-nineteenth-century narrative modes have become mysterious, succumbing to an age of interpretation, of epistemological uncertainty, that Homer no less than James was the master of. This doubt, too, this openness to interpretation, the vain search for a meaning definitive and clear—to this day we do not know how the *Maine* blew up—is all appropriate too. Homer represents it in the searchlights: the doubt-driven quest at the mute, mild, haunted place where something awful happened—where you can see, *all but see*, the skeleton and the soldiers sleeping their sleep. Focusing on what cannot exactly be seen no matter how hard we look, Homer found the right Jamesian mode for the story of the Spanish-American War to be told.

These examples are ways then of siding with the governess. What is out there on the parapet requires acuity and not just invention to see. It is out there even though the raking beams of a searchlight could never reveal it. How, even so, might the connections between the story and the news coverage be explained? The illustrations, for example—is there some logical way to account for the *Maine* allusions in at least some of them? Was Pape responding to events, making pictures that sometimes accommodated recent circumstances, if only unconsciously? This is doubtful. Are the resonances merely signs of a *Collier's* idiom, a "house style" down at the basement in which the journal kept its raw materials—rows of spike-edged paper explosions, stacks of weeping women, cartons of graveyard mourners, shelves full of wrinkle-nosed cute little children—that could be transformed, shaped to fit particular stories, given a smile or a frown, a smite of shock or a flounce of jubilation, depending on the case, so that they would each convincingly portray specific events and tales and yet still reveal their common material, that genteel fabric compounded always of the same graphic boldness and sentimental appeal? Probably so.

That would mean that in the pages of *Collier's* the *Maine* would explode and Quint would materialize in basically the same way, and that little Miles and Zolnay's orphan boy would be—deep down in that common journalistic basement where they too were made—brothers of a certain generic stripe. There would be nothing more to the connections than that. Yet all this savors too much of a rational explanation for a more inexplicable phenomenon: the unwonted vision of the *Maine* in these pictures.

Could we say instead—turning now to the story itself—that the Cuban connections make sense because deep down James's tale, like so much nineteenth-century fiction, is preoccupied with the sea? The governess fancies that she and the other residents of Bly are "a handful of passengers in a great drifting ship" with her "strangely at the helm."[30] James met Joseph Conrad early in 1897, getting from him "a vivid sense of long lonely vigils on ships in distant waters," as James's biographer Leon Edel puts it, and from Conrad's fiction a pleasure James described as a form of "surrender."[31] The tale's celebrated title has a nautical connotation as of churning propellers—"screw propellers," as they were called in several publications of that era[32]—enough to make one think that James's title refers to the story's own powers of forward momentum, what the literary historian Mark Seltzer calls "The Mechanics of Fiction," citing the tide of a Frank Norris essay of 1899. If poorly wrought fiction is for Norris a "liner with hastily constructed boilers," James's story—his "pot-boiler," he deprecated it—is a more relentless nautical machine.[33] *The Turn of the Screw* is a yarn, like so many nineteenth-century stories, even ones that contain no sailors, and the fact only adumbrates the stranger naval connotations that ended up residing in James's tale. By a kind of gluing or laminating effect, the account of the *Maine* naturally affixed to his story, like attaching to like.[34]

All of this too makes sense, but again the explanation is a little too rational. The greatest value of the governess's method is that she sees something so strange that it can never be fully explained even once we too come to see it and understand it a bit. The presence of the *Maine* in

James's story, and vice versa, makes ideological sense—we see more deeply into the complex of late-nineteenth-century political and cultural discourse because of these links. Maybe, professionally speaking, for historians that is their primary value: to show the smoke of connections that more than any lucid taxonomy (dividing "politics," "fiction," and the like, or even sometimes "before" from "after") is the very thickness of the historian's element. But these meanings do not surpass the phenomenon of the first sight itself, the initiating strangeness—amounting to a phenomenology of historical realization, the instant when we come to see the past in the shape of something odd—that the governess models for us so wonderfully. And though we may move hastily onward from the wonder of these clarion epiphanies—these glimmers and intuitions, amounting to visions, on which we stake our historical claims, though we may place considerable professional pride in having developed and explained them, making them visible and understandable to other people—we do so often by disavowing the sharp startling weirdness of these first sights. The *reconcentrado* on the far shore at Bly will always be more vivid than the meanings we ascribe to his presence there.

The governess stands for the frightening singularity of these visions in an especially intense way, one that I cannot and probably would not want to emulate. She casts the historian as a person who perceives an explosion that finally can *never* be seen by others—the person to whom alone the trauma comes to haunt the cheerful evening. She is like William James's diner, who alone among the revelers sees the skeleton at the banquet. The horror she perceives is no less real for the fact that she is the only one who perceives it. The implausibility of her storytelling is only the crude outward form of an experience so incredible and vivid, so disturbing, that were it to be told it could assume only such an outlandish shape inviting our scorn and superiority. Being a historian in the governess' sense is a matter of turning, swiveling, pointing, just like her, to direct the attention of those around you to a spot atop the tower or on the shore where something devastating and terrible stands "as big as a blazing fire," as plain as day, only to have those others ask, and never stop asking because they never will see, "*Where?*"[35]

This is a graver way, to be sure. It is silent and more awful, since it means never being able to convince others of what you know to be true, since it means being locked with the secrets others can never see. Conrad's Kurtz, in *Heart of Darkness*—a book written less than a year after *The Turn of the Screw* and owing a lot to it, claims Edel—beholds something unbelievable: He "cried in a whisper at some image, at some vision"; he sees a horror that makes his features into "the appalling face of a glimpsed truth."[36] No one can see what Kurtz sees. No one can see what the governess sees. Envisioning the past, maybe in the most profound sense, is to be alone in possession of the fact.

Notes

1   Henry James, *The Turn of the Screw* (1898), ed. Deborah Esch and Jonathan Warren (New York: W. W. Norton, 1999), 49.

2   Ibid., 15.

3   Ibid., 38–9 and 17.

4   Ibid., 4.

5   Edmund Wilson, "The Ambiguity of Henry James," *Hound & Horn* 7 (1934): 385–406.

6   James, *Turn of the Screw*, 15.

7   For more on James and history, see, for example, Roslyn Jolly, *Henry James: History, Narrative, Fiction* (Oxford: Clarendon Press, 1993). Jolly quotes James's view of 1883: "It is impossible to imagine what a novelist takes himself to be unless he regard himself as an historian and his narrative as a history" (1). James means that the novelist must write as though the events and people he describes are real.

8   James, *The Sense of the Past* (published posthumously in 1917), quoted in Simon Schama, *Dead Certainties (Unwarranted Speculations)* (New York: Knopf, 1991), 319–20.

9   On the relation of *The Sense of the Past* to *The Turn of the Screw*, see Leon Edel, *Henry James: A Life* (New York: Harper & Row, 1985), 504.

10 William Todd, "The Brothers Karamazov and the Poetics of Serial Publication," *Dostoevsky Studies* 7 (1986): 91–2.

11 William Todd, "Contexts of Criticism: Reviewing *The Brothers Karamazov* in 1879," *Stanford Slavic Studies* 4 (1991): 294. Todd quotes Trilling, *The Liberal Imagination: Essays on Literature and Society* (Garden City, NJ: Anchor Books, 1953), 200. See also Todd's further work on serialization, including "Anna on the Installment Plan: Teaching *Anna Karenina* through the History of Its Serial Publication," *in Approaches to Teaching Tolstoy's Anna Karenina*, ed. Liza Knapp and Amy Mandelker (New York: Modern Language Association of America, 2003), 53–9: and his forthcoming book *In the Fullness of Time: Serialization of the Russian Novel*.

12 Edith M. Thomas, "One Woman's Voice Against War," *Collier's Weekly*, 19 March 1898, 8.

13 James, "The Turn of the Screw," *Collier's Weekly*, 19 March 1898, 9.

14 The full proposed monument is illustrated and described in *Collier's Weekly*, 2 Apr. 1898, 5.

15 Adeline R. Tintner, *The Museum World of Henry James* (Ann Arbor, MI: UMI Research Press, 1986), 223–4. My thanks to Marc Simpson for calling my attention to this book.

16 James, *Turn of the Screw*, 55.

17 Ibid.

18 Ibid., 39.

19 Michael Blow, *A Ship to Remember: The "Maine" and the Spanish-American War* (New York: William Morrow, 1992), 127.

20 "Naval Divers," *Frank Leslie's Popular Monthly*, December 1898, 170.

21 James, *Turn of the Screw*, 40.

22 Ibid., 70.

23 "The Destruction of the *Maine*," *Collier's Weekly*, 5 March 1898, 2.

24 Randall C. Griffin, *Winslow Homer: An American Vision* (London: Phaidon, 2006), 205–6. For the construction of the fort during the reign of Philip II, see Maria Luisa Lobo Montalvo, *Havana: History and Architecture of a Romantic City* (New York: Monacelli Press, 2000), 52.

25 Eino Railo, *The Haunted Castle: A Study of the Elements of English Romanticism* (New York: Humanities Press, 1964), 7.

26 The photograph, captioned "Entering Havana, past Morro Castle," appears in *Collier's Weekly*, 12 March 1898, 4.

27 Griffin, *Winslow Homer*, 230, n. 19.

28 For more on this painting, see *Seeing America: Painting and Sculpture from the Collection of the Memorial Art Gallery of the University of Rochester* (Rochester, NY: Memorial Art Gallery of the University of Rochester, 2006), 81–84.

29 "A Masterpiece by Mr. Henry James," *New York Tribune Illustrated Supplement*, 23 Oct. 1898, quoted in *Turn of the Screw*, 151.

30 James, *Turn of the Screw*, 9.

31 Edel, *Henry James: A Life*, 526–7.

32 See D. W. Taylor, *Resistance of Ships and Screw Propulsion* (New York: Macmillan, 1893); I. McKim Chase, *Screw Propellers and Marine Propulsion* (New York: John Wiley & Sons, 1895); and A. E. Seaton, *The Screw Propeller: And Other Competing Instruments for Marine Propulsion* (London: Charles Griffin, 1909).

33 Frank Norris, "The Mechanics of Fiction," quoted in Mark Seltzer, *Bodies and Machines* (New York: Routledge, 1992), 44. James refers to *The Turn of the Screw* as a "pot-boiler" in a letter to H. G. Wells, 9 December 1898, quoted in *Turn of the Screw*, 116. In this context, the rotating propeller of a Holland submarine boat in Sonntag's center spread illustration for the 2 Apr. *Collier's Weekly* makes sense in the vicinity of that week's installment of James's advancing tale. See the "Holland Submarine Boat Ejecting Shell" in Sonntag, "Our Submarine Defenses" in *Collier's Weekly*, 2 April 1898, 12–13.

34 The sea does indeed haunt James's accounts of his own writing and his descriptions of his characters. Two brief examples illustrate the point. In the New York Edition preface to *Roderick Hudson*, James recalls that this "first attempt at a novel ... permitted me at last to put quite out to sea. I had but hugged the shore on sundry previous small occasions; bumping about, to acquire skill, in the shallow waters and sandy coves of the 'short story' and master as yet of no vessel constructed to carry a sail. The subject of 'Roderick' figured to me vividly this employment of canvas, and I have not

forgotten, even after long years, how the blue southern sea seemed to spread immediately before me and the breath of the spice-islands to be already in the breeze." Henry James, *The Art of the Novel: Critical Prefaces* (New York: Charles Scribner's Sons, 1947), 4. My thanks to Nicholas Jenkins for calling my attention to this passage.

In *The Golden Bowl* (1904) James describes Adam Verver's proposal of marriage to Charlotte Stant in Brighton as a figurative burning of ships: "They were walking thus, as he felt, nearer and nearer to where he should see his ships burn." The proposal made, Verver stands before the "definitely blazing and crackling" ships of "his committed deed." James, *The Golden Bowl* (London: Penguin, 1987), 192, 195. Here, as elsewhere, the oceangoing allusions are not a kind of theme or content but more like irruptions of the novelistic preoccupation with the sea, as if that preoccupation were bound to manifest itself—in phrases, metaphors, and extended descriptions—even in texts that have very little to do with ships and oceans.

For *why* the novel and the sea would so want to belong together, I turn to Fredric Jameson's account, in *The Political Unconscious*, of the ocean in Joseph Conrad's fiction as a blank and purely aesthetic space on the one hand and as a vivid arena of labor, capital, and empire on the other: "The sea is the empty space between the concrete places of work and life"—that is, an abstraction outside the zones of social activity—"but it is also, just as surely, itself a place of work and the very element by which an imperial capitalism draws its scattered beachheads and outposts together, through which it slowly realizes its sometimes violent, sometimes silent and corrosive, penetration of the outlying precapitalist zones of the globe." The artistic prose of Conrad transforms the ocean's "realities into style," making the actions of labor, capital, and empire "available for consumption on some purely aesthetic level." But those actions remain vivid in his fiction in ways sometimes repressed, sometimes not. Jameson, *The Political Unconscious* (Ithaca, NY: Cornell University Press, 1981), 213–14. The oceanic allusions in James's fiction perhaps could be read in this way. For a further account of the ocean and the novel, see Margaret Cohen, "Chronotopes of the Sea," in Franco Moretti, ed., *Forms and Themes*, vol. 2, *The Novel* (Princeton, NJ: Princeton University Press, 2006), 647–66.

35 James, *Turn of the Screw*, 69, 85.

36 Joseph Conrad, *Heart of Darkness* (Harmondsworth, England: Penguin, 1973), 100–1. Edel, *Henry James: A Life*, 527–8. Edel writes, "Both tales begin in the same way—the quiet circle, the atmosphere of mystery and gloom, with the hint of terrible evil, the reflective narrator, the retrospective method, the recall of crucial episodes. And perhaps from the 'Mr. Quint is dead' of the ghostly tale there sounds in Conrad a powerful echo, 'Mistah Kurtz—he dead.' The stories are as different as their authors, but they suggest that Conrad went to school to the works of Henry James and notably learned James's devices for obtaining distance from his materials." Edel links the governess and Marlow as tale-tellers, with the ghosts and Kurtz as the subjects of their stories. I would only add that Kurtz owes something also to the governess's special powers of envisioning terrible things.

INDEX